59/3

OTTO KLINEBERG

COLUMBIA UNIVERSITY

Social
Psychology

REVISED EDITION

New York: HENRY HOLT & COMPANY

To M. G.

with gratitude and affection

Preface to the Second Edition

The publication of this second edition of my textbook gives me a great deal of satisfaction, since it results directly from the cordial response extended by many of my colleagues and their students to the first. I must confess, however, that I hesitated a long time before writing it. In the first place, the appearance of so many excellent textbooks in this field during the years since 1940 raised in my mind a real question as to whether I had anything significant to add. In the second place, I felt that I had already said my say; if my point of view had any value it was now in the public domain, for others to accept or reject as they saw fit.

I changed my mind not only because of the friendly insistence of the publishers but also for a more basic reason. The field of social psychology is developing so actively and changing so rapidly that no writer can expect a textbook published in 1940 to be acceptable today. Since I found several chapters inadequate even at that time, I was eager to present the material more fully and to bring it up to date. The point of view may have remained relatively intact, but the specific implications needed to be brought into line with more recent developments.

I have indicated in the text that, in the fluid situation in which social psychology finds itself today, the organization and presentation of topics will inevitably vary with the viewpoint of the writer. The same holds true for the actual content, which necessarily involves a selection out of a large amount of available material. In making such a selection, I have undoubtedly failed to do justice to many investigations and viewpoints, and I know that I have left out almost altogether some very important developments. This is true, for example, for the field of industrial relations, which receives only brief and inadequate mention.

For those who are familiar with the first edition, I should like to indicate the major changes which have been introduced. No chapter has remained unaltered, but the first half of the book represents only moderate changes from the original; the same is true for chapters 15 and 16, which are slightly modified from the earlier chapters 19 and 20. The rest of the book has been largely rewritten, and chapters 14 and 20 are completely new. I have tried to do more justice to the study of attitudes and opinions, group dynamics, and the whole field of culture and personality, in the light of new data. The last chapter, on the implications of social psychology for international relations, may seem a little out of place in a textbook, but I was eager to present some ideas for classroom discussion of this important problem.

My acknowledgments are many and varied. My greatest debt is to my colleagues in the social sciences whose work is described in the following pages and without whom, in the most literal sense, this book could not have been written. I have used in the text, in slightly altered form, materials from several of my own articles published in the *American Journal of Orthopsychiatry,* the *American Journal of Psychiatry,* and the *International Social Science Bulletin* (Unesco) and I am grateful for the permission to do so. My students at Columbia University have helped through their friendly criticisms of the first edition, and a group of them—Mrs. Macleod, Miss Davidowitz, and Messrs. Salzinger, Leeds, Koponen and Viktor—were kind enough to work with me late into the night in preparing the index of names. My secretary at Unesco, Miss Nora Curran, most generously contributed her spare time to last-minute typing. My children, Rosemary, John, and Stephen, helped not only in the mechanical tasks requiring scissors and paste, but also in the more complex one of preparing the index of subjects.

My wife once again worked at my side through every stage of the preparation of this book.

O. K.

Paris
February 20, 1954

Preface to the First Edition

The rapid changes which have occurred in the content of social psychology, both in its concepts and in its data, have seemed to me to justify the appearance of a new textbook in the field. More particularly, the increasing concern of psychologists with other cultures has suggested that there might be some interest in an attempt at integration between psychology and ethnology. This integration is by no means complete, but I have the hope that some at least of the findings of ethnology and comparative sociology have been brought within the psychologist's frame of reference. At the same time the traditional content of social psychology has also been taken into consideration, although to a somewhat reduced extent because of the inclusion of materials from neighboring social sciences.

With the increasing variety of courses offered in psychology, it is inevitable that social psychology will trespass upon related fields. As far as the present text is concerned, this is true especially of the sections dealing with Differential Psychology and with Personality. In spite of possible overlapping it was decided that these materials do belong legitimately within the scope of social psychology.

References have been appended rather liberally at the end of each chapter for the convenience of the student or teacher interested in supplementary reading. It may be worth while to mention some of the texts which I would regard as particularly helpful. Among the writings of psychologists the revised edition of *Experimental Social Psychology* by Murphy, Murphy and Newcomb is especially valuable, but there is excellent material also in *A Handbook of Social Psychology*, edited by Murchison, in G. W. Allport's *Personality*, in Anastasi's *Differential Psychology*, and in Doob's *Propaganda*. The 39th Yearbook of the National Society for the Study of Education, *Intelligence: Its Nature and Nurture*, was published too late for inclusion in the present text, but it should be consulted. For data from ethnology and comparative sociology, Thomas' *Primitive Behavior* and Sumner and Keller's *The Science of Society* are rich source-books, and the writings of Boas, Linton, Benedict, Lowie, Mead, Malinowski and Goldenweiser give an understanding of culture which is of real value to the psychologist.

In connection with the actual preparation of this book, it is a pleasure to record my indebtedness to Gardner Murphy, who read the first draft of the manuscript and made valuable suggestions for its improvement; to G. W. Allport, who performed a similar service at a later stage; to Ralph Linton, J. G. Peatman, George Herzog and E. L. Horowitz, who read portions of the manuscript in proof; to Edward Arluck, who assisted with the bibliographies; and to Lillian Dick, Allan Fromme and Louis Long, who gave so generously of their time in the painstaking tasks of proof-reading and preparing the index.

Throughout this undertaking my wife has been my partner. She has collaborated at every stage from the writing of the first draft to the completion of the book in its present form. Her name should really appear as co-author.

O. K.

April 15, 1940
Columbia University

Contents

Part One. Introductory

Part Two. Social Factors in Human Nature

Part Three. Differential Psychology

Part Four. Social and Cultural Factors in Personality

Part Five. Social Interaction

Part One

INTRODUCTORY

Background and History

1

INTRODUCTION

Psychology has been defined (1) as the scientific study of the activities of the individual. Social psychology may be defined as the scientific study of the activities of the individual as influenced by other individuals. These "others" may exert their effect singly or in groups; they may act directly through their presence in the immediate environment, or indirectly through the medium of traditional or expected modes of behavior which affect the individual even when he is alone. Whether he moves positively in the direction indicated by a group of which he approves, or negatively in the opposite direction because the group is one which he rejects, his behavior is still socially determined. Even when he reacts not to the actual characteristics or behavior of others, but in terms of an image or stereotype which may be entirely false, he is still being influenced by other individuals as he sees them; this phenomenon is also social-psychological. If he in turn affects those who have affected him—which is usually the case—we may speak of interaction, regarded by a number of recent writers as the essence of social psychology (2, 3). Since this may not always be the case, however, it seems preferable to adopt the more inclusive definition suggested above.

To speak of a situation as social when the individual is alone may seem at first somewhat paradoxical, but it is not difficult to find confirmation of this view. When an American encounters something which he did not anticipate, he is likely to open his eyes wide in surprise; a Chinese under similar circumstances is much more likely to stick out his tongue. In both cases the reaction is certainly determined by the respective groups to which the individuals belong. Others—parents, teachers, associates—have helped to shape this particular bit of behavior, even though it may occur in an individual unseen by others. To take another example, when someone is faced with a difficult decision, perhaps related to the choice of a new occupation or a new home, though he may have shut himself up alone in his study to consider the alternatives, he is being influenced by others—by those from whom he acquired his standards of value, by his judgment of what the change would do to his wife and children, by his views of the attitudes of his former and future associates, by his estimate of the effect on his social position within the community, etc. Every experiment in psychology in which human beings are used as subjects involves a social component to the extent that the observed behavior is determined by previous social experience.

Conceived so broadly, social psychology is not always easy to separate from neighboring disciplines. Usually it is distinguished on the one hand from general psychology, which deals at least in theory with the activities of the individual as such, and on the other hand from sociology, which is concerned primarily with the group and with social institutions.

Actually both of these distinctions are difficult to maintain. In connection with the former, there is a growing recognition among psychologists of the importance of the group in determining the characteristics of the individual. In particular the discoveries of the ethnologists have revealed the extent to which personality is shaped by the cultural and social environment in which it develops. It would be difficult to point to any substantial amount of psychological description of the individual which does not reveal social influences to some degree. It may not be entirely true that "all psychology is social psychology," but we shall have occasion to see that this statement contains little exaggeration.

It has been said that the psychoanalysts have not been sufficiently aware of the part played by culture in the formation of the individual. It is probably true that they have paid too little attention to the varieties of behavior for which culture may be responsible. Freud himself does, however, admit that the activities of the individual can be understood only in relation to the group.

> The contrast between Individual Psychology and Social or Group Psychology, which at a first glance may seem to be full of significance, loses a great deal of its sharpness when it is examined more closely. It is true that Individual Psychology is concerned with the individual

man . . . but only rarely and under certain exceptional conditions is Individual Psychology in a position to disregard the relations of this individual to others. In the individual's mental life someone else is invariably involved, as a model, as an object, as a helper, as an opponent, and so from the very first Individual Psychology is at the same time Social Psychology as well—in this extended but entirely justifiable sense of the words (4, pp. 1-2).

For purposes of convenience, however, some line will have to be drawn between the material usually included in a textbook of general psychology and that which will be our concern in the present volume. In the descriptions, for example, of many of the phenomena of memory or of sense perception, the social component enters only indirectly, and much of the material may be understood with little reference to social factors. Even in these areas, however, evidence has accumulated to indicate that social influences are more important than was formerly realized, and research is being actively directed toward determining the nature and extent of such influences. Our procedure will be to take for granted on the part of the reader a knowledge of the usual textbook material, and emphasize here those aspects which are primarily social-psychological.

It may perhaps be helpful to think of psychological phenomena as representing a continuum extending from a minimum to a maximum of social determination. At one extreme may be found data relating to after-images, dark-adaptation, conditioning of the patellar reflex to electric shock, for example; at the other, a study of the effects of an interracial housing project on the attitudes of the participants, or the extent to which the behavior of an individual is shaped by his status in the community or by the role which he is expected to play. It would be difficult if not impossible to determine the exact point on the continuum at which social factors become important. No sharp break is to be expected, nor can it be discovered. At the same time the phenomena do change in character as we go from one extreme to the other, and different techniques are required for their investigation even though the scientific principles may remain the same. Perhaps the safest conclusion to reach is that the student of social psychology deals with phenomena which are *more* social and the student of general psychology with those which are *less* social.

This absence of any sharp dividing line holds also for the relation between social psychology and sociology. It is true that sociology supposedly deals with groups and institutions, and psychology with individuals, but as groups are obviously made up of individuals, overlapping is inevitable. It is not surprising that textbooks in social psychology have been written with almost equal frequency by men who are technically sociologists or psychologists, respectively. In some American universities social psychology is offered in the department of psychology; in others, in the department of sociology; in still others, it is taught in both departments. It would be interesting to make a careful analysis of the content of social psychology as understood by representatives of these two different disciplines. We would undoubtedly discover a great deal of overlapping, but also some clear indications of a difference in emphasis, in point of view, and in the problems which are regarded as most important.

If a distinction must be made, it may be helpful to look at the problem in this manner. Suppose, for instance, our interest is in the problem of gangs and gang behavior. The sociologist would presumably be concerned with the social and economic causes of gang life, the relation of the gang to law and order and institutions like the school and the church, the geographical distribution of gangs, their effect on the life of the community. The social psychologist, on the other hand, might be expected to study the nature of the individuals in the gang, their intellectual and personal characteristics, the effect of the gang on the individuals composing it, the life history of individual members, etc. When, however, a sociologist writes a book on "The Gang" (5), he certainly makes no such artificial distinctions, and many of his findings belong properly in the field of social psychology. Similarly, when the Lynds (6) give us a sociological account of "Middletown," they tell us a great deal also about the attitudes and personality of the individuals in that community.

Nowhere is the distinction between social psychology and sociology more difficult to draw than in the field of attitude measurement and public opinion surveys. Major contributions have been and are being made by representatives of both disciplines. Psychologists and sociologists alike man the staffs of the research centers connected with various universities, as well as the commercial polling organizations and market research agencies. At this empirical level the two disciplines come so close together as to be for all practical purposes indistinguishable. At the same time it remains true that the primary concern of the sociologist is group behavior, and that of the social psychologist is the behavior of the individual in the group situation.

The science of anthropology, particularly cultural anthropology or ethnology, bears a similar relation to social psychology. Wissler (7) regards psychology as concerned with individual performances, and anthropology with group behavior. The anthropologist, according to him, is not especially interested in the function of the individual in the group; if he were, he would be indistinguishable from the psychologist. There can be no doubt, however, that on occasions the individual may be of great importance to the anthropologist. The description of the Ghost Dance, a religious movement among the Plains Indians during the latter part of the last century, is clearly incomplete without some attention to the personality of Wovoka, its founder (8). The autobiography of Crashing Thunder, a Winnebago Indian, though edited by the anthropologist Paul Radin (9), is obviously concerned at least as much with the individual as with the group. The growing literature dealing with the life histories of members of many different cultural groups bears ample testimony to the ever-increasing interest of anthropologists in the individual as well as in the culture.

The writings of many ethnologists reveal this difficulty of separating their material and their problems from those of social psychology. Radin (10, p. 267) writes: "Let me refer . . . to what is perhaps the core of all investigations of cultures: can we ever arrive at any satisfactory knowledge of what constitutes human nature?" It is clear, however, that the knowledge of what constitutes human nature is also the central problem of the social psychologist. Seligman (11) states that he "has become convinced that the most fruitful development—perhaps indeed the only process that can bring social anthropology to its rightful status as a branch of science and at the same time give it the full weight in human affairs to which it is entitled—is the increased elucidation in the field and integration into anthropology of psychological knowledge" (p. ix). Linton (12) in *The Study of Man,* a textbook in social anthropology, devotes considerable space to a discussion of such problems as the relation between instinctive and learned behavior, and the nature of man's inherent qualities—problems usually associated with the content of psychology. Rivers (13), who was himself both psychologist and ethnologist, expresses the belief that "the ultimate aim of all studies of mankind, whether historical or scientific, is to reach an explanation in terms of psychology, in terms of the ideas, beliefs, sentiments, and instinctive tendencies by which the conduct of man, both individual and collective, is determined" (p. 3).

We have here sufficient proof of the intimate relation between these two sciences. Three aspects are important. In the first place, the materials collected by ethnologists may be of tremendous value in clarifying many psychological problems. Kantor (14) pointed out in 1925 that psychologists were oblivious of the fact that much of the data they required could be found in the writings of the ethnologists, but it is safe to say that at the present time this oblivion no longer exists. Psychologists have become increasingly "culture-conscious." They have made considerable use of such materials in their own writings, and when they have reported the results of an experimental study conducted in one society, they have come to realize that the conclusions may legitimately be applied only to that society, and that further evidence is required before the findings may be generalized.[1] More and more psychologists are familiarizing themselves with anthropological research and are insisting on its importance in connection with the attempt to separate the accidental from the universal in "human nature."

The second aspect of the relation between the two sciences lies in what psychology can do to explain certain ethnological problems. Lowie (16), for example, makes use of some of the findings of abnormal psychology in his interpretation of primitive religion. In some cases, psychologists [2] and psychoanalysts [3] have applied their theories and their techniques to the understanding of ethnological phenomena; in other cases, ethnologists [4] have taken from psychology those modes of interpretation which they have found most useful.

A third major area of contact between psychology and anthropology is to be found in the increasing application of psychological techniques to the comparative study of cultures. The use of experimental methods for the investigation of cultural differences in memory processes, and the administration of the Rorschach and other projective techniques in the study of personality in other cultures

---

[1] See Terman & Miles (15).
[2] For example, Bartlett (17) and Köhler (18).
[3] Freud (19), Abraham (20), Rank (21), Roheim (22), Kardiner (23).
[4] Benedict (24), Mead (25), Malinowski (26), Murdock (27), etc.

as well as of the phenomena of culture change or acculturation, may be mentioned as representative of this trend. Psychologists and anthropologists have cooperated in this development, in some instances combining their techniques and points of view in carrying out joint research undertakings.

This account of the way in which psychology and social anthropology are interrelated may perhaps serve as an introduction to the present textbook and as a justification for the method which is here adopted. The writer has for some years felt the need of a closer integration between the contents of these two disciplines; he is here attempting to write a social psychology mainly from the standpoint of the relation of the individual to his culture, and to effect at least a partial synthesis of the science which deals with culture and the science which deals with the individual. That seems to him to be the only way in which one can write a "social psychology" which may legitimately be termed "social."

It follows that in one important respect this textbook differs from others in the same field. The usual concern is with the constants of human behavior, whereas the present concern is at least as much with its varieties. The method is comparative, but the purpose of the comparison is to show the wealth of possible social patterning as well as to inquire into the common human denominator. There is no real opposition between these two points of view. Social psychology does have implications for all societies, but at the same time the cultural variations which influence human behavior must not be neglected. In a sense then, this book may be described as an attempt to write a comparative social psychology.[5]

Linton (28) has written as follows: "The individual has been assigned to psychology, society to sociology, and culture to cultural anthropology. . . . It is now becoming apparent that the integration between the individual, society and culture is so close and their interaction so continuous that the investigator who tries to work with any one of them without reference to the other two soon comes to a dead end . . . the next few years will witness the emergence of a science of human behavior which will synthesize the findings of psychology, sociology and anthropology" (pp. 4-5). Although we

[5] The word "comparative" has acquired a special meaning because of its use by animal psychologists. It is applied with at least equal propriety to a comparative study of human behavior. The term "comparative sociology," which is devoid of animal implications, may be regarded as setting the necessary precedent.

have not yet achieved this goal, it is precisely the hope of contributing toward such a synthesis which motivated the writing of this book.

HISTORICAL OUTLINE

As psychology grew out of philosophy, so were many of the problems of social psychology anticipated by the philosophers. More particularly, speculations as to "human nature" or "the original nature of man" are apparently as old as philosophy itself. Aristotle and Plato, for example, were both very much interested in this problem. The former looked upon man primarily as a biological animal, to be explained largely on the basis of hereditary organic dispositions; Plato, on the other hand, thought that man was mainly a product of a certain type of society, and in his Utopian "republic" believed it possible to mold human nature in any direction by the proper use of educational and social institutions. It is not a very comforting reflection that after the lapse of so many centuries we are still debating this same problem.

In more recent times, interest was directed to the problem of original human nature by the writings of the English philosopher Thomas Hobbes, who published his *Leviathan* in 1651. Hobbes described the "natural" state of man without organized society as "solitary, poor, nasty, brutish and short." Although his concern was primarily with the problems of politics, he did seek to understand human nature, and he has sometimes been called the first social psychologist [Murphy (29)]. Somewhat after the manner of the modern "instinct" psychologist he lists the dominant motives of man—according to him, hunger, thirst, sex, fear and the desire for honor; through all of these runs the search for pleasure and the avoidance of pain. Original human nature is selfish and self-interested, and must be curbed and controlled by society if men are to live together in peace.

It is usual to contrast Hobbes with Jean Jacques Rousseau. The latter also was concerned with the problem of original human nature, which was of importance to him from the point of view of educational as well as political theory. His portrait of the "noble savage" is too well known to require much comment; it is perhaps sufficient merely to mention that his theory was in many ways the opposite of that of Hobbes. For Rousseau natural man is essentially good, unselfish and pure and it is only when civilization has had its effect upon him that vice and defect appear. It may be of interest to add that this conflict of opinion as to whether man is originally good or bad occurs also among other peoples; in ancient Chinese philosophy Mencius adopted on this point a position similar to that of Rousseau, and Hsün Tsu anticipated Hobbes.

The publication of Darwin's *Origin of Species* in 1859 was of great significance in the development of social psychology. Among other things it stimulated Francis Galton's study of hereditary factors in individual mental differences (*30*). Galton was particularly interested in the hereditary transmission of genius, but he believed also that individuals are born to imbecility, criminality and other defects as well as to virtues. He was responsible for the use of the pedigree method of studying mental endowment and his emphasis resulted in the genealogical histories of the Jukes (*31*), the Kallikaks (*32*), the Edwards family (*33*), and others. Although there has been great criticism of Galton for his relative indifference to social and environmental factors, and especially for his one-sided emphasis on a rather narrow theory of eugenics, he must still be regarded as the founder of the study of individual differences, which now represents an exceedingly important subdivision of social psychology.

Another important effect of Darwin's theory was the introduction of the evolutionary viewpoint into social science. There had been attempts to develop such a viewpoint before Darwin, as in Auguste Comte's *Law of the Three Stages* (*34*) and in the theory of economic evolution suggested by Marx (*35*), but it is not probable that these had any very important influence on the main stream of social psychology. Darwin's theory, particularly as it was developed by Herbert Spencer (*36*), for a long time played a decisive part in shaping the theoretical approach to the social sciences.

In general Herbert Spencer's view was that social behavior is to be understood as a series of stages the succession of which obeys certain fundamental laws of development. Just as in biology the later more evolved forms may be understood only in the light of what has preceded them, so in social science the complex institutions of modern society require an evolutionary explanation. Largely as a result of Spencer's influence it became fashionable to erect schemes of evolution in connection with the various aspects of culture. Tylor (*37*) explained the development of religion from its origin in animism, through polytheism to the ultimate belief in one God; Morgan (*38*) attempted to demonstrate that economic life passed through stages of hunting, pastoral life and agriculture; Haddon (39) believed that geometric art grew out of realistic; Lubbock (40) thought that marriage began with primitive promiscuity which was followed by group marriage, polygamy and finally monogamy. Although this evolutionary standpoint is not now widely accepted, it has had unmistakable historical significance.

A more direct contribution to the development of social psychology was made by a number of French writers toward the end of the nineteenth century. Their aim was to explain the way in which groups control the behavior of the individuals of whom they are composed as well as the way in which individuals act upon one another. Tarde's (41) discussion of the laws of imitation and Gustave LeBon's analysis of crowd mentality (42) may be taken as representative of this trend. Both were very much influenced by the psychiatry of Charcot, especially by his studies of extreme cases of suggestibility and hypnosis. Suggestion was regarded as furnishing the key to the explanation of mass behavior, and it was so used by these and other French writers. Tarde believed that a proper application of the laws of imitation was all that was needed to understand the phenomena of social change, progress, religious movements and all other varieties of group effects. LeBon, on the other hand, gave impetus to the notion of a crowd psychology, relatively independent of the psychology of the individuals of whom it is composed, and constituting an entity *sui generis*. His book marks a turning point in the discussion of the relation between the group and the individual, and it initiated a controversy which continued throughout the later history of social psychology and to which we shall have occasion to refer later. Some indication of LeBon's influence may be seen in the fact that when the term "social psychology" is used by the layman, he usually thinks of a "crowd psychology" in LeBon's sense of the term.

A particularly important figure in this area is that of the sociologist Durkheim (43), for whom the individual had no existence except as a member of society. Although Durkheim and Tarde were in violent opposition with regard to the relationship between psychological and sociological principles of explanation, they have been regarded [Blondel (44)] as making parallel contributions toward the understanding of human behavior in social terms. In particular Durkheim's study of suicide (45) represents one of the first significant analyses of the manner in which social influences enter into a highly "individual" aspect of human activity.

The first book to be titled *Social Psychology* was written by Professor E. A. Ross, and appeared in 1908 (*46*). Ross was greatly influenced by Tarde, and his book consists largely of an application of the "laws of imitation" to the events of his day. Almost at the same time there appeared William McDougall's *Introduction to Social Psychology* (*47*), which gave a tremendous impetus to the development of this field. The book is one of the most popular ever written in the field of psychology and went through fourteen editions in the first thirteen years. Greatly influenced by the evolutionary point of view, McDougall postulated certain primitive urges or "instincts" which were the prime movers of action both in animals and man. Whatever we may think now of McDougall's instinct theory (see Chapter 4) the fact remains that in its time it laid the foundation of much of the work in the social sciences and became the guiding concept in the application of psychology to the understanding of social phenomena.[6]

There gradually developed a marked reaction against the use of instinct as a fundamental concept in social science. Many writers particularly among the sociologists have emphasized the social factors in human behavior, as contrasted with the biological ones upon which McDougall insisted. The attack by the behaviorists probably went too far, but they helped to bring about a re-examination of McDougall's assumptions and a rephrasing of the problem. Still more important in this connection has been the contribution of the anthropologists, who have given to the psychologists an insight into the variations in human behavior and into the manner in which culture may determine activities formerly regarded as instinctive.

Perhaps the most important development in the field of social psychology has been the gradual extension of the applicability of experimental, empirical and quantitative methods. There were early attempts in the direction of social-psychological experimentation by German educators who compared the work done by school children when alone and in the presence of others. Moede (*50*) was probably the first to make careful experimental studies of the effects of rivalry and competition, and F. H. Allport (*51*) carried this whole trend further in an important series of experiments, the results of which

[6] The books by Graham Wallas (*48*) and Ordway Tead (*49*) are examples of this tendency.

were published in 1920. The development of the experimental method in this and related fields was shown in the analysis of this material in *Experimental Social Psychology* by Murphy and Murphy (52) in 1931, and particularly in the revised edition by Murphy, Murphy and Newcomb (53) in 1937. An illuminating account of the large number of empirical techniques now applicable to the field of social psychology is to be found in the recent publication by Jahoda, Deutsch and Cook (54). The prospects are encouraging for the further development of social psychology as an empirical and objective branch of science.

In the recent history of social psychology three major trends may be identified. First, it has become more and more *comparative*. The conviction has grown that psychological behavior cannot be satisfactorily understood if it is studied in one cultural context alone, and increasing use has been made of ethnological and sociological materials dealing with a variety of cultures and societies. In the second place, it has become increasingly *experimental*. More and more areas of social psychology are being explored by techniques which may be labeled objective, experimental and (as far as possible) quantitative. Finally, social psychology has taken on much more markedly the character of an *applied* science, with practical implications and applications in the field of human relations. These three trends are, of course, not mutually exclusive, but clearly complementary; the study of race relations, to take only one example, represents a field in which all three of these trends—comparative, experimental and applied—are unmistakably present.

THE FIELD OF SOCIAL PSYCHOLOGY

It is evident from the above that the scope of social psychology is wide, and growing ever wider. New techniques develop, or new applications of old techniques are discovered; contact with neighboring disciplines increases constantly; practical problems arise—at the local, national and even international level—to which social psychologists direct their attention. Although the field grows in one direction, it may contract in another. Any listing of problem areas must therefore have a somewhat fleeting quality. It may be reasonably accurate for today, but it will undoubtedly have to be changed in the not-so-distant future. This is no reason for discouragement;

on the contrary, it should give us confidence in the vitality and growth of our discipline.

With these considerations in mind, the following problem areas may be identified as among those with which social psychologists are now directly concerned. They will be more fully discussed in subsequent chapters of this book.

(1) *The interpenetration of general psychology and social psychology.* This involves on the one hand an examination of the manner in which social factors enter into activities which are not usually considered social—motivation, emotional behavior, perception, memory, etc.; it involves on the other hand [Bruner (55)] the translation of traditional social-psychological concepts—imitation, suggestion, prejudice, etc.—in terms of basic psychological concepts—learning, perception, etc.

(2) *The socialization of the child; culture and personality.* Closely related to the first area, but with a somewhat different orientation and making use of different methods, is the study of the manner in which the child becomes a socialized adult. This involves primarily the comparative approach, since it has long been clear that if the socialization process is to be studied adequately, it must be studied under differing conditions and in a wide variety of cultural situations.

(3) *Individual and group differences.* The field of "differential psychology" represents a continuing interest on the part of social psychologists. There has been a particularly active development in recent years of the study of the characteristics of contemporary national groups—the problem of "national character."

(4) *Attitudes and opinions; communications research, content analysis, propaganda.* This whole area represents one of the most active fields of concentration on the part of social psychologists and of many sociologists as well. It includes the measurement of attitudes, the use of polling devices and other survey techniques, investigations of the effects of the various mass media, the development of quantitative methods for the analysis of the content of these media, the study of attitude change through propaganda and other methods, the study of trends in public opinion, and many other related problems.

(5) *Social interaction, group dynamics, sociometry, leadership.* This, too, includes an interrelated group of techniques and problems which are attracting great attention among psychologists. The approach represented by group dynamics has been especially active

in the study of social interaction, particularly in small groups, and in the process of group formation, group functioning, group decision, and in the analysis of the phenomenon of leadership. Another important development is represented by the increasing emphasis on the concept of social role as contributing to the understanding of the behavior of the individual in the group situation.

(6) *Social pathology*. There has been a continuing concern with the pathological aspects of social life, and with the development of adequate therapeutic methods. This interest has been directed particularly to the problems of mental abnormality, of delinquency and crime, and of the forms of intergroup hostility reflected in prejudice and discrimination and in industrial conflict.

(7) *Politics, domestic and international*. As one aspect of the practical orientation of contemporary social psychology may be mentioned the growing concern with political behavior, both at the national and the international level.

It is clear that these seven major problem areas are by no means mutually exclusive. The question of cultural influences on the development of personality runs through most if not all of them; communications research plays a part in the study of national characteristics, in the analysis of prejudice and discrimination, and in the field of politics and international relations. Group dynamics enters into the understanding of the decision-making process in international conferences, and also into the question of attitude formation and attitude change in a boys' club or an industrial plant. Whenever possible, the interrelationships of these various fields will be indicated, even though for purposes of an orderly presentation the field as a whole must be classified and subdivided. It will be helpful to keep in mind, however, that any form of subdivision does violence to the integrated nature of the material.

SUMMARY

Social Psychology is concerned with the scientific study of the individual as influenced by other individuals. There is, however, no strict line of demarcation from general psychology on the one hand or from sociology and anthropology on the other. For this reason the attempt is here made to bring about an integration between the material collected by students of society, particularly the anthropologists, and the material referring more directly to the individual.

The aim is not merely to arrive at the constants of human nature, but also to indicate the variations in behavior resulting from social and cultural factors. The method may be described as that of a Comparative Social Psychology.

The history of this field of investigation begins with the speculations of the philosophers. Later developments include the application to society of evolutionary and hereditarian principles, the emphasis on the psychological characteristics of groups as distinct from individuals, the instinct theory and the reactions against it, the application of the experimental method to the problems of social psychology, and the increasing realization of the part played by society in determining the behavior of the individual. More recently, three important trends have acquired primary importance: social psychology has become increasingly comparative, experimental, and applied. At the present time, the major problem areas may be listed as follows: (1) The interpenetration of general psychology and social psychology. (2) The socialization of the child; culture and personality. (3) Individual and group differences. (4) Attitudes and opinions. (5) Social interaction, group dynamics, sociometry, leadership. (6) Social pathology. (7) Politics, domestic and international.

REFERENCES

1. Woodworth, R. S. *Psychology*. Rev. ed. 1929
2. Newcomb, T. M. *Social Psychology*. 1950
3. Hartley, E. L., and Hartley, R. E. *Fundamentals of Social Psychology*. 1952
4. Freud, S. *Group Psychology and the Analysis of the Ego*. 1922
5. Thrasher, F. M. *The Gang*. 2d ed. 1937
6. Lynd, R. S., and Lynd, H. M. *Middletown*, 1929; *Middletown in Transition*, 1937
7. Wissler, C. *Introduction to Social Anthropology*. 1929
8. Mooney, J. "The Ghost-Dance Religion," *Annual Report of the Bureau of Ethnology*, vol. 14, Part 2, 1896
9. Radin, P. *Crashing Thunder: The Autobiography of an American Indian*. 1926
10. Radin, P. *The Method and Theory of Ethnology*. 1933
11. Seligman, C. G. Introduction to J. S. Lincoln's *The Dream in Primitive Cultures*. 1935
12. Linton, R. *The Study of Man*. 1936
13. Rivers, W. H. R. *Kinship and Social Organization*. 1914

14. Kantor, J. R. "Anthropology, Race, Psychology and Culture," *Amer. Anthrop.*, 1925, 27: pp. 267-283

15. Terman, L. M., and Miles, C. C. *Sex and Personality.* 1936

16. Lowie, R. H. *Primitive Religion.* 1924

17. Bartlett, F. C. *Psychology and Primitive Culture.* 1923

18. Koehler, W. "Psychological Remarks on Some Questions of Anthropology," *Am. J. Psychol.*, 1937, 50: pp. 271-288

19. Freud, S. *Totem and Taboo.* 1927

20. Abraham, K. "Dreams and Myths," *Nerv. and Ment. Dis. Mono.*, Ser. 15, 1913

21. Rank, O. "The Myth of the Birth of the Hero," *Nerv. and Ment. Dis. Mono.*, Ser. 18, 1914

22. Roheim, G. "Psychoanalysis of Primitive Cultural Types," *Internatl. J. Psychoanal.*, 1932, 13: pp. 2-224

23. Kardiner, A. *The Individual and His Society*, 1939; *The Psychological Frontiers of Society*, 1945

24. Benedict, R. F. *Patterns of Culture.* 1934

25. Mead, M. *Coming of Age in Samoa*, 1928; *Growing up in New Guinea*, 1930; *Sex and Temperament in Three Primitive Societies*, 1935

26. Malinowski, B. *Sex and Repression in Savage Society.* 1927

27. Murdock, G. P. *Social Structure.* 1949

28. Linton, R. *The Cultural Background of Personality.* 1945

29. Murphy, G. *An Historical Introduction to Modern Psychology.* 3d ed. 1932

30. Galton, F. *Hereditary Genius.* 1869

31. Dugdale, R. L. *The Jukes*, 1910; Estabrook, A. H. *The Jukes in 1915.* 1916

32. Goddard, H. H. *The Kallikak Family.* 1912 and 1921

33. Winship, A. E. *Jukes-Edwards.* 1900

34. Comte, A. *Cours de Philosophie Positive.* 6 vols. 1835-1852

35. Marx, K., and Engels, F. *The Communist Manifesto,* 1848; Marx, K., *Zur Kritik der Politischen Oekonomie,* 1859

36. Spencer, H. *Principles of Sociology.* 1880-1896

37. Tylor, E. B. *Primitive Culture.* 1874

38. Morgan, L. H. *Ancient Society.* 1907

39. Haddon, A. C. *Evolution in Art.* 1914

40. Lubbock, J. *The Origin of Civilization.* 1870

41. Tarde, G. *Les Lois de l'Imitation.* 1890

42. LeBon, G. *La Psychologie des Foules.* 1895

43. Durkheim, E. *Les Formes Elémentaires de la Vie Religieuse.* 1912

44. Blondel, C. *Introduction à la Psychologie Collective.* 1928

45. Durkheim, E. *Le Suicide.* 1912

46. Ross, E. A. *Social Psychology.* 1908

47. McDougall, W. *An Introduction to Social Psychology.* 1908

48. Wallas, G. *Human Nature in Politics.* 3d ed. 1921

49. Tead, O. *Instincts in Industry.* 1918

50. Moede, W. *Experimentelle Massenpsychologie.* 1920

51. Allport, F. H. *Social Psychology.* 1924

52. Murphy, G., and Murphy, L. B. *Experimental Social Psychology.* 1931

53. Murphy, G., Murphy, L. B., and Newcomb, T. M. *Experimental Social Psychology.* Rev. ed. 1937

54. Jahoda, M., Deutsch, M., and Cook, S. W. *Research Methods in Social Relations.* 2 vols. 1951

55. Bruner, J. S. "Social Psychology and Group Processes." In Stone, C. P., ed. *Annual Review of Psychology.* v. 1. 1950

The Social Behavior of Animals

2

INTRODUCTION

In *A Handbook of Social Psychology*, edited by Murchison in 1935
(*1*), there are no fewer than eight chapters out of twenty-two
devoted directly to aspects of sub-human social behavior. In the
plans for a new *Handbook* to be published shortly under the editorship of Gardner Lindzey, material on the social psychology of animals is reduced to one chapter out of twenty-five. This striking
difference may be due to the interests and judgment of the respective editors, or to a change in emphasis through time, but it also
raises in clear form the question of the degree to which the social
behavior of men and of animals is related. Is the social psychology
of animals relevant to the understanding of human social behavior?
In what manner? And to what extent?

The argument in favor of studying the social behavior of animals may be presented along several different lines. In the first
place, social phenomena may be observed in rather simpler form,
and it is possible to study the development of in-groups and out-
groups, of leadership, of habits of courtship and mating, of social
habituation and other forms of social behavior common to animals
and man. In the second place, the study of animal behavior may
be particularly useful as an aid in the separation of hereditary and
environmental factors in human life. It seems reasonable to suppose
that whenever a form of behavior is found which man shares with
a number of animal species, and particularly with those most closely
related to him, such behavior may with some certainty be regarded
as having a biological basis. On the other hand, when a form of
behavior is found in man and is completely lacking throughout the
rest of the biological kingdom, it is more probably the result of cul-

tural factors. Such an approach is exemplified in a recent book by Ford and Beach (2) on sexual behavior; comparisons are constantly drawn between human and animal behavior for this purpose.

In addition, the fact that social psychological experiments of various kinds may be carried out on animals much more quickly than among human beings, and that controlled changes may be introduced into the conditions of their life much more effectively, makes it possible to conduct among them investigations which would be difficult to reproduce among human beings. This point has been made by Carpenter (3) and Harlow (4), both of whom have designed a series of interesting experimental procedures in this connection. Harlow writes: "We may study in these animals the forces operating in the formation, maintenance, and dissolution of their social groups, and we may study by appropriate experimental procedures the social forces operating to influence the formation of basic social and personality traits. But the study of the behavior of sub-human animals will make a less direct but equally important contribution to social psychology in its service of analyzing, under rigidly controlled experimental conditions, the fundamental nature of neuroses, personality mechanisms, motivation, and learning" (p. 139).

It has also been argued that psychology is concerned with the discovery of general principles of behavior, and that such principles, when established for even relatively simple organisms like the white rat, may be extrapolated with a high degree of probability to human behavior, including social behavior as well. This approach has been developed particularly by Skinner (5) and by Keller and Schoenfeld (6).

Finally it may be urged that animal social psychology is of interest for its own sake, just as is animal psychology in general, and not merely for the comparisons which it makes possible.

It has also been pointed out, however, that in certain fundamental respects the behavior of animals and of men is so different that any inference from one to the other is always dangerous and may frequently be misleading. If it is true that animal behavior is primarily determined by physiology and biology, and human behavior by social and cultural factors, the extrapolation to which reference was made above cannot be scientifically justified; Schneirla (7), for example, regards the differences between animal and human social behavior as so vast that a new set of concepts is required when we move from one to the other. In connection with learning theory Gibson (8) points out that what has been discovered through research with animals fails to take into consideration what is specifically social in human behavior.

We shall return to this problem later. As a first step, it should be helpful to have before us a brief survey of some of the more important findings in the field of animal social psychology. It would be an artificial division, however, to separate the animal material completely from the human, since in so many cases both are relevant to the examination of a particular problem. As a consequence much of the data collected from observation and experiment among animals will be included in later chapters whenever pertinent.

GROUP BEHAVIOR

If we adhere strictly to our definition of social psychology as dealing with the influence of others on the behavior of the individual, we find the rudiments of a social psychology among the very simplest biological forms. It may seem farfetched to speak of a social psychology of plants, yet Clements (9) states that the first definite families are found among the unicellular algae, arising as the result of multiplication by fission, accompanied by sufficient pressure to prevent separation, or by the production of a mucilage that serves a similar purpose. Such families may be temporary, but while they last there is among them something approaching a division of labor, with special cells developing for the tasks of dividing the thread, of apical growth, and of spore production. There is even among plants a rudimentary parental care in some cases, as may be seen in juvenile families enclosed within the adult *volvox* and in many other species in which the young remain attached to the parents until they are able to support themselves. Among bacteria also (10) may be seen some of the simplest examples of living things working together to their mutual advantage, as well as all grades of parasitism and antagonism.

These examples are of course "social psychological" only in a very broad sense. When we turn, however, to relatively simple biological forms like the insects, we find social phenomena of the greatest intricacy and complexity. Wheeler (11) expresses the opinion that human and insect societies are so similar that it is difficult to detect really fundamental differences between them. Warden (12), on the other hand, believes that the differences are so great that the similarities appear altogether trivial and superficial. Whether they are similar to human societies or not, however, the study of insect societies is of particular interest. Ants, for example, show very definite lines of demarcation between the in-group and the out-group, the distinction apparently being due to scent, since ants of the same species will devour each other if some have been bathed in the juices extracted from an enemy group. Ants also have many "guests" in their territory. These are usually plant lice or aphids, which supply their hosts with a sweet excretion in exchange for care and food; this excretion is exuded in drops at a signal from the "host," and immediately imbibed. The "guests" are carefully guarded and reared in large numbers.

Even below the level of the social insects, group behavior of a highly integrated type may be observed. The degree of integration within a group varies widely, and its beginnings may be difficult to perceive. It is shown most clearly when the individuals composing the group give reactions over and above those which they would give as individuals. As Allee (13) points out, some of the most primitive integrations are shown in the modification of the timing of individual behavior to give rise to group synchronization. This is observed in the synchronist flashing of fireflies as well as in the singing of tree crickets.

At a higher level social behavior may be seen in the life of birds. The migration of birds in groups is difficult to explain, but represents a highly integrated pattern of group activity. The intricate courtship and mating activities of birds, as well as the frequent occurrence of family relationships among them, are further evidence of the importance of social life. Reports from zoological gardens also describe behavior in birds which is strikingly similar to what we regard as nostalgia or homesickness in ourselves (14).

In the case of the great apes, there appears to be wide variation in the amount of social behavior. The gibbons are said to be gregarious and to move about treetops in groups. The orang-utan, on the other hand, is not very sociable, and males apparently keep away from the females except in the mating season. The gorilla is found in groups which are said to consist of a single adult male with one or more females and their offspring; other observers insist that bands numbering as many as thirty individuals and including several adult males may be found together.

The social behavior of the chimpanzee has been described in considerable detail, and it has been pointed out (*14*) that social dependence is a fundamentally important fact in chimpanzee existence. From birth through infancy and into early childhood it may or actually does powerfully direct development and expression. Enforced separation from customary companions may bring about marked physiological reactions comparable to loneliness or homesickness in man. This condition may even lead to a disturbance in the processes of digestion, and in extreme cases not relieved by restoration to companionship, serious illness or even death may result. Köhler (*15*) states that a chimpanzee kept in solitude is not a real chimpanzee at all. When taken from the group the smaller animals are terribly frightened and the larger ones cry and scream in rage. When an animal is returned to the group, the other members rejoice; they put their arms around him and greet him with enthusiasm.

One important form of social relationship found in chimpanzees as well as in other animals is the habit of grooming. It has been urged that grooming in the chimpanzee is a form of social service accompanied by strong feelings and a definitely altruistic quality. This service may be eagerly and persistently solicited. The social relation which it establishes favors the development of disinterestedness, friendliness and confidence; among captive chimpanzees it is a favorite and engrossing occupation. "It is our opinion that no pattern of social behavior which involves the cooperation of at least two individuals is at all comparable with it in social significance" (*14*, p. 1027).

Tinklepaugh (*16*) lists the factors which he regards as important in determining social relationships. There is in the first place the physical environment; for example, protozoa with negative phototropism will respond similarly to the presence of light and will therefore be found in groups wherever there are shadows. Climatic factors will bring about the common behavior of migration or hibernation in many species. In the second place, social behavior may be determined by structure. The complex social organization of the ants, for instance, is to be understood in the light of their morphology; the anatomical differences between the egg-laying queens, the males, and the sterile females or workers determine the pattern of social relationships. Thirdly, physiological factors may be important, as in the courtship and mating relationships determined by the mutual attractiveness of the sexes. Finally, there may be psychological factors, particularly of an emotional type. One sheep in a herd may become startled and throw all the others into a panic.

THE IN-GROUP AND THE OUT-GROUP

The phenomenon of friendliness within the group and hostility against those outside it has been described for many species of animals. It has already been referred to in the case of ant societies in which lines of demarcation seem to be due to differences in odor. Among birds it has been noted (17) that there is almost invariably fighting against a newcomer. As among human beings, this common attack upon the stranger may obliterate hostilities within the group and at least temporarily unite all its members. The in-group phenomenon has been noted among chimpanzees who immediately attacked a newcomer introduced among them (15). Little by little, however, they tolerated her and finally became friendly.

Harlow (4) has observed groups of monkeys in adjacent cages. He states: "No matter how much quarreling there is within cages, all members of a cage group put up a common front when threatened by the foreigners in the next cage. When the common enemy threatens, a 'cage consciousness' quickly develops. . . . This 'cage consciousness' is an obviously learned process, and its study under experimental conditions should provide information concerning the forces operating in the formation and maintenance of basic primate social groups" (p. 130).

This hostility against the stranger has sometimes been regarded as evidence for the biological nature of the "consciousness of kind" (18), or the "ethnocentrism" or "dislike of the unlike" (19), which is alleged to exist among human beings. It is important to note, therefore, that the in-group among animals is not necessarily made up of members of the same species. It has been pointed out that in a great many instances a herd may be composed of very heterogeneous elements. Wild zebras may follow domestic horses and graze among them, or they may accompany various species of gazelles and ostriches. Wild buffaloes may be found with elephants, and horses with antelopes of different types. If there is an "urge to company" among animals it is not necessarily for company of their own biological kind. Alverdes (20) cites the case of a young captive rhinoceros which was apparently much comforted by being given a grown-up goat as a companion; the two animals soon were such good friends that the goat frequently rested on the rhinocerous. It would seem that familiarity rather than "consciousness of kind" is the basis for the in-group relationship.

Alverdes further illustrates this artificial determination of the in-group in connection with sexual behavior. A young donkey brought up with mares will later mate only with mares, and not with donkeys. Whitman (21) has shown that a male passenger-pigeon reared by ring-doves will always be ready to mate with ring-doves and not with other passenger-pigeons. In these cases also, familiarity rather than biological similarity determines the pattern of social relationships.

LEADERSHIP AND DOMINANCE

The phenomenon of leadership has been observed among a large variety of animal species. Anecdotal material is rich in examples of the manner in which two members of a mammalian herd may fight for dominance, the victor usually being accepted as the leader of the whole group. In the case of gorilla societies, the leader is almost invariably the adult male who is followed by a number of females with their immature offspring, and in this case the sexual relationship is undoubtedly the most important factor determining dominance. This is, however, not necessarily the case in other groups, and the pattern of following a leader is widespread altogether apart from the sexual factor.

The question of dominance has been studied most carefully in the case of birds, among which Schjelderup-Ebbe (17) noted a definite order of precedence or social distinction. Between any two birds of each species in a large number of different species examined, one individual invariably had precedence over the other, which was thus forced into a subordinate position. "A generalization may be made from the observation of these various species to the effect that there are no two individual birds of any given species which, when living together, do not know which of the two has precedence and which is subordinate" (p. 949). Both birds display characteristic reactions. The subordinate one shows apprehension, fear, and occasionally even terror of the other. There is also a pattern of avoidance and a distinctive variety of vocalization. The despot, on the other hand, may completely ignore the other's existence, but more frequently will peck at him and drive him away. The order of despotism is decided at the first meeting, and revolts rarely occur.

Strength is an important factor in the hierarchy, but it is by no means the only one operative. This is demonstrated by the curious fact that the pecking may be of a triangular variety, that is to say, bird A will peck B, B will peck C, and C in turn will peck A. There is evidently, as among human beings, a specific personality relationship which makes an individual act differently in different company.

Dominance is not primarily a matter of sex. In some species of birds, for example the silver pheasant and the turkey, it is the male which is the despot over the female, whereas in many sparrow species it is the female which is dominant. Among certain birds, for example the half-wild mallards of Sweden, the remarkable circumstance is found that the female has the upper hand at one time of the year, and the male at another.

Older birds are usually dominant over younger, and this despotism may continue even after the older ones have lost their strength. The wrath of the old birds gives them so martial and so uninviting an appearance that this acts as a substitute for their former strength. Force of habit also appears to keep the young in a subordinate position. "We can in this connection not help thinking of how many analogies there are between the position of the old human in social life and that of the old among birds" (17, p. 961). This whole question has been subjected to careful analysis by Murchison (22) in a series of experimental investigations upon domestic fowl. By varying the conditions in a number of ways, Murchison was able to determine with greater precision the factors creating dominant and subordinate behavior.

In an interesting series of studies Maslow (23) has described the patterns of dominant and submissive behavior among baboons. In their case also, two animals placed together will quickly determine which one is to be the despot. The relationship shows itself not only in the harsh physical punishment often meted out to the subordinate, but also in the despot's tendency to take the greater share of the food placed in the cage and in the supplicant behavior of the subordinate animal. One of the most important of Maslow's observations shows the manner in which dominant behavior may be altered by the social situation. He tells of the case of one animal,

A, who was dominant over animals *B* and *C.* Once when all three animals were placed in the same cage, *B* and *C* joined forces and gave *A* a severe pummeling. Ever after, *A* was subordinate to the others even when alone with either one of them. Personality characteristics of this type seem therefore to be determined not merely by the nature of the individual, but by the whole social situation.

Among chimpanzees also it is a matter of common observation that every group of captives more or less promptly and definitely displays the principle of dominance. Yerkes and Yerkes (*14*) mention age, sex, vigor, alertness, resourcefulness, and temperamental characteristics as determiners of this relationship. It is not merely a matter of leadership of one individual over the group, but a system of relationships extending to all individuals and constituting an order or hierarchy.

Yerkes (*24*) has shown how the patterns of dominance and submission may be influenced by the sex relation; when female chimpanzees are in heat they exercise definite dominance over the males, although under other conditions the reverse holds true. This may perhaps best be explained as a voluntary submission on the part of the males in order to obtain the desired cooperation of the females. Just as dominance in most instances fulfills the purpose of giving the animal certain privileges—for example, access to food—so in this specific case it is submission which is more effective in reaching the goal, that is, access to the female. Dominance and submission may thus both be regarded as means to an end. In this connection Carpenter (*3*) has demonstrated the striking fact that rhesus monkeys show a strongly developed dominance hierarchy and at the same time the phenomenon of the exclusive possession of females by certain males; among howling monkeys, on the other hand, generalized relations between the sexes are much more prevalent and differences in dominance are found to be small.

Another type of "leadership" phenomenon has been demonstrated by Mowrer (*25*) in a learning experiment which involved three rats placed in a cage so constructed that if a bar were pressed at one end of the cage food appeared at the other end. Under these circumstances, when one animal pressed the bar, the other animals obtained the food. This situation reduced bar-pressing to a minimum, and the impasse continued until one animal solved the problem by pressing the bar with such vigor and frequency that enough food was released for all three animals. This division of labor continued for a considerable period of time. Here again we see among animals a complex pattern of interpersonal relations which, superficially at least, is not unlike that frequently found among human beings.

THE INDIVIDUAL IN THE GROUP SITUATION

In a later chapter we shall have occasion to summarize the experimental material bearing upon the manner in which the behavior of one human being is modified by the presence of others. It may be of interest here to note that in the case of a number of animal species, comparable modifications have been described. Katz (26) has shown, for example, that when a domestic hen has eaten her fill of seed, she may start to eat all over again when another hungrier animal begins to eat in her vicinity. A chimpanzee which has refused to eat cellulose may accept a piece after he has seen the experimenter eat it (14).

In experiments on conditioning, the effect of the group situation seems to vary from species to species and from one situation to another. A cockroach when isolated may be conditioned with less time and fewer errors per trial than when the same cockroach is a member of a pair or of a group of three. In the paired and group condition activity is reduced and the number of errors per trial is increased (27). There is a similar group retarding of conditioning when mud-minnows are trained to jump out of the water if a red light is turned on and to seize a bit of earthworm loosely impaled on a wire. In this case there was apparently a direct interference in motor activity, since it often happened that as one fish would assume a jumping attitude, another would attack it with a vigorous jab (28). On the other hand, common goldfish become conditioned more rapidly to run simple mazes in the group situation than when alone. The larger the group, the quicker the conditioning. This appears to be due in part to group cohesion, as well as to interstimulation or the quieting effect of the presence of others.

Allee (13) concludes from this material that the only safe generalization to be drawn is that the nature of the group effect, even in fish, depends in part on the problem set and in part on the experimental conditions. He believes that when research in this field will have been completed, a similar relation may be found to hold with regard to the effect of group size upon the rate of learning in man.

In his opinion animal and human social psychology are intimately related and exhibit the same fundamental tendencies.

ANIMAL "CULTURE"

There is a difference of opinion as to whether animals may be regarded as possessing culture, or whether culture is rather to be thought of as an exclusively human product. This question has considerable significance in connection with the possibility of using animal psychology in order to determine the relative importance of hereditary and cultural factors in human behavior. It has frequently been suggested that if any activity is found both in human beings and the higher apes, this activity must be due mainly to biological causes, without any appreciable cultural influence. For example, F. H. Allport (29) writes:

> In order to discover what part human beings really do play in forming and using their culture pattern, we must discover what the behavior of human beings might be if divested of all culture. We cannot learn this directly because there are no human tribes without a culture of some sort. Recourse must therefore be had to a comparative study using as control groups the lower animals, particularly those most closely related to man (p. 459).

Although not explicitly stated, the underlying assumption in Allport's position is that animals have no culture. This point of view is expressed more directly by Warden (12) in a book dealing with the "emergence" of human culture. Warden proposes a threefold criterion of culture—invention, communication, social habitation. That is to say, culture involves some new form of behavior which is communicated to other members of the species so that it becomes a habit common to a large number of them. This is not found in his opinion among any animals below man. What seems like culture among them is "biosocial" in character. determined phylogenetically or by heredity, whereas culture in man is ontogenetic, developing during the lifetime of individuals as the result of social factors. Although it is true that domestic animals display marked social traits and a high intelligence in submitting to man's cultural regime, they are unable, says Warden, to take over human cultural traits and impress them upon their progeny by social habituation. They are the wards of human culture and would revert to the wild state if man cast them off.

Kroeber (30) expresses similarly the opinion that not even the beginnings of culture are found in existing anthropoid apes. Boas (31), on the other hand, believes that phenomena analogous to those of human culture occur in animal society. He regards culture as embracing "all the manifestations of social habits of a community, the reactions of the individual as affected by the habits of the group in which he lives, and the products of human activities as determined by these habits" (p. 79). In spite of the inclusion of the word "human" in this statement, Boas states that the nature of animal social behavior is such that "there is no absolute gap between many of the aspects of human culture and the life habits of animals" (p. 79).

The decision in this question may turn out to be a matter of terminology, but the more reasonable position appears to be one which finds the same continuity in animal and human social behavior as has been demonstrated in animal and human morphology. There is evidence that in many cases a new pattern of animal behavior is established in a manner which is in some ways parallel to social change among human beings. Such an instance has been reported in the case of African lions, though the relevant evidence is somewhat anecdotal in character. All African lions belong to a single species, and throughout most of Africa they hunt alone or at most in pairs accompanied by their partly grown offspring. In Kenya, however, they have taken to hunting in packs with a regular division of function. The pack spreads out in a surround and closes in, roaring, thus driving the game within the circle to a point where one lion lies quietly in ambush. "Old hunters say that this is a recent development and that, within the memory of persons still living, the Kenya lions hunted in the ordinary way" (32, p. 78). Why the change occurred is not entirely clear, but the fact that it did occur is significant.

A similar modifiability of group behavior has been noted in the case of beavers, apparently in response to the nature of their environment. It is stated that the few beavers still found in Europe usually live in couples, but beavers in rather quiet countries, for instance in Canada, may live in small or large groups. In thickly populated countries they usually live in simple underground tunnels, but in sparsely settled regions they frequently build houses (20).

The evidence in the case of bird society is perhaps the most striking. In the classical experiment by Scott (33), very young orioles were separated from the parents and were given no opportunity to learn the usual oriole song from them. The result was that they developed a song of their own, what Scott calls "a new school of oriole music." When other young orioles were placed among these, they too learned this new song. It is true that in this case there has been some human interference, but the results do indicate the possibility of invention, communication and social habituation, and therefore satisfy Warden's criteria. The equally important experiment by Conradi (34) showed that when sparrows are placed among canaries they imitate the canary song, and in spite of their vocal limitations there is an unmistakable resemblance. It is of course well known that canaries, nightingales and other birds all improve their song when in the presence of a good "teacher," and that such teachers are kept by bird fanciers for this very purpose. It seems a reasonable conclusion that the song of birds has ontogenetic as well as phylogenetic elements, or in other words that learning and "culture" do play at least a modest part.

The statement that domestic animals are unable to impress human cultural traits upon their progeny cannot be accepted without some question. Unfortunately we have here only anecdotal material, but it has frequently been pointed out by those who have had experience with domestic animals that the mother does "train" the young to observe certain of the rules which have been imposed upon her. Apart from such human rules of behavior, there are many ways in which animal mothers of various species train their young. The bird mother teaches her offspring to fly, and in the case of the eagle the training period may be long and arduous. Both the orang and the chimpanzee mothers have been observed teaching their offspring to walk.

Yerkes and Yerkes (14), in referring to this and similar material, insist that to "refrain from the use of such terms as educate, teach, train, merely because the subject is infrahuman would seem indefensible, since as a fact the chimpanzee mother, apparently with definite intent, encourages and in many ways aids her infant to achieve locomotor independence, to walk, climb, and eventually to run about and play in a variety of ways and freely" (p. 1013). Systematic exercise of the infant by the mother may appear during the first year of its life, continue for a time and then disappear. The youngster may be restrained from doing certain things until he has reached a definite stage of development, and then he is encouraged and aided to do them. These writers conclude that if we are unwilling to attribute the beginnings of culture to the anthropoid apes, we must at least admit that tradition and experience function in the social life of the chimpanzee as do cultural accumulations in man.

It was stated above that this problem may depend upon the definition of culture. Even if we accept Warden's criteria, there can be no doubt that the phenomena of invention and social habituation are certainly found in animal societies. There may be some argument, however, about the fact of communication. Is it communication when a sparrow learns a song from a canary? Or does communication depend upon the existence of a language? At this point it may be of interest to examine the whole question of the language of animals.

COMMUNICATION AMONG ANIMALS

It is helpful in connection with the following discussion to make a distinction between "active" and "passive" language. By the latter, we mean the ability of an animal to respond with appropriate behavior to sounds, including those made by a human being. We know that a dog, for example, may quite easily be trained to carry out orders of various kinds and to distinguish clearly between some of the auditory impressions he receives from the human voice. In the case of the young chimpanzee studied by the Kelloggs (35) this passive language reached a high degree of complexity, and the investigators give an impressive list of the words and phrases which the chimpanzee "understood." By "active" language we refer rather to the sounds made by the animals themselves as a means of communication or of control of the action of other animals. This presents a more serious problem, and it is important to understand its extent and its limitations.

Alverdes (20) points out that animals frequently produce sounds in common; these may be regarded as due to imitation, to rivalry in the case of males, or to the expression of greeting. When two or more animals meet, it is by no means rare for them to make some sound. When a lion roars, others nearby usually join at once in the roaring. One donkey may cause all the donkeys in the neighborhood to bray. Two bats may call to each other in passing.

Sounds of this type may have no "meaning," that is to say, they may not partake of the nature of language as we understand it. There is, however, a large group of vocal expressions which may in certain situations serve to elicit characteristic responses in other animals. These have been called "signalling reflexes" (36). It must be noted that the effect of such cries is due only in part to the cry itself; the total context is also important. This is true of human language also, but not to the same extent as in the case of animal cries. Their biological significance lies in the fact that they make possible the coordination of activities of two or more individuals. As the result of the cry, stimuli acting on one individual may indirectly act on others, so that the sense organs and motor organs of one individual are placed at the disposal of other members of the group. Esper (37) describes four main type-responses in this connection. (1) The Flight Response—certain sights and smells may cause flight plus a cry; other animals respond to the cry with flight. The striking phenomenon of "sentinels" is an example of this form of behavior and makes it possible for a large number of animals to be calmly feeding while one of their number stands on guard. (2) Feeding Behavior—the cry on finding food or prey brings other animals to the scene. (3) Sex Behavior—the cries of one animal prepare another for sex responses and coordinate such behavior. (4) Aggressive Behavior—the cries may be preliminary to or substitutes for combat.

In the case of the infrahuman primates, there are several careful studies of the most important types of vocalization. Carpenter (38) was able to distinguish a large variety of separate sounds in the "vocabulary" of the howling monkey. (1) The males give a low-pitched and sonorous barking roar, and the females a terrier-like bark in response to disturbing stimuli. (2) In connection with group progression, the leading male may produce at regular intervals a deep metallic cluck. (3) When slightly disturbed or apprehensive, the animal may give a series of gurgling grunts or crackling sounds which prepare the group for defensive behavior. (4) If the offspring falls to the ground, the mother may produce a wail ending in a grunt or groan. (5) A youngster out of its mother's reach may utter a series of cries, usually consisting of three notes. (6) A young infant may emit a prolonged purr which influences the mother-young relation. (7) In play, the young howling monkeys utter low chirping squeals. (8) When the youngsters play at fighting, an old male may make a grunting sound of reprimand or warning. (9) When confronted by a strange situation, the males grunt who! who! who!

Baboons (39) make a low chattering sound as part of their friendly advances. In sex activity as well as in all states of well-being there is a series of deep grunts; in case of danger the young animals and the female give a high-pitched screech, and the adult male makes a similar sound in anger. After the death of a baby its mother was heard making a series of deep barking sounds.

For the chimpanzees, Nissen (40), who made a careful study of them in French Guinea, describes (1) an excitement or panting cry, (2) a fear-pain cry—a high-pitched scream, (3) a loud barking cry —anger, defiance or exasperation, (4) a whimper or a whining cry —disappointment or frustration, (5) food muttering—a low soft bark expressive of satisfaction. There is also much noise-making by "drumming" on hollow logs or trees, but Nissen was not able to discover its precise significance.

In connection with his investigations of various species of monkeys, Harlow (4) writes: "Casual observations in our own laboratory have indicated a very considerable ability of cage-mates to communicate with each other. Thus, calls of one member of a pair restrained in the living quarters will cause an animal in a test-room to cease work even though these sounds are only faintly audible to the human tester. . . . Equally striking results have been observed in the response to vocalizations of separated mothers and infants. It is more than possible that primates make far more use of vocalizations in the wild than is commonly recognized . . ." (p. 135).

These studies show that animals below man can and do make a number of distinct sounds in a variety of situations. It may be added that at least as far as chimpanzees are concerned, there are so many phonetic elements in their vocal expression that any limitations to their articulate speech cannot be ascribed to deficiencies in the glossolabial apparatus. That is to say, there is nothing in their vocal cords, the mouth, the larynx, etc., to prevent their using language as human beings do; if there is a deficiency it appears to be somewhere in the higher nervous centers. Even this deficiency, however, is apparently not complete. A report of an investigation in progress at the Yerkes Laboratory of Primate Psychology on a young chimpanzee, "Viki," indicated that this animal had been taught to use actively three simple English words, though the meanings associated with them were not always precise [Hayes and Hayes (*41*)]. The main difference between human language and that of all other animals seems to lie in the fact that the language of animals can express only what is present at the time; it occurs mainly in response to an emotional situation; it may on occasions indicate desires or types of object or action (*14*). As far as we can tell, however, it can have no abstract or symbolic meaning, nor can it to any extent describe what has happened in the past or what is to happen in the future.

It must be admitted that this last conclusion is difficult to document with complete certainty. How can we be sure that the apparently aimless chattering of a group of chimpanzees is not really an argument about what one of them claims he saw the day before yesterday, or even a discussion of the nature of the universe? At least we can say that on the basis of what we have learned about animal communication it is much more probable that all the sounds made by animals are indeed restricted to the *here* and *now*.

In this connection, Esper (*37*) concludes that the deficiency in animal language imposes two limitations of the utmost importance. In the first place, cooperation in communal undertakings is radically limited; and in the second, social tradition, the accumulation of useful techniques and discoveries, is possible only to a slight degree. This means that in certain fundamental respects human society differs so greatly from that of all other animals that any inference from one to the other remains questionable. Comparisons between animals and men will still be important, but all conclusions will have to be tempered by the realization that although some significant similarities may be found, and animal experimentation may supply us with important principles of behavior, most of the characteristics of human society cannot be duplicated elsewhere in the animal world. The differences are not absolute; the rudiments of culture certainly have pre-human beginnings. Differences of degree, however, if they are sufficiently great, become differences of kind. The special qualities of human communication, particularly as this affects what Korzybski (*42*) calls its "time-binding" aspect, namely, the fact that each generation builds upon the accumulated traditions of the past, give to human social life its unique character.

We must urge great caution, therefore, in the application to human social behavior of the findings of research based on laboratory experimentation, or even field observations, on animals. The farther down we go in the phylogenetic scale, the more doubtful will be the inferences which we draw. Even in the case of the anthropoids, we are faced with important limitations which derive from two inter-related conditions, first, that animals have at most only the rudiments of what may be called culture, and second, that their linguistic behavior is inadequate for the forms of interaction characteristic of human societies. In conjunction with other evidence, animal material may make a significant contribution to the total sum of our knowledge; it can provide useful leads; it can help in verifying or disproving many of the hypotheses which are prevalent in psychology. The real advances, however, toward the understanding of human social behavior require the study of human beings.

SUMMARY

Social interaction of varying degrees of complexity is found among the simplest as well as the more advanced biological species. Although the most striking phenomena occur among the social insects, many other animal forms also illustrate the dependence of individual behavior on the group situation. Among the conditions determining social relationships are the physical environment, the morphological structure of the individual, physiological and psychological factors. In-groups are formed, but these may consist of members of different species. Within any one group, particularly among the vertebrates, the individuals frequently arrange themselves in a hierarchy with well-defined patterns of dominance and submission. These and allied phenomena indicate some of the close parallels to be found between human and animal social groups.

There is no sharp dividing line between the social behavior of animals and the culture of human societies. The suggested criteria of culture—invention, communication and social habituation—are satisfied in rudimentary form by the observed changes in the song of birds, as well as in the behavior of lions, beavers and other species. Special studies have been made of communication among infrahuman primates, and these have shown that baboons, howling monkeys and chimpanzees make a number of distinguishable sounds in a variety of different situations. It seems certain, however, that animal language occurs mainly if not exclusively in response to stimuli in the external or internal environment, and that it does not refer to the past or the future. The superiority of human language in this respect creates the possibility of a definite accumulation of social traditions, and is responsible for the most important differences between animal and human societies.

REFERENCES

1. Murchison, C., ed. *A Handbook of Social Psychology.* 1935

2. Ford, C. S., and Beach, F. A. *Patterns of Sexual Behavior.* 1951

3. Carpenter, C. R. "Characteristics of Social Behavior in Non-human Primates." *Trans. N. Y. Acad. Sci.* 1942, 4, Ser. II: pp. 248-258

4. Harlow, H. F. "Levels of Integration Along the Phylogenetic Scale." In Rohrer, J. H., and Sherif, M., eds. *Social Psychology at the Crossroads.* 1951

5. Skinner, B. F. *Science and Human Behavior.* 1953

6. Keller, F. S., and Schoenfeld, W. N. *Principles of Psychology.* 1950

7. Schneirla, T. C. "The 'Levels' Concept in the Study of Social Organization in Animals." In Rohrer, J. H., and Sherif, M., eds. *Social Psychology at the Crossroads.* 1951

8. Gibson, J. J. "The Implications of Learning Theory for Social Psychology." In Miller, J. G., ed. *Experiments in Social Process.* 1950

9. Clements, F. E. "Social Origins and Processes among Plants." In Murchison, C., ed. *Hdbk. Soc. Psychol.* 1935

10. Buchanan, R. E. "Population Behavior of Bacteria." In Murchison, C., ed. *Hdbk. Soc. Psychol.* 1935

11. Wheeler, W. M. *Social Life Among the Insects.* 1923

12. Warden, C. J. *The Emergence of Human Culture.* 1936

13. Allee, W. C. "Relatively Simple Animal Aggregations." In Murchison, C., ed. *Hdbk. Soc. Psychol.* 1935

14. Yerkes, R. M., and Yerkes, A. W. "Social Behavior in Infrahuman Primates." In Murchison, C., ed. *Hdbk. Soc. Psychol.* 1935

15. Köhler, W. *The Mentality of Apes.* 1925

16. Tinklepaugh, O. L. "Social Psychology of Animals." In Moss, F. A., ed. *Comparative Psychology.* 1934

17. Schjelderup-Ebbe, T. "Social Life of Birds." In Murchison, C., ed. *Hdbk. Soc. Psychol.* 1935

18. Giddings, F. H. *The Principles of Sociology.* 1896

19. Sumner, W. G. *Folkways.* 1906

20. Alverdes, F. "The Behavior of Mammalian Herds and Packs." In Murchison, C., ed. *Hdbk. Soc. Psychol.* 1935

21. Whitman, C. "The Behavior of Pigeons," *Carnegie Inst. Publ.,* 1919, No. 257

22. Murchison, C. "The Experimental Measurement of a Social Hierarchy in *Gallus domesticus,*" *J. Gen. Psychol.,* 1935, 12: pp. 3-39; *J. Soc. Psychol.,* 1935, 6: pp. 3-30; *J. Genet. Psychol.,* 1935, 46: pp. 76-102

23. Maslow, A. H. "The Role of Dominance in the Social and Sexual Behavior of Infra-Human Primates," *J. Genet. Psychol.*, 1936, 48: pp. 261-277

24. Yerkes, R. M. "Social Dominance and Sexual Status in the Chimpanzee," *Quart. Rev. Biol.*, 1939, 14: pp. 115-136

25. Mowrer, O. H. "Animal Studies in the Genesis of Personality," *Trans. N. Y. Acad. Sci.*, 1940, 3: pp. 8-11

26. Katz, D. *Hunger und Appetit.* 1932

27. Gates, M. F., and Allee, W. C. "Conditioned Behavior of Isolated and Grouped Cockroaches on a Simple Maze," *J. Comp. Psychol.*, 1933, 13: pp. 331-358

28. Welty, J. C. "Experimental Explorations into Group Behavior of Fishes," *Physiol. Zool.*, 1934, 7: pp. 85-128

29. Allport, F. H. "Introduction: The Hanover Round Table—Social Psychology of 1936," *Soc. Forces*, 1937, 15: pp. 455-462

30. Kroeber, A. L. "The Superorganic," *Amer. Anthrop.* N.S., 1917, 19: pp. 163-213

31. Boas, F. "Anthropology." *Encycl. Soc. Sci.*, 1930, 2: pp. 73-110

32. Linton, R. *The Study of Man.* 1936

33. Scott, W. E. D. "Data on Song in Birds," *Science.* N.S., 1901, 14: pp. 522-526

34. Conradi, E. "Song and Call-Notes of English Sparrows When Reared by Canaries," *Amer. J. Psychol.*, 1905, 16: pp. 190-199

35. Kellogg, W. N., and Kellogg, L. A. *The Ape and the Child.* 1933

36. Meyer, M. F. *Psychology of the Other-One.* 1922

37. Esper, E. A. "Language." In Murchison, C., ed. *Hdbk. Soc. Psychol.* 1935

38. Carpenter, C. R. "A Field Study of the Behavior and Social Relations of Howling Monkeys," *Comp. Psychol. Monog.*, No. 10, 1934

39. Zuckerman, S. *The Social Life of Monkeys and Apes.* 1932

40. Nissen, H. W. "A Field Study of the Chimpanzee," *Comp. Psychol. Monog.*, No. 8, 1931

41. Hayes, K. J., and Hayes, C. "Vocalization and Speech in Chimpanzees." Cited by H. F. Harlow in Rohrer, J. H., and Sherif, M., eds. *Social Psychology at the Crossroads.* 1951

42. Korzybski, A. *Science and Sanity.* Rev. ed. 1941

Language

3

INTRODUCTION

The field of language has long intrigued scholars from many different disciplines; its specifically psychological components have not, however, at least in the opinion of the present writer, received the attention which they deserve. Some valuable psychological research has indeed been conducted, but there remain many aspects of linguistic behavior which are still imperfectly understood. This chapter is therefore not to be regarded as in any sense definitive. It raises a number of problems in connection with which the available data are inadequate. In many instances conclusions must remain tentative and questions are asked to which no definite answers can be given. At the same time the problem of human communication is so important, and enters into so much of the material to be considered in later chapters, that at least some attempt must be made at an introduction to the subject.

Nothing can be said with certainty about the origin of human language. As we have seen in the last chapter, there is reason to believe that the beginnings of language are pre-human, and that some at least of its important aspects find their counterparts in the communicative behavior of animals. There are several theories, however, as to how human speech originated.

One of the best known of these is the onomatopoeic theory, usually attributed to the German philosopher Herder. According to this theory, words arose in imitation of natural sounds. So, to use familiar English examples, we speak of the "hiss" of a snake or of escaping steam, the "twitter" of birds, the "rustling" leaves, "whirring" wings and the sound of a "gong." It is suggested that out of these beginnings a language might very well have arisen. Boas (1) points out in this connection that in some languages, for example Chinook (American Indian) and many Bantu (South African) dialects, the formation of new words by sound imitation is a very live process.

In criticism of this theory, however, it has been urged in the first place that only a small proportion of the words in any known language appear to have an onomatopoeic derivation, and secondly that this theory does not account for the symbolic or abstract quality which is characteristic of human speech.

Similar criticisms may be leveled against the interjectional theory. It is true that there are certain sounds and words in our language which have an interjectional quality; we say "oh" and "ah" and "whew," but it is difficult to see in these examples a general basis for language. On the other hand, it seems reasonable to regard the vocalization of animals as having at least in part an interjectional quality, and as predisposing to similar linguistic activity among human beings.

A third theory suggests that man possesses a faculty which makes it possible for every impression from without to receive its vocal expression within the body by a kind of predetermined resonance. This has been called the "natural ringing" theory. It was first proposed by the philologist Max Müller but was later abandoned by him and has today very little scientific support.

John Dewey (2), commenting on these theories, expresses the opinion that they are not true theories of language, but mere "accounts, of some plausibility, of how and why certain sounds rather than others were selected to signify objects, acts, and situations." In other words, they may explain the nature of the sounds used, but not the reason why sounds were used in the first place, nor the manner in which they attained any symbolic significance.

Another theory of a somewhat different type is that the first language was a language of gestures, which gradually gave way to vocal speech. Paget (3) suggests that there were probably fully developed gesture languages which served as the first means of communication. He points to the sign language of the American Indians, of the Cistercian monks and of deaf-mutes as examples of the extent to which communication may be carried on by gesture alone. His theory is that after the gestures were developed, occasions would arise when men were busy working with their hands, and yet wished to communicate with their fellows; they would then make the great discovery that this could be done by means of the voice. The many advantages of vocal communication would soon become apparent and gradually supersede pantomime or gesture. The fact that gestures are obviously useless in the dark, for example, would impose an immediate limitation upon their use.

There is of course no doubt that gestures may be used effectively as a means of communication. One of the best known of all sign languages, that which developed among the American Indians of the Plains, served as a sort of international language common to a large number of American Indian tribes, whose spoken languages were mutually unintelligible. The sign language was valuable in all intertribal contacts, especially in commerce. It probably served as an important agent in the process of culture contact and the transmission of culture traits from one tribe to another. To the White man in his first dealings with the Indians of the Plains it proved particularly valuable, since it made it possible for him to learn one language which would serve over a wide area. It is important to note that this language, in spite of its pantomimic character, was not restricted to the expression of concrete situations, but by means of metaphors was able to convey abstract ideas as well. Thus a gesture signifying that the sun was in the heart was a symbol of happiness. There is no indication, however, that this gesture language antedates the spoken languages of the Plains. It is not possible to use its occurrence as evidence for the priority of gesture language, since there are so few parts of the world in which such a language appears, even in legend. There is, however, one argument in favor of Paget's theory, namely, that the expression of meaning through gesture is much more direct than through voice and may very often be understood even when we have had no previous experience with these particular gestures. It is possible, for example, because of its pantomimic character to understand something of the Indian sign language, though by no means all, the first time it is seen. On the other hand, perhaps the strongest argument against the theory is that animals below man make some use of vocal expression for communication.

This last point requires some qualification. In social insects communication results mainly from a direct transmission of excitement from individual to individual through tactual encounters by means of the antennae [Schneirla (4)]. Among animals more closely related to man, it is recorded that mature chimpanzees are able to use gestures such as shoulder tapping as a means of influencing the behavior of other chimpanzees in cooperative activities [Crawford (5)]. These examples indicate that gesture language may also have its pre-human beginnings, although in the cases reported it is gesture through direct contact, rather than as perceived visually, which apparently makes communication possible.

That the interest in the origin of language is by no means a recent one is shown by a report of the Greek historian Herodotus (6). He tells of an Egyptian king Psammetichus who was interested in discovering whether Egyptian was really the first language of mankind. He therefore had two young children put by themselves on an island before they had a chance to learn to speak, and had them cared for by a deaf-mute. After the passage of some years they were visited, and they ran up to the newcomers shouting the word "becos." Unfortunately the Egyptian scholars could not find that word in their language. They did, however, discover that this sound means "bread" in the Phrygian language, so they reluctantly decided that this must be the oldest language, and Egyptian the second. It is reported that a similar experiment was tried by the Mogul emperor Akbar in order to determine the first religion of mankind, but the children isolated by him had no speech at all when they were discovered.

PHONETIC SYMBOLISM

Allied to the onomatopoeic theory of the origin and nature of language is the fact that certain words appear to convey something of their meaning by the nature of their sound. This phenomenon has been called phonetic symbolism. Jespersen (7), for example, has pointed out that the vowel "i" serves very often to indicate what is small, insignificant or weak, or, on the other hand, what is refined and dainty. It is also symbolic of brief duration. Paget (3) believes that the "i" sound also indicates what is near; he cites the example of the Javanese "iki," "ika" and "iku," representing respectively three degrees of distance from the speaker.

The anthropologist Edward Sapir (8) subjected this theory to an experimental investigation. One of his studies was concerned with the contrast between the ideas "large" and "small." He presented to his subjects two monosyllables, "mal" ("a" as in German "Mann"), and "mil" ("i" as in French "fini"). He arbitrarily assigned to these two nonsense syllables the meaning of "table," but one of them was to mean a large table and the other a small one. The subjects were asked to decide which was which, and in the great majority of cases "mal" was chosen as the larger. There were seven

Chinese students among the subjects and their choice was also in the same direction. Newman (9) carried this experiment further and established a scale of size for a number of different vowel sounds. He found that "i" was the smallest, with the other vowels following in this order: "e" (as in French "été"), "ɛ" (as in English "met"), "ä" (as in English "hat"), "a" (as in German "Mann"), "u" (as in English "put"), "ɔ" (as in English "note"), and finally "o" (as in French "tôt").

Newman also conducted experiments on other types of phonetic symbolism, in connection with consonants as well as with vowel sounds. He found, for instance, that vowel sounds had a "symbolism" with reference to the opposition between bright and dark, as well as between small and large; "i" was the brightest vowel, and "u" the darkest. Among the consonants, "p" apparently was smallest and "br" the largest; "s" was the brightest and "br" the darkest.

It has been suggested that many of these results may be due not to phonetic symbolism as such, but to some sort of assimilation to the sounds of actual familiar words expressing the meaning of "large," "small," etc. For example, the French words "petit" and "grand" or the English words "little" and "large" might conceivably be responsible for the findings in the "mil, mal" experiment. Boas (1), while admitting some relation between sound and concept, regards it as by no means certain that the same impressions are conveyed by all languages through the medium of similar phonetic elements. He gives several illustrations of the manner in which size or intensity may be expressed by variations in sound.

> Thus Nez Percé, an Indian language spoken in Idaho, changes "n" to "l" to indicate smallness; Dakota has many words in which "s" changes to "sh," or "z" to "j," indicating greater intensity. . . . Undoubtedly the particular kind of synesthesia between sound, sight and touch has played its role in the growth of language (p. 132).

What is clearly needed here is a series of studies on subjects ignorant of any of the common European languages. Sapir did have a small group of Chinese subjects, but they were familiar with English; in any case a larger number of subjects would be needed. It is important to keep in mind that there are many words in English as well as in related languages which would tend to have an influence in the opposite direction—for example, "big" and "small," "infinity," and others. Newman made a careful survey of a number of English words denoting largeness and smallness, and concluded that they take practically no account of the magnitude symbolism revealed by his and Sapir's experiments. He concludes that experience with actual language probably plays little or no part in the phenomenon of phonetic symbolism. In any case the investigation should be carried further.

In explanation of these results, three possible factors have been invoked. There may be a difference in the kinesthetic sensations arising from the size of the oral cavity; in making the "i" sound the resonance chamber (the mouth, etc.) is smaller than in the case of the vowel "a." A second possibility is that the difference is acoustic, due to unequal vibration frequencies in the actual sounds. A third, which is allied to the first, is the difference in the position of the tongue in the mouth. The first of these suggestions seems by far the most reasonable. Mauthner, for instance, writes:

> If we are in a foreign country and, not knowing its language, want to express bigness, we shall open our arms wide; if the opposite, we shall press the palms of the hands together. Now suppose the whole vocal apparatus desired to share in the gesture; suppose the glottis and the mouth pressed themselves together to articulate an "i" in imitation of a small space, or opened wide into an "o" to imitate a big one (10, p. 237).

There is no doubt that the actual sensations experienced in the two cases are quite different, and they would certainly help to account for the "feeling" of size which these vowel sounds give us.

One related investigation which yielded promising results was conducted by Mosel (11), using real words from four living languages rather than manufactured "nonsense" material. The languages were Chinese, Japanese, Hungarian, and one language from West Africa; none of these were at all familiar to the college students who served as subjects. The technique consisted of presenting lists of twenty pairs of opposites in each language, followed in every case by the English equivalent, sometimes in the same order, sometimes in reverse. To take the case of Chinese as an example, the subjects were given the words "ta, hsiao: large, small"; "yuan, chin: near, far," etc., and asked to guess whether the order in English was the same as that in Chinese, or different. In the first case, the correct answer would be "same" and in the second, "different." In the absence of any knowledge of the language, the proportion of correct guesses would indicate whether or not the phenomenon of phonetic symbolism exerted any effect on the recognition of meaning. The experimenter obtained the cooperation of speakers who were completely familiar with these languages and who spoke the words from behind a screen so that their facial expression would give no clue to the correct answers. Chance expectation would of course be fifty percent correct responses; the results showed better than chance success in the case of all four languages, with the correct responses in the case of Japanese, where the results were most successful, reaching seventy-eight percent.

It is not suggested that phonetic symbolism plays any important part in the origin of language, or of the characteristics of the specific languages now in use. In all probability it does not account for the actual nature of more than a small part of our vocabulary. The fact that it occurs at all, however, does constitute an important psychological problem, and shows the possibility that sound in itself may have "meaning" apart from the conventional significance which attaches to it. In poetry this may have special importance. Coleridge spoke of the "loud bassoon," and was later criticized because actually the bassoon is not an especially loud instrument. There is, however, something about the word which suggests loudness, and which at least explains, if it does not justify, his use of this expression.

There is an allied problem which may be mentioned at this point. Languages differ very markedly in the phonetic elements out of which words are composed, although there is of course a great deal of overlapping between one language and another. When a language contains a large number of words with the same vowel or consonantal sound, it is probable that the facial expression of the speaker may to some extent be affected by this constant repetition. In other words, if the muscles of the face are used habitually in a certain manner, the consequence is that even in repose there is still sufficient contraction of these muscles to differentiate the members of one linguistic group from another. For example, as Bloomfield (12) points out, English, in contrast to French or German, retracts the jaw; German and French advance the jaw and use the muscles more vigorously—German in large sweeping movements, French in smaller and more precise ones, especially in the front of the mouth; Danish draws the muscles in toward the median line. It is obvious that such language habits would affect facial expression only after a considerable period of time, and it is therefore not likely that a person who merely learned another language in addition to his own would show any such influence. Nor is it suggested that this is the only factor which determines facial expression. It is, however, probable that when a German is recognized as different from an Englishman of the same "racial" stock, one feature which makes this recognition possible—in addition to such extraneous factors as posture, clothing, haircut, etc.—is the expression of the face due to the effect of language on facial musculature.

LANGUAGE AND THOUGHT

The problem of the exact relation between language and thought has been the subject of considerable discussion by psychologists. The behaviorist Watson (13) has even gone so far as to regard them as identical. For him thinking is merely speech which remains subvocal; it is laryngeal rather than vocal language. When we think, we really speak, though this speech cannot be heard. Watson's theory has stimulated a number of experimental studies in this field, which have demonstrated that during the process of thinking, movements do take place in the tongue, the palate, and other portions of the vocal and laryngeal apparatus. Against Watson it has been urged, however, that even though we habitually think by means of language, it is also possible to think in images and without giving expression to the thought in words; it has been pointed out also that we may be thinking of one thing while saying another, so that subvocal speech is not a prerequisite of the thought process.

Whether or not language is to be identified with thought, there can be no doubt that thinking in the large majority of cases does require the use of language, and that the nature of language has an important influence on the nature of thought. Sapir (14) points out that the forms of our language predetermine for us certain modes of observation and interpretation; we must learn in a great many cases to fight the implications of language. When we use the expression "the grass waves in the wind" or "friction slows up a moving body," we are in danger of personalizing or reifying words which have no such meaning. This process is clear also in much of the work of Piaget (15) on the relation between the language and thought of the child. Piaget finds among children a marked tendency to personalize inanimate objects, and to speak of them as if they were living things. This "animistic" tendency is regarded by him as universal among children and gradually overcome as they grow older. He himself recognizes, however, that linguistic habits are at least in part responsible. If we speak of the sun as "rising" and "setting," or ask, "What are the wild waves saying?" or refer to a ship as "she," we are clearly encouraging children in our society to give expression to this personalizing or anthropomorphic tendency. Margaret Mead (16) has suggested that the absence of this tendency among the Manus children of New Guinea may be due at least in part to the relatively more matter-of-fact language they speak. Piaget believes that the tendency would persist even if the language did not encourage it, but he admits that language does have some influence.

It is a somewhat similar linguistic tendency which led Max Müller (17) to view mythology as a "disease of language." When we speak of the sun as *trying* to break through the clouds, or the wind as *shaking* the trees, and the trees *bowing* before the wind, we fall into linguistic habits which predispose us to personify these inanimate objects. This leads directly to the development of myths and story plots concerning such "persons" and their "interpersonal relations," culminating in the complicated adventures of Phoebus Apollo, Diana, and other figures of mythology. A further contributing factor may have been the use in many languages of masculine and feminine gender to apply to inanimate objects as well as to living beings of different sex. In French, for instance, the distinction between "*le* soleil" and "*la* lune" may suggest a sexual differentiation between the sun and the moon, and prepare the way for myth-making. (Curiously enough, in German the genders are reversed; it is "*die* Sonne" and "*der* Mond.") This suggestion is not too convincing, since there is no evidence that mythology develops more easily in French or German, than, for example, in English, in which the genders apply only to pronouns which make "logical" distinctions between male and female, and animate and inanimate objects. In any case it must be remembered that there are many other proposed explanations of the origins of mythology, none of them entirely satisfactory [Benedict (17)].

Language may affect the nature of thought in many ways. It has been pointed out, for example by Trendelenberg, that Aristotle's categories and similar distinctions which play a large part in his system cannot be studied apart from the peculiarities of the Greek language. Mauthner states that Aristotle was superstitiously devoted to words. In his logic he is absolutely dependent on the accidents of his mother tongue. "If Aristotle had spoken Chinese or Dacotan, he would have had to adopt an entirely different logic, or at any rate an entirely different theory of categories" (*10*, p. 50).

In this connection it is not always possible to determine the exact nature of the causal relationship. It may be that language determines thought; it may also be that the thinking of a people and the problems which interest them determine the form and character of the language. Dr. Hu Shih believes [1] that the relatively concrete and matter-of-fact character of the Chinese language is unfavorable to the development of metaphysical subtleties or hair-splitting distinctions, and that this accounts for certain characteristics of Chinese philosophy. It might be argued, however, that a lack of interest in such subtleties could be responsible for a vocabulary defective in this respect. At the other extreme it has been pointed out that Sanskrit is a particularly rich language from this point of view. With reference, for instance, to the training in concentration there is a special word for the state of concentration "when the name of the object alone is in the mind, another when the object is thought of with its predicate relations, still another when it is merely a point, and so on. It is significant that more words for philosophical and religious thought are to be found in Indian literature than in the Greek, Latin and German languages combined" (*18*, p. 93).

We shall probably never be able to decide which came first. It is likely that an interest in certain problems or objects develops a vocabulary capable of dealing with them adequately; but it is also likely that an individual born into any particular culture will think in terms of the medium of expression current in his society, and that the nature of his thinking will be affected thereby. For the culture as a whole, however, it does seem possible to learn something about the mental life of the people from an analysis of its language. Dunlap (*19*) says:

> In studying the structure of the language of a people, we are studying the forms and methods of their thinking. In studying their vocabulary, we are finding their types of discrimination. The description of a language as the crystallized thought of a people is far from wrong (p. 310).

This may seem a somewhat extreme statement, but there can be no doubt that differences in the vocabulary of peoples tell us some-

[1] Personal communication.

thing about their culture. In some languages, for example, it is impossible to differentiate between "to kill" and "to murder" (14). The distinction that we make in this regard is based on a certain legal philosophy which considers intent or motivation to be an important aspect of the act; that is to say, killing accidentally or without intent is entirely different from deliberate murder. Other societies emphasize the result; intentionally or not someone has been killed, and that is the only thing that matters.

One of the most striking examples of the manner in which vocabulary may mirror the interests of a people is to be found in the words for "camel" in Arabic (20). There are said to be about six thousand names connected in some way with "camel," including words derived from the camel and attributes associated with it. These include, for instance, names of classes of camels according to function—milk camels, riding camels, marriage camels, slaughter camels, etc.; names of breeds of different degrees of nobility of lineage, derivation from different lands, etc.; names of camels in groups, as several, a considerable number, innumerable; and with reference to their objectives—grazing, conveying a caravan, war expedition, etc.; as many as fifty words for pregnant camels, states of pregnancy, stage at which movement of the fetus is first felt, mothers who suckle and those who do not, those near delivery, etc. This list might be continued almost indefinitely, and it is hardly necessary to point out that it reflects the exceptional importance of the camel in Arab civilization.

In the same manner the large variety of words for "snow" among the Eskimos clearly results from the need to discriminate between numerous aspects of what is to most of us a single phenomenon. "In the life of the Eskimo *snow* means something entirely different as falling snow, soft snow on the ground, drifting snow or snowdrift. Fresh water ice, salt water ice, an iceberg, play quite different rôles in their life and all these are designated by distinctive terms" (1, p. 130). Similarly the Chuckchee of Northeastern Siberia have a wide array of designations for the reindeer.

There are other types of linguistic distinction which are important in this connection. For example, in the Hupa (California Indians) language whenever a statement is made a suffix is employed to indicate the source of authority. There is one suffix for what is perceived by hearing, another when the occurrence has been seen, another for things conjectured from circumstantial evidence (21). We cannot conclude that the Hupa are necessarily more accurate than we are, but it is probable that their language does avoid certain misunderstandings which are common in English.

It has frequently been argued that the absence of certain words from a vocabulary may point to a deficiency in the type of thinking represented by such words. More particularly, the fact that many of the languages of primitive peoples have few or no abstract words has occasionally led to the conclusion that the thinking of these peoples is restricted to the concrete, and that they have no power of abstraction. This is undoubtedly a faulty conclusion. The paucity of certain abstract terms is probably due to a lack of interest in these abstractions, rather than to an inability to deal with them. Boas (22) has shown that it is possible to convey an abstract notion to a member of a tribe whose language normally makes no use of it; the native may on such occasions even decide what the word should be in order to express such a notion. The present writer had a similar experience among the Huichol Indians. Their language has words for "my father," "your father," "his father," but no word for "father." The informant, however, was perfectly capable of understanding the idea of "father," and supplied a word which he thought could be used with that meaning.

In general we may conclude that language and thought are intimately related and mutually influence each other. The vocabulary in particular can give us valuable information as to the content and the interests of the culture. The argument from the absence of certain words to corresponding defects of the intellect is, however, more than questionable. Vendryès (23), for instance, notes that modern Greek and Bulgarian have no infinitive, and yet no one could possibly say that Greeks and Bulgarians therefore lack the faculty of conceiving a verbal action in an abstract way.

At a somewhat more complex level, the emotional vocabulary of contemporary nations has sometimes been interpreted as furnishing clues concerning prevailing national attitudes. In his analysis of the relationship between a German boy and his father, Schaffner (24) found that the word most frequently used was "Ehrfurcht," which is compounded of the ideas of "honor" or "respect" and "fear." There is no single word in English which serves as an adequate translation, and it is highly probable that the particular combination of emotional responses represented by "Ehrfurcht" is much more common in Germany than in the United States or Great Britain. Thorner (25) was impressed by the existence of the German word "Schaden-freude" (which may be translated as joy resulting from a misfortune that has befallen someone else), and by the absence of any similar word in French or English. Unfortunately for the argument that this is indicative of a specifically German response, the same word is found in the Scandinavian languages. Thorner discounts this fact because the Scandinavians "borrowed" the word from the German, but as anthropologists have frequently pointed out, cultural borrow-ing is a selective process, not a mechanical one, and if a word is found in a particular language the question of its origin may be relatively unimportant. We may not legitimately give an explana-tion of the existence of a word in one language and refuse to accept a similar explanation when it is found in another. Much more work is needed before we can depend on vocabulary as a clue to these more subtle aspects of interpersonal relations in a particular national community, although even in these cases the technique appears to be a promising one.

SEMANTICS

In connection with the psychological aspects of language be-havior, one of the most important developments is associated with the field of *semantics*, which is concerned with the critical analysis of symbols and the manner in which words are—and should be—used. The classics of semantics are *Science and Sanity* by Alfred Korzybski (26) and *The Meaning of Meaning* by Ogden and Rich-ards (27), which represent two different approaches to the same problem. The main thesis of the latter book can perhaps best be epitomized in the phrase "find the referent," which serves as a reminder to us that if we are to use words in order to convey mean-ing, we must keep constantly in mind the objects or acts to which the words refer. Confusion and misunderstanding arise whenever we use words for which the referent is not clearly specified; this may be particularly dangerous in the case of emotionally toned symbols like "democracy," "patriotism," "socialism," "appeasement," etc., which may signify different things to different people. This does not necessarily mean that such words should not be used, but rather that when they are used, their "referents" should be indicated in such a fashion as to make true communication possible. One of the interesting by-products of the work of Ogden and Richards has been the development of Basic English, which makes use of a total of 850 words, allegedly sufficient to permit translation into this simplified language of everything from tabloid newspapers to Lincoln's Gettysburg address and *Hamlet*. Although conceived in part as an international language, Basic English also forces us to express ourselves in terms which make it easy to find the "referent."

Korzybski and his followers make a somewhat similar point in different terms. They distinguish between "extensional" or denotative meanings of words, and "intensional" or connotative meanings. Confusion arises when a word has a particular intensional meaning for the speaker and a different extensional meaning in terms of the specific object or acts to which it refers—or should refer. Korzybski also argues against the use of the copulative *to be* as misleading; it suggests a degree of identity which may not correspond with reality. Instead of saying, "John *is* smart," we should rather say "John *appears* smart," or better, "John *appears* smart *to me*," or, still better, "John can solve arithmetic problems more quickly and more accurately than any other boy in his class at school." Another device suggested for increasing the accuracy of our language is the use of subscripts, for example, "pencil$_1$" and "pencil$_2$," since what we say about one pencil may not necessarily be true of the second. Hayakawa (28) indicates the importance of this mechanism in our relations with different members of a particular group; what holds for Jew$_1$ or Negro$_1$ may be entirely inapplicable to Jew$_2$ or Negro$_2$, and serious mistakes may occur when we speak of "Jew" or "Negro" without further specification. Still another device regarded as important is the mechanical model of an Abstraction Ladder; definitions are useless if we go up the ladder from less to more abstract; they are useful only if we go down, specifying in more concrete terms what it is that the word really indicates.

Great claims have been made for the salutary effect of training in semantics. It has allegedly increased the intelligence quotients of sub-normal children; in view of the large part played by linguistic ability in most intelligence tests, it is not too surprising that training in the use of words may have a favorable effect on the scores. It is reported to have contributed to the cure of many psychotic and neurotic patients by teaching them not to attach the wrong meanings to the words in which they phrase their emotional responses. Korzybski goes so far as to regard his system as a means of restoring sanity to society and of removing the causes of misunderstanding not only between individuals, but even between nations, thus reducing if not eliminating the possibility of war.

It is difficult to arrive at a just evaluation of these ambitious claims until more empirical research has been conducted, but there can be little doubt regarding the extent to which we are subject to what Stuart Chase (29) has called "the tyranny of words." Hayakawa gives an illuminating example of what words can do. Two men have tried three times unsuccessfully to solve a particular problem; one of them says to himself, "I have failed three times"; the other, "I am a failure." As we shall see later, words play an important part in interpersonal relations at all levels of complexity, including the phenomena of suggestion, of propaganda, of attitudes in general. It does seem highly probable that some at least of the ills of human society might be reduced if we all remained constantly concerned with the "referents" of our own speech and that of others.

LANGUAGE DEVELOPMENT IN THE CHILD

Esper (30) describes five stages in the acquisition of language. The first is the stage of screaming, which begins with the birth cry; this was formerly interpreted as expressing the infant's wrath or joy at entering the world, but it is now more prosaically regarded as a reflex activity, an incidental result of the mechanism of blood oxygenation. In the early period of life the sounds are reflex in character and uttered without any conscious intent. It has been suggested that in this early stage various organic conditions—hunger, pain, anger, etc.—are each accompanied by its own specific cry, and may be distinguished from one another. An interesting series of experiments by Sherman (31) demonstrated, however, that observers were not able to tell from the cry what condition it accompanied. When they heard the cry but could not see what caused it, they were just as likely to be wrong as right in their interpretation. It is quite possible, however, that whereas there is no common "language" for all infants, each particular infant may have a specific and characteristic cry for each condition, and that this cry may be successfully interpreted by the mother or nurse.

The second or babbling stage occurs usually toward the end of the second month, when consonantal sounds appear for the first time. During the whole of the first year the infant makes use of a great multiplicity of sounds, many of which do not occur in the adult language. This large variety of sounds shows that any infant could with equal facility learn any human language, and that "racial" heredity is of no importance in this connection. The babbling of these early months is probably due to intra-organic stimulation, and occurs especially after meals, after waking from sleep, etc.

The third is the stage of sound imitation, which usually begins during the second six months of life, but may occur somewhat earlier. One aspect which has received particular attention is the so-called circular reaction, characterized by the child's repetition of the same sound over and over again. This has been explained on the principle of the conditioned response (32). Some organic condition causes the child to make the motor response resulting in the sound; at the same time he hears the sound of his own voice, so that this auditory experience may become the conditioned stimulus setting off the same motor response. The following diagram may serve as an illustration.

$$S_1 \text{ (organic condition)} \rightarrow R_1 \text{ (producing the sound)}$$

$$S_2 \text{ (hearing the sound)}$$

The hearing of the sound, which is the consequence of the motor response, may at the same time serve as the conditioned stimulus because of its coexistence with the original unconditioned stimulus. It may therefore bring on the motor response; this in turn results in the hearing of the sound, which again produces the motor response, and so on in this circular fashion until some new condition intervenes.

$$S_2 \text{ (hearing the sound)} \rightleftarrows R_1 \text{ (producing the sound)}$$

At the age of eight or nine months there may be imitation of sounds made by others. This may be understood on a basis similar to the preceding. Once the sound itself has served as a stimulus for the associated vocal reaction, the same or associated sounds made by the parents may have a similar effect. It has been pointed out by the Sterns (33), however, that what has been called "sound imitation" in the speech development of children refers to a number of distinct forms of activity, of which that described above is perhaps the simplest. True imitation of new vocal patterns introduced by adults appears usually toward the end of the first year or at the beginning of the second. The Sterns describe also a type of "imitation" to which they have given the name *metalalia;* when the child has had frequent experience with a complex situation which includes certain sounds produced by the adults (e.g., "good night"), he may himself in a similar context supply the sound before anyone else has spoken it. This phenomenon is closely associated with the origin of true vocal utterance—the final stage in the developmental process.

The fourth has been called the stage of verbal understanding, and has its beginnings toward the latter part of the first year. The child now begins to respond with specific movements to sounds made by others. This stage also may be explained on the principle of the conditioned response. For example, the child may be playing in the bath and splashing, and at the same time the parent says, "Splash, splash!" In time, this word becomes the conditioned stimulus which sets off the same response. In the same way such a conditioned response may be established when the child is put through certain movements which are invariably accompanied by the same words. This stage may also be described as the acquisition of a passive vocabulary, and as was pointed out in the preceding chapter, it may reach a high degree of complexity among many species of animals.

The final stage is that of verbal utterance, usually beginning in the first half of the second year. It is the stage of the acquisition of an active vocabulary and is described by Esper as "the establishment of conventionalized speech reactions as specific responses to socially presented stimulus patterns" (p. 442). It may perhaps best be explained as the result of a combination of the conditioning process described above and the pattern of imitation which was noted in the third stage. The child, for instance, hears the sound "bow-wow" when he sees a dog, and later produces it by himself in the same situation. Further development in language is essentially a continuation of the same process, as well as of the processes of sound imitation and of verbal understanding which have had an earlier start.

Other psychologists and sociologists have postulated a somewhat different sequence of events. For Kimball Young (34), for example, there are four distinct stages: (1) a pre-linguistic stage of random vocalization, followed by a period of babbling in which the same sounds may be frequently repeated; (2) a stage of self-imitation; (3) the stage of imitation of others; and (4) the final stage of verbal comprehension or real speech.

Still another approach to the learning of language is represented by Skinner (35), who starts from the fact that in the first stage of speech the child makes use in random fashion of a large variety of different sounds. Some of these, because they resemble at least superficially the accepted sounds of certain words like "milk" or "mama," etc., are rewarded through encouragement or demonstrations of affection or through the receipt of the designated objects, and as a consequence are reinforced; other sounds do not receive such reinforcement and therefore become "extinguished." One of the difficulties with this theory would seem to be the unlikelihood that in this first babbling there would be a sufficient number of different sounds to enable this particular form of learning to bear the brunt of the explanation of language development. Skinner's description of the psychology of language also introduces a distinction between the "mand," which acts like an imperative, obtaining for the speaker that which he requests or demands from others, and the "tact" which has a declarative function. "Meaning" is to be understood in terms of the way in which speech controls various aspects of the environment. The present writer can only echo the judgment of Sargent (36), who writes: "Whether or not this new behavioristic, learning-centered approach will answer the major questions about symbolism and symbolic communications remains to be seen" (p. 281).

THE IMPORTANCE OF LANGUAGE IN SOCIAL PSYCHOLOGY

It is hardly possible to overestimate the part played by language in the development and control of social behavior. It represents what is specifically human in social life. It is an instrument of thought and of communication. It serves as a cohesive force uniting human groups and setting them apart from others; as Sapir (14) points out, the fact of common speech is an index of the social solidarity of a group. Much of the opposition between the in-group and the out-group reported for the most primitive as well as for the most complex societies may probably be explained by the fact that the groups cannot understand each other. This is of course the principal motivation for the movements which have developed in support of Esperanto and other international languages as a means of uniting mankind; there can be no doubt that language acts as either a cohesive or a divisive force, depending upon the degree of understanding. It would be difficult to exaggerate the importance of language in human social behavior.

SUMMARY

There are several theories of the origin of language, but they account for the particular sounds used rather than for the phenomenon of communication. The suggestion that the first language was a language of gestures conflicts with the fact that vocal expression occurs in animals below man. The experimental evidence for phonetic symbolism supports the theory that onomatopoeia may account for some of the actual sounds used in spoken language. More important is the demonstration of a relationship between language and thought; the forms of language determine certain modes of observation and interpretation. This may be seen not only in the animistic thinking of young children, but also in the complex speculations of philosophers. The development of semantics represents an important area of exploration into the manner in which language habits affect not only thought processes, but also the whole field of interpersonal relations. The content of a vocabulary reflects the interests of the corresponding culture, but does not justify any conclusions as to the intellectual capacity of a people.

In the acquisition of language by the child, five stages of development may be distinguished—(1) the stage of screaming, which begins with the birth cry; (2) the babbling stage, toward the end of the second month; (3) sound imitation, beginning usually during the second six months of life, characterized by the circular conditioned response, resulting also in imitation of sounds made by others; (4) verbal understanding toward the end of the first year; (5) verbal utterance, or the acquisition of an active vocabulary, usually beginning in the first half of the second year.

Language serves as an instrument of thought and of communication, as a means of controlling the actions of others, and as a force which unites the members of a particular community, at the same time separating them from others.

REFERENCES

1. Boas, F. *General Anthropology.* 1938

2. Dewey, J. *Experience and Nature.* 1925

3. Paget, R. *Human Speech.* 1930

4. Schneirla, T. C. "The 'Levels' Concept in the Study of Social Organization in Animals." In Rohrer, J. H., and Sherif, M., eds. *Social Psychology at the Crossroads.* 1951

5. Crawford, M. P. "The Cooperative Solving of Problems by Young Chimpanzees," *Comp. Psych. Monogr.,* 1937, 14: pp. 1-88

6. Kroeber, A. L., and Waterman, T. T. *Source Book in Anthropology.* Rev. ed. 1931

7. Jespersen, O. *Language, Its Nature, Development and Origin.* 1923

8. Sapir, E. "A Study in Phonetic Symbolism," *J. Exp. Psychol.,* 1929, 12: pp. 225-239

9. Newman, S. S. "Further Experiments in Phonetic Symbolism," *Amer. J. Psychol.,* 1933, 45: pp. 53-75

10. Mauthner, F., quoted in Rank, O., *Art and Artist.* 1932

11. Mosel, J. N. Unpublished Master's Essay, Columbia University. 1942

12. Bloomfield, L. *Language.* 1933

13. Watson, J. B. *Behaviorism.* 2d ed. 1930

14. Sapir, E. "Language," *Encycl. Soc. Sci.,* 1933, 9: pp. 155-169

15. Piaget, J. *The Language and Thought of the Child.* 1926

16. Mead, M. "An Investigation of the Thought of Primitive Children with Special Reference to Animism," *J. Roy. Anthrop. Instit.,* 1932, 62: pp. 173-190

17. Benedict, R., "Folklore," in *Encyclopaedia of the Social Sciences.* 1931

18. Behanan, K. T. *Yoga.* 1937

19. Dunlap, K. *Civilized Life.* 1934

20. Thomas, W. I. *Primitive Behavior.* 1937

21. Goddard, P. E. "Life and Culture of the Hupa," *Univ. Cal. Publs. Amer. Archaeol. & Ethnol.,* 1903, I: pp. 1-88

22. Boas, F. *Handbook of American Indian Languages. Bull. Bur. Ethnol.,* No. 40, 1911

23. Vendryès, J. *Language.* 1925

24. Schaffner, B. F. *Father Land.* 1948

25. Thorner, I. "German Words, German Personality and Protestantism." *Psychiatry,* 1945, 8: pp. 403-417

26. Korzybski, A. *Science and Sanity.* Rev. ed. 1941

27. Ogden, C. K., and Richards, I. A. *The Meaning of Meaning.* 2d ed. 1927

28. Hayakawa, S. I. *Language in Action.* 1941

29. Chase, S. *The Tyranny of Words.* 1938

30. Esper, E. A. "Language." In Murchison, C., ed. *Hdbk. Soc. Psychol.* 1935

31. Sherman, M. "The Differentiation of Emotional Responses in Infants," *J. Comp. Psychol.,* 1927, 7: pp. 265-284; 335-352

32. Allport, F. H. *Social Psychology.* 1924

33. Stern, W., and Stern, C. *Die Kindersprache.* 1922

34. Young, K. *Personality and Problems of Adjustment.* 1941

35. Skinner, B. F. *Science and Human Behavior.* 1953

36. Sargent, S. S. *Social Psychology.* 1950

Part Two

SOCIAL FACTORS IN HUMAN NATURE

The Concept
of Human Nature

4

INTRODUCTION

It is not unusual for textbooks in social psychology, as well as many in the fields of sociology, anthropology and other social sciences, to include a discussion of the characteristics of human nature. This has presumably been done on the theory that any science which deals with the behavior of groups of individuals, or with that of the individual in the group situation, should begin with some statement of the nature of the individual as such. In other words, it is assumed that this problem belongs primarily in the field of general psychology, but that some consideration of it is essential as a preliminary to all social science.

There is an alternative point of view which holds that the very problem of human nature and its characteristics belongs to the social at least as much as to the individual aspects of psychology. If human nature is in whole or in part created or affected by social factors, then the characteristics of human nature are of direct, and not only of indirect, concern to the social psychologist.

Theories of human nature have of course practical as well as theoretical implications. Discussions of possible changes in our economic system frequently center upon the question of whether "acquisitiveness" is natural to man, or whether he would be willing to work in other than a competitive system. The possibility of the abolition of war is frequently questioned on the ground that "aggressiveness" is a fundamental human trait. It becomes of the greatest importance therefore to discover what are the essential characteristics of human behavior, as well as the limits of their variability. There is implicit here the controversy between those who believe in an original human nature relatively fixed and immutable, and those

63

who hold that what we call human nature is socially determined and modifiable. As has already been pointed out, this controversy is not a new one; Aristotle and Plato defended the opposing viewpoints many centuries ago.

The statement that social factors play a part in determining the characteristics of human nature may seem at first to be a contradiction in terms. When we speak of human *nature*, are we not specifically excluding the contributions of the social environment? In view of the contrasted meanings attached to *nature* and *nurture*, respectively, are we not committing the paradox of assuming that the latter may influence the former, in spite of the fact that the two are mutually exclusive? Does not human nature refer to the constants, the universals, rather than to what is variable in human behavior?

The apparent paradox may be resolved, at least in part, if we keep the following considerations in mind. Whatever else human nature may include, a fundamental and universal characteristic of man is his variability, his malleability in the face of the social and cultural conditions under which he grows and develops. A child gradually becomes a man because of the processes of growth and maturation which are physiologically and biologically determined, but he grows and matures into a particular kind of man largely as the result of what he learns from others in his society. This learning process may itself occur according to laws which are very similar for all human beings, perhaps even for all biological organisms; there may be similar responses to rewards which provide reinforcement of the learning, or to punishments which act as deterrents; there may be a similar process of generalization from what has been learned to other situations which seem to the subject to be similar to those which he has previously encountered [Hull (1), Keller and Schoenfeld (2)]. *What* he learns will, however, vary enormously, and the consequent effect on his behavior will be correspondingly great. Man's capacity for socialization—the process by which he becomes a member of a particular society—and what has been called "enculturation" [Herskovits (3)]—by which he becomes adapted to and incorporates within himself a substantial portion of the culture by which he is surrounded—must therefore be seen as an essential characteristic of human nature. It may be exceedingly difficult to prove that because of human nature man will act thus and so; it is much less difficult to demonstrate that precisely because of human nature man will act in many different ways according to his social and cultural environment.

In spite of these considerations, the question continues to be raised: are there constants in human behavior? Can we determine their nature? What meaning can be attached to the notion of the "psychic unity of mankind" [Goldenweiser (4)]?

THE INSTINCT THEORY

In the past, much of the discussion of these questions centered upon the theory of instincts. In the earliest uses of the concept of instinct, it was regarded as referring to the behavior of animals, not of men. For Descartes, for example, there was a sharp dichotomy between the instinct of animals and the intelligence of man; man alone had intelligence because God had given him a soul. Descartes' successors, says Brown (5), left God out of it. "In place of God, gradually, came the concept of heredity" (p. 86). The question of the origin of behavior was passed on to the biologists. It was noted that animals might show the same type of modifiability of behavior that was called intelligence in human beings, and that conversely, men sometimes behaved like the beasts. The transition between human and animal behavior, or between intelligence and instinct, was seen to be a gradual one, and the Darwinian viewpoint was extended to the continuity of behavior as well as of morphology.

The instinct theory in its modern form is usually associated with the name of William McDougall, whose *Social Psychology* was first published in 1908 (6). He presented the theory that instincts are the prime movers of all human activity; take them away and the organism would be incapable of activity of any kind. They are the forces that shape the life of individuals and societies. An instinct was described as an innate disposition which determines the organism to perceive or to pay attention to any object of a certain class, to experience in its presence a certain emotional excitement, and to act or have an impulse to action which finds expression in a specific mode of behavior in relation to that object. An instinct, therefore, had three aspects—cognitive, affective and conative; the association between instinct and emotion was of particular importance.

McDougall gave a list of thirteen major instincts, including such activities as curiosity, self-assertion, submission, food-seeking, mating, acquisitiveness, and others, and six minor instincts, such as sneezing, coughing, laughing and eliminating waste products from the body. In making up this list he looked on the one hand at the behavior of animals, and on the other to the exaggeration of instincts found in psychopathic individuals; he turned, according to his critics, "to the menagerie and the insane asylum" for his material. It has also been said that "he does a great deal of packing for a journey on which he never starts"; for he describes his instinct theory as an "introduction" to social psychology, but he makes almost no use of it when he deals with social phenomena. This last criticism is not quite fair, since McDougall's treatment of group behavior is associated with his theory of "sentiments," which are more complex systems of behavior and attitude erected upon an instinctive basis. He may be said, therefore, to have continued the journey in *The Group Mind* and other volumes.

Many psychologists accepted the instinct theory with one modification or another. Thorndike (7) and Warren (8), for instance, gave their own lists of instincts, somewhat longer and more complicated than McDougall's. It became fashionable in psychology to use instinct as a principle of interpretation of all sorts of behavior. As one critic of this theory (9) put it:

> Man is impelled to action, it is said, by his instincts. If he goes with his fellows, it is the "herd instinct" which actuates him; if he walks alone, it is the "anti-social instinct"; if he fights, it is the instinct of pugnacity; if he defers to another, it is the instinct of self-abasement; if he twiddles his thumbs, it is the thumb-twiddling instinct; if he does not twiddle his thumbs, it is the thumb-not-twiddling instinct. Thus everything is explained with the facility of magic—word magic (p. 4).

As was pointed out in the first chapter, there has been a marked reaction against the instinct hypothesis. Serious criticisms have been leveled against it on the basis of observations of animals and young children who apparently showed simple reflex patterns of behavior rather than the more complex ones which McDougall had postulated. Many social scientists came to a similar negative conclusion in the light of their sociological analysis of the various factors influencing and determining the so-called instincts.[1] Because of these

---

[1] Cooley (10), Bernard (11), and others.

and other criticisms the very term "instinct" has fallen into disrepute as denoting something mystical and intangible which has no place in the field of science. The one important exception is to be found in the writings of Freud and his followers, who continued to make use of the concept of instinct as an explanation of behavior. Even among psychoanalysts, however, there has been a distinct reaction against Freud's biological and "instinctual" orientation.

Although the term instinct was almost completely discarded by academic psychologists, it continued to be the fashion to speak of certain underlying motivating factors in behavior common to human beings in general. Dunlap (12) uses the term "desires"; according to him, the primary desires are important everywhere for the preservation of the life and welfare of the individual and the life of the race. They have an organic basis and are subject to perversions. He lists the primary desires as alimentary, excretory, protection, activity, rest and relaxation, amorous or erotic, parental or philopedic, pre eminence and conformity. This list may certainly be criticized in the same manner as McDougall's and it hardly seems as if much has been gained by the substitution of "desire" for "instinct." The same may be said for Gurnee's (13) discussion of "motives," which are described as internal stresses disposing the organism to restless activity until that stress is relieved. These motives include food-seeking, temperature, escape and avoidance, sex, protection of other living things, gregarious tendencies, social approval and disapproval, self-assertion, negativism and submission.

Many other terms have been used in this same connection, frequently without any preconception as to the innate or instinctive nature of the corresponding behavior. The word "drive," for example, is preferred by Holt (9) in his *Animal Drive and the Learning Process* as well as in the studies of animal motivation by Warden and his associates (14). Woodworth (15) speaks of "dependable motives" and we shall later make use of this expression in our own analysis. Murray (16) has used the word "need," and distinguishes between *viscerogenic* needs, which are presumably "provoked by internal conditions regardless of the environment," and *psychogenic* needs, which "though found to operate without obvious dependence upon the viscerogenic needs, were perhaps once subsidiary to the latter," and are influenced to a great extent by cultural forms (pp. 74-75). As we shall see later, however, the line between these two is difficult to maintain, since cultural factors affect the specific expression of viscerogenic phenomena as well. Murray's list is a long one and includes most, if not all, of the motives which have been described in other publications. He discards the term "instinct" because it is limited to those needs which can be proved innate. Murphy, Murphy and Newcomb (*17*) list four groups of motives or drives: visceral drives (hunger, thirst, etc.), activity drives (exercise, novelty, and exploration, etc.), esthetic drives (color, tone, rhythm, etc.), and emotions.

All attempts to define the fundamental characteristics of human nature have been challenged by Brown (*5*), who has written a social psychology from the point of view of the "field theory" developed by Kurt Lewin (*18*). In essence, the field theory maintains that behavior is to be understood as due not so much to the nature of the individual as to his relationship to the physical and social environment acting upon him and in which his behavior occurs. From this standpoint, says Brown, there is no such thing as human nature independent of the existing structure of the social field. There are no specific reaction forms inherent in the human as such. "From our primitive ancestors to us as modern men, change in 'human nature' has occurred and it seems only reasonable to suppose that change will continue to occur in the lives of our issue" (p. 261). Even such apparently fundamental tendencies as those toward self-preservation and race-preservation may not be said to belong to human nature. Suicides and homosexuals are still human and cannot be explained away as special cases; under selected field conditions any individual may be caused, according to Brown, to develop homosexuality or to commit suicide.

Although much of Brown's criticism of the usual concept of human nature is justified, his own point of view appears to go too far in the other direction. There can be no doubt as to the great importance of the "field" in shaping human behavior. It is still necessary, however, for us to inquire into the nature of this human animal who is part of the field. To put it another way, we might say that if the human organism were different, behavior would differ accordingly; the social field itself would be changed as a result. In a brilliant essay by Clarence Day (*19*) there is some amusing speculation as to what human beings would be like if they were descended from the great cats or from the social insects, instead of from a primate stock. Many of the characteristics of "this simian world" are to be understood precisely in the light of our biological ancestry.

In all fairness to Brown, it should be pointed out that in a later statement (20) he did emphasize clearly the biological characteristics of man as important aspects of the total field. "Implicit in field theory is the idea that social behavior depends on the biological nature of the individual as an integral part of groups whose characteristics are intimately connected with cultural phenomena" (p. 863). In that case, the problem of the essential characteristics of human nature remains a real one. We may prefer the term "fundamental drive" to that of "instinct," but we have still to ask what drives there are, and what evidence there is that they are fundamental. In what follows we propose to examine those forms of behavior which have been alleged to be fundamental or dependable and attempt to determine to what extent they may be so regarded.

Criteria of Dependability. In general the procedure will be to employ a threefold criterion. The first is the existence of continuity between a particular form of behavior in man and that of other biological species, particularly the anthropoid apes. In the light of the close biological relationship as well as the similarity observed in their activity, it seems reasonable to assume that such continuity may be used as evidence for an unlearned component in such behavior. In the second place, the discovery of a biochemical or physiological basis for any specific activity will also be evidence in the same direction; it will show that there is in the organism a condition predisposing to such an activity. Finally, a significant criterion will be that of universality. The discovery of a form of behavior common to all human societies in spite of the variations in their culture will constitute strong evidence in favor of its dependability. This last criterion need not be applied too strictly. If the universality is disturbed by no more than a few exceptions which may be explained in the light of special circumstances operative in those communities, the behavior may still have a fundamental basis. To return to one of Brown's examples, the fact that some individuals or even some groups commit suicide by no means proves that it is as "natural" to wish for death as for life.

In connection with this third criterion, liberal use will be made of the material collected by anthropologists, whose reports show something of the varieties of human behavior determined by culture. It is important to point out that examples from primitive communities are not employed in an evolutionary sense; that is to say, they are not to be regarded as stages of behavior prior to our own. The evolutionary point of view with reference to culture is in general no longer accepted by the large majority of competent anthropologists. In other words, we use primitive material as illustrating *varieties,* not *stages,* of human behavior.

The question may arise as to the need for three different criteria. Would not any single one of these three, if fully and adequately applied, be sufficient for our purposes? In particular, would not the third criterion, that of universality, give us all the information we require concerning the degree of dependability of the various motives? Our answer might be in the affirmative, if we had before us scientifically acceptable data concerning all human societies and if we had the opportunity to examine all the data, from all societies, relative to the aspect of human behavior which we are investigating. This is obviously an impossibility. Even the most extensive available catalogue of the characteristics of human groups, namely that included in the Human Relations Area Files at Yale University, inevitably falls short of such an ideal. Under the circumstances, since no single criterion can be applied with complete confidence owing to the limitations of the available data, it will be scientifically much safer to apply all three, so that each may exert the necessary corrective to the results obtained from the others.

The use of this threefold criterion makes possible a treatment of the problem of motivation which differs in one important respect from previous analyses with which the writer is familiar. The customary procedure has been to present lists of drives or motives on what may be described as an "all or none" basis. That is, a particular motive was either dependable or not; there was no intermediate ground. The view adopted in the present text is that dependability is a relative concept, permitting of marked variations in degree. For any particular motive we must determine not merely wheather it is dependable or not, but also how dependable it is. We must place it somewhere in a hierarchy of dependability, so that we may know how it stands in comparison with other motives. To put it another way, motives differ in their degrees of compulsion; some have an imperative character, others may be more easily suppressed or neglected. In this connection the amount of variation found in different cultures will be of special significance.

THE ORIGINS OF CULTURE

Culture may be defined as consisting of the capabilities and habits acquired by man as a member of society (21). How culture arose and how it developed are problems outside the scope of this discussion; we must take culture for granted. It may perhaps be sufficient to point out that those cultural phenomena which are universal have been explained on the basis of (1) the psychic unity of man (to be discussed in the following chapters), (2) the identity in the basic needs of life, (3) the fact that man's physical environment, broadly speaking, is always the same (4). Linton (22) also speaks of the constants (to be found mainly in human nature) which affect the development of all social systems. The cultural phenomena which are variable, on the other hand, must be understood historically.

> The specific form of any pattern or institution is mainly the result of social inventions, culture contacts, and the total environment, natural as well as cultural, in which the pattern or institution develops and functions. Since all these factors are inherently variable, patterns and institutions, when treated as discrete phenomena, can only be explained on a historic basis (p. 268).

Linton points out further that pure chance may also enter. The Mohammedan rule that a man may marry the divorced wife of his adopted son is due to the fact that the Prophet wished to marry the divorced wife of his adopted son and had a revelation that this was permissible. There is a clan among the Tanala in Madagascar which prohibits the taking of sisters as plural wives, although all other clans (as well as most polygynous peoples) permit it; this prohibition resulted from an actual case of poisoning among sisters who were plural wives in this group about fifty years ago.

Variations in culture may thus be due to differences in the physical environment, to economic factors, to contacts with other peoples, to accident, perhaps also to the nature of the individuals composing the group. Whatever their origin, however, our concern is with the variations in human behavior for which they are responsible, and with the uniformities that may still be found in spite of the cultural variations.

MAN WITHOUT CULTURE

At least in theory, the simplest and most direct method of separating cultural from biological determinants in human behavior would be to look at human beings "in a state of nature," that is to say, remote from the influence of social and cultural factors. It goes without saying that no actual "primitive" group satisfies these conditions. In fact, the very label "primitive" is inappropriate, since all societies of which we have any knowledge possess cultures of varying degrees of complexity. Some of the societies which have been termed primitive, may in some respects, as in the well-known example of kinship terminology among the aboriginal Australians, show a form of cultural development more complex than our own.

It has been suggested that some approximation to the state of nature in man may be found in the case of certain children who have grown up by themselves far from human society, either in complete isolation, or reared by animals. Many years ago the Swedish naturalist Linnaeus included "feral man" in his classification of human types. *Homo ferus,* according to him, was characterized by three principal traits—he was *mutus, hirsutus* and *tetrapus,* that is to say, he had no intelligible language, he was hairy, and he walked on all fours. Linnaeus based his description on tales brought back by travelers, and in the present more critical age his anecdotal data cannot be taken too seriously. Over a period of years, however, a considerable amount of evidence regarding the characteristics of these feral children has accumulated, and although much of it is still of the anecdotal variety, there are a few cases which have been carefully observed, and which have attracted the critical attention of social scientists.

In his summary of more than thirty cases, Zingg (23) has indicated that these wild children develop no vocalization resembling human speech, and that they almost invariably move about on all fours. (They were therefore in Linnaeus' terms *mutus* and *tetrapus,* but there was no indication of the third alleged characteristic, *hirsutus.*) They usually ate like animals, smelling the food before eating, lowering the mouth to the food instead of raising the food to the mouth; they wore no clothing; their expressions of emotion were usually not understood by other human beings; they showed little or no desire for human company.

Among the best authenticated and most fully documented cases are those of the Wild Boy of Aveyron, who was studied over a period of five years by the French psychiatrist Itard (*24*), and the Wolf Children of Midnapore, described by Singh and Zingg (*25*). The first was the case of an eleven- or twelve-year-old boy found in a French forest in 1799; the second was that of two girls, one approximately two to four years old, the other eight or nine, discovered in India in 1921 living in a cave with wolves. In essentials they showed the same general characteristics which Zingg regards as typical for the total sample of cases examined.

There has been much argument concerning the interpretation to be put on these data. It is difficult to know how long the children were separated from human society; it is impossible to determine whether they were normal or feeble-minded to start with. Both the boy studied by Itard and the elder of the two Indian girls (the younger one died within a year after discovery; the elder lived eight years) made considerable progress under tuition, but in neither case did they reach the level which could be anticipated for normal children of the same age. One might argue that the depressive environment of the early years had produced an "isolation amentia," the effects of which were irreversible; but the possibility cannot be excluded that the children were sub-normal from the first.

It is not easy to see how sub-normal children could have survived under such difficult conditions. Further it might be pointed out that even sub-normal children usually behave very differently from those discovered far from human society. To the extent that we can accept the accumulated evidence—and there is at least some of it which deserves to be taken seriously—the cases of feral children argue strongly for the overwhelming influence of society in making a human being "human."

SUMMARY

The determination of the characteristics of human nature, as well as of the limits within which they may vary, is of practical as well as theoretical importance; attempts to bring about fundamental changes in social institutions or to eliminate war and other evils must meet the challenge that "human nature" makes certain forms of behavior inevitable. The instinct theory of McDougall assumes the existence of innate dispositions to specific modes of behavior, but there has been a marked reaction among social scientists against this view, and the term *instinct* is now rarely used. Later texts speak of *desires, motives, drives, needs,* etc., but the assumption of underlying common human characteristics often continues to be made.

The procedure followed here is to examine the allegedly dependable motives through the use of a threefold criterion: (1) phylogenetic continuity, (2) physiological basis, (3) universality. Motives may differ in their degree of dependability, and this procedure makes possible a decision not merely as to whether a motive is dependable, but also as to how it compares with other motives in this respect. Ethnological material helps to make such a comparison possible, since the variations in culture, whatever their origin, are responsible for a wide range of human activities. The extent of this range, and the existence of uniformities in spite of it, must be determined before any decision may be reached about the nature of human motivation. The evidence from the study of "feral children" indicates the tremendous importance of social factors in the development of characteristically "human" behavior.

REFERENCES

1. Hull, C. L. *Principles of Behavior: An Introduction to Behavior Theory.* 1943
2. Keller, F. S., and Schoenfeld, W. N. *Principles of Behavior.* 1949
3. Herskovits, M. J. *Man and His Works.* 1948
4. Goldenweiser, A. A. *Anthropology.* 1937
5. Brown, J. F. *Psychology and the Social Order.* 1936
6. McDougall, W. *Introduction to Social Psychology.* 1st ed. 1908
7. Thorndike, E. L. *Educational Psychology.* 3 vols. 1913
8. Warren, H. C. *Human Psychology.* 1919
9. Holt, E. B. *Animal Drive and the Learning Process.* 1931
10. Cooley, C. H. *Human Nature and the Social Order.* 1922
11. Bernard, L. L. *Instinct.* 1924
12. Dunlap, K. *Civilized Life.* 1934
13. Gurnee, H. *Elements of Social Psychology.* 1936
14. Warden, C. J. *Animal Motivation.* 1931
15. Woodworth, R. S. *Psychology.* Rev. ed. 1929
16. Murray, H. A., et al. *Explorations in Personality.* 1939
17. Murphy, G., Murphy, L. B., and Newcomb, T. M. *Experimental Social Psychology.* Rev. ed. 1937
18. Lewin, K. *Principles of Topological Psychology.* 1936

19. Day, C. *This Simian World*. 1936

20. Brown, J. F. "Individual, Group, and Social Field," *Amer. J. Sociol.*, 1939, 44: pp. 858-867

21. Tylor, E. B. *Primitive Culture*. 1874

22. Linton, R. *The Study of Man*. 1936

23. Zingg, R. M. "Feral Man and Extreme Cases of Isolation," *Amer. J. Psychol.*, 1940, 53: pp. 487-517

24. Itard, J. M. G. *The Wild Boy of Aveyron*. (Trans. from the French by G. and M. Humphrey.) 1932

25. Singh, J. A. L., and Zingg, R. M. *Wolf-Children and Feral Man*. 1942

Motivation

INTRODUCTION

In the preceding chapter reference was made to the wide variety of terms which have been applied to human motivation in place of the original—and controversial—term *instinct*. It is not easy to make a choice between *motive, drive, urge, need, desire, press, prepotent reflex,* and a host of other suggested substitutes. Assuming that other considerations are more or less equal, it would appear preferable to do as little violence as possible to established usage in this field. On this basis the terms which seem to have the most secure place in the literature are, first, *motive,* and second, *drive.*

Frequently these two terms are used interchangeably; occasionally the attempt is made to distinguish between them. On the one hand, Hartley and Hartley (1) speak of physical activities which "are variously called drives, motives and needs—physical states of imbalance within the organism which impel it to activity" (p. 234). On the other, Newcomb (2) defines motive as a "state of the organism in which bodily energy is mobilized and selectively directed toward parts of the environment"; drives are "bodily states felt as restlessness, which initiate tendencies to activity" (p. 80). Motive would therefore include a state of drive and a direction of behavior toward some goal. Krech and Crutchfield (3) make a somewhat similar point when they stress the fact that the proper unit of motivational analysis is molar behavior, that is, whole behavior acts, involving both needs and goals. Newcomb believes that it is preferable to label any particular motive according to its goal rather than according to its state of drive. He therefore speaks of a hunger drive and a food motive, and not of a food drive or a hunger motive.

Helpful though it is to stress the broad and inclusive nature of the motivational process, the distinction between motive and drive is difficult to maintain. A drive in Newcomb's sense of a "bodily state" is probably never found without a direction of behavior towards some goal, except possibly in the diffuse, undifferentiated reactions of the new-born, and perhaps not even then. There is no simple way of separating a "hunger drive" in its pure state from a "food motive" in which the drive is directed toward food. The relationship becomes even more complicated when the sight of food (the goal) induces hunger (drive or motive?), or the presence of a female rat in heat results in sexual excitement in the male. Conceptually the distinction can be made, but it does not appear to be valid for actual behavior.

As the organism develops, the bodily state and the goal become even more closely interrelated through the process of *canalization*. Murphy (4) defines canalization as "the process by which general motives (which are at first rather non-specifically related to a class of stimuli) tend, upon repeated experience, to become more easily satisfied through the action of a specific satisfier than of others of the same general class" (p. 162). In other words, we rarely encounter a "hunger drive" directed toward food, but rather toward certain kinds of food; the "sex drive" similarly is usually directed toward specific kinds of satisfaction.

For these reasons no attempt will be made here to draw a line of demarcation between motive and drive. These terms will be used interchangeably to refer to the motors of action, the dynamic conditions either within the organism, or in the environment, or both, which lead us to seek to reach certain goals.

We turn now from the theoretical discussion of motivation in general to a specific examination of individual motives, particularly in their social implications. The procedure will be to apply to each motive in turn the criteria developed in the preceding chapter, and to determine in that way the nature and the extent of its dependability. The presentation does not follow any systematic order, because it seems preferable to postpone the classification of motives to the end of the discussion after the pertinent material has been reviewed. The motives are then assigned their position in the list on the basis of the assembled evidence. The reader who wishes to know in advance the precise nature of the classification will find it on page 164.

The concept of *dependability* should not be confused with the concept of *strength*. In general it is probably true that the more dependable the motive, the more powerful it tends to be. In specific individuals or groups, however, this is not necessarily the case. The motive of acquisitiveness, as we shall see in greater detail later, shows only a low degree of dependability, but it may sometimes become so strong as to dominate the whole of an individual's behavior. The motive of self-preservation has high dependability, but in one particular society it may be subordinated to a concept of honor which is entirely unknown in another. The question of the relative strength as contrasted with that of the relative dependability of motives is an important one, but it requires different techniques and a different approach from those used here; furthermore, it would have to be investigated separately in every society. In American culture E. L. Thorndike (5) has made an approach to the problem by using the common denominator of money. He asked his subjects to indicate how much money it would take to persuade them to forego a particular satisfaction. In this fashion the relative attractiveness or strength of two different goals could be compared.

Dependability is indicated by the probability with which the appearance of a particular motive may be predicted, in the absence of specific knowledge of the person about whom the prediction is made. If we know only that he is a healthy adult, what can we say about his probable behavior? Since one of the major tasks of all science is prediction, this appears to be a legitimate and important goal.

In what follows, the stress is on dependable behavior at the conscious level. We have all been made familiar through psychoanalysis with the concept of unconscious motivation, and no one can now deny its great significance. An attempt will be made at the conclusion of Chapter 6 to show some of the points of contact between the psychoanalytic point of view and the investigation into motivational *behavior* to which we now turn.

THE PARENTAL DRIVE

The Maternal Drive. The maternal drive constitutes one of the forms of behavior for which universality has been claimed. Obviously it is not peculiar to our own society. As a matter of fact there are probably many cultures in which it has a strength and importance greater if anything than among ourselves. There are many peoples among whom the respect in which a woman is held is proportionate to her fecundity, and as Westermarck (6) points out, a barren wife is frequently despised as an unnatural and useless being.

In this as well as in what follows, it is important to keep in mind that there is a distinction, psychologically, between the desire to have children and the urge to care for them. These have both been included in most discussions of the maternal drive, but they are by no means identical. Although clearly related biologically, they are distinct as motives. For convenience, we shall use the terms *pre-maternal* motive for the attitude or behavior related to the desire for children, and *post-maternal* motive for that which follows conception and comes to its fullest expression after the child is born. There is reason to believe that the latter is a far more dependable motive.

As far as concerns the care of offspring, there is ample evidence for its existence among many animals besides man. In fact, it has been shown in a series of experiments by Warden and his associates (7) that in the white rat this drive at its height is stronger than any other. The strength of the drives was measured by means of an apparatus composed of three compartments, the central one consisting of an electric grill. The experimental animal was placed in the compartment on one side of the grill, and the object representing its "goal" on the other. The number of times the animal crossed the grill to the goal measured directly the amount of punishment it received, and therefore indirectly the strength of its drive toward the goal. In this way comparison could be made of the strength of various drives by putting in at different times a hungry animal separated from food, a thirsty animal separated from drink, a mother from her young, a female in heat from a male, etc. The results were as follows:

Drive	Av. No. of Crossings (optimum conditions)
Maternal	22.4
Thirst	20.4
Hunger	18.2
Sex	13.8
Exploratory	6.0
No incentive	3.5

It is important to add that although at its maximum the maternal drive is the strongest, it decreases as the age of the mother increases, and even more markedly as the age of the litter increases. While it lasts, it includes also a strong urge to retrieve the young when they have wandered away, and to bring back even members of other litters and small lifeless objects. It begins to decrease in strength from twelve to twenty days following parturition, and usually has disappeared by the twenty-fifth day. It apparently parallels closely the duration of the lactation period. As P. T. Young (8) points out, the demand of the mother for her offspring seems to be due to the fact that the young are required for the free and normal functioning of the mammary glands; without them a congested condition of the breasts arises which the animal finds painful. This need normally persists until the young are weaned, and it largely explains the urge of the mother to return to her litter.

There are undoubtedly other physical or biological factors operative. "Maternal behavior" was induced, for example, in adult male rats through the implantation of anterior pituitary. These animals made nests, cared for young rats, licked them in a maternal way, etc. There was no apparent development of the mammary glands (9). There is also some indication of the production in the female organism of certain hormones which may contribute to the strength of the drive. In any case, there can be no doubt that post-maternal behavior satisfies our first two criteria—continuity with lower animals and a physiological basis.

Adoption. When, however, we turn to an examination of maternal behavior in various human societies, we find a number of striking phenomena which require consideration. In our culture, for example, parents prefer to have their own rather than adopted children; adoption occurs, but it is definitely a second-best. There are many societies among which this is apparently a matter of complete indifference. Rivers (10) reports that it was very difficult to obtain genealogies in Murray Island in the Torres Straits and that the islanders were reticent about this whole subject. The chief difficulty arose from the great prevalence of adoption. It was a common practice to adopt a child, in some cases the arrangement being made before its birth, and it was customary then to keep the child ignorant of his true parents. Even after reaching adult life, the child would give the name of his adoptive father. After Rivers left the island, one of the White residents continued the effort to determine true family relationships, but with little success.

In the Andaman Islands, adoption was similarly prevalent. In an early account by Man (11) it is reported to be of rare occurrence to find any child above the age of six or seven residing with its parents, "because it is considered a compliment and also a mark of friendship for a married man, after paying a visit, to ask his hosts to allow him to adopt one of their children. The request is usually complied with, and thenceforth the child's home is with his (or her) foster-father" (p. 125). In this case there is apparently no ignorance of the true parentage, but it seems a matter of little moment. A man may adopt as many children as he pleases on the understanding that he will treat them kindly.

Adoption was also very common in Borneo (12). Frequently it was the child of a relative who was adopted, but it might also be a captive or a slave child whose parents were willing to relinquish him. The adoption was always accompanied by an elaborate ceremony. For some weeks the adoptive mother observed all the prohibitions of pregnancy; at the end of that time the child was pushed forward between her legs, and if very young was put to her breast. So complete was the adoption that the new parents regarded the child as entirely their own, and it was very difficult to obtain from them any admission to the contrary.

There were also cases in which adults were adopted. Among the Omaha Indians, when a war party took a captive, he might be adopted by anyone who had lost a child or who was childless. In an early account by Tanner (13) it is reported that there was among many Indian groups a strong feeling about the replacement of lost members. He cites one incident which in our own society would certainly seem incredible, namely, that an Indian mother proposed to adopt a young man who had murdered her son in a drunken brawl. When we consider how a mother among us would feel about having in her own home the man who had killed her son, we realize the extent to which the manifestations of "maternal love" may vary from one community to another.

The many instances of adoption reported in ethnological literature appear to indicate that the attachment of parents to their own children is determined by the folkways of the community. It is important to note, however, that the ethnologist frequently fails to inform us of the attitudes of the persons involved. If adoption occurs because of the dictates of the community and in spite of the objections of the parents, it would constitute no argument against the universality of the maternal drive. For example, adoption occurred with considerable frequency in the Gilbert Islands (13), and the request to adopt a child could not be refused by the parents. It is reported, however, that "the parents are often extremely unwilling to part with their child, and it is probably only the force of native custom and the fear of social ostracism which makes them do so" (p. 141). This is of course an interpretation by the ethnologist, and it may be the correct one, although it is not made clear why the custom should persist if it conflicts with the wishes of the people.

It must not be assumed that all primitive peoples are alike in their attitude toward adoption. There are many communities in which it is relatively rare, and others in which a sharp distinction is made between adoption and blood kinship. This is true of Dobu, for instance, where a foster-parent will refer freely and publicly to an adopted child as a "bastard" or an "orphan," and where the relationship is not regarded as particularly binding (14).

Infanticide. The prevalence of adoption has been interpreted by Lowie (15) as due to the fact that "savages commonly have a generic love of children in no way dependent on the sense of consanguinity" (p. 460). This interpretation is in conflict, however, with the existence of another behavior pattern which was widespread among primitive peoples, namely, infanticide. This occurred so frequently that it is easy to multiply examples (16). The reasons for infanticide varied. In the Murray Islands in the Torres Straits it was considered proper to have the same number of boys and girls in the family, and if there were too many of the same sex, some were put to death. In the New Hebrides women had a great deal of work and could not attend to more than two or three children; they buried the rest as soon as they were born. Infanticide was practiced in Australia for similar reasons of convenience. In other cases, as in China, infanticide appears to occur only as a last resort when economic conditions have made it impossible to rear all the children.

Here also the psychologist would like to know much more about the emotions and attitudes of the parents who put their children to death. If they are driven to it by economic necessity and are unhappy as a result, their action by no means implies that children are not wanted, or that the parents are indifferent to them. If on the other hand they do it calmly and willingly, the probability increases that the nature of the maternal drive in general is socially determined. Some of the examples in the literature appear to point in this latter direction. It is reported that an Australian woman was asked why she had killed her baby; she pointed to a child two years old and said with apparent indifference that she could not look after two babies at once (16). There is no indication that any great emotional conflict was here involved, but negative evidence is not satisfactory. In a case of this kind it is of the utmost importance to know how the woman felt about the act she had committed. Unfortunately the ethnologist who made the report was more interested in the behavior than in the emotion which may have accompanied it. One must also consider the possibility (see Chapter 7) that the expression of emotions varies so much from one culture to another that it may not always be a simple matter to determine the exact nature of the emotional reaction.

It might be argued that infanticide is by no means absent from our own society. The practice of abortion is not uncommon. In the eyes of the Catholic Church at least it is in exactly the same category. It seems certain, however, that psychologically the two acts are entirely different. Many people who calmly proceed with an abortion would be completely revolted at the thought of killing the child after it was born. The fact that infanticide does occur in the case of births out of wedlock is to be explained by the social disapproval of illegitimate motherhood rather than by the absence of a maternal impulse. There is certainly nothing in our society to parallel the attitude of the Arioi in Tahiti, among whom special privileges were acquired by membership, but who had a rule enforced without exception that all their children should be immediately put to death (17). A woman who failed to kill her child was known as "a bearer of children," which was a term of reproach, and she was immediately expelled from the society. It seems clear that if there is a maternal drive, the customs of a people may not only alter its direction, but even cause its apparent disappearance.

Even apart from ethnological evidence of the type which we have just summarized, the existence of a maternal instinct has been questioned on the basis of an analysis in terms of our own society. Bernard (18), who has made one of the most thorough criticisms of the whole concept of instinct, expresses the opinion that social and traditional factors have been mistaken for apparently instinctive behavior. A little girl, for instance, may play with dolls not because of the presence of an incipient biological drive, but because she imitates her mother. Boys do the same until they learn that such behavior is not fitting for them. This observation is borne out by the experience of Margaret Mead (19) in the Manus tribe in New Guinea. In this community the women are usually occupied with regular work in the house and the fields, whereas the men are busy for a time with their hunting and fishing, but have more leisure. As a consequence, after the initial care of the baby it is the father rather than the mother who spends time with the child. These children have no dolls. It happened, however, that Miss Mead brought them some small wooden figures from a neighboring tribe, and found that it was the boys rather than the girls who showed an interest in them and a desire to play with them. Apparently in this case social factors have produced behavior in boys which in our community is often regarded as "instinctive" in girls. Bernard believes further that the mother's affectionate behavior toward the child grows out of her contact with it and that an initial biological basis for this affection is of no great importance.

In summary it may be said that there is a physiological or biochemical basis for post-maternal behavior in the changes occurring in the maternal organism during the period of gestation and after parturition. The enlargement of the mammary glands, as well as other glandular changes affecting the presence of hormones and other products in the organism, prepare the expectant mother for maternal behavior. In any case, however, this physiological condition explains the presence of a maternal drive only in those cases where the child is expected or where it has already arrived. It offers no basis for the desire to have children, i.e., for what we have called the pre-maternal drive.

The Desire for Children. If we apply to this pre-maternal drive the criteria of dependability, we find no evidence either for continuity with animals below man or for a physiological basis. The presence of such a drive in female animals might be expected to reveal itself in a willingness to accept punishment in order to get to the young of the species before parturition or even conception. In the studies by Warden and his associates no such tendency was observed. Among human beings, on the other hand, the desire for children is widespread.

Leta Hollingworth (20) has discussed what she calls "social devices for impelling women to bear and rear children." She mentions the forces of public opinion; the fact that governmental leaders like Mussolini, Theodore Roosevelt and the German Kaiser encouraged and in some cases subsidized large families; the law that sterility in the wife may be a cause for divorce; the law against dissemination of birth control information; the drastic laws against abortion, infanticide and infant desertion. She believes that the very existence of these laws testifies against the "instinctive" nature of the maternal drive, and that we cannot imagine laws forcing us to feed ourselves or to give ourselves sex satisfaction.[1] She points also to the religious forces behind the bearing of children as well as to the myriad madonnas by means of which art holds up the ideal of motherhood. In the light of this and similar material she concludes that the maternal drive would not be very effective if left to itself.

Sumner (21) comes to a similar conclusion for somewhat different reasons. "Children add to the weight of the struggle for existence of their parents. The relation of parent to child is one of sacrifice. The interests of parents and children are antagonistic. The fact that there are or may be compensations does not affect the primary relation between the two. It may well be believed that if procreation had not been put under the dominion of a great passion, it would have been caused to cease by the burden it entails" (p. 309).

There is an apparent contradiction in this point of view. To the biologist, for example, the causal relationship would appear to be exactly the reverse of that which Sumner suggests. That is to say, the biologist would regard the sexual impulse as subordinate to the preservation of the race, or in other words, to the bearing of children. It may still be true, however, that for the *individual* the primary motivating force is the sex drive, and that at least in a large number of cases procreation is a by-product.

When children are desired, either by men or women, a variety of reasons may be operative. In a great many instances an economic motive is clearly responsible, for the child may be a practical asset to the entire family. Stefansson (22), for example, writes that "the nearest thing to an investment among the Stone Age Eskimos, the one means of providing against old age, is children. For that reason a widow without a child would have to be loved for herself alone. A widow with one child would be a desirable match. To marry a widow with three or four children was, among the Stone Age people of Coronation Gulf, the New York equivalent to marrying the widow of a millionaire" (p. 164).

The motive may not always be directly economic. The women of the Pilaga tribe in the Gran Chaco of the Argentine are said not to care very much for children but they are glad when children

---

[1] It should be pointed out, however, that we do have laws against homosexual practices, so that on this basis we should have no right to assume that heterosexual behavior is innately determined.

come, because they know that is the best way to keep their husbands.[2] This mechanism is of course not unknown in our own society.

The material from primitive societies is not to be understood as indicating that maternal love is always subservient to practical considerations. It is rather that culture determines the extent to which children are loved and the reasons for which they are desired.

Paternal Behavior. So far we have said little about the attitude of the father and the existence of a "paternal" drive. There is considerable evidence that the father's interest in the offspring is found far down in the animal scale, and is by no means confined to human beings. In the case of many species of birds the male usually remains with the female even after the breeding season, helps build the nest, brings food for the young and defends the mother and the offspring against enemies. In mammals the male commonly does not concern himself with the progeny, though there are many exceptions. The evidence regarding the anthropoids is contradictory on this point. Some observers describe the male parent as relatively indifferent to the welfare of the offspring. Yerkes (23), however, states that the chimpanzee father helps look after the young one, amuses and exercises him, protects him and supplies him with food. There appears to be some indication therefore that the human family may be an inheritance from anthropoid ancestors.

On the other hand, the anthropologist Malinowski (24) states that at least in higher cultures the necessity for imposing the bond of marriage is practically and theoretically due to the fact that a father has to be made to look after his children. Culture forces the male to keep guard over the pregnant female and to share in her anticipatory interest in the child. Once forced into this position, however, the male responds with strong interests and positive feelings for the offspring. This furnishes the raw material out of which culture fashions paternal love. In other words, society imposes upon the man the duty of caring for his children as a sort of payment for the rights he has in his wife.

This theory offers an explanation of paternal behavior which does not depend upon the presence of any biological factors. Malinowski is himself inconsistent on this point. He insists that there must be an anatomical basis for behavior before it may be regarded as instinctively determined. Without finding such a basis, he still concludes that paternal motives are due to biological elements, and

2 Jules Henry, personal communication.

that culture merely emphasizes natural tendencies. If we apply our threefold criterion, we see that paternal behavior must be denied the status of complete dependability, since no visceral or biochemical basis has ever been discovered which might explain its existence.

The criterion of universality is also not fulfilled. Whereas most families do consist of mother, father and offspring, there are a few striking exceptions. It is reported of a warrior tribe in India, the Nayars (25), that immediately after marriage divorce occurs on the theory that warriors must not be burdened by wives and families who might constitute a responsibility for them. After the divorce the wives are permitted intimacies with any number of other men and the children belong to the mothers alone. The institution of "professional husbands," also found in India (13), is another exception. As one aspect of the caste system there exists the practice of "hypergamy," which means that a woman may marry a man of her own or of a superior caste, but not of an inferior one. Frequently her father may not be able to pay the dowry needed to obtain a husband who can satisfy this requirement. In that case he may marry his daughter to a professional husband who has a number of wives, and who makes periodical visits to each one of them. The children belong entirely to the mother and her family. It is true that these exceptions to the more usual family pattern are rare and due to special circumstances, so that they should not be overemphasized. The absence of any known physiological basis for the paternal drive, however, constitutes a more serious objection to the assumption that it is an innate part of human nature.

The desire for children is of course present in men as well as women. It may perhaps be adequately explained on the basis of the values attached to children by the particular culture. These values may be economic, as mentioned above; they may be religious, as in China, where sons are necessary to insure the immortality of the parents by attending to their shrines and burning incense to their memory. Children may be desired as a form of immortality in another way, by insuring the continuity in others of what is really ourselves. They may also be welcomed by men as a tangible proof of their virility. It is interesting to note in this connection that in our society the inability to procreate is usually regarded as much more "shameful" in a man than in a woman; this is in direct contrast to the attitude in many other cultures where the worst thing that may be said of a woman is that she is unable to bear children.

A behavior pattern similar in some respects to the phenomenon of adoption and also expressive of an attitude diametrically opposed to our own is the claim of the husband to all the offspring of his wife, even when he knows that he is not the father. This has been reported for a large number of communities in Africa, Melanesia, Siberia, etc. (16). An especially interesting case is found in the Sakalava tribe in Madagascar. There the bride price is considerable, and in case of divorce there is no refund or substitution. The divorced wife may not remarry, however, without the permission of her husband, who usually enters into an agreement with the new husband by which he receives the first three children of the new union. He is said to take as much interest in them as if they were his own (25). The fact that children are an economic asset undoubtedly explains this attitude, but for our present purposes the cause is less important than the existence of a point of view which seems to be opposed to "human nature" as we know it.

In connection with the attitude toward children, there is a final point to be made. The familiar adage "spare the rod and spoil the child" played a more prominent part in the life of our society a hundred years ago than it does today, but it still reflects a not-uncommon practice. To a large number of "primitive" groups it represents something quite unthinkable. Among many American Indians, for example, corporal punishment in any form was severely condemned. It is reported that Eskimos do not consider that White people deserve to have children, since they are so heartless as to strike them. In Tahiti a White man who beat his own child was almost put to death by the natives. Among the Buka people in Melanesia (26) any kind of punishment of children was unknown. It is interesting to speculate on what an Eskimo or Melanesian psychologist would say about such behavior in our society; he might decide that we were lacking in the parental instinct.

The evidence here assembled permits the following conclusions. What we have called the post-maternal drive has a physiological basis, shows continuity with animal behavior and a very wide, though not universal, distribution among human beings. The pre-maternal drive, on the other hand, has apparently no physiological basis, cannot be demonstrated in animals below man, and its distribution among human societies appears to be determined by the economic and social motives operative in the community. The same is true for the attitudes of the father. In any case, whether they have a physiological basis or not, the functioning of these motives is clearly influenced by cultural patterning and conditioning.

AGGRESSIVENESS

The problem of the innateness or universality of aggressive behavior is one of obvious practical significance. It would probably be agreed that the occurrence of war and the threat of war in our society represent its worst feature—one which may even contain the germs of the destruction of our whole civilization. The assertion is sometimes made that war will never be abolished because it is rooted in an instinct of pugnacity which is natural to man. Psychology and ethnology have an important contribution to make in connection with this problem.

Aggressive behavior is of course found widely in the animal kingdom. It must be borne in mind, however, that it is by no means an invariable rule of behavior. Cases of mutual help and cooperation also occur in abundance, even between members of different species. When aggressiveness is found it is frequently in association with other drives, such as self-preservation, sex, and maternal love, and probably is not to be regarded as an end in itself.

On the physiological side no basis has been discovered for the existence of aggressiveness as such. It has been amply demonstrated by Cannon (27) that in anger there is a whole series of biochemical and physiological changes under the influence of the sympathetic nervous system and the adrenal glands. These changes prepare the organism for an emergency; they include the liberation of glycogen from the liver so that in the form of glucose it may be used as a source of energy; the more rapid elimination of the products of fatigue; the quicker clotting of blood, so that wounds will not be so dangerous; the movement of blood from the digestive system to the muscles, so that these may act more efficiently, and so on. The general result of these changes is that in the presence of an enemy the organism may respond with an unusual output of energy over an unusually long period of time. These changes do occur in anger, but they occur also in fear and in excitement; they constitute an organic basis for violent emotional behavior in general, rather than for aggressiveness itself (see also Chapter 7).

War. There are some human groups among whom aggressive behavior was apparently indulged in for its own sake. An Iroquois chief is reported to have proposed to a neighboring ruler that their young men be allowed to have a little war. On the second chief's refusal, he was asked, "With whom then can my children play?" (28). However, this may not be an example of aggressiveness as such, since the Iroquois chief was concerned with the need of his young warriors for practice. Of the Lango it is said—"They are brave and venturesome warriors, who have won the fear and respect of their neighbors, delighting in war not only for the plunder which it brings, but also for its own sake" (29, p. 68).

These examples do not necessarily prove that aggressive behavior is innately determined. It may become an end in itself even though it originated as a means to an end. In all cases we have a long previous history of warfare and the possibility therefore that warlike habits have been developed. As we shall see later much of the warfare of primitive peoples is to be understood as similar to athletic contests or trials of strength, and that may be the primary motivation responsible.

On the other hand, it has been noted that warfare is by no means universal and that there are many societies to which it is foreign. In their survey of the cultural characteristics of a large number of groups, Hobhouse and his associates (30) report that there were at least ten tribes which had no war. The Arctic explorer Nansen quotes an Eskimo letter of 1756 which is pertinent to this discussion. The writer of the letter cannot understand how it is that men of the same faith are hunting each other like seals and stealing from people they have never seen or known. Fighting about land seems to him sheer greed. He apostrophizes his own country. "How well it is that you are covered with ice and snow! How well it is that, if in your rocks there are gold and silver, for which the Christians are so greedy, it is covered with so much snow that they cannot get at it. Your unfruitfulness makes us happy and saves us from molestation" (31, p. 180). The writer was surprised that the Europeans had not learned better manners among the Eskimo and proposed to send medicine men as missionaries to the Whites to teach them the Eskimo way of life.

There are many writers who feel that aggressive warfare, far from being native to man, develops only when culture has reached a certain degree of complexity. Letourneau (32) states that at the beginning of society, when men were few in number and did not trouble each other, war was as strange to them as until recently it was among the Eskimo of the far north. Van der Bij (33) also believes that the simplest and most primitive peoples were not warlike; they had no offensive war and were even unwilling to engage in defensive wars. He cites cases from a number of very simple societies in support of this point of view, and believes that war comes only with greater cultural development and an increase in the size of the groups. Elliot Smith (34) is substantially of the same opinion. It may be that these writers tend unduly to glorify the "noble savage" and to attribute all the ills of mankind to an interference with the state of nature, and we must certainly be careful not to exaggerate the purity and nobility of primitive man. There is no doubt, however, that there were many groups who were not at all warlike, and that therefore aggressiveness, at least to the extent that it expresses itself in war, does not satisfy our criterion of universality.

Wars do of course occur with great frequency, but they may usually be understood in terms of certain very definite motives. Obviously, most peoples will defend themselves when attacked. Clearly too, they will fight for food and in many cases for plunder. Examples of this type of warfare are numerous. As Bunzel (35) indicates, war raids for profit are characteristic of many primitive societies; even the peaceable Zuñi formerly conducted raids on the sheep of their Navajo neighbors. The Crow raided for horses, as this was their favorite form of wealth, and a stolen horse was the only acceptable bride gift. Among the Kiowa, the whole economic system hinged upon warfare, the objective of which was the acquisition of horses; the enemy was killed only when it was absolutely necessary. In parts of West Africa slave-raiding was one of the main causes of war. Hobhouse and his associates (30) found also that in forty or more peoples, where marriage by capture occurred, the possession of women was the direct object of a warlike raid.

War has often been due to religious causes. Eating a dead man was interpreted by many peoples as giving the conqueror his virtues. Among the Yoruba, hearts were regularly sold in order to give courage, and the procuring of them often led to battle. In Aztec Mexico religious factors were responsible for the major part of warlike behavior. One of the important beliefs was that the gods, particularly the Sun, would die if deprived of food, and the only satisfying nourishment consisted of human hearts. The victim of the sacrifice was identified with the god, and his killing and eating meant a resurrection of the god and the renewal of his strength. There was a Mexican legend to the effect that the gods themselves had formerly been sacrificed to the Sun in order to endow him with strength to do his work, and they bequeathed the duty to the human representatives, directing them to fight and kill each other to provide the necessary food. There was almost perpetual warfare with the neighboring Tlaxcalans for the sole purpose of obtaining captives to serve as sacrificial victims (36).

> When the great temple of Huitzilopochtli was dedicated in 1486, the chain of victims sacrificed on that occasion extended for the length of two miles. In this terrible massacre the hearts of no less than 70,000 human beings were offered up. . . . These victims were nearly always captive warriors of rival nations. . . . (37, p. 41.)

Among the Wyandot Indians it was believed that an increase in the size of the clan would please the animal god from which it was descended. Every effort was made to keep the clan full, that is, to keep in use the complete list of names belonging to it. For this purpose war was carried on in order to secure women and children, and occasionally men, for adoption. Connelley (38) writes:

> The old Wyandots have often told me that their tribe made war on the Cherokees for the express purpose of securing women and children with which to make good the wasting clans. To allow a clan to become extinct was sure to call down the displeasure of the animal-god for which the clan was named and from which it was supposed it was descended (p. 237).

The glory motive, or the quest for prestige, is one of the most frequent causes of aggressive behavior. Head-hunting, for example, although sometimes the result of religious practices, may also be due to the intense desire for a trophy which will elevate its possessor to a higher position in the community. Among the Asaba on the Niger River a man receives the honorary title of Obu if he has done a brave deed, and he most clearly earns this title if he has killed another man (39). In parts of New Guinea a youth must have "fetched a head" before he may be counted an adult, and the badges of distinction for warriors depend on the number of lives taken (40). Distinguished Masai warriors had the right to wear bracelets and bells. Among the Bagobo of the Philippines a man's clothing indicated his status, which was determined by the number of deaths for which he was responsible (41).

Among the Plains Indians the desire for military renown was hypertrophied. The Crow, for example, regarded four events as honorable and as conferring the title of chief upon the warrior—(1) cutting loose and stealing a horse picketed in the camp of the enemy, (2) taking an enemy's bow or gun in a hand-to-hand encounter, (3) striking "coup"—touching an enemy with a weapon or with the hand, and (4) leading a victorious occupation or attack. A man's standing was proportional to his war record, and at tribal gatherings he recounted his exploits and was honored by his fellows. Warriors often courted death in foolhardy adventures, and a coward was the object of supreme contempt (41). In Plains Indian warfare in general, killing an enemy was relatively unimportant; the bravest act was to count coup by touching or striking a living unhurt man without killing him. It was an evidence of bravery to go into war without any weapon that could harm the enemy at a distance, and the most courageous warrior was the one who was armed only with a coup stick. This does not prove the absence of economic motives, since booty was also the frequent reward of the warrior, but there can be no doubt that the added prestige concerned him most.

It should be pointed out further that when primitive peoples do fight they seem not to be giving expression to a spontaneous and uncontrolled pugnacious drive, but rather to a form of behavior which is regulated and modified by social conventions. In general, primitive warfare was not very destructive of human life, and the casualties were frequently insignificant. When two groups of Australian aborigines fought, the battle was over as soon as one warrior on either side had been killed. Sometimes the first wound ended the combat. Sumner and Keller (40) state that conflicts among primitive people were generally brief and relatively bloodless. "A savage would stand aghast before the wholesale slaughter of civilized warfare, and beside some of its methods his own are those of a gentleman" (Vol. I, p. 370).

As a matter of fact, war was really in many cases a sort of duel or game, and the attitude toward it was frequently sportsmanlike. It is said that the Arkansas Indians once gave a share of their powder to the Chickasaw with whom they were at war; an Algonquin tribe refrained from pressing an attack upon the Iroquois when it was pointed out that night had fallen. Australian tribes have been known to provide unarmed Europeans with a set of weapons before attacking. The Maori are reported to have filled canoes with food for their hungry enemies so that they might fight on more equal terms. On the other hand, sudden raids without any warning are by no means unknown in primitive warfare. [For a comprehensive review of the causes of war as seen by a political scientist, see Quincy Wright (42).]

Quarrels Between Individuals. William James (43) once spoke of a "moral equivalent for war." There are many primitive communities which have worked out some such equivalent, particularly in the case of quarrels between individuals. The Indians of the Northwest Coast settle disputes by means of the institution of the potlatch. If two men have a quarrel one of them may give a potlatch or feast, at which the aim is to give away or destroy as large an amount of property as possible. His rival is humbled as a consequence and regarded as having lost status in the community until he can do likewise. A Kwakiutl chief once said, "The White man fights with his hands, but we fight with property" (44). This fighting with property may also take place under much more informal conditions. There is a story to this effect told of the Tlingit of Alaska. "Two women were quarreling. In a rage one of them said to the other, 'I'll shut you up!' At that she rushed into her house, came out with both hands full of silver money, and scattered it to the crowd that was watching the proceedings. This did shut the mouth of her opponent as she could not do likewise" (45, p. 95). Goldman (46) reports a case among the Alkatcho Carrier Indians in which a man had been insulted by being placed in a position of inferiority at a feast. He went out with his relatives and returned with a number of articles which he presented to his host, thereby humbling him and wiping out the insult.

A particularly interesting method of settling a quarrel is reported for various groups of Eskimos, from the Aleuts at one geographical extreme to the Greenland tribes at the other. An Eskimo who has suffered some injury may compose a satirical song in mockery of his enemy and challenge him to a public singing contest. The village group assembles, and the two contestants take turns mocking each other to the best of their ability. The spectators decide the victor. Sometimes this is not possible until the contestants have been re-called many times.

One example of this Eskimo "duel" may be of interest. Eqerko had married the divorced wife of Marratse. The marriage reawakened the old love and jealousy of Marratse, who challenged his rival to a singing contest. Marratse sings:

> Words I shall split
> little sharp words, like wood splinters
> from under my axe.
> A song of olden days
> a breath of the ancestors.
> A song of longing
> for my wife.
> A song that brings
> forgetfulness.
> A cheeky braggart
> has stolen her.
> He has tried
> to belittle her.
> Miserable wretch
> who loves human flesh.
> A cannibal
> from famine days.

Eqerko answers:

> Cheek which amazes one!
> Laughable fury
> and sham courage.
> A song of derision
> which proclaims my guilt.
> You want to frighten me!
> Me who defy death
> with indifference.
> Hei! You sing to my wife
> who once was yours.
> Then you were not so worthy
> of love.
> While she was left alone,
> you forgot to exalt her
> in song,
> in challenging, fighting
> song.
> Now she is mine,
> nor will she ever be visited
> by song-making, false lovers,
> abductors of women
> in strangers' tents (47, pp. 97-99).

These examples indicate that aggressiveness, whether or not it has an innate basis, may be modified by the culture in many ways. It may be stimulated in one society and relatively lacking in another. It may arise as the result of any one of a number of different causes. It may express itself in violent physical combat or in a socially regulated contest in which no one is harmed. There is no justification, therefore, for the attempt to explain any specific type of aggressive behavior on the ground that it has a biological basis. To the question as to whether war is inevitable because of the existence of such an aggressive instinct, the ethnologist and the social psychologist have reason to give a categorical negative. War is an institution, and must be explained in relation to the whole social structure in which it occurs. After a somewhat similar survey of the pertinent material, Sumner and Keller (40) come to the conclusion that "There is no 'instinct of pugnacity.' What there is is a set of life conditions demanding adjustment" (Vol. IV, p. 369).

To the more specific question as to what does cause war in our society, it is not easy to give a definite answer. There is a growing conviction backed by a large amount of concrete evidence, that economic factors play a very important part. It has also been suggested that within our culture the marked development of the sentiment of patriotism easily leads to a supernationalism committed to the ideal of expansion and aggrandizement. In our own time this has been particularly noticeable in Fascist countries where an attitude of almost religious adoration of the Fatherland was accompanied by readiness to resort to war. In any case we may say with certainty that the causes of war are to be found in society and not in human nature.

In the writings of the psychoanalysts the notion of an aggressive instinct—sometimes called the death instinct—has been utilized in a somewhat different form. The Freudians believe that there is in all of us an unmistakable, though often latent, aggressiveness. This may express itself during infancy in the hostility against the father; later it may be directed against a whole group. It is stimulated and aggravated by the controls and inhibitions which society imposes upon the individual, and it develops in him the desire to "get even." War may furnish a socially approved outlet for this aggressiveness, and may therefore be welcomed by a substantial proportion of the community. One writer (48) states that during a long process of sublimation the anger and resentment of a child toward the father becomes successively directed upon various substitute objects.

> In some cases the sublimation may be carried on and on until at last the hatred becomes directed upon an object that the whole community agrees in disliking. What more likely object is there than "the enemy," who thus fulfils the extremely important function of providing intense expression for the repressed father-hate of childhood? The desire to "punish" the enemy then becomes a consuming passion, and a harmless citizen becomes a fanatical supporter of a ruthless war policy (p. 129).

Other psychoanalysts stress the fundamental character of aggressiveness without such direct reference to father-hatred.

We shall return to this theory later in the discussion of group conflict as it is expressed in the phenomenon of prejudice. At this point it may suffice to say that the Freudian explanation of war is definitely inadequate. Perhaps the best disproof of the theory is to be found in the fact that in every modern war the number of those who volunteer for service (and who may therefore be expressing this latent aggressiveness) always represents a small minority. Every large nation has had to depend upon some form of conscription or draft to form its armies. Hostility between nations, as expressed in war, is clearly far from universal; when it does occur, it has usually been stimulated by every artificial means at the disposal of governments and army staffs and propaganda experts. Aggressiveness as an end in itself is of no help as a principle of explanation, either in the form of one of McDougall's instincts or in the formulation of Freud and his followers. It should be added that the statements of certain psychoanalysts, particularly Horney (49) and Kardiner (50), lay less emphasis upon the innateness and inevitability of aggressive behavior and more upon the socially determined conflicts and strains which lead to violence.

Frustration and Aggression. A somewhat modified version of the psychoanalytic approach is represented by the theory that aggression is caused by frustration, and that frustration always leads to aggression (51). An impressive array of evidence has been collected, including materials from animal behavior, ethnology, experiments with children, phenomena in the field of prejudice and discrimination, crime and delinquency, etc. As we shall see in greater detail later, the theory is a useful and fruitful one, which has contributed to the understanding of many psychological phenomena. Controversy has arisen, however, as to the regularity of the postulated causal relationship. Does frustration *always* lead to aggression? And is aggression *always* the result of frustration?

One investigation which has cast doubt on the one to one correspondence between frustration and aggression is reported by Barker, Dembo, Lewin and Wright (52). A group of children were given some attractive new toys, and observers rated the degree of maturity which the children showed in their play. The new toys were then placed behind a transparent screen so that the children could see them, but not touch them; instead they were given older, less attractive toys. When the observers again rated the maturity of the play, they noted in a number of cases the phenomenon of regression rather than aggression; that is to say, the frustration resulted in a return to more primitive, infantile behavior, of a kind which these children had outgrown. The investigators concluded that aggression *may* follow frustration, but that it is not inevitable.

As a matter of fact, frustration may apparently have many different consequences, depending upon the previous experience of the individual, his personal characteristics, the circumstances in which the frustration occurs, etc. Krech and Crutchfield (3) mention a number of possibilities: (1) intensification of effort in the attempt to overcome the barriers; (2) reorganization of the perception of the problem, with frustration leading to new insight, and the discovery of new paths to the goal; (3) substitution of new goals, which serve in place of the goals which cannot be reached; and (4) maladaptive consequences, which may include aggression, regression, withdrawal, repression, etc.

The safest conclusion therefore to draw in this connection is that frustration may frequently, but not necessarily, give rise to aggression, and that aggression may frequently, but not necessarily, result from frustration. Two of the authors who contributed to the original volume on *Frustration and Aggression*, namely Miller and Dollard (53), have in fact expressed their belief that learning may play a much greater part in the relationship than was previously realized; in the process of socialization, some individuals and some cultures may learn to react with aggression; others may learn to respond in some alternative fashion. The anthropologist Bateson (54) makes a somewhat similar point with regard to the behavior of the Balinese. The fact that children are so frequently "frustrated" by the Balinese mother, who stimulates her child emotionally and then abruptly turns away when the child reaches for her, may develop in the Balinese adult an expectation of certain forms of frustration which as a consequence are not taken too seriously. Apparently we can learn to accept frustration without any aggressive response, depending on the experiences to which our culture has accustomed us. The phenomenon of "frustration tolerance," described in detail by Rosenzweig (55), may hold for cultures as well as for individuals.

These considerations make it impossible to accept the frustration-aggression theory as an adequate explanation of international hostility or war. They apply also to the thesis defended by Durbin and Bowlby (56), who find in the frustrations of childhood the major cause of adult aggressiveness, furthered by the operation of certain psychoanalytic mechanisms—displacement, which leads us to direct our aggression against a group which is not responsible for our frustration; projection, which permits us to ascribe to others the aggression which has its source in us; rationalization, which results in attempts to justify our aggression as based entirely on lofty, ethical considerations, etc. It seems clear that these various mechanisms do play a part. We fall back, however, on our previous queries. If war is due to latent aggressiveness resulting from early frustration, and if this is something we all experience, why are so many of us reluctant to go to war? Why must we be forced to fight?

One additional point should be made. Modern warfare includes a great many essential activities far removed from the battlefield—problems of logistics, the building of roads and bridges, the manufacture of weapons, the maintaining of communications, and a host of others—so that the proportion of our military personnel who ever see the enemy, and the still smaller proportion who actually engage in combat, represent only a tiny fraction of the total. It is impossible to explain this complicated machinery on the basis of individual aggressiveness.

A Question of Definition. In connection with the argument concerning the universality of aggression, the suggestion has occasionally been made that the problem may be one of definition of terms. Bender (57), for example, believes that aggression in its original meaning refers to the tendency to "go forward or approach"; this is instinctive, in her view, whereas the inborn or instinctive nature of *hostility* has never been demonstrated. Similarly, Allen (58) regards aggression as "a fundamental characteristic of all living organisms," expressing itself in "the will to assert and to test our capacity to deal with external forces." Aggression may therefore be either positive or negative; in the latter case it is synonymous with hostility.

If aggression is defined as broadly as has been suggested, it will clearly include many forms of behavior which have usually been listed under other headings—curiosity, exploration, self-assertiveness, activity drives (59) in general. Without quarreling with the facts as presented by these investigators, the present writer is of the opinion that only confusion can result from the use of a single term to encompass so many different psychological operations. It is difficult to specify on every occasion whether the aggression of which we speak is positive or negative, whether it takes the form of mastery over inanimate nature or over other human beings, whether it is constructive or destructive. The all-embracing use of the term may make aggression more respectable, but it is misleading. That is our justification for continuing to use the word *aggression* as synonymous with hostility, and to use other terms to designate different, though possibly related, forms of behavior.

We may conclude that aggressive behavior shows continuity with animals, that it has an indirect though probably no direct physiological basis, and that in one form or another it has a wide distribution. The exact nature of its expression varies from one group to another, and no particular form of aggressiveness, e.g., war, may be regarded as inevitable. Social factors determine the amount, the nature and to a large extent the very existence of aggressiveness.

ACQUISITIVENESS

The phenomenon of acquisitiveness may with considerable justification be regarded as central to the social structure of the Western world. It is probable that a large number of our institutions are to be understood only in connection with acquisitive behavior. As we noted in the preceding section, the institution of war may be partly explained from this standpoint. It becomes of prime importance therefore to analyze the nature of this phenomenon from both ethnological and psychological points of view.

The problem of variations in acquisitive tendency was noted by W. H. R. Rivers (60), who in a great deal of his work applied ethnological categories to the understanding of psychological behavior. He took the position, which is in complete agreement with our own, that only that behavior may be regarded as instinctive which is common to mankind in general. He then analyzed the attitudes toward property among the people of Melanesia, and reported that there are a great many objects, particularly those made by the united efforts of the community, which are regarded as owned in common. A canoe, for example, is the common possession of the group, and land, though individually cultivated, is always common property.[3] There are rules concerning the use of produce taken from land which has been cultivated by others, and disputes do not arise. Even those objects like weapons and utensils produced by an individual and regarded as his own are used by others much more frequently than would be the case in our society. Rivers concludes: "Melanesia shows that the instinct of acquisition in the interest of the individual can be so greatly modified in response to gregarious needs that it practically disappears or only appears under special circumstances" (p. 272).

If it "practically disappears," should we still speak of it as an instinct? Since Rivers himself applied the criterion of universality and found it not to be satisfied by his Melanesian data, it would have been more reasonable to question the instinctive nature of the phenomenon. This is precisely what is done by Beaglehole (61), who has written the best analysis of this whole question. In his introduction to a very careful survey of the pertinent literature, he writes:

> That, in general, my conclusions are not favorable to the acquisitive instinct theory I should perhaps state at the outset. The biological facts are too complex to be explained away in terms of an innate acquisitive tendency. One is sometimes tempted to wonder how many more of McDougall's instincts would survive an equally rigid biological examination! (p. 28)

Beaglehole begins with an examination of the evidence for acquisitive behavior among various animal species, from insects up to anthropoids. His general conclusion is that although acquisitive behavior is found in considerable frequency it is to be explained not as an end itself, but as a means of satisfying the more fundamental needs of the organism. Objects are appropriated when they are required for some specific purpose. The fundamental forms of acquisi-

---

[3] It may be noted here that whereas primitive groups differ widely from one another in the distinctions made between private and common property, it is rare for land to be owned outright by an individual.

tive behavior have to do with the demand for food, for a mate, for a nest or territory. Most cases of acquisitiveness among animals are due to the operation of the more powerful drives of hunger, sex and care of offspring.

An exception to the above is noted in the behavior of certain birds like the magpie and the raven, who apparently collect objects for their own sake. Beaglehole's explanation of this phenomenon is not entirely satisfactory. He believes that in the case of these intelligent birds, their curiosity and interest are easily aroused by bright portable objects. "Curiosity rather than a blind desire to collect is the motive of their behavior" (p. 119). In the meantime, curiosity has not been established as a "dependable motive," and until we have subjected it to the same critical analysis which Beaglehole has directed toward the concept of acquisitiveness, we can hardly use it as a principle of explanation.

As far as our first criterion of dependability is concerned, namely, continuity with lower animal forms, we conclude that such continuity undoubtedly exists. With a few rare exceptions, however, the acquisitive behavior of animals may be shown to be subordinate to other apparently more fundamental drives.

On the physiological side we can find no basis whatsoever for acquisitive behavior, except in the indirect manner referred to in the preceding paragraphs; that is to say, to the extent that acquisitiveness is subordinate to the hunger drive as it clearly is in the case of squirrels, for example. The hunger contractions might then be regarded as the visceral basis of the behavior. It is clear, however, that we have here an organic basis for hunger and not for acquisitiveness, and it seems safe to conclude in general that our second criterion is definitely not fulfilled in this case.

The question of the universality of acquisitive behavior has already been mentioned in connection with Rivers' analysis. There can be little doubt that culture may determine any degree of emphasis on the principle of private ownership, from its almost complete absence in one society to its all-pervasiveness in another. It was formerly believed, largely as the result of the work of Morgan (62), that primitive peoples were communistic and that there had been a gradual evolution from that condition to our present one of private property. This evolutionary scheme is no longer taken seriously by the majority of ethnologists. In the Torres Straits Islands, for example (63), private property was present in an extreme form.

Every rock and water hole had its owner, the only piece of common land being the village street. There were, however, many societies in which the economic system could be described as partial or complete communism.

Attitudes Toward Property. One example of a society in which the essentials of life are communally owned is to be found in the people of Lesu (64). In this Melanesian group there is abundance of land and no private ownership of it, nor are there any private fishing or hunting rights. Food may be obtained by a moderate amount of industry, shelter is easy to provide, and clothing is so scanty that it presents no problem. There is a certain amount of private property in connection with ornaments, implements of work, ceremonial currency, pigs and knowledge. Everyone lives in about the same style and there is no poverty. The private property that does exist in this community allows a man to make elaborate rites for his dead ancestors and so gain prestige for himself. Wealth is not hoarded, but is always being put in circulation by these frequent ritual feasts. Old people are well looked after by the community and have no need to save anything. Powdermaker describes the economic organization as well-integrated and as providing adequately for the needs of all the members of the community. The underlying social forces are the principle of reciprocity, the desire for prestige, respect for the old, and a closely knit kinship system—these take the place of any individual competition for the necessities of life, and the result is security for all. In this system even the lazy man is not allowed to starve, but he has no importance in the community, no influence in discussion; it is difficult for him to secure a wife, he is unable to give big feasts and he lacks prestige. This is admitted to be a serious handicap, and it is a rare individual who will not do the work which is ordinarily required.

After a survey of the economic organization of a large number of primitive societies, Goldenweiser (47) concludes that complete communism is rare if not entirely absent, and that the theory which regards primitive communism as a prelude to the individual ownership that developed later must as a consequence be rejected.

It contains, however, the germ of a truth, to this extent: in modern Western society, individual ownership has, as we know, acquired a significance and a role far beyond the importance of this institution among most primitives. . . . On the other hand, ownership of the essential articles needed for life or of the territories from which these are derived, in other words, just those things which in later times came to represent the most coveted of individual property, constitute among primitives the prerogative of the group: what is needed and used by all is held in common (pp. 148-149).

Even if, therefore, we never encounter complete communism, we may still say that many societies show a great deal more communism than our own, and it is clear that any insistence upon the psychological inevitability of economic competition to the extent that we know it is unwarranted.

For primitive man in general it has been suggested (*61*) that objects acquired or made by personal exertion are regarded as private property, whereas those acquired or made through the combined labor of a group are usually the common property of the individuals forming that group. There are, however, numerous exceptions. Among the Siberian tribes as well as among the Eskimo the seal or the whale killed by an individual was still divided with the other members of the community. The Eskimo had in addition the interesting rule that if one man borrowed something from another and failed to return it, nothing was done about it. The assumption was that the borrower needed it more and that the lender must have a surplus if he was able to part with it in the first place.

Among the Kaingang Indians of Brazil (*65*) when a hunter brings down a tapir he neither keeps the meat nor distributes it. He gives the whole animal to a close relative, who butchers it, giving some to the hunter and some to the other members of the camp, and keeping the greater part for his own use. The cleverest hunter has only slight economic advantages, since in the long run the product of the hunt is shared evenly.

Among the Arapesh also, it is not true that what a man acquires with his own hands belongs to him alone (*66*). The society has a system of exchanges and reciprocity rather than one in which every man works for himself. An Arapesh man hunts only to send most of his kill to his mother's brother, cousin or father-in-law. "The lowest man in the community, the man who is believed to be so far outside the moral pale that there is no use reasoning with him, is the man who eats his own kill—even though the kill be a tiny bird, hardly a mouthful in all" (p. 29).

One other economic attitude of the Arapesh deserves a word of comment. They are very closely attached to their ancestral lands, but they do not conceive of themselves as owning the lands; rather they belong to the lands, and they feel none of the proud possessiveness of owners.

> On a neighboring hilltop, the village of Alipinagle was sadly depleted. In the next generation there would not be enough people to occupy the land. The people of Alitoa sighed: "Alas, poor Alipinagle, after the present people are gone, who will care for the land, who will there be beneath the trees? We must give them some children to adopt, that the land and the trees may have people when we are gone." Such generosity had of course the practical consequences of placing a child or so in a more advantageous position, but it was never phrased in this way, nor did the people recognize any formulations based upon possessiveness about land (p. 18).

In this case, however, the difference between the Arapesh attitude and our own seems to be a matter of phrasing rather than a real difference in behavior.

Differing attitudes toward private property are illustrated in the experience of Rivers, who reports that after he had questioned his Melanesian subjects about their various customs, one of them put a question to him. He asked what Rivers would do if he found a sum of money which did not belong to him. Rivers answered that if he could not discover the rightful owner, he would naturally keep it for himself. When the Melanesians learned that he would not divide it equally with other members of his group, they were greatly disappointed at his evident greediness. It might be added that stinginess in any form is one of the greatest crimes among Melanesians, as it is among many other primitive peoples.

We noted above that in the case of animals the acquisition of property is usually subordinate to some other motive. The same holds for man, although of course the motives are quite different. The desire for prestige is undoubtedly one of the most significant in this connection. Among the Trobrianders, for example, food was collected not only for use as nourishment, but for purposes of display. This food was placed in large storehouses in such a way that through the openings others might see how much the owner had been able to acquire. Prestige rose and fell according to the amount. It was the greatest insult to say of someone that he was a "man with no food" (67). The possession of hunting trophies, of badges and ornaments testifying to the valor of the possessor, are all easily understood on the basis of the prestige motive. The most striking instance of the determination of property attitudes by the desire for prestige is undoubtedly found among the Indians of British Columbia and the Northwest Coast in general. Reference has already been made to the institution of the potlatch which centered upon the ability of the host to give away or to destroy a large amount of property. There was a tremendous, one might almost say an hypertrophied interest in property, but not in acquisition; property was merely a means to an end, that end being prestige. It is true that the property given away had to be returned later, often with about one hundred percent interest (44), but the primary consideration was clearly prestige, and was so understood by the Indians themselves. The fact that the most valuable property was so often destroyed or "thrown into the fire" without any possibility of concrete return, testifies to the correctness of this interpretation. Here, even more than in Melanesia, the greatest social sin was keeping all of one's property, and the man who gave no potlatches had no standing in the community. It is only fair to point out that in our own society as well some form of "conspicuous waste," as Veblen (68) long ago insisted, may have a definite prestige value, and may therefore constitute an important motive in the acquisition of property. With us it is secondary, however, whereas for the Kwakiutl and other Northwest tribes it represents the very core of the social and economic structure.

Among the herders of South Africa, the acquisition of large amounts of property may best be understood in terms of prestige. The man who owns great flocks usually puts them to no economic use whatsoever. He needs for his family only a fraction of what he possesses, and he might profitably dispose of the remainder in return for something else. This however he refuses to do, because his status depends on the size of his herd. "As a wealthy and successful herder, he is a great and admirable man, envied by those less fortunate. But this is where the matter ends. From the economic standpoint the whole business represents little but waste of energy and effort; but our standpoint is not that of the Africans" (47, p. 153).

The prestige motive played a similarly important part in certain of the economic practices of the Comanche (25). A leader of a war party could theoretically keep what he wanted, but he rarely kept more than a small share. It was generally believed that success in war was due to the leader's "medicine." If the leader kept the bulk of the spoils, this was confession that he felt his power was leaving him. The selfish leader thus lost prestige, and would have difficulty getting men for his next war party. If he gave freely, it was apparently because he knew that his medicine was strong, and his prestige rose accordingly. In this case if he had any marked acquisitive tendencies, they would have to be subordinated to his desire for status among his potential followers. It may be argued that the acquisitive drive is really primary here and that the leader is merely renouncing it temporarily for a later gain. It appears more likely, however, that the principal motive is the desire for prestige.

An analysis of acquisitive behavior in our own society regards it as motivated principally by some form of self-assertiveness.

> Wherever acquisitiveness does appear it is not primary, as an instinct must by definition be, but secondary. . . . It is noteworthy that the fundamental, and therefore universal, human tendency of which it is but a particular expression, is the desire for pre-eminence, dominion, approbation, and the obverse of these, the eagerness to escape the contempt of one's fellows (69, p. 311).

Freeman believes that such apparently opposed forms of behavior as destruction of property on the one hand, and accumulation on the other, are both to be understood on the basis of a common psychological factor underlying them, namely, the desire for prestige or pre-eminence. Whether this desire for prestige is in its turn instinctive, he does not attempt to decide. "We may regard it as an instinct or not, just as we please, so long as we recognize that it is *prior* to and more fundamental than acquisitiveness. It is quite likely that it, too, is not an instinct. . . ." (p. 319) We shall return to this problem in a later section.

William James (70) also saw property in our society as an extension of the personality—as giving a sort of increase in psychic stature.

> It is clear that between what a man calls *me* and what he simply calls *mine* the line is difficult to draw. . . . In the widest possible sense . . . a man's Self is the sum total of all that he can call his, not only his body, and his psychic powers, but his clothes and his house, his wife and children, his ancestors and friends, his reputation and works, his land and horses and yacht and bank account. All these things give him the same emotions. If they wax and prosper, he feels triumphant, if they dwindle and die away, he feels cast down—not necessarily in the

same degree for each thing, but in much the same way for all (Vol. I, pp. 291-292).

It must be added, however, that this relationship between a man and his property is important only as a result of the folkways of the group. It is because a society attaches significance to property that a man feels his Self to increase and decrease with his possessions.

In the case of many primitive peoples this intimate connection between a man and what he owns is carried even further as a result of magical and religious ideas. It is stated that for the native Australian, property is so charged with the owner's personality that when changing camp a man may leave his valuable stone utensils lying about the ground, since he is absolutely sure of finding them whenever he returns. The other members of the group will regard these objects as bound to their owner so closely that they would not think of appropriating them. Similarly, land belonging to one Australian group was never taken by another, since it was the home not only of a people, but also of the spirits of their ancestors, and therefore could not possibly be used by anyone else. The Maori also recognized a similar identification with the land on which they lived (61).

It is sometimes argued on the basis of economic behavior in our society that some form of acquisitiveness in the shape of a profit motive is essential to a system of trade and economic exchange. From this point of view it is interesting to note the many cases in which trade occurs with the profit motive conspicuously absent. In the Marquesas, for example, trade was carried on by the exchange of objects of equivalent value, and was phrased in terms of the exchange of gifts. The initiator of the deal visited the other and made him a gift with expressions of good will and respect. In later conversation, he mentioned his own need very casually. After a polite interval, the other made a return visit presenting him with an object of exactly equivalent value. To give too much would be ostentation; too little would mean that he deprecated the value of the original gift. Both were social errors showing that the offender was unfamiliar with polite usage, and exposed him to ridicule (25).

On the island of Lesu similarly there seems to be no profit motive. The usual objects of trade are pigs, which are almost always purchased in connection with some ritual feast. The man buying a pig holds up a string of *tsera*, or ceremonial currency, and makes a short speech during which the tsera are in full view of all the bystanders. Payment is always made in this public manner for two reasons —first, everyone has witnessed the transaction; second, everyone knows what has been paid for the object, and should the owner ever wish to resell it, he must get for it exactly the same amount. There is no buying or selling for profit. There is of course a real purpose to the exchange, since each person presumably gets what he needs at the time, but apparently no permanent gain or loss is possible (64).

Many other non-economic motives may play a part in behavior that we usually term economic. It is reported of the Malagasy, for example, that they are shrewd traders, but count the amusement of bargaining an integral part of their commerce. Linton (25) tells of bargaining with a native at Tananarive for a piece of cloth and closing with the merchant for about a fourth above the regular price. He then offered to buy the whole stock at the same rate, but his offer was promptly refused. The merchant explained that if he sold out he would be left with nothing to do. A somewhat similar story is told of a Chinese merchant, although the motive was different. A European, satisfied with the knife he had purchased, offered to buy the merchant's whole stock at the same price. The Chinese demurred, asking a proportionately higher price if he disposed of all his knives, explaining that they were his specialty and that if other purchasers asked for them, he would lose face if he no longer had them to sell. Here again a prestige motive is stronger than any desire for profit (71).

Within our own society similar examples are not lacking. A salesman is reported to have remarked, when offered a position paying an unusually large salary on condition that he keep his income a secret—"What's the use of having a swell job, if I can't talk about it?" An expert carpenter engaged in building target floats for the gun practice of battleships, after seeing the destruction of his work, quit his job for one paying only half as much but where his products had a chance to last (72). These instances from primitive as well as from our own culture show that Adam Smith's (73) classical concept of the "economic man" who was apparently interested only in getting as much as possible and paying as little as possible for it, is far removed from man as studied by the ethnologists and the psychologists. It seems fair to conclude that any economic theory which is in harmony with the facts will have to pay considerable attention to motives which are not primarily in the economic sphere.

A further significant fact about the economic life of primitive peoples is the frequency with which the concept of property is attached to incorporeal objects. In the Andaman Islands, utensils such as cooking vessels are treated as communal property. No such latitude holds, however, with regard to the songs composed on the occasion of a tribal gathering. A song that has been received with applause may be repeated by request at later gatherings, but irrespective of its popularity no one dares sing it except the composer himself. Similarly, the concept of "property" applies to magical formulae and incantations among the Koryak of Siberia, local legends among the Torres Straits islanders, rituals among the Nootka Indians, the right to plant sacred tobacco among the Crow and membership in military organizations among the Hidatsa. All of these things may be bought and sold and are therefore property in a real sense, even though they are not embodied in any material object. It has been suggested (35) that there are many examples among ourselves of "incorporeal property," for example, patents on inventions, words of songs and stories, the "good will" of a business establishment, etc. It should be kept in mind, however, that these constitute property because they may be translated into goods of a more material kind. No such transformation is necessary in the case of primitive incorporeal property, although it may also occur; a Kwakiutl Indian may pawn his name if he has no other way of paying his debts.

This raises the interesting problem as to whether, granting for the sake of argument that there is an acquisitive drive, this might be sublimated in many different ways. There might, in other words, be some sort of "moral equivalent" of acquisitiveness, to paraphrase William James' phrase concerning war. The particular form that the drive takes would then be determined by the culture patterns, even if the drive itself has some more basic significance. We have seen, however, that there is ample justification for questioning the dependability of the drive itself, although there can be no doubt that in our own society it has been erected into a value which may dominate the behavior of many individuals.

Acquisitiveness in Children. The nature of acquisitive behavior has also been investigated by a study of the collecting tendencies of children. It has been argued that if such tendencies occur with great frequency, this would constitute an important argument in favor of the innateness of the drive. In 1900 Caroline F. Burk (74), working under the direction of G. Stanley Hall, made a survey of 1214 children in California between the ages of three and fourteen, and found that about 90% of them were making some sort of collection at the time. In 1927, however, Lehman and Witty (75) studied 5000 children in the Middle West between the ages of eight and twenty and found hardly more than 10% so engaged. At no age level were as many as 15% of the boys making collections at the time of the study. They explain the discrepancy between their results and those of Burk as due to a change in social patterning in the meantime. With new interests and different types of leisure activity, collecting simply became less popular.

Two years later, however, Whitley (76) received four thousand replies to a questionnaire sent to children from the ages of seven to eighteen and found that the great majority had made some sort of collection during the preceding period. Below the age of twelve the motive was apparently play; after that age, girls said that they kept their collections in order to look at them, boys because they wanted to show them to others, or because they thought they might need them. In spite of the frequency of the collections, the investigator does not ascribe them to any collecting instinct, but points out that there is a whole web of complex influences in which the child's age, intelligence, amount of leisure, economic status, stimulus by playmates and a number of other factors participate. In this same connection, Murphy, Murphy and Newcomb (59) stress the specificity of the collecting activity, and the consequent impossibility of explaining it in terms of any general "collecting instinct." "The collector of stamps need not collect newspapers or Japanese prints, as would be the case if he were simply a man with a 'strong collecting instinct'" (p. 104). In other words, the collections are due to interest, previous experience, perhaps also the desire for prestige as well as the enjoyment of the objects, and many other possible motives.

As far as primitive children are concerned, Margaret Mead (19) reports that the Manus children of New Guinea made no collections and did not pass through any "collecting stage" of the type regarded by G. Stanley Hall as a necessary aspect of development. She found no child under thirteen or fourteen with any possessions except his canoe or the bow and arrow which were furnished him by adults.

He might be interested in a new toy for a very short while and then seem to have no further use for it. It would be worth while to extend this type of investigation to other societies and to note specifically how the acquisitive tendency develops, how it differs in "communistic" and "capitalistic" societies, and how the child absorbs the economic practices of his community. It is probable that the tendency to collect and to hoard would by no means be universal, and that when it occurred it could be explained by the general structure of the society.

In conclusion a word should be said about the Freudian explanation of acquisitive behavior. The Freudians, particularly Ernest Jones (77), regard this behavior as an outgrowth of the interest in the products of one's own body. The child is said to be naturally delighted with these products and to be anxious to play with them and to possess them as long as possible. His education and training reverse this primitive attitude of delight into one of disgust; furthermore, his desire to retain the products of his body is thwarted by both physiological and social factors. There is a consequent sublimation of the interest, which now becomes attached to the accumulation of money and other socially acceptable objects. One writer (48) even goes so far as to explain both our own acquisitive society and its socialistic counterpart on this basis.

> Anal retentiveness will be credited with giving us misers, thrift, our banking systems and capitalist, co-operativist and collectivist ventures in cheap production and marketing. . . . It also underlies the interest in manipulation and construction which is of an importance in industry at least comparable with the love of gain and which interests people in such things as Five-Year Plans, and in reconstructing our whole industrial order (p. 136).

This omnibus application of the theory probably goes far beyond the opinions of other psychoanalysts.

The Freudians believe that those individuals who have received a particularly repressive toilet training in their childhood develop also certain character traits, for instance, obstinacy, procrastination and parsimony, which may similarly be regarded as sublimations. This interpretation does not seem to the writer to be particularly significant, since there are so many children for whom such a primary interest in their bodily products cannot be demonstrated. Even if there are anal character traits of the type described, it is not very likely that all acquisitiveness is to be explained on that basis. In any case, the theory is capable of verification or disproof through field work in different cultures. A beginning in this direction has been made by Roheim (78), who finds that the complete naturalness of the excretory processes among the Australian Arunta is accompanied by an indifference to private property and a generous attitude to one's fellows. Comparable material must be collected from other societies if we are to determine whether or not the alleged relationship among the Arunta is more than a coincidence.

We may summarize by saying that for acquisitiveness the criterion of continuity with animal forms is satisfied, but that the acquisitive behavior of animals may almost always be explained on the basis of other, more fundamental motives; the criterion of a visceral or physiological foundation for the drive is not satisfied; the criterion of universality is similarly not satisfied. The conclusion seems clear that acquisitive behavior is not to be regarded as innate or instinctive, and that important though it may be for certain societies, its nature and extent are culturally determined. It has a moderate degree of dependability because of the structure of certain types of society.

SELF-ASSERTIVENESS

One of the tendencies regarded by McDougall as instinctive is the desire to assert oneself, to obtain standing and position in one's community, to achieve superiority. In the system of psychology developed by Alfred Adler and his followers, this tendency is not merely an instinct, it is *the* instinct—that is to say, it is the principal motive of behavior, and the one most frequently used as a principle of explanation.

The question of the existence among animals of a self-assertive tendency similar to that which has been postulated for human beings is difficult to answer. There is ample evidence that the stronger males in many mammalian communities fight for leadership. The studies of social relationships among monkeys and anthropoids by Zuckerman and Maslow, and among birds by Schjelderup-Ebbe and Murchison, referred to in Chapter 2, point to an apparent striving for dominance among these animal forms. Since this type of self-assertiveness usually means that the dominant animal obtains for himself special privileges with regard to food and the possession of females, the behavior is to be interpreted as a means to these ends. In his earlier work Maslow regarded dominant behavior as an end in itself, but in his more recent statements, he adopts an interpretation more nearly in line with this one.

There is no known direct organic or physiological basis for self-assertive behavior. Adler, however, has indicated the possibility of an indirect basis, which in his opinion explains the universality of this tendency. Self-assertiveness is in his interpretation a reaction to, or a compensation for, a feeling of real or fancied inferiority. In cases of organic defect, for example, there may be a strong compensatory reaction which makes up for the defect, and in some cases leads to unusually successful achievement in the same direction. The classical example is that of Demosthenes, who conquered his stammering to become one of the greatest orators of all time. Most people do not have such a striking inadequacy to overcome, but there is one type of inferiority which no one may escape, namely, that of once having been a child. This may seem too obvious to mention, but for the Adlerian it has a definite significance. The feeling of inferiority in the child is built up out of three related groups of experiences: first, the feeling of helplessness, second, the feeling of being weaker than adults, and third, the feeling of dependency upon adults. Every child wishes to be "grown-up" and strives for superiority in order to remove his feeling of inadequacy. This striving thus has a universal organic foundation, and the habits set up in this manner continue to play an important part in the life of the individual long after the inferiority has been removed by the natural process of growth. Self-assertiveness becomes in this manner a universal phenomenon.

This ingenious analysis has a certain amount of plausibility. In any case there is little doubt as to the strength and the prevalence of this particular motive for behavior. In the preceding account of aggressive and acquisitive motives, it was necessary on many occasions to refer to the desire for prestige as the underlying drive. "Counting coup" among the Crow, giving potlatches among the Kwakiutl, displaying food among the Trobrianders, collecting cattle and even children among the Bantu, may all apparently be explained on this basis.

The prestige motive is almost but not completely universal. There are at least a few communities among whom it plays no important part. One is the Zuñi of New Mexico (79, 80) who do not welcome evidences of outstanding ability or originality among their members. The best thing to be said about any individual is that no one ever hears anything about him. So far do they carry their negative attitude against individual superiority that if a man wins a race in their annual athletic contest, they do not permit him to run again the next year. A modest amount of prestige may be obtained by buying one's way into certain secret societies, or by learning a great deal of ritual material, but even this confers no great honor or merit. Competition in general is reduced to a minimum. For the neighboring Hopi, Kennard (81) has reported that the children play no competitive games. Similarly, Asch (82) states that the Hopi school children will not compete against one another, and that all of the efforts of the teachers to make them do so are unavailing. One teacher once tried the new method of lining them up against a blackboard with instructions to complete their sums as quickly as possible and to turn to the front as soon as they had finished. She observed that as each child finished, he looked surreptitiously along the line to see how far the others had advanced, apparently unwilling to turn around until the others were also ready. These children grow up without any incentive to compete, and self-assertiveness, at least in our sense, seems to be almost completely lacking.

Another group for whom a similar lack of self-assertiveness has been noted is the Arapesh tribe of New Guinea (66). There are leaders, but it is assumed that no one really wants to be one. Those who are in a position of authority "have to plan, have to initiate exchanges, have to strut and swagger and talk in loud voices, have to boast of what they have done in the past and are going to do in the future. All this the Arapesh regard as most uncongenial, difficult behavior, the kind of behavior in which no normal man would indulge if he could possibly avoid it. It is a role that the society forces upon a few men in certain recognized ways" (p. 27). When his eldest son reaches puberty, the "big man" can retire from the active competitive life which he has had to lead and which the society assumes, usually correctly, to be eminently uncongenial and distasteful to him.

These examples may seem rather extreme, and it is true that few societies, primitive or civilized, have limited self-assertiveness to this extent. The analysis of cooperative and competitive behavior in a large number of different societies has shown (83), however, that there may be almost any degree of this tendency, varying from the cooperative, submissive behavior of the Arapesh to the highly competitive, violently self-assertive attitudes of the Kwakiutl. These variations are not always easy to explain, but for our present purposes the fact that they occur is more important than the factors which are responsible.

Our own society is perhaps not the most self-assertive in the world (the Kwakiutl, for example, are probably more extreme in this respect), but it certainly ranks near the top in the emphasis which it places on this motive. It seems likely that Adlerian psychology owes some of its success to the fact that it fits so well the patterns of our own particular social structure. This is the point of view of Dollard (84), who writes:

> It seems to the writer that Adler's psychology could be characterized as peculiarly bound by our culture and as emphasizing in psychology the motive which is most characteristic of it. This is certainly a value which will recommend it to many observers, but it also imposes a limitation on its use as a generalized social psychology which must be adapted to use in cultures which do not exhibit our powerful status and money competition and which do not put such a premium on fighting (pp. 70-71).

The Status of Children. From this point of view there is an important problem which requires study in the field, that is to say, by actual investigation of children in many communities different from our own. As we have seen, Adler bases the universality of the self-assertive drive on the weakness and dependence of children. This dependence, however, while probably always present to some degree, is not equally marked everywhere. It has frequently been pointed out that primitive children are usually given much more freedom and much fuller control of their own activities than is the case in our community. Among American Indians, for example, it was usual to regard the child as completely master over whatever property had been given to him. If a White man wished to buy something that belonged to a small child, the parents would regard it as entirely the child's affair whether it should be sold or not, and what price it should bring. If the child did not wish to sell, that ended the matter. Linton (25) makes a similar statement with reference to the Tanala of Madagascar and reports that he had to strike a bargain with a child of five in order to buy some of his toys for a museum collection. It is highly probable that this complete control over property reduces the feeling of dependence in the child, and in line with Adler's theory, it might as a consequence reduce the later tendency toward self-assertiveness. It may be added that the total period of "childhood" is shorter among primitive peoples, largely because the things they must learn in order to become full-fledged members of the community are so much simpler, and their economic problems usually so much easier of solution.

There is also an allied phenomenon to be found in primitive societies, namely, that children are rarely punished. We have already referred to the horror with which groups like the Eskimos, the Tahitians and others react to the habits of the Whites in this regard. This, too, will mean that the physical inferiority of the child will not be felt so keenly, and will not constitute such a great handicap. Blackwood (26) points out that among the Melanesians of Buka Passage, children are subject to little or no discipline. A child will take or be given anything he wants, even if it is dangerous and likely to hurt him. It a father tells his daughter to do something and she refuses, he does nothing about it. His society does not grant him the right to punish her for her disobedience. In this setting it is not likely that a child would feel his inferiority nearly so much as where he is forced to do the bidding of his elders.

Given this wide variation in the treatment of children by adults, and in the control which children may exercise over their own destiny, it would be important to discover whether there is any relationship between the amount of dependence in early life and the degree of self-assertiveness in the adult. The organic inferiority of the child may still make it possible to understand the prevalence of this self-assertive tendency, but if Adler is right, the compensation for it will be much greater in some societies than in others. It is quite certain, however, that over and above any Adlerian mechanism there is the important influence of the folkways which makes itself felt throughout the lifetime of the individual. In some societies, asserting oneself is simply "the thing to do"; in others, it is condemned.

Additional evidence of the "learned" character of competition and self-assertiveness is to be found in the fact that this tendency is absent in very young children in our own society. One investigator (85) found that she could not use children below the age of five in a study of the effects of praise and competition on persistence, or cite the performance of other children to motivate them. The five-year-olds, however, were good subjects for this type of experiment. In another study (86) no evidence was found for the existence of competition at the age of two years, whereas at five years 75.4%, and at six years 86.5%, of the children responded to competition. This suggests that the child must be well "socialized" before the prestige drive, at least in its competitive aspect, plays an important part. It would be interesting to conduct similar studies in other societies.

There is one other standpoint from which the self-assertive tendency may be viewed, and which in the opinion of the present writer makes it most clearly understandable. It is obvious that in every society it is to a man's interests to be well regarded, to have relations with others that will make it possible for him to carry out those activities with which he is most concerned. As Malinowski (87) has pointed out, a man acts in conformity with the customs of his community, not as a result of the mystical strength of custom, nor because he fears punishment, but mainly because otherwise he would be left out of all the social and economic exchanges which are necessary for well-adjusted behavior. If this is so, it is clear that a man would wish to stand well with his fellows, to have their respect and approbation. If he can best obtain this approbation by success in war, as among the Indians of the Plains, that will be the goal of his self-assertive behavior; similarly, he will give potlatches if he is a Kwakiutl, and collect herds if he is a Bantu. On the other hand, if he is a member of the Zuñi community, he will refrain from doing anything spectacular or outstanding, since such behavior would bring him condemnation. Stated differently, this means that there is no tendency toward self-assertiveness as such, but there is for very practical reasons the need to be approved by others. Self-assertiveness then becomes the means toward the acquisition of as large an amount of such approval as is possible. It is obvious that in many cases, too great concern with such approval defeats its own ends.

The interpretation of the prestige drive as a means to an end is in agreement with the view of Blatz (88), based on his observations of young children, and particularly of the Dionne quintuplets. Dominance (as well as submission) is sought when it serves as an efficient method for gratifying a need.

To summarize, we have seen that dominant behavior or self-assertiveness does occur in animals, but probably in the interests of more fundamental organic drives; it has no organic basis except possibly the indirect one postulated by Adler, namely, the universal organic inferiority of childhood; it is widespread, but not universal, and shows great variations in degree. It is probably to be explained as due mainly to a desire for social approbation for practical and utilitarian purposes.

SELF-PRESERVATION

The so-called instinct of self-preservation is in a quite different category from the others which we have so far discussed. It might better be regarded as the general goal which many of the drives have in common. In other words, the hunger motive, pugnacity, flight, the need for rest and elimination of waste products, all contribute to the preservation of the individual. On the basis of biological evolution it is possible to understand why all existing species should have patterns of behavior directed to this end; if these patterns worked in the opposite direction, they would obviously result in the destruction of the individual and therefore of the species. The same considerations hold for those forms of behavior like sex and maternal care, which are directed to the preservation of the species rather than of the individual.

On this basis one would expect those tendencies responsible for self-preservation to be found throughout the animal kingdom, as of course they are. We may therefore regard our first criterion as satisfied. As for an organic basis, this is to be found in connection with the individual motives which play a part in self-preservation, rather than for self-preservation in general. There is obviously a physiological foundation for hunger, thirst, fatigue, elimination and so on.

The question of the universality of this motive presents special problems. It is of course rare for a group deliberately to destroy itself, or to act for any length of time in a direction hostile to the continuity of its existence. It does happen that a military group may sacrifice itself in the interests of patriotism, as in the case of the Spartans at Thermopylae, and the "suicide squads" of recent military engagements. It has also been observed (89) that many groups of South Sea Islanders, both Melanesian and Polynesian, as a result of the encroachment of the Whites on their territory and their culture, had no longer any desire to keep alive. Many of these groups have disappeared not as the result of any specific disease or infection or because their livelihood has been interfered with, but apparently because they felt they had nothing left to live for. A similar explanation has been given for the disappearance of the Tasmanians, a number of whom were placed on a sort of reservation after their disastrous defensive against the British, and who, in spite of being given all the sustenance they needed, died out in one generation. It seems therefore that on certain abnormal but by no means rare occasions a whole group may in this manner "commit suicide." It should be pointed out, however, that this is not the type of suicide in which an individual does away with himself. It seems rather to be due to a failure to marry or to have children, out of a more or less conscious conviction that future generations would be destined to a life of unhappiness. The individuals preserve themselves, but they allow their community to die.

As has already been mentioned, J. F. Brown (90) points out, in a criticism of the concept of "human nature" as something common to all individuals, that even self-preservation is not to be regarded as common-human irrespective of the social field, since a man may be led to commit suicide as the result of certain social and cultural factors. There is no doubt that cultures differ widely in their attitude toward suicide, and that its frequency will vary markedly from group to group. Suicide, therefore, is not to be regarded as exclusively, perhaps not even mainly, an individual abnormal phenomenon, but as one which also is under the control of custom and convention. In a careful survey of the prevalence and causes of suicide among primitive peoples, Dublin and Bunzel (91) show clearly the wide variations in the attitudes which prevail; in some regions it is unknown, in others it is common and fits into the general cultural pattern. Among the groups for whom no cases of suicide have been reported are the Yahgans of Tierra del Fuego, the Andaman Islanders, the natives of western and central Australia, and the Zuñi of New Mexico. At the other extreme the Kamchadals of Siberia commit suicide at the least apprehension of danger, being convinced that the future life is much happier than this one; a Cherokee Indian committed suicide because his face had been disfigured by smallpox; the Ojibway often killed themselves after capture or disappointment, and the Navajos upon the death of a loved one or as the result of jealousy. Among the Melanesians of Buka Passage (26), the reasons given for actual or attempted suicide include the following—(1) the wife was angry and insulted him, (2) the husband beat her, (3) his wife refused him intercourse on the grounds that it was too soon after childbirth, (4) his father would not get him a wife, (5) someone stole his ceremonial currency, (6) he was angry with another man. There seems in general to be a close correspondence between the frequency of suicide and the attitudes toward it held by the community in general.

It should be added that the fate of the suicide after death is viewed differently in various societies, and this, too, undoubtedly helps to determine the frequency of this type of behavior. The Catholic attitude on this point is well known; the body of the suicide may not be buried in consecrated ground and the soul is punished in the after-world. A similar stigma is attached to suicide in many other societies. The Ossetes of Siberia believed that punishment followed after death, and buried the body of the suicide apart. The Kayans of Borneo were taught that the spirits of suicides remained poor and wretched. The Paharis of India said that such souls could not be admitted to heaven and hovered eternally between heaven and earth. For the Omahas, the soul of a suicide ceased to exist. The Ashanti of Africa decapitated the body and believed that the headless ghost would wander in search of his head until his destined time had run out, when he would return to the world as a cruel spirit who also would come to an unhappy end (91). It is obvious that these beliefs would have a deterrent effect upon any individual contemplating such behavior.

In all probability the culture which most encouraged suicide was that of ancient Japan, and the attitudes which developed have persisted in somewhat slighter degree to the present day. A typical example from history is a case reported by Brinkley (92): "Nobunagu caused so much solicitude to his tutor and showed so much indifference to his remonstrances that finally the tutor committed suicide—the faithful vassal's last expedient" (p. 474). As for modern Japan, in World War II there were a number of Japanese who committed suicide because they would not face the dishonor of capture or because they disapproved of some of the Japanese war measures, and there was one non-combatant who left his insurance money to the army. Some time ago it was reported that a Japanese tennis player committed suicide because he felt that he could not adequately represent his country in the forthcoming Davis Cup matches.

In ancient Japan the cult of Bushido, a code of moral conduct practiced particularly by the samurai, demanded suicide under certain well-established conditions (93). The type of suicide prescribed, known as *seppuku* or *kappuku* and more popularly as *hara-kiri*, consisted of self-immolation by disembowelment. The bowels were regarded as the seat of the soul, and this form of suicide meant: "I will open the seat of my soul and show you how it fares with it. See for yourself whether it is polluted or not." Death was considered the solution to many complex problems, particularly those involving a question of honor; to an ambitious samurai a natural departure from life seemed colorless. Seppuku was not mere suicide, but a legal and ceremonial institution, a process whereby warriors could expiate their crimes, apologize for their errors, escape disgrace, redeem their honor, or prove their sincerity. None could perform it without the utmost coolness of temper and composure of demeanor. For a variety of causes, often from our point of view entirely unreasonable, many young men thus ended their lives, and there were at various times in Japanese history veritable epidemics of hara-kiri. Life was unimportant compared to the conventionally accepted meaning of honor. It is clear that in this case a motive which has its root in the fundamental nature of biological processes, namely the preservation of the self, may give way completely to an attitude which has purely social and cultural definition.

Self-preservation, therefore, is not a single "fundamental drive," but a group of them. At the same time there is probably a desire to preserve the self, apart from the contributing motives. It has itself no organic basis but is the goal of many motives which do have such a basis. In that sense it is common to all species of animals. Among human beings it may be absent in whole communities under special circumstances, and in the case of individuals it may be subordinated to other motivating forces. In spite of its biological nature, therefore, it may within certain limits be controlled by the folkways of a community.[4]

SUMMARY

In connection with the maternal drive, a distinction must be made between the desire to have children (the pre-maternal drive) and the urge to take care of them (the post-maternal drive). The latter satisfies the criterion of continuity with animals below man, and has

[4] The classical studies by Durkheim (94) and Halbwachs (95) discuss the relation between suicide and the patterns of culture.

a physiological basis; it is apparently found in all societies, though not in all individuals; the phenomena of adoption and infanticide indicate the manner and the extent of possible cultural patterning. In the case of the pre-maternal drive, there is no evidence either for phylogenetic continuity or for a physiological basis; when children are desired, a variety of reasons, many of them practical in character, may be operative. The attitude of the father appears to be determined mainly by the values which the culture attaches to children rather than by innate biological factors.

Aggressive behavior is found among many animal species. It has an indirect physiological basis in terms of the "emergency theory" of emotional reactions. In the form of warfare it is widespread but by no means universal, and its occurrence may be explained as a means to an end rather than as an end in itself. Aggressiveness between individuals may be similarly explained and is increased or decreased in amount or altered in its expression under different social and cultural conditions. Its occurrence and extent appear to be related to frustration, which may, however, have other consequences as well.

Acquisitive behavior shows some continuity with animals below man, but has no definite physiological basis, and is far from universal. It bears a close relation to the prestige drive, as, for example, in the case of the potlatch and other culture patterns. It occurs with some frequency, not because of innate factors, but as a reflection of certain varieties of socio-economic structure.

Self-assertiveness, or the prestige drive, has certain parallels among animal groups, particularly in the establishment of a dominance hierarchy. On the physiological side, Adler has suggested with some plausibility that it may be due to a striving to overcome the inferiorities of early childhood, and it may therefore be regarded as having an indirect organic basis. It is found in the large majority of human societies, but shows marked variations in degree. It may be understood in large measure as an extension of the need for social approbation, which is required for the satisfaction of fundamental needs.

Self-preservation is really the end-result of a group of motives, such as hunger, thirst, the elimination of waste products, and so forth. On the other hand, the phenomenon of suicide shows that in spite of the biological nature of the desire for self-preservation, it is still subject to variations under the influence of the folkways.

REFERENCES

1. Hartley, E. L., and Hartley, R. E. *Fundamentals of Social Psychology.* 1952

2. Newcomb, T. M. *Social Psychology.* 1950

3. Krech, D., and Crutchfield, R. S. *Theory and Problems of Social Psychology.* 1948

4. Murphy, G. *Personality.* 1947

5. Thorndike, E. L. *Human Nature and the Social Order.* 1939

6. Westermarck, E. A. *The History of Human Marriage.* 5th ed. 1921

7. Warden, C. J., et al. *Animal Motivation.* 1931

8. Young, P. T. *Motivation of Behavior.* 1936

9. McQueen-Williams, M. "Maternal Behavior in Male Rats," *Science,* 1935, 82: pp. 67-68

10. Rivers, W. H. R. *Report of the Cambridge Anthropological Expedition to Torres Straits.* 1904, vol. 5

11. Man, E. H. "On the Aboriginal Inhabitants of the Andaman Islands," *J. Roy. Anthrop. Instit.,* 1882, 12: pp. 69-116, 327-434

12. Hose, C., and McDougall, W. *The Pagan Tribes of Borneo.* 1912

13. Thomas, W. I. *Primitive Behavior.* 1937

14. Fortune, R. F. *Sorcerers of Dobu.* 1932

15. Lowie, R. H. "Adoption, Primitive," *Encycl. Soc. Sci.,* 1930, 1: pp. 459-460

16. Miller, N. *The Child in Primitive Society.* 1928

17. Handy, E. S. C. "Polynesian Religion," *Bernice P. Bishop Mus. Bull.,* 1927, 34: pp. 1-342

18. Bernard, L. L. *Instinct.* 1924

19. Mead, M. *Growing Up in New Guinea.* 1930

20. Hollingworth, L. S. "Social Devices for Impelling Women to Bear and Rear Children," *Amer. J. Sociol.,* 1916, 22: pp. 19-29

21. Sumner, W. G. *Folkways.* 1907

22. Stefansson, V. "Lessons in Living from the Stone Age," *Harper's,* 1939, 179: pp. 158-164

23. Yerkes, R. M., and Yerkes, A. W. "Social Behavior in Infrahuman Primates." In Murchison, C., ed. *Hdbk. Soc. Psychol.* 1935

24. Malinowski, B. *Sex and Repression in Savage Society.* 1927

25. Linton, R. *The Study of Man.* 1936

26. Blackwood, B. *Both Sides of Buka Passage.* 1935

27. Cannon, W. B. *Bodily Changes in Pain, Hunger, Fear, and Rage.* 1929

28. Lafitau, J. F. *Moeurs des Sauvages Amériquains, Comparées aux Moeurs des Premiers Temps.* 2 vols. 1724

29. Driberg, J. A. *The Lango.* 1923

30. Hobhouse, L. T., et al. *The Material Culture and Social Institutions of the Simpler Peoples.* 1915

31. Nansen, F. *Eskimo Life.* 1893

32. Letourneau, C. *La Guerre dans les Diverses Races Humaines.* 1895

33. Van der Bij, T. S. *Ontstaan en Eerste Ontwikkeling van den Oorlog.* 1929

34. Smith, G. E. *Human History.* 1929

35. Bunzel, R. L. "The Economic Organization of Primitive Peoples." In Boas, F. *General Anthropology.* 1938

36. Payne, E. J. *History of the New World Called America.* 1892-1899

37. Spence, L. *The Mythologies of Ancient Mexico and Peru.* 1907

38. Connelley, W. E. *The Wyandot Folk-lore.* 1899

39. Parkinson, R. "Notes on the Asaba People (Ibos)," *J. Roy. Anthrop. Instit.*, 1906, 36: pp. 312-324

40. Sumner, W. G., and Keller, A. G. *The Science of Society.* 4 vols. 1927

41. Lowie, R. H. *Primitive Society.* 1920

42. Wright, Q. *A Study of War.* 2 vols. 1942

43. James, W. "The Moral Equivalent of War," *Pop. Sci. Mo.*, 1910, 77: pp. 400-412

44. Boas, F. *Contributions to the Ethnology of the Kwakiutl.* 1925

45. Jones, L. F. *A Study of the Thlingets of Alaska.* 1914

46. Goldman, I. "The Alkatcho Carrier of British Columbia." In Linton, R., ed. *Acculturation in Seven American Indian Tribes.* 1940

47. Goldenweiser, A. A. *Anthropology.* 1937

48. Hopkins, P. *The Psychology of Social Movements.* 1938

49. Horney, K. *New Ways in Psychoanalysis.* 1939

50. Kardiner, A. *The Individual and His Society.* 1939

51. Dollard, J., et al. *Frustration and Aggression.* 1939

52. Barker, R. G., Dembo, T., Lewin, K., and Wright, M. E. "Experimental Studies of Frustration in Young Children." In Newcomb, T. M., and Hartley, E. L. *Readings in Social Psychology.* 1947

53. Miller, N. E., and Dollard, J. *Social Learning and Imitation.* 1941

54. Bateson, G. "The Frustration-Aggression Hypothesis and Culture." In Newcomb and Hartley, *Readings in Social Psychology.* 1947

55. Rosenzweig, S. "Outline of Frustration Theory." In Hunt, J. Mc. V., ed. *Personality and the Behavior Disorders.* 1944

56. Durbin, E. F. M., and Bowlby, J. *Personal Aggressiveness and War.* 1939

57. Bender, L. "Genesis of Hostility in Children," *Amer. J. Psychiatry*, 1948-9, 105: pp. 241-245

58. Allen, F. H. "Aggression in Relation to Emotional Development," *Proc. Int. Conf. on Child Psychiatry.* 1948, pp. 4-11

59. Murphy, G., Murphy, L. B., and Newcomb, T. M. *Experimental Social Psychology.* Rev. ed. 1937

60. Rivers, W. H. R. "The Instinct of Acquisition," *Instinct and the Unconscious.* 1920

61. Beaglehole, E. *Property: A Study in Social Psychology.* 1931

62. Morgan, L. H. *Ancient Society.* 1907

63. Haddon, A. C. *Report of the Cambridge Anthropological Expedition to Torres Straits.* 1904, vol. 5

64. Powdermaker, H. *Life in Lesu.* 1933

65. Henry, J. *The Kaingang of Brazil.* Unpublished MS.

66. Mead, M. *Sex and Temperament in Three Primitive Societies.* 1935

67. Malinowski, B. *Argonauts of the Western Pacific.* 1922

68. Veblen, T. *The Theory of the Leisure Class.* 1899

69. Freeman, E. *Social Psychology.* 1936

70. James, W. *The Principles of Psychology.* 2 vols. 1890

71. Burgess, S. Personal communication.

72. Husband, R. W. *Applied Psychology.* 1934

73. Smith, A. *An Inquiry into the Nature and Causes of the Wealth of Nations.* 2 vols. 1776

74. Burk, C. F. "The Collecting Instinct," *Pedag. Sem.,* 1900, 7: pp. 179-207

75. Lehman, H. C., and Witty, P. A. "The Present Status of the Tendency to Collect and Hoard," *Psychol. Rev.,* 1927, 34: pp. 48-56

76. Whitley, M. T. "Children's Interest in Collecting," *J. Educ. Psychol.,* 1929, 20: pp. 249-261

77. Jones, E. "Anal Erotic Character Traits," *J. Abn. & Soc. Psychol.,* 1919, 13: pp. 261-284

78. Roheim, G. "Psychoanalysis of Primitive Cultural Types," *Internatl. J. Psychoanal.,* 1932, 13: pp. 2-224

79. Bunzel, R. L. "Introduction to Zuñi Ceremonialism," *Bur. Amer. Ethnol.,* 1932, 47: pp. 467-544

80. Benedict, R. F. *Patterns of Culture.* 1934

81. Kennard, E. Personal communication

82. Asch, S. E. Personal communication

83. Mead, M., et al. *Cooperation and Competition Among Primitive Peoples.* 1937

84. Dollard, J. *Criteria for the Life History.* 1935

85. Wolf, T. H. "The Effect of Praise and Competition on the Persisting Behavior of Kindergarten Children," *Institute of Child Welfare Monograph,* University of Minnesota Press, 1938, No. 15

86. Greenberg, P. J. "Competition in Children: An Experimental Study," *Amer. J. Psychol.*, 1932, 44: pp. 221-248

87. Malinowski, B. *Crime and Custom in Savage Society.* 1926

88. Blatz, W. E. "The Individual and the Group," *Amer. J. Sociol.*, 1939, 44: pp. 829-838

89. Pitt-Rivers, G. H. L-F. *Clash of Cultures and Contact of Races.* 1927

90. Brown, J. F. *Psychology and the Social Order.* 1936

91. Dublin, L. I., and Bunzel, B. *To Be or Not To Be: A Study of Suicide.* 1933

92. Brinkley, F. *A History of the Japanese People from the Earliest Times to the End of the Meiji Era.* 1915

93. Nitobe, I. *Bushido: The Soul of Japan.* 1905

94. Durkheim, E. *Le Suicide.* 1912

95. Halbwachs, M. *Les Causes du Suicide.* 1930

Motivation (Continued)

6

SEX

That there is an innate or "instinctive" basis for sex behavior may be taken for granted. It is obviously a form of activity which is shared with all animal species above the very simplest forms. It has certainly an organic basis in the bodily changes which take place in the male and female organisms at the time of puberty and which prepare them for the act of reproduction. It is highly probable that even before adolescence, as the Freudians in particular have emphasized, there is a drive toward sexual manipulation and experimentation, presumably due to the special sensitivity of certain zones of the body, as well as to the stimulus of hormones active from early childhood. As Dollard (1) expresses it, it seems to be one of our cherished beliefs that the sex impulse emerges in adolescence; this is due in his opinion to the error of identifying sexual life with the capacity for reproduction. The frequency of pre-adolescent sexual play in many communities, the early development of interest in erotic books and pictures, as well as the sexual significance of Freudian mechanisms operating in early childhood testify to the appearance of the sex drive before it may be put to direct biological use.

As in the case of the motive of self-preservation, it may be said that sex behavior is found in all cultures, but not in all individuals. Where it is absent, custom regards such individuals as abnormal, but as we shall see later, the concept of abnormality varies widely from group to group—homosexuality, for example, being permitted in certain communities. The various religious orders which enforce chastity in their members testify to the possibility that the folkways may counteract this organic drive. That sex impulses often have considerable strength even under these circumstances is amply demonstrated by the stories of the temptations that beset the members of such groups. There are, however, individuals in whom the sex drive appears to be completely lacking. In the well-known report by Kinsey and his associates (2) there is not only indication of a wide variation in the amount of sex activity reported by different men, but also evidence that the range goes down to zero, that is, that some men deny the existence of any such behavior altogether. They are of course exceptions, and do not cast serious doubt on the fact that sex behavior has an organic function and a high degree of dependability.

Even in the case of such an innate drive, however, the importance of cultural patterning may hardly be overestimated. A survey by Ford and Beach (3) of patterns of sex behavior, based on the findings of biology, psychology and ethnology and making extensive use of the data collected in the Human Relations Area Files at Yale University, bears ample testimony in this direction. As each aspect of human sex activity is examined, the variations from group to group emerge so strikingly that the authors, an ethnologist and a comparative psychologist respectively, express over and over again their conclusions regarding the overwhelming importance of culture and "learning" in this connection. Groups may differ, for example, in the importance which they attach to relations between the sexes. In our own society, it is usually regarded as the most important of all social relationships and the source (even though the Freudians may exaggerate) of a great deal of our literature and art and other forms of creative activity. In other societies it may be taken rather more for granted, and relationships of a different order may receive greater emphasis. In China (4), for example, lyric poetry tended to celebrate the great and lasting friendships between men rather than the romantic attachments between men and women; the latter relationship was by no means left out, but it was apparently less significant. Among the Comanche Indians, the most important social relationship was that of "brother-in-arms," a voluntary association with reciprocal rights and duties exactly defined, and with an emotional context deeper than all others. "It was to his brother-in-arms that a man turned first in any difficulty, and it was his brother-in-arms whom he saved first in time of danger" (5, p. 256).

The emotional attitude toward sexual matters varies widely. In the Western world, probably as the result of religious influences, the usual feeling about sex, at least in public, is one of shame, although there has been a marked change in this connection in recent times. McDougall (6) believed that the feeling of shame was due to the proximity of the sexual and the excretory zones of the body, and that the disgust aroused by the latter was extended to include sexual matters as well. This explanation can have no universal significance, since there are many groups for whom neither sex nor excretion is associated with shame in any manner. The native Australians, for example, are completely "natural" about relieving themselves, and quite indifferent to the presence of others during the act. As for sex, although primitive cultures differ widely, the attitude is frequently one in which shame plays little or no part. In Buka (7), for instance, myths and stories with sexual incidents are told without any special comment, and are not made subjects of jest. Children's questions on these subjects are always answered directly, and there is no suggestion that such matters should not be discussed. There are taboos regarding sex, but there are taboos also regarding eating and conversing, and they are taken for granted in the same manner. In Lesu (8) children from about the age of four will imitate the sexual play of their parents. This is done openly, and the adults smile indulgently and regard it as natural. Children have full knowledge of almost everything pertaining to sex. There is only one rigid taboo in connection with it, namely, that there must be no sex play between children of the same moiety, that is, of the same subdivision of the tribe. "If this rule should be broken the children would be lectured, beaten, and thoroughly ashamed" (p. 85).

This variation in the attachment of shame to the tabooed relationships is paralleled by other variations in the situations giving rise to this emotion. In Buka the taboos regarding food appear to be much more serious than those concerned even indirectly with sex behavior. Two people who are "wagun" to each other, that is to say, in-laws of the same generation but of opposite sex, may not eat in each other's presence. If this cannot be avoided the woman must cover her face with a hood. A man may sleep in the same hut as his "wagun," but goes elsewhere for his meals, "thus precisely reversing the taboos observed among ourselves" (7, p. 65).

In Western society the emotion of shame is frequently associated with the exposure of the body, but it is easy to multiply examples from primitive peoples indicating their complete lack of concern on this point. There were many groups who went absolutely naked, or who wore clothing which did not cover those parts of the body which we regard it as modest to conceal (9). A feeling which with us is so strong as to appear "instinctive" may be entirely lacking in other communities. It is interesting in this connection to note the rapidity with which folkways may change, and the manner in which a former custom may come to be regarded with horror. In Buka, before the advent of the Whites, men wore no clothing of any kind, and women only a waist string of thin fiber, from which a bunch of leaves hung down in front, scarcely concealing anything. This is still true of certain of the mountain natives. When the ethnologist spoke to a woman in the village of Kurtatchi about it, the latter seemed quite horrified, and "hastened to explain that the Kanua people were only 'bush Kanakas' who did not know any better. Yet scarcely more than a few years ago they were following exactly the same fashion themselves" (7, p. 133).

The attitude toward pre-marital chastity in the woman shows similar variations. There were many groups among whom it was prized, others to whom it was a matter of indifference, still others to whom it was an actual drawback. Among the Bagesu, a Bantu people, "it is no disgrace to a young woman to become a mother before marriage, nor does it prevent her from obtaining a husband; indeed men like to know that a woman can bear children, and her fault thus rather adds to her value than detracts from it" (10, p. 171). Among the African Bushongo, the little girl remains with her parents until she is past puberty. "Then she is promiscuous until she has borne a child, when she goes to live with her husband, saying, 'Now I have passed my test and it will not be my fault if I do not give you children.' The child already born is left with her parents and regarded as theirs. No shame attaches to this" (11, p. 271). A Bontoc Igorot in the Philippines will not marry a girl until she is pregnant, because he wants proof that she is not sterile. If a girl should be deserted by the father of her child, her chances for a good marriage are better than if she had no child (12).

Throughout large parts of Melanesia and Polynesia promiscuity is permitted before marriage and in many cases is accompanied by the rigid enforcement of monogamy after marriage. In some groups, as for example the Trobrianders, unmarried girls are allowed as many affairs as they desire, but bearing an illegitimate child is a disgrace; Malinowski states that illegitimacy is rare, either because they have methods of birth control the nature of which he could not discover, or because the very fact of promiscuity is in itself a kind of contraceptive (*13*). In the island of Dobu, an affair may turn into marriage at the wish of the boy. The rule is for a boy at puberty to leave his parents' house at night and roam about until he finds a girl who will let him sleep with her. He prefers to sleep with a different girl every night to avoid permanent entanglement, but he must leave the girl's house before dawn. If he oversleeps and is caught publicly, he has to marry the girl, and so if and when he wishes to marry, he may deliberately stay later. It goes without saying that neither the boy nor the girl is condemned for this promiscuity. Here as elsewhere the line between right and wrong is seen differently in different cultures. On this point Lowie (*14*) makes an illuminating comment. "A Crow interpreter once twitted me with the indecency of the Caucasians who dare reproach the Indians with looseness of morals while themselves so shameless as to speak freely with their own sisters" (p. 99).

Closely related to the problem of sex behavior is the question of the standard of beauty, particularly with reference to women. It seems clear that what is sexually stimulating in one society may be a matter of indifference or even of disgust in another. There is, for example, a fatting-house for girls in Central Africa, where feminine beauty is largely dependent on obesity. On reaching puberty a girl is segregated sometimes for years, fed with sweet and fatty foods, and her body is rubbed assiduously with oils. Her seclusion ends with a parade of her corpulence that is followed by her marriage to the proud bridegroom (*15*). The Batoka tribe in South Africa has the custom of knocking out the upper front teeth at the age of puberty. "This is done by both sexes; and though the under teeth, being relieved from the attrition of the upper, grow long and somewhat bent out, and thereby cause the underlip to protrude in a most unsightly way, no young woman thinks herself accomplished until she has got rid of the upper incisors" (*16*, p. 571). The people of Buka admire the effect produced by cicatrization; they say, "That is a fine girl, she has marks all over her body" (*7*, p. 108). A servant of the king of Cochin China is reported to have spoken with contempt of the wife of the English ambassador because "she had white teeth like a dog, and a rosy color like that of potato flowers" (Waitz; see *17*, p. 31).

The phenomenon of romantic love, which with us represents the ideal if not the most frequent type of relation between the sexes, may in other societies be relatively unimportant. Even in Europe, as

Linton (5) points out, it did not appear until the time of the thirteenth century troubadours, who, though they glorified it, believed
it was unattainable by married couples. As late as the eighteenth
century it played only a small part in European marriage. "All
societies recognize that there are occasional violent emotional attachments between persons of the opposite sex, but our present
American culture is practically the only one which has attempted
to capitalize these and make them the basis for marriage" (p. 175).
In many primitive societies such individuals are regarded as unfortunate, and the victims of these attachments are held up as bad
examples. Margaret Mead (18) writes: "These Samoans condone
light love-affairs, but repudiate acts of passionate choice, and have
no real place for any one who would permanently continue, in spite
of social experiences to the contrary, to prefer one woman or one
man to a more socially acceptable mate" (p. 114). Linton goes on
to say that the rarity of such romantic attachments in other societies
suggests that they are psychological abnormalities to which our own
culture has attached great value. It must appear strange to describe
romantic love as an abnormality, but our usual belief that one
woman and that woman alone will be satisfactory as a marriage
partner must seem very odd to those groups who do not have the
romantic tradition.

The prevalence of marriage by purchase among primitive communities illustrates the marked contrast between their attitude and
our own. A girl in our society would feel forever ashamed if she
were "bought and paid for"; where marriage by purchase is the
prevailing form, she is proud of the price she brings. She would be
despised if she cost nothing. It would mean that she or her parents
regarded her as having so little value that she was willing to go to
a man without a bride-price. There were many groups among whom
this was the greatest degradation (19). An interesting example of
a difference in attitude determined by the folkways is cited by
Powdermaker (8). She states that when she described our own
marriage customs to the natives of Lesu they were scandalized at
the lack of payment for the bride, and asked how that could be a
true marriage. They were almost equally shocked at the Continental
custom of the bride's bringing a dowry. One native compared a
Christian marriage without payment to the mating of pigs.

It should be made clear, however, that marriage by purchase
does not permit a man to regard his wife as his own property in

the same sense that inanimate objects are considered property. It is not the woman who is bought outright, but the privilege of using her body for the satisfaction of the husband and for the procreation of children by him. The woman still has rights of her own, and marriage by purchase is not in any way detrimental to her dignity. The wife's family still retains a definite interest in her welfare and the right to insure that she will be treated properly. In Buka the regulations governing divorce of the wife, as well as the procedure to be followed on her death, show that the having of children is regarded as the most important aspect of wife-purchase. If a woman refuses to perform the duties of a wife, a man may divorce her and his money will be returned. If she has cause to divorce him, nothing is returned. If she dies without giving him a child, he will expect to be repaid unless he receives a sister in her place. If there is one child repayment is made in part. If she dies having borne more than one child no repayment is expected—"the husband has had his money's worth, so to speak" (7, p. 99).

Jealousy. The phenomenon of sexual jealousy has attracted considerable attention and opinions differ as to whether or not it is an inevitable concomitant of the sex relation (20, 5). Shand (21) defines jealousy as "that egoistic side of the system of love which has as its special end the exclusive possession of the loved object, whether this object be a woman, or other person, or power, reputation, or property" (p. 260). There is a great deal of evidence from primitive communities to show that such exclusive possession is by no means the rule, and apparently not even the goal of the relationship between the sexes. The wide prevalence of multiple marriage—in the form of group marriage, in which several husbands are married to several wives; or polygyny, in which one man has several wives; or polyandry, in which one woman has several husbands—is the best proof of this statement. Of these by far the most frequent is polygyny, and most reports agree that jealousy among the wives is a relatively rare occurrence. Driberg (22) states that among the Lango, a Nilotic African tribe, the women on the whole live in amity one with another. Jealousies are apt to occur if one wife thinks that the other receives undue favors or is preferentially treated in the matter of land for cultivation or gifts of food, and the husband may have to exercise considerable tact as a consequence. It is rare that any serious difference of opinion arises. "Indeed, instances are not wanting in which a woman, on growing old, of her own instances presses her husband to marry a younger and more attractive wife, and it is certainly true that the womenfolk would be the first to resent the institution of monogamy, as in a polygynous establishment, not only is the woman's work lessened, but in their husband's absence his wives avoid the solitude inherent in a monogamous union" (p. 155). In this community the women are treated with great courtesy and consideration, and they may if they wish prevent the husband from contracting a second marriage; it is said that this veto is rarely if ever exercised.

Among the Tanala tribe of Madagascar (5) the institution of polygyny is accompanied by a number of regulations which will appear strange to most of us. The first marriage is usually a love match. The second occurs three to four years later and in a large number of cases is instigated by the wife on the ground that there is too much work for her in looking after the fields and the children. The man and woman talk it over and decide on a second wife acceptable to both. When a man is detected in an affair with an unmarried woman his wives may insist upon his marrying her, on the principle that she should share in the labors if she has also a share in the privileges of marriage. When a man has three wives, each one has a separate house, and he spends one day with each wife in succession. If he spends one wife's day with another, it is adultery, and the slighted wife is entitled to divorce with alimony. If he really commits adultery in our sense, that is, with a woman to whom he is not married, it is the concern only of the wife on whose day the offense was committed. In other words, the issue is one of marital status rather than of sexual jealousy. There is always a tendency for the wives to present a united front against the husband, and if one of them is carrying on a love affair she can be certain that none of her fellow wives will betray her.

In Lesu (8) marriage may be polygynous, polyandrous or monogamous. In the case of polyandry, the woman will sleep alternately with her husbands and "there appears to be no quarreling between the two men" (p. 227). In this community also sexual life is not confined to marriage, and it is the socially accepted custom for a wife or a husband to have affairs with a number of other people. Either one if young would be considered abnormal otherwise. "A young married woman without lovers would be in the same social position as a young girl in our society who never has any beaux and is never invited to parties" (p. 244). In all cases of extramarital intercourse the man makes a payment of *tsera* or ceremonial currency to the woman, who hands it over to her husband. The woman would consider it disgraceful if no money were paid, since that would lower her prestige and position in the community. This is not a form of prostitution; a woman does not sleep with her lover for the payment, but the payment is part of the relationship. The husband accepts his wife's children as his own and no disgrace is attached to illegitimacy. Jealousy occurs, but it is exceptional.

Among the Kulus and other tribes in the Himalayas, polyandry occurs with some frequency and is usually of the fraternal type, that is to say, a number of brothers have one wife in common. When all the brothers stay at home, the wife usually bestows her favors on each of them equally in turn. The house usually has two rooms, one for the wife, the other for the husbands. "When one brother goes into the wife's room, he leaves his shoes or hat at the door, which is equivalent to the notice 'engaged' " (*Census of India;* see 17, p. 119). In the Jat tribe of the Punjab when women quarrel one may say to the other, "You are one so careless of your duty as not to admit your husband's brothers to your embraces" (23, p. 86).

The phenomenon of wife-lending—the so-called "prostitution of hospitality"—is well known and occurred in a number of widely scattered communities. Perhaps the most familiar instance is that of the Eskimos, among whom it was the custom for the host to lend his wife for the night and sometimes for longer periods to a guest toward whom he wished to be gracious (24). It must be clearly understood that the wife did not have the right to go to another man of her own initiative; this was adultery and was severely punished. This does not mean, however, that the husband was jealous in our sense. He apparently did not feel the need for exclusive possession of his wife's favors. What he objected to was not any infringement on his sexual prerogatives, since he freely shared these with others, but rather the infringement on his status and property rights.

Linton (5) is of the opinion that sexual jealousy does have some universal basis. He cites in support of this view cases in which jealousy is theoretically outlawed but tends to crop up on occasions in which the control by the folkways is temporarily in abeyance. In the Marquesan Islands, for example, an unusual degree of sexual freedom is allowed both sexes before and after marriage. There appears to be little opportunity for the development of the notion of exclusive sexual possession, since group marriage is the normal form and sexual hospitality is commonly practiced. There are rarely any signs of jealousy when the natives are sober. When they are drunk, however, such jealousy frequently manifests itself and may lead to numerous squabbles. These are considered breaches of good manners and the participants are ashamed of themselves as soon as they are sober. Among the Comanche an elder brother would lend his wife freely to his unmarried younger brother, and would expect the latter to return the compliment after his marriage. This is interpreted by Linton as a voluntary restraint of jealousy, partly by the social approval of his act, partly by his expectation of a return in kind. In both these cases it is suggested that jealousy would develop if it were not for restraining influences.

The present writer is not prepared to accept this interpretation. The fact that jealousy does crop out on occasions even though it conflicts with the *mores* seems no proof of its innate universality. The prevalence of polygyny and polyandry, and the smoothness with which these institutions work in the large majority of instances, show that exclusive possession is not a necessary component of harmonious sex relations; the habit of wife-lending testifies in the same direction. It seems certain that only in some societies, notably our own, is the relation between the sexes regarded as ideally monogamous, and jealousy appears to develop principally in that context. Even in our own society there are many instances in which adultery would go unpunished and officially unnoticed, except that it has come to the attention of other people so that prestige and honor are also involved.

We may summarize the discussion of the sex drive up to this point. Sex has clearly an organic basis, and is also clearly common to animals and man. It is universal, with the exception that certain small groups and many individuals have voluntarily renounced sexual satisfaction in the interests of what they regard to be a greater value. In spite of the innateness of the sex drive, the importance of cultural patterning may be seen in the varying emotional attitudes which it arouses; in the differing standards of beauty or perfection looked for in the sex partner; in the contrast between romantic love and a more matter-of-fact relationship; and in the many institutions which testify to the absence or at least to the relative unimportance of exclusive possessiveness or sexual jealousy. We turn now to another aspect of sex behavior which has sometimes been regarded as instinctive, namely the incest taboo.

The Incest Taboo. In every community known to us there are certain restrictions on the choice of the marriage partner. Usually, as we shall see, these restrictions apply particularly to other members of one's immediate family, and are accompanied by strong feelings opposed to any relaxation of the taboos. The term "incest" is ordinarily applied to such consanguineous matings, and the horror of incest appears to be so widespread that many writers have suggested that it may have an innate or instinctive foundation.

There is no indication of any such "instinct" among animals other than man. Pliny (9) tells of a horse which on discovering that it had unwittingly been guilty of incest committed suicide by throwing itself over a cliff! This isolated anecdote is hardly convincing. On the contrary we know that inbreeding is common throughout the animal kingdom and is often the method used in order to develop certain desired characteristics in the offspring.

Lowie (25) states that in every part of the world there are restrictions on mating based upon propinquity of relationship. He cites Hobhouse's theory that this is instinctive and expresses his agreement with it. Wissler (26) also believes that all primitive peoples show a deep disgust over the marriage of brothers and sisters; it is also repugnant to them for a mother to marry her son and only slightly less so for a father to marry his daughter. The rules permit of certain exceptions, but these refer only to a few individuals in the community and are nowhere practiced by a whole tribe or nation. He believes this aversion to incest to be fundamental, since it is universally condemned in all types of culture. In his opinion it may be instinctive, but there is nothing impossible in the idea that it is only a convention. Linton (5), on the other hand, believes that the prohibition of marriage between mother and son is the only one universally present. Marriage between father and daughter is permitted in at least one society, the Azande, while several groups have recognized or even required marriage between brother and sister.

This last type of marriage, for example, has been reported for a number of scattered communities. In Egypt, particularly during the nineteenth and twentieth dynasties, the king was expected to marry his own sister. Among the Incas of Peru, "so insistent was the feeling that the sovereign was raised far above everyone—nobleman or commoner—that he was compelled to marry into his immediate family" (27, p. 129). His official wife was either his sister or his half-sister. The ancient kings of Hawaii had a similar practice. In certain districts of Finland a tradition is preserved that in the old days a brother could marry a sister. Even within fairly recent times a story is told of a very pretty and hard-working girl who lived in the village of Dubensk. "Her parents were reluctant to part with her and give her in marriage to a stranger. So they sent her to pay a long visit to her relatives at a distance, and on her return they received her as a complete stranger. From that day they obliged her to consider her brother as her husband" (28, p. 183). The chiefs among certain tribes of the Nilotic Sudan similarly object to their sisters and daughters going to commoners; they prefer to keep them for themselves, saying that they are more beautiful than the women in the remainder of the tribe. Marriage to a sister—more frequently a half-sister—is common (29). It is also stated that in former times the Veddas of Ceylon frequently married their younger sisters, although marriage with an elder sister seemed to them as horrible as it does to us (30).

The theory of the nature of the incest taboo which has received perhaps the most attention is that of Westermarck (31). In his opinion there are two reasons why this taboo has developed. In the first place, there is no innate aversion to marriage with near relatives, but there is an innate aversion to marriage between persons living very closely together from early childhood. Since such persons are in most cases members of the same family, the horror of incest manifests itself principally in connection with the marriage of near kin. It is not by degree of consanguinity, but by close living together that the prohibitory laws against incest are determined. In the second place, says Westermarck, the incest taboo becomes instinctive as the result of the harmful effects of inbreeding.

The first part of this theory was anticipated by Bentham (32), who wrote: "It is very rare that the passion of love is developed within the circle of individuals to whom marriage ought to be forbidden. There needs to give birth to that sentiment a certain degree of surprise, a sudden effect of novelty. . . . Individuals accustomed to see each other and to know each other, from an age which is neither capable of conceiving the desire nor of inspiring it, will see each other with the same eyes to the end of life" (p. 220).

Westermarck reports that he asked his Berber teacher from the Great Atlas whether marriages between cousins were frequent in his tribe, and the answer was: "How could you love a girl whom you have always seen?" (Vol. II, p. 194). In ancient Japan brothers and sisters might be permitted to marry provided they had not been brought up together.

On the other hand, among the Siberian Chuckchee a great many marriages between relatives are concluded at an early age, some-times when the bridegroom and the bride are still infants. The marriage ritual is performed, and from that time on the children play together and spend as much time as possible in each other's company. Bogoras (33) here takes a view opposite to that of Wester-marck and states that "Of course, the ties between them grow to be very strong, often stronger even than death; when one dies, the other also dies of grief, or commits suicide" (17, p. 183). Among the Arapesh also there were early betrothals, and the two people des-tined later to marry grew up together in terms of closest intimacy. Here again it is reported that affection developed rather than decreased as a result of this contact (34).

It should be added that incest is by no means so rare within our own society as is sometimes supposed. The reports from isolated mountain communities indicate that it occurs with considerable frequency, in spite of the intimacy of family life—or possibly because of it. Another argument against this portion of Westermarck's theory is to be found in the fact that there are many communities in which brother-sister incest is rigidly taboo, and where brothers and sisters do not grow up together. This is particularly true in many parts of Melanesia where there are special communal houses in which the boys live, and which make close intimacy with their sisters impos-sible. In general it is safe to conclude that the theory is not borne out by the facts and that on the contrary the intimacy within the family circle would lead to many more incestuous relationships if these were not restrained by the folkways of the group.[1]

---

[1] This is precisely the point made by Knight Dunlap (35), who argues that the lack of erotic attraction in housemates is not the cause, but the result of the incest prohibition. His own explanation is that the taboo is necessary in order to prevent sexual relations between persons in the same household. One wonders, however, why this need should ever have arisen. Dunlap's suggestion that otherwise sexual inter-course would begin early and be dangerously excessive is hardly convincing in view of the amount of sexual freedom permitted by many primitive communities. Unless incest can be shown to have some special danger, the origin of the taboo is still unexplained.

The other aspect of Westermarck's theory, namely, that the incest taboo develops as a result of the dangers of inbreeding to the off-spring, and that it consequently becomes instinctive, may also be rejected. The most common opinion among biologists at the present time is to the effect that inbreeding as such has no harmful effects, and it is only when there are latent defects in the parents that the marriage of close relatives will result in defective offspring. To cite one outstanding historical example, the pedigree of Cleopatra is remarkable from this point of view.

> Not only had she nothing but royal blood in her veins . . . but over and over again, in the royal pedigree, she was derived from full brother and sister marriages. . . . Yet this woman, descended from a series of closely inbred ancestors, is not only handsome, vigorous, in-tellectual, but also prolific. Apart from her moral standard, which in any case was far removed from ours, or even from that of the great Greeks and Romans, she was as perfect a specimen of the human race as could be found in any age or class of society (Mahaffy; see 17, p. 195).

To take a more recent example, Leipoldt (36) tells of examining twin children, a boy and a girl of nine, whom he describes as about the most perfect specimens of juvenile humanity he had examined in a long series of 150,000 cases. He was told by the father with much embarrassment that his great-grandparents were brother and sister; that his father and mother were cousins, and that his wife was his own second cousin. Leipoldt comments: "I know of no scientific reason why two persons, both physically and mentally sound, should not marry and breed equally sound progeny" (p. 78). It is stated also that certain Fijian stocks require first cousins to marry, and the ethnologist who studied them found no harmful effects of this practice (37). It is certainly difficult to imagine that any instinct should be based upon a biological principle so uncertain as that of the danger of inbreeding. In any case, Murdock (38) has pointed out that in no fewer than fifty-six of the sample societies included in the Human Relations Area Files, extreme inbreeding (for example, with first cousins) may actually coexist with strong incest taboos directed toward other members of the "family."

Perhaps the best argument against the instinctive nature of the incest taboo is to be found in the fact that although some form of marriage prohibition is universal, its exact character varies from group to group. In Dobu (39) mother-son incest is regarded as a great contamination, whereas father-daughter incest is not taken so seriously; biologically, of course, the two relationships are equally close. The greatest of all crimes is adultery between a man and his mother's brother's wife. In Buka the worst form of incest is between a man and his sister's daughter. Mother-son incest is rare; father-daughter incest more frequent. While disapproved of, it is not viewed with the same horror as intercourse between a man and his sister's daughter. From the point of view of this people, the father is a member of a different lineage from that of his daughter, but is of the same lineage as his sister and her daughter; this helps to explain the difference between their attitude and our own (7). In Lesu brother-sister incest is rigidly taboo, and there are a number of women whom a man calls "sister," even though from our point of view there is no biological relation between them. The taboo against these classificatory sisters is regarded just as strictly as the taboo against the real sister. It is clear that biological relationships can have little to do with the origin of the taboo in this case.

There are many instances of contrasting attitudes toward incest which show that social rather than biological factors are operative. The greater number of primitive groups are exogamous, that is, they disapprove of marriage within the group (or sib). Some sibs are endogamous, and require marriage within the group. "The rightness of sib endogamy was expressed by the scorn of the Bella Bella of the Northwest Coast of America who said, 'Who ever heard of a Raven marrying an Eagle?' in contrasting their own custom with that of their exogamous northern neighbors, the Tsimshian" (40, p. 417). Mention was previously made of the brother-sister marriages among the Egyptian and Peruvian rulers. On the other hand, among the Loango of the Congo region (41) the king may not marry any princess, because all princesses are considered his sisters. There are a great many societies which forbid marriage with parallel cousins (that is, with children of the mother's sister or father's brother) but permit, and on occasions prefer, marriage with cross cousins (children of the mother's brother or the father's sister). Here a similar biological relationship assumes diametrically opposite forms, and is associated with contrasting emotional attitudes because of the folkways of the community.

In England until recently it was regarded as a very great crime to marry the sister of one's deceased wife. This was looked upon in the same manner as marriage with one's own sister, and was spoken of as "psychic incest." A bill repealing this law was adopted in 1850, but came into effect only in 1907. Before that time, this prohibition was spoken of as "a law of God" and any breach of it was considered unnatural (17).

This last illustration makes it clear that not only does the nature of the incest prohibition vary from one group to another, but that even within the same group the passage of time and the consequent alteration in the folkways may make perfectly acceptable a union previously regarded as impossible. There seems to be no way of reconciling this variability with the notion that the incest taboo is instinctive.

Another approach to the incest prohibition would regard it as arising out of certain practical considerations. Tylor (42) maintains that exogamy, or marrying outside of one's own community, would enable a tribe to establish friendly relations with any number of other intermarrying groups, and would thereby give it an advantage in a struggle with an isolated community that lacked similar relationships with other groups. "Again and again in the world's history, savage tribes must have had plainly before their minds the simple practical alternative between marrying out and being killed out" (p. 267). Since exogamy would give the group this practical advantage, any incestuous marriage would be regarded as detrimental to the group's interests, and would be condemned. Fortune (43) develops this theory a little further on the basis of his experience in Melanesia. He states that in small communities social organization depends on the performance of obligations attached to family relationships. If the consanguineous relatives differ from the affinal relatives (the "in-laws") there is a wider recognition of social obligations, since the affinal relationship carries with it such duties as alliance in war and cooperation in hunting and in the mourning ceremonial. Marriage outside one's own family assures therefore a large group of allies in economic and other activities. "Any incestuous alliance between two persons within a single consanguineous group is in so far a withdrawal of their consanguineous group from the alliance and so endangers the group's survival" (p. 620). This theory has considerable plausibility. It may be objected, however, that it is not always true that such affinal relationships play a part in the economic and ceremonial life of the community, and that Fortune's account applies better to Melanesia than to groups in other parts of the world.

In the case of the Arapesh, a Melanesian tribe, there appears to be a conscious realization of the practical drawbacks to incest of the type which Fortune describes. In answer to a question regarding the possibility of marrying one's own sister, a native replied:

> What, you would like to marry your sister? What is the matter with you anyway? Don't you want a brother-in-law? Don't you realize that if you marry another man's sister and another man marries your sister, you will have at least two brothers-in-law, while if you marry your own sister you will have none? With whom will you hunt, with whom will you garden, whom will you go to visit? (*34*, p. 84)

In this case, however, incest is regarded not with horror and repulsion, but as a stupid negation of the value of increasing the number of people whom one can love and trust, and with whom one may cooperate.

Another native explanation of a somewhat different type is given by the African Chagga (*44*). An informant expressed it as follows:

> At first people married their own sisters, but they noticed that they were beating their wives excessively, so they determined: We will not marry our own sisters but each will marry the sister of another, so that everyone will say: "If I beat my wife I shall be called to account by her brother and he will take my property away." If they had continued as they began they would have killed their wives, for they said: "If she dies what difference does it make, whose business is it?" (p. 38)

Malinowski (*13*) believes that the objection to incest arises from the fact that it would be a disruptive element within the family. The sensual approach of a son toward his mother would disturb the normal mother-son relationship, since it would be incompatible with the submission and reverence which a son would be expected to show his mother. It would also introduce an active hostile rivalry between father and son instead of the harmonious relationship otherwise to be expected. If incest were allowed, therefore, the family could not exist, and the aversion to incest is due to a complex scheme of cultural reactions dependent upon the interrelationships within the family. This point appears to be a sound one and is helpful as a principle of explanation. Even in the case of brother-sister incest, which Malinowski does not discuss in this connection, it is also applicable in certain instances. If a man married his sister, for example, his mother would also be his mother-in-law. Since in many communities there is the custom of mother-in-law avoidance (see below, p. 147), the intimate relationship with the mother would conflict with the expected attitude toward the mother of one's wife, and the normal family life would thereby be disrupted.

This whole approach to incest on the basis of its practical disadvantages is not always applicable. There are some cases in which brother-sister marriage in particular would be a real convenience. In our own society especially, the frequent difficulty of finding a husband for one's daughter could be met most easily by marriage with her brother. In justice to the theory, however, it must be added that this type of difficulty is a relatively new phenomenon due to the structure of our society and that it probably occurs rarely if at all in primitive communities.

In his *Totem and Taboo*, which represents the first important attempt to apply psychoanalytic principles to the interpretation of ethnological phenomena, Freud (45) suggests another explanation for the attitude toward incest. He starts from the Darwinian hypothesis of a primal horde, conceived after the analogy of gorilla society, in which a violent jealous father (the dominant male) keeps all the females for himself, and drives away the growing sons. These younger males would resent the power of the father and would of course desire possession of some of the females. One day, says Freud (although it is doubtful whether he thought this happened at a particular moment in history), the expelled brothers slew their father and thus put an end to the father horde. They had, however, as in the case of all sons, an ambivalent attitude toward their father; they hated him and resented his authority, but they also loved and admired him. They satisfied their hate by his removal, but then their suppressed tender impulses asserted themselves, and took the form of remorse and a sense of guilt. They tried therefore to undo their deed by declaring that the killing of the father substitute, the totem,[2] was not allowed, and they renounced the fruits of their act by denying themselves their father's women. This is the origin of the incest prohibition, as a result of which all men renounce the women of their own family group.

The urge toward incestuous relationships still remains, however; Freud approves Frazer's statement that the existence of a legal prohibition against it shows that many men have a propensity in that direction. "If the law represses it, it does so because civilized men

[2] The institution of totemism frequently, but not invariably, includes the prohibition against killing or eating the totem animal.

have come to the conclusion that the satisfaction of these natural instincts is detrimental to the general interests of society" (p. 206). There is no innate aversion to incestuous relations; as a matter of fact the first sex impulses of the young are, according to Freud's theory, regularly of an incestuous nature. In this connection, the important part played by the Oedipus complex (see below) is well known. For Freud, therefore, it is not the dread of incest which is instinctive, but rather the desire for it, and this desire is kept in check by the folkways which have arisen as the result of the murder of the primal father by his sons.

It is difficult to criticize this theory of Freud's because the "crime" upon which it rests is so entirely hypothetical that any direct proof or disproof of it is unobtainable. It is possible to say, however, that there is no group of human beings among whom a primal horde such as Freud postulates has ever been discovered. In addition, the theory may conceivably explain why a man should deny himself his mother or his sisters, but it does not explain the extension of the incest prohibition to his daughters, a relationship which is forbidden as strictly as the others. Although undoubtedly there is some truth to the notion of an Oedipus complex and its derivatives, its extension backward into a particular point in time from which all incest prohibitions all over the world have originated is an assumption which ethnologists in general are not prepared to accept. The theory as a whole must be regarded as unproven.

A significant approach to the understanding of the incest taboo has been made by Murdock (38), who has attempted to combine the insights of several different disciplines into an overall scheme of clarification. Psychoanalysis, he feels, has accounted for the emotional quality of the taboos against incestuous behavior by stressing repressed impulses and the unconscious defenses against genuine temptation. Sociological theory, through the analysis of many forms of social organization, has helped to reveal the disruption of family relationships which would result from incest, and the many practical advantages which accompany "marrying out." Behavioral psychology accounts for the extension of the incest taboo beyond the bounds of the immediate family; the principle of "stimulus generalization" developed by Hull (46) holds that an habitual response developed in connection with one stimulus will tend to be evoked by other stimuli to the extent to which they are perceived as similar; in this context the principle helps to explain why avoidance behavior is extended to others who are not members of one's immediate (or nuclear) family. Cultural anthropology, finally, provides the knowledge of specific customs and relationships which helps us to understand why such extension takes one form in one society and a very different form in another.

Although granting the value of applying to a complex social phenomenon the insights obtained from as many different sources as possible, the present writer feels that of all the suggested theories, by far the most helpful is that which explains the incest taboo in terms of its social utility. That utility has been recognized by many writers, as has been indicated above, and Murdock (38) also attaches considerable significance to it. The ethical and religious sanctions with which the taboo becomes gradually surrounded probably obtained their initial impetus from such practical considerations.

In summary it may be said that of the various explanations suggested, the most probable is that the incest taboo arose from very practical considerations. Marrying out would have definite advantages, and incest definite disadvantages. It is natural therefore that the latter should be universally condemned. This theory does not adequately explain the nature of the prohibition in every case, but it is likely that it represents the principal consideration, with additions and alterations resulting from historical factors. There is no real evidence that the incest prohibition is instinctive.

Patterns of Avoidance. Allied to the problem of incest is the prevalence among primitive communities of certain patterns of avoidance. These are rules of relationship which may forbid any kind of social contact between certain individuals, and which are usually regarded as very important. Of these, by far the most widespread is the mother-in-law taboo. Whereas among ourselves, the mother-in-law relationship has been the object of a considerable amount of ridicule and occasionally of unpleasantness, among a great many primitive communities it is characterized by an attitude of respect and avoidance. The taboo against speaking to one's mother-in-law is so strict among the native Australians that in former times the penalty for breaking it was death. Among the African Baganda a greater sanctity attached to the mother-in-law taboo than to the taboo against incest. A Navajo believed he would go blind if he saw his mother-in-law's face (9). In Buka it is the strictest of all taboos. The mother-in-law always carries with her a kind of pointed hood made of pandanus leaves; if she learns that her son-in-law is approaching she immediately covers her face. They must not eat together nor sleep in the same house nor speak to each other directly (7). A missionary in New Britain tells of trying to translate the passage in the Gospel of St. Mark in which Herod swears to give Salome whatever she asks, even to the half of his kingdom. When he investigated the natives' idea of what it meant to swear, he found that the most solemn oath a man could take was—"Sir, if I am not telling the truth, I hope I may shake hands with [touch the hand of] my mother-in-law" (47, p. 17). The taboo between father-in-law and daughter-in-law also exists but is not nearly so widespread nor so strict.

Several theories have been suggested in explanation of these avoidance patterns (3). Lubbock, for example, believes that in cases of marriage by capture the husband would fear the anger of the parents of his bride, and would consequently stay as far from them as possible. This theory is difficult to accept, first because marriage by capture occurs quite rarely, and second, because on this basis the husband would be expected to avoid his father-in-law at least as much as his mother-in-law, and this is not the case. A somewhat similar explanation is that of Tylor (42), who believes that the husband is regarded as an outsider and is "cut" by his wife's family. He cites in support of this the fact that often when a child is born the avoidance taboo no longer exists. This also fails to explain why the mother-in-law avoidance should be stricter than all the others.

Freud's theory is as follows: The mother-in-law is unwilling to give up possession of the daughter; she distrusts the stranger and wishes to retain her own dominant position. The man in his turn is determined not to subject himself to any foreign will, and is jealous of those who preceded him in his wife's affections. He is also averse to any disturbance in his "illusion of sexual over-evaluation," that is to say, the sight of his mother-in-law reminds him that his wife, too, will some day grow old, that she will not always possess the charm and the youth that he now sees in her. There are also unconscious factors at work. The mother-in-law lives again in the emotional experiences of her children and identifies herself with them; this may go so far that she also falls in love with the man her daughter has married. The avoidance would remove from her any possible temptation. In the case of the man, there may be identification of the mother-in-law with the mother, and since there is an ever-present incest temptation with regard to the latter, mother-in-law avoidance also develops as a protection against it.

This theory is part of the whole Freudian structure and cannot properly be criticized in isolation from it. It seems probable that in our own society difficulties do develop as the result of the unwilling-ness of the parents to surrender control over their children, and of the young husband to submit to such control. It should be noted, however, that in those primitive communities in which the avoid-ance is found, it is expressed not in terms of hostility, but in terms of respect. As far as one can tell from the reports of the ethnologists, the two parties to the avoidance may have the highest regard for each other. Lowie (*14*) tells of an incident among the Crow in which one man said to another, "What's the matter with your mother-in-law, Joe? She does not seem to have any respect for you at all!" (p. 88).

Another frequent type of avoidance pattern is that between brother and sister. This may be regarded as an extension of the incest taboo, since the attitude toward it is determined by the fear that it may lead to incest. It is found in the most extreme form in Melanesia. So great is the objection to any degree of intimacy be-tween brother and sister that there are parts of Melanesia where one of twin siblings of different sex may be put to death immedi-ately on account of their objectionable contacts before birth (*48*). In the Trobriand Islands boys are separated from their sisters at a very early age and live in their own communal house. Malinowski (*13*) states that in this community by far the worst type of incest is that between brother and sister. This taboo relationship extends, however, to all other types of intimacy as well. Although complete sexual freedom is permitted before marriage, sex must not even be mentioned in the presence of a sister. Some of the consequences of this taboo will be discussed in greater detail below.

In Buka there is a feeling of "shame" between brother and sister which persists through life. They are ashamed to talk to each other unless other people are present. If a man's sister calls to him to come and take some food from her, he may do so, but more probably he will pretend not to hear her. Jokes on sexual subjects may not be told by anyone to a woman in the presence of her brother. It is not even permitted under such circumstances to use certain slightly improper words which otherwise are looked upon much as we con-sider slang (*7*). In Lesu, on the other hand, there is only semi-avoidance between brothers and sisters, and the most rigid taboos are reserved for the relationship between cross cousins of the opposite sex. Between these two, contacts are regulated by many ritual prohibitions. Personal names must never be mentioned between them; they must not go near each other; if they must speak, they do so briefly at a distance. Food may be exchanged, but only through the medium of a third person (8). These reports indicate that the avoidance relationships, like the incest taboos, may vary markedly from group to group and may apply to different members of the family. A relationship which is a familiar one in one group may be surrounded by the most rigid taboos in another. These variations appear to be due to cultural and historical factors and probably do not depend upon any fundamental or common human psychological attitudes. They may, however, have important implications for the personal relationships among members of a particular family.

The Oedipus Complex. This consideration leads to another problem within the general framework of sex relationships. Mention was previously made of the Oedipus complex, which Freud regards as one of the very foundations of our psychological structure. As is well known, this complex gets its name from the story of Oedipus, King of Thebes, of whom it was prophesied before his birth that he would kill his father Laius and marry his mother Jocasta. He was as a consequence exposed to die in the woods, but was saved and brought up in ignorance of his parentage. Eventually the prophecy was fulfilled. On his return to Thebes Oedipus killed Laius in a skirmish on a narrow road, and then married the widow. When the true relationship was discovered after many years, Jocasta killed herself and Oedipus put out his eyes. This tragic story moves us particularly, says Freud, because there is in every one of us the submerged desire to kill the father and possess the mother. In the development of the personality, the Oedipus stage is one through which all boys pass on their way to complete heterosexual maturity, but the incestuous wishes which form part of it are never completely lost. In dreams and in neuroses they may come to definite expression.[3] The hostility against the father may manifest itself in a host of ways, for example in the development of a general revolt against authority, and the consequent determination of one's economic and political attitudes. In general it may be said that these two aspects of the

[3] They have found their way into literature, as the writings of D. H. Lawrence, Sidney Howard, and Eugene O'Neill testify.

Oedipus complex, the hostility against the father (tempered by attitudes of love and respect as well) and the excessive love of the mother, are among the foundations of psychoanalytic interpretation.

For Freud the Oedipus complex is regarded as a universal phenomenon. It is present in varying degree in all boys, and plays an important part throughout their psychological development. The ethnologists, however, have been skeptical of this universality and have thought it worth while to see whether it exists in similar form in all societies. There are, apparently, many groups besides our own in which it has been observed. Herskovits (49), for example, asked one of the Bush-Negroes of Suriname, or Dutch Guiana, the following question: "When a man dies, do they destroy his house?" The reply was: "Not unless he has done black magic. If he is an ordinary man, his widow lives there with his daughters." "What happens to his sons?" "They are sent away for a long time." "Why?" "Because the soul of a man loves his daughters but hates his sons, and if they remained in his house, his ghost would kill them." "And if a woman dies?" "Then the husband continues to live there with his sons, for if it is a woman's ghost, she will destroy her daughters. But her sons, she loves them and watches over them" (50, p. 139).

On the other hand, Malinowski's (13) observations indicate that there may be an intimate connection between the nature of the family and the social organization on the one hand and the characteristics of the Oedipus or "nuclear" complex on the other. He believes that this complex is to be understood as a reaction to the family in which the individual develops rather than as an inevitable stage through which every boy must pass. The Trobriand family, in which these observations were made, differs in certain fundamental respects from the family in our society. Fatherhood, for example, is a purely social relationship, which does not involve the presence of any authority over the children. It is the duty of the father "to receive the children into his arms"; he assists in looking after them and attending to their natural needs. He is much more active in caring for the child than is the father in our society. The attitude of the child to him is one of friendship and affection. There can be no fear of him, nor rebellion against him, since he never issues orders nor asks obedience of the child. Authority is vested instead in the mother's eldest brother, who is idealized by his nephew and regarded as a model to be followed. He introduces into the life of the boy social ambition, glory, pride of lineage, promises of future wealth, power and social status. On his death he leaves to his nephew his most important possessions, including his most powerful magic. If there is any struggle against authority, therefore, it must be against the maternal uncle and not the father.

The relationship to the mother also differs from our own. Weaning, for instance, may be sudden and painful for a child in our society, and may constitute a very disturbing experience. The separation from the mother may leave a gap in the child's life and cause him to long for a return to her. Among the Trobrianders weaning takes place much later, when the child himself decides that he prefers other food. There is no great wrench from the mother, and the desire for her consequently does not loom so large in later life.

The important taboo, as was indicated above, is that between brother and sister, who are separated at an early age and are never together socially with any intimacy. Most important of all, neither one must ever show the slightest interest in the love affairs of the other. There is completely free play given to sexuality with the exception of this taboo. The sister is a mysterious being, therefore, with whom no intimacy is permitted. She is "the only spot in the sexual horizon permanently hidden," and any incipient tenderness toward her is immediately cut short. As the result of this family constellation, the nuclear complex is quite different from what it is in our society. "In the Oedipus complex, there is the repressed desire to kill the father and marry the mother, while in the matrilineal society of the Trobriands the wish is to marry the sister and to kill the maternal uncle" (p. 81).

Malinowski cites as additional evidence in favor of his interpretation the fact that the Trobrianders were unwilling to discuss with him the question of brother-sister incest, and showed considerable emotional disturbance when he questioned them about it. They were amused rather than disturbed at any reference to incest between mother and son, referring to the difference in age as an adequate barrier to any such relationship. No one admitted dreaming of incest with the sister, but many of them claimed to know that others had had such dreams. In addition, Malinowski found that the mythology of the Trobrianders furnished evidence in the same direction. One legend, for example, explains the origin of the most powerful of all love potions as resulting from a case of brother-sister infatuation; another describes the exploits of a hero whose principal adversary is his mother's brother.

This position has been subjected to considerable criticism on the part of orthodox psychoanalysts. Roheim (51), for example, questions Malinowski's competence in the application and interpretation of psychoanalytic method, characterizing him as little more than an amateur in this field. It must certainly be admitted that the manifestations of the Oedipus complex in our society are not always obvious, and it requires considerable practice in the interpretation of dreams as well as of overt behavior to be certain of its existence. There is always the possibility, therefore, that it does exist in the Trobriands in a form analogous to our own, but that Malinowski was simply not sufficiently well trained to observe it. The probability remains that this complex does vary with the cultural setting, and that in the form in which we know it, it is not universal. The analysis by Fromm (52) of the relation of various forms of parental authority to the family pattern points in the same direction.

This whole discussion of sex behavior has led into a number of bypaths not directly connected with the question of sex as a fundamental drive. These additional considerations have been important, however, in showing the manner and the degree to which a drive which is clearly organic in nature may still be controlled by cultural factors. Even those aspects of human nature which are universal and biologically determined are not understood unless they are seen in their social setting.

ORGANIC NEEDS

A number of the instincts included in McDougall's list refer to the satisfaction of definite organic needs, or "visceral drives." In this category we find hunger and thirst, the need for rest or sleep, the elimination of waste products from the body, etc. These are primary urges which cannot be ignored if the organism is to continue in a healthy state. Their satisfaction is essential for life. When any one of them is unsatisfied a tension is set up in the organism which demands relief, and some kind of activity is undertaken until the relief is obtained. These needs have of course an organic basis. The most acceptable explanation of hunger is that it is experienced as a consequence of the rhythmic contractions of the stomach wall, resulting from the diminution of the sugar content in the blood. These contractions take place long before the organism is actually in a state of starvation, and constitute a sort of danger signal indicating that the energy requirements of the body are being depleted. The sensation of thirst is apparently set up by the drying of the tissues at the back of the throat and similarly indicates somewhat ahead of time that the tissues require more fluid. The need for sleep has been accounted for in various ways; one theory, for which there is experimental evidence, regards it as the result of the accumulation of certain chemical products in the cerebro-spinal fluid and the blood stream, these products being decreased after a period of sleep. The need for elimination of waste products is accompanied by a sensation of distension in the bladder or in the lower part of the large intestine. Although the exact mechanisms are in some cases debatable, these organic needs are obviously present also throughout the animal kingdom, except in the simplest species. We may speak of them therefore not only as "human nature," but more broadly still as "animal nature."

These organic needs have also, however, their social aspect. The elimination of waste products, for example, is in many societies subject to certain customs and conventions. In our case it must be carried out in strict privacy, but there are groups like the native Australians among whom no such taboo is observed. In the case of our children a long and sometimes painful period of training is necessary before the social requirements are properly satisfied. There are general rules also for the time and place for sleep, but these are not nearly so rigid nor so universally enforced.

In the case of hunger and thirst social factors play an exceedingly important part. The fact that we eat at least three meals a day at prescribed intervals is not due to any organic rhythm. In many primitive communities there are only two meals, and no one suffers particularly as the result of this different pattern. If we get hungry at meal-time, this is due at least in part to our previous socially determined habits of eating. As Malinowski (53) expresses it, "Appetite or even hunger is determined by the social milieu. Nowhere and never will man, however primitive, feed on the fruit of his environment. He always selects and rejects, produces and prepares. He does not depend on the physiological rhythm of hunger and satiety alone; his digestive processes are timed and trained by the daily routine of his tribe, nation, or class" (p. 943).

The kind of food we eat is also in large measure due to social factors. It may be that certain individuals, because of the chemical constituents of their tissues or their blood stream, have special food requirements which they try as far as possible to satisfy. One person may need more sugar, another more protein, and his diet may vary accordingly. Although individual differences in food preferences may partly be explained in this manner, this is not true of differences between groups. Wissler (26) states that there is probably no community which does not consistently refrain from eating certain available foods. This is not peculiar to primitive man; in our society there is a practical taboo against the eating of snakes, dogs, cats, rats and insects. These food aversions are held usually for no obvious reasons and are probably not based on practical considerations. As a rule there is no aversion to the most abundant and accessible foods in the habitat of a tribe; for example, many American Indian tribes which tabooed the eating of fish lived in regions which were not well watered and where the streams contained only small fish which were difficult to catch.

In an interesting article on "food prejudices" Townsend (54) gives many examples of the variations in food preference in different parts of the world. Clams and mussels, for example, are of the same family; in Europe mussels are eaten and clams are not, whereas in America the reverse holds true. Clams are actually shipped from England to Newfoundland to be used for bait; the English will not taste them. In England and the United States various species of flat fish—sole, plaice and flounder—are regarded as good and delicate eating; in Gaspé, Newfoundland and Labrador, they are used only as fertilizer. All along our coasts dogfish are thrown away as soon as caught, but in the Hebrides they are called "gray fish" and "rock salmon" and there is no prejudice against them. The Algonquin Indians were fond of skunk, which the Whites would not consider eating. Similar examples might be multiplied. It is important to keep in mind, however, that these food prejudices may be overcome as a result of necessity. It is said that the first Europeans and Americans to visit the Indians of British Columbia and the Northwest Coast found the food so saturated in fish oil that it was quite unpalatable. After a time they were able to eat it with relish. This means that biological necessity may counteract the force of socially determined food habits as well as of personal preference, but it is evidently only in an emergency situation that this takes place.

In this connection Katz (55) stresses the important distinction between hunger and appetite. In a series of interesting experiments he has shown how animals of different species can be made to eat even when they are not "hungry," that is to say, immediately after they have finished eating all they could of a certain food. The introduction of another food or of a hungry animal would stimulate the appetite and the apparently satiated animal would start eating again. Exactly the same observation has been made in the case of human beings. We may perhaps conclude that the hunger drive is organic and universal, but that appetite, which plays an exceedingly important part in our food habits, is socially determined. The same considerations apply to thirst, which therefore does not require a separate discussion. In general these organic needs are completely "dependable"; they must be satisfied at all costs.

GREGARIOUSNESS

The drive toward gregarious activity, sometimes called the herd instinct, has special significance in the field of social psychology. If there is such a drive, it makes it possible to understand why groups are formed and how a group behavior as distinct from individual behavior develops. In the psychological literature it has loomed largest in the writings of Trotter (56), for whom it is one of the four instincts which play the most important part in the life of man, the others being self-preservation, nutrition and sex.

Gregariousness, says Trotter, is a phenomenon of profound biological significance. "The only medium in which man's mind can function satisfactorily is the herd, which therefore is not only the source of his opinions, his credulities, his disbeliefs, and his weaknesses, but of his altruism, his charity, his enthusiasms and his power" (p. 47). The gregarious characteristics of man are shown by the fact that he is intolerant and fearful of solitude, physical and mental; that he is more sensitive to the voice of the herd than to any other influence; that he is subject to the passions of the pack in his mob violence and of the herd in his panics; that he is remarkably susceptible to leadership; that his relations with his fellows are dependent upon their recognition of him as a member of the herd. If this analysis of Trotter's is correct, the gregarious motive would stand in the very forefront of the mechanisms which we are here considering.

To return to the criteria which we have previously employed, we find first that there is continuity with the behavior of the lower animals, but that this continuity is difficult to interpret. It is well known that among certain of the insect species gregarious activity is carried to remarkable heights of complexity and thoroughness. Among higher species, however, particularly in mammalian groups, the gregarious behavior may be absent or reduced to a minimum. This is particularly true of the more ferocious animals like lions and tigers, who are almost invariably found singly or in pairs. Among the higher anthropoids, although accounts of their behavior in this respect differ, it is frequently recorded that single individuals are encountered.

There is considerable evidence to the effect that social behavior, even among animals, involves learning and experience. A study by Scott (57) indicates that a female lamb which was isolated from other sheep until nine days of age showed little subsequent tendency to play with other lambs, and never became a fully integrated member of the group. Similar results have been reported in the case of a chimpanzee (58). Carpenter (59) believes that monkeys reared in isolation and then brought together will not form a unified group, because they have not been conditioned to one another. "They have not been socialized, i.e., they have not learned to make fitting responses to each other as complexes of stimuli" (p. 256).

Still another factor which may play a part in the social behavior of animals is to be found in the survival value of such behavior under certain conditions. Allee (60) has observed, for example, that rats in isolation are more subject to certain diseases than those reared in groups, because when they huddle close together the warmth of their bodies serves as a valuable means of keeping the temperature of all of them at an optimum level.

In general we may conclude that the criterion of continuity with animals gives ambiguous results in this case, since species may be found either with or without gregarious behavior, and since its occurrence may frequently be explained by other factors which are operative in the immediate environment.

The second criterion, namely that of a known physiological basis for the drive, is not satisfied in the case of gregariousness. It may be that further research will some day uncover such a foundation, but that is unlikely. In the light of our present knowledge of physiology it is difficult to conceive of a neurological or endocrine pattern which would directly lead to gregarious activity. It is possible, however, that in the early experiences of the child the faces and persons of adults have a high stimulus value, partly because they actually con-stitute a large part of the environment and partly also because they are related to the satisfaction of fundamental needs. This might represent a very indirect physiological basis, not in the form of a visceral or tissue need, but determined by the perceptual primacy of other human beings.

As far as the universality of this drive is concerned, it seems clear that a certain minimum amount of interaction between individuals would be necessary everywhere, although it is important to note that the extent of this association varies greatly. Certain groups have been described as "atomistic," in the sense that individuals or small family groups live in practical isolation. This is said to be true of many tribes in the Sahara and in Madagascar, as well as of the Jibaro Indians of Ecuador. The African pygmies are reported to be very anti-social even toward members of their own group, and in some of the Indian tribes of Brazil each family lives by itself (*61*). Relatively small isolated groups, consisting at the most of a few families, have been reported for the Veddas of Ceylon, the Semang of the Malay Peninsula, several Australian tribes, and others (*62*). There are apparently many groups among whom gregarious tend-encies are limited to the members of one's own family, although there may be larger assemblages on special occasions.

This leads to a possible interpretation of gregarious behavior as an extension of the interrelationships within a family. Malinowski (*63*), for example, states that there is no herd instinct in man, but that common sociability develops by extension of the family bonds and from no other sources. The endurance of family ties is the pattern of all social organization and the condition of cooperation. As an additional argument against the existence of a gregarious instinct as such, Malinowski points to the fact that as culture advances, individual activities, economic and otherwise, gradually disappear and are replaced by collective behavior. We should then have a case of an instinct increasing with the greater complexity of culture, which is a manifest impossibility. In other words, if we have a form of behavior which is relatively rare among more "primitive" groups and much more developed in complex societies, it is not very likely that it may be explained in biological terms. We may add here that Darwin (*64*) was also of the belief that "the feeling of pleasure from society is probably an extension of the parental or filial affec-tion" (p. 80).

Hobhouse (62) makes the suggestion that groupings could have arisen out of the need to find mates outside of one's family. "The simplest social organization, therefore, postulates two or more families living together, but constantly united by cross ties of inter-marriage" (p. 43). This would mean that a certain minimum amount of gregariousness would be necessary in order not to do violence to the incest taboo. The interpretation here given depends, how-ever, upon the assumption that this taboo is primary, whereas in a previous section (see page 138) we have seen that in all probability the taboo develops as a result of practical considerations, included among which is the desirability of friendly cooperative relations with other people.

This suggests that gregariousness also may be understood in terms of practical advantages. Sumner and Keller (61) deny the existence of a herd instinct and state that association has become a charac-teristic habit of mankind because of its high survival value. Not only is it possible to carry on in the group certain economic and religious activities which would not be possible for an individual—for ex-ample, trade and exchange of goods at a common market, compli-cated ritual ceremonies, division of labor, united defense against an enemy, etc.—but it also makes life generally easier and more secure. In such associations the individual must inevitably give up a certain amount of his liberty, but the cooperation that results more than repays him for his loss. Life in society may consequently be regarded as a species of insurance, in which a small recurring cal-culable loss is substituted for a possible ruinous and incalculable one.

This theory makes it possible to understand gregarious activity as a means to a very practical end. The minimum amount of gregari-ousness found everywhere may be explained as the consequence of family life, which is in turn the effect of sex activity and the rela-tionship between parents and children. Any extension beyond this family group is probably due originally to the mutual advantages resulting from this extension. Here as elsewhere, a mechanism may become a drive, to use an expression of Woodworth's (65); that is to say, a means to an end may become an end in itself. In this way it is easy to see why an individual may be unhappy when he is alone, or even why he may develop definite mental disturbance as a result. Even if the need for association is not a biological one, the fact that he has been accustomed to it all his life may make sudden and complete deprivation quite unbearable. The strength of a drive, as we have seen before, is no proof of its innateness.

It should be added that Woodworth (66) rejects the theory that gregarious activity is the result of practical considerations. He believes that the individual derives great satisfaction from participation in selected external processes, both physical and social. "Social participation is not forced on the individual as a necessary means to satisfying other needs. It is, rather, a primary characteristic of his behavior" (p. 827). On the other hand, Blatz (67) has observed the manner in which the Dionne quintuplets as they grow older have gradually increased their social contacts with one another, and concludes that such contacts are not imperative to start with. "The social behavior and experience of individuals are wholly derived and cannot be said to be basic" (p. 829).

Our own conclusion with reference to gregariousness is that it has a possible though doubtful continuity with the behavior of animals; it has no known physiological or anatomical foundation; it is universal in a minimum form, but this minimum can probably be adequately explained on the basis of family relationships. The extensions beyond this are determined by practical considerations.

OTHER MOTIVES

There are a number of additional motives or "instincts" in the lists given by McDougall and others upon which we shall comment briefly. One of these is the form of behavior known as curiosity. In a previous section it was noted that the acquisitive tendencies of certain birds were explained as due to their interest in strange and curious objects (19). It seems certain that the tendency to explore one's environment with some care is found among many animal species. As for a physiological basis, it is probable that exploratory behavior represents one of a group of activity drives, or "trends toward active motor response to the environment" (68, p. 94). There is apparently a good deal of activity for the sake of exercise, as is shown by the behavior of the rat in an activity cage, as well as in the apparently random muscular movements of the young child. When this activity is in response to some external stimulus which through its sensory qualities or novelty attracts "attention," there may be exploratory behavior in connection with it. At a more complex level, a great deal of exploratory activity is directed toward the mastery of the environment for practical or utilitarian purposes. In the satisfaction of a great many of the impulses common to animals and man, namely, sex, hunger, preservation from danger, it is clearly important to know the nature of one's environment. Exploration may lead to any one of these goals, and may best be understood on that basis. The study by Warden and others (69) of the strength of the various drives in the white rat showed curiosity to be much weaker than the other incentives measured. Although it is of course dangerous to apply this result to human beings, it seems probable that curiosity as such has no great power, unless it contributes in some way to the mastery of the environment.

Another group of motives has been labeled "esthetic drives," described as "the positive response of the little child to color and tone, to tactual stimulation, and to all those sensory attributes of the world which appeal to him, lead him to act, i.e., motivate him" (68, p. 94). In their elemental form, these drives seem to be direct responses to sensory stimuli, and are not always clearly distinguishable from activity drives, such as exploratory behavior. At a more complex level, however, they may be responsible for the vivid enjoyment of artistic creation, and for the positive pursuit of esthetic satisfactions.

The problem of the flight motive is very similar to that of aggressiveness, and many of the same considerations apply. There is of course throughout the animal world the tendency to escape as quickly and as effectively as possible from the menace of danger. On the physiological side, as far as we can tell at present, we have no direct flight mechanism; we have rather a general preparedness for activity in the face of an emergency situation. Whether this activity will be aggression or flight will be determined by the previous experience of the individual as well as by the conditions of the moment. There are almost certainly organic differences among animal species in this respect, some like the lion showing more readiness for aggression, and others like the deer showing a greater propensity to flight. This may also be connected, however, with the probabilities that aggression will be successful. Social factors will enter, both in the determination of what will cause flight and in the readiness with which it occurs. The fear of ghosts or of the dead will be great in one community and practically absent in another. Flight may be permitted to women and not to men under the same circumstances, and so on.

The so-called instinct of self-submission has been a special target for McDougall's critics, since it apparently exists side by side with its opposite, the instinct of self-assertiveness. It is argued that to explain two diametrically opposed types of behavior as due equally to instinct removes from this whole concept any claim to scientific validity. This criticism seems a sound one. On the other hand, we cannot deny the existence of a widely prevalent tendency for individuals to submit themselves to the will of someone else. When this occurs, however, whether in private, interpersonal relations or in the submission of a whole people to a dictator, there are undoubtedly very practical reasons which enter into the decision to submit. There may be force or the threat of force on the part of the individual or group in a position to dominate, or there may be voluntary submission to a leader because of the resulting protection or economic gain—or even psychological gain—which comes from identification with power. In the case of the Nazis, Erich Fromm (70) has described what he calls "escape from freedom" characterizing those Germans who were unwilling to take their future into their own hands, who were unable to determine their course for themselves, and who took refuge in blind obedience to a leader whom they thought they could trust. Young children will submit to parents or elders from fear of punishment or out of a desire to win their love and approval. It is safe to conclude that submissive behavior, when it occurs, is to be understood as a means to an end.

THE DEPENDABLE MOTIVES IN GENERAL

As was pointed out in Chapter 4, the problem of dependable motives is not merely one of deciding which motives should appear on our list, but also of determining their degree of dependability. It is not sufficient to ask whether or not a certain drive is present in man, whether acquisitiveness or curiosity or self-submissiveness, for example, should or should not be included among the dependable motives; it is also important to know how dependable these motives are. There are undoubtedly some motives which are truly universal, others which permit of occasional exceptions, still others whose dependability is extremely limited.

In a discussion of this problem by Malinowski (53) it is stated:

Taking man as a biological entity it is clear that certain minima of conditions can be laid down which are indispensable to the personal welfare of the individual and to the continuation of the group. All human beings have to be nourished, they have to reproduce, and they require the maintenance of certain physical conditions. . . . (p. 940)

Actually, however, for each individual the need for nourishment has a degree of imperativeness much greater than the need for reproduction. The continuation of the group obviously depends upon sex activity, but many members of the group may under certain conditions dispense with this form of behavior, not without discomfort, perhaps, but probably without any fundamental injury to their "personal welfare." Hunger and sex have, therefore, differing degrees of dependability.

As was indicated above, the concept of dependability as here employed refers to the likelihood with which a particular form of *behavior* may be predicted. This approach will certainly be regarded as unduly narrow by those who have concerned themselves with some of the indirect, subtle and even hidden ways in which a particular motive may conceivably be expressed. If individuals who show no overt sex behavior produce a poem or a painting which represents a sublimation of the sex impulse, should that be regarded as in any way limiting or reducing the dependability of the sex motive? Such an argument rests on the reality of sublimation as a psychodynamic process, and this has been challenged by Kinsey and his associates (2), who find that artistic creativity does not result from any lack of opportunity for the full expression of the sex impulse; on the contrary, artists appear to be above average in the frequency with which they utilize physiological outlets for sex satisfaction. Artistic activity is not a substitute for sex, in their view, but is added to it.

If Kinsey and his colleagues are correct, and there is no validity to the concept of sublimation, then our conclusion is certainly justified that sex is less dependable as a motive than the need for food or rest. If the Freudians are correct, and sublimation does exist as a psychological phenomenon (and the present writer inclines to this position), this means that sex may express itself also in ways which are not overtly sexual. In that case, and in that sense, it may be correct to grant to the sex motive the highest degree of dependability. There remains then one fundamental difference between sex and, for example, the hunger motive; the former may be sublimated, the latter not. From the point of view of the prediction of behavior, therefore, the two motives are not in the same category.

Some of the same considerations apply to the case of aggressiveness, although here the decision is made more difficult by doubt as to the precise meaning of the term. As has already been indicated, there is a tendency among some writers to use the word so broadly as practically to make it coincide with the whole realm of activity, exploration, mastery of the environment. If we were to accept such a definition, aggression would clearly have to be included among the most completely dependable motives. We have preferred to speak separately of activity drives, and to reserve the term *aggressiveness* for those forms of behavior which are aggressive in the sense of being hostile. This restriction reduces the degree of dependability to be ascribed to this motive.

With these considerations in mind, the following classification is tentatively presented:

1. Motives which are absolutely dependable, have a definite physiological basis and admit of no exceptions. Social factors play a part in their manifestations, but do not determine their existence. These include hunger, thirst, the need for rest and sleep, the elimination of waste products from the body, and similar organic requirements; also activity drives and "esthetic" drives.

2. Motives which have a definite physiological basis, are found in all societies, but admit of exceptions in the case of individuals. Social factors not only determine the manner of their expression, but may also in certain circumstances cause them not to appear. These include sex, post-maternal behavior, and possibly also self-preservation.

3. Motives which have an indirect physiological basis and occur with great frequency, but admit of exceptions both in groups and in individuals. These include aggressiveness, flight and probably also self-assertiveness.

4. Motives which have no known physiological basis, but which occur with some frequency either because of social factors common to the majority of human communities, or as a means to the satisfaction of practical interests. They are primarily means to an end, but may come to function as ends in themselves. These include gregariousness, the paternal motive, the pre-maternal motive, the filial motive, acquisitiveness, and self-submission.

The list of possible motives is not complete, and many others might certainly be added. The extension of our knowledge in the fields of animal behavior, physiological mechanisms, and ethnological observation may lead not only to a more adequate list, but also to a rearrangement of the individual motives in the hierarchy. It may also result in a finer discrimination between the motives now included within a single category of dependability. For these reasons the present classification is regarded as tentative, and subject to modification in the light of further analysis and more complete information.

This classification may in one sense be regarded as a compromise between those who have looked upon human nature as somewhat rigidly determined by a group of fundamental motives, and those at the other extreme who have seen it entirely as a by-product of social factors. The view here taken is that there are characteristics found among human beings all the world over, and others which though they loom large in our own society, have no such universality. It is of the utmost importance to stress the social and cultural influences entering into behavior, but we must not lose sight of the fact that these act upon a human being with essentially human (as well as animal) qualities.

It should be kept in mind that few instances of human behavior are to be explained on the basis of a single motive. A man may acquire property as a means of guarding himself against privation, or to gain prestige, or to obtain a suitable wife, or to make his children happy. Several of these motives may function simultaneously. A list of separate motives will therefore fail to do justice to the complexity of human activities.

One final point should perhaps be made. Motives are not clearly separable from other aspects of social behavior. As we shall see in the following chapter, the intimate connection between motivation and emotion has long been recognized; some psychologists have even subsumed the latter concept under the former. Problems of motivation enter into the study of personality; they are closely allied to attitudes, as Newcomb (71) has clearly pointed out; they are relevant to the understanding of social factors in abnormality. These last two chapters, therefore, relatively lengthy though they have been, represent only an introduction to a topic to which we shall have occasion to return frequently.

SUMMARY

The sex drive satisfies the criteria of phylogenetic continuity and of physiological basis; it is found in the overwhelming majority of individuals, although direct sexual satisfaction may be renounced under certain conditions. Cultural influences determine varying attitudes toward the importance of the sex relation, the emotions associated with it, the values attached to chastity, standards of attractiveness in the sex partner, methods of acquiring a mate, desire for exclusive possession and other aspects of sexual behavior. The taboo against incest cannot be regarded as innately determined, since the exact nature of the prohibition varies from group to group. It is best explained on the basis of the practical advantages resulting from marriage with someone outside the immediate consanguineous family. The inevitability of the Oedipus complex, with its hostility against the father and incestuous attachment to the mother, is challenged by the material from the matrilineal Trobrianders, among whom the nuclear complex takes the form of hostility against the maternal uncle and desire for the sister. The complex, like other aspects of social and sexual relationships, varies with the cultural setting.

Visceral drives or organic needs belong in the category of complete dependability, since they satisfy the threefold criteria. They include hunger, thirst, the need for rest or sleep, the elimination of waste products, and probably the need for activity and exercise. Social factors in part determine the time, the place and the conditions for the satisfaction of these needs, but their existence is independent of society.

Gregarious behavior shows some continuity with the behavior of animals below man, but it has no known physiological foundation; some degree of social interaction is found among all human beings, but is probably to be explained on the basis of family groupings as well as of the practical advantages growing out of a larger range of social activities.

The classification of motives in a hierarchy of dependability has the advantage of indicating with what degree of assurance we may expect a given motive to appear in any given individual. Hunger, sex, aggressiveness and acquisitiveness, for example, belong in four different categories, arranged in a descending order of dependability. The classification is based on overt behavior, and is not directly concerned with unconscious motivation. It also leaves out the interconnections among the various motives. Further investigation may alter the exact nature of the classification.

REFERENCES

1. Dollard, J. *Criteria for the Life History.* 1935
2. Kinsey, A. C., Pomeroy, W. B., and Martin, C. E. *Sexual Behavior in the Human Male.* 1948
3. Ford, C. S., and Beach, F. *Patterns of Sexual Behavior.* 1951
4. Waley, A. *The Temple, and Other Poems.* 1923
5. Linton, R. *The Study of Man.* 1936
6. McDougall, W. *Introduction to Social Psychology.* 1908
7. Blackwood, B. *Both Sides of Buka Passage.* 1935
8. Powdermaker, H. *Life in Lesu.* 1933
9. Briffault, R. *The Mothers.* 3 vols. 1927
10. Roscoe, J. *The Northern Bantu.* 1915
11. Torday, E., and Joyce, T. A. "Notes ethnographiques," *Ann. du Musée du Congo Belge.* Quoted in Thomas (*17*)
12. Jenks, A. E. *The Bontoc Igorot.* 1905
13. Malinowski, B. *Sex and Repression in Savage Society.* 1927
14. Lowie, R. H. *The Crow Indians.* 1935
15. Van Gennep, A. *Les rites de passage.* 1909
16. Livingstone, D. *Missionary Travels and Researches in South Africa.* 1858
17. Thomas, W. I. *Primitive Behavior.* 1937
18. Mead, M. *Male and Female: A Study of the Sexes in a Changing World.* 1949
19. Beaglehole, E. *Property.* 1932
20. Mead, M. "Jealousy: Primitive and Civilized." In Schmalhausen, S. D., and Calverton, V. F., eds. *Woman's Coming of Age.* 1931
21. Shand, A. F. *The Foundations of Character.* 2d ed. 1920
22. Driberg, J. A. *The Lango.* 1923
23. Kirkpatrick, C. S. "Polyandry in the Panjab," *The Indian Antiquary,* 1878, 7: p. 86
24. Boas, F. "The Central Eskimo," *Sixth Annual Report of the Bureau of Ethnology.* 1888
25. Lowie, R. H. *Primitive Society.* 1925
26. Wissler, C. *An Introduction to Social Anthropology.* 1929
27. Radin, P. *The Story of the American Indian.* 1934
28. Abercromby, J. *The Pre- and Proto-historic Finns.* 1898
29. Seligman, C. G., and Seligman, B. Z. *Pagan Tribes of the Nilotic Sudan.* 1932
30. Bailey, J. "An Account of the Wild Tribes of the Veddahs of Ceylon," *Ethnol. Soc. Trans.* N.S., 1863, 2: pp. 278-320
31. Westermarck, E. A. *The History of Human Marriage.* 5th ed. 1921

32. Bentham, J. *The Theory of Legislation* (ed. by C. K. Ogden). 1931

33. Bogoras, W. "The Chuckchee," *Amer. Mus. Nat. Hist. Mem.*, 1904, 11: pp. 1-733

34. Mead, M. *Sex and Temperament in Three Primitive Societies.* 1935

35. Dunlap, K. *Civilized Life.* 1934

36. Leipoldt, L. C. "The Wages of Sin," *Magazine Digest,* 1938, 16: pp. 77-78

37. Thomson, B. H. "Concubitancy in the Classificatory System of Relationship," *J. Roy. Anthrop. Instit.*, 1894-95, 24: pp. 371-387

38. Murdock, G. P. *Social Structure.* 1949

39. Fortune, R. F. *Sorcerers of Dobu.* 1932

40. Reichard, G. A. "Social Life." In Boas, F., ed. *General Anthropology.* 1938

41. Bastian, P. W. A. *Die Deutsche Expedition an der Loango-Küste.* 1874

42. Tylor, E. B. "On a Method of Investigating the Development of Institutions," *J. Roy. Anthrop. Instit.*, 1888-1889, 18: pp. 245-269

43. Fortune, R. F. "Incest," *Encycl. Soc. Sci.*, 1932, 7: pp. 620-622

44. Gutmann, B. "Die Frau bei den Wadschagga," *Globus*, 1907, 92: pp. 1-4

45. Freud, S. *Totem and Taboo.* 1927

46. Hull, C. L. *Principles of Behavior: An Introduction to Behavior Theory.* 1943

47. *Proc. Roy. Geo. Soc.* N.S. 9. Quoted in Thomas (*17*)

48. Goldenweiser, A. A. *Anthropology.* 1937

49. Herskovits, M. J. "Freudian Mechanism in Negro Psychology," *Essays Presented to C. G. Seligman.* 1934

50. Lincoln, J. S. *The Dream in Primitive Cultures.* 1935

51. Roheim, G. "Psychoanalysis of Primitive Cultural Types," *Internatl. J. Psychoanal.*, 1932, 13: pp. 2-224

52. Fromm, E. *Autorität und Familie.* 1936

53. Malinowski, B. "The Group and the Individual in Functional Analysis," *Amer. J. Sociol.*, 1939, 44: pp. 938-964

54. Townsend, C. W. "Food Prejudices," *Sci. Mo.*, 1928, 26: pp. 65-68

55. Katz, D. *Hunger und Appetit.* 1932

56. Trotter, W. D. *Instincts of the Herd in Peace and War.* 1919

57. Scott, J. P. "Social Behavior, Organization, and Leadership in a Small Flock of Domestic Sheep," *Comp. Psychol. Monogr.*, 1945, 18: pp. 1-29.

58. Jacobsen, C. F., Jacobsen, M. M., and Yoshioka, J. G. "Development of an Infant Chimpanzee During Her First Year," *Comp. Psychol. Monogr.*, 1932, 9: pp. 1-94

59. Carpenter, C. R. "Characteristics of Social Behavior in Non-Human Primates," *Trans. N.Y. Acad. Sci.*, 1942, 4, Ser. II: pp. 248-258

60. Allee, W. C. *The Social Life of Animals.* 1938

61. Sumner, W. G., and Keller, A. G. *The Science of Society.* 4 vols. 1927

62. Hobhouse, L. T., et al. *The Material Culture and Social Institutions of the Simpler Peoples.* 1915

63. Malinowski, B. *The Father in Primitive Psychology.* 1927

64. Darwin, C. *The Expression of the Emotions in Man and Animals.* 1873

65. Woodworth, R. S. *Dynamic Psychology.* 1918

66. Woodworth, R. S. "Individual and Group Behavior," *Amer. J. Sociol.*, 1939, 44: pp. 823-828

67. Blatz, W. E. "The Individual and the Group," *Amer. J. Sociol.*, 1939, 44: pp. 829-838

68. Murphy, G., Murphy, L. B., and Newcomb, T. M. *Experimental Social Psychology.* Rev. ed. 1937

69. Warden, C. J., et al. *Animal Motivation.* 1931

70. Fromm, E. *Escape from Freedom.* 1941

71. Newcomb, T. M. *Social Psychology.* 1950

Emotional Behavior

7

INTRODUCTION

There is no sharp line of demarcation between motivation and emotional behavior. In the theory of McDougall which formed the starting point for our discussion of the dependable motives, there was postulated an intimate relationship between instinct and emotion. Each instinct was regarded as having a specific emotion which accompanied it, for example, the instinct of flight and the emotion of fear, the instinct of pugnacity and the emotion of anger, the sex instinct and the emotion of love, and so on. That the line between the two is difficult to draw is evident from the fact that in our preceding discussion there were several instances in which the physiological changes occurring in emotion were pertinent to an understanding of the drive itself. Murphy, Murphy and Newcomb (1) include the emotions in their classification of motives.

Since we are concerned primarily with social aspects of behavior, we may pass quickly over the physiological factors involved in the emotions. It is now well established, largely as the result of the experiments of Bard (2) on dogs, that the impulse to rage and probably also to other emotional activity comes from that region of the mid-brain known as the hypothalamus. Bard found that cutting through the brain above this region increased the amount of overt emotional behavior, evidently because the restraining influence of the cortex was thereby removed. On the other hand, section below the level of the hypothalamus caused a complete disappearance of the external bodily manifestations of emotion, thus clearly indicating that this was the region responsible. The hypothalamus initiates a series of internal changes which are more immediately under the control of the sympathetic nervous system and the adrenal glands. Cannon (3) has shown that in emotional excitement this sympathico-adrenal system brings on a number of reactions which prepare the organism to deal with an emergency. These include the flow of blood from the internal organs to the muscles of the arms and legs, which are enabled to exert additional strength; an increase in the coagulability of the blood so that wounds are less dangerous; a mobilization of the stored glycogen in the liver and its transformation into glucose which is a source of available energy; the chemical counteraction of the fatigue products in the blood, and other changes acting in the same direction. As was pointed out in a preceding section (see p. 89) the total group of emergency reactions is characteristic of emotional excitement, but does not distinguish one emotion from another. In spite of repeated experiments, Cannon and his collaborators have not found any difference between the glandular and visceral processes associated with fear, anger, and excitement, respectively. There may possibly be minute physiological differences which have not yet been discovered. As far as our present knowledge is concerned, however, we must depend upon social and situational factors in order to explain the differences in the manifestations of one emotion and another.[1]

An interesting example of the possible effects of these physiological changes is given by Collip (4). A diabetic taking insulin treatment found while walking on the street that he was being overcome by the physical and mental condition which follows the reduction of the amount of blood sugar. Having forgotten to provide himself with the sugar, he staggered into a drug store and incoherently demanded a bar of chocolate. The druggist thought he was drunk and threw him out. This of course enraged the man, and with his anger he suddenly recovered, and was then able to acquire the sugar which he needed to restore the equilibrium of his body fluids. Anger had so stimulated the output of the adrenals that there was a temporary increase in his blood sugar content sufficient to bring him through the crisis.

When we turn to the social aspects of emotional behavior, we find, as has been indicated elsewhere (5), that there are at least three distinct ways in which these are important. They may play a part first in determining the situations in which one emotion or another will be aroused; they may condition also the amount of overt emotional behavior occurring under these conditions; finally they may influence the manner in which the emotions manifest

[1] This brief discussion of the physiology of emotions should be supplemented by the account in any one of the standard textbooks in physiological psychology.

themselves. In this as in the preceding discussion, we depend largely on the findings of the ethnologists for pertinent material.

THE CAUSES OF EMOTIONAL BEHAVIOR

There are obvious differences between communities as to the situations which give rise to the various emotions. The same set of conditions may elicit diametrically opposite reactions. Thomas (6) has collected examples illustrating the varying emotional responses to the birth of twins. Among the Murngin of Australia (7) the mother kills one of the twins because it makes her feel like a dog to have a litter instead of one baby. With the Negroes of the Niger Delta the rule is that the mother and the twins are put to death. "In some cases the mother is allowed to live; but her life is little better than a living death, for she becomes an outcast and must live the remainder of her days in the forest" (8, p. 57). Less than a thousand miles away from this group live the Bankundo of the Congo valley, among whom at the other extreme the mother of twins is the object of honor and veneration throughout her life. "She is entitled to wear a special badge around her neck, and her name is changed to 'Mother-of-twins'" (9, p. 190).

In our society the failure to have children may be a source of great regret, but certainly anyone may mention the fact without conveying an insult. Among the African Lango (10) infecundity brings more shame and disrepute to a woman than the most riotous living. Many African tribes have a similar attitude, and life is said to become intolerable for a woman whose barrenness has been mentioned in public.

Death is a source of grief not only in our society, but probably in the majority of known cultures. There are cases, however, when it is an occasion for rejoicing. It has been reported of certain groups of Siberian natives and Eskimos, as well as of the Fiji Islanders, that people were actually anxious to die before they became too old. These Islanders believed that life on earth was merely a prelude to an everlasting life in which they would possess the bodily and mental powers which they had when they died. If they lived until they were decrepit, they remained so forever. For this reason a dutiful son might kill his parents, secure in the conviction that he was doing them the greatest possible favor. A belief in immortality is present also among ourselves, but evidently we do not hold it with quite so much conviction.

The Bontoc Igorots of the Philippines (*11*) are reported not to take death very sorrowfully nor very passionately. A mother weeps one day for a dead child or husband. There is no self-mutilation, no somber colors, no earth nor ashes on the body. When a child or a young person dies, the women assemble, wail a melancholy dirge, and ask the departed why he went so early. For the aged there are neither tears nor wailing, but only a grim philosophy. "You were old," they say, "and old people die. You are dead and now we shall place you in the earth. We too are old and soon we shall follow you" (p. 74).

One further example of what to us would seem an unusual attitude toward death is reported for the Lango (*10*). On the death of a suicide there is very little mourning, and that is restricted to the closest relatives. This is due to their idea that "the self sought death proves that the deceased wished to leave the world, and consequently an elaborate display of sorrow would be superfluous" (p. 169). Among ourselves the sorrow at the death of a suicide is usually no less acute for this reason, although there might be added to it a sense of shame, especially where there is a religious proscription against it.

The discussion of jealousy in a preceding section may also be taken as illustrative of this variability in the causes of an emotion. The fact that a man takes a second wife may be welcomed in one society and unthinkable in another. The same variation holds for pre-marital chastity, wife-lending, illegitimacy, incestuous relationships, and the other aspects of sex activity; these may arouse quite different emotional reactions in different parts of the world, and even in the same society at different times.

It is possible that many of these differences are more superficial than real, and that a fundamental similarity underlies them. Shame, for example, may be the emotional reaction to the realization that one is condemned by his fellows; this may be universal, even though the specific act condemned may differ in each case. Jealousy may follow any failure to receive from one's marriage partner what the society regards as due, and this principle may be general in spite of the variations in detail. It is not always possible, however, to find such underlying similarities, although more intimate knowledge of the particular cultures might reveal them. In any case, in terms of overt behavior patterns, similar situations may arouse entirely different emotions according to the dictates of the folkways.

As an example of the manner in which these emotional reactions may be changed as a result of new habits, the case is reported of a missionary among the Carrier Indians, who have a strict taboo of the names of the dead. The missionary writes: "I, for instance, distinctly remember how, after many years spent in the closest intimacy with my Carriers, having gone to attend the funeral of my Bishop, I was indescribably shocked at the freedom with which his name was pronounced by the mourners and others, and felt prone to consider that sans-gêne as something little short of sacrilege" (12, p. 645).

THE AMOUNT OF EMOTIONAL BEHAVIOR

It is obviously difficult if not impossible to make any comparisons between groups as to the strength of subjectively felt emotions. Our comparisons must be restricted to the overt emotional behavior. In this respect we find that cultures differ widely from one another in the amount of emotional expression which is permitted. We speak, for example, of the imperturbability of the American Indian, the inscrutability of the Oriental, the reserve of the Englishman, and at the other extreme of the expressiveness of the Negro or the Sicilian. Although there is always some exaggeration in such clichés, it is probable that they do correspond to an accepted cultural pattern, at least to some degree.

In connection with the Oriental, the suggestion has been made that there may be an anatomical basis for the lesser degree of expression. Dr. Mêng (13), formerly connected with the Peking Union Medical College, and later with the Army hospital in Nanking, showed the writer many of his dissections of the Chinese face. He observed several peculiarities in the Chinese facial anatomy as distinct from that of the White European. The most important of these is the fact that one of the facial muscles, the quadratus labii superioris, is in the European face divided into three distinct parts, each of which may act semi-independently of the others, whereas in the Chinese face they are much more nearly fused together. In Dr. Mêng's opinion, this allows much freer play to the muscular contractions in the White face, and gives to the Chinese face an appearance of immobility. The other anatomical differences refer to the orbicularis oculi (the muscle surrounding the eye), which is larger and flatter in the Chinese; and the platysma muscle in the neck, which in the case of the Chinese extends much higher over the region of the lower jaw. These two muscles do not, however, play a very important part in facial expression.

These findings are of importance, but as yet they cannot be regarded as conclusive. Dr. Mêng's comparisons are between his own dissections of Chinese faces and the textbook descriptions of White facial musculature. In view of the great technical difficulty of making accurate anatomical dissections in a region of the body in which the muscles are so small and so numerous, a controlled study of White faces by the same investigator is essential.

Even if these anatomical characteristics of the Chinese face can be demonstrated, it is not probable that they compare in importance with the influence of cultural factors. Part of the education of the young Chinese consists of training in restraint. A Chinese girl is admonished—"do not show your unhappiness easily and do not smile easily," and "do not let your teeth be seen when you smile" (14). The boys are taught that it is unbecoming to the conduct of a gentleman to show anger or to be too boisterous. It may be, however, that the Chinese with whom we have had most contact, namely, residents of our large American cities, show an unusual amount of reserve because they are in an alien environment, and because they are not quite certain of their reception. Schrieke (15) has suggested that much of their apparent inscrutability is merely a precaution against embarrassment.

> [The Chinese] do not want to go anywhere unless they are sure that no restrictions will be imposed. They are being forced to stay together as a group, separated from the American community. As a result of the rebuffs they have experienced, they have become more cautious, even suspicious, in their dealings with white Americans. They have learned the wisdom of keeping their thoughts to themselves and, consequently, seem cold and expressionless (p. 18).

This interpretation is borne out by the fact that when the Chinese are in an environment to which they are not alien, they give an impression of liveliness and vivacity in marked contrast to the usual stereotype. Somerset Maugham (16) writes: "You watch their faces as they pass you. They are good-natured faces and frank, you would have said, if it had not been drilled into you that the Oriental is inscrutable" (p. 83). Similarly, Gilbert (17) states that "the code of face often dictates that a Chinese should be restrained, calm and expressionless in the thick of trouble . . . but in the ordinary run of events his vivacity makes a Latin seem a restful companion" (p. 34). This is probably an exaggeration, since the precepts and admonitions to which we referred clearly encourage a certain degree of reserve in the Chinese which is not entirely due to his discomfort in a strange environment. The truth probably lies somewhere between the extremes which regard him on the one hand as "vivacious," and on the other as "inscrutable."

It is sometimes suggested that there may be "racial" factors responsible for differences in expressiveness. The whole question of ethnic differences will be discussed in Chapter 11; for the present it may merely be pointed out that the probability is against this hypothesis, in spite of the anatomical features which have been described. The most telling argument against a purely physical explanation is the fact that Chinese and Japanese vary so greatly in the degree of their "inscrutability" when they live in different social environments. Professor Romanzo Adams (18) of the University of Hawaii describes his observations in a rural district in Japan from which many of the Hawaiian Japanese had come. He met close relatives of those he had known in Hawaii, and had the opportunity of observing them and their children closely. He writes:

> The mannerisms of the old country villagers seemed to an American to show a constraint not characteristic of the Hawaiian Japanese. There was less self-assertiveness, less expression of individuality. Their faces, especially those of girls, were less expressive. It seemed that the numerous little muscles about the eyes and the mouth that have to do with facial expression were relatively undeveloped from lack of use (p. 256).

In spite of its anecdotal character this observation is of great significance in this connection, since it indicates that inborn anatomical factors may not be nearly so important as Dr. Mêng has suggested.

Adams goes on to describe the marked difference in the behavior of the Oriental in Hawaii and on the mainland of the United States. Referring particularly to the Chinese, he makes an observation which tends to corroborate Schrieke's interpretation of Chinese inscrutability. He states that when a White man from Hawaii goes to California and meets the Chinese living there, he is impressed with a reserve on their part. The normal attitude of a Chinese in San Francisco and elsewhere on the west coast toward a White stranger, even though he may have a friendly manner, is one of distrust. "The Hawaiian Chinese are, in the presence of Whites, more given to laughter and when in sorrow they may weep. In an interracial group they act as if they have a sense of really belonging" (p. 319). This difference is explained as due to the more satisfactory social status of the Chinese in Hawaii, and their consequent freedom from restraint. In their tastes, mannerisms and loyalties, they are becoming Americanized or "acculturated" much more rapidly and more effectively than is the case in California. This interpretation seems a highly plausible one, and indicates that the so-called Oriental reserve is dependent upon previous training and the social situation, rather than upon innate factors.

In connection with the amount of expression permitted in a culture, it is important to note that this may differ greatly according to the nature of the emotion involved. In the two most "inscrutable" cultures we know, the American Indian of the Plains and the Chinese, overt expression of grief was not only permitted, but demanded. The Chinese, who feel that a display of anger is never warranted and that affection should be shown only in strict privacy, insist upon a public manifestation of grief or sorrow. One piece of advice to young girls reads: "If your father or mother is sick, do not be far from his or her bed. Do not even take off your girdle. Taste all the medicine yourself. Pray your god for his or her health. If anything unfortunate happens cry bitterly" (*14*). Not only is grief expressed, but there is an elaborate set of rules and regulations which ensure that it will be properly expressed. One of the Chinese classics is *The Book of Rites*, a considerable portion of which is devoted to the technique of the mourning ceremonial, with elaborate instructions as to just what procedure should be followed in order that the expression of the grief may be socially acceptable (*19*). The Plains Indians, in spite of their deserved reputation for imperturbability, expected a man literally to wail and howl for hours at a stretch at the death of his wife or child. It is reported of many African tribes that any public show of affection between husband and wife was regarded as disgraceful, although other emotions might be quite freely expressed. The same holds true for parts of

Melanesia. It is clear that the repressive influence of a culture with regard to emotional behavior is not applied equally in all directions. It is perhaps unnecessary to add that the absence of the manifestation of an emotion does not prove that it is not experienced. It merely prevents our direct knowledge of its existence.

Even within our own society there are tremendous individual variations in the amount of expression. These may to some extent be due to organic factors, for example, to a relative stability or lability of the sympathico-adrenal system. There may be differences in the threshold for emotions generally, or for one or another emotion in particular, making one person angry and another frightened more easily than the average. Individual training and experience will also play a part. In addition, there are undoubtedly great variations in this respect between different social and economic classes, as well as between different regions of the same country. In the United States there are marked contrasts between New England and the South on the one hand and the Middle West on the other. Probably in all countries the urban population is much livelier and more expressive than the rural. As for socio-economic classes, it is usual to find more obvious emotional expression in the poorer than in the wealthier groups. In the latter, there frequently develops the ideal of the "gentleman" who does not wear his heart on his sleeve. The traditional reserve of the Englishman is apparently the product of the most exclusive schools, just as the self-control of the Chinese scholar was largely due to his education in the Confucian manner. In both cases other classes of the society were also affected, but not nearly to the same degree, so that a class distinction exists here as in other aspects of behavior.

An experiment (20) on the judgment of facial expression of emotions indicates the smaller amount of expression in the Chinese as compared with the American face. Chinese and American subjects posed for the illustration of different emotions, and these photographs were given to both Chinese and American students to judge. The results showed that both groups of judges were somewhat more successful with the American than with the Chinese pictures. The conclusion appears warranted that the American face is more expressive, at least in these artificial situations; the proof is not absolute, since the two groups of persons photographed could not be regarded as "equated" in every way. The result is in keeping, however, with general observations of the amount of expression normally permitted to Americans and to Chinese, respectively.

THE NATURE OF EMOTIONAL EXPRESSION

There are undoubtedly certain types of expressive behavior which are common to all human societies. Apparently most children cry considerably during the early years of life, when they are hungry or in pain, or when they require some attention. Apparently, also, at the outset the cry subserves a great many uses, expressing anger, for example, just as readily as it does physical pain; but with the passage of time it becomes associated with certain unpleasant emotions more than with others. The occurrence of the cry in grief or in "mental pain" is probably a still later extension from this origin. Laughter, too, is in all probability universal as a sign of joy or well-being, although the exact physiological mechanism involved is still in doubt (see below, p. 100). There are certainly other expressions which are universal, but in all of these, including the two which have been mentioned, social factors enter to a considerable degree.

The attempt was made by Darwin (21) to explain the origin and nature of emotional expression in terms of the following three principles: (1) *The principle of serviceable associated habits* may be illustrated by the violent start which usually accompanies hearing a sudden noise. Originally this was due to the need to jump away as quickly as possible from danger, so that now even though the sound may not mean danger the same behavior ensues. The sneer which accompanies anger or contempt is similarly explained; it represents a survival from the time when teeth were bared as a preparation for their use in fighting. Darwin writes:

> Certain complex actions are of direct or indirect service under certain states of the mind, in order to relieve or gratify certain sensations, desires, etc.; and whenever the same state of mind is induced, however feebly, there is a tendency through the force of habit and association for the same movements to be performed, though they may not then be of the least use (p. 28).

This principle is a significant one, but not so much may be said for (2) *the principle of antithesis*. According to this, when the opposite state of mind to the above is induced, there is a strong and involuntary tendency to the performance of movements of a directly opposed nature, though these may be of no possible use. A dog, for example, assumes the opposite attitude when at the feet of his master from that indicating an intention to fight. There appear to be few expressions to which this principle is applicable. Finally there is (3) *the principle of actions due to the constitution of the nervous system.* This would apply to the loss of pigmentation of the hair after extreme terror or grief, the trembling which accompanies various types of emotional excitement, perspiration, blushing, etc. Many of these phenomena can now be explained on the basis of the physiological changes described by Cannon and others.

Emotional expression has been studied in a variety of ways. We are here not primarily concerned with the many investigations of the purely physiological changes accompanying the emotions. There have been measurements of changes in blood pressure, respiratory rate and the nature of the breathing curve, pulse rate, changes in volume in various parts of the body, electrical phenomena accompanying the psycho-galvanic reflex, the electroencephalogram, etc. These studies, important though they are, concern themselves primarily with problems in individual psychology, and are not directly social except in regard to the causes of the emotions. More pertinent to the field of social psychology is the problem of the recognition of emotional expression by others. The observations of Bühler (22) have shown that such recognition is not present at birth, but develops gradually through the first years of life. A very young child cannot distinguish a friendly tone of voice or a scowling face from their opposites and must learn the difference. In the case of the adult many investigations have been conducted on the recognizability of emotional expressions, particularly in the face. The pioneer work of Feleky (23) was followed by that of many others. Feleky showed that emotions differ widely in their recognizability, joy and surprise being judged with ease, anger and disgust with greater difficulty.

In the judgments of facial expression in general, although there are always a great many errors, the judgments are more frequently right than wrong. Dunlap (24) used the interesting technique of joining the upper portion of one facial expression to the lower portion of another in order to see which part of the face is of greater importance in determining the perception of the emotion. He found that the lower portion of the face was dominant. There was apparently a Gestalt or configurational effect, since the combination of the upper part of a "disgust" picture and the lower part of a "mirth" picture not only combined to give a judgment of mirth, but the eyes were actually seen to convey the same expression.

Studies have also been carried out on the recognizability of emotions as expressed in the voice. Gates (25) reports that when the letters of the alphabet are spoken with varying intonation, the voice may in a very large number of cases convey the meaning correctly. It is also possible to recognize emotions to some degree from posture (26), and from the position of the hands (27).

Pertinent to this whole problem is the question of the relationship between emotional expression in man and in the higher anthropoids. If expression is largely biological and innately determined, we should expect considerable similarity between these two closely related species. If, on the other hand, culture is largely responsible for expression, we should expect marked differences, since the anthropoids are presumably exposed to a culture only of the most rudimentary sort. Köhler (28), who had the opportunity of observing chimpanzees closely over a period of years on the island of Teneriffe, states that he was able without too much difficulty to understand the emotions which these animals were expressing. Similarly, Mrs. Ladigina-Kohts (29) of the Laboratory for Zoopsychology in Moscow regards the emotional expression of chimpanzees and of human beings as essentially the same. This view has been subjected to an experimental check by Foley (30), who made Ladigina-Kohts' pictures the basis for a study of the recognizability of chimpanzee expression. The pictures allegedly represented the following emotional states—quietude, sadness, laughter, weeping, anger, excitement. They were presented to a group of students who judged each picture by choosing one out of a mimeographed list of sixteen emotions. The results showed great individual differences. The main finding of the investigation was that the number of correct judgments was just about what would be expected by pure chance. In other words, the judges failed to recognize the emotional expression in the face of the chimpanzee. In particular there was frequent confusion between the pictures representing physical pain, anger and joy. Foley points out that this type of confusion entered into a popular motion picture, "School Pals," depicting some curious antics of the chimpanzee.

At the conclusion of this picture, when the chimpanzee had just "played a trick" upon his adversary, it was desired to convey to the audience the impression that the chimpanzee was laughing. The animal's hand, hidden from direct view behind a board fence, was pinched or otherwise painfully stimulated. This immediately elicited the typical facial expression of rage or anger, which was interpreted by the audience as joy or laughter (p. 58).

Foley concludes that there are enormous differences in emotional expression between the chimpanzee and man, as well as a demonstrated inability of man to judge the expressive reactions of the chimpanzee.

The discrepancy between these results and the view of Köhler, referred to above, has a number of possible explanations. It may be that Köhler's rich experience made possible for him a recognition of the emotions hardly to be expected from the untrained judges in Foley's experiment. It is also probable that if one sees the live active animal and knows the context of his behavior, one receives many cues not present in a photograph of the face alone. Finally it should be pointed out that Köhler's success may not necessarily be due to any essential similarity in the expressions of the chimpanzee and man; even if the expressions differ, continued observation of the animals in a variety of situations, as well as of the associations between these and their expression, might still make it possible that such recognition would occur. It is clear that further research on the emotional expression of the anthropoids is needed. Our tentative conclusion is that the weight of evidence is against any real similarity between anthropoid and man in this respect, and in favor therefore of the hypothesis of cultural or social determination of emotional expression.

The Language of Emotional Expression. Emotional expression is to be viewed not merely as a spontaneous result of inner physiological processes, but also as a means of social communication, a language. Among psychologists this has been most clearly recognized by Dumas (31), who indicated that most expressions, whether they are explained in terms of psychology, physiology or physics, have become language in that we use them constantly in social life to convey information to others. It has frequently been noticed that if a little child hurts himself, he will usually cry very little or not at all if there is no one in his immediate environment. In the presence of a possibly sympathetic adult it is much more likely that the child will cry in order to be comforted. As adults we voluntarily put on an interested expression when we are taking part in conversation or listening to a lecture, we smile upon meeting an acquaintance we care nothing about, we put on a "long face" as we listen to bad news which does not concern us in the least. In all these cases the expression has exclusively the function of communication, and the signs are understood by others as clearly as if we had spoken. This of course does not mean that we never feel the particular emotion expressed, but it does mean that we do not need to feel it in order to express it. The ethnologist Tylor (32) correctly refers to physical expression as an important adjunct to spoken language.

There is another sense in which emotional expression is comparable to spoken language, namely, in the fact that it, too, must be learned. This is not true of both to the same degree, but there can be no doubt that acquired as well as innate mechanisms play a part. Other societies besides our own have recognized this aspect of emotional expression. Rank (33) states that the first attempts to systematize human gestures are found among the Babylonians, who recorded their knowledge of the psychology of expression in the so-called "twitching books." The recognition of the conventional aspect of emotional expression is clearest among the Chinese. There is an interesting story in this connection included in *The Book of Rites.*

> Yu-tze and Tze-yu (third to fourth century B.C.) saw a child weeping for the loss of his parents. The former observed, "I never could understand why mourners should necessarily jump about to show their grief, and would long ago have got rid of the custom. Now here you have an honest expression of feeling, and that is all there ever should be." "My friend," replied the other, "the mourning ceremonial, with all its material accompaniments, is at once a check upon undue emotion and a guarantee against any lack of proper respect. Simply to give vent to the feelings is the way of barbarians. That is not our way. The due regulation of the emotions is the function of a set ceremonial" (34, pp. 45-6).

There are certain expressions which are so obviously cultural that they present no special problem. This category includes, for example, thumbing the nose as a sign of contempt or defiance. It is not likely that an act of this kind has any biological meaning. The Maori have a sign of friendship made by doubling the forefinger of the right hand, and putting the projecting second joint to the tip of the nose, a somewhat similar act with exactly opposite significance. A Chinese mother pushes her child's head back with her forefinger to show that she is angry with him, or rubs her cheek with her finger instead of calling "shame." Acts like these will obviously vary from group to group.

The same holds true in all probability for the habit of kissing, although Crawley (35) speaks of it as "instinctive" in the higher societies and very rare among lower or semi-civilized races! It need hardly be pointed out that we know of no instinct present in some societies and not in others. The region of the lips is usually included among so-called erogenous zones which are capable of giving sensual satisfaction; in spite of this fact, the kiss is far from universal. In other societies it may be replaced by the rubbing of noses, touching the nose to the cheek, rubbing faces, touching the right nostril of the other person with the right index finger, and other forms of contact. In Japan, the kiss is (or was) restricted to the relationship between mother and child, and the Western habit of kissing between adults was regarded as disgusting. Crawley observes that not only is the kiss absent in many parts of the world, but that where it does occur, it has a wide variety of uses and applications. He refers to the early Christian habit of promiscuous kissing as a symbol of fellowship; the kiss of charity; kissing of knights after they were dubbed, and of persons elected to office; kissing the hands or breast or feet of superiors, kissing the feet of the monarch by his vassals; the kiss on the forehead conveying blessing or reverence; the kissing of sacred objects. It is of course still used, notably in France, in the ceremony of conferring special honors. It may be added that the religious significance of the kiss is by no means restricted to Christian and Jewish practice; Cicero observes that the lips and beard of the statue of Hercules at Agrigentum were almost worn away by the kisses of the devout. It is clear that the kiss is not necessarily a sign of sexual affection, although it might be argued that it is always an extension from an erogenous origin. For our purposes it is sufficient to point out that it is not universally used with the same significance that it has among us. It may be added that when visitors to primitive communities remark on the lack of affection between husband and wife, their reaction may be due to differences in the manner of expression. Here as elsewhere we must be familiar with the language of emotional expression in the group we are trying to understand.

In the case of other expressions, apparently more fundamental, the same variation may be noted. The occurrence of tears as a sign of grief is probably universal. Cultural factors enter, however, in the determination of the time, the place and even the amount of the crying which is expected. Mauss (36) has pointed out that among the native Australians the expression of grief upon the death of a relative was socially regulated in this manner. In China, as was mentioned above, there were elaborate ceremonial rules which made certain that the grief would be expressed in a manner acceptable to the society. As Granet (19) points out, there was the development of a true language of grief, with rules as exact as those of any grammar. A mourner was forbidden to show a grief which could not be expressed in terms of the required symbolism. There were certain rules associated with the ceremonial which seem strange to Western observers. For example, the severity of the mourning increased with the importance of the person mourned; a young woman should mourn more for the death of her mother in law than for her own mother; mourning may be discontinued if no visits of condolence are received. The mourning required tears at certain stated times and under definite conditions. The same has been reported for Montenegro, where during mourning men weep at one time and women at another. At the funeral there is a period of wailing which is soon followed by tears, even in the case of those villagers who are not even related to the person whose death they are bemoaning. Of one such occasion, Durham (37) writes: "The Vrbica men mostly did not know the poor boy's name and had to be coached in the details before beginning to wail, but within a minute or two of beginning they were sobbing bitterly. Coming home people compared notes as to who had cried best" (p. 298). This ability to cry at stated times is by no means absent among ourselves, but it is not common. In other societies there has apparently occurred a sort of conditioning process which has associated tears with specific situations, and the occurrence of such situations directly results in the appropriate shedding of tears. It may be added that in China and Montenegro, and undoubtedly in many other countries as well, men weep as readily as women on these occasions.

Apparently with the ability to weep at will under definite conditions, there goes also the capacity of recovering quickly from this display of emotion. Among the Huichol Indians of Mexico the writer noted that when weeping occurred as part of the religious cere-

monial, it was possible for the man who wept to stop at will, and as
soon as it was over he returned to his usual cheerfulness. A similar
observation is made by Blackwood (38) for the people of Buka,
among whom there is much weeping at funerals. She tells of a girl
whose grief seemed very profound and who had to be dragged away
from the coffin when it was finally taken to the burial ground; but
almost immediately after, she was talking and laughing with the
other girls of the village.

More striking still is the weeping which occurs in several communities under conditions unconnected with either pain or sorrow.
For both the Andaman Islanders (39) and the Maori (40) it has
been reported that tears are shed when two persons meet after a
long absence, and when peace has been declared between two war-
ring parties. An early account of this practice among the Andaman
Islanders by Man (41) interprets it as follows:

> Relatives, after an absence of a few weeks or months, testify their joy
> at meeting by sitting down with their arms around each other's necks
> and weeping and howling in a manner which would lead a stranger to
> suppose that some great sorrow had befallen them; and, in point of
> fact, there is no difference observable between their demonstrations
> of joy on these occasions and those of grief on the death of one of
> their number (pp. 147-8).

It is probably not correct, however, to regard weeping on these
occasions as a sign of joy. The natives themselves say that it is
weeping for the loss of those who have died during the time that the
friends were separated. From our point of view it is important to
note that even if no one has died in the interval, weeping still is the
correct form of greeting.

Radcliffe Brown believes that this form of ritual weeping does
have an emotional significance, even though it may not necessarily
be an expression of sorrow. It represents the individual's emotional
reaction to the notion of group solidarity, which has been threatened by absence or war and which has now again been restored.
Even this degree of emotional response seems unnecessary, however,
since Radcliffe Brown reports that when he asked the natives to show
how it was done, two or three of them sat down and were immediately weeping real tears at his request. This means that we have here
a complete divorce of weeping from true emotional expression, and
its use as a conventional rite or ceremony. These natives do weep

on painful and sorrowful occasions, as we do, but a process of conditioning has taken place which makes possible the association of the response of the tear glands to a secondary stimulus or situation. This phenomenon is of particular importance in the present discussion, since it indicates the possibility of cultural conditioning of a physiological response which is evidently universal and which has a biological basis. For further discussion of this problem see (5).

In this connection an interesting observation was reported to the writer by Dr. Peter Buck, the director of the Bernice P. Bishop Museum in Honolulu. Dr. Buck is himself part Maori and has been able since his childhood to produce tears at will. He stated, however, that the young Maori now growing up in New Zealand with a thoroughly Anglo-Saxon type of education are rapidly losing this ability. They are finding it difficult to weep at the times indicated by the traditional ceremonials. This is an example of the manner in which a change in cultural pattern may affect deep-seated behavior tendencies. It shows incidentally that the relative facility in weeping is not an inherited trait, as the Maori are losing it under changed conditions.

The emotion of anger and its manifestation have already been touched upon in connection with the discussion of aggressive behavior. It was pointed out that anger might be expressed by means of a potlatch, by the singing of satirical songs, by striking at a rock with a piece of wood, and so forth. We may mention here as an additional example the habit of the Melanesians of Buka, whose usual way of showing anger is to break up their own personal possessions. This occurs not in a fit of blind temper, but intentionally (38). It is similarly reported for the natives of Nicobar that in a serious quarrel a man may set fire to his own house (42). It seems evident that in anger there is a strong urge to do something, but that the outward expression of this urge will vary markedly according to one's previous training and experience.

The expression of anger among the Chinese shows interesting variations from our own behavior, and raises a number of important problems. A search through Chinese novels revealed many literary expressions of anger which might not readily be understood by a reader unfamiliar with them (14). We find, for example, "her eyes grew round and opened wide," or "he made his two eyes round and stared at him." Although the Chinese condemn any outburst of anger, staring with fixed eyes seems to be an acceptable method of indicating one's reaction. Incidentally, the Chinese find that the faces of Europeans seem constantly to be expressing anger or irritation; this is probably due to the fact that the normally larger and rounder eyes of the European resemble the Chinese eyes in anger. Other expressions of anger are: "he laughed a great ho-ho"; "he smiled a chill smile"; "he looked at them and he smiled and cursed them." Both the laugh and the smile of contempt do occur in our own culture, but apparently not nearly so frequently as in China and in the Chinese literature. More striking still, one may read, "he was so angry that several times he fainted from his anger." When the writer expressed wonder at this, Chinese friends said that they in their turn could never understand why European ladies fainted so frequently in the mid-Victorian literature, and with so little cause. Certainly the delicately nurtured young lady of not so long ago did faint with astonishing ease and regularity; there were even rules of fainting which had to be followed. "Etiquette books taught them the correct way to faint elegantly. The emotions of women during the Victorian age were arranged and ordered for them, and they accepted these restrictions gracefully" (43, p. 202). This is certainly no less surprising than that the Chinese should faint in anger. The conclusion seems clear that fainting, like tears, may be conditioned by social custom to appear on entirely different occasions.

In connection with the Chinese expression of anger, undoubtedly the most striking phenomenon is the fact that death is alleged to be a possible consequence. We read in the literature: "his anger has risen so that he is ill of it and lies upon his bed, and his life cannot be long assured." " 'To-day am I killed by anger' . . . and when he had finished speaking he let his soul go free." This is reported as still occurring, and the writer saw a patient in a Peking hospital who stated in his family history that his father had died of anger after losing a lawsuit. It is important to note that this death cannot be explained as due to anything like an apoplectic stroke; it does not occur suddenly as a stroke would. When someone is very angry but forced to suppress his anger because there is nothing he can do about it, he may become ill, faint many times and take to his bed; death may follow after the lapse of some days or weeks. This can best be explained in terms of suggestion; the belief that people die of anger under these conditions may succeed in causing the death of an impressionable person. The case is similar to that of death in many primitive societies as a result of black magic or from the consciousness of having broken a serious taboo.

In connection with contempt, which is closely related to anger, Darwin suggested that spitting is an almost universal expression of it; it represents the rejection of anything offensive from the mouth, this sign then being extended figuratively to other types of rejection. There are, however, many cases which do not fit this theory. In a great many different communities spitting is a kind of blessing in critical situations and may be used to bring good luck and to ward off or cure disease. "Travellers report that in the ceremonial attending the birth of a child among the Arabians the priest, after invoking the blessing of God upon the child, whispers a few sentences in the child's ear and spits three times on its face" (43, p. 22). Even in Europe it was firmly held during the Middle Ages that spittle applied to the forehead or other parts of the body would ward off evil. It seems unlikely therefore that Darwin's explanation is the correct one.

Accounts of the expression of fear in different communities show a substantial degree of similarity. In the Chinese literature, for example, we find the following: "everyone trembled with a face the color of clay"; "every one of his hairs stood on end, and the pimples came out on the skin all over his body"; "a cold sweat broke forth upon him, and he trembled without ceasing"; "they stood like death with mouths ajar"; "they were so frightened that their waters and wastes burst out of them" (14). Allowing for the Chinese literary style, these expressions might just as easily have been used by Europeans. It is possible that in the case of fear the expressions are much more directly controlled by physiological processes, and that cultural patterning has played little or no part. Another possibility is that fear is an emotion which has an asocial character and is thus less subject to control by social factors. Anger, love, surprise, interest, and most remaining emotional states are conveyed to others; they have at least in part the character of communication. Fear, however, is primarily a form of withdrawal, and as a consequence may have fewer social components.

Laughter. As far as joy and happiness are concerned, the smile and the laugh appear to be a universal expression. In no ethnological account familiar to the writer is there any indication of a people who fail to express their good spirits in this way. Although it is true that the infant passes through a short period before the smile appears, this indicates more probably a lack of muscular control than a need to be taught how to smile. It certainly is not long before the child laughs purely to express his happiness, and education appears to play only a small part in the process.

Before we turn to comparative material pertinent to this problem, some mention should be made of the various explanations and theories of laughter and a sense of humor. One of the most famous of these theories is that of Thomas Hobbes (*44*), who believed that laughter arises out of a feeling of sudden glory induced by the misfortunes of others and the consequent conviction of our own superiority. This would explain our laughter at all forms of slapstick comedy and similar occurrences in everyday life, as well as our amusement at the manners and customs of people different from ourselves. Apparently Hobbes' theory helped to spread the notion that it was somehow mean and rude to laugh, and one of Lord Shaftesbury's letters to his son urges him never to indulge in such ungentlemanly behavior. Another theory is that of Schopenhauer (*45*), who believed that laughter arises as a result of any perception of incongruity in a situation. We laugh when things are seen together which do not belong together, or when two lines of action are indulged in simultaneously in spite of being mutually incompatible. There is certainly a good deal of humor which would fit into this category, but it is possible also to see in the theory merely a more specific instance of the wider principle which Hobbes expressed. Incongruity may be regarded as one variety of defect or inferiority in the objects or situations which arouse our amusement. The same may be said of Bergson's theory (*46*), which holds that we laugh whenever we see anything living acting like something mechanical or dead. This is the reason we laugh at the pompous gentleman who stubs his toe and falls. In all probability, however, this is also the perception of inferiority in someone else; it may also serve as a social corrective.

On the physiological side the important theory is that of Herbert Spencer (*47*), who regarded laughter, like play, as due to surplus energy. This arises principally in those cases in which we are all set for a difficult situation which suddenly and surprisingly turns out to be very simple, or when we are prepared for an emotional reaction which is no longer applicable. In such situations we have been prepared for a considerable expenditure of energy, and we find that this is no longer needed. The energy has been mobilized, however, and demands some kind of outlet. Since the muscles of the face and throat are among those most easily stimulated, the sounds and movements constituting laughter are the result. This theory explains in a similar manner laughter resulting from tickling; the outstretched finger or hand of another person originally signified danger, but in the case of tickling this danger becomes dissipated into nothing. The energy with which the danger would have been met is transformed into laughter.

Freud (48) has developed a theory of wit and humor which contains some of the elements of Spencer's view, and some more closely allied to Hobbes'. For Freud there are two kinds of wit. The first is "harmless wit," in which puns and plays on words, for example, are pleasing because of the economy which they effect in the expenditure of energy. Suppose, for example, we hear the Christmas vacation described as the "alcoholidays." In this case two words have been combined into one, and there is a consequent saving. This economy results in a surplus of energy which is released as laughter. This portion of Freud's theory does not carry very much conviction, since the amount of energy so saved is infinitesimal. The second type of wit is called *Tendenzwitz*, which might best be translated as tendentious wit, that is to say, wit which has some sort of barb or point and which serves as a means of expressing one's true opinions. In the form of a joke this type of hostility is socially permitted, but it none the less expresses the real (sometimes unconscious) hostile attitudes of the speaker.

We may give as an example of *Tendenzwitz* the famous story of the conversation between Whistler and Oscar Wilde. The former made some brilliant remark and Wilde said enthusiastically, "That's wonderful. I wish I had said that." "You will, Oscar, you will," was the reply. Presumably in this case Whistler meant what he said and the witticism gave him a chance, although in a friendly manner, to point out Wilde's tendency to repeat as his own the clever remarks made by his friends. The familiar expression "there's many a true word spoken in jest" illustrates this mechanism. In any case we see that this portion of Freud's theory of wit fits in perfectly with Hobbes' explanation of the nature of laughter, since the humor is clearly directed against somebody.

As Goldenweiser (49) has pointed out, it is very difficult for an ethnologist to become sufficiently well acquainted with the language and the customs of the group he is studying to understand the nature of their sense of humor. It seems clear, however, that although in many respects their humor may differ markedly from ours, laughter of the Hobbesian variety occurs everywhere. The specific examples from primitive societies are sufficiently rare to warrant a somewhat detailed description of some of them at this point. Blackwood (38) tells of the children in Buka that after the annual visit of the British governor they enacted the whole occasion, taking the salute and going through all the remaining official ceremonies. They ended by throwing to the other children bits of stick and pigs' teeth for which they scrambled just as the adults had scrambled for the governor's tobacco and sweets. It was all done very solemnly until the final scramble which ended with shrieks of laughter. Among the Ontong Java of the Solomon Islands, individuals are betrothed when very young. Hogbin (50) reports that on one occasion when assisting the medical officer to make an examination of the whole population, he called up a betrothed boy and girl at the same time to see what would happen. They seemed very shy and uncomfortable; the rest of the people were intensely amused at their embarrassment.

Among the Pueblo Indians of New Mexico there are a number of individuals who play the part of clowns or "delight-makers" (51). Their humor consists mainly of a mimicry or burlesque of the ceremonies as well as of other varieties of behavior which customarily are taken very seriously. Mimicry of the Whites, accompanied by considerable ridicule, occurs frequently. One of the Pueblo clowns once called out from the housetop that he had a message from the Indian agent that if any man or woman talked to another's husband or wife he would be brought up for trial. It seems clear that many of the agent's regulations must from the Indians' point of view have been just as ridiculous as this imaginary one, and their laughter indicated their attitude. In general, ridicule is used by primitive societies largely for purposes of social control. This use is of course present in our society also, as Bergson (46) pointed out, but in other groups it may take the place of more drastic forms of coercion. In Lesu, for example, it is the weapon employed by the wife to keep her husband at his appointed duties. If he should fail in these, she makes a speech before the villagers ridiculing him for not knowing how to work, for strolling about all the time, and for leaving it to her to mend the garden fence or to clear the ground where the taro is to be planted. The loud laughter with which this announcement is greeted is of course directed against the husband, who is shamed into doing what is required of him (52).

Wissler (53) states that in general primitive people are especially sensitive to the ridicule and the adverse opinions of their fellows, and that this more than anything else keeps the members of the community true to the principles of their elders. Particularly among the American Indians the rule was that most crimes were punished only by laughter and ridicule. Lowie (54) reports that among the Crow, when a man had committed a serious breach of morality, nothing would be done to him directly, but in the evening some-one might call out to the whole group· "Did you hear about so-and-so?" Then amid great laughter his transgression would be com-mented upon in terms of the most scathing ridicule, and this might go on for a long time. The transgressor would be so shamed by the laughter of his fellows that he might even be driven to leave the community and not return until he had in some way redeemed himself.

There were some American Indian tribes which made use of ridicule as a means of social control through the institution of the "joking relatives." Although the exact relationship varied consid-erably, it conferred both the right and the duty of reciprocal ridi-cule and criticism. This served effectively to prevent any important deviations from the mores, since one's joking relatives always seized the occasion for merriment at the expense of the wrongdoer. The Pueblo clowns performed a similar function for the whole commu-nity. They would stand before the various houses in the pueblo, calling the inmates by name in song and twitting them for their stinginess, laziness, domestic infelicity, excessive fondness for Ameri-can ways, and so forth (55).

On the basis of this and similar material, it seems safe to conclude that laughter is everywhere used with the meaning of ridicule and that this argues in favor of Hobbes' theory. It is also true, however, that laughter in young children, if not in adults, apparently expresses "pure joy" without any reference to the inferiorities and inadequacies of others. It is still "sudden glory," but it does not necessarily have the origin which Hobbes ascribed to it. If we broaden the theory to include all forms of joy or sudden glory no matter what their origin, we shall probably account for the majority of cases in which laughter is the means of expression. This would fit in also with Spencer's explanation in terms of surplus energy, since joy may exercise a dynamogenic effect, whether it is due to the feeling of well-being or to the consciousness of our own superiority over others.

There are cases, however, in which joy is not expressed in this manner. We have already mentioned the use of tears as a ceremony of greeting, on what would appear to us as a festive rather than a sad occasion. Wilson (56) reports the following experience in Tahiti:

> In passing a few houses, an aged woman, mother to the young man who carried my linen, met us, and to express her joy at seeing her son, struck herself several times on the head with a shark's tooth, till the blood flowed plentifully down her breast and shoulders, whilst the son beheld it with entire insensibility (p. 70).

Williams (57) describes a festive ceremony among the Melanesian Orokaiva as follows:

> The guests, arriving in their several parties, come striding single file into the village, each party headed by its man of first importance, befeathered club on shoulder. No smile adorns his face, but rather an expression of fierceness, which, however unsuited it may seem to the hospitable occasion, is nevertheless Orokaiva good form (p. 29).

Porteus (58) reports that the native Australians whom he studied inflict injuries upon themselves on both joyous and sorrowful occasions, and he saw no difference between the expressions of these two diametrically opposed emotions.

Not only may joy be expressed without a smile, but in addition the smile may be used in a variety of situations in a manner quite different from what appears to be its original significance. Even in our own society, we know that a smile may mean contempt, incredulity, affection, and serve also as part of a purely social greeting devoid of emotional significance. In China as we have noted, it accompanies anger much more frequently than among ourselves. In China also, as in Japan, the smile is the correct expression for a person who is announcing to his superior some calamity that has befallen him. He smiles in order to minimize the importance of his misfortune, so that the other should not be troubled by it. The Chinese servant smiles also when he is being scolded, apparently so as to reduce the accompanying unpleasantness.

Lafcadio Hearn (59), who spent many years among the Japanese, was perhaps the first to point out to Westerners the meaning of the

Japanese smile. He gives many examples which illustrate principles similar to those which hold for the Chinese. In some instances, the misunderstanding of Japanese by Europeans on this account may even have tragic consequences, as in the case of the samurai whose smile when he was scolded by his employer so infuriated the latter that he struck him; in order to expiate this insult the samurai committed hara-kiri, or honorable suicide.

Hearn states that it was the Emperor Iyeyasu who first required that an inferior when reproved should not only not sulk, but should actually show pleasure. It gradually became a mark of disrespect to betray any feeling of grief or pain in the presence of a superior, and with it there arose an elaborate code of deportment which had to be followed.

> It required not only that any sense of anger or pain should be denied all outward expression, but that the sufferer's face and manner should indicate the contrary feeling. Sullen submission was an offense; mere passive obedience inadequate; the proper degree of submission should manifest itself by a pleasant smile, and by a soft and happy tone of voice (60, p. 192).

Even the quality of the smile was regulated. It was a moral offense, for example, so to smile in addressing a superior that the back teeth could be seen. Among the samurai these rules of conduct were rigidly enforced. "Samurai women were required, like the women of Sparta, to show signs of joy on hearing that their husbands or sons had fallen in battle; to betray any natural feeling under the circumstances was a grave breach of decorum" (p. 193).

In these cases the smile obviously does not stand for sorrow, even though the occasions may be unhappy ones. It is rather that the sorrow may not be expressed, and that an appearance of joy must be maintained. In practice it does mean, however, that among the Chinese and Japanese the smile appears in circumstances which we would regard as quite foreign to it, and there is no doubt that serious misunderstandings arise as a consequence. In order to understand the behavior of a people we need to know not only their spoken language, but also their language of bodily expression.

Emotional Expression in General. This survey has shown the wide variety of expressive behavior related to the emotions. Many other examples have been cited by LaBarre (61). This does not mean that all emotional expression is to be regarded as artificial and flexible to the same extent as spoken language. Apparently all degrees are possible. At the one extreme we have the crying of the child in pain—an expression common to all individuals no matter what their culture. At the other extreme we have the language of emotional expression on the Chinese stage, in which standing on one foot means surprise, and fanning the face with the sleeve means anger. In this same category also we may put the custom of the Blackfoot Indians to express their mood by the color of the paint used on their faces. "If we felt angry, peaceful, in love, religious, or whatever the mood was, we painted our faces accordingly, so that all who should come in contact with us would know at a glance how we felt" (62, p. 244). Between these extremes we find every possible degree of cultural patterning. In those cases in which culture has not interfered too greatly with physiological processes, or where such interference has proceeded along lines similar to our own, we can understand the emotional behavior of other peoples with some success. Otherwise, we may be led far astray if we interpret their behavior patterns as necessarily having the same significance which they would have among ourselves. It should be added that this type of misunderstanding may apply to linguistic as well as to bodily forms of expression. This is illustrated by the comment of an aged Omaha Indian on the White people's custom of addressing one another by name, particularly if they were members of the same family. "It sounds as though they do not love one another when they do not use terms of relationship" (63, p. 335), that is, when they do not express in their speech the exact relationship between them. In this instance it is a member of another culture who is mistaken in his interpretation of us, but we are just as likely to err in a comparable manner.

Between any two groups of different culture it will almost certainly be found that their patterns of emotional expression show considerable overlapping as well as a definite amount of diversity. This was the result of the experiment referred to above (20), in which Chinese and American photographs were compared. Both groups of judges recognized a substantial proportion of the expressions in both groups of pictures, indicating that there must be many common factors. It was true, however, that the American judges recognized the American pictures better than did the Chinese, and that the Chinese in turn were better judges of the Chinese pictures than were the Americans. The factor of familiarity or acquaintance with the patterns of expression has an unmistakable effect. This is much more noticeable in certain emotions than in others. In surprise, for example, it is common for the Chinese to stick out the tongue; since this pattern is rare among Americans, the picture corresponding to it was more easily recognized by the Chinese. Allowing for all possible variations between the individual judges and the specific emotions, the experiment indicated clearly the existence of cultural patterning, as well as of aspects of expression common to the two cultures.

In the interpretation of the kind of evidence presented in this chapter, some writers have been more impressed by the similarities in emotional expression in various cultures, others by the differences. The anthropologist LaBarre (61), for example, may be taken as representative of the latter view; he comes to the conclusion that "there is no 'natural' language of emotional gesture." On the other hand, the psychologist Asch (64) insists that much emotional expression has a direct quality which is not dependent on learning. "We would say that leaping, dancing, elevating the body are intrinsic expressions of joy and mastery; bowing the body is the intrinsic expression of grief; and prostrating the body is the expression of abject submission" (p. 188). Asch cites in support of his view two studies of emotional expression of the blind. The first, by Thompson (65), used photographs of blind and seeing children in a number of spontaneous situations, and found that the expressions of emotion revealed essentially the same pattern The second, by Fulcher (66), made a similar comparison, but of voluntary or posed facial expressions, and also found many aspects in common. Asch concludes: "These findings are presumptive evidence that the expressions are in large part innately determined" (p. 189).

The position we prefer lies somewhere between these extremes. In opposition to the view of LaBarre, the evidence seems to be definitely in favor of the existence of at least some common aspects of emotional gesture, presumably determined by common anatomical structure and physiology. The evidence points with equal strength, however, in favor of the great importance of culture or learning in this context. Even the study by Fulcher, on which Asch leans heavily, did find some differences. There was more variation in the expression of different emotions in the case of the seeing children; there was an increase in their facial activity with age, and a corresponding decrease in the blind, whose facial expressions were in general judged to be less adequate in conveying information concerning the emotion represented. The safest conclusion appears to be that there are some common expressions of emotions, and some culturally determined variations in such expressions. The writer has attempted to give some examples of both types. He would, however, agree with Asch that more research in this important field is needed, and that there should be further exploration of the possibility (discussed above in connection with the situations giving rise to the various emotions) that there may be underlying similarities of meaning in expressions which superficially, at least, are conspicuous for their variety. The fact remains that in order to understand fully what the people of other cultures are trying to communicate, we need to know not only their spoken or written language, but also the significance which we may safely attach to their gestures. In this sense it is correct to speak of a language of emotional expression.

It should be added that even for the understanding of emotional expression in members of our own cultural group, some previous experience with those particular individuals is also helpful. A scowl on the face of a person who habitually looks cheerful will convey an entirely different meaning from that of a scowl by a person who is chronically irritated. Hebb (67) points out, for example, that one can recognize the presence of shyness or embarrassment only against the general background of the individual's customary behavior. Such recognition becomes all the more difficult when the individual is differentiated from us not only through his own idiosyncratic experience, but also by what he has acquired as a member of a cultural group whose patterns of behavior are far removed from our own.

On the physiological side it is possible to understand the observed variations in emotional behavior on the basis of Cannon's (3) emergency theory. We know the physiological concomitants of emotion generally, but not of the specific emotions. The consequence may be that whereas in emotional excitement the organism is prepared to do something, the exact nature of the act will be influenced by social factors. This makes it possible to understand why, for example, a sudden death may be the cause of fighting among the members of the bereaved group, or why anger may be accompanied by such a variety of responses. The true limits of the physiological as contrasted with the social factors have not as yet been exactly determined, and further research in this field is needed from both points of view.

THE NATURE OF EMOTIONAL EXPERIENCES

There is still another possible way in which social factors may enter into the emotions, namely, in determining their subjective content and the meaning they have for the individual who is experiencing them. It may be that the very names and labels we give to the emotions have an entirely different connotation in one social setting and another. A few examples make this clear. Among the Kwakiutl Indians the death of a wife or a child is as among us an occasion for grief. They have the conviction, however, that this misfortune is not accidental, but is a kind of "insult" directed against them by the forces of nature. As with other insults, they feel shamed as a consequence, and seek some method of restoring their prestige by striking back (68). Grief in their case is accompanied by shame and anger, united in a configuration which would be extremely rare among ourselves. (With us also, grief may occasionally be associated with resentment, and under special circumstances with shame.) This certainly will alter the quality of the grief, which becomes a different emotion in the two cases. The emotion of love shows the same type of variation. In one society it is inevitably associated with the desire for exclusive possession of the loved one, so that jealousy becomes an important component of it; in other societies jealousy is apparently absent. The complex emotion known as "face" also shows the importance of social factors. Although the desire for prestige is present almost everywhere, in China and Japan it has become associated with a whole complex of relationships, in which prescribed forms of etiquette are of the greatest importance. The nature of "face" differs markedly in the East and in the West, so that it is doubtful whether the same term may appropriately be applied in the two cases.

In this direction, also, more research is needed. Ethnologists in the field would contribute to the further understanding of this problem by a careful description of the behavior accompanying every emotional situation, and of the manner in which the individuals concerned describe their experiences. A strictly behavioristic point of view in this field would lose sight of some of the most important implications of the response. Although the social setting must in every case be described in full, it must also be supplemented by information of a more personal kind. Linguistic research may turn out to be even more significant in this connection; that is, a detailed study of a people's emotional vocabulary, of the distinctions drawn between shades of emotion or between different kinds of grief or anger, of figurative expressions used in the descriptions of the emotions, and so on. This information would be of real value in clearing up the manner and the degree to which even the nature of an emotional experience is subject to social control. The genetic approach, revealing the gradual alterations both in the character of the emotional experience and the nature of emotional responses with increasing age, would also have great value, particularly if comparable data could be obtained from several different societies.

SUMMARY

Emotional behavior is accompanied by a series of physiological changes which presumably occur in all individuals. Social factors may, however, affect the emotions in various ways. There are, for example, differences in the situations which will arouse the various emotions in different societies; the contrasting reactions to the birth of twins, to death, to sex activity may be cited in this connection. There are differences also in the amount of overt emotional behavior, as well as in the specific emotions which are permitted expression. Although it has been suggested that anatomical characteristics may play a part, it is certain that cultural influences are much more important; the variations in the emotional behavior of the Chinese under different conditions are particularly striking.

Emotional expressions apparently common to all societies are the occurrence of tears in pain or sorrow, of laughter as a sign of joy or well-being and perhaps of feelings of superiority, of trembling and pallor in fear, and possibly others. On the other hand, the great difficulty experienced by untrained human observers in recognizing the emotions of chimpanzees from their facial expressions strengthens the hypothesis of cultural or social determination of the expression of the emotions in man. Emotional expression is analogous to language in that it functions as a means of communication, and in that it must be learned, at least in part. Examples of cultural patterning are the variations in the means of expressing affection, the occurrence of tears in greeting among the Maori and others, of fainting in anger among the Chinese, of the smile of submission among the Japanese, and many others. For different emotions and in different situations there may be all possible degrees of cultural patterning. Even the content of a particular emotional experience requires analysis in terms of folkways and traditions.

REFERENCES

1. Murphy, G., Murphy, L. B., and Newcomb, T. M. *Experimental Social Psychology*. Rev. ed. 1937

2. Bard, P. "Emotion: I. The Neuro-humoral Basis of Emotional Reactions." In Murchison, C., ed. *Hdbk. Exper. Psychol.* 1934

3. Cannon, W. B. *Bodily Changes in Pain, Hunger, Fear, and Rage*. 1929

4. Collip, J. B. *Factors Determining Human Behavior*. 1937

5. Klineberg, O. *Race Differences*. 1935

6. Thomas, W. I. *Primitive Behavior*. 1937

7. Warner, L. *A Black Civilization*. 1937

8. Cardi, C. N. de. "Ju-ju Laws and Customs in the Niger Delta," *J. Roy. Anthrop. Instit.*, 1899, 29: pp. 51-61

9. Faris, E. "Are Instincts Data or Hypotheses?" *Amer. J. Sociol.*, 1921, 27: pp. 184-196

10. Driberg, J. A. *The Lango*. 1923

11. Jenks, A. E. *The Bontoc Igorot*. 1905

12. Morice, A. G. "Carrier Onomatology," *Amer. Anthrop.* N.S., 1933, 35: pp. 632 658

13. Mêng, Dr. Personal communication

14. Klineberg, O. "Emotional Expression in Chinese Literature," *J. Abn. & Soc. Psychol.*, 1938, 33: pp. 517-520

15. Schrieke, B. *Alien Americans*. 1936

16. Maugham, W. S. *On a Chinese Screen*. 1922

17. Gilbert, R. *What's Wrong with China*. 1926

18. Adams, R. *Interracial Marriage in Hawaii*. 1937

19. Granet, M. "Le langage de la douleur d'après le rituel funéraire de la Chine classique," *J. de Psychol.*, 1922, 19: pp. 97-118

20. May, H. S. "A Study of Emotional Expression Among Chinese and Americans," *Unpublished Master's Essay*, Columbia University, 1938

21. Darwin, C. *The Expression of the Emotions in Man and Animals*. 1873

22. Bühler, C. "The Social Behavior of Children," *Hdbk. Child Psychol.* (ed. by C. Murchison). 1933

23. Feleky, A. M. "The Expression of the Emotions," *Psychol. Rev.*, 1914, 21: pp. 33-41

24. Dunlap, K. "The Role of Eye-Muscles and Mouth-Muscles in the Expression of the Emotions," *Genet. Psychol. Monog.*, 1927, 2: No. 3

25. Gates, G. S. "The Role of the Auditory Element in the Interpretation of Emotion," *Psychol. Bull.*, 1927, 24: p. 175

26. Blake, W. H. "A Preliminary Study of the Interpretation of Bodily Expression." *Teachers Coll. Contribs. to Educ.*, 1933, No. 574

27. Carmichael, L., et al. "A Study of the Judgment of Manual Expression as Presented in Still and Motion Pictures," *J. Soc. Psychol.*, 1937, 8: pp. 115-142

28. Köhler, W. *The Mentality of Apes.* 1925

29. Kohts, N. *Infant Ape and Human Child (instincts, emotions, play, habits).* 2 vols. 1935

30. Foley, J. P., Jr. "Judgment of Facial Expression of Emotion in the Chimpanzee," *J. Soc. Psychol.*, 1935, 6: pp. 31-67

31. Dumas, G. *Traité de Psychologie.* 2 vols. 1923-1924

32. Tylor, E. B. *Primitive Culture.* 1871

33. Rank, O. *Art and Artist.* 1932

34. Giles, H. A. *A History of Chinese Literature.* 1901

35. Crawley, E. *Studies of Savages and Sex* (ed. by T. Besterman). 1929

36. Mauss, M. "L'Expression Obligatoire des Sentiments," *J. de Psychol.*, 1921, 18: pp. 425-434

37. Durham, M. E. "Some Montenegrin Manners and Customs," *J. Roy. Anthrop. Instit.*, 1909, 39: pp. 85-96

38. Blackwood, B. *Both Sides of Buka Passage.* 1935

39. Brown, A. R. *The Andaman Islanders.* 1922

40. Best, E. *The Maori.* 1924

41. Man, E. H. "On the Aboriginal Inhabitants of the Andaman Islands," *J. Roy. Anthrop. Instit.*, 1882, 12: pp. 69-116, 327-434

42. Westermarck, E. A. *The Origin and Development of the Moral Ideas.* 2 vols. 1908-12

43. Bromberg, W. *The Mind of Man.* 1937

44. Hobbes, T. *Human Nature* and *Leviathan, Works* (ed. by Molesworth). 11 vols. 1840

45. Schopenhauer, A. *The World as Will and Idea.* 5th ed. 1906

46. Bergson, H. *Laughter.* 1911

47. Spencer, H. "The Physiology of Laughter," *Essays.* 2 vols. 1863

48. Freud, S. *Wit and Its Relation to the Unconscious.* 1917

49. Goldenweiser, A. A. *History, Psychology, and Culture.* 1933

50. Hogbin, H. I. "The Sexual Life of the Natives of Ontong Java (Solomon Islands)," *J. Polynesian Soc.*, 1931, 40: pp. 23-34

51. Parsons, E. C. "Notes on Zuñi," *Memoirs, Amer. Anthrop. Assn.*, 1917, 4: Pt. II

52. Powdermaker, H. *Life in Lesu.* 1933

53. Wissler, C. *An Introduction to Social Anthropology.* 1929

54. Lowie, R. H. *The Crow Indians.* 1935

55. Bunzel, R. L. "Introduction to Zuñi Ceremonialism," *47th Annual Report, Bur. Amer. Ethnol.*, 1932

56. Wilson, J. *A Missionary Voyage to the Southern Pacific Ocean.* 1796

57. Williams, F. E. *Orokaiva Society.* 1930

58. Porteus, S. D. *The Psychology of a Primitive People.* 1931

59. Hearn, L. "The Japanese Smile," *Glimpses of Unfamiliar Japan.* 2 vols. 1894

60. Hearn, L. *Japan: An Attempt at Interpretation.* 1904

61. La Barre, W. "The Cultural Basis of Emotions and Gestures," *J. of Pers.*, 1947, 16: pp. 49-68

62. Long Lance. *Long Lance.* 1928

63. Fletcher, A. C., and La Flesche, F. "The Omaha Tribe," *Bur. Amer. Ethnol., Ann. Rep.*, 1905-1906, 27: pp. 15-655

64. Asch, S. E. *Social Psychology.* 1952

65. Thompson, J. "Development of Facial Expression of Emotion in Blind and Seeing Children," *Archives Psych.*, 1941, No. 264

66. Fulcher, J. P. "Voluntary Facial Expression in Blind and Seeing Children," *Archives Psych.*, 1942, No. 272

67. Hebb, D. O. "Emotion in Man and Animal: An Analysis of the Intuitive Processes of Recognition," *Psych. Rev.*, 1946, 53: pp. 88-106

68. Benedict, R. F. *Patterns of Culture.* 1934

Social Factors in Perception and Memory

8

SENSE PERCEPTION

One of the most conspicuous research developments in recent years is represented by the extent to which sense perception has become a social-psychological problem. This is perhaps the clearest indication of what has been described in an earlier chapter as the "invasion" of general psychology by social psychology. It is no longer possible to approach perception as a purely individual phenomenon, the nature of which is determined by the pattern of neurones which bring impulses from the outside world to the central nervous system. Although it is true that the process of vision is made possible by the impingement of certain vibrations on the optic nerve, and the transmission of the impulse through the optic thalamus to the occipital part of the cortex, there are aspects of vision which are determined by the previous experience of the individual, in connection with which group-membership plays an important part. Considerable evidence has accumulated which indicates that social factors must be considered if the phenomena of sense perception are properly to be understood.

Malinowski (1) gives an interesting example of the cultural patterning of visual experience. Among the Trobrianders, the idea of resemblance between parents and offspring, or between children of the same parents, is controlled by strict social norms. These may at times go counter to the evidence of one's senses. In the first place, resemblance to the father is regarded as natural and proper, and such similarity is always assumed and affirmed to exist. It is a great offense to hint that the child resembles his mother or any of his maternal relatives. "It is a phrase of serious bad language to say 'thy face is thy sister's,' which is the worst form of kinship similarity" (p. 88). In the second place it is taken for granted that brothers do not resemble each other. This is dogma; although both may resemble the father, everyone will deny that they look at all alike. Malinowski once commented on the likeness of two brothers, and "there came such a hush over all the assembly, while the brother present withdrew abruptly and the company was half-embarrassed, half-offended at this breach of custom" (p. 92). In this example it is difficult to know with certainty whether the sense perception has actually been interfered with, that is to say, whether the Trobrianders actually *see* the two brothers as different even though to us they would obviously resemble each other, or whether they are merely unwilling to acknowledge such a resemblance even when they do see it. It is probable, however, on the basis of our knowledge of the degree to which we see what we are looking for, that the Trobrianders fail to note any resemblance because they do not want or expect to find it. It may be added that the Trobriander belief in the resemblance between father and child is all the more surprising since according to Malinowski they are ignorant of the father's part in procreation; they assume that the father's function is the mechanical one of opening up the mother, and that any other mechanical means may be substituted for it.

To turn to a more specific visual phenomenon, the perception of color and of variations in hue may be shown to vary from group to group, largely under the influence of the color terminology. The apparent inability of the members of certain groups like the Torres Straits Islanders and others to recognize certain colors, and their tendency to combine colors which seem to us unrelated, are probably linguistic in origin (2). Wallis (3) writes:

> Not infrequently the savage ignores distinctions observed by us or cross-sections our distinctions. This frequently happens in color designations. The Ashantis have distinct names for the colors black, red and white. The term black is also used for any dark color, such as blue, purple, brown, etc., while the term red does duty for pink, orange and yellow (p. 421).

Of the New Guinea natives Margaret Mead (4) writes: "Their color classifications are so different that they saw yellow, olive-green, blue-green, gray and lavender as variations of one color" (p. 638). Strange as this confusion may seem to us, it is a perfectly natural response under the conditions imposed by their particular nomenclature. There can be little doubt that when the same name is used for two colors, they may be seen to resemble each other as a consequence.

This is not always the case, however, as the observations of Seligman (5) in New Guinea indicate. He gave to his subjects the task of sorting colored wools, and they did not necessarily put together those wools to which the same name would be applied. Members of the Takitaro tribe were especially quick and correct, in spite of their very incomplete color vocabulary. Color names do not necessarily affect perception, therefore, but it is highly probable that in many cases they would operate in that direction.

A significant experiment on the effect of social factors on visual experience has been carried out by Sherif (6). The study was undertaken in order to test the importance of social norms or "frames of reference," that is to say, standards which serve as means of judging the experience in question, or placing it in a proper framework. He was interested in seeing what would happen to a visual experience when there was no such frame of reference, and when the subject had therefore to create one. He experimented with the "auto-kinetic" phenomenon, produced by looking at a single point of light in a room which is otherwise completely dark; this point has no external frame of reference which determines its position in the visual field, and is consequently seen to move, probably as the result of physiological factors. The distance through which it moves varies considerably from one subject to another. Sherif found that when he placed two or three subjects together in the experimental situation, after having determined the average distance through which the point had previously moved for each one of them separately, there was a definite tendency for their reports to converge. The effect may in part be explained by suggestion, since the words first spoken by any one subject usually influence the others, but in any case a social norm was set up under these conditions. In a second portion of the experiment, the subjects were first tested together and then separately; the social norm established in the group situation persisted, so that the reports made by each subject individually tended to approximate those previously made in the presence of others. In other words, the group norm is effective even when the subject is tested in isolation. This result parallels in certain respects the effect of cultural patterning on the sense perception of the individual, and is a significant attempt to bring such patterning within the field of laboratory experimentation.

The study has, however, one apparent limitation. It deals with a form of sense experience in which the stimulus is itself in part subjective, since the spot of light does not really move. The extension of the results to those cases in which the eye or ear is actually stimulated by known wave lengths might therefore conceivably be questioned. Evidence has since accumulated, however, which indicates that similar results are obtained even with "real" stimuli. Schonbar (7), for example, was able to demonstrate the same phenomenon of convergence and the formation of social norms in an experiment in which the subjects were asked to judge the distance through which light actually moves. The results were not so striking as in Sherif's case, but they were in the same direction.

Recent developments in this field have been marked by the extensive exploration of the influence of individual and social factors on perception in a variety of situations. Cantril (8), for example, has experimented with a series of illusions resulting from the perception of "distorted rooms," first devised and constructed by Ames (9). When the observer looks into a room of this kind, his previous experience and what Cantril calls his "values" or "purposes" determine his perceptions to such an extent that he may, for example, "see" people get larger or smaller as they move from one corner to another. Cantril regards this as demonstrating a fundamental principle of perception, namely, that it is largely determined by previous, rather than by present, experience. Since such past experience will differ according to our cultural background or group membership, it follows that cultural or group factors will have to be included among the variables by which perception is influenced.

Krech and Crutchfield (10) divide the determinants of perception into two major categories, *structural* and *functional*. "By *structural* factors are meant those factors deriving solely from the nature of the physical stimuli and the neural effects they evoke in the nervous system of the individual. . . . The *functional* factors of perceptual organization, on the other hand, are those which derive primarily from the needs, moods, past experience, and memory of the individual" (pp. 81-82). Much of the recent history of experimentation in the field of perception has been concerned with establishing the relative contribution of these two groups of factors and the nature and extent of their interrelationship. Some indication of the interest aroused by this set of problems is given by the recent publication of two volumes of studies dealing with the interdependence of personality and perception (*11, 12*).

It is important to note that not all functional factors in perception are social in the usual sense of the term. In one experiment, for example, Levine, Chein and Murphy (*13*) presented a series of ambiguous drawings to hungry college students, and found a marked tendency for such drawings to be perceived as food objects—sandwiches, salads, roasts, etc. There was no such effect when the same drawings were shown to students who had just finished eating. In this case it is individual experience rather than culture or group membership which altered the perception of stimuli that are structurally the same for both groups of subjects.

More directly social in its implications is the experiment by Bruner and Goodman (*14*), in which thirty ten-year-old children were given the task of adjusting a circular patch of light so as to equate it in size to that of various objects. They were first asked to estimate in this manner, from memory, the size of coins from a penny through a half dollar; this experiment was repeated with the coins present. A control group performed the same task, not with coins, but with gray cardboard disks of identical size. In the presence of the objects, the results showed that the coins, which are socially valued, are judged larger in size than the gray disks; secondly, the greater the value of the coin, the greater the degree of overestimation of size (with the exception of the half dollar, which according to the investigators might have a lesser reality value for these ten-year-olds). When the total group was divided into a rich sub-group, from prosperous business and professional families, and a poor sub-group from a settlement house in one of Boston's slums, it was demonstrated that the poor children overestimated the size of the coins considerably more than did the rich. The difference in the relative value of the coins for the two groups is regarded as the explanation of this finding. (The results when the estimates were made from memory were less clear.)

To take one more example from a series of important investigations, Postman, Bruner and McGinnies (*15*) explored the relation between perception and the value systems of the individual. Students were classified according to their scores on the Allport-Vernon Study of Values, which is based on the Spranger typology, and which makes it possible to describe subjects in terms of the relative pre-dominance of religious, social, theoretic, economic, political and esthetic values. The subjects were shown a series of words, but the tachistoscopic presentation was at such a speed and at such low illumination that the words were at first "ambiguous" in many cases. With an increase in both the illumination and the frequency of presentation, the words were gradually recognized, but with vary-ing degrees of difficulty. The major finding of the study was that those words were more easily recognized which were congruent with the predominant values of the subject; people with high religious values, for example, saw religious words more quickly and more accurately. Value systems are interpreted therefore as playing a significant part in determining the ease and selectivity of perception.

These studies, and others in the same area, have aroused great interest and have focused increasing attention on the functional aspects of perception. It is possible, however, that although such functional aspects undoubtedly have an effect, the extent of that effect may have been exaggerated. A repetition of the Bruner-Good-man study regarding the estimation of the size of coins has been made by Carter and Schooler (16) with results that do not entirely bear out the original conclusion. The findings regarding the effect of value systems on perception have been questioned by Howes and Solomon (17), who believe that the familiarity of the words used may affect perception more than the value-systems themselves. A replication of this study by Dohrenwend (18), using frequency of exposure of words before recognition as a criterion of perception, failed to substantiate the results of the original study. Much more research will be needed before the exact contribution of functional factors to perception can be estimated with any degree of accuracy.

One of the best known and most widely used techniques for the study of personality characteristics is the Rorschach, in which a series of ten ink blots is presented to the subject for his interpreta-tion. The theory underlying this technique is that what the subject perceives in the ink blots is really a projection of his own person-ality; what one sees is a reflection of what one is. The application of the Rorschach to groups of differing cultural background reveals in clear fashion the manner in which such perceptual responses may be affected by the culture. Samoan subjects, for instance, gave fewer original responses than are found in other communities. Cook (19) points out that this is due to a general disparagement of any form of deviation or originality, particularly in children. The Samoan subjects also gave an unusually large number of responses to the white spaces on the Rorschach cards, rather than to the black or colored portions of the figure. Such responses are usually interpreted as signifying negativism or a tendency to opposition, but Cook believes that in the case of the Samoans the explanation is to be found in the high value attached to the color white. These findings indicate that the application to two different cultural groups of a personality test based on perception, even when the test appears to be "culture-free," may create serious difficulties unless the cultures concerned are understood by the investigator and taken into account in his interpretation of the results.

A significant study of social influences on perception was conducted by Asch (20), who presented to his subjects the apparently simple task of choosing from three lines the one which was equal in length to the standard line. The crucial feature of the situation is that out of the group of seven to nine individuals, *all but one* co-operated with the experimenter by giving at certain times unanimously wrong judgments, calling two clearly unequal lines equal. In each of these groups there was only one naive, critical subject. Some of these critical subjects remained entirely independent of the group; at the other extreme there were some who agreed with the majority in every case. When they yielded, in spite of the evidence of their own eyes, they did so for various reasons. Some yielded because they did not wish to appear different; some assumed that their own perceptions were defective; there were a few subjects, however, who reported a real change in their perception of the lines. In these last instances the conclusion is justified that perception was actually altered because of the pressure exerted by the group.

In an important experiment, Zillig (21) was able to demonstrate the extent to which social attitudes may determine what one sees. In a preliminary survey of friendships within a classroom she discovered that certain children were almost universally liked, and others disliked to the same degree. In the experiment proper she took an equal number of pupils from these two extreme groups, and had them stand up in front of the class and perform calisthenic exercises under her direction. She had previously instructed the "liked" children to make mistakes, and had trained the "disliked" ones to follow her instructions exactly. At the end of the experiment, she asked the class to indicate which group had done the exercises correctly, and the majority of votes went to the popular group. It seems unlikely that the children designated the favored group as superior even though they saw them make the errors; Zillig believes on the basis of conversations with them that they actually "saw" the differences as they reported them. This experiment raises in a significant manner the whole problem of the relation of prejudice to sense perception. There is no doubt that a mental set of favor or prejudice toward a particular group may influence the observer in his perception of their behavior.

Among the interesting observations by E. L. and R. E. Horowitz (22) there is one which is particularly significant in this connection. They showed a picture of a fine home to southern children. Later the children were questioned about the picture, and many of them "saw" a Negro woman engaged in some sort of domestic occupation, although this was not in the original. Here the stereotype of the Negro and of his place in the socio-economic scale determined the perception, or at least the later report of it.

A study by Razran (23) also demonstrates the effect of stereotypes on our perceptions. A group of college students were shown photographs of thirty girls and asked to rank each photograph on a five-point scale, indicating their general liking of the girl, her beauty, her intelligence, her character, her ambition and her "entertainingness." Two months later, the subjects were again shown the same photographs, but with surnames added. For some of the photographs Jewish surnames were given, such as Rabinowitz, Finklestein, etc.; a second group received Italian surnames such as Scarano, Grisolia, etc.; a third received Irish surnames such as McGillicuddy, O'Shaughnessy, etc.; and a fourth, "old American" names like Adams and Clark. Razran was able to demonstrate that the mere labeling of the photographs with these various surnames had a definite effect upon the manner in which the photographs were perceived. The addition of Jewish and Italian surnames, for example, resulted in a substantial drop in general liking, and a smaller drop in beauty and character; it also resulted in a rise in the ratings for ambition, more marked in the case of the Jewish surnames. It seems clear that in these cases the stereotypes associated with ethnic groups had a very definite effect upon the perception of the photographs, and upon the consequent judgment of the characteristics possessed by these girls.

An essentially similar mechanism is apparent also in the experiment of Goring (24), who showed that because of the popular belief that intelligent people have high foreheads, those who were judged intelligent were also "seen" to have high brows; actual measurement showed the reverse relationship to hold true.

Another experiment dealing with social factors in perception is that of Ansbacher (25). Using ordinary postage stamps, the investigator found that those which were greater in value seemed larger than the others; Canadian stamps, with which the subjects had had less experience, seemed smaller than the American of the same denomination and actually of the same dimensions, apparently because they did not have the same value for the subject.

Sense perception, no matter which receptor is stimulated, involves the question of selectivity. In other words, no one sees or hears everything in the environment; rather, we make a choice dependent upon previous training and acquired powers of observation. There are marked individual differences in this respect determined by occupational and other interests; it is obvious that a college professor, a dealer in antiques, and a prospective bride may "see" entirely different things in the same shop window. Selectivity enters also in other types of observation, as when a mother notices the cry of her child when no one else hears it. There are cultural as well as individual differences in this respect. The reputedly greater sensory acuity of primitive peoples is undoubtedly due to training, and a White man may learn to make the same discriminations as do the natives. Conversely, a member of a primitive community would be confounded by the multiplicity of noises in any metropolitan center and would undoubtedly need some experience with automobile horns and the sounds made by street-cars and airplanes before these could stand out as recognizable stimuli.

The principle of selectivity is also illustrated by an experiment conducted by Allport and Kramer (26) in connection with their study of some of the significant components of prejudice. They presented photographs of students to their subjects, who were given the task of separating the Jewish from the non-Jewish students. On the whole, the proportion of success was not much greater than would be expected by chance. Those subjects, however, who showed themselves to be anti-Semitic in their answers to a previously administered attitude questionnaire, were definitely more successful in recognizing the Jewish photographs than were the subjects who were friendly toward Jews. Evidently the anti-Semitic attitudes resulted in greater sensitivity to those features which aided the recognition. It is obviously important for anti-Semitic persons to be able to distinguish Jews from non-Jews, and this fact explains the added selectivity of their perceptual responses in this context.

The same considerations apply to auditory as to visual phenomena, although considerably more work has been done on the latter. We know that the combination of tones into various intervals may be regarded as consonant in one community and dissonant in another. Herzog [1] reports the occurrence of two-part singing in Melanesia one note apart, an interval which to us is the most dissonant imaginable. Even in the history of our own music the same discrepancy may be observed, and it is well known that Beethoven's harmonies were regarded as most unpleasant when they were first heard. Moore (27) has demonstrated experimentally that an interval which is heard as dissonant may become agreeable after it has been heard a number of times, and that conversely one which is at first pleasant may become disagreeable as the result of constant repetition. In this connection it is important to note that the theories of consonance like that of Helmholtz (28) which explain it on the basis of the physical relationships between the individual tones and their overtones, require at least to be modified so as to include the effect of previous training and experience.

The perception of intensity of sound may also, but probably to a lesser degree, show the effect of similar factors. Those who hear Chinese music for the first time, or who listen to the musical accompaniment to a Chinese play, are usually much disturbed by its intensity. They may even express their amazement that the Chinese can stand it. Lin Yu-t'ang (29) in discussing this point makes a suggestion that the hearing of the Chinese may actually be different, and that loud noises may not affect them to the same degree as they affect us. This is highly improbable. It is much more likely that one's ear becomes accustomed to certain combinations of sounds so that they seem natural and satisfying. In support of this interpretation is the fact that many Chinese have complained that they found American popular music, as well as Wagnerian brasses, much too loud for them at first hearing.

[1] Personal communication.

We have already referred to the variations in taste which make the same food palatable or disagreeable in two different communities. Similar considerations apparently apply to the phenomena of smell. It has been pointed out, for example, that the odor of valerian, which we regard as most unpleasant, has actually had a vogue as a sort of perfume. Junker (30) writes of the A-Barmbo tribe in Africa that they were "disgusted at the smell of some genuine old Edam (Dutch) cheese, of which I had eaten a few scraps, and gave out that the White people eat 'the foulest muck.' Many smells affect them differently from us, and they turn with loathing from eau de cologne, for example, and from scented soap" (p. 101). As far as the cheese is concerned, there are enough individual differences among ourselves to make this a doubtful example of cultural patterning, but the other cases clearly indicate the variations in the pleasantness and unpleasantness of odors.

The degree of adaptation to painful stimuli also shows wide variations between individuals and groups. There is undoubtedly a marked subjective component in the experience of pain, as hypnotic phenomena amply demonstrate. In our society, there is a sex difference in this respect (although with considerable overlapping), since it is regarded as more legitimate for a woman than for a man to give expression to pain. The training which many American Indians received seems to have resulted in an actual ignoring of the pain stimuli and the consequent diminution in the pain experience. Blackwood (31) gives an example of a similar effect among the people of Buka.

> These people will put their hands into water that is only just off the boil, and take out a taro so hot that when they passed me my share I invariably dropped it. . . . Similarly they will plunge a hand into a potful of shellfish immediately it has been taken off the fire (p. 292).

These various instances combine to demonstrate the importance of social factors in perception. Not only as between different cultures, but also between sub-groups (occupational, national, class, etc.) in our own society and between individuals within the sub-groups, the whole pattern of previous experience, training and interest enter very definitely. As Freeman expresses it:

> In a very literal sense, we tend to observe more after the manner of our own natures than photographically after the properties of the external world. This fact . . . explains not only why individuals from

different classes of society with different common segments of apperceptive mass and response cannot think, feel, and believe alike, but why they cannot, in principle, even perceive alike (32, p. 49).

This does not mean that there are not certain aspects of perception which are common to all normal individuals, as a result of the nature of our neurological organism, but we must not neglect those social factors which create the differences to which we have referred.

A final example from the Maori is pertinent to this discussion, although it might be regarded as illustrating a conceptual difference, rather than one in sense perception properly so-called. An English painter while traveling through New Zealand made a number of portraits of the natives, including one of an old chieftain whose face was covered with the spiral tattooing typical of his rank. The artist showed the model his picture, expecting his hearty approval. The old man looked at the portrait, then declined it with the words, "That's not what I am." The artist then asked the chief to draw his own portrait. "When he handed the White man the result, with the words: 'That's what I am!' the latter could see nothing but the old chief's tattoo pattern which signified his tribal connection" (33, p. 44). Lips comments that this indicates that the world of Western thought with its emphasis on the individual is foreign to this Maori, for whom the concept of the community is paramount. This may be the correct explanation. For our purposes it is sufficient to point out that he apparently "saw" himself in a manner quite different from the White artist because of what he and his people regarded as important.

Perception of Time. There has been considerable discussion as to whether the perception of time is based upon organic or upon social factors. The fact that we get hungry at stated intervals, that we become sleepy at about the same time each evening, and awaken at about the same time each morning (some individuals acquire great precision in this latter respect), has suggested the possibility of internal organic rhythms serving as clues to the passage of time. Just what these rhythms are and where they are located it is not yet possible to say. Certainly they are notoriously defective for short intervals of time, although, as has been shown (34), they are rather more dependable in connection with the major physiological requirements of the organism. There can be no doubt, however, that social factors are also important. In the first place the importance of time will vary from one culture to another. Our own machine age has made speed a matter of utmost importance but this attitude is not shared by groups whose activities do not require completion at any stated time. As Dollard (35) points out, time is a concept with social implications, and "especially in our culture it is one of the most vigorously felt and imposed basic concepts . . . and it has certainly 'social' as well as organic factors" (p. 103). One example of the relative indifference to time is that given by Kroeber (36) in the case of the California Indians. Among them no one knew his own age, nor how remote an event was that had happened more than half a dozen years ago; they kept no record of the passage of long intervals of time.

In the writer's study of intelligence test performance among the Yakima Indians of the State of Washington, he discovered that the instruction to "do this as quickly as possible" simply did not have the effect anticipated. These Indian children saw no reason to hurry; they were not persuaded that solving a problem in forty-five seconds was really "better" than using up a full minute in the process.

Among the Saulteaux Indians, Hallowell (37) found relatively crude indications of time intervals, in which the positions of the sun throughout the day served as the reference points. The seasons were indicated by the occurrence of natural events, such as the melting of the ice, the first appearance of birds, etc. Past events were located in terms of the individual's own life history, such as "when I was a youth" or "when my father was a child," etc. Such a "clock" or "calendar" was perfectly adequate to meet the needs of the Saulteaux, but the result would certainly be a perception of the passage of time different from that to which we are accustomed.

In this connection Sorokin and Merton (38) make use of the concept of "social time" to indicate the variations between one society and another.

> The category of astronomical time is only one of several concepts of time. Social phenomena are frequently adopted as a frame of reference so that units of time are often fixed by the rhythm of collective life. The need for social collaboration is at the root of social systems of time. Social time is qualitatively differentiated according to the beliefs and customs common to the group (p. 629).

These writers give a number of examples to illustrate the variations in social time. In Madagascar the natives speak of doing something in a "rice-cooking," the equivalent of about half an hour; in the "frying of a locust," or a moment. The Cross River natives use an expression such as "the man died in less than the time in which maize is not yet completely roasted," that is, in less than fifteen minutes; or "the time in which one can cook a handful of vegetables." The Khasis name their months according to the activities which take place in each; there is a "month for weeding the ground," "a month when cultivators fry the produce of their fields," and so forth. Radcliffe Brown (39) states that in the Andaman Islands it is possible to recognize a distinct succession of odors throughout the year as the various trees and plants come into bloom. "The Andamanese have therefore adopted an original method of marking the different periods of the year by means of the odoriferous flowers that are in bloom at different times. Their calendar is a calendar of scents" (p. 311).

There are of course individual as well as group differences in time perception, and also in the attitude toward time generally. William Storn (40) speaks of a personal space and time, differing from one individual to another. Personal space refers to the region of possible movement and contact, and will obviously be different in the case of an international banker and in that of a farmer in the hills of Kentucky. Personal time refers to the tendency to see things in terms of their immediate or deferred consequences, differences in thought for the future and in the need for haste, etc. What causes these differences is difficult to decide, and need not concern us here. It is clear that the reaction to time, like other forms of sense perception, is by no means solely an organic matter. A clear example of the manner in which social factors may enter is given in the study by Lazarsfeld and others (41) of a little community outside of Vienna in which unemployment had affected the whole population. There were many consequences of this unemployment, among others the development of complete indifference to the passage of time and to the desirability of doing anything within a stated period. People would come hours late to an appointment as the result of this attitude.

Although not directly in the field of sense perception, a study by Asch (20) on the "perception" of traits of personality is relevant here, because it illustrates the importance of the context in which social perception occurs. Two lists of personality traits were read to two different groups of subjects. The first group received the following list: kind, wise, honest, *calm, strong*. The second group heard: cruel, shrewd, unscrupulous, *calm, strong*. It will be noted that the first three words of the two lists are different, whereas the last two are identical. The subjects were then told: "Suppose you had to describe this person in the same manner, but without using the terms you heard, what other terms would you use?" There were striking differences in the synonyms given by the two groups. The word "calm" was translated by words such as *cold, frigid, calculating*, in the case of the second group; this never occurred in the responses of the first group. The latter used instead such words as *soothing, peaceful, gentle*. Comparable differences were obtained in the case of the word *strong*. The meaning of the words changed because of the set induced by the pattern of the words as a group. A parallel with important social implications can be found in the interpretation of traits attributed to ethnic groups. Words like *ambitious, frugal, practical* will have a very different flavor when applied to a group with which we identify ourselves, or on the other hand to a despised or disliked minority.

It is important to note that our patterns of perception are acquired in the course of our personal and social experience, and that therefore we must expect them to follow the principles established for other instances of learning. One of these principles is that when responses are rewarded, they are reinforced and tend to become firmly established; conversely, when they are not accompanied by rewards, they tend to be extinguished. Mausner (42) tested this principle in the case of the auto-kinetic effect. When the subjects responded in the alone situation, some of them had their responses reinforced by being told eighty percent of the time that their judgments were correct; other subjects were told eighty percent of the time that their judgments were incorrect. The subjects were then tested together in a variety of combinations. When both subjects had been previously reinforced, there tended to be very little convergence; they persisted in the responses they had previously given. When both subjects had been told earlier that their judgments were wrong, there was usually marked convergence in the group situation. When the group consisted of one subject who had been reinforced, and one who had not, there was convergence, which took the form of an acceptance by the latter of the judgments made by the former. This study shows the extent to which group phenomena of the type investigated by Sherif may be dependent upon the previous experience of the individuals who constitute the group.

MEMORY

There is no clear dividing line between the phenomena of perception which we have just reviewed, and many of the phenomena usually dealt with under the head of memory. If a subject is presented with a picture and asked to describe its contents immediately after its removal, it is difficult to determine whether any failures of reproduction are due to faulty perception or to faulty recollection. When some time has elapsed between the original presentation and the attempted reproduction, the distinction can be made with greater certainty. In any case, it would appear that many of the principles which have been described as operating in the case of perception, also apply to memory.

It is probable that a large number of facts discovered by psychologists in connection with learning and memory are due to the nature of the nervous system and are valid for human beings everywhere. We have no reason to believe that the shape of the learning curve and the principles of reinforcement or extinction, for example, are greatly affected by the nature of the society in which the individual develops. Social factors clearly enter, however, in determining what one remembers. Here again an experiment of Zillig's is pertinent (21). She presented to a number of subjects, male and female, a list of statements that had been made at various times about the nature of women. Some of these were favorable, others, mostly from the writings of Schopenhauer and Oscar Wilde, were distinctly unfavorable. A week after this presentation, the subjects were asked to record from memory the statements that had been previously presented to them. The results showed a decided tendency for the women to remember more of those items which favored them, and for the men to remember relatively more of the unfavorable items. This simple but conclusive experiment demonstrates clearly that memory may be determined by other than neurological factors.

The effect of sex identification on what is remembered was also demonstrated by Clark (43), who presented to high-school boys and girls a passage to be reproduced from memory as accurately as possible. The passage dealt with a conflict situation between a man and a woman; a brawny, hard-working woman taunts the man with not being able to perform even once a task which she is required to do every day. The incident is related from the point of view of the man, but entirely in the third person. The male subjects frequently identified with the man to such an extent as to reproduce the story in the first person; this never happened in the case of the girls. There were other differences reflecting a contrast in the impression which the story made on the girls and boys respectively, including the fact that the girls remembered the story better.

The relation between memory and attitude has been explored in a number of investigations. Margolies (44) gave to a group of students an attitude scale designed to measure the extent of their prejudice against the Negro. She then read to them a number of statements concerning the Negro, some of them favorable, and others unfavorable. A week later she asked her subjects to reproduce from memory the statements they had heard. Although the results were not conclusive, they showed on the whole a tendency for those with favorable attitudes to remember more of the favorable statements.

More conclusive results were obtained by Levine and Murphy (45), who were interested in the learning and forgetting of controversial material relating to the Soviet Union. In this study, which was conducted in 1941, the subjects consisted of two groups of college students, one pro-communist, the other, anti-communist. They were first tested for memory of a neutral passage, and in this respect were very much alike. They were then given two passages to read, one opposed to communism, the other in favor. The results indicated the superior memory of the pro-communist group for the pro-Soviet selection, and of the other group for the anti-Soviet selection. This result is parallel to the common observation that when people read articles or books of a controversial nature, they show a definite tendency to remember those points which are in agreement with their own opinions, and conveniently to forget those that differ.

These facts are also in definite agreement with the Freudian theory of repression as the cause of forgetting. In general this theory holds that we forget those things the memory of which is unpleasant. This does not mean that the forgetting is pleasant or satisfactory, since it may result in considerable inconvenience; it does mean that in spite of such inconvenience, forgetting takes place because of the repression of the unpleasant memory into the unconscious.

Prejudice in favor of one's own sex, or for or against the Negro, would then serve as the emotional basis of the repression.

Among the first to recognize the phenomena of memory as problems in social psychology were William Stern (46) and Bartlett (47). Stern undertook a series of experiments on the psychology of rumor and testimony, one of the results of which was to demonstrate the frequency of errors in the reporting of what one has actually seen or read. Even when the subject was willing to take an oath upon his evidence, errors both of omission and of distortion still occurred. Social influences were studied by the method of chain reproduction, a story being transmitted through several subjects, each of whom attempted to repeat the account given him by his predecessor in the chain. The results show strikingly that even with a few transmissions (five, in one experiment) rumor becomes extraordinarily unreliable. There is, in general, a progressive abbreviation of the account, with the phrasing becoming more general and less definite. Errors occurring most frequently include those of confusion, substitution, alteration of temporal and spatial setting, and of names and dates. In another experiment, a comparison was made between the reliability of testimony when the subject gave his own coherent report, and when he was subjected to cross-examination. The accuracy is much reduced in the latter case; when the witness does not have the correct answer in mind, he prefers to give an incorrect one rather than admit that he does not know. Here the social relationship between the "lawyer" and the "witness" plays a significant part.

In Bartlett's investigation, the subjects were asked to reproduce stories, usually of a mythological nature, which had previously been presented to them. Two principal methods were used. In the first, known as the Method of Repeated Reproduction, the subject is given a passage to study under prescribed conditions, attempts a first reproduction usually after an interval of fifteen minutes, and thereafter gives further reproductions at intervals of increasing length. In the second, the Method of Serial Reproduction, the reproduction by the first subject is presented to Subject B, and his version to C, and so on, as in the case of Stern's studies. The results of the second series are of greater interest to us as they carry Stern's analysis somewhat further. They show the substantial change which may take place in the nature of the original material, including the forgetting or distortion of proper names, a tendency to make the material concrete wherever possible, a loss of individual characteristics of style and content, an abbreviation of the length of the story, an attempt at rationalization or explanation, and frequently startling and radical alterations in the actual material. We have here an experimental verification of what happens in the case of rumor or gossip in which an original story is distorted far beyond recognition. As Bartlett points out, this is clearly a social process, the reproductions being influenced by the fact that individuals are communicating to one another.

In connection with cultural or group differences, Bartlett cites a number of interesting examples in the social psychology of memory, taken mainly from his observations among the Swazi of South Africa. He states that some years ago the Swazi chief and a number of his followers visited England in connection with a long-standing land dispute. On their return, they were asked what they remembered best among their English impressions; and the one thing that remained most vividly fixed in their recollection was their picture of the English policeman regulating the traffic with uplifted hand. This may be explained by the fact that the Swazi greets his friend or his visitor in a somewhat similar manner, and he was therefore impressed by the use of this gesture in a foreign country with such marked effect. It was one of the few things which fitted directly into the Swazi social framework, and so it was remembered.

The Swazi, in common with most Bantu-speaking tribes, are said to possess a remarkable memory. Bartlett subjected this to experiment, and found that their retentiveness as such was apparently not superior to that of the Whites. They did, however, remember certain things exceedingly well, for example the characteristics of the cattle which they owned or which they were tending, because of the importance which this had for their social and economic life and because of their previous training. We have here an example similar to that of the allegedly superior sensory acuity of so-called primitive peoples; it is not a matter of innate superiority, but of socially determined attitudes and acquired techniques.

Even the manner of remembering may be socially determined to a considerable degree. Bartlett reports that when he talked to a Zulu about the former military exploits of his people, the Zulu lived through his memories with the greatest vividness and emotional excitement. A Swazi would tell about similar incidents in a stolid and unmoved manner. It was not a matter of difference in temperament, since the Swazi also could be aroused to violent interest by other questions, particularly those dealing with cattle, women, marriage and children. The memories showed a marked difference in emotional tone in the two cases. One other characteristic of the Swazi manner of remembering may be mentioned. There is a definite tendency to recall in a recapitulatory or rote manner, with the introduction of a mass of apparently irrelevant detail. This may be particularly trying to all listeners in the case of a lawsuit, during which the Swazi witness will insist on telling the story in his own detailed way no matter how long it takes. He seems in fact often to be incapable of coming to the end of his account without going through all the intervening steps.

One of the most significant demonstrations of the effect of culture on the processes of memory is to be found in a study by the anthropologist Nadel (48), who applied the techniques of experimental psychology in connection with his field work in Africa. Two groups of school children from the Nupe and Yoruba tribes, respectively, were presented with the same tasks, namely, to repeat from memory a story which was read to them and to describe from memory the contents of a picture they had just seen. The differences between the two groups were striking. The Nupe responded in a piecemeal, enumerative manner, listing the items in the story and the objects in the picture one after the other, with little attempt at organization or integration. The Yoruba, on the other hand, showed much less concern with detail, emphasizing instead the general meaning of what had been presented to them, and the interrelationships of the individual parts. There appeared to be a definite difference in the manner in which memory functioned in the two groups. Nadel notes a parallel between this finding and other aspects of the two cultures. The Nupe pantheon, for instance, consists of a number of different gods and spirits, whose relationship to one another is never clearly defined, and whose functions are relatively independent; among the Yoruba, the gods constitute an organized whole, with a clear hierarchy and a well-understood division of power and responsibility. Nadel's use of objective, experimental methods in the exploration of cultural differences represents a promising and fruitful approach which should be more widely developed.

The study of rumor by Allport and Postman (49) is a significant further development in this field. An analysis of rumors circulating among the American public during 1942 led to the establishment of certain principles regarding the circumstances which facilitated the development of rumors and the reasons why they were accepted and believed. In addition, the authors conducted a number of experiments along the lines suggested by Bartlett's Method of Serial Reproduction. A slide was thrown upon a screen, usually a semi-dramatic picture containing a large number of related details. The experimenter described the picture to the first subject, who could not himself see the screen. A second subject entered the room, and the first subject proceeded to tell him all he could about the picture. This was continued through a "chain" of six or seven subjects. The authors rightly point out that the situation does not exactly reproduce the conditions of rumor-spreading in actual life; among other factors, there is the striving for accuracy on the part of the subjects, which prevents them from acting like spontaneous rumor agents.

Nevertheless, the authors were able to identify three major tendencies which apparently operate in both real life and laboratory rumors. The first is labeled *leveling;* as rumor travels, it tends to grow shorter and more concise. (This appears to contradict the popular impression that rumor grows as it spreads, and it may be that here the real life situation and that in the laboratory do differ.) Secondly, there is the process of *sharpening*, which may be defined as the selective perception, retention, and reporting of a limited number of details from a larger context; it is the reciprocal of leveling. Finally, the principle of *assimilation* has to do with the powerful attractive force exerted upon rumor by the habits, interests and sentiments of the listener.

One of the most convincing examples of the phenomenon of assimilation is found in the successive reproductions of the contents of one picture, representing a subway scene in which two of the passengers are conversing; one of them is a Negro and the other a White man in working clothes. The White man is holding an open razor in his left hand. In over half of the experiments with this picture, the final reproduction located the razor in the hand of the Negro; in some cases the Negro was even reported as "brandishing" it, or as "threatening" the White man with it. It seems clear that the widespread acceptance of the stereotype that the Negro uses a razor in an aggressive fashion is responsible for this result. This does not mean that half the subjects reacted in such a fashion, since one such shift in a rumor chain might be reproduced by all who followed. It does mean that in fifty percent of the *groups* this phenomenon was observed. [Levitt (50) has shown that individuals differ markedly in the degree of distortion which they contribute to the final outcome of the rumor chain.]

There were two striking exceptions to this finding. When Negro subjects were used, there was no such distortion, for obvious reasons; nor did it occur in young children, who had not yet learned the stereotype. A subsequent study by Muhyi (51) indicates that the "movement" of the razor from the White man to the Negro begins to occur in White American children around the twelfth to the thirteenth year. The Allport-Postman study is particularly important as indicating the extent to which our prejudices may distort our perception and recollection of the facts with which we are presented.

It is difficult to exaggerate the importance of the materials reviewed in this chapter for the understanding of certain aspects of social relationships. If what we see is dependent on our wishes as well as on the objective stimuli to perception; if reality is distorted to fit in with our preconceptions; if our group membership determines, at least in part, what the world looks like to us; it follows that a good deal of misunderstanding between individuals, and possibly also between nations, may be due to such group-determined differences in what we perceive. It is not enough to "see ourselves as others see us"; it is at least equally important to see external reality as others see it, or perhaps more accurately, to understand how and why others see external reality as they do. This is not an easy task, but it is an important one, if cooperation is to take the place of misunderstanding. Fundamental differences of interest and opinion may persist, but they will be reduced to the extent that they are now based on lack of knowledge of the way in which functional factors enter into perception and memory.

We may summarize this discussion in Bartlett's words:

> This means that the group itself, as an organized unit, has to be treated as a veritable condition of human reaction. It means that, even if we said everything that theoretically could be said about experience and conduct from the point of view of its determination by external stimulation, or by internal factors of individual character and temperament, we should still leave wholly unexplained some—very likely a large number—of the most important human responses (p. 241).

SUMMARY

Although many of the phenomena of sense perception are undoubtedly due to the nature of the sense organs and of the nervous system, social and cultural influences also play an important part. Examples that may be mentioned in this connection are the socially determined resemblances between members of the Trobriand family, the relation of color perception to color nomenclature, the establishment of social norms in the experimental study of the autokinetic phenomenon, the place of values and needs in determining perception, the variations in the perception of harmony in sound and of the affective qualities of tastes and odors, the degrees of adaptation to pain, the phenomenon of "social time," and many others.

The same considerations apply to the field of memory. Social factors may determine what one remembers, and the studies of testimony and of chain reproduction show the manner and the degree to which reproduction is influenced by the social situation. Ethnic stereotypes may play an important part in causing distortions in both our perception and our recollection of the behavior of members of other groups. Observations among the Zulus and the Swazis indicate that even the manner of remembering may be at least in part socially determined. In the absence of research on memory in a variety of cultures, it is not possible to state whether the "laws" of learning and of forgetting would be equally valid under all social conditions; it seems probable that some of them are related to the nature of the nervous system and would hold true universally.

The effect of social factors on perception and memory has implications of the greatest practical significance.

REFERENCES

1. Malinowski, B. *Sex and Repression in Savage Society.* 1927
2. Klineberg, O. *Race Differences.* 1935
3. Wallis, W. D. *An Introduction to Anthropology.* 1926
4. Mead, M. "The Primitive Child." In Murchison, C., ed. *Hdbk. Child Psychol.* 1933
5. Seligman, C. G. "The Vision of the Natives of British Guinea," *Report of the Cambridge Anthropological Expedition to Torres Straits.* 1901, vol. 2
6. Sherif, M. *The Psychology of Social Norms.* 1936

7. Schonbar, R. A. "The Interaction of Observer-Pairs in Judging Visual Extent and Movement," *Arch. Psychol.*, 1945, No. 299: pp. 1-95

8. Cantril, H. *The "Why" of Man's Experience.* 1950

9. Ames, A. *Some Demonstrations Concerned with the Origin and Nature of Our Sensations: A Laboratory Manual.* 1946

10. Krech, D., and Crutchfield, R. S. *Theory and Problems of Social Psychology.* 1948

11. Bruner, J. S., and Krech, D., eds. *Perception and Personality, A Symposium.* 1950

12. Blake, R. R., and Ramsey, G. V., eds. *Perception: An Approach to Personality.* 1951

13. Levine, R., Chein, I., and Murphy, G. "The Relation of the Intensity of a Need to the Amount of Perceptual Distortion," *J. Psychol.*, 1942, 13: pp. 283-293

14. Bruner, J. S., and Goodman, C. C. "Value and Need as Organizing Factors in Perception." In *Readings in Social Psychology*, T. M. Newcomb and E. L. Hartley, eds., 1947, pp. 99-108

15. Postman, L., Bruner, J. S., and McGinnies, E. "Personal Values as Selective Factors in Perception." In *Readings in Social Psychology*, rev. ed., G. E. Swanson, T. M. Newcomb, and E. L. Hartley, eds. 1952

16. Carter, L. F., and Schooler, K. "Value, Need, and Other Factors in Perception," *Psychol. Rev.*, 1949, 56: pp. 200-207

17. Howes, D. H., and Solomon, R. L. "Visual Duration Threshold as a Function of Word-probability," *J. Exp. Psychol.*, 1951, 41: pp. 401-410

18. Dohrenwend, B. S. Unpublished Ph.D. Dissertation, Columbia University. 1953

19. Cook, P. H. "The Application of the Rorschach Test to a Samoan Group," *Rorschach Res. Exch.*, 1942, 6: pp. 52-60

20. Asch, S. E. *Social Psychology.* 1952

21. Zillig, M. "Einstellung und Aussage," *Ztschr. f. Psychol.*, 1928, 106: pp. 58-106

22. Horowitz, E. L., and Horowitz, R. E. "Development of Social Attitudes in Children," *Sociometry*, 1937-38, I: pp. 301-338

23. Razran, G. "Ethnic Dislikes and Stereotypes: A Laboratory Study," *J. Abn. & Social Psych.*, 1950, 45: pp. 7-27

24. Goring, C. *The English Convict.* 1913

25. Ansbacher, H. "Perception of number as affected by the monetary value of the objects: A critical study of the method used in extended constancy phenomena," *Arch. Psychol.*, 1937, No. 215

26. Allport, G. W., and Kramer, B. M. "Some Roots of Prejudice," *J. of Psychol.*, 1946, 22: pp. 9-39

27. Moore, H. T. *The Genetic Aspect of Consonance and Dissonance.* 1914

28. Helmholtz, H. v. *On the Sensations of Tone as a Physiological Basis for the Theory of Music*. 4th ed. 1912

29. Lin Yu-t'ang. *My Country and My People*. 1935

30. Junker, W. J. *Travels in Africa*. 3 vols. 1890-92

31. Blackwood, B. *Both Sides of Buka Passage*. 1935

32. Freeman, E. *Social Psychology*. 1936

33. Lips, J. E. *The Savage Hits Back*. 1937

34. MacLeod, R. B., and Roff, M. F. "An Experiment in Temporal Disorientation," *Acta Psychol.*, 1936, I: pp. 381-423

35. Dollard, J. *Criteria for the Life History*. 1935

36. Kroeber, A. L. "Elements of Culture in Native California," *Univ. Calif. Publ. Archaeol. & Ethnol.*, 1917-1923, 13: pp. 260-328

37. Hallowell, A. I. "Cultural Factors in the Structuralization of Perception." In *Social Psychology at the Crossroads*, J. H. Rohrer and M. Sherif, eds. 1951, pp. 165-195

38. Sorokin, P. A., and Merton, R. K. "Social Time," *Amer. J. Sociol.*, 1937, 42: pp. 615-629

39. Brown, A. R. *The Andaman Islanders*. 1922

40. Stern, W. "Raum und Zeit als personale Dimensionen," *Acta Psychol.*, 1935, I: pp. 220-232

41. Lazarsfeld, P. F., Jahoda, M., and Zeisl, H. *Die Arbeitslosen von Marienthal*. 1933

42. Mausner, B. "The Effect of Prior Reinforcement on Interaction of Observer Pairs," *Amer. Psychologist*, 1950, 5: pp. 296-297

43. Clark, K. B. "Some Factors Influencing the Remembering of Prose Materials," *Arch. Psychol.*, 1940, No. 253

44. Margolies, H. "The Effect of Race Attitudes on Memory and Perception," Unpublished Master's Essay, Columbia University, 1938

45. Levine, J. M., and Murphy, G. "The Learning and Forgetting of Controversial Material." In *Readings in Social Psychology*, T. M. Newcomb and E. L. Hartley, eds. 1947, pp. 108-115

46. Stern, W. *Beiträge zur Psychologie der Aussage*. 2 vols. 1903-1906

47. Bartlett, F. C. *Remembering*. 1932

48. Nadel, S. F. "A Field Experiment in Racial Psychology," *Brit. J. Psychol.*, 1937, 28: pp. 195-211

49. Allport, G. W., and Postman, L. J. *The Psychology of Rumor*. 1947

50. Levitt, E. Unpublished Ph.D. Dissertation, Columbia University.

51. Muhyi, I. Unpublished Ph.D. Dissertation, Teachers College, Columbia University.

Part Three

DIFFERENTIAL PSYCHOLOGY

Individual and Class Differences

9

INTRODUCTION

We turn now to a different branch of the field of social psychology. In the preceding chapters we have been discussing the problem of the "common human" and have reviewed the material pertinent to the discussion of what constitutes human nature. In the process of this review we have had to pay attention also to differences between groups and cultures, but mainly in order to distinguish between what is common and what is variable. Our concern in the succeeding chapters will be more directly with the problem of variations among human beings—a field which has received the name of Differential Psychology.

This field was for a long time largely neglected. The concern of the earliest psychologists was with the establishment of laws in psychology which should hold good for all individuals. To the extent that individuals differ, their behavior and their introspections can less easily be stated in terms of general principles; consequently these differences were formerly regarded as largely outside the scope of the science of psychology. They might be of practical interest to the social engineer or to the foreman of a factory, perhaps, but not of immediate concern to the psychologist.

It is usual to regard differential psychology as originating mainly in the work of Francis Galton (1). Although there were many precursors, Galton's study of individual differences in imagery, as well as his examination of the genealogies of men of genius, may be regarded as the real starting point. The succeeding development of techniques and approaches in this field, notably the work of Binet (2) in testing intelligence, of Cattell (3) in the study of motor and sensory abilities, of Thorndike (4) in the development of statistical measures, and of William Stern (5) in his analysis of differential psychology as a whole, laid the foundation for further research. Interest in this field has grown enormously, and the careful surveys of the literature (6, 7) indicate its present scope and importance.

It is not usually realized that individual differences in "abilities" are found all the way down the animal scale, even in the simplest biological organisms. Razran (8) reports that in an experiment in which protozoa were conditioned to respond to light, the average number of combinations of stimuli required to produce the conditioned response in 82 cases was 138.5; the range was tremendous, from 79 to 284 combinations. In another study, in which fish were conditioned to respond to sound stimuli, the average number of combinations required in 59 cases was 12.7, and the range from 3 to 35. In all animal experiments comparable variations are found, whether the "problem" to be solved is to respond to a conditioned stimulus, escape from a puzzle box, or learn to run a maze [see Anastasi and Foley (6), p. 95].

HEREDITY AND ENVIRONMENT

The problem of individual differences in psychology cannot be discussed apart from the general and apparently perennial question of heredity and environment. It is obviously outside the province of this book to attempt a complete analysis of this complicated matter, and we shall have to restrict our treatment to certain of the more essential aspects.

In the first place it is important to note that there has been a marked change in the formulation of this problem. It was formerly customary to ask concerning any specific trait or capacity whether it was caused by heredity *or* environment, by nature *or* nurture. There were many discussions, for example, as to whether musical ability was due to the one or the other. The individual was regarded as a sum total of characteristics and capacities, some of which he had inherited, whereas others had been acquired during the course of his lifetime. As an indication of a more constructive and accurate point of view, we may take the treatment of this problem by Woodworth (9). He stresses the fact that both heredity and environment are effective. The influence of heredity may be demonstrated in the case of hybrids; though the mule and the colt both develop in the same prenatal environment, they have different characteristics which may be explained only in terms of a different genetic constitution. On the other hand, a change in the environment of the developing embryo may markedly affect characteristics normally under the control of heredity; for example, an alteration in the chemical content of the fluid in which young fish develop may cause the eyes to be formed closer together, and in some cases even to fuse into one central eye.

Every individual is the resultant of both of these factors. It is inaccurate, however, to say that he is so much heredity plus so much environment. He is not merely the sum of two groups of determinants. Since heredity and environment act upon each other, Woodworth suggests the analogy of a rectangle in which they represent the two dimensions. Individuals may differ from each other in either dimension or in both, and conversely, two individuals may show the same present capacity even though both their heredity and their environment are different.

The analogy of the rectangle must not be pressed too far. The relationship between nature and nurture is a phenomenon of interaction rather than of multiplication. It is probable, however, that no single characteristic is exclusively the result of the one or the other. Stature, for example, has usually been regarded as mainly genetic in origin, and yet we know that the nature of the living conditions may make a substantial difference in this respect. A study by Shapiro (10) has shown that Japanese born in Hawaii grow to be taller than their own relatives born in Japan. The field of botany is full of examples in which the same plant shows entirely different external characteristics if conditions of soil, light and moisture are made to vary. Conversely, the environment cannot act unless there is an organism which can respond to it and can be affected by it, and it is obvious that the nature of the response will differ from one organism to another. This constant interaction is much more complex than Woodworth's analogy would indicate.

Since both nature and nurture are always present, a proper formulation of the controversy would appear to be the one given by Murphy, Murphy and Newcomb (11). They state the problem to be essentially one of "variance," that is to say, the amount of variation between individuals that may be ascribed to nature, and the amount that may be ascribed to nurture. Every individual is the resultant of both, but the differences between individuals may be due more to variation in the one than to variation in the other. The same formulation applies also in the case of group differences; we do not ask whether, for example, the intelligence of Negroes and Whites is due to heredity or environment, but rather whether the apparent differences between the two groups are due to variations in one or the other. It is obvious, therefore, that the field of differential psychology depends in a very direct manner upon the correct answer to the nature-nurture question.

There appears to be some tendency in current social-psychological literature to ignore this whole problem, or to treat it as if it had already been solved. A search through the index of several recent textbooks reveals only sparse and sketchy treatment of what was once regarded as one of the central questions facing the social psychologist. The present writer is convinced that the problem requires more rather than less attention than it has received in the recent past, and that we must direct to it all our ingenuity and scientific skill, in cooperation with our colleagues in genetics and related disciplines, in order to arrive at a clearer understanding of a most important practical, as well as theoretical, issue.

As for the exact nature of the hereditary mechanism, we can do no more than mention a few of the more important principles. The transmission of inherited characteristics takes place through the medium of the chromosomes—microscopic but observable bodies within the germ cells. To explain the manner in which a single chromosome may transmit a number of characters, there has developed the theory of genes, of which there are presumably a large number in each chromosome. It is important to bear in mind that genes are not actual bodies which may be seen under the microscope, although small particles have been observed within each chromosome. At the same time the theory of the gene (12) best fits the complicated facts of genetics. Human characteristics are each determined by a great number of genes—either as a result of their numerical combination, or of their pattern or arrangement within the chromosome. This multiplicity of determining factors makes it difficult to apply directly to human heredity the Mendelian principles.

Of these Mendelian principles, the distinction between dominant and recessive characters must be kept in mind. Dominant characters are those which will be present in the somatoplasm (or the observable organism) if they occur in the germ plasm (i.e., the germ cells); recessive characters are those for which the genes exist in the germ plasm without revealing themselves in characteristics of the body if the corresponding dominant genes are also present. These recessive genes may have an observable effect under certain conditions of mating. Their occurrence explains in part the distinction that has been drawn between phenotype and genotype; the latter refers to genetic constitution, the former to the observable characteristics of the organism. The Mendelian theory makes it possible to see how two individuals might have the same phenotype and still differ in their genetic make-up. This imposes an important limitation in the inference from observable characteristics to the genes underlying them. One person with brown eyes, for example, may have genes which make it possible for him to have blue-eyed children; another brown-eyed individual may have no genes for blue eyes.

Inheritance of Acquired Characters. Although chromosomes and genes are found in all cells of the body, those that are handed on from one generation to another through heredity are located only in the germ cells. This has led to the well-known theory of Weismann (*13*), which states that in hereditary transmission, the only influences which count are located in the germ cells, which are sharply separated from the other cells of the body. This leads directly to the consideration of the inheritance of acquired characters. On the basis of Weismann's theory, such inheritance is impossible since what happens to the somatoplasm does not directly affect the germ cells. Weismann did believe, however, that it might be possible for these modifications to have secondary or indirect effects, and so influence the offspring to some degree.

The problem is of vital importance. If acquired characters can be inherited, the results of education and training may be handed on not only through the social environment, but also in the genetic make-up of future generations. The whole process of evolution might be differently interpreted as a result. As is well known, Lamarck (*14*) based his theory upon it, as in the famous example of the giraffe whose neck became so long as the result of continued stretching to reach the food at the tops of trees, the cumulative effects of this stretching being transmitted from one generation to another. The most direct expression of the opposite view is that of DeVries (*15*) who regarded sudden mutations, which happened to be adapted to the environment, as responsible for the changes which have taken place throughout the animal kingdom.

Research in this field has an interesting history. The earlier experimenters tried cutting off the tails of successive generations of rats, but each generation was born without any obvious change resulting from this method. Later, the work of Kammerer (16), who believed he had proved the inheritance of characteristics induced in the parents by changes in the chemical composition of their environment, attracted great attention. Kammerer wrote and lectured on the basis of these results, and for a time there was a tendency to regard his theory as proven. It then developed that one of his assistants, perhaps in his zeal to prove his master correct, had introduced similar changes in the environment of each succeeding generation, so that no inheritance of this type was involved. Kammerer was so overcome at this revelation that he committed suicide. Pavlov (17) has reported the application of his conditioned reflex method to this problem. It is well known that after repeated association of food with the sound of a bell, the bell alone will elicit salivation in the animal. In this experiment the conditioned reflex was established in a group of rats, and they were then inbred; the next generation acquired the conditioned response after a smaller number of presentations, and so on with each succeeding generation. Pavlov believed it might be possible to breed rats which would salivate at the sound of the bell without any training whatever. This startling result is surrounded by a certain amount of mystery, since in his later publications Pavlov no longer referred to it, and he refused to answer any further questions about it. It is usually believed to be a repetition of what happened in the case of Kammerer, although fortunately without the same tragic consequences. At any rate, the result has not been verified.

A striking investigation in this field has been reported in a series of papers by McDougall (18). The procedure was similar to that used in Pavlov's study, except that the ability to solve a simple water maze was substituted for the formation of a conditioned response. Each generation of rats was taught to run the maze and then inbred, and for each succeeding generation the average number of trials, as well as the average time required to run the maze successfully, were substantially reduced. The results appear clear and incontrovertible. Serious criticisms of a methodological nature have, however, been leveled against McDougall's procedure. The principal objection has been that since in each generation it was obviously impossible to interbreed all the rats, McDougall chose from among them a limited number for this purpose; the question arises as to whether, quite unconsciously, he might have chosen in each generation those rats which had superior maze-running ability, so that the results might have been due not to the inheritance of acquired characters, but to selective breeding.

That this is at least a possibility is indicated by the work of Tryon (19), who used a more complex type of maze, and from each generation of rats chose those with very superior or inferior maze-running ability. These he bred separately, the superior with the superior and the inferior with the inferior. When this procedure had been repeated for several generations, he found that he had developed, by means of such selective breeding, two distinct "races" of rats, differing so clearly in maze-running ability that there was almost no overlapping between them. This study indicates that a result similar to McDougall's may be obtained without the intervention of any inheritance of acquired abilities. Although McDougall states that in his experiments he was careful to choose the poorer rather than the better rats for purposes of inbreeding, and that therefore his results cannot be explained on the basis of selection, this can hardly be regarded as an adequate refutation of an important methodological criticism.

The theory of inheritance of acquired characters has been given political overtones in the Soviet Union, where it has been adopted as official scientific truth, and where all opposition to it is condemned as bourgeois and reactionary. As Huxley (20) points out, genetics in the sense in which we know it, often referred to as neo-Mendelism, was actively developed in the U.S.S.R. after 1922, and first-rate experimental work was conducted in many Soviet laboratories during approximately a decade. The research was stopped by politics around 1932, mainly because a theory was wanted which assigned the chief role to the environment. Earlier, a variant of Lamarck's theory had been developed by Michurin; and one of his followers, Lysenko, succeeded around 1935 in having his master's views adopted as state policy. The Academy of Sciences in Moscow passed the appropriate resolutions, and opponents were forced either to recant or to give up their scientific and academic posts. Incidentally, a motion picture was made glorifying the life and works of Kammerer.

It is hardly necessary to point out that truth cannot be established by governmental fiat, and that a final answer to the question as to whether acquired characteristics can be inherited must be given by further independent, objective research. In the meantime, the conclusion that appears to be justified on the basis of all the available evidence, is that such inheritance has never been satisfactorily demonstrated. It should be added, as Huxley indicates, that attempts to duplicate in other countries the results obtained by Lysenko have failed, and that many geneticists have concluded that Lysenko must have used impure genetic strains in his experiments.

There is one curious aspect of this controversy that should be mentioned. The Soviet followers of Michurin and Lysenko have applied the epithet "racist" to those who have accepted the view of Weismann and Morgan that the germ plasm does not transmit the qualities acquired from the environment. This accusation apparently stems from the view that if we believe in the persistence of hereditary traits, we must also accept the notion that ethnic groups now inferior in achievement will always remain so. Lysenko's position would presumably permit us to hope for an improvement in the germ plasm, once the environment had been changed for the better. A little reflection, however, should have shown the Soviet "geneticists" that they were arguing against their own case. If the germ plasm is affected by the environment, then centuries of living under inferior conditions should surely cause a marked *inherited* degeneration, whereas if the germ plasm is not affected, the hereditary potentialities would remain the same as ever. From this point of view, there would appear to be more "racialism" inherent in the Soviet view than in that of traditional genetics. It is true that, for Lysenko, if and when the environment improved, "heredity" would improve with it, but at any given time the germ plasm of a group of southern Negroes living under backward conditions would, according to this theory, necessarily be inferior; for neo-Mendelian genetics, the germ plasm would be just as sound as ever because it would remain unaffected. It is of course possible for a belief in the immutability of the germ plasm to accompany "racialism," but there is no necessary connection between them.

Eugenics. The fact that improvement may be brought about in a stock by selective breeding, if not by the transmission of training, raises the important question of the applicability of a eugenics program to man. Such a program has attracted the attention and devotion of a number of biologists and geneticists, and in many parts of the world societies have been formed for the purpose of its advancement. It is customary to divide the eugenics platform into a positive and a negative aspect. The positive is the attempt to improve the quality of the stock by selective mating of its superior members. In connection with man, the valid objection has been raised that marriage has become associated with so many factors of an emotional and sentimental nature that the direct application of the same breeding principles used with other animals seems impossible. It seems safe to say that in general relatively few men and women would lend themselves to a breeding experiment of the type which some eugenists have advocated.

On the negative side the eugenics program stands mainly for the elimination of the unfit in a population by preventing their procreation. The method advocated is usually that of sterilization of those who are judged unfit in any serious manner, with the hope that in a generation or two such individuals may appear rarely or not at all. There are many countries and many states in this country which have sterilization laws of this type, although in the majority of cases it is a voluntary sterilization and takes place only with the approval of the persons most concerned. This form of eugenics has usually been received much more favorably than the other. It is important to point out, however, that the objections to it are in some ways at least as serious as those which apply to the more positive program. In the first place, the determination of what is fit or unfit is difficult to make with any objectivity; in one society the physically defective and in another those who criticize their government might seem to be the ones who should be eliminated. In any eugenics program, positive or negative, the community is at the mercy of those who establish the standards of fitness. It is obvious that this possibility leads into such serious danger that the greatest caution is necessary in its application. This danger becomes a real one when we think of the number of outstanding men of genius in our history who have had defects which would lead to their inclusion among the unfit from certain points of view. In the second place, such individuals might not only have defects themselves, but come of families similarly defective. A eugenics program would have prevented their birth, and the loss would have been incalculably greater than any conceivable gain. Third and most important, the reduction in the amount of defect by this method is so small that it would take many generations to effect a perceptible improvement. As Jennings (21) and others have pointed out, although there may be rather more defective offspring proportionately among defective than among normal parents, the large majority of defectives come from parents who are perfectly normal as far as all our tests make it possible to determine. The distinction between phenotype and genotype is pertinent at this point. A great many persons who appear healthy may still be capable of breeding defective children, and since there is no way of determining this in advance, negative eugenics would be of little help in improving the population. Hogben (22) has made a statistical study of the possibility of reducing defects in this manner, and he shows clearly that it is remote.

As a summary standpoint of the views of careful biologists on the questions of eugenics, we may cite the conclusion of Pearl (23):

> In absolute numbers the vast majority of the most superior people in the world's history have in fact been produced by mediocre people or inferior forebears; and, furthermore, the admittedly most superior folk have in the main been singularly unfortunate in their progeny, again in absolute numbers. . . . In human society as it exists under present conditions of civilization, many a gaudy and imposing pheno-type makes a very mediocre or worse genotype . . . and most eugenic selection of human beings is, and in the nature of the case, must be based solely upon phenotypic manifestations (p. 266).

We may add that even in connection with negative eugenics, the report of Myerson and his associates (24) indicates that steriliza-tion must not be expected to effect any substantial reduction in the amount of mental defect and abnormality in the general population.

This problem is on the borderline between biology and social psychology. It is obviously not the province of the psychologist to determine directly the facts or the mechanism of heredity. It is, however, his very serious concern to devise measures of population quality in connection with mental abilities, and to use these as far as possible to indicate the presence or absence of genetic relation-ships. The work of Galton (25) on hereditary genius may be re-garded as a first step in this direction. His results show that there is a definite tendency for ability to run in families, so that eminent men have eminent relatives in a proportion far greater than would be expected by chance. This study inspired the family histories of the Kallikak family by Goddard (26) and of the Jukes family by Dugdale (27) and Estabrook (28); both of these showed the frequency with which defects of a mental and physical nature occurred among the descendants of individuals who were themselves defective. At the other extreme the detailed study of the Edwards family by Winship (29) apparently showed a similar tendency for superior ability and mental adjustment to be found consistently in the same family. All of these studies, however, suffer from a fatal methodological defect, namely, that these families were relatively homogeneous not only in their heredity, but also in their environment. Family histories of this type fail to separate the two factors and are of little help in this problem. More pertinent is the study by Voss (30) of a musician whose first wife was musical and whose second was not; his children by the first wife showed more than the average interest and ability in a musical direction, and those by the second showed nothing outstanding in this respect. It is to be noted that both groups of children lived under the same socioeconomic conditions. Even in this case, since the mother constitutes an important part of the environment of the child, we cannot be certain that the effect is due solely or even primarily to heredity.

STUDIES OF TWINS

In the attempts to devise a technique for the separation of hereditary and environmental factors, the greatest attention has been directed to the question of twins. A distinction is made between identical twins who originate from the division of a single fertilized ovum, and non-identical, or fraternal twins, who develop from two separate fertilized ova. In the case of the former, the heredity is presumed to be identical; in the latter, it is as much alike as in the case of ordinary siblings (i.e., brothers and sisters). Obviously, identical twins must be of the same sex, whereas the non-identical may be of the same or of opposite sexes. It is the sex ratio which constitutes the greatest argument in favor of the existence of identity in twins. If there were no identity, one would expect by chance that there should be just as many like-sex as unlike-sex twins. Actually there are about 63% of like-sex twins, which is due to the fact that 25% of all twins, or 40% of like-sex twins, are identical (31).

Even in the case of identical twins slight differences may be observed, due either to certain asymmetries or to late division of the ovum. The rare cases of Siamese twins and of monsters of various kinds are due to very late and incomplete division. The diagnosis of identity is made on the basis of the general close resemblance, as well as by specific similarities in the prints of the fingers, the palms of the hands, and the soles of the feet. They also have the same shape and arrangement of teeth, belong to the same blood group, and show identical brain wave patterns (6). Identical twins may in addition look like mirror images of each other, so that the left side of the one resembles the right side of the other, and vice versa. In some cases, there may be only one sac or chorion, which makes the diagnosis of identity certain. There are a great many instances, however, in which the diagnosis is exceedingly doubtful, since the similarity may be very close, and yet not close enough to result in any confusion of the two individuals. It is important to keep in mind, therefore, that the distinctions between identical and fraternal twins, upon which so much research has been based, must be used with considerable caution. If we accept the distinction, as most investigators have done, the issue may be put in this way: if variations in heredity are more important than variations in environment, identical twins should resemble each other more closely than do the non-identical in any psychological measures which we use for purposes of comparison; if variations in the environment are more important, the results should be the same for the two groups, since the environments in both cases are presumably identical.

This last point requires a word of comment. The assumption that the environment of twins is necessarily identical has not gone unchallenged. Certainly in the case of unlike-sex twins, the cultural pattern of treatment of boys and girls may play an important part from infancy on. In the case of like-sex twins, the chances for an essential similarity in the environment are much greater, but the very fact of great similarity in appearance may also be responsible for a greater similarity in treatment than would be the case for non-identical twins. With these sources of error in mind, it may still be of interest to summarize a few of the more important studies in this field.

Tallman (32) gave the Stanford-Binet to 162 pairs of twins and to 199 siblings. She found an average difference in I.Q. of 13.14 in the case of siblings, and 7.07 in the case of the twins. This might be regarded as an argument in favor of heredity except for the fact that the environment of siblings, due to the difference in age and to possible changes in the domestic situation or in the family fortunes, may differ much more than in the cases of twins. In order to answer this question, Tallman reports that siblings less than two years apart had an average difference of 11.96, slightly less therefore than that for all siblings, but still substantially greater than the difference in the case of twins. When the group of twins was further subdivided, the following results were obtained:

Opposite-sex twins,	84 pairs, average difference	8.48
Like-sex	78	6.42
Identical	63	5.08
boys	29	5.82
girls	34	4.22
Non-identical	39	7.37
boys	17	7.56
girls	22	7.14

Tallman concludes that among the like-sex twins those who look alike (identical twins) resemble one another more closely in their I.Q. than those who look distinctly different. She regards her results therefore as indicating the greater importance of hereditary factors.

There is, however, the significant fact that the non-identical twins, whether of the same or of opposite sex, resemble each other much more closely in their test scores than do ordinary siblings, in spite of the fact that the hereditary resemblance is the same in the two cases. This in turn seems to point to the significance of environmental factors, although it must be borne in mind that the results of an intelligence test given at different age levels are not strictly comparable.[1] There appears to be only the small difference between 5.08 (for the identical twins) and 7.37 (for the non-identical), i.e., a little more than two points in I.Q., which may safely be ascribed to the greater similarity in heredity. This study may therefore be interpreted as having indicated that heredity does have an effect upon the intelligence test scores, but not as having demonstrated that this effect is a marked one.

The degree of relationship between twins as compared with siblings can be expressed also in terms of the correlation coefficient. The following table from Viteles (33) is based upon results ob-

---

[1] This is due to the tendency for the I.Q. to decrease slightly with age, particularly in the case of the brighter children, because of the manner in which the Binet is constructed.

tained by Thorndike (*34*), Merriman (*35*), Lauterbach (*36*), and others. The correlations refer to intelligence test scores.

Identical twins	.90
All twins	.75
Fraternal twins	.70
Siblings	.50
Cousins	.20
Unrelated	.00

These results apparently demonstrate the effect of both hereditary and environmental factors. The difference in the correlation coefficients for identical twins and fraternal twins argues in favor of hereditary factors; the difference between the latter and siblings, in favor of environment.

The relationship between twins has also been studied in connection with other psychological characteristics. McNemar (*37*) gave five tests of motor skill to 93 pairs of male twins, including 46 nonidentical and 47 identical twins in a junior high school. The correlations ranged from .39 to .56 for the non-identical, and from .71 to .95 for the identical twins. The investigator concludes that hereditary factors play a major part in twin resemblance in motor abilities. It seems probable that heredity would be more important in these than in more intellectual activities, because of the closer dependence upon sensory and muscular development.

A study of the handwriting of a pair of male identical twins and of female Siamese twins has been made by Seeman and Saudek (*38*). A detailed examination showed a marked degree of similarity in both cases. It is interesting to note that Newman (*39*), who examined the same pair of Siamese twins, found them to differ rather markedly in their personalities. This seems to be at the same time an argument against graphology as a means of personality diagnosis and in favor of the possibility that identical twins may develop in different ways.

One of the most striking studies in this field is that by Lange (*40*), who in the Bavarian prisons found 30 men with twin brothers. There were 13 who were identical twins, and of these, 10 had twin brothers also in prison. Of the 17 fraternal pairs, only 2 men had twin brothers also in prison. Lange states that even in the detailed nature of their criminal careers there was a close resemblance within each pair of identical twins. He concludes that crime is due primarily to destiny, which in turn has its basis in the germ plasm and not the environment. These results have apparently received a certain degree of confirmation in the study by Rosanoff (41) of twin resemblances in psychosis. The only questions which we must ask are whether the environment of the identical twins was any more similar than that of the non-identical, and whether on the average they were separated at about the same time of life. If the results cannot be explained on the basis of this environmental difference, Lange's study must be regarded as an important argument in favor of the hereditary basis of similarities in personality. This does not mean, however, that criminality as such is inherited. There remains the possibility that certain personality tendencies are inherited, and that under certain social conditions these will readily lead to crime.

What is probably one of the most important series of investigations in this field is that conducted by Kallmann (42) on the inheritance of schizophrenia. In one study carried out in the mental hospitals of New York State, 174 identical twin pairs were located, among whom one twin was schizophrenic; in 85.8% of the cases, the other identical twin was schizophrenic also. The concordance was considerably lower in the case of non-identical twins. When a number of additional varieties of family relationship were explored, it was found that the greater the degree of biological affinity, the greater the chance of concordance in the incidence of the disease. Kallmann concludes that the hereditary factor in schizophrenia has been amply demonstrated. The results which he obtained are certainly striking; it should not be overlooked, however, that the closer the degree of biological relationship, the more similar (in most cases) will be the environmental influences to which the individuals concerned will be subjected. With reference to identical twins, for example, Carter (43) expresses the opinion that their environments "are on the average much more similar than those of fraternal twins" (p. 246); he cites a number of facts to support this conclusion. This cannot be interpreted as disproving Kallmann's thesis, but it does indicate the need for caution before regarding the matter as entirely settled. It may very well be that hereditary factors exert an influence, but the extent as well as the precise nature of that influence require further investigation.

In most of the cases studied, the identical twins were reared together; and as has been mentioned, some of the striking similarities between them may be explained on that basis. For that reason, the interest of investigators in this field has been aroused particularly by the cases of identical twins reared apart. Newman (44) and his collaborators report on twenty such cases, all of them studied with great care and in considerable detail, with special reference to any differences in the environment which might be expected to affect ability or personality. They had all been separated early in life and saw little or nothing of each other until they had become adults. From the point of view of the present discussion, the analysis of the educational experience of the separated twins has special importance. Newman writes: "It was found that whenever the educational experiences of a pair of twins differed to a marked extent, the twin with the greater amount of education had a distinctly higher score in all ability and scholastic achievement tests, while in those cases where there was no difference in education, or only a small difference, the scores of the twins of a pair tended to be about as similar as the average of one-egg twins reared together" (p. 1).

The case of twins Gladys and Helen is particularly instructive. Gladys stopped school after the third grade, whereas Helen went on through college. In the Stanford-Binet, there was a difference of 24 points in I.Q.; Helen scored 116, and Gladys, 92. A second pair differed by 19 points. [A similar investigation in England (6) also revealed a pair of identical twins with a difference of 19 points in I.Q.] In the majority of cases, the differences in educational opportunities were small, and the differences in I.Q. correspondingly so. Newman concludes: "From this we may draw the conclusion that small differences in education do not appreciably affect ability, but that large differences in education may induce important differences in ability" (p. 3).

Taking the group as a whole, the average difference in I.Q. was 7.95 with a range from 0 to 24. This means that twins reared apart may resemble each other very closely, but that there may also in some cases be marked differences between them, and the results are therefore difficult to interpret in connection with the nature-nurture controversy.

One of the reasons for the difficulty in interpretation is the fact that the environments to which the separated twins went were in some cases similar, and in others dissimilar. If the twins grow up in separate but more or less equivalent environments, the similarities between them may be due to that fact in addition to the similar heredity. Differences in age at the time of separation may also have had an effect. The problem is further complicated by the fact that in the case of identical twins reared together, whereas the average difference between the individuals in each pair is only 5.3 I.Q. points, the range of the differences is from 0 to 20. Why there should ever be a difference of 20 points in I.Q. between two individuals whose heredity and environment are both presumably identical (or nearly so) is difficult to explain. The Dionne quintuplets are also reported (45) to show definite individual variations, in spite of their biological and environmental "identity." A similar range was found also in the case of the Morlok quadruplets, among whom personality differences were especially conspicuous (46). It is of course probable that the social environment does differ to some degree for each individual even in such closed groups. What is needed in this whole field is a much more careful analysis of the nature of the environment in each case and of the manner in which the individual and his environment interact.

Newman and his collaborators (47) maintain a middle-of-the-road position in their interpretation of the data. They feel rightly that any dogmatic conclusion is unwarranted. In the writer's opinion, the study of twins indicates the presence of both hereditary and environmental influences in the causation of individual differences, with the latter playing the larger part.

It should be added that in a large number of investigations reported, the twin correlations on personality tests tend to be considerably lower than on tests of ability; there is also considerable variation depending on the particular personality tests used. Newman believes that "there are many evidences that environmental differences have caused greater differences in personality than in any other traits" (44, p. 6).

Before leaving the field of family resemblances in mental test performance, mention should be made of an approach by Thorndike (48) to this problem. He gave intelligence tests to 1800 pairs of siblings and found a positive correlation between them of .60. It happens, however, that in a previous study by Pearson (49) of family resemblances in physical traits the correlations obtained were .52 for eye color, .55 for hair color, and .49 for cephalic index. Thorndike argues that since the relationship in intelligence is approximately the same as for physical traits known to be determined by heredity, it is reasonable to assume that intelligence is similarly determined. This inference appears on the surface to be reasonable, but it is not really justified. There are many possible reasons why two similar correlations, even in the case of the same individuals, may be due to entirely different factors. The similarity between them may be largely a matter of chance.

This does not mean that there is no genetically determined family relationship in intelligence; it merely means that this argument cannot be accepted as it stands. In all probability intelligence is to a certain degree inherited along family lines, although there is no doubt that social and environmental factors exercise a constant and important influence.

OCCUPATIONAL DIFFERENCES

A great many investigations agree in their demonstration that occupational groups differ markedly from one another in their mental test performance (6). The individual studies differ in the details of their procedure and in the tests used, but show substantial agreement in their results. The investigation by Collins (50) may be taken as representative, and his results are presented in the following table.

Occupation	No. of Families	Range of Middle 50%	Median I.Q.
Professional	90	106-126	116
Clerical	131	105-122	113
Managerial	165	104-123	112
Trade	413	100-120	110
Foreman	106	98-118	109
Skilled labor	569	94-114	104
Unskilled labor	377	85-108	95

It may be added that results of this type are found not only in the case of school children (as in Collins' study and many others), but also among adults (51) and among pre-school children (52). They were not demonstrated to exist in the case of children below one year of age (53), but in view of the difficulty of equating these tests of infants with those used in the case of older children, the interpretation of this study is doubtful. In general we may say that the evidence conclusively demonstrates a relationship between socioeconomic status as indicated by occupation and the scores obtained on the standard intelligence tests.

In the study of gifted children by Terman and his associates (54), it was also revealed that extraordinary ability was found much more frequently in the upper than in the lower economic groups. The following table shows the distribution of occupations of the fathers of the gifted children, compared with the proportion of these occupations in the whole population of Los Angeles and San Francisco, where the study was conducted.

Occupation	Percentage of Gifted Children	Occupations in General Population
Professional	29.1%	2.9%
Public Service	4.5	3.3
Commercial	46.2	36.1
Labor	20.2	57.7

A study among Negro college freshmen at West Virginia State College showed a similar hierarchy (55). The results follow:

Occupation	Number	%	Median	Range of Middle 50%
Professional	49	11.1	98.15	72-150
Commercial	18	4.1	94.99	68-157
Artisan	28	6.4	93.50	80-135
Skilled labor	182	41.3	87.50	60-126
Unskilled labor	164	37.1	73.10	52-103

The test used was the American Council Psychological Examination, and the results are not directly comparable with those reported above. The occupational hierarchy, however, is similar. [For additional references see Anastasi and Foley (6) and Tyler (7).]

The results are clear, but the interpretation is very difficult. There are at least two ways of explaining the data. One may argue that these differences point to variations in the hereditary intelligence of the occupational groups, that those in the upper socioeconomic levels are there because of their superior intelligence, which is transmitted to their children. On the other hand it might be argued that the difference in "intelligence" as measured by the tests is not the cause, but the effect of the socioeconomic variations, and that the superior home and school environment of the more favored groups is responsible for their better performance. It is of course also possible that both factors are operative. As the results stand, they lend themselves equally well to either of these interpretations. It is important to see what additional light may be thrown upon them by other pertinent material.

THE EFFECT OF SCHOOL TRAINING

A direct approach to this problem is the investigation of the degree to which a change in the environment will effect a change in the test scores. If we can study the same children in both favorable and unfavorable environments, we may hope to determine to what extent the environment is responsible. Obviously the environment is a complex of a great many factors and requires the most careful analysis, but we shall be most concerned here with the effect of a change in education and a change in the economic status of the home.

In connection with the effect of school training, several significant studies have been conducted by Wellman. In one of these (56) she observed the effect of nursery school training on the intelligence test scores of children. She had of course a control group, matched with the experimental group in every way except that it did not receive this training. The results showed significant and marked gains in I.Q. in the case of the experimental group—gains which were maintained over a period of four to eight years during which the children were studied. Wellman concludes: "A permanent change in intellectual standing can be effected in one to one-and-one-half years that will last four to eight years." In a later study (57), in which the same subjects were followed throughout their educational careers, the differences were so pronounced that the author concluded that "pre-school attendance permanently affected mental ability, resulting in higher scores at high-school and college ages."

The I.Q. may move downward as well as up. Wellman (58) reports the results of a three-year study of pre-school age children who were placed in an orphanage, with subsequent decreases in I.Q. ranging in amount up to 43 points. One child dropped from an initial I.Q. of 103 to one of 60; another, from 98 to 61. Twenty-six such children in less than two years dropped on the average from 90 to 74. Although this study does not deal with schooling in the strict sense, it represents an aspect of Wellman's important investigation of changes in I.Q. resulting from environmental influences, and has therefore been included at this point.

An extensive study by Schmidt (59) on the effect of education on the I.Q.'s of mentally retarded children has attracted considerable attention because of the remarkable results reported. The subjects of the investigation were 254 boys and girls between the ages of twelve and fourteen with an initial average Stanford-Binet I.Q. of 52.1, ranging from 27 to 69. In the course of a three-year especially-devised training program, an average gain of almost 41 points in I.Q. was obtained, with a corresponding improvement in educational achievement. This result is so extreme that it is not surprising to find the study subjected to careful and searching criticism. It should be added that the results of Wellman's investigations have also been queried on the basis of the techniques used, and more especially because of some of the statistical problems involved. These criticisms must of course be taken seriously, but it seems probable that although they may throw doubt on the *extent* of the changes reported, they do not disprove the *fact* of change. In some instances negative results have been reported by investigators working in this area, which may mean that some varieties of educational experience do exert a positive effect, and others do not. As Anastasi and Foley (7) conclude, "it is apparent that both the nature of the training and the nature of the subjects determine the degree to which intellectual performance level can be raised by training" (p. 224).

Since there can be no doubt that in general the schooling of children in the higher occupational levels is of a superior type, this fact may certainly account for part of the obtained differences among socioeconomic groups in mental test performance. The further fact that the superior schooling of the higher economic groups continues for a much longer period of time than in the case of the investigations reported above, would appear to strengthen this conclusion.

THE INTELLIGENCE OF FOSTER CHILDREN

As for the second approach, namely, by a study of changes in the home environment, the most satisfactory technique has been developed in the study of foster children. If children are taken from poor to good, or at least better, home environments, a direct indication of the extent of the environmental effect should be obtainable. There are at least four important investigations in this field, differing in their approach and, as we shall see, in their interpretation, but all of sufficient importance to warrant somewhat detailed consideration.

The first of these to be described is the well-known study by Freeman, Holzinger and Mitchell (*60*) on foster children in and near the city of Chicago. One part of the study dealt with 130 pairs of siblings who had been separated four years or more. The homes to which these children went were rated by field workers, and were found to differ considerably. The investigation showed that the average test score for siblings in poorer homes was 85.7, and for those in better homes, 95.0—a difference of 9.3 points. Various factors make a correction necessary, and the investigators estimate that the real difference is about six points. If we could assume that on the average the intelligence of siblings is about the same, this difference would be attributable to the nature of the home environment.

A more direct method was applicable in the case of 74 children who were retested after they had lived four years in their foster homes. On the first test their average score was 91.2, and on the second, 93.7—a gain of 2.5 points, which in this case is statistically significant. This result appears much more striking when it is further analyzed. It was found, for example, that those children who went to better homes gained 5.3, and those in poorer ones, 0.1. Those who were adopted at an early age gained more; children who were under twelve at the age of re-test gained on the average 5.2, and those over twelve showed an insignificant loss of 0.4.

Correlations were calculated for the degree of resemblance between siblings. It was found that when they had been separated before either one was six years old, the correlation coefficient was .25; when the foster homes were of different grade, it was .19. As was indicated above (see p. 244), there is a correlation of at least .50 for siblings brought up together, and the results of Freeman and his collaborators show the extent to which this resemblance may be decreased when the home environments differ.

Finally, the test scores of the foster children were compared according to the occupations of the foster fathers, with the following results.

Occupation	Average I.Q.	No. of Cases
Professional	106.8	61
Semi-professional and business	101.1	160
Skilled labor	91.6	149
Semi- and slightly-skilled	84.9	19

There were no unskilled laborers among the foster parents. The table shows a hierarchy similar to that reported for occupational groups in general, although the figures are somewhat lower for foster children than for those born into homes of corresponding quality. This discrepancy in the scores argues in favor of native factors, if it were certain that the treatment accorded the two groups of children was the same in every particular, and that their social environments were identical. This assumption is questionable, however, since we have no data concerning the very early training of the children before they were placed in the foster homes, nor as to the frequently unintended but nonetheless existent differences in the attitudes of many of the parents. The knowledge that a child is "of one's own blood" may give rise to certain expectations, and therefore to a certain kind of treatment, which may not be operative in the case of foster children. It is difficult to ascertain with any definiteness the force of this argument, but it is probable that it has considerable significance.

The fact that the hierarchy of occupational groups exists among foster children would seem to be a strong argument in favor of the environmental hypothesis. It seems difficult otherwise to understand why children going into professional homes should differ so markedly (on the average by more than twenty points in I.Q.) from those going to homes of semi- and slightly-skilled laborers. It may be added that since there were no really "poor" homes among the foster parents, even this large difference may still not represent the whole possible environmental effect. The significance of this argument is weakened, however, by the possibility that another factor is operative, namely, a selective effect upon the placement of children. It has been suggested that professional people will either demand or be given the brighter children; they may ask for some indication of the mental level of the children they propose to adopt, or the placement bureau of the orphanage may attempt to "match" the children with their prospective parents. That this procedure is followed in many institutions is certain. Freeman and his associates are of course aware of this possibility and discuss it at considerable length, but point out that from their knowledge of the conditions of placement in the institutions from which they obtained their children, there seems little possibility that selection entered to any important degree. If that can be regarded as certain, the strength of the environmental explanation of the results is greatly increased.

It would undoubtedly aid the final evaluation of results of this kind, however, if more direct information could be obtained as to the degree to which selective factors related to intelligence may enter into the placement of children in one foster home or another— whether, for example, similarity of appearance is more or less important than mental level, whether foster parents ask for I.Q.'s and whether the institution furnishes such information, whether they are content to know that the child is "intelligent" or insist upon knowing just how intelligent he is, and so on.

In summary it may be stated that this investigation constitutes an important argument in favor of an environmental explanation of occupational differences in intelligence. The improvement in the scores of the children after re-test, the fact that children in superior homes rank considerably higher than their siblings in poorer ones, and the occupational hierarchy found among the foster children, all point in that direction. On the other hand, the fact that the foster children do not do so well as children born into similar homes argues in favor of hereditary factors. The investigators themselves interpret their results as indicating that the environment is much more important than is usually realized.

Another important study in this field was made by Burks (61). The approach in this case was to compare the degree of resemblance between parents and their children on the one hand, and foster parents and their foster children on the other. The subjects were homogeneous as to ethnic background and educational opportunity, and the study was conducted in three California cities, San Francisco, Los Angeles and San Diego. The children were all placed in the foster homes before the age of twelve months, with three months as the average age of placement. The experimental group consisted of 214 children and 342 foster parents, and the control group, of 105 children and 205 parents. The environments of the two groups were carefully matched by field workers. The correlation of test scores of parents and children gave the following results: foster father and foster child, .07; foster mother and foster child, .19; own father and child, .45; own mother and child, .46. There is obviously a much greater resemblance in intelligence when there is also a greater similarity in heredity, with the environment presumably held constant. The results are interpreted therefore as arguing definitely for the operation of hereditary factors. The question arises here again, however, as to whether the environment of a foster child is really identical with that of an own child. As was pointed out above, the very fact that parents will look for resemblances to themselves in their own children may be regarded as helping to create such resemblances.

In a second portion of the study correlations were calculated between the I.Q.'s of the foster children and the quality of their environment, measured by a rating scale which took into account a large number of the characteristics of the home. The correlation coefficient was .42; since this figure is squared in order to indicate the factors common to the two variables, it was concluded that the total contribution of the measurable home environment to the intelligence of the child is about 17%. The remaining 83% presumably represents the contribution of heredity. This conclusion of Burks has attracted considerable attention and has been subjected to criticism from various quarters. Apart from the doubtful procedure of attaching definite statistical figures to the relative importance of nature and nurture, there is the more important objection that the home does not constitute the totality of the child's environment. There may be many other factors—the school, the neighborhood, friends, recreations, etc.—which may also play a significant part and account for a portion of the 83% ascribed to heredity. There is the additional fact that *measurable* home environment is not the same as total home environment, and that an error consequently enters into the result which makes the use of actual percentages a still more doubtful procedure. Burks recognizes that the measures she uses do not exhaust the scope of environmental influence, and it is all the more surprising therefore to find her giving so much weight to this one correlation.

In this connection, it is necessary to keep in mind Freeman's conclusion that the environment may raise or depress the mental level of a child by ten points or more in the I.Q. Since, however, the occupational differences referred to above show a disparity of about twenty points in the I.Q. of the best and the poorest groups, the addition of the ten points to those of low economic status, and the subtraction of an equal amount from those most favorably situated, would result in the complete disappearance of the difference between them. If this analysis is correct, and it seems a logical one, the conclusion is justified that there is nothing in the occupational hierarchy that cannot be explained on the basis of the environmental hypothesis.

There is an additional point which requires consideration. The conclusion that occupational differences in intelligence may be explained on an environmental basis does not mean that there are no inherited differences in intelligence as regards individuals. Within each occupational group there is still a wide variation. The son of one lawyer may have a very much higher I.Q. than the son of another. Although we are not suggesting that one professional home is necessarily the equal of another, the great range of differences within the professional group in all probability requires at least in part an explanation in terms of heredity. Adlerian psychologists may point to position in the family and to compensatory mechanisms as explaining these differences, but it is much more likely that they have also a biological basis.

The importance of the distinction between individual and group differences in the nature-nurture problem comes out clearly in connection with an interesting third study in this field. Leahy (62) approaches the problem somewhat as Burks did, through the comparison of two groups of children living in approximately identical environments. One group consisted of adopted children, unrelated to the persons who shaped the environment; the other consisted of children living with their own parents. Both heredity and environment operate to produce resemblances in the latter group, only environment in the former. It is argued that with measurable environment identical for both groups of children, differences in the relationship of the child's intelligence to that of the parents must be the result of the presence of a common heredity in the case of true parents and offspring, and the result of the absence of hereditary likeness in the case of adopted parents and children. The problem of selective placement does not enter into this study, since the two groups of subjects were not compared with each other, but were deliberately matched for a number of factors—sex, race and nationality, size of community, mental age, paternal occupation, and fathers' and mothers' schooling. The adopted children had all been in the foster homes from the age of six months or younger. At the time of the study the age range was from five to fourteen, with the average 9:3 for the adopted group and 9:4 for the controls. There were 194 subjects in each group.

The main results of this study refer to the degree of relationship between the child's I.Q., as measured by the Otis Self-Administering

Test, Intermediate Form, and various aspects of the environment, including the characteristics of the parents. They are presented in the following table.

Correlated Factor	Adopted Children	Control Children
Father's Otis score	.15	.51
Mother's Otis score	.20	.51
Mid-parent Otis score	.18	.60
Father's vocabulary	.22	.47
Mother's vocabulary	.20	.49
Mid-parent vocabulary	.24	.56
Environmental status	.19	.53
Cultural index of home	.21	.51
Child training index	.18	.52
Economic index	.12	.37
Sociality index	.11	.42
Father's education	.16	.48
Mother's education	.21	.50
Mid-parent education	.20	.54
Father's occupational status	.12	.45

The differences between the degree of relationship for the two groups are impressive, and appear to point to a much greater resemblance between children and parents when there is a hereditary as well as an environmental factor at work. The most pertinent question that arises is the one referred to above, namely, the possibility that true parents look for greater resemblances in the case of their own children, and that this may play a part in determining such resemblances. It is doubtful, however, whether it should be regarded as affecting the findings to any great extent. Leahy's contention that the results of this study show the hereditary component in intelligence tests to have a greater significance than the environmental component would seem justified, with the important limitation that it has been shown to apply in the case of a group with relatively homogeneous background, and that the results are not to be extended beyond these limitations without further proof.

This restriction in the validity of Leahy's results is not merely the one commonly expressed in psychological research, namely, that the conclusion must not be extended beyond the scope of the actual data. In this particular case it has a different meaning. The environments included in this study were all of a superior type, and we find none of the marked discrepancies in home background and educational opportunity characterizing the occupational groups pre-viously discussed. Children are rarely adopted into homes comparable to those of the day laborer or farmer group in the occupational hierarchy. It is highly probable therefore that whereas the average differences between occupations are best explained in terms of environmental factors, the individual or family differences within the occupation, or within any relatively homogeneous background, may be strongly influenced by heredity. That parents and children should resemble each other is to be expected; that day laborers as such are inferior and have inferior children has never been proven, and cannot be until the economic system gives them exactly the same opportunities for advancement as it does to the sons and daughters of professional and business men.

A fourth important study in this field is represented by the long-range project conducted by Skodak and Skeels (63), who investigated the intellectual development of foster children over a period of thirteen years. One hundred of the original sample of 306 children were followed throughout this whole period, and they consistently obtained a high average I.Q., varying between 112 and 117. This result was regarded as especially noteworthy, since 80 of the true mothers, in all probability representative of the entire group, averaged only 93. The investigators therefore concluded that the more favorable environment in which these foster children were placed was responsible for a substantial rise over the average I.Q. which might have been anticipated if inherited factors were alone responsible. This result has been questioned, in part because the majority of these children were illegitimate, and there was no way of determining the inherited capacity of the fathers.

It is a striking and somewhat discouraging fact that in these four studies, the investigators responsible for two of them (Freeman et al., Skodak and Skeels) favor an explanation of their results in environmental terms, whereas the remaining two (Burks and Leahy) prefer to account for theirs on the basis of inheritance. The writer has given his reasons for concluding that the range of individual and family variations *within* the same socio-economic group requires an appeal, at least in part, to hereditary factors. The variations *among* socio-economic groups appears, however, to be much more adequately explained by the manifest differences in educational opportunities (in the widest sense) available to such groups.

THE CUMULATIVE EFFECTS OF INFERIOR ENVIRONMENT

This last conclusion is strengthened by the results of a series of investigations which indicate that when environmental opportunities are inferior, there is a gradual deterioration in intelligence-test scores. Reference has already been made to one of Wellman's studies, in which it was shown that children placed in an orphanage underwent such a deterioration. Other studies in this field did not follow up the same children, but relied mainly on a comparison of the test performance of children of different ages living in an inferior environment. The results are impressive.

One of the earliest of these studies, but one which is still pertinent, is that by Gordon (64) on canal-boat and gypsy children in England. The parents of the canal-boat children traveled about a great deal, and the children went to special schools only when the boats were tied up at the docks; their average school attendance was about five percent of that of ordinary school children. The average I.Q. of the 76 subjects in this group was 69.6; more striking was the fact that it declined sharply with age, dropping from 90 in the case of the four-to-six year group to 60 for children over twelve. A similar, though less marked decline was noted in the case of the gypsy children.

This decrement with age has been reported for several groups of American children living in relatively isolated and underprivileged environments, usually in the mountain areas of southern and border states. One such study was conducted by Sherman and Key (65) on 102 children in the "hollows" of the Blue Ridge Mountains of Virginia, about 100 miles from Washington, D.C. On the Pintner-Cunningham test the average I.Q. dropped from 84 at ages 6-8 to 53 at ages 10-12. For the Goodenough Draw-a-Man test, it went from 80 to 71 during the same period, dropping to 49 at ages 14-16. Similar results were obtained by Hirsch (66) in various mountain regions of Kentucky, where the average I.Q. based on the Pintner-Cunningham and Dearborn tests showed a drop from 87 at ages 5-6 to 73 at 13. Asher (67), also working with mountain children in Kentucky, reported that with the Myers Mental Measure, I.Q.'s declined from 83.5 at age 7 to 60.6 at 15. In the case of East Tennessee mountain children, Wheeler (68) compared the results obtained from the administration of group tests to children in 40 mountain schools on two different occasions, first in 1930 and again in 1940. During that period there was a substantial improvement in conditions of schooling, and the median I.Q. showed a corresponding rise from 82 to 93. In both years the usual decrement with age was noted; in 1930 the I.Q. dropped from 95 at age 6 to 74 at age 16; in 1940, from 103 at age 6 to 81 at age 15.

The evidence along these lines is so overwhelming that the cumulative effect of inferior environment on reducing intellectual achievement as measured by mental-test scores can hardly be questioned. In this case no alternative explanation of the results carries conviction. Taken together, the studies constitute a powerful argument in favor of the important part played by educational factors in determining group variations in the level of the I.Q.

THE PROBLEM OF "RACIAL DEGENERATION"

In connection with the occupational hierarchy in intelligence test performance, a number of writers have expressed concern over the existence of a differential birth rate, with a tendency for wealthier and more successful families to have comparatively fewer children than those at lower economic levels. There has been talk of race suicide, of degeneration, of a gradual decrease in the level of intelligence and ability. A number of years ago R. B. Cattell (69) analyzed this occupational hierarchy in the city of Leicester, England, and in rural Devonshire, and related the data to the average size of family at different I.Q. levels. He estimated that this would result in a decline in average I.Q. for the total population of about three points per generation, or one point per decade. "If this were to continue for 300 years half of the population would be mentally defective" (p. 43). Cattell expresses great concern over what he calls "the decline of British intelligence," and urges the immediate adoption of eugenic measures to counteract this disturbing and potentially disastrous trend.

Burt (70) is also concerned with the negative correlation between "innate intelligence" and size of family, and concludes that the average level of intelligence in the general population is declining. He is considerably less pessimistic, however, than Cattell, mainly because the examination of actual data obtained from London school children shows the decline to be much less alarming than had been anticipated. He points out that the actual figures for recent years compared with those obtained a generation ago reveal changes in the proportion of bright and dull children decidedly smaller than the anticipated rate of decline would imply. Regarding the decline, Burt writes: "If required to make a guess at the most probable figure for London, I would be disposed to put it as nearer 1.5 I.Q. points per generation than 3.0 points. I should be surprised if it was much lower than 1.0 points or much higher than 2.0 points" (p. 26).

Burt wisely points out that what we need in this field is less speculation and more collection of objective data by trained psychologists and statisticians. Thomson (71) makes the same suggestion, and he and his colleagues (72) found it possible to analyze just such data in connection with two very extensive surveys of the mental test performance of Scottish school children. A remarkable aspect of these surveys was the fact that they included extremely large and truly representative samples of one age group, namely eleven-year-old children; there were 87,498 in the 1932 survey, and 70,805 in 1947. On the group test used, the average score in 1932 was 34.5 points, and in 1947 it was 36.7 points. In other words, there was no deterioration, and no verification of the dire predictions regarding the "decline of racial intelligence." On the contrary, there was if anything a slight improvement. A supplementary study using the individual Binet scale gave comparable results. One thousand children in 1932 obtained an average I.Q. of 101.6; 874 children in 1937 scored 100.1; 1,215 children in 1947 scored 102.5. In the United States, an analysis of the test scores obtained by army recruits in the First and Second World Wars, using the same measuring instrument, again showed no deterioration, but rather a marked improvement in performance on the second occasion (73).

These results fit in with our thesis that fear of a decline in intelligence, based upon the occupational hierarchy and a differential birth rate, is not warranted. (It should be added that recent statistical studies have indicated a partial reversal in the trend of the birth rate, with the wealthiest families having a relatively large number of children.) The apparent inferiority of those in poor economic classes will in all probability disappear as soon as their cultural and educational environment is raised to a satisfactory level. A wise eugenics program in that case would focus attention upon such an environmental improvement rather than upon the hypothetical dangers arising from differences in the birth rate. An improvement of this type would have also the direct eugenic effect of improving the community by increasing the chances of bodily as well as of mental health.

Whatever the final conclusion may be regarding the causes of the occupational hierarchy, it must be kept in mind that there is a tremendous amount of overlapping between the groups. In other words, in spite of the difference in averages between the children of professional men and laborers, there is a substantial number in the latter group superior to the professional average. A consistent eugenics program would concern itself therefore not merely with occupational groups as such, but would be obliged to choose from within each group those most capable of producing superior off-spring. It becomes again a matter of superiority of families or of individuals rather than of groups. A further correction would have to be made by the addition to the scores of those in a poor environment of an amount corresponding to their handicaps, and by a corresponding subtraction from the scores of the superior groups. That this is hardly feasible goes without saying. In the light of these various considerations, it is not difficult to understand why some eugenics societies have altered their original program substantially in the direction of working toward an improved environment instead of attempting first to improve heredity, and why they are laying more and more stress on individual rather than on group differences.

Throughout this account of occupational differences, the criterion used for the measurement of intelligence is the intelligence test. The use of this measure raises a number of important questions, only a few of which may be touched upon here.[2] It is, however, important to mention at this point that psychologists do not regard the intelligence test as a measure of native intelligence independent of environmental factors, but rather as a measure of achievement into which both native and acquired factors enter. If the test is given to a group of children all of whom have had approximately equal environmental opportunities, the differences in test scores will probably correspond roughly to differences in native ability. If, on the other hand, the background differs markedly, the test scores may be affected by it to such a substantial degree that any conclusion as to variations in native intelligence would be unwarranted. Tests may still be of use in vocational guidance or in school placement, but they will have to be interpreted with caution until the necessary corrections have been made for the element of nurture.

[2] For further discussion of the uses and abuses of intelligence tests see 7, 73, 74.

There is one final point that should be made. Studies (75) have shown that at least part of the superiority in the test performance of upper economic groups may be due to the specific content of the tests. The questions asked often deal with upper- or middle-class experiences; the objects referred to may be found much less frequently in lower-class environments. A careful item analysis has shown in detail just how the upper economic groups are favored and their superior performance facilitated as a result. This finding should serve as an additional criticism of the assumption that the occupational hierarchy is necessarily to be explained in hereditary terms. It is scientifically safer to conclude that the occupational differences in measured intelligence depend certainly to some degree, and probably entirely, on the relative opportunities created by the background for the acquisition of the information and the techniques which aid in the solution of the problems presented by the tests. (We shall return to the problem of socioeconomic differences in connection with the discussion of Culture and Personality.)

REGIONAL DIFFERENCES IN INTELLIGENCE

Similar considerations apply to differences in mental test performance among children in different regions, and particularly in the case of rural and urban communities. Extensive studies by Book (76), Pressey (77), and others find definite evidence for the superiority of urban groups in this respect. As in the case of the occupational hierarchy, there is the difficulty of knowing what is the cause and what the effect in the explanation of the findings. It is possible to argue that the city environment, with its better schools and more varied opportunities for education, creates the difference between the two groups; it may also be urged on the other hand that there has been a selective migration of the superior individuals from the country to the city, resulting in the better showing of the urban group.

That environmental factors undoubtedly play a part has been pointed out by Shimberg (78), whose investigation showed the important influence of previous information in certain types of intelligence tests. The study indicated that for the usual test the questions asked were such as to give to city children a definite advantage. It was possible to devise an information test based upon the experience of rural children in which urban children were at a definite disadvantage and showed themselves to be inferior. Shimberg's opinion is that one procedure is as reasonable as the other, and that neither one warrants any conclusion as to superior or inferior native intelligence. As an extreme example of the manner in which background factors may enter into test performance, Pressey (79) cites the experience of an investigator among the Kentucky "poor whites." He presented the familiar Binet problem: "If you went to the store and bought 6 cents' worth of candy and gave the clerk 10 cents, what change would you receive?" One youngster replied, "I never had 10 cents and if I had I wouldn't spend it for candy, and anyway candy is what your mother makes." The examiner made a second attempt and reformulated the problem as follows: "If you had taken 10 cows to pasture for your father and 6 of them strayed away, how many would you have left to drive home?" The child replied: "We don't have 10 cows, but if we did and I lost 6, I wouldn't dare go home." The examiner made one last attempt: "If there were 10 children in a school and 6 of them were out with measles, how many would there be in school?" The answer came even more promptly, "None, because the rest would be afraid of catching it too" (p. 237).

This example is of course not conclusive in itself, but it raises the whole question as to the familiarity of rural children not only with the content of the test, but with the very procedure of testing. If they are unaccustomed to the need for imagining these hypothetical situations and answering questions concerning them, their whole attitude may be completely negative. It goes without saying that such unfamiliarity is not equally marked in all rural communities, and that the Kentucky mountaineers represent an extreme case of isolation.

The theory of selective migration has attracted considerable support. Probably its first clear formulation occurred in the work of Otto Ammon (80), who tried to establish the thesis that superior individuals, who are also dolichocephalic, migrate to the cities, whereas the relatively inferior brachycephals remain on the land. He based his conclusion mainly upon measurements made in and near Karlsruhe, where he found the urban population had longer heads than their rural neighbors. This theory was checked by Livi (81) in Italy and by Beddoe (82) in England, and no such anthropometric difference between city and country was noticed. It is not usually realized that certain of Ammon's own results argue against the theory of a selective migration with reference to innate superiority. Among other things, he compared the occupational distribution of immigrants to Karlsruhe with that of their own descendants and obtained the following results.

Generation	Lowest Economic Group	Middle Group	Professional Group
Immigrants	82%	14%	4%
Their sons	41	49	10
Their grandsons	40	35	25

This would seem to show that the immigrants themselves are not a superior group to start with, but that with the passage of time they improve their economic status and become much like the average city population. It seems more likely that this is to be explained on the basis of a gradual assimilation to the environment than through the original superiority of the migrants.

In more recent discussions of this problem, Ammon's anthropometric linkage plays little part, but the theory of selective migration is still appealed to in order to explain observed differences in population quality. Pintner (83), for example, summarizes the results of the testing of rural children and concludes that "in general . . . it would appear as if the urban districts rate higher in intelligence than rural districts and that this is due to the migration of superior intelligence to the cities" (p. 253). In connection with the mountaineers of Kentucky, Hirsch (66) concludes that close inbreeding in conjunction with selective migration is responsible in large part for the low general intelligence of the East Kentucky mountaineers today. Plant (84) expresses the opinion that "the stream coming from rural areas into our metropolitan districts represents a group highly selected as to ability and general stability. There are, it is true, other factors at work but a persistent tendency for the more venturesome, the more able, to move towards city life is an outstanding characteristic of this movement" (p. 147). Finally, Doob (85), writing of the poor Whites in the South, states that "moving from a known area into an unknown one requires courage, intelligence, and initiative in meeting new economic conditions and in establishing new social ties" (p. 457). Although he has no data applicable to his particular community, he feels that the presumption is in favor of this generalization, since it has been found to be true for other communities in the past.

In spite of the prevalence of the belief in selective migration, there is little direct evidence in its favor. In the case of the writers mentioned in the preceding paragraph, the argument appears to be based on logic rather than on objective data. It is believed that certain qualities are necessary for migration and that therefore the migrants must be in possession of such qualities. Neither half of this proposition has so far been proved. On a priori grounds one can make as good a case for the inferiority as for the superiority of the migrants. During an investigation of Negro migration in the South (see below, Chapter 11) the present writer found many southerners, both Negro and White, who did point out that it requires energy and initiative to start over again in a new community, as well as intelligence to see the advantage of the new environment over the old. There were just as many, however, who argued that those who are more successful in the old environment, who have achieved a certain social and economic position, who possess property and friends, are less likely to wander off in search of fresh opportunities than those who are shiftless and unsuccessful and have nothing to lose by leaving. It was rare to hear the opinion that those who left were neither better nor worse than those who stayed behind. It is clear that in this whole field there is need for objective information, and that the argument from logic is not to be relied upon.

In a study which did make use of objective data, Gist and Clark (86) analyzed the results obtained by migrants and non-migrants, respectively, among high-school students in rural communities in Kansas. Of the large group investigated, 35% (over 2,500 cases) had moved to cities. Of the migrant group, 27% obtained an I.Q. of 105 and over; only 17% of the non-migrants were in the same category. I.Q.'s under 95 were found in 39% of the migrant and 53% of the non-migrant group. This study does give evidence in favor of selective migration, although the overlapping between the two groups is clearly very great.

On the basis of their analysis of migration from the tidewater region of Virginia, Gee and Corson (87) conclude that those who migrate are slightly better educated than those who remain, but that there is some tendency for those who own their own farms, and who therefore are presumably more successful, to stay where they are. The results are therefore inconclusive as far as selective migration is concerned. Zimmerman (88) has studied migration in Iowa and is of the opinion that the very successful and the unsuccessful groups migrate, and that those in an intermediate position remain in their original homes.

An investigation was made of White migrants from rural New Jersey to urban centers in the vicinity (89). There were several New Jersey counties in which intelligence tests had been given in the rural schools during the past years, and it was possible to find a considerable number of migrating children for whom test records were available. The scores of 597 migrants were studied, and they were found to be slightly below those of the general non-migrating group. These scores were made by children who were taken to the city by their parents, and who did not themselves initiate the migration, but since we are interested in the quality of the stock rather than of any particular individual, the use of the children's test scores would seem justified. A second study was, however, made of adult migrants in South Germany, although in their case it was necessary to use school records rather than intelligence test scores. The total number of cases in this study is very small, but their average school standing was slightly above that of the non-migrant group and therefore appears to represent a moderate degree of selection.

In the present state of our knowledge it is impossible to make a definite statement as to whether or not the migrants as a whole are superior to the non-migrants as a whole. In the German group the migrants were slightly superior; in the New Jersey study they were average or slightly inferior. Any blanket concept of "selective migration" with respect to intelligence is not justified by the evidence.

The problem is much too complicated to be stated in terms of intelligence alone. There must be some selection, since not everyone migrates, but this selection may be determined by a number of different causes. Economic factors undoubtedly play an important part, and bad conditions at home and good conditions elsewhere will certainly provide a definite spur to migration. A study by Raper (90) has shown how the boll weevil caused an exodus of Negroes from one county in Georgia, whereas there was little or no migration from a neighboring county which had not been similarly affected. It is probable that economic factors operate usually in a much more complicated manner; it may be that differing economic conditions will cause an exodus of a different type of migrant in each case. Careful study is required of the manner in which such factors may operate. A second group of factors relates not so much to the intelligence as to the personality of the migrants. Such characteristics as a desire for novelty or adventure, adaptability to the speed and noise of the city, lack of emotional attachment to the home—these and allied qualities may determine migration quite apart from intelligence. A third group of factors may be regarded as accidental. The inducements held out by friends or relatives in the city, misdemeanors committed at home, failure in social adjustment, may all play a part. Migration is by no means always the result of a spontaneous decision to move. This complexity in the factors involved, as well as the objective data to which reference has been made, indicate that we have no right to interpret the apparent superiority of urban over rural groups as due to selective migration. It seems much more probable that it is the city environment which is responsible.

Further evidence in this direction is furnished by the results of a study of rural Negroes who migrated to the city of New Orleans (91). It was found that those children who had lived longer in the city were superior in their intelligence test scores to those who had been there a shorter time; there was in fact a close correspondence between length of residence and average test score. This would seem to indicate that the environment is clearly responsible, and that when favorable conditions are introduced into the life of the rural child, there is a notable improvement in his mental level.

Indirect confirmation of this position comes from a study by Rusk (92), in which the Binet I.Q.'s of rural and urban children in Scotland were compared; no differences were found. This is most probably due to the fact that educational opportunities differ relatively little throughout Scotland; even the more isolated rural areas have schools which are said to be just as good as those in the large cities. The conclusion appears justified that when educational opportunities are equalized, the usual differences between rural and urban groups in intelligence test scores disappear completely.

The problem of selective migration will come in for further consideration in connection with the studies of Negro intelligence, and particularly with reference to the differences between southern and northern Negroes (see Chapter 11). At this point it will suffice to state that migrants may apparently be superior, inferior, or equal to the non-migrants in intelligence, and that we have no right to use selective migration as an explanation of the observed differences unless we have direct evidence that it is at work in the specific situation under discussion.

SUMMARY

The field of differential psychology is closely related to the nature-nurture problem. The present position is that both nature and nurture are responsible for the characteristics of all individuals; the question is rather as to the amount of variation between individuals that may be ascribed to nature and nurture, respectively. The number and complexity of genes within the human germ-plasm make the direct application of Mendelian principles difficult, but the distinction between dominant and recessive characters is especially important.

The experimental studies of the inheritance of acquired characteristics have not succeeded in demonstrating such a possibility The apparent success of McDougall is probably due to selective breeding, as Tryon's studies suggest. This does not mean, however, that artificial control of breeding, in the form of either positive or negative eugenics, is capable of producing any marked improvement in the human stock. Positive eugenics is not feasible, and negative eugenics not especially promising. The lack of any acceptable standard of population quality adds danger to a eugenics program.

Research on identical and non-identical twins has demonstrated that the former resemble each other somewhat more closely; this points to a demonstrable, though not a very marked, effect of heredity on intelligence test scores. Identical twins reared apart usually continue to have approximately equal scores, but substantial differences have been found in certain cases. Both hereditary and environmental factors must therefore play a part.

An occupational hierarchy in test scores has frequently been demonstrated. That this is at least in part due to environmental influences is indicated by the marked effect of school training, by the gains reported for foster children placed in homes of good economic level, and also by the marked decrease in I.Q. with increasing age under poor economic and educational conditions. In view of the known effects of variations in the environment, the occupational hierarchy may be explained adequately without the assumption of inherited differences. On the other hand, individual variations within a particular occupational group clearly point to the importance of heredity, partly because the range of variations is too great to be ascribed to nurture, and partly because of the much greater resemblance between true parents and children than between foster parents and children in comparable environments. Variations between groups, therefore, are almost certainly environmental in origin; variations between individuals within a homogeneous group are due to a combination of hereditary and environmental factors. The fear of a decline in general intelligence because of the differential occupational birth rate appears to be groundless.

Similar considerations apply to the differences between urban and rural groups. The explanation in terms of selective migration has not been substantiated. In some cases it is a superior group which migrates to the city; in others, an inferior group. There are many factors—economic, personal, accidental—which determine the nature of the migration. The superiority of the city groups is much more probably due to the nature of the urban environment.

REFERENCES

1. Galton, F. *Inquiries into Human Faculty and Its Development.* 1883
2. Binet, A., and Henri, V. "La Psychologie Individuelle," *Année Psychol.,* 1895, 2: pp. 411-463. See also subsequent volumes of the *Année Psychologique.*
3. Cattell, J. McK. "Mental Tests and Measurements," *Mind,* 1890, 15: pp. 373-380
4. Thorndike, E. L. *An Introduction to the Theory of Mental and Social Measurements.* 1904
5. Stern, W. *Die Differentielle Psychologie in Ihren Methodischen Grundlagen.* 1921
6. Anastasi, A., and Foley, J. P., Jr. *Differential Psychology.* 1949
7. Tyler, L. E. *The Psychology of Human Differences.* 1947
8. Razran, G. "Conditioned Responses in Animals Other than Dogs," *Psychol. Bull.,* 1933, 30: pp. 261-324
9. Woodworth, R. S. *Psychology.* 3d ed. 1934
10. Shapiro, H. L. *Migration and Environment.* 1939
11. Murphy, G., Murphy, L. B., and Newcomb, T. M. *Experimental Social Psychology.* Rev. ed. 1937
12. Morgan, T. H. *The Theory of the Gene.* 1926
13. Weismann, A. *The Evolution Theory.* 2 vols. 1904
14. Lamarck, J. B. *Philosophie Zoölogique.* 2 vols. 1809
15. DeVries, H. *Species and Varieties, Their Origin by Mutation.* 1905
16. Kammerer, P. *The Inheritance of Acquired Characteristics.* 1924

17. Pavlov, I. P. "New Researches on Conditioned Reflexes," *Science,* n.s. 1923, 58: pp. 359-361

18. McDougall, W. "An Experiment for the Testing of the Hypothesis of Lamarck," *Brit. J. Psychol.,* 1927, 17: pp. 267-304

19. Tryon, R. C. "The Genetics of Learning Ability in Rats"—a preliminary report, *Univ. Calif. Publ. in Psychol.,* 1929, 4: pp. 71-89; "Studies in Individual Differences in Maze Ability: I. The Measurements of the Reality of Individual Differences," *J. Comp. Psychol.,* 1930, 11: pp. 145-170

20. Huxley, J. S. *Soviet Genetics and World Science.* 1949

21. Jennings, H. S. *The Biological Basis of Human Nature.* 1930

22. Hogben, L. T. *Nature and Nurture.* 1933

23. Pearl, R. "Biology and Human Trends," *J. Wash. Acad. Sci.,* 1935, 25, No. 6: pp. 265-266

24. Myerson, A., et al. *Eugenical Sterilization.* 1936

25. Galton, F. *Hereditary Genius.* 1869

26. Goddard, H. H. *The Kallikak Family: A Study in the Heredity of Feeblemindedness.* 1912

27. Dugdale, R. L. *The Jukes: A Study in Crime, Pauperism, Disease, and Heredity.* 1877

28. Estabrook, A. H. *The Jukes in 1915.* 1916

29. Winship, A. E. *Jukes-Edwards: A Study in Education and Heredity.* 1900

30. Voss, G. See Reference 33.

31. Schwesinger, G. C. *Heredity and Environment.* 1933

32. Tallman, G. G. "A Comparative Study of Identical and Non-Identical Twins with Respect to Intelligence Resemblances," *Twenty-Seventh Yearbook Nat. Soc. Stud. Educ.,* 1928, Part I: pp. 83-86

33. Viteles, M. S. *Industrial Psychology.* 1932

34. Thorndike, E. L. "Measurement of Twins," *Arch. Psychol.,* 1905, No. 1

35. Merriman, C. "The Intellectual Resemblance of Twins," *Psychol. Monog.,* 1924, No. 5

36. Lauterbach, C. E. "Studies in Twin Resemblance," *Genetics,* 1925, 10: pp. 525-568

37. McNemar, Q. "Twin Resemblances in Motor Skills, and the Effect of Practice Thereon," *J. Genet. Psychol.,* 1933, 42: pp. 70-99

38. Seeman, E., and Saudek, R. "Self-Expression in Twins' Handwriting and Drawing," *Char. & Pers.,* 1933, 1: pp. 91-128

39. Newman, H. H. "Differences Between Conjoined Twins," *J. Hered.,* 1931, 22: pp. 201-216

40. Lange, J. *Crime and Destiny.* 1929

41. Rosanoff, A. J., et al. "The Etiology of So-called Schizophrenic Psychoses," *Amer. J. Psychiat.,* 1934, 91: pp. 247-286

42. Kallmann, F. J. "The Genetic Theory of Schizophrenia," *Am. J. Psychiatry*, 1946, 103: pp. 309-322

43. Carter, H. D. "Ten Years of Research on Twins: Contributions to the Nature-Nurture Problem." *39th Yrbook. Nat. Soc. Stud. Ed.*, 1940, Part I: pp. 235-255

44. Newman, H. H. "How Differences in Environment Affected Separated One-egg Twins." In *Readings in Social Psychology*, T. M. Newcomb and E. L. Hartley, eds. 1947, pp. 1-6

45. Blatz, W. E. *The Five Sisters*. 1938

46. Gardner, I. C., and Newman, H. H. "Studies of Quadruplets," *J. Hered.*, 1943, 34: pp. 259-263

47. Newman, H. H., et al. *Twins: A Study of Heredity and Environment*. 1937

48. Thorndike, E. L., et al. "The Resemblance of Siblings in Intelligence," *Twenty-Seventh Yearbook Nat. Soc. Stud. Educ.*, 1928, Part I: pp. 41-53

49. Pearson, K., and Lee, A. "On the Laws of Inheritance in Man: Inheritance of Physical Characters," *Biom.*, 1903, 2: pp. 357-462

50. Collins, J. E. "The Intelligence of School Children and Paternal Occupation," *J. Educ. Res.*, 1928, 17: pp. 156-169

51. Yerkes, R. M. "Psychological Examining in the U. S. Army," *Memoirs Nat. Acad. Sci.*, 1921, 15

52. Goodenough, F. L. "The Relation of the Intelligence of Pre-school Children to the Occupation of their Fathers," *Amer. J. Psychol.*, 1928, 40: pp. 284-294

53. Furfey, P. H. "The Relation Between Socio-economic Status and Intelligence of Young Infants as Measured by the Linfert-Hierholzer Scale," *J. Genet. Psychol.*, 1928, 35: pp. 478-480

54. Terman, L. M. *Genetic Studies of Genius*. Vol. I: *Mental and Physical Traits of a Thousand Gifted Children*. 1925

55. Canady, H. G. "The Intelligence of Negro College Students and Parental Occupation," *Amer. J. Sociol.*, 1936, 42: pp. 388-389

56. Wellman, B. L. "Growth in Intelligence under Differing School Environments," *J. Exper. Educ.*, 1934, 3: pp. 59-83

57. Wellman, B. L. "Mental Growth from Preschool to College," *J. Exper. Educ.*, 1937-38, 6: pp. 127-138

58. Wellman, B. L. "Iowa Studies on the Effect of Schooling," *39th Yrbk. Nat. Soc. Stud. Educ.*, 1940, Part II: pp. 377-399

59. Schmidt, B. G. "Changes in Personal, Social, and Intellectual Behavior of Children Originally Classified as Feebleminded," *Psychol. Monogr.*, 1946, 60, No. 5: pp. 1-144

60. Freeman, F. N., Holzinger, K. J., and Mitchell, B. C. "The Influence of Environment on the Intelligence, School Achievement, and Con-

duct of Foster Children," *Twenty-Seventh Yearbook Nat. Soc. Stud. Educ.*, 1928, Part I: pp. 103-217

61. Burks, B. S. "The Relative Influence of Nature and Nurture upon Mental Development, etc." *Twenty-Seventh Yearbook Nat. Soc. Stud. Educ.*, 1928, Part I: pp. 219-316

62. Leahy, A. M. "Nature-nurture and Intelligence," *Genet. Psychol. Monog.*, 1935, 17: pp. 235-308

63. Skodak, M., and Skeels, H. M. "A Follow-up Study of Children in Adoptive Homes," *J. Genet. Psychol.*, 1945, 66: pp. 21-58

64. Gordon, H. *Mental and Scholastic Tests Among Retarded Children.* 1923

65. Sherman, M., and Key, C. B. "The Intelligence of Isolated Mountain Children," *Child Dev.*, 1932, 3, pp. 279-290

66. Hirsch, N. D. M. "An Experimental Study of the East Kentucky Mountaineers," *Genet. Psychol. Monogr.*, 1928, 3: pp. 183-244

67. Asher, E. J. "The Inadequacy of Current Intelligence Tests for Testing Kentucky Mountain Children," *J. Genet. Psychol.*, 1935, 46: pp. 480-486

08. Wheeler, L. R. "A Comparative Study of the Intelligence of East Tennessee Mountain Children," *J. Educ. Psychol.*, 1942, 33: pp. 321-334

69. Cattell, R. B. *The Fight for Our National Intelligence.* 1937

70. Burt, C. *Intelligence and Fertility.* 1946

71. Thomson, G. H. "The Trend of National Intelligence," *Eugen. Rev.*, 1946, 38: pp. 9-18

72. Thomson, G. H. (ed.) *The Trend of Scottish Intelligence.* 1949

73. Tuddenham, R. D. "Soldier Intelligence in World Wars I and II," *Amer. Psychologist*, 1948, 3: pp. 54-56

74. Klineberg, O. (ed.) *Characteristics of the American Negro.* 1944

75. Davis, A., and Havighurst, R. J. "The Measurement of Mental Systems," *Scient. Monthly*, 1948, 66: pp. 301-316

76. Book, W. F. "Variations in Mental Ability and Its Distribution among the School Population of an Indiana County," *Bull., Ext. Div., Indiana Univ.*, 1918, 4, No. 4: pp. 100-131

77. Pressey, L. W. "The Influence of Inadequate Schooling and Poor Environment upon Results with Tests of Intelligence," *J. Appl. Psychol.*, 1920, 4: pp. 91-96

78. Shimberg, M. E. "An Investigation into the Validity of Norms with Special Reference to Urban and Rural Groups," *Arch. Psychol.*, 1929, No. 104

79. Pressey, S. L. *Psychology and the Newer Education.* 1933

80. Ammon, O. *Zur Anthropologie der Badener.* 1899

81. Livi, R. *Anthropometria Militare.* 1896

82. Beddoe, J. *The Races of Britain: A Contribution to the Anthropology of Western Europe.* 1885

83. Pintner, R. *Intelligence Testing; Methods and Results.* 1923

84. Plant, J. S. *Personality and the Cultural Pattern.* 1937

85. Doob, L. W. "Appendix I" in J. Dollard's *Caste and Class in a Southern Town.* 1937

86. Gist, N. P., and Clark, C. D. "Intelligence as a Selective Factor in Rural-Urban Migration," *Amer. J. Sociol.*, 1938, 44: pp. 36-58

87. Gee, W., and Corson, J. J. "Rural Depopulation in Certain Tidewater and Piedmont Areas of Virginia," Univ. of Va., *Soc. Sci. Monog.*, 1929, No. 3

88. Zimmerman, C. C. "The Migration to Towns and Cities," *Amer. J. Sociol.*, 1926, 32: pp. 450-455; 1927, 33: pp. 105-109

89. Klineberg, O. "The Intelligence of Migrants," *Amer. Sociol. Rev.*, 1938, 3: pp. 218-224

90. Raper, A. F. *Preface to Peasantry.* 1936

91. Klineberg, O. *Negro Intelligence and Selective Migration.* 1935

92. Rusk, R. R. "The Intelligence of Scottish Children," *39th Yrbk. Nat. Soc. Stud. Educ.*, 1940, Part II: pp. 269-273

Sex Differences

10

INTRODUCTION

In spite of the tremendous amount of research which has been devoted to the question of psychological sex differences, it is difficult to summarize with confidence the conclusions that have been reached. The psychological significance of the obvious physical differences between the sexes has been the subject of almost endless discussion. Not so long ago the assumption was usually made that the psychological differences between the sexes were fundamental and biologically determined, and that as a consequence men had certain intellectual capacities that could not be matched by women; it is only in comparatively recent times, for example, that women have been regarded as having brains capable of coping with higher education and that they have been admitted to colleges and universities on terms of equality with men. As recently as 1935, Alexis Carrel (1) wrote: "The same intellectual and physical training, and the same ambitions should not be given to young girls as to boys. Educators should pay very close attention to the organic and mental peculiarities of the male and the female, and to their natural functions. Between the two sexes there are irrevocable differences. And it is imperative to take them into account in constructing the civilized world" (p. 92). On the other hand, Huxley and Haddon (2) expressed the view that the apparent differences between the sexes are probably due mainly to upbringing, and they cite as an instance of changed habits in this respect the exclamation of the third century Greek gossip writer, Athenaeus, "Whoever heard of a woman cook?" (p. 69).

In this connection Margaret Mead (3) points out that although most societies assume some psychological difference between the sexes, the exact nature of this assumption varies from group to group.

With the paucity of material for elaboration, no culture has failed to seize upon the conspicuous facts of age and sex in some way, whether it be the convention of one Philippine tribe that no man can keep a secret, the Manus assumption that only men enjoy playing with babies, the Toda prescription of almost all domestic work as too sacred for women, or the Arapesh insistence that women's heads are stronger than men's (p. xix).

As we shall see later, her own study of the relation between sex and temperament in several primitive societies has indicated some of the patterns of sex differences for which culture may be responsible.

In deciding upon the relative importance of nature and nurture in the determination of sex differences, several lines of evidence require examination. These include the material collected by means of actual physical and psychological measurement of the two sexes in our own society, the comparative data collected by the anthropologists, and the related material from biology.

QUANTITATIVE STUDIES

Between men and women in our own society and probably in most other groups as well, there are certain physical differences apart from those relating to the primary or secondary sex characters. Men are taller and heavier than women, the average height of English males being 67.5 inches and of females 62.7 inches. Men weigh on the average twenty percent more than women, although women usually have relatively more fat on their bodies; Dunlap (4) cites the observation that their "bodies are said to burn more readily on funeral pyres." Both in absolute and relative brain weight women are inferior to men, although the overlapping is considerable, as it is with all of the measures cited. The basal metabolism of women is usually somewhat lower. Girls mature more rapidly than boys, and as a result may exceed boys of the same age in stature and weight until after puberty. Males have a higher mortality rate than females; this is true even prenatally, and the difference in life expectancy is found at all ages.

Of these various differences, the only ones which may have psychological significance are those referring to brain size, metabolism and rate of maturation, but the experimental work relating to these three characteristics has so far shown little direct relationship to psychological functions.

More direct psychological measurements have revealed the presence of a number of points of difference. From earliest childhood on, for instance, girls show superiority in language development—in the age at which they begin to talk, in the size of their vocabulary, in sentence structure, in the number of speech sounds used, etc. There is some indication that this superiority in language ability persists in later life. Though there have been some studies which have failed to demonstrate such a superiority (5), they are the exception; the evidence is overwhelming in favor of a linguistic advantage in the case of females.

In connection with language ability the interesting observation has been made that stuttering is much more frequent among boys than girls, the ratios reported varying from 2:1 to 10:1. The reason for this clear-cut difference is not entirely certain, but Dunlap (6) has suggested a possible explanation. He believes that one of the important causes of stuttering is the fear on the part of the child that he may say something bad, or use tabooed and naughty expressions for which he may be punished. Boys, playing on the streets more frequently, are much more likely to pick up such expressions than are girls, and the fear will consequently be greater in their case. This theory is in need of further verification before it can be accepted; it is possible that the discrepancy between the sexes in knowledge of naughty words is not so great as Dunlap imagines. Even if there is such a discrepancy, it has not been proven that this is responsible for the difference in the frequency of stuttering.

Studies of sensory capacities have shown women to be slightly superior in color discrimination, and to have a much smaller incidence of color blindness. Men are superior in motor and mechanical abilities, and on the average obtain much higher scores on spatial tests, mazes, construction tests, the Stenquist mechanical aptitude test, etc. In tests involving number ability, men do somewhat better, but the difference is not consistent. In most tests of general intelligence, girls are slightly superior until about the age of fourteen, beyond which there is substantial equality. This equality may be to some degree an artificial consequence of the construction of the tests, which are usually standardized on both boys and girls, and which would not be regarded as satisfactory if there were a marked sex difference in the results. At the same time the test scores indicate an apparent female superiority in linguistic ability, and a male superiority in numerical, spatial and mechanical abilities. In scholastic achievement, in tests of memory, and in the Social Intelligence test girls are somewhat superior. In the Allport-Vernon (7) Study of Values, girls more frequently obtained high scores in esthetic, social and religious values, and men, in economic, political and theoretic values.

The most careful and elaborate experimental study of sex differences in personality is that of Terman and Miles (8), who devised a "masculinity-femininity" index based upon their examination of many hundreds of subjects, including elementary and high school children, college and graduate students, unselected adults, members of several occupational groups, athletes, juvenile delinquents and homosexuals.

The sexes were compared in terms of (1) a word association test, (2) ink-blot association, (3) information, (4) emotional and ethical responses, (5) interests, (6) opinions, and (7) introversion-extraversion. The investigators are careful to state that their conclusions apply to men and women in our culture only; they may be true for other societies as well, but that remains to be demonstrated. With that limitation clearly understood, the results indicate that the males, in the main group studied, showed a distinctive interest in exploit and adventure, in outdoor and physically strenuous occupations, in machinery and tools, in science, physical phenomena, and inventions; usually also in business and commerce. The females showed more interest in domestic affairs and in esthetic objects and occupations; they preferred more sedentary and indoor occupations, and those more directly ministrative, particularly to the young, the helpless, the distressed.

> The males directly or indirectly manifest the greater self-assertion and aggressiveness; they express more hardihood and fearlessness, and more roughness of manners, language, and sentiments. The females express themselves as more compassionate and sympathetic, more timid, more fastidious and esthetically sensitive, more emotional in general (or at least more expressive of the four emotions considered), severer moralists, yet admit in themselves weaknesses in emotional control and (less noticeably) in physique (pp. 447-8).

The extent of the differences found is sometimes very marked, and indicates the reality of a relationship between sex and temperament, although it leaves open the question as to the factors determining this relationship.

The application of the masculinity-femininity index to men and women in various occupations reveals some interesting results. Among the most "masculine" men were engineers and architects; among the least masculine were journalists, artists and clergymen; policemen and firemen were also close to the lower end of the range of scores for masculinity. Among women, domestic servants obtained the highest "feminine" scores, and high school and college teachers, the lowest. Needless to say, the overlapping between the various occupational groups was very great.

In a supplementary study, the masculinity-femininity of a group of male homosexuals was also investigated. The 71 *passive* homosexuals (those who took the female role in the relationship) obtained significantly more "feminine" scores than the average; the 46 homosexuals described as *active* were slightly more "masculine" than the normal subjects. Physical measurements did not differentiate the homosexuals from the normals, and on this basis Terman and Miles regard environment rather than constitutional factors as responsible for the deviant behavior.

Statistics for crime and delinquency show a tremendous discrepancy between the sexes. Scheinfeld (9) reports that in one typical year the ratio of males to females sent to federal and state prisons and reformatories in the United States was in the neighborhood of 25 to 1. Part of this difference may of course be due to greater leniency in the treatment of women, but the discrepancy is too great to be explained away entirely on this basis. It must be kept in mind that a large proportion of delinquent and criminal behavior is aggressive in character, and there is evidence to the effect that aggressive behavior is more common among males, perhaps in part due to biology, and in part to differences in what is regarded as "acceptable" for boys and girls, respectively. (See also Chapter 16.)

With regard to the incidence of abnormality, statistics collected by Landis and Page (10) show a marked difference, with substantially more admissions of males to hospitals for mental diseases in general, and for all specific diseases except involutional melancholia, manic depressive insanity and psychoneurosis. The greater frequency of mental disorder among males is not easy to interpret. It may be that the male in our society is subject to somewhat more stress and strain, especially because of his greater responsibility as a breadwinner; it may also be that the incidence of mental disease is merely another instance of the greater morbidity of the male.

Anastasi and Foley (5) summarize the results of various studies dealing with sex differences in school achievement, play behavior, personality, neuroticism, etc. Although such differences do emerge from the data they are usually small in amount, with the overlapping correspondingly great. The fact that on almost every measure such overlapping can be demonstrated has suggested that any strict line of demarcation in connection with education, economic opportunity, occupational selection, even "role" in general, is unjustified. This conclusion is strengthened by the material collected by anthropologists.

THE ETHNOLOGICAL APPROACH

A survey of the available ethnological data indicates that at least one sex difference in behavior is widely prevalent, namely, that power is usually in the hands of the males. There is a theory in anthropology developed by Bachofen (11) and followed by Briffault (12), that society was originally a matriarchate, with the authority vested in a woman. The opinion of most modern anthropologists is, however, against this view. Lowie (13) states that a genuine matriarchate is nowhere to be found, though in a few places feminine prerogatives have evolved to a marked degree in certain directions. The Iroquois Indians probably furnished the closest approximation to the matriarchal condition. Women arranged marriage, owned houses and land, managed some of the most important ceremonial organizations, furnished three out of six of the ceremonial officials of each sib, nominated the candidate for a vacancy in the council of chiefs, and had the right to impeach or admonish an unworthy chief-elect. Even among the Iroquois, however, no woman had a place on the supreme council of the League, and it may not be said that more power was in the hands of women than of men. In other alleged matriarchates, their power was considerably less. In societies like those of Melanesia, where matrilineal descent prevailed, and where authority over the children was vested in the mother's family, it was the men and not the women of the family who had this authority. It was the maternal uncle rather than the father whom the boy was obliged to obey; the mother had considerably less authority over him. As far as economic prerogatives are concerned, there are instances in which those of women were on a par with those of men (for example, the Iroquois, the Zuñi, the Khasi of Assam, etc.), but these are exceptions. In general the lesser power of women shows itself also in certain disabilities in property rights (14).

It has been suggested that the reason for the greater power of men is to be found in their physical superiority (15). Since man was strong enough to force woman to obey him, it may seem natural that he should have kept the greater authority in his own hands. There are, however, a few communities in which women are reputedly stronger and physically more capable than men.

Work is to the Mkamba nothing short of a misfortune; when he does take to it a very little discomfort, such as he would otherwise not notice, will completely incapacitate him, while he has then the appearance of undergoing the deepest misery. . . . But if the men are unfit for hard work, the women are exceedingly tough and hardy, and whereas a man can rarely carry more than a 45-lb. load, most women will easily shoulder 60 lbs. I have seen women carrying as much as 140 lbs. At an early age the men become useless for work, while the women will continue to labour up to a great age (16, pp. 490-1).

This instance is not entirely convincing, since it may have been unwillingness rather than incapacity for work which prompted the men to behave as they did. It is reported that Arapesh women regularly carry heavier loads than men because their heads are regarded as much harder and stronger. These exceptions to the general rule are so rare, however, that it seems highly probable that men are usually stronger than women, and that to a certain extent the relation between the sexes is determined by male superiority in this direction.

In this same connection Sumner (17) believes that the physiological differences between the sexes place the woman at a definite disadvantage. "No amount of reasoning, complaining, or protesting can alter the fact that woman bears children and man does not" (p. 112). This apparently obvious remark also points, however, to the disabilities of maternity and menstruation, which result in a periodical weakness on the part of women and handicap them in any struggle with the other sex. That these disabilities exist is undoubted, but it is certain that they have been greatly exaggerated

by the mode of life imposed upon women by our folkways. Seward
(18), for example, points out that at least some of the consequences
of menstruation can be explained by the attitudes toward it which
have developed in our society; the expectation of certain effects
itself contributes toward their realization. There can be no doubt
that child-bearing has become for women in our society a much
more troublesome and complicated undertaking than it is in most
primitive groups and peasant communities. The accounts of the
way in which women in such groups continue working in the fields
until the last possible moment, and resume their work almost immediately after childbirth, indicate that the disability need not be
nearly so great as is usually supposed. The literary accounts by Knut
Hamsun and Pearl Buck about Norwegian and Chinese peasants,
respectively, have received ample corroboration from the observations of ethnologists among primitive peoples.

This raises the whole question of sex differences in occupation,
and the degree to which they are to be explained by the biological
nature of the two sexes. A survey of the available material by
Goldenweiser (19) reveals few if any occupations which are exclusively practiced by either one sex or the other. It is commonly,
but not uniformly true, that agriculture was formerly in the hands
of women and that it became the work of man only after the introduction of domesticated animals. The allotment of agriculture to
women in primitive societies may in many cases be due to the notion
of their greater fertility. It is reported that an Indian in Orinoco said
to a missionary, "You must remember that our women know how to
bring forth, and we do not. If they sow the seed . . . everything
is increased. Why is this? Because women are able to bring forth,
and are able to command the seed they sow to be productive" (20,
p. 318). At any rate, there are also exceptions among primitive
groups to the rule that agriculture is woman's work, so that even its
indirect relation to the biology of woman is by no means a necessary one. In general, there is no obvious division of labor among
pastoral and agricultural peoples.

In other arts and handicrafts there seems to be little consistency
in this respect. In British Columbia and southern Alaska, men are
responsible for the elaborate wood industry—totem poles, memorial
columns, boxes, canoes, etc.—and women make the blankets. The
California baskets and Pueblo pots are made entirely by women,

although in many other parts of North America this is the work of men. The rule that men do the more difficult manual labor and that women engage in domestic occupations has a great many exceptions. In the Marquesas, for example, even cooking, housekeeping and baby-tending are proper male occupations. Among the Tasmanians, the difficult work of seal-hunting was done by women. "They swam out to the seal rocks, stalked the animals, and clubbed them. Tasmanian women also hunted opossums, which required the climbing of large trees" (15, p. 117). It is probable, however, that the physical differences between the sexes do play a definite part in the division of labor in some communities.

Among people who hunt large roving animals with spear or bow and arrow women's physical disabilities are most conspicuous. A woman who is carrying a child or nursing an infant cannot pursue animals hour after hour. To women fall the more sedentary occupations, frequently just as difficult and arduous, but requiring less muscular strength, and fleetness of foot (21, p. 369).

Even warfare is not exclusively practiced by men. In certain of the complex societies of Africa regiments of women were occasionally formed, as for example, the famous bodyguard of the King of Dahomey. These women were especially trained for the warrior profession and acquired sufficient expertness in it to enjoy a high reputation both for their proficiency in the art and for their ferocity (22). We know also that in the various resistance movements that opposed the Nazis during World War II, as well as in the ranks of the Israelis who fought against the Arabs over Palestine, women frequently participated on terms of practical equality with men.

One of the most amusing examples of a difference in attitude toward what should be woman's occupation comes from British Central Africa. Among these natives sewing was man's work, upon which no woman ever thought of encroaching; there was therefore considerable feeling against the missionaries who instructed the women in an art which "ought" not to be feminine (23). Similarly in Samoa, men did all the cooking, even the chiefs taking part in the preparation of meals for the community (24).

An extensive analysis of the division of labor according to sex has been made by Murdock (25) on the basis of the files of the Cross-Cultural Survey initiated at Yale University in 1937 and now known as the Human Relations Area Files. A study of the distribution of economic activities between the sexes in 224 tribes scattered throughout the world indicates that in 75% of the societies the tasks assigned to women include grain-grinding, water-carrying, cooking, the gathering of fuel and vegetable products, the manufacture and repair of clothing, the preservation of meat and fish, pottery-making, weaving, and the manufacture of mats and baskets. Murdock points out that "most of these tasks can be carried on in the house or its immediate vicinity, and that none of them requires an intimate knowledge of the tribal terrain. The tasks assigned to men in more than 75% of the sample societies include the following: herding (84%), fishing (86%), lumbering (92%), trapping (95%), mining and quarrying (95%), hunting (98%), and the catching of sea mammals (98%). All of these activities, as well as the characteristically masculine pursuit of war carry the men far from the dwelling and demand a thorough knowledge of the environs of the community and of the location of all its usable resources" (p. 213). He believes that these facts may be related to the tendency for more and more communities to become patrilocal, with the man remaining in his original residence instead of going to live with his wife's family.

The most thorough ethnological study of sex differences in personality characteristics is that by Margaret Mead (3) in her analysis of the relation between sex and temperament in three Melanesian societies. She was interested in discovering whether the differences in temperament popularly supposed to hold true for men and women generally would also be found in societies with an entirely different cultural background. More particularly she wished to test the assumption that men were naturally more aggressive, and women more passive and submissive in their usual social reactions. She summarizes her conclusions as follows:

> We found the Arapesh—both men and women—displaying a personality, that, out of our historically-limited preoccupations, we would call maternal in its parental aspects, and feminine in its sexual aspects. We found men, as well as women, trained to be cooperative, unaggressive, responsive to the needs and demands of others. We found no idea that sex was a powerful driving force either for men or for women. In marked contrast to these attitudes, we found among the Mundugumor that both men and women developed as ruthless, aggressive, positively sexed individuals, with the maternal cherishing aspects of personality at a minimum. Both men and women approximated to a personality type that we in our culture would find only in an undisciplined and

very violent male. Neither the Arapesh nor the Mundugumor profit by a contrast between the sexes; the Arapesh ideal is the mild, responsive man married to the mild, responsive woman; the Mundugumor ideal is the violent aggressive man married to the violent aggressive woman. In the third tribe, the Tchambuli, we found a genuine reversal of the sex-attitudes of our own culture, with the woman the dominant, impersonal, managing partner, the man the less responsible and the emotionally dependent person (p. 279).

There are of course many deviants from this pattern, and Miss Mead describes these in some detail, but she regards her descriptions as true of the large majority of the men and women in these three communities. With the inclusion of our own society her data indicate that man's aggressiveness may be equal to, greater or less than that of woman, and that both sexes may resemble either the "masculine" or "feminine" types to which we are accustomed in our own community. There appears to be little left in temperament that may safely be ascribed to the direct biological or physiological influence of sex.

Several specific examples from Miss Mead's study may be mentioned as illustrative of this general thesis. The "maternal" attitude of Arapesh men is associated with the belief that a father "bears" children just as the mother does. After children are conceived, the father must "work" sexually in order to build them, the semen is regarded as food for the developing embryo and as essential for its proper growth. Later on the father takes care of the children in the same way as the mother. ". . . if one comments upon a middle-aged man as good-looking, the people answer: 'Good-looking? Ye-e-s! But you should have seen him before he bore all those children'" (p. 39). Among the Tchambuli there was a widow who indulged in a series of sexual affairs during the period pending her remarriage; she was excused on the grounds that women are so highly sexed that any other type of behavior would be difficult for them. "Are women passive sexless creatures who can be expected to wait upon the dilly-dallying of formal considerations of bride-price? Men, not so urgently sexed, may be expected to submit themselves to the discipline of a due order and precedence" (p. 259).

As far as the contrast between the active and the passive role in sex behavior is concerned, the ethnological material shows that variations in this respect may occur. Powdermaker (26) reports that in Lesu when the man desires his wife he goes to her bed, and when he has finished returns to his own bed almost immediately. "The woman never takes the initiative in going to her husband's bed, and when asked the question my women friends regarded such a procedure with horror, and asked if the woman should be a man" (p. 240). It is probable that in most societies the man does take the lead in sex relationships. In Buka on the other hand (27), it appears that the reverse may be true. The Whites who have lived there express the view that the woman was more frequently the instigating partner in love affairs. The folk tales commonly contain incidents in which a woman pretends to be ill in order to persuade the attending medicine-man to have sex relations with her. It is difficult to be certain of the facts in matters of this kind, and in any case this may be an exception to the general rule.

The ethnological material which has just been reviewed justifies the conclusion that culture plays a great part in determining the patterns of behavior prevailing among men and women respectively. A comprehensive volume on this subject by Margaret Mead (28) documents the point fully. Even within our own society, marked changes have occurred in what are regarded as the typical characteristics of women. The delicate fragile lady of the 1800's is almost extinct. We know that many forms of behavior which at that time were regarded as "unnatural" to women have since then been practiced by them with conspicuous success. There has clearly been a growth in self-reliance and independence, and with these a willingness to engage in the kinds of work which used to be regarded as exclusively masculine in character. With all that, however, the known organic differences due to the effect of the male and female hormones respectively, and the fact that these determine not only morphological but also physiological and functional characteristics, must cast considerable doubt upon the theory that sex differences in behavior are entirely due to culture. The evidence from zoology and experimental biology is especially pertinent in this connection.

SEX DIFFERENCES AMONG ANIMALS

There is considerable research indicating that among most species of animals aggressiveness is found more typically in the male than in the female. Some exceptions to this generalization have been reported; Anderson (29), for example, showed female rats to be less timid than males, and Tryon (30) found female rats also to be more active. These are exceptions, however, to a rule which holds true in a large majority of cases.

The experimental work on animals by means of the removal of the sex glands or the implantation of those of the opposite sex have shown that the animal is altered not only with reference to its anatomical development, but also in its behavior. If the sex glands of a young stag are removed, the horns do not develop, and in addition the animal shows none of the typical combative tendencies in the presence of the female, but remains quiet and peaceable. The capon does not crow like a cock, nor will he fight with other male birds. Examples of this type could easily be multiplied. On the other hand, when male glands are implanted into a castrated female guinea pig, there develops not only a hyper-masculinization in external appearance, but the animal also pursues females in heat, calls like a male, and fights with normal males (31). Experiments of this type indicate that not only the direct sexual behavior but the general nature of the social responses of the animal, including combativeness and self-assertion, have a definite organic basis in the nature of the particular sex hormone which is operative. Although there is always some danger in applying the results of animal experimentation to man, it is unlikely that such behavior could be entirely cultural among human beings in the light of this clear indication that among other animals it is organically determined.

An additional argument in this direction is the indication that among animals close to man, but without human culture, masculinity and femininity are well developed. This has been reported by Carpenter (32) in the case of the howling monkeys. He describes the male as more aggressive, protective and defensive than the female. On the other hand, Carpenter indicates that some at least of the sex differences ascribed to human beings do not hold for the howling monkeys. When in the sexually receptive state, for example, the female may either approach or be approached by a mature male; either sex may initiate the sexual advances preparatory to copulation. There is no indication that in this particular respect the male is necessarily more active. Apparently there are organically determined sex differences in aggressiveness, but these do not always or necessarily apply to the actual sex relationship.

WOMEN OF GENIUS

The intelligence tests have revealed no dependable difference in the level of intellectual performance of the two sexes, and it is now customary among psychologists to assume that there is no sex difference in this respect. It has frequently been pointed out, however, that among persons possessing the outstanding ability and achievement which we term "genius," women are relatively rare. Goncourt (33) wrote, "There are no women of genius; all the women of genius are men" (p. 138). He meant by this that even when there are women who are in the genius class, they have probably within them a definite masculine component; cases like those of Rosa Bonheur, George Sand and George Eliot come to mind in this connection. An alternative explanation is possible. We know that it is only in very recent times that women have been given opportunities comparable to those of men; even in our own generation they suffer from definite handicaps with regard to appointments and promotion to positions of importance. The statement that women constitute the largest "minority group" in the world, in terms of status and opportunity, undoubtedly contains more than a grain of truth. It is exceedingly likely that this discrimination may explain their relatively rare appearance in the statistics for outstanding achievement. As for Goncourt's dictum, there are of course many cases of distinctly feminine women, like Marie Curie or Elizabeth Barrett Browning, with undoubted standing in their own field; it is also probable that some at least of the masculine characteristics of women of genius were deliberately cultivated in order to improve their chances in a man's world.

One other possible explanation of the difference in the frequency of genius in the two sexes in spite of the similarity in average intelligence, is that men are more variable, with a larger number of deviations at both ends of the scale. Many investigations have included data on male and female variability, and the differences found are not only inconsistent, but too slight to be of any real significance in this connection. The most probable explanation of the observed differences is that they are due to the relative opportunities for advancement, as well as to the respective roles ascribed to the two sexes by the patterns of our culture.

We shall return to this question in connection with the discussion of Culture and Personality.

SUMMARY

In addition to the primary and secondary sex characters, there are differences between the sexes in rate of growth and development which appear to have implications for behavior; the earlier maturation of girls is especially significant. Other observed differences, as for example in the metabolic rate, have not been shown to affect behavior to any marked degree. In these as in other comparisons there is great overlapping between the sexes. The fundamental biological difference in connection with child-bearing results in a periodical incapacitation of woman which may have an effect on other social and occupational relationships, but undoubtedly this has been exaggerated in our culture.

The ethnological material shows the wide variations in the behavior of the sexes under the influence of social and cultural factors, even with regard to aggressive and submissive attitudes. There are also marked differences in the nature of the occupations regarded as typically masculine or feminine, respectively. It seems probable, however, on the basis of the data furnished by zoology and experimental biology, that in spite of these variations, temperamental characteristics are to some degree dependent upon the respective sex hormones.

The results of psychological studies showing sex differences in interests, linguistic and mechanical ability, memory and information, etc., may best be explained in terms of the social environment of boys and girls in our society. The discrepancy in the frequency of occurrence of "genius" in the two sexes may also be ascribed to differences in training and opportunity.

REFERENCES

1. Carrel, A. *Man, the Unknown.* 1935
2. Huxley, J. S., and Haddon, A. C. *We Europeans.* 1935
3. Mead, M. *Sex and Temperament in Three Primitive Societies.* 1935
4. Dunlap, K. *Civilized Life.* 1934
5. Anastasi, A., and Foley, J. P., Jr. *Differential Psychology.* 1949

6. Dunlap, K. "The Stuttering Boy," *J. Abn. Soc. Psychol.*, 1917, 12: pp. 44-48

7. Allport, G. W., and Vernon, P. E. "A Test for Personal Values," *J. Abn. Soc. Psychol.*, 1931, 26: pp. 231-248

8. Terman, L. M., and Miles, C. C. *Sex and Personality; Studies in Masculinity and Femininity.* 1936

9. Scheinfeld, A. *Women and Men.* 1943

10. Landis, C., and Page, J. D. *Modern Society and Mental Disease.* 1938

11. Bachofen, J. J. *Das Mutterrecht.* 1861

12. Briffault, R. *The Mothers.* 3 vols. 1927

13. Lowie, R. H. *Primitive Society.* 1925

14. Goldenweiser, A. A. *Early Civilization.* 1926

15. Linton, R. *The Study of Man.* 1936

16. Dundas, C. "History of Kitui," *J. Roy. Anthropol. Inst.*, 1913, 43: pp. 490-491

17. Sumner, W. G., and Keller, A. G. *The Science of Society.* Vol. I. 1927

18. Seward, G. H. *Sex and the Social Order.* 1946

19. Goldenweiser, A. A. *Anthropology.* 1937

20. Lévy-Bruhl, L. *Primitive Mentality.* 1923

21. Bunzel, R. L. "The Economic Organization of Primitive Peoples." In Boas, F. (ed.), *General Anthropology.* 1938

22. Seligman, C. G. *Races of Africa.* 1930

23. Werner, A. *The Natives of British Central Africa.* 1906

24. Turner, G. *Samoa: A Hundred Years Ago and Long Before.* 1884

25. Murdock, G. P. "Comparative Data on the Division of Labor by Sex," *Soc. Forces,* 1937, 15: pp. 551-553

26. Powdermaker, H. *Life in Lesu.* 1933

27. Blackwood, B. *Both Sides of Buka Passage.* 1935

28. Mead, M. *Male and Female.* 1949

29. Anderson, E. E. "Sex Differences in Timidity in Normal and Gonadectomized Rats," *J. Genet. Psychol.*, 1941, 59: pp. 139-153

30. Tryon, R. C. "Individual Differences." In Moss, F. A. (ed.), *Comparative Psychology.* 1942

31. Scharpey-Schafer, E. *The Endocrine Organs.* Parts I and II. 1924

32. Carpenter, C. R. "A Field Study of the Behavior and Social Relations of Howling Monkeys," *Comp. Psychol. Monogr.*, 1934, No. 10

33. See Lombroso, C. *The Man of Genius.* 1891

Ethnic Differences

11

INTRODUCTION

The problem of psychological differences between ethnic groups—"races" and nations—has always been of interest to the social psychologist. At various times and in many countries it has obtained a practical application and a political significance which have made it far more than an academic question. Since these practical applications have been justified in the name of science, it is especially important to know with some precision the findings of scientists who have worked in this field. It is a field in which objectivity is rare, but for that reason all the more important, and it has become the real duty of the student of social science to inform himself as to what may legitimately be said on so controversial a topic.

THE ANTHROPOLOGICAL APPROACH

To the anthropologist the popular use of the concept of race is seen to be accompanied by an almost hopeless confusion of terms. Hogben (1) points out how frequently the term "race" is employed without any precise understanding of its significance. Geneticists, he states, use it because they believe that the anthropologists know what it means, and the anthropologists use it because they are sure the geneticists can give it an exact definition.

Although it is probable that not all anthropologists would agree on a definition, the following statement would be accepted by most of them, namely, that a *race* is a large subdivision of mankind, "the members of which are distinguished by possession of similar combinations of anatomical features due to common heredity" (2). A similar idea is expressed more briefly by Boas (3), who regards a race as "a group of common origin and of stable type."

The geneticists approach the problem of definition from a somewhat different direction, stressing not so much the observable physical characteristics, but rather the genetic bases of differences among populations. As Dobzhansky (4) puts it: "The fundamental units of racial variability are populations and genes, not the complexes of characters which connote in the popular mind a racial distinction" (p. 78). Krogman (5) combines the two approaches in his statement that "A race is a sub-group of peoples possessing a definite combination of physical characters, of genetic origin; this combination serves, in varying degree, to distinguish the sub-group from other sub-groups of mankind, and the combination is transmitted in descent, providing all conditions which originally gave rise to the definite combination remain relatively unaltered" (p. 49).

Essentially, therefore, race is expressed as an aggregate or complex of physical characteristics, of genetic origin. The application of racial terms to groups not so characterized is scientifically unacceptable.

In actual practice, the most frequent confusion is found between the concepts of race and nation, and race and language. There is no nation which is physically sufficiently homogeneous in inherited type so that it may be described as "racially pure." As Retzius (6) pointed out long ago, even the Swedes, who are regarded as unmixed representatives of the Nordic or North European physical type, show such marked divergences among themselves that only a minority actually possesses the combination of physical features usually regarded as Nordic. This is of course even more marked in other European nations, and Dixon (7) refers to the fact that anthropometric research in Germany was once stopped because it revealed so many individuals who did not conform to the alleged German type.

This means that the attempts by the Germans during the period of the Nazi dictatorship to keep their nation "pure" in the anthropological sense represented an impossibility. Many German writers saw how difficult it was to reconcile their political aims with accepted anthropological doctrine, and had as a consequence to create an anthropology of their own. The identification in the popular mind between "German" and "tall, blond and blue-eyed" was officially condemned because of the tremendous number of obvious exceptions. One writer (8) insisted that many people who look like Nordics do not have Nordic souls, and that conversely there may be a Nordic soul within a non-Nordic body. This served as a political expedient, but it is scientifically meaningless. The comparable insistence of a group of Italian professors, during the Fascist regime, on the homogeneity of the Italian "race" because of its isolation during the last thousand years is also untenable. The North Italian is blonder and taller and has a rounder head than the Italians farther south, and resembles the Frenchman of Auvergne much more than he does the Sicilian. Anthropologists of other nations have not been so blind to the facts, and British and French writers have frequently stressed the heterogeneity in the physical characteristics of their respective peoples.

The confusion between race and language is even more frequent. To the anthropologist, for example, there is no "Latin race," but a group of languages of Latin origin; these languages may be spoken by people differing greatly from one another in their physical appearance. The term "Semitic" also has a linguistic significance; the fact that Semitic languages include not only Hebrew and Arabic, but also Amharic, the official language of Ethiopia, indicates clearly the variations in the racial constitution of the Semites. Even these subgroups cannot be spoken of as racially pure; the Jews, for example, show physical variations almost as great as those found in all Europeans taken together. Huxley and Haddon (9) point out that in the Caucasus, for example, the large majority of Jews are roundheaded or brachycephalic, whereas among the Yemenite Jews dolichocephaly is the rule. In parts of Poland and Lithuania the average stature of Jews is 5′ 4″, and in certain districts of London it is 5′ 8″. Similar variations have been reported for color of the skin and of the eyes and hair. There is no Jewish race. This statement represents the opinion of the majority of American and British anthropologists who have written on this question. The work of Huxley and Haddon (9), Dixon (7), and Boas (10) may be mentioned as representative. The UNESCO "Statement on Race" points out that "Moslems and Jews are not races, nor are groups who speak English or any other language thereby definable as a race" (11).

By far the most striking misuse of the term "race" occurs in connection with the "Aryans." This term more than any other has been given political significance and was at one time made the basis of legislation in Germany. The word "Aryan" was probably first introduced to the West by Sir William Jones, a British philologist who lived for some time in India and made a special study of Sanskrit and other Asiatic languages (9). He used the word "Aryan" to apply to these languages. Later the problems of linguistic relationship were taken up in Germany by the Schlegels, Bunsen, and others, and in England by a young philologist of German origin, Max Müller. Research showed that there were certain similarities in vocabulary between these Asiatic languages and the overwhelming majority of languages spoken in Europe, and they were together referred to as the Aryan or Indo-European or Indo-Germanic family of languages. It was probably Max Müller who first spoke of an "Aryan race" to refer to that group of people who originated the Aryan language; he thought of them as a superior people because of their discovery of such an efficient and flexible means of linguistic expression. In the years which followed, speculation as to the homeland of the Aryans occupied the attention of many anthropologists and historians, and a large number of different hypotheses were defended. The origin of the Aryans was variously ascribed to the Baltic region, Germany, Russia, central Asia, India, Persia and even North Africa. This uncertainty regarding the place of origin of the Aryans was paralleled by the uncertainty as to their physical appearance. For these reasons Max Müller came to realize that the term "Aryan" could legitimately be used only in a linguistic sense, and that any racial implications were entirely unwarranted. In a famous passage in a later book (12), which appeared in 1888, he stated that when he used the word "Aryan" he posited nothing about the physical appearance of the Aryans, about their status as conquerors or conquered, or about their place of origin; the word "Aryan" was used in a linguistic sense alone. "To me an ethnologist who speaks of Aryan race, Aryan blood, Aryan eyes or hair, is as great a sinner as a linguist who speaks of a dolichocephalic dictionary or a brachycephalic grammar" (p. 120).

This complete recantation of an earlier position came too late. In the meantime the concept of a superior Aryan race had been seized upon by a number of writers, and had received its most thorough development in Gobineau's *Essay on the Inequality of Human Races.* Gobineau was not the first to speak of superior and inferior races; as Barzun (13) points out, this type of thinking goes back as far as Tacitus, who for political reasons glorified the Germanic tribes at the expense of the Romans. In its modern form, however, the race theory owes most to Gobineau and his followers, although his *Essay* depends upon a concept which its originator correctly repudiated.

The Classification of Races. Even if we are careful to restrict the term "race" to hereditary physical characteristics, we still find considerable difficulty in discovering an acceptable criterion for racial classification. In the past many criteria have been used—skin color, shape of the head, stature, color of the eyes and hair, shape of the hair in cross section, and many others. The difficulty arises from the fact that the use of different criteria gives mutually contradictory classifications. Blumenbach (14), for example, is responsible for the familiar classification into five races according to skin color—the White or Caucasian, the Yellow or Mongolian, the Black or Ethiopian, the Red or American and the Brown or Malayan. Many writers speak of three major "races" or stocks—the White or Caucasian or European, the Yellow or Mongoloid or Asiatic, and the Black or Negro or African. The specialists called in by UNESCO state that at the present time "most anthropologists agree on classifying the greater part of present-day mankind into three major divisions, as follows: the Mongoloid Division; the Negroid Division; and the Caucasoid Division" (11). Sergi (15), on the other hand, prefers to employ head shape, and speaks of two main species or races, the Eurasiatic, or roundheaded, found in Asia and Central Europe, and the Eurafrican, or long-headed, originating in Africa, but found also in Northern and Southern Europe. This classification unites in one category the blondest Scandinavian and the darkest Negro, because both are long-headed, and it ignores all the differences between them. Since there seems to be no way of deciding whether skin color or head shape is the more significant criterion, and since the two divisions are mutually incompatible, considerable doubt is thrown on the whole process of racial classification among human beings. The difficulty is not removed if we use a number of criteria in combination. This was attempted by Deniker (16), who arrived at 17 main races and 29 sub-races by this method; the process could be carried on indefinitely, depending upon the aim and interest of the classifier.

The notion that racial classifications may be artificial and arbitrary is not a new one. In 1843 Pritchard (17) expressed the opinion "that all mankind constitute but one race, or proceed from a single family." The French naturalist Buffon (18) wrote "species, orders, and classes exist only in our imagination. They are merely conventions. Nothing really exists but the individual. Nature does not recognize our definitions: she has never classified her work by group or kind." The German philosopher Herder (19) also protests against the use of the term "race" in connection with man, since there are always transitional forms between one alleged race and another. Even Blumenbach insists that "the various types of men differ from each other in degree and not in kind and are connected with each other by innumerable gradations" (9, p. 27).

The discrepancies in the racial classifications, the fact that transitional forms may always be discovered, and the marked degree of overlapping in physical characteristics between one group and another, appear to justify the conclusion that human races, in any strict sense of the term, exist only in the mind of the classifier. It may be that at some future date new methods in the field of physical anthropology or genetics may make it possible to reach a sound differentiation, but the techniques at present available hold little hope in this direction. When the method of blood groupings was first applied to race by the Hirszfelds (20) it was thought that it might eliminate the difficulties inherent in other approaches and make it possible to arrive at an objective and scientifically acceptable classification. This hope has now been shown to be unfounded, and the complications in the use of the blood groups are at least as great as those found with the more usual physical criteria. Although many anthropologists insist upon retaining the concept of human races, and many new classifications still appear, by far the most reasonable position seems to be that there is only one human race, and that the distinctions found within it are relatively unimportant. For that reason the present writer prefers, when referring to existing populations, to use the term "ethnic group," which may be distinguished by inherited physical type, or by culture, or by nationality or by any combination of these.

Even if this position is accepted, however, the problem of the meaning of physical differences still exists, and requires more direct consideration. Although the usual distinction between the Negro and the Caucasian may have little significance in terms of a scientifically valid classification, it is certainly taken seriously by the large majority of people. On the basis of the customary racial classification, a great deal of research has been carried on, and there is now a voluminous literature on the question of the psychological and cultural implications of race differences. Most of this has centered upon the problem of ethnic differences in ability, and we turn now to an appraisal of the arguments which have been used in this connection.

THE BIOLOGICAL ARGUMENT FOR "RACIAL" SUPERIORITY

One type of argument heard with some frequency is that "races" differ in their degree of "primitiveness"—more specifically, that one physical type, for example, that of the Negro, may have developed earlier from the ancestral anthropoid stock and represents therefore a species inferior to the later evolved Caucasian or Mongolian. This assumption determines the nature of the developmental or genealogical trees found in books by Osborn (21), Warden (22) and others. It rests upon the observation that in certain physical characteristics, for instance, the wide flat nose, the long arms, etc., the Negro resembles the anthropoid more than do either of the other two racial stocks. This argument has been examined in detail by Boas (23), Kroeber (24), and others. As they have pointed out, this hierarchy of physical types depends upon the nature of the criteria used. There are many characteristics in which the Negro resembles the anthropoid less than do other physical types. As Kroeber (24) points out, there is an approximately equal number of ape-like characteristics in the three stocks, and no decision is possible as to which is the most primitive.

It is frequently argued that the physical differences create a presumption in favor of psychological differences. Kroeber (25) states that there is "no sound reason to expect anything else but that races which differ anatomically also differ in some degree physiologically and psychologically" (p. 352). Franz Boas (26) wrote in the first edition of the *Mind of Primitive Man* in 1911: "It does not seem probable that the minds of races which show variations in their anatomical structure should act in exactly the same way. Differences of structure must be accompanied by differences of function, physiological as well as psychological; and as we found clear evidence of differences in structure between the races, so we must anticipate that differences in mental characteristics will also be found." It is significant that this passage does not appear in the later edition (1938) of the book, and it seems highly probable that Boas changed his mind on this point.

The fact is that there is no sound reason to expect any such relationship. Races differ anatomically by definition; if they did not differ anatomically, they would not be different races. Before we may assume that this has any psychological significance, however, we must have independent evidence of some genetic or other relationship between psychological characteristics and those anatomical features used in racial classification. Differences in skin color, for example, may have arisen in response to the direct or indirect effect of the physical environment. It is possible, as Linton (27) suggests, that the different skin color in tropical and in cold regions may be related not to differences of heat, but of light intensity. The actinic rays of the sun are beneficial in small quantities, but harmful in large ones. The skin pigment seems to act as a ray filter, its efficiency being related to the depth of color. In the tropics a dark skin color is an advantage since it prevents the absorption of too great a quantity of actinic rays; in cold regions a light skin color aids in the absorption of the necessary amount. Under these conditions a process of natural selection may help to fix one or the other skin color as a racial trait. If this interpretation is correct, there is no reason to suppose that psychological factors are in any way involved in the process of selection. The dark skin would simply be more advantageous in one physical environment and would therefore survive. Unless there is some other reason to assume an original relationship between skin color and psychology, the probabilities are that this form of natural selection would have no psychological significance whatsoever.

In the second place, Kroeber's argument assumes that there is in general some necessary connection between physical and psychological characteristics. This is a problem which has interested psychologists and physiologists throughout the history of their research, and a large amount of material has been accumulated. There have been studies of the possible psychological significance of various physiognomic features, including skin color, shape of the head, size of the nose, height of forehead, convexity and concavity of facial profile, glandular make-up and general bodily constitution. Some of these attempts, for example the last, have for a time held out promise of the establishment of a positive relationship, and in particular the theories of Kretschmer (28) and Sheldon (29) concerning the relation between constitution and personality have received considerable attention (see Chapter 12). In any case, such constitutional typologies do not involve to any important degree the specific characteristics—skin color, head shape, hair texture, etc. —that have been used in racial classifications. As far as such characteristics are concerned, the careful examination of the research data by Paterson (30), Anastasi and Foley (31) and others justifies the conclusion that not a single one of them has proved any positive relationship between physique and mentality. This means that we have no right to assume a relation between physical and psychological differences, and to treat the problem of race differences as if this assumption had been verified. (The problem of sex differences is, of course, in a different category.)

There is one physical feature which requires somewhat more detailed consideration—namely, the size and shape of the brain. As far as size is concerned, the earlier studies apparently demonstrated certain differences in averages, the brain of the Negro being somewhat smaller than that of the White. Some significance has been attached to this difference. It must be borne in mind, however, that the overlapping is very great, so that there are a great many Negro brains larger than the White average. In addition, the fact that the brains of certain Negro groups like the Kaffirs and the Amaxosa are on the average larger than those of certain White groups like the Scots makes it difficult to assume any significant "race" difference in this respect. It is probable that general body contours as well as physical well-being also play a part in determining brain size. Most important of all, a very careful study of Negro and White brains from similar (low) socio-economic status made by Todd and Lindala (32) revealed "no significant stock differences." Finally, the fact that studies of brain size within the White group have failed to show any close correspondence with level of mentality, and the added fact that the brain size of women is both relatively and absolutely inferior to that of men, throw further doubt on the psychological significance of possible group differences in this respect.

In connection with the qualitative characteristics of the brain, the early investigations of Bean (33) have focused attention upon possible Negro-White differences. In a series of studies Bean arrived at the conclusion that the frontal area of the brain was less well-developed in the Negro than in the White, and the posterior area better developed. He believed that this difference paralleled the "known fact" that the Negro is inferior in the higher intellectual functions and superior in those concerned with rhythm and sense perception. Another important difference was in the depth of the convolutions of the cortex, those of the Negro being much shallower and more "childlike" than those of the White. There were also differences in the shape of the corpus callosum, which connects the two hemispheres of the cerebrum, and in the temporal lobe, but these were not regarded as having any direct psychological significance. It happened that these studies were carried out at Johns Hopkins University under the direction of Professor Mall, head of the Department of Anatomy. Mall was for some reason uncertain of Bean's results, and he repeated the whole study (34) on the same collection of brains on which Bean had worked; he took the precaution, however, of comparing the brains without knowing in advance which were Negro and which were White. When he and his associates placed in one group those brains which had rich convolutions, and in another those with convolutions which were shallow, they found exactly the same proportion of Negro and White brains in the two groups. When further they measured the size of the frontal and posterior lobes in the two groups of brains, they found no difference in their relative extent. As a consequence Mall came to the conclusion that Bean's findings had no basis in fact, and that it had not been demonstrated that Negro brains differed in any essential manner from those of Whites. Incidentally, these two studies taken together illustrate in a very significant manner the importance of stereotypes and "mental set" in determining what one will see in any given situation. There can be no doubt that Bean was sincere in his belief that he had observed these differences between the two groups of brains. It seems clear, however, that because of the expectation of finding signs of inferiority in the Negro, and because of his knowledge of the origin of the brains he was examining, he actually "saw" differences which did not exist. In any case Mall's more carefully controlled study testifies to the fallacy of the popular assumption that one can recognize a Negro brain by the presence of certain definite inferiorities.

THE CULTURAL ARGUMENT

A second group of arguments in favor of the superiority of certain ethnic groups over others centers upon the question of their relative contributions to culture or civilization. This is the type of argument made popular by Gobineau and used by many writers who more or less followed his example. Gobineau spoke of the superior "race" as the Aryans; Houston Stewart Chamberlain (35) glorified the Teutons; Madison Grant (36) and Lothrop Stoddard (37) and many others have spoken of the supremacy of the Nordics. Throughout the variations in terminology there is the common tendency among these writers to regard as superior the North European, usually conceived as tall, blond and blue-eyed; the other European groups are regarded as having made relatively inferior contributions, but they are still superior to the Mongolians, and even more markedly to the African Negroes. This point of view has been developed so frequently during the past century that it is customary to think of the problem mainly in terms of the alleged superiority of the Nordics.

The first important consideration in connection with this type of evaluation is the need to place it in proper historical perspective. It is necessary to keep in mind that we have no right to argue from a temporary to a biological and permanent superiority. It is illuminating in this connection to examine some of the judgments of "racial" ability found in the earlier literature. We know that Aristotle (38), for example, basing his argument mainly upon the effects of climate, regarded the North Europeans as barbarians incapable of a creative culture, particularly in the field of politics. The Roman Vitruvius (39) took a similar position. At the time these men wrote, no one could possibly have made a reasonable case for the superiority of the Nordics. Even in fairly recent times there is by no means unanimity in connection with this judgment. Writers like Huntington (40) and Dixon (7) regard the contributions of the Alpines as superior. Sergi (41), Elliott Smith (42), and Huxley and Haddon (9) believe that the Mediterraneans had laid the foundations of European civilization long before the Nordics came upon the scene, and that the contribution of the latter is relatively insignificant. Elliott Smith in particular thinks of civilization as having originated among the Mediterranean Babylonians, Sumerians and Egyptians, and having later traveled through the world from that source. W. I. Thomas (43) points out that our Western European civilization is a composite containing contributions from peoples all over the world, including those of Asia and Africa, and that to think of it as exclusively or predominantly Nordic in origin indicates merely regional or national chauvinism. We see that even within the framework of our contemporary Western civilization there is by no means unanimity of judgment as to which group has made the most important contribution.

In the second place, however, the argument becomes even more tenuous when we remember that other groups may legitimately protest against our judging them in terms of our own criteria. We tend to think of the Eskimos or the Africans as inferior because they have failed to develop our type of civilization. There is, however, no universal criterion which enables us to determine the superiority of one culture or civilization over another. Marco Polo may have ridiculed the Chinese for wasting their discovery of gunpowder on firecrackers, but they with at least equal right might have questioned the intelligence of using it for the destruction of human beings. Rivers (44) in an amusing passage imagines the effect of our civilization upon a Melanesian; he suggests that to the Melanesian our failure to keep clearly in mind the degrees of consanguinity of all our relatives would certainly indicate our incapacity, since to him nothing is more important than social and family relationships. Lips (45) has collected many illuminating examples of the manner in which members of primitive groups have reacted to the presence of Whites among them. There are cases in which the Whites are admired, but frequently they are despised and hated as criminals and oppressors. LaPiere and Farnsworth (46) quote from a letter written by a Chinese of the 17th century, following upon the firsts visits of Jesuits to his country, in which doubt is expressed that these "Ocean Men" are human in the same sense as are the Chinese. Nansen's example of the Eskimo who wished to send medicine men as missionaries to the Whites in order to teach them the advantages of peace, may again be cited in this connection (see p. 90). As has been pointed out many times, Western man has shown the greatest skill and ingenuity in his mechanical inventions and in his conquest of physical nature generally, but he has so far not succeeded in devising a satisfactory formula for living. The one fact that we are in constant fear of the destruction by war of everything we have created makes it impossible in any objective sense to regard our civilization as superior.

A third reason for questioning any intimate relation between physical type and culture is the great amount of variability found within any one type in this respect. The most cultivated Chinese and the simplest tribes of Siberia are of the same inherited physical type; the same is true of the Incas of Peru and the Mayas of Yucatan on the one hand, and the rude communities of the California Indians on the other. These wide divergences make it impossible to assume that physical type is in any direct way the cause of culture. They indicate rather that we must take into account a whole host of geographical and historical factors which are relatively independent of physique, which make it possible for one society to reach the height of complexity in its cultural and social life, and which keep another at a relatively simple level. Individuals within various groups may differ in their biological make-up, but in the examples cited above they are "racially" homogeneous.

The frequent contrast in the data supplied by social statistics regarding different sub-groups of the same inherited physical type also argues in this direction. McDougall (47) believed that suicide occurs with greater frequency among peoples of Nordic ancestry because of their tendency toward introversion, which causes action to be directed to oneself in any crisis situation. He cited figures to prove that this was an essential Nordic characteristic. More complete statistics showed, however, that this was by no means necessarily true; the figures for Norway, to take only one example, were among the lowest, in spite of the marked predominance of the Nordic component among Norwegians; both France and Switzerland, with the Alpine the most frequent physical type, had very high rates of suicide (48). The alleged frequency of homicide among Mediterranean peoples has also been linked to their genetic origin, but quantitative studies have shown (49) that the apparent homicidal tendencies of Italians in America are markedly reduced after the passage of one generation, and that American-born sons of Italian parents have a homicide rate closely approaching that of the American population in general.

The same variability within each group holds for other characteristics of culture and of personality. The American Indians of the Plains were warlike, and their whole social structure depended upon war as an institution; the Pueblos of the Southwest, at least in recent times, were a peaceful group who fought only in self-defense. The American Negroes are said to be musical, but there are many tribes in Africa for whom ethnologists have reported little or no music. The plastic art of Benin and Dahomey is famous the world over, but there are large areas in Africa where this type of art is unknown. It is difficult to understand this great variability on the assumption that these aspects of culture are directly associated with inherited physical type.

The discussion up to this point has been somewhat "subjective" in the sense that the judgments which have been discussed and described depend to a considerable degree upon personal bias and point of view. One writer may be impressed by the similarities between the Plains Indians and the Pueblos, and another by the differences; one person may judge the civilization of the Hindus to be inferior to that of the Germans, and another may regard it as superior. It is obviously desirable to make use of more objective criteria whenever they are available, and among these the intelligence test has received the most attention in this field.

TESTS OF INTELLIGENCE

There have been many reviews of the literature dealing with the application of mental tests to the study of racial and national differences in intelligence. The reader will find extensive discussion of the techniques and results in the books by Anastasi and Foley (31) and Klineberg (50). At this point we shall attempt only a brief summary of what seem to be the more important considerations.

Marked changes in viewpoint may be noted among the investigators in this field since the work of testing group differences in intelligence on a large scale was begun during World War I. The analysis of the results of this study by C. C. Brigham (51) came to the conclusion that there was clear evidence for the innate intellectual superiority of Whites over Negroes, and of North Europeans or Nordics over Alpines and Mediterraneans. These conclusions were widely quoted and generally accepted by psychologists at the time of their appearance, although criticism, especially at the hands of anthropologists, was by no means lacking. As the result of further critical analysis, doubt was thrown not only upon the racial distinctions used in the study, but also on the capacity of the tests themselves to measure native intelligence apart from the effect of environment. More refined statistical analysis of the nature of the Army Alpha tests supported the growing conviction that these conclusions were invalid. Brigham himself in a later publication (52) carried certain of these criticisms to their logical conclusion, and with fine scientific and objective candor withdrew completely from his earlier position, stating that all the studies which had appeared to demonstrate racial differences by means of intelligence tests, including his own, fell completely to the ground. In Brigham's own change of attitude may be seen the reflection of a change typical of a great many psychologists. It is unfortunate that so many people have been influenced by the original study, whereas relatively few know of the recantation.

A further example of this change in point of view is represented by Goodenough (53), who published an article in 1926 on ethnic differences in the intelligence of school children. She used her own "Draw-a-Man" test, in which achievement is measured in terms of how accurately the figure is drawn, without regard to the esthetic qualities of the drawing. Since the test makes no use of language or information, she believed it could be regarded as a measure of native intelligence, independent of culture or previous experience. Her groups did differ in economic background, but she regarded this fact as irrelevant. She wrote: "It seems probable upon the whole, that inferior environment is an effect at least as much as it is a cause of inferior ability. . . . The person of low intelligence tends to gravitate to those neighborhoods where economic requirement is minimal. . . . His children inherit his mental characteristics."

In 1950 Goodenough, writing with Morris (54) reviews many of the investigations made with her test and concludes that there is a definite indication of the influence of culture and previous training on the results obtained. The test is not so "culture-free" as was formerly believed. The investigators state that they "would like to express the opinion that the search for a culture-free test, whether of intelligence, artistic ability, personal-social characteristics, or any other measurable trait is illusory, and that the naive assumption that the mere freedom from verbal requirements renders a test equally suitable for all groups is no longer tenable." In a brief footnote Goodenough adds that her own earlier study reporting differences among the children of immigrants to the United States is "certainly no exception to the rule. The writer hereby apologizes for it!"

These honest and courageous admissions on the part of distinguished scholars are mentioned here because they represent in clearest form the development which has taken place in this whole field of inquiry. When the tests were first applied to representatives of different ethnic groups, it was usually in the belief that the method was capable of measuring native ability, and that the results could be so interpreted. Voices of caution and criticism were raised from the beginning, but for a time, at least among psychologists, they were in the minority. The history of the mental testing of ethnic or "racial" groups may almost be described as a progressive disillusionment with tests as measures of native ability, and a gradually increasing realization of the many complex environmental factors which enter into the result. As between Terman's (55) earlier position that the tests were a true measure of native capacity and the insistence of Garrett and Schneck (56) that "the examiner must always remember that comparisons are permissible only when environmental differences are absent, or at least negligible" (p. 24), there can be no doubt that at present most psychologists would accept the latter position. As was pointed out in an earlier chapter, it is essential to keep in mind the effect of previous experience.

In the field of ethnic comparisons, a number of environmental considerations have been regarded as important. The relationship of the subjects to the tester, or the degree of rapport between them, may obviously differ in the case of two ethnic groups. Their motivation, or their anxiety to do well on the test, cannot always be presumed to be similar. The discussion of occupational differences in intelligence in Chapter 9 has shown that even within one race, socioeconomic and educational factors are of importance; their weight is all the greater in any comparison, for example, of Negroes and Whites, who differ so greatly in economic opportunities and in the nature of schooling and other education available. The frequent reliance in the intelligence test upon speed as a measure of capacity has also been shown to be unfair to those groups outside of our own culture who place no premium upon getting things done in a hurry. There may also be, as Porteus has pointed out (57), an actual misunderstanding of the purpose of the test on the part of those who are not accustomed to being tested. There are varying attitudes and points of view which we collectively call "culture," which may produce such different reactions as to make direct comparison of two racial or cultural groups scientifically valueless.

We are not suggesting that there are many studies of ethnic differences in which all of these environmental factors enter. It is hard to imagine an investigator so naive that he would compare two groups differing in all of the above respects. It is more probable that some of these factors operate in one investigation, but not in another; one group may be handicapped by linguistic disability, a second by poor schooling, a third by lack of adequate motivation, a fourth by a combination of any of these, and so on. Taken all together, these environmental factors may account for a good part if not all of the differences found in the mental test performance of racial and national groups.

Even if the two groups are adequately equated in these respects, there still remains an important source of error—namely, the factor of sampling or selection. Obviously an investigator or a team of investigators cannot test all the members of any two groups which are being compared, and only a relatively small proportion of each may possibly be examined. This raises the question as to the degree to which this sample is truly representative. To take a specific instance, the comparison of Scottish and Italian children in New York City, even if all of the environmental factors have been adequately considered, may still not hold for Scots and Italians generally, since the migrants to this country may not represent similar samples of the total Scottish and Italian populations. This makes it necessary to restrict the conclusions to the particular samples studied. An investigation by Franzblau (58) indicates that the superiority of Danish over Italian children in this country does not extend to Danish children in Copenhagen as compared with Italian children in Rome. In spite of statistical and other checks on the validity of a sample, this remains a constant problem and a possible source of error in all group comparisons.

This question of the nature of the migrants within any given population has already been discussed in Chapter 9 in connection with rural-urban comparisons. It has special significance with reference to the Negro. The investigation by the Army testers showed the superiority of White recruits over Negroes in general, but they also indicated that Negroes of certain northern states during World War I were superior to the Whites of certain southern states. This was especially true for those who took the Army Alpha examination, which is a test involving the use of language. In this test the Negro recruits from Ohio, Illinois and New York obtained higher scores than did the Whites, for example, from Mississippi, Kentucky and Arkansas. In previous discussions of this comparison (including those by the present writer), it was not made sufficiently clear that these comparisons referred only to the Army Alpha. Since this is a "language" test which was not taken by all the recruits, a fairer statement would run somewhat as follows: that the literate Negroes from certain northern states, who took the Army Alpha, obtained higher average scores than the literate Whites from certain southern states who were examined by means of the same test.

The fact is, however, that the scores obtained with the Army Beta, a non-language test, support the conclusions indicated above. In some cases, groups of northern Negroes were superior to groups of southern Whites on both tests. This was true for Negroes from

Ohio and Indiana, for example, in comparison with Whites from Kentucky and Mississippi. The conclusion is therefore justified that the Negro recruits from some of the northern states did obtain higher scores on the Army intelligence tests than the Whites in some of the southern states.

This raised the question as to whether the superiority of the northern Negroes was due to the better educational and economic opportunities available to them in the North, particularly in the large cities, or whether there had been a selective migration of superior Negroes from South to North. The Army testers did not commit themselves to either of these alternatives. A study by Peterson and Lanier (59) of twelve-year-old Negro and White boys, found the Whites superior in Nashville, slightly superior in Chicago and equal to the Negroes in New York. The investigators decided that selective migration to New York was responsible, although their evidence does not seem to support this conclusion. In a more direct attack upon this problem (60) there appeared to be no indication of a selective migration to the North, since the school records of the migrants were not in any way superior to those of the non-migrants; on the other hand there was definite indication of an improvement in the intelligence test scores of southern Negro children living in New York City, which was clearly related to the length of time during which they had lived in the superior environment. There was direct evidence of an environmental effect, but no indication of selective migration. Since the average test scores of the Negroes even in New York City were slightly inferior to the White norms, this study cannot be regarded as disposing of the question of group differences. It must be borne in mind, however, that even in New York City the environment of Negroes cannot be regarded as completely equal to that of Whites. The study does at least indicate that as the environment of the Negro improves, his test scores rise correspondingly. It seems to the writer highly probable, if not certain, that with complete environmental equality, the present difference in test scores between Negroes and Whites would entirely disappear. It should be added that an investigation by Lee (61) in Philadelphia, closely paralleling the study just described, but following the *same* pupils for several years after their migration from the South to that city, also demonstrated a gradual improvement in test scores accompanying the longer sojourn in a more favorable environment.

An approach designed to avoid the difficulties discussed above is represented by a study of very young children, presumably before they have been subjected to any influences from the social environment. This was attempted by McGraw (62), who studied White and Negro infants in the first year of life, administering to them the "Baby Tests" devised by Hetzer and Wolf under the direction of Charlotte Bühler at Vienna. The results showed the White babies to be on the average definitely superior to the Negro. The author concludes: "It is significant that with even the very young subjects when environment factors are minimized, the same type and approximately the same degree of superiority is evidenced on the part of the White subjects, as that found among older groups."

The difficulty with this conclusion is that environmental factors, even at this early age, are by no means "minimized." The performance of an infant on these tests is markedly influenced by general physical development, which in turn depends on adequate nourishment. In this respect the Negro children were definitely at a disadvantage. They came from economically inferior homes and were relatively deficient in weight. These facts are not irrelevant simply because the children were young; on the contrary, the linkage between physical and mental development should be at least as striking at the beginning of life as later.

This interpretation is supported by a study of Negro and White babies in New Haven, Connecticut, by Pasamanick (63) under the direction of Arnold Gesell of Yale University. This time the Negro infants revealed a physical and psychological development equal to that of the Whites; the tests showed no significant differences between the two groups. The investigator points out that, as the result of careful dietary controls introduced during World War II, the Negro mothers in this group received adequate nourishment and in fact were not markedly different from the White mothers in this respect. The general economic level of the Negro group had also improved as a consequence of the opportunities opened up by defense industries. These Negro infants started out, physically, on equal terms with the Whites; they also, in parallel fashion, showed no inferiority or retardation in psychological development. With the equating of environmental opportunities, the difference between the two groups disappeared.

It is important to remember that when it is alleged that Whites are superior to Negroes, it is a superiority *on the average* which is being defended. In other words, even if there is a difference of this type, it is still true that a great many Negroes are superior to a great many Whites. Any restrictions therefore upon the education or occupation of Negroes on the basis of the results of psychological studies is unwarranted. In this connection it is interesting to consider some of the cases of gifted Negro children described by Witty and Jenkins (64). One of these, a young girl of nine, of almost unmixed African ancestry, had a Binet I.Q. of 200 with correspondingly high scores in a number of other intelligence tests. This score has been matched by very few indeed of the thousands of White children tested. It goes without saying that any restrictions placed upon this girl on grounds of race have no foundation in the science of psychology.

American Indians in general obtain low test scores; on the average, the Indian I.Q. is in the neighborhood of 80. This result is not difficult to understand. Not only do most American Indians occupy an inferior economic position in comparison to the rest of the population; but in addition, their whole background and culture are so different from that of White Americans that they can hardly be expected to do equally well on tests that have been standardized on the latter group.

In an important study, Garth (65) attempted to discover what would happen if American Indian children were placed in a "White" environment. He reported that a group of Indian foster children living in White homes obtained an average I.Q. of 102, which is certainly a remarkable improvement over the general Indian average of 80. This result would be conclusive evidence of the effect of the environment on group differences, if it were not for the possibility that the Indian children living in White homes were exceptional to begin with. It may be that when White families pick Indian children, they choose those who have superior intelligence. This is the hypothesis of "selection" in a different context and in another form. Garth attempted to answer this criticism by testing also the brothers and sisters of the foster children; these siblings were still living on the reservation. Their average I.Q. was only 87.5. This suggests that the superiority of the foster children is in fact due to their more favorable environmental opportunities, but the proof is not complete.

An even more convincing result is represented by Rohrer's (66) study of Osage Indians in Oklahoma. These Indian children live under social and economic conditions quite similar to those of the White children with whom they were compared. This is largely due to the fortunate accident that on the land which was ceded to them by the American Government as a reservation, oil was later discovered. As a consequence, these Indians became relatively well-to-do, and were able to create for themselves and their families living conditions far superior to those of other Indian communities. With this fact in mind, it is illuminating to look at the results obtained by Rohrer. On one test, the Goodenough "Draw-a-Man" test, the White children obtained an average I.Q. of 103, and the Indian children, 104. On a second test, which made use of language, the White score was 98, the Indian, 100 (these differences are of course so small as to be insignificant).

There can be no doubt in this case that when American Indian children have environmental opportunities comparable to those of Whites, their apparent inferiority disappears completely. Nor can this result be explained by selection. It was *after* they had been given their land that oil was discovered; they did not seek out this particular region. Their good fortune gave them opportunities denied to other Indians. This is reflected not only in their economic success, but also in their ability to solve the problems presented by the intelligence tests.

As far as nations within the White race are concerned, there is almost complete unanimity among psychologists that biologically determined differences between them have never been proven. As we have seen above, the most extensive investigation in this field has been repudiated by its author. It may be added that an attempt to compare groups of Nordic, Alpine and Mediterranean children, selected in Europe according to the most rigid anthropological criteria, failed to demonstrate any significant differences between them. To speak of national instead of racial differences really begs the question, since nations are political and not biological entities.

As an indication of the change in attitude among social scientists on this question, we may cite in conclusion a statement by Odum (67) that among "the errors of sociology" is "the assumption that races are inherently different rather than group products of differentials due to the cumulative power of folk-regional and cultural environment" (p. 338). This statement is all the more significant in view of the fact that Odum himself in an earlier work on the social and mental traits of the Negro (68) expressed the very definite conviction that Negroes are constitutionally inferior to Whites.

The conclusion of this discussion is that there has as yet appeared no adequate proof of inherent "racial" differences in ability. The various arguments used in support of such differences are not scientifically valid. This does not mean that we rule out heredity as an explanation of certain individual and possibly even group differences. As was pointed out in Chapter 9, it is perfectly consistent to regard the differences between large groups, socio-economic or ethnic, as due to environmental factors, while insisting that within each of these groups the individual differences may at least in part be determined by heredity. In connection with race, the differences between Whites and Negroes in present achievement may be explained in terms of the background of the two groups, but the tremendous variations within the Negro and within the White group may still reveal the influence of hereditary factors. Expressed differently, a White superiority of ten or twenty points in average I.Q. may be explained by the environment, but a range of at least 100 points between the best and the poorest members of each group may hardly be accounted for in the same manner. This does not mean that the environment plays no part in the causation of these individual differences, but it is certainly not entirely responsible for them.

THE MEASUREMENT OF NON-INTELLECTUAL TRAITS

It has sometimes been argued that the essential differences related to inherited physical type are in the realm of personality rather than intelligence. The criticisms that we have leveled against the use of intelligence tests in this field apply even more strongly in the case of tests of non-intellectual characteristics. In addition, the results conflict to such a degree, that any conclusion from them is unwarranted. This is true, for example, of tests of musical ability, in which even the alleged superiority of the Negro in rhythm is by no means a consistent finding. There are, however, a few studies in this field which raise problems of special interest in this connection.

One of the most significant of these is the investigation by Efron (69), which deals with the gestural patterns sometimes regarded as being inborn group characteristics. By means of very careful sketches and motion picture recordings it was possible to compare in great detail the gestures used by Jews and Italians in a large variety of social conditions. There were marked differences between the two groups, the Italian gestures being much more frequently symbolic and conveying a definite meaning, whereas those of the Jews were rather a running accompaniment to speech, but without significance when taken by themselves; there were differences also in the nature of the movements employed, those of the Italians tending to extend laterally away from the body, and those of the Jews forward toward the person addressed. The interesting finding was, however, that in spite of these marked differences between the immigrant Jews and Italians, the gestures almost entirely disappeared with the passage of one generation. There was clear indication therefore of the temporary and cultural rather than of the native character of the gestures.

The problem of speed is also of interest in this connection. Not only is it of significance in relation to intelligence test scores, but it has also some direct bearing on the general question of personality differences. It has been suggested that groups may differ in this respect because of the direct effect of physiological factors. In connection with the apparently more easy-going tempo of the Chinese, for example, Earle (70) has suggested that a difference in basal metabolic rate between the Orientals and the Whites may be responsible. This seems unlikely for several reasons—first, because the basal metabolism is affected by factors of diet, climate, occupation and other environmental circumstances; second, because the metabolism of members of the same race living in different environments may vary greatly; and third, because experimental methods have failed to reveal any direct relation between basal metabolism and speed of behavior in normal subjects.

The more direct approach to the question of differences in speed by means of reaction-time experiments as well as measurement of rate of movement have revealed marked variations between groups, but apparently not determined by inborn factors. Indians on the Yakima reservation, for example, moved very slowly in the test situation and showed a corresponding decrease in the number of errors during the solution of a performance test; this qualitative difference between Indians and Whites did not obtain in the case of pupils at the Haskell Institute, where the Indian children are brought up in a manner comparable to Whites generally (71). The conclusion that differences in speed are cultural, not innate, is supported by the careful study by Foley (72), who showed a relationship between type of occupation and speed of movement in a variety of test situations. It is true, however, that this study did not entirely control the factor of selection, and there is the possibility that those who prefer a quicker tempo find their way into certain occupations. Foley prefers the conclusion that tempo is determined by habits acquired by the individual.

The use of personality tests of the usual type, including those of the paper-and-pencil and of the performance variety, have failed to reveal any significant group differences. One study (73) involved the application of the Bernreuter inventory, the Allport-Vernon Study of Values, a persistence test, a test of suggestibility, and an honesty test to students in a number of academic institutions in New York City and vicinity. These were divided according to their "racial" characteristics into Nordic, Alpine and Mediterranean groups, as well as into Jews and non-Jews. The results showed these "racial" differences to be insignificant, although there were rather marked variations among sub-groups of the same "race" in different academic institutions and different socio-economic classes. This result finds support in an earlier observation by Hartshorne and May (74) who in their *Studies in Deceit* noted that Jewish children in a poor neighborhood cheated more frequently than the average, and those in a good neighborhood less frequently. Their conclusion is that honesty in these situations appears to be a function of intelligence and background and not of ethnic origin.

Personality tests are so deeply impregnated with the culture in which they have originated that their direct application to other groups and other cultures yields results that may be very misleading. To mention one specific example, the Pressey X-O Test, which is designed to measure emotional responses, was administered to Indians of varying tribal origin, now living in Nebraska, Montana, California, New Mexico and Oklahoma (75). The investigators report that the Indians were less mature emotionally than the Whites with whom they were compared. "The Indian tends to remain immature; either he is incapable of a more mature adjustment, or else his environment has been so simplified that adjustment on a childish level is good enough." In view of the obvious cultural relativity of the concept of emotional maturity, this statement does not seem especially meaningful. The investigators themselves realize this at least in part, for in a subsequent study (76) they point out that the tribes with the greatest degree of White contact (like the Crow) are "less retarded emotionally" than those who have remained relatively isolated (like the Hopi). This conclusion closely parallels the findings in the case of intelligence tests, that the more similar the environments of the groups compared, the smaller the difference in their average test scores. Any inference to inherited group differences is completely unjustified.

There is, however, as in the case of measures of intelligence, ample room for heredity to exert a significant effect upon the range of variations among individuals within any community and in all probability these variations do have in part a biological origin. Our negative conclusion with regard to hereditary factors applies again therefore not to individual, but to group differences.

In what has been said here, there is no implication that all ethnic groups are alike in their behavior. Obviously they are not alike; or rather, they are alike in some respects and not in others. The differences that emerge, however, cannot be attributed to the physical or anatomical characteristics associated with racial classifications. It is not easy to determine just what is responsible. The causes may lie deep in history; they may be due to socio-economic factors; they may be related to the physical environment, to contacts with surrounding peoples, to the inventions and discoveries of individuals, to the problems which had to be solved, and to the ways hit upon, sometimes by accident, for their solution. In any case, there is no evidence that they are innate. We shall return to the problem of differences in the culture and the personality of ethnic groups in a later chapter (see Chapter 14).

THE PROBLEM OF MISCEGENATION

The question of miscegenation or race mixture has aroused a great deal of acrimonious discussion. There are people who advocate such mixture as the best solution for all inter-group conflicts; there are others who look upon it as equivalent to degeneration. In fairly recent European history the cult of the "pure race" has been a cornerstone of national politics, and it plays a similar role now in South Africa. The previous discussion of the relation between "race" and nation should have made it clear that biological purity in any strict anthropological sense is impossible of attainment by any nation today. Huxley and Haddon (9) go so far as to suggest that there may never have been any such thing as "racial purity," since the earliest prehistoric evidence already indicates the concomitance in one geographical area of many different physical types.

The attitude toward miscegenation may to a considerable extent depend on the attitude toward one's own ethnic group. If we regard our own group as biologically superior, we shall probably consider any mixture with an "inferior" group as equivalent to mongreliza-tion or degeneration. Our survey of the material pertinent to the question of ethnic differences has indicated the lack of evidence for the innate superiority of any one group over any other, and we may therefore dismiss this as an argument based on sentiment rather than on science.

If the notion of the inherited inequality of different groups is rejected, there are still two possible points of view toward miscege-nation. On the one hand it may be regarded as desirable because of the phenomenon which has been termed "hybrid vigor." It is argued that since inbreeding is bad, the maximum of outbreeding is clearly desirable, and this is most easily attained in marriages of individuals of different inherited physical type. There is some direct evidence in favor of hybrid vigor, as for example, in Boas' (77) finding that American Indian and French Canadian hybrids had larger families and seemed physically more robust than either of the two parent groups. Shapiro (78) has demonstrated a similar phenomenon in his study of the Polynesian-English descendants of the mutineers of the *Bounty;* they, too, showed marked superiority over the parental stocks both in physical size and in birth rate. Against the theory of hybrid vigor it is urged that inbreeding is not necessarily bad except when there are defects in the parents, and that in any case it is possible to find sufficient disparity in genetic constitution between two members of the same race without resort-ing to race mixture.

Those who argue against miscegenation have usually stressed the possibility of disharmonies arising in the offspring. Davenport (79) and his associates have been most active in support of this point of view. He points, for example, to the fact that since Negroes have on the average longer arms and legs than the Whites, the hybrid may inherit the disharmonious combination of the long legs of the Negro and the short arms of the White. This may have the practical dis-advantage to the hybrid of making him unfit for occupations which require picking things off the ground. Similar disharmonies are regarded as occurring in other aspects of the body. There is the possibility, he suggests, that if one parent is a robust, well-built Nordic, and the other a short, slender Mediterranean, the offspring may inherit the large bony structure of the former and the small internal organs of the latter; this might result in his having a heart or a stomach too small to do the work for a large organism, or there might be a visceroptosis or a dropping of the organs of the body because of insufficient support. Conversely, the inheritance of a small frame and large internal organs would cause congestion and consequent internal damage. Another possible disharmony is a discrepancy between the size of the teeth and of the jaw, and Davenport believes that excessive miscegenation is responsible for much of the dental trouble in America.

This argument depends entirely upon the theory that size is inherited separately for different organs in the body, so that the genetic basis for length of leg would be entirely distinct from that determining length of arm. This theory has been effectively disproved in a series of experiments by Castle (80), who showed among other things that in the crossing of two breeds of rabbits of markedly different size, the hybrids were harmonious in every respect. There is an apparent confirmation of Davenport's point of view in the experiments by Stockard (81) which showed that the crossing of dogs might result in very unsatisfactory combinations, as, for example, a large body upon legs too short to support it adequately. It must be kept in mind, however, that the differences between these dogs are immeasurably greater than those found between any two human physical types, and that therefore the argument from one to the other is not tenable. The direct observation and measurement of human hybrids show only an occasional disharmony probably of no more frequent occurrence than among members of a single unmixed group. The mulattoes in America are certainly not conspicuous for any excessive frequency of disharmonies in their physical constitution.

On the biological side therefore we may conclude that neither the arguments for nor those against race mixture have any special cogency. It is not necessary to go outside of one's group in order to marry someone whose genes are sufficiently different to avoid any possibly harmful effects of inbreeding. On the other hand, the disharmonies alleged to follow miscegenation seem to be for the most part imaginary, and constitute no valid argument in favor of racial purity. Mixture in itself is neither good nor bad; its results depend upon the nature of the individuals who enter into the crossing.

From the sociological point of view, however, the problem is a much more serious one. If there is general objection to miscegenation, and if as a consequence the hybrids find it difficult to fit into the social and economic life of either of the parent groups, the effect upon them as individuals may be very unfavorable. As Castle points out in this connection, the real problem of race mixture is not one of biology, but of personal and social relationships. This becomes clear if we contrast the descriptions of Chinese-White crosses in Shanghai and in Hawaii; the former are described by Lamson (82) as maladjusted, unfortunate individuals who are found mainly in the less savory occupations of the city, whereas Romanzo Adams (83) speaks of the healthy integration of this group with every aspect of life in Hawaii. It is clearly the attitude toward the hybrids, not their biological make-up, which determines their place in the community. For this reason many valid objections may be raised against race mixture within any society in which the half-caste is looked upon with contempt or finds adjustment difficult. It must be kept clearly in mind, however, that in these cases it is not race mixture which is harmful, but the treatment accorded to the hybrids.

The problem of race mixture has also been studied by means of the application of intelligence tests to the hybrids. It has been urged by Herskovits (84), Witty and Jenkins (85), and others that this approach might help to settle the problem of innate group differences; if, for example, Whites are superior to Negroes, then among the mulatto group there should be a direct correspondence between level of intelligence and degree of White admixture. This argument depends, however, upon the assumption that the mixture is made up of comparable samples of both groups. This has not so far been demonstrated. As a matter of fact Reuter (86) has suggested the possibility that the mixture is composed of an average White but a superior Negro component, owing to the fact that within the social framework of slavery White men would choose the best Negro girls for their mistresses. This also has not been proved, especially since there is no known relation between beauty and intelligence, but it does raise the problem of selection or sampling in this whole connection. Until we know more of the nature of this sampling, we cannot argue from the characteristics of the mulatto to the nature of the component groups.

The actual results in this field were formerly regarded as indicating clearly the relationship between degree of White intermixture and standing on the intelligence tests. The early study by Ferguson (87) came to this conclusion, but made use of relatively crude measures both of mental level and of racial constitution. The later studies by Herskovits (84), Peterson and Lanier (59), and Klineberg (71) used more careful measurements of Negroid characteristics such as skin color, nose width and lip thickness, and found that within relatively homogeneous socio-economic groups of Negroes the correlations of these measures with intelligence test scores were negligible. Garth's (88) studies on American Indian crosses were also formerly interpreted as indicating the importance of degree of White mixture, but he later concluded that there is no proof of such a relationship.

It is true, however, that among the American Negroes there has in the past been a definite tendency for leadership in the fields of art, science and business to be largely in the hands of the lighter-colored mulattoes. The suggestion was frequently made that this was due to the admixture of White genes. It is much more likely, however, that the true cause is to be found in the fact that in the past mulattoes have had much better opportunities for education and advancement than darker Negroes. There have been many reasons for this. In the first place, at the time when Negroes were prohibited by law from acquiring an education, this did not apply to the mulatto children of White men, and they thus secured a definite advantage; in the second place these lighter-colored Negroes were given the preference in those jobs which brought them into contact with Whites; and finally Negroes themselves, accepting to a large extent the notion of White superiority, regarded the mulattoes as an intermediate group and treated them accordingly. This last point is particularly significant, since it has led to a tendency among Negroes to rate high those physical characteristics which are least Negroid, and the success of cosmetic establishments emphasizing preparations for bleaching the skin and straightening the hair is indicative of this trend. This attitude is prevalent even at the present time, and as Herskovits has shown (89), it expresses itself also in the preference of successful Negroes for light-colored wives. As far as leadership among the Negroes is concerned, however, it is not nearly so true now as it was in former days that the mulattoes preponderate. In the Negro universities, for example, there has been a progressive "darkening" in the complexion of the average student. It seems clear that the superiority of the mulatto is a temporary one and that it also is rooted in social and educational rather than in biological factors.

SUMMARY

The word *race* refers to a group of people of similar physical type and common heredity. In popular usage it is frequently confused with nation, which is a political grouping consisting of individuals heterogeneous in origin and in physical characteristics; there is no German or Italian or American race. Another type of confusion is with language; the terms *Latin, Semitic,* and *Aryan* all refer to families of languages, and not to race. Similarly, there is no Jewish race.

The very concept of race as applied to man has been challenged because of lack of agreement as to the criteria of classification. Subdivisions based on skin color are in conflict with those based on cephalic index, and there appears to be no means of deciding which is to be preferred. This supports the notion that "all mankind constitute but one race."

The physical differences which do exist have often been regarded as having psychological implications. It has been urged, for example, that the characteristics of the Negro are more primitive than those of other races, but ape-like features occur with equal frequency in all groups. The brains of Negroes and Whites appear to be approximately equal in size and to have the same conformation. In general, there has been no demonstration that psychological differences of any significance are associated with the physical features used in race classification.

The cultural argument for racial superiority is unsatisfactory because of the great variations in the cultural level of the same ethnic group at different times in history, as well as of different sub-groups of similar physical type, and also because there is no acceptable criterion which may be used in judging all cultures. As far as intelligence tests are concerned, it was formerly believed by many psychologists that racial differences had been demonstrated, but the present consensus is to the effect that so many environmental factors enter into the comparisons that no conclusion as to innate ability is justified. The superiority of northern over southern Negroes argues in favor of the environmental determination of the test scores, since there is no definite evidence for the selective migration of a superior group. The discovery of individual Negro children with intelligence quotients at the extreme upper end of the distribution, the excellent showing made by American Indian children adopted into superior White homes, as well as the marked improvement following a rise in economic level and educational opportunities, also testify to the absence of innate ethnic differences in intelligence.

The measurement of traits of personality has yielded mainly negative results in this field, partly because of the nature of the tests used, and partly because of the inconsistency of the findings. In this respect also, sub-groups within the same ethnic population differ markedly according to variations in the socioeconomic and cultural environment.

Miscegenation has been on the one hand opposed because of the physical disharmonies which are alleged to result, and on the other hand advocated because of the phenomenon of hybrid vigor. Neither argument appears to be particularly significant. The results of mixture depend upon the nature of the individuals who participate in the crossing, and upon the attitude which society adopts toward the hybrid.

There has been a striking change in the position adopted by social scientists with regard to inherited ethnic differences. Many investigators who formerly accepted the idea of such innate differences now regard them as unproven.

REFERENCES

1. Hogben, L. *Nature and Nurture.* 1933
2. Hooton, E. A. *Apes, Men and Morons.* 1937
3. Boas, F. *General Anthropology.* 1938
4. Dobzhansky, T. *Genetics and the Origin of Species.* Rev. ed. 1941
5. Krogman, W. M. "The Concept of Race." In R. Linton (ed.), *The Science of Man in the World Crisis.* 1945
6. Retzius, G., and Fürst, C. M. *Anthropologia Suecica.* 1902
7. Dixon, R. B. *The Racial History of Man.* 1923
8. Kossinna, G. *Ursprung der Germanen.* 1928
9. Huxley, J. S., and Haddon, A. C. *We Europeans.* 1935
10. Boas, F. "Aryans and Non-Aryans," *American Mercury,* 1934, 32: pp. 219-223

11. *Statement on Race,* published by UNESCO (UNESCO Publication 769)

12. Müller, F. M. *Biographies of Words and the Home of the Aryas.* 1888

13. Barzun, J. *Race: A Study in Modern Superstition.* 1937

14. Blumenbach, J. F. *Anthropological Treatises.* 1865

15. Sergi, G. *L'Uomo, secondo le origini, l'antichità, le variazioni e la distribuzione geografica.* 1911

16. Deniker, J. *The Races of Man.* 1900

17. Pritchard, A. *The Natural History of Man.* 1843

18. Buffon, G. L. *Histoire Naturelle.* 36 vols. 1749-1788

19. Herder, J. G. *Ideen zur Philosophie der Geschichte der Menschheit.* 1784-1791

20. Hirszfeld, L., and Hirszfeld, H. "Serologic Differences Between the Blood of Different Races," *Lancet,* 1919, 2, No. 5016: pp. 675-678

21. Osborn, H. F. *Men of the Old Stone Age.* 1918

22. Warden, C. J. *The Evolution of Human Behavior.* 1932

23. Boas, F. *Anthropology and Modern Life.* 1928

24. Kroeber, A. L. *Anthropology.* 1923

25. Kroeber, A. L. "Cultural Anthropology," *The Problem of Mental Disorder* (ed. by M. Bentley and E. V. Cowdry), 1934

26. Boas, F. *The Mind of Primitive Man.* 1911

27. Linton, R. *The Study of Man.* 1936

28. Kretschmer, E. *Physique and Character.* 1925

29. Sheldon, W. H., Stevens, S. S., and Tucker, W. W. *The Varieties of Human Physique.* 1940. Sheldon and Stevens. *The Varieties of Temperament.* 1942

30. Paterson, D. G. *Physique and Intellect.* 1930

31. Anastasi, A., and Foley, J. P., Jr. *Differential Psychology.* 1949

32. Todd, T. W., and Lindala, A. "Dimensions of the Body; Whites and Negroes of Both Sexes," *Amer. J. Phys. Anthrop.,* 1928, 12: pp. 35-119

33. Bean, R. B. "Some Racial Peculiarities of the Negro Brain," *Amer. J. Anat.,* 1906, 5: pp. 353-432

34. Mall, F. P. "On Several Anatomical Characters of the Human Brain," *Amer. J. Anat.,* 1909, 9: pp. 1-32

35. Chamberlain, H. S. *The Foundations of the Nineteenth Century.* 2 vols. 1911

36. Grant, M. *The Passing of the Great Race.* 1916

37. Stoddard, T. L. *The Rising Tide of Color Against White World Supremacy.* 1920

38. Aristotle. *The Politics of Aristotle.* 1885

39. Vitruvius, P. *The Ten Books on Architecture.* 1914

40. Huntington, E. *The Character of Races.* 1924

41. Sergi, G. *The Mediterranean Race.* 1895

42. Smith, G. E. *Human History.* 1929

43. Thomas, W. I. *Primitive Behavior.* 1937

44. Rivers, W. H. R. *Psychology and Ethnology.* 1926

45. Lips, J. *The Savage Hits Back.* 1937

46. LaPiere, R. T., and Farnsworth, P. R. *Social Psychology.* 1936

47. McDougall, W. *Is America Safe for Democracy?* 1921

48. Hankins, F. H. *The Racial Basis of Civilization.* 1926

49. Stofflet, E. H. "A Study of National and Cultural Differences in Criminal Tendency," *Arch. Psychol.,* 1935, No. 185

50. Klineberg, O. *Race Differences.* 1935. *Characteristics of the American Negro.* 1944

51. Brigham, C. C. *A Study of American Intelligence.* 1923

52. Brigham, C. C. "Intelligence Tests of Immigrant Groups," *Psychol. Rev.,* 1930, 137: pp. 158-165

53. Goodenough, F. L. "Racial Differences in Intelligence of School Children," *J. Exper. Psychol.,* 1926, 9: pp. 388-397

54. Goodenough, F. L., and Morris, D. B. "Studies in the Psychology of Children's Drawings," *Psychol. Bull.,* 1950, 47: pp. 369-433

55. Terman, L. M. *The Measurement of Intelligence.* 1916

56. Garrett, H. E., and Schneck, M. R. *Psychological Tests, Methods and Results.* 1933

57. Porteus, S. D. *Primitive Intelligence and Environment.* 1937

58. Franzblau, R. N. "Race Differences in Mental and Physical Traits: Studied in Different Environments," *Arch. Psychol.,* 1935, No. 177

59. Peterson, J., and Lanier, L. H. "Studies in the Comparative Abilities of Whites and Negroes," *Ment. Meas. Monog.,* 1929, No. 5

60. Klineberg, O. *Negro Intelligence and Selective Migration.* 1935

61. Lee, E. S. "Negro Intelligence and Selective Migration: A Philadelphia Test of the Klineberg Hypothesis," *Am. Sociol. Rev.,* 1951, 16: pp. 227-233

62. McGraw, M. B. "A Comparative Study of a Group of Southern White and Negro Infants," *Genet. Psychol. Monog.,* 1931, 10: pp. 1-105

63. Pasamanick, B. "A Comparative Study of the Behavioral Development of Negro Infants," *J. Genet. Psychol.,* 1946, 69: pp. 3-44

64. Witty, P. A., and Jenkins, M. D. "The Case of 'B,' a Gifted Negro Girl," *J. Soc. Psychol.,* 1935, 6: pp. 117-124

65. Garth, T. R. "A Study of the Foster Indian Child in the White Home," *Psychol. Bull.,* 1935, 32: pp. 708-709

66. Rohrer, J. H. "The Test Intelligence of Osage Indians," *J. Soc. Psychol.,* 1942, 16: pp. 99-105

67. Odum, H. W. "The Errors of Sociology," *Soc. Forces,* 1936-37, 15: pp. 327-342

68. Odum, H. W. *Social and Mental Traits of the Negro.* 1910

69. Efron, D. *Gesture and Environment.* 1941

70. Earle, H. G. "Basal Metabolism," *The Caduceus,* 1922, I: pp. 81-85

71. Klineberg, O. "An Experimental Study of Speed and Other Factors in 'Racial' Differences," *Arch. Psychol.,* 1928, No. 93

72. Foley, J. P. "Factors Conditioning Motor Speed and Tempo," *Psychol. Bull.,* 1937, 34: pp. 351-397. "An Experimental Study of the Effect of Occupational Experience upon Motor Speed and Preferential Tempo," *Arch. Psychol.,* 1937, No. 219

73. Klineberg, O., Fjeld, H., and Foley, J. P. Unpublished study

74. Hartshorne, H., and May, M. A. *Studies in Deceit.* 1928

75. Pressey, S. L., and Pressey, L. C. "A Comparative Study of the Emotional Attitudes and Interests of Indian and White Children," *J. Appl. Psychol.,* 1933, 17: pp. 227-238

76. Pressey, S. L., and Pressey, L. C. "A Comparison of the Emotional Development of Indians Belonging to Different Tribes," *J. Appl. Psychol.,* 1933, 17: pp. 535-541

77. Boas, F. "The Half-Blood Indian," *Pop. Sci. Monthly,* 1894, 14: pp. 761-770

78. Shapiro, H. L. *Heritage of the Bounty.* 1936

79. Davenport, C. B., and Steggerda, M. *Race Crossing in Jamaica.* 1929

80. Castle, W. E. "Race Mixture and Physical Disharmonies," *Sci.,* 1930, 71: pp. 603-606

81. Stockard, C. R. *The Physical Basis of Personality.* 1931

82. Lamson, H. D. "The Eurasian in Shanghai," *Amer. J. Sociol.,* 1936, 41: pp. 642-648

83. Adams, R. *Interracial Marriage in Hawaii.* 1937

84. Herskovits, M. J. "On the Relation Between Negro-White Mixture and Standing in Intelligence Tests," *Ped. Sem. and J. Genet. Psychol.,* 1926, 33: pp. 30-42

85. Witty, P. A., and Jenkins, M. D. "Intra-Race Testing and Negro Intelligence," *J. Psychol.,* 1936, I: pp. 179-192

86. Reuter, E. B. *Race Mixture.* 1931

87. Ferguson, G. O. "The Psychology of the Negro," *Arch. Psychol.,* 1916, No. 36

88. Garth, T. R. *Race Psychology.* 1931

89. Herskovits, M. J. "Color Line," *American Mercury,* 1925, 6: pp. 204-208

Part Four

SOCIAL AND CULTURAL FACTORS IN PERSONALITY

12

The Development of Personality

INTRODUCTION

There is no sharp line of demarcation between the materials to be reviewed in the following section, and the contents of the three preceding chapters on Differential Psychology. In this new section we will continue our exploration of individual and group differences, but with a change of emphasis. Our attention shifts from the nature-nurture controversy to a more direct concern with social and cultural factors, and from differences in intellect and achievement to differences in personality. We shall try to rediscover the individual, who has been partially lost in the consideration of central tendency, of range and variability, and whom we shall now examine more closely and directly. The two sets of problems are so interconnected, however, that they should be considered as a unit, with the subdivisions into sections and chapters understood as due to convenience rather than to any rigorous logic of classification. As a matter of fact, this is true of the book as a whole, as has already been indicated. The same problems keep recurring in different contexts, and have relevance at various points in the development of the total argument. This is perhaps one reason why two different textbooks in Social Psychology may show such wide discrepancies in organization and arrangement; the interdependence of the data makes any organization somewhat arbitrary.

This section has been entitled "Social and Cultural Factors in Personality." In what follows there will be no attempt to keep the *social* and the *cultural* sharply separated. It is of course possible to make the distinction; society refers to groups of people, and culture to modes of behavior. Culture is, however, created, transmitted and modified by people; groups react as they do at least in part because of their culture. When two individuals engage in competitive activity, we speak of the phenomenon as social, but the manner and the degree of competition cannot be understood apart from the folkways or culture by which these individuals have been influenced. A family is a social unit, but the interpersonal relations within the family, the patterns of child rearing, the distribution of responsibility and authority, the nature and extent of family integration, are all at least in part cultural phenomena. In this context, therefore, social and cultural factors are considered together.

There is considerable difference of opinion as to the extent to which problems of personality fall within the scope of the social psychologist. Theories range all the way from those of Kretschmer (1) and Sheldon (2), who see personality as determined almost entirely by inherited body constitution, to F. H. Allport's (3) view that personality traits are entirely social, and that a hermit has no personality. As is usual in controversies of this kind, the truth probably lies somewhere between these extremes. It will be clear in what follows that the writer inclines more to a social than to a biological interpretation, but without going so far as to adopt Allport's position. Granting that what we call personality emerges mainly in a social situation and in terms of reactions between individuals, the fact remains that two hermits are not exactly alike and that they have some individuality in spite of their isolation. Biological factors undoubtedly play a part in shaping the individual, and they require the attention even of those psychologists whose concern is mainly with the social aspects of personality. As we shall see, however, constitutional factors are also to a considerable extent social in their implications, and can only be completely understood in relation to the fate they undergo in the process of social development. As Murphy (4) expresses it, personality is neither biological nor social alone, but *bio-social*.

There have been many definitions of personality, and many different uses to which the term has been put. G. W. Allport (5) lists a total of 50 different ways in which the words "person" and "personality" have entered into our common speech; with original meanings derived from the use of "persona" as a theatrical mask, the terms have been extended to the physical self, to a moral ideal of perfection, to legal relationships, to esthetic qualities of attractiveness, and to many other uses, popular as well as academic. Among the attempts to define personality more adequately for scientific purposes, there are several which regard personality as the sum total of innate and acquired dispositions; this "omnibus" approach has been rightly criticized on the ground that the individual is not a mere addition, but represents some form of integration or organization. Allport suggests the following: "Personality is the dynamic organization within the individual of those psycho-physical systems which determine his unique adjustments to his environment."

The question of the "uniqueness" of the personality is in need of further clarification. Obviously, the individual is not unique in everything. Kluckhohn, Murray and Schneider (6) point out that: "Every man is in certain respects (a) like all other men, (b) like some other men, (c) like no other men" (p. 53). He is like all other men to the extent that his responses are determined by a common-human biological heritage, or by universal features of social life; he is like some other men if he belongs to the same cultural group, or performs a similar role in society, possibly also if he inherits a similar bodily constitution; he is unique, because no other person has undergone exactly the same sequence of experiences; "there is uniqueness in each inheritance and uniqueness in each environment, but, more particularly, uniqueness in the number, kinds, and temporal order of critically determining situations encountered in the course of life" (p. 55).

In that sense, everyone has personality. When popularly we say "he has personality," we usually mean that he has some positive quality which makes his presence felt by others, or which makes him attractive to others. May's (7) suggestion that an individual who has "personality" is one whose presence or absence "makes a difference" to the group, is apparently an extension from this popular view. He would presumably ascribe "personality" in this sense equally to the individual who is heartily disliked and to the one who is liked by others. We would go further and insist that a person whom no one notices still has personality in the same sense as anyone else. There is something in him as an individual which describes him, which marks him off from others, even though he may have little social-stimulus value. The great differences in the "attractiveness" or "noticeability" of individuals are important and demand the attention of psychologists, but they are not part of the definition of personality.

THE CONSTITUTIONAL APPROACH TO PERSONALITY

Kluckhohn, Murray and Schneider have listed four groups of determinants of personality—constitutional, group-membership, role and situational determinants. They also point out that these are interrelated and interact with one another. We turn first to a brief examination of the constitutional determinants of personality and of the manner in which they may be affected by the social environment.

The popular view that personality is reflected in physiognomy has had a long history, going back at least as far as Aristotle. When subjected to careful scientific evaluation, however, the assumption that specific facial characteristics have any validity for the diagnosis of personality has been proven to be completely untenable (8). Even physiognomy as a whole seems to be of very little value in this context. Healy (9), for example, has reported a series of studies by means of composite photographs of individuals well known to him and his associates. He writes as follows:

> I found that no one could distinguish the young sadist from a kindly youth, and often not even a misanthrope from a jovial fellow. By taking group photos I found . . . that feeble-minded adolescents in the picture could not be differentiated from the others. Kretschmer, the great student of body and personality types, once spoke of the face as the visiting card of the individual constitution . . . he should have remembered that it is quite possible to find many misrepresentations recorded on even a visiting card (p. 132).

In one sense, however, physiognomy may be important. We may safely rule out characteristics like the shape of the head, the color of the skin and eyes, the size of the nose or the presence of warts or other blemishes. It is still possible that the face may reflect the personality to the extent that facial expression is affected by previous experience and habitual emotional reactions. The muscles of the face are used differently to express joy and sorrow, and the frequency of their use in one direction or the other will leave its imprint upon the face even under conditions of repose. It is even possible that in a society which regards a jaw thrust forward as a sign of determination, an individual may unconsciously put on a sort of bulldog expression whenever he is faced with difficulties, and as a result this physiognomical sign may have real significance.

This type of physiognomical diagnosis applies, however, only to the soft parts of the face which may be affected by experience, or to movements which may be consciously made. The face then serves as a medium of expression rather than as an indication of an original biological relationship. It seems highly probable that varying facial expressions would in that case be differently interpreted in different cultures. (See Chapter 7.)

The approach to personality in terms of the functions of the endocrine glands also reveals the intimate connection between constitutional and social influences. Most of the available material comes from pathological cases, and as far as normal individuals are concerned, the argument appears to depend upon an extension from the known changes which occur in diseased conditions. The fact that cretins, who are hypothyroid, show a sluggishness in behavior and low intelligence has led to the belief that even slight deficiencies in these respects may also be explained as conditioned by the thyroid. The actual experimental investigations, however, of the relationship between thyroid activity as measured by basal metabolic rate on the one hand, and differences in speed of reaction on the other, have failed to yield any conclusive results. Lanier (10) gives evidence for a positive relationship, but Steinberg (11) and Levy (12) have reported findings in the opposite direction. The case of the thyroid is particularly important, because it is the only gland whose degree of activity may adequately be measured by experimental methods applicable to normal individuals.

In connection with the attempt to explain personality in terms of the endocrine glands, two critical considerations must be kept in mind. The first is that endocrine functioning is not entirely hereditary, but that social and environmental factors may enter to a considerable degree. In the case of the thyroid, for example, it is known that great emotional excitement of the kind experienced during an air raid may raise the basal metabolism considerably and involve a permanent change in the condition of the gland. We know also that even less drastic experiences like a change in diet and habits of exercise may modify thyroid functioning to an appreciable degree. The fact that puberty may occur earlier in life in the tropics or under the influence of stimulating experiences indicates that the glandular changes accompanying adolescence may also be in part environmentally conditioned. The pituitary gland allegedly determines stature, but it is well known that more favorable socio-economic circumstances may cause an increase in stature, so that in all probability the pituitary is also affected by the environment. These facts illustrate the impossibility of completely separating biological from social influences in glandular functioning.

Margaret Mead (13) illustrates this point in connection with the incidence of Graves' disease, which is due to the hyperactivity of the thyroid gland. She cites data to indicate that the disease increased greatly in frequency during the First World War, then decreased, and increased again during the critical period of 1939-40. She comments that "the increase in anxiety may be seen as a function of the general social situation in which a large number of persons, individually vulnerable to Graves' disease, developed positive symptoms. If we now further postulate not a passing emergency like a depression or a threat of war, but a type of culture which systematically exerts upon the developing organism this sort of anxiety-producing pressure at critical stages in maturation, we might expect an alteration in thyroid metabolism which would become chronic . . ." (pp. 533-4). Additional evidence regarding fluctuations in the incidence of psychosomatic disorders in response to the social situation is furnished by Halliday (14).

The second important consideration is that no endocrine gland functions in isolation, and that consequently the description of a personality in terms of the functioning of a single gland is undoubtedly misleading. The rate of sexual maturation, for example, appears to be influenced by the changes in the thymus and by the activity of the sex glands, as well as by the secretion of the adrenal cortex. Maturation may also be disturbed by hypofunction of the thyroid as well as in many cases of pituitary involvement in which the sex glands are also affected. Energy or "drive" is probably affected by the adrenal cortex, the thyroid and the gonads. Emotional excitability may be influenced by the adrenal medulla, the thyroid, the parathyroids, and in some cases also, the pituitary. This means that we must always consider the endocrine glands as an organized system, in which no element can be disturbed without the involvement of the remainder. Thyroid disturbance is not restricted to that gland, but alters the inter-relationships of all the glands with one another. It is probable that future research on the relation between the endocrine glands and personality will concern itself not so much with measures of the activity of single glands as with a technique for the study of the glandular system as a whole.

Constitutional Types. This has in a sense been attempted in the approach to personality in terms of general bodily constitution. The approach is clinical in origin, and has arisen from the observation of medical men that different individuals are not equally susceptible to various diseases. Hippocrates was probably the first to suggest a typology on this basis when he spoke of an "habitus phthisicus" predisposing to pulmonary tuberculosis, and an "habitus apoplecticus" predisposing to diseases of the heart and circulatory system. Since then many attempts have been made to relate physical type to the incidence of disease—for example, by Draper (15), whose careful measurements have yielded some evidence in favor of a "gall bladder type," a "gastric ulcer type," etc.

For the psychologist an important constitutional typology is that of Ernst Kretschmer (1), a German psychiatrist who has postulated a relationship between physical type and susceptibility to mental disorder. Taking as his starting point the two most common functional psychoses, dementia praecox, or schizophrenia, and manic-depressive or circular insanity, Kretschmer presents evidence for the theory that those who suffer from one or the other of these two diseases differ markedly in their physical constitution. There are four main constitutional types—the pyknic, who is relatively short and round, has considerable weight in relation to his height, and whose sitting height is a relatively large proportion of his standing height; the leptosome, tall for his weight, with a short trunk and long arms and legs; the athletic or muscular type, with a heavy frame and well-developed musculature; and the dysplastic, who shows some asymmetry, or physical deformity. The relationship between physique and personality may be expressed in the following table:

Constitutional Type	Mental Disease	Borderline Cases	Normal Biotypes
Pyknic	circular insanity	cycloid	cyclothyme
Leptosome ⎤			
Athletic ⎬	schizophrenia	schizoid	schizothyme
Dysplastic ⎦			

The description of the cycloid and schizoid temperaments is based upon the case histories of the early life of patients who later develop one or the other of the two psychoses. Cyclothyme and schizothyme are roughly equivalent to extravert and introvert types with the addition of other allied psychological tendencies.

With reference to the psychoses, Kretschmer's original data have been supplemented by a series of subsequent investigations in various parts of the world, the general result of which has been in favor of this theory. A number of serious objections have, however, been raised. The most important of these has to do with the effect of the age factor; it is argued that as people grow older they tend to become more pyknic. It is also true that schizophrenia usually appears early in life, and circular insanity relatively late. There might therefore be more leptosomes and more schizophrenia among young people, and more pyknics and manic-depressive insanity among older ones, without any necessary causal relationship between physique and mental disorder. This view has been tested by Garvey (16) and Farber (17), who found that when they equated the patients for age, Kretschmer's theory no longer held. A thorough study was made by Burchard (18) in which the psychotic subjects were divided into ten-year groups. The results showed that although much of the difference between the two psychotic groups may be attributed to age, there is still within each decade a slight difference in the direction favorable to Kretschmer's theory. The conclusion would be that age is an important factor which Kretschmer has unduly neglected, even though it may not account entirely for his findings.

A second serious criticism lies in the relative frequency of exceptions. In the various studies which Kretschmer reports, from one-quarter to one-third of the patients failed to fit into his scheme. Kretschmer explains this discrepancy in terms of mixed heredity, the constitution being inherited from one parent and the disease from the other. This explanation appears to be in flat contradiction to the rest of the theory. If there is a causal relation between physique and psychosis, it is difficult to understand how a case of schizophrenia could ever appear with a pyknic constitution.

As for normal personalities, a large amount of material has been accumulated by Kretschmer and his colleagues indicating that pyknics and leptosomes differ in a wide variety of psychological activities. Klineberg, Asch and Block (19) give the following summary of the main conclusions of the German studies.

> Pyknics (cyclothymes) as contrasted with leptosomes (schizothymes) have a greater perception span, are more distractible, have less power to abstract, less "cleavage capacity" or "Spaltungsfaehigkeit," better incidental memory, respond "synthetically" (leptosomes "analytically")

in the case of a difficult perception, are more sensitive to colors (lepto-somes to forms), see colors as blends more quickly, respond as "extra-verts" to the Rorschach test (leptosomes, "introverts"), diagnose them-selves as cyclothyme (leptosomes, schizothyme), give more chain asso-ciations in the word association test (leptosomes more perseveration and more meaningless associations), show less marked psychogalvanic reactions except to pain stimuli, and are superior in motor tasks except those which require fine and delicate movements. The handwriting differences are not clear, and the differences in intelligence negligible (p. 156).

This imposing list of differences appeared to make it worth while to repeat these experiments under controlled conditions, and this was done in two separate investigations (19, 20). The attempt was made to adhere as closely as possible to the psychological categories involved in the studies of the German psychiatrists and even to use identical techniques wherever possible. The greatest care was exer-cised to choose those subjects who could unmistakably be diagnosed as pyknics or leptosomes. As all the subjects were students, it was possible to equate the two groups for age, intelligence and socio-economic status, as well as sex, and in that way to avoid some of the errors of the German studies. The results showed not a single psy-chological category in which the differences between two consti-tutional groups were statistically reliable. The first of the two in-vestigations concludes: ". . . the results of the present investiga-tions, with the use of methods more careful than those of Kretsch-mer's group, have consistently failed to provide evidence for the existence of types which they claim to have found" (19, p. 215).

It is important to note that Kretschmer's description of types does not follow those cases which occur with the greatest frequency, and the conventional criticism that pure types are rare does not really affect his theory. Kretschmer willingly admits that the "classical cases occur only rarely" and states that the type as he understands it refers to the most "beautiful" cases (p. 16). One may draw an analogy between his procedure and that of medical books which describe a disease in terms of what is frequently referred to as the "text-book picture," and which may be rarely encountered in the actual experience of the physician. Just as the diagnosis of gastric ulcer may still be made even though some of the expected signs and symptoms are lacking, so Kretschmer makes the diagnosis of lepto-some constitution in spite of the presence of certain pyknic or athletic characteristics in the individual. This is a concept of type which is difficult to handle statistically, and which is not in favor among most scientists.

From this point of view, the system of classification proposed by Sheldon and his associates (2) represents a definite step in advance. The *somatotype* (or constitutional type) is determined by the relative strength of each of three primary components; these are: *endomorphy*, in which the digestive viscera are massive and highly developed, while the somatic structures are relatively weak and undeveloped; *mesomorphy*, in which the somatic structures (bone, muscle, and connective tissue) are in the ascendancy; and *ectomorphy*, which means fragility, linearity, flatness of the chest, and delicacy throughout the body. The somatotype is expressed as a series of three numerals indicating the strength of these three components in the above order. Thus a 7-1-1 is the most extreme endomorph, a 1-7-1 is the most extreme mesomorph, and a 1-1-7, the most extreme ectomorph. The 4-4-4 would fall at the midpoint for all three components.

There are three correlated groups of temperamental traits. *Viscerotonia*, the first component, is characterized by general relaxation, love of comfort, sociability, conviviality, gluttony for food, for people and for affection. *Somatotonia*, the second component, is indicated by a predominance of muscular activity and of vigorous bodily assertiveness. *Cerebrotonia*, the third component, means a predominance of the elements of restraint, of inhibition and of desire for concealment. Data accumulated by means of detailed interviews and rating scales indicate a close relationship between the physical and temperamental components in the order in which they have been presented above. Correlations are in the neighborhood of +.80.

In commenting on Sheldon's theory, Harsh and Schrickel (21) point out that the research to date has been conducted by investigators very sympathetic to the theory, and that we cannot be certain of the extent to which unconscious bias may have entered into the results. This appears to be a sound criticism, since both the physical and the psychological data have been collected by investigators closely identified with Sheldon's viewpoint, and their observations might therefore be influenced, although of course quite honestly, by their expectations. Sheldon himself discusses this possibility, and suggests that his awareness of it should have been sufficient to rule out its influence, but this cannot be accepted as an adequate answer to the methodological question raised. There have, however, been a few additional investigations of the theory. Seltzer and his colleagues (22) conclude from their study of Harvard men that Sheldon's correlations hold for the extremes of somatotype and temperament, but do not hold very clearly for the less extreme cases. Using objective test scores instead of personality ratings, Child and Sheldon (23) obtained much lower correlations, the highest being +.21. Fiske (24) gave a series of personality tests to boys aged 13 to 17, and found no significant relationship with bodily constitution. Sheldon's theory requires further confirmatory evidence before it may be regarded as proven.

In connection with the approaches of Kretschmer and Sheldon, there is an important question which must be raised in the present context. Are the personality characteristics associated with constitutional type due to an original, inherited relationship, or to the social expectations to which a particular constitution gives rise, as well as the differential treatment accorded by others in the social environment? An example should make the issue clearer. Cabot (25), for instance, found that the "athletosomes" (Kretschmer's athletics) possessed certain personality traits that have high social value. Because their physique is regarded as the most desirable, they tend to develop an ascendant, influential and extraverted personality. This finding, though in conflict with the theory of Kretschmer, for whom "athletics" were schizothyme or introvert, is in substantial agreement with the position of Sheldon, who attributes to the mesomorphs a dominant, aggressive type of extraversion. The explanation given by Cabot is, however, entirely different. He speaks of a "sociobiological advantage" accruing to the individual because his physique gives him status and prestige among his fellows, with consequent effect on his personality. In another culture, where a different variety of constitution or somatotype is preferred, the effect might be entirely different.

Similar considerations apply to a study by Seltzer (26) of variations in physical "masculinity" among Harvard students, and accompanying variations in personality characteristics. The relationship is demonstrated, without doubt, but its meaning is subject to argument. Seltzer believes that his results are due to a direct relation between physique and personality; it is at least as likely that the more "masculine" students are treated differently by their colleagues and develop differently as a consequence.

This interpretation of the relation between physique and personality is not unlike that of Alfred Adler (27), who attempted to explain personality formation as in part a reaction to bodily characteristics, particularly those related to organ inferiorities. This approach is only indirectly biological. Excessively short stature, ugliness, and a humped back do not directly determine personality characteristics, but are effective because of the attitudes held in connection with them. Short stature, for example, would have an entirely different effect upon personality if it were generally regarded as a desirable characteristic.

In his review of the effect of constitutional and prenatal factors on child health, Montagu (28) makes the important point that constitution is a process rather than an unchanging entity; it is "not a biologically *given* structure predestined by its genotype to function in a predetermined manner. The manner in which all genotypes function is determined by the interaction of the genotype with the environment in which it undergoes development" (p. 149). What we have emphasized here is one aspect of this interaction, namely, that which is due to the way a particular constitution is evaluated by society, the extent to which it is accepted or rejected, the characteristics attributed to it by others, etc. Whether we are dealing with red hair, short stature, excessive weight or general body type, the *social meaning* is probably more important than the inherited relationship to personality. This should not be taken to mean the denial of inherited predispositions to a particular form of personality development; what we are emphasizing is the interpenetration of constitutional and social factors.

As a matter of fact, personality differences appear so early in life that it is difficult to deny the existence of a constitutional or hereditary basis. R. W. Washburn (29), for example, studied the reactions of fifteen babies to various laughter stimuli, the experiment being repeated at four-week intervals from the eighth to the fifty-second week level. There were very marked individual differences in the strength and frequency of the reactions. In another connection similar differences are reported by Charlotte Bühler (30), who observed the behavior of nursing children put together in small social groups. Some of the children were embarrassed and inactive; others were openly delighted; some pounced on the toys and paid no attention to the other children; others explored the general environment; some robbed their companions of all their toys, while others attempted to exchange their own toys for those of other children; some were furious in the new situation and showed definitely negativistic attitudes even in the first year of life. It is difficult to be certain whether these differences are due to early association with the mothers and other people in the social environment, or to inherited dispositions. Bühler regards the latter as the more likely explanation.

It appears to be true that individual differences in personality appear so early that drastic differences in conditioning have not yet had time to play an important part. The weight of evidence is definitely in favor of some sort of hereditary predisposition which plays a part in the causation of individual differences in very young children.

It is important, however, to keep in mind the fact that environmental factors may exert an influence even before birth. Sontag (31), summarizing the results of long-range research being conducted by the Fels Institute at Antioch College, reports that the mother's anxieties or fears may have certain somatic effects which prove irritating to the fetus. This may lessen his adaptability to his post-natal environment, and digestive disturbances may follow. "In addition, his behavior may be further modified by causing him to be an irritable, nervous, and crying infant, a less desirable child in the eyes of the new mother" (p. 490). A pattern of interpersonal relationships has now been set up which may have important consequences for the future development of the child's personality. What looks like "constitution" may therefore turn out to be the effect of prenatal environment, and this effect may show itself in many different ways.

Much more attention has of course been directed to the experiences of the child after birth, and we turn now to the important question of the relation between early child training and the development of the adult personality.

"FATHER OF THE MAN"

The fact that personality differences may be observed in very young children does not necessarily mean that these characteristics persist through life. Bonham and Sargent (32) studied the relationship between the personality of the newborn and that of the same child twenty-four to thirty months later. They originally obtained ratings on 120 babies by the head nurse of the maternity ward, the traits rated including good-naturedness, restless motion, frequency of smiling and good looks. The correlations with the later measures of personality were very low, good looks being the only one of the characteristics which showed definite consistency.

The possibility of altering personality characteristics by a change in the accompanying circumstances has been demonstrated by Jack (33) in an ingenious study of ascendant behavior among four-year-old children. Ascendant behavior is defined to include the pursuit of one's own purposes against interference and direction by others. After careful observation, 18 children were divided into three groups —ascendant, moderately ascendant, and non-ascendant. The differences between them seemed to be mainly a matter of self-confidence. The five most non-ascendant children were selected and given information regarding the opportunity to use certain materials, including complicated toys, etc. They were then put back with the others, and they made a tremendous gain in their ascendance scores. Apparently, the acquisition of new information and the ability therefore to take the lead in social situations altered their "personalities." The problem remains as to the permanence of this change and its transfer to other social situations. Jack's conclusions were verified in a subsequent study by Page (34), who found that ascendance could be increased by a "training series" and by attendance at a nursery school. There was some tendency, however, for the effect to be less marked after the passage of time. The results show clearly, nevertheless, the manner in which personality characteristics may be influenced by experience, and it is highly probable that the change would be permanent if the experience continued to act in the same direction.

At the same time there persists, in scientific as well as in popular writing, the belief that the child is father of the man; the material in this field is extensive, and raises a number of important problems [see for example Davis and Havighurst (35)]. Only a brief review of some of the relevant data will be possible at this point.

Goldman-Eisler (36) writes: "The description of adult character in terms of childhood experience is one of the basic principles of psychoanalytic characterology, and indeed the ontogenetic approach to human personality is the essence of the theory and method of psychoanalysis" (p. 147). Her own research on the relation between breast-feeding and character formation, based on a statistical analysis of the data obtained from questionnaires and interviews with 115 adults in London, lends support to the view that early weaning is related to "oral pessimism," characterized by a profoundly pessimistic outlook on life, a tendency to withdrawal, feelings of insecurity, etc., whereas late weaning is more likely to be found in cases with the opposite syndrome of traits.

Ribble (37) has stressed the deleterious effects of the lack of "mothering" of young children, and believes that some of the consequences may be lasting. Spitz (38), who has conducted some of the most significant research in this area, was able to demonstrate that when mothers had to abandon their infants in a foundling home, there frequently followed a marked depression, with mental and physical retardation; a follow-up study showed that the effects might be irreversible, with permanent damage to personality development. The presence of mother-substitutes may of course reduce the severity of the effect, but lack of adequate attention to the emotional and social needs of the child may cause the disease of "hospitalism" even when all the physical and hygienic requirements are fulfilled.

These investigations refer, however, to rather extreme cases, and the question remains as to the effect of varying procedures of child training on the development of the normal adult personality. Orlansky (39), reviewing the available research material, concludes that the effects ascribed to specific aspects of child care—for example, breast- versus bottle-feeding, early versus late weaning, severe versus permissive toilet training, etc.—have so far not been adequately demonstrated. It seems probable that the general aspects of the mother-child relationship are more significant than any one of the above factors taken by itself; whether the child gets the breast or the bottle is less important than whether he is given love and affection and develops a feeling of trust and security [see Erikson (40)].

The studies by anthropologists in different cultures represent a particularly fruitful source of information in this connection, because the variations in both child training and in adult personality make it possible to examine more adequately the extent of the relationship between these two factors. Sometimes, however, the data brought back from the field are not entirely satisfactory to the social psychologist because they leave some rather crucial questions unanswered. We are told a great deal, for example, about the training procedures which adults direct to the child, but not always enough about their effect on the child. Perhaps the best illustration of this is to be found in reports concerning a form of discipline reported among the Pueblos of the Southwest, particularly the Hopi and the Zuni. The Hopi father rarely if ever uses corporal punishment to socialize his child; he relies on precept, example and admonition. Occasionally a Hopi child refuses to be socialized. The father may then threaten him with the kachinas, the masked dancers who are often of genuinely terrifying appearance, and who are interpreted to the child as being spirits or gods. If the child continues to misbehave, he is approached by a kachina on the occasion of the next feast, and told that now he will be severely punished. The father "tries" to protect the child; he may beg the kachina not to hurt him, promising that there will be no further trouble. The kachina usually remains adamant, however, and the child is punished, sometimes severely. The child of course remains unaware of the fact that it is the "protective" father who is himself responsible for the whole painful procedure.

From the point of view of parent-child relationship this appears to be a good arrangement. The father remains the friend, the protector; there is no paternal punishment to threaten the friendly atmosphere; hostility comes from and is projected upon impersonal, supernatural beings. We need also to know, however, what happens when the slightly older child makes the discovery that the kachinas are only men with masks, and that his own father has betrayed him.

In the Hopi biography *Sun Chief* by Leo Simmons (*41*), we find that the discovery of the real nature of the kachinas may come as a devastating and disillusioning experience. Eggan (*42*) quotes a Hopi informant as saying, "I cried and cried when I found out that the kachinas were real people instead of gods" (p. 154). Goldfrank (*43*) suggests what the effects of this experience might be. "A Pueblo child, upon discovering his parents' duplicity at initiation, feels considerable resentment towards them to be sure, but . . . he knows that it is the supernaturals and the priests who exercise the final authority, and that his parents despite their intrigues against him, must also defer to them" (p. 538). It is still not clear from this account, however, whether the net result of this whole experience is a friendlier or a more hostile relation between father and child. Goldfrank goes on to suggest that the disillusionment may help to account for the fact that Pueblo adults may frequently accuse their closest associates of practicing witchcraft against them.

At a simpler and more direct level, we do have evidence that in certain cultures specific traits may be introduced early in childhood and developed consistently into adult life. This seems true, for example, of the trait of generosity among the Sioux; it was one of the cardinal virtues of the old Dakota society and is still strong today. Macgregor (44) writes: "Modern Dakota children are carefully trained in this tradition. . . . Children of five, six and seven give freely and pleasantly to their younger brothers and sisters. Small children learn the more formal type of giving by observing their elders" (p. 126). A similar example of continuity is to be found in the relative absence of competitiveness among the Hopi, old and young alike. Laura Thompson (45) writes: "In marked contrast to the competitive norms of the general American culture, there is a strongly entrenched attitude among the Hopi against singling out one individual for special recognition or praise. A teacher who is herself a Hopi considers it undesirable to praise a child in the presence of other children" (p. 115). The adult pattern is transmitted to the child early in life.

A problem is raised however by the observations of Kluckhohn (46) among the Navaho. Infants are well treated and well fed, weaning is late and gradual, toilet training is neither strict nor premature; theoretically, there should be little tension or anxiety in Navaho childhood. Kluckhohn concludes: "The most striking theoretical question which emerges from this consideration of some of the main aspects of Navaho infancy is this: how can this picture be reconciled with the facts on Navaho witchcraft, on the states of morbid melancholia and endemic uneasiness which have been well documented for adult Navaho. . . . If the writings of certain psychoanalysts were literally true (and the whole truth) adult Navahos ought to have calm and beautifully adjusted personalities. However, this is certainly not the case" (p. 86). With reference to the Hopi, Dorothy Eggan (47) similarly makes the point that in spite of optimal treatment in infancy, they show extreme anxiety and maladjustment in later life. Evidently we do not always find in early childhood all the seeds of later growth and development. Benedict (48) has pointed out that there are continuities and *discontinuities* in cultural conditioning.

Even when child training and adult personality are congruent, this does not necessarily mean that the former is the cause, and the latter the effect. In connection with Mead's (49) description of the Mundugumor (see Chapter 10), it is not easy to determine whether the hostile and assertive behavior of adult women is the cause or the effect of the relatively unfriendly treatment of children. Shaffner (50) has suggested that the insistence upon obedience within the German home is the origin of the widespread emphasis on discipline and obedience in German society generally, but it is equally possible that the home is the reflection rather than the cause of the broader cultural patterns. In Kardiner's (51) view, patterns of child training (primary institutions) give rise to the basic personality structure, and this in turn becomes projected into the secondary institutions (for example, religious beliefs and practice). One of the major questions raised in connection with this stimulating approach deals precisely with the direction of the causal relation. It is logical to assume that basic personality will also affect child training, and that religious attitudes may help to shape both the family relationships and the common traits of personality. The best way out of this difficulty is to assume a circular relationship. Newcomb (52), for example, states that "Different practices in child training are *consequences* of differences both in culture and in personality," and that "Different practices in child training also *lead* to differences both in culture and in personality" (p. 429). This appears to be the soundest and most acceptable position regarding the causal relationship.

In their important exploration of this relationship, Whiting and Child (53) make use of ethnographic accounts of 75 communities included in the Human Relations Area Files at Yale University, to which reference has already been made. Taking psychoanalytic theory as their starting point, but reinterpreting many of the principles in terms of behavioral psychology, they have used the method of correlation between certain reported aspects of child training and the beliefs current among adults in the same culture. Their results offer corroboration for some of the aspects of the Freudian approach, but not for others. They examine five systems of behavior—oral, anal, sexual, dependence and aggression—from the point of view of *fixation,* that is, whether "events occurring in childhood with respect to a particular system of behavior, e.g., oral or sexual behavior, may bring about a continued importance or prepotency of that system of behavior, in comparison with the importance it would have had in the absence of those events" (p. 130).

Positive evidence was found in connection with the oral, dependence and aggressive systems of behavior; the results were less clear with regard to training in the anal and sexual systems. There is a close relation, for example, between Oral Socialization Anxiety (indicated by relative absence of early nursing indulgence, by early and severe weaning, etc.) and Oral Explanations of Illness (that is, that illness is caused by ingestion, or by verbal spells and incantations). This means, in somewhat oversimplified form, that people who have experienced worry about food in early life later explain illness in oral terms. There is, on the other hand, practically no relation between Anal Socialization Anxiety (determined by amount of initial indulgence, age and severity of toilet training) and Anal Explanations of Illness (that is, that illness is caused by excreta, by the failure to perform some ritual, etc.).

One may perhaps argue about some of the criteria used for the determination of socialization anxiety and of fixation, but the investigators are careful to define their terms, and to present all the data on which their conclusions are based. A more important question concerns the adequacy of the original ethnographic reports on the basis of which the ratings had to be made. In any case, the correlational method, as the investigators themselves indicate, has the defect "that it can provide no conclusive evidence about the direction of causal relationships" (p. 319). We are left with the possibility that either child training or adult personality may be cause or effect, or that the relation between them may be—as seems most probable—a reciprocal one.

Another difficulty regarding the effect of child training on adult personality is that it may in part depend not on the absolute, but on the relative treatment received by the child. Lewis (54), for example, indicates that the women in the Mexican village which he studied had an attitude toward children which is at least suggestive of "rejection." He writes: "Women for the most part 'accept' children fatalistically as a burden to be endured. . . . It is common for women to complain at having to bear many children, which they believe to be a punishment of God" (p. 228). The point we are now making is that the effect on the child of a certain amount of maternal rejection will be very different if he sees all around him other children who are welcomed and wanted by their mothers, as compared with the situation in which other children are "rejected" to the same degree. This represents a real problem in connection with the attempts to apply to other cultures some of the principles of developmental psychology which work reasonably well in our own.

This brief survey does not lead to the conclusion that child training is unimportant, but rather that its importance has sometimes been exaggerated, and that the relationship to adult personality is more complex than has frequently been realized. Child training is indeed important; as McClelland (55) has indicated, what we know regarding the principles of learning does justify the belief that the earliest experiences in life may in many ways be the most significant. Learning may also take place later, however, and those aspects of our culture to which we become exposed as we grow older should not be neglected. Sometimes they may supplement and reinforce the results of early experience; sometimes they may modify or even supplant them. Our culture affects us throughout life, not just at one stage of our development. We may accept the statement that the "child is father of the man," but there may be various degrees of resemblance between the child and its father.

The relation of an individual to his culture may be further clarified by the examination of biographical material; we now turn to that aspect of our analysis.

CULTURE AND THE LIFE HISTORY

The materials collected through biographies and autobiographies furnish a rich source of information as to the variations between personalities, and the manner in which these variations may express themselves. Since, however, these biographies have been written from many different points of view, and usually with little concern for those aspects of personality in which the psychologist is primarily interested, the approach through biography has not usually been regarded as a scientifically acceptable method. Use has been made of biographical material, but for the most part in piecemeal fashion, as illustrative of one or another general theory of personality.

An attempt has been made by Dollard (56) to place the writing of biographies upon a more scientific basis through the use of certain "criteria" for an acceptable life history. These criteria represent the most significant systematization in this field and will therefore be presented in detail with some critical comments.

1. *The subject must be viewed as a specimen in a cultural series.* Much is known about an individual merely from the fact that he is born into a certain community. We can foretell a great deal about the later personality of any individual at birth if we know the nature of the culture of his group. This is a criterion which has on

the whole not received adequate consideration in the biographies which we possess. Most writers have taken for granted the folkways of the community and have not stressed sufficiently their direct effect upon the personality. The writings of the anthropologists satisfy this criterion better than do any others.

2. *The organic motors of action ascribed must be socially relevant.* Here Dollard, in spite of his predominantly cultural and sociological approach, gives some weight to the organic basis of personality. As a matter of fact, the organic motors of which he speaks appear to be those which are common to all individuals, rather than those which account for personality differences. There are of course biological motives related to hunger and sex, which to a considerable extent condition the individual's response to his social environment and which play an important part in his personality development. There are also, however, inherited constitutional and physical factors which distinguish one individual from another, which are "socially relevant," and which Dollard completely neglects. Although it is true that the organic basis of personality differences is not adequately understood, there seems little doubt that it exists, and it should be taken into account wherever possible. The biographical analyses of the endocrinologists and of Kretschmer and others who stress the significance of constitution may be said to satisfy this criterion, although the manner in which they do so is not universally regarded as valid.

3. *The peculiar role of the family group in transmitting the culture must be recognized.* There can be no doubt that the family is of the greatest importance in the development of personality, and it has been stressed by most biographers. Among the psychological systems, the Adlerian, and to a lesser extent the Freudian, have given to the family a very great significance. It should be kept in mind that this significance will vary in degree according to the nature of the culture. It is likely that in ancient China the large family really constituted the social environment of the individual to such an extent that outside influences were relatively unimportant (57). In our society also the influence of the family is undoubtedly very great. In Samoa (58), where a child who is dissatisfied with his own home may find a more congenial one with some of his relatives, there are obvious limitations to the role of the family. The hostility against the father, for example, which allegedly plays a dominant role in the development of certain types of per-

sonality, will not occur to nearly the same extent if the son may leave his father's house whenever he is so inclined. In this same connection it is important to keep in mind that the nature of the family may vary in different cultures; we have already referred to the Trobriand Islanders (see p. 151), among whom authority is vested in the uncle, not the father. In the American Negro family it is probable that in large sections of the country the mother is the real head of the household, and the whole pattern of inter-family relationships may be altered as a consequence (59). We should add, therefore, to Dollard's criterion our insistence upon the recognition of variations both in extent and in kind of family influence, and upon the fact that the family is of importance not only in transmitting the culture, but also in terms of the personal relationships which develop within its framework.

4. *The specific method of elaboration of organic materials into social behavior must be shown.* It is a little difficult to see why this criterion should have been separated from the second. The emphasis here seems to be on the need to show how the organic materials work, instead of remaining satisfied with their mere description or enumeration. The two criteria could easily be combined into one which has reference to the inclusion of the organic or biological approach to the understanding of personality.

5. *The continuous related character of experience from childhood through adulthood must be stressed.* This is an insistence upon seeing the total personality in terms of its development through life. The genetic approach should be carried back as far as possible so that any explanation of later behavior in terms of early experiences will have an adequate basis. We have already given reasons for believing that although there must be some continuity, new experiences may alter the pattern of development. Inconsistency, real or apparent, must be explained in terms of the specific situations which give rise to them. This criterion has on the whole been fairly well satisfied by most biographers, and has been stressed in particular by the Freudians, who see personality characteristics as directly related to the experiences of early childhood.

6. *The "social situation" must be carefully and continuously specified as a factor.* Behavior is not understood except in relation to the social situation; Dollard insists, however, that the social situation as seen by an outside observer may not be the same as that seen by the

subject himself. It is important always to keep in mind the standpoint from which the subject interprets his social environment.

7. *The life-history material itself must be organized and conceptualized.* This criterion is perhaps the most controversial. Dollard is suggesting that a life history can be written only in terms of some conceptual system, and that it must not be a mere collection of facts. It is of course true that no biographer can write down everything that has occurred in the lifetime of his subject, and therefore he must make a selection of the materials he wishes to present. Such a selection would undoubtedly be more coherent and logical if undertaken from the standpoint of a certain theory of personality which serves as a framework into which the details may fit. On the other hand it is precisely this conceptualization which has troubled the readers of biographies written, for example, from the Freudian or Adlerian point of view. In Freudian biographies, the choice of materials related to early sex life or to attitudes toward the parents may be stressed, with a relative neglect of experiences which a non-Freudian might regard as having a decisive influence. There is no doubt that the same life history written from the Freudian and Adlerian standpoints, respectively, would stress different factors and that the actual content of the biography would differ markedly as a consequence. If a biography is to be generally useful, it seems clear that it ought not to be tied too closely to any one system of psychological interpretation. Perhaps here a compromise position is possible, permitting the organization of the material in terms of one particular system, but with the inclusion of materials which might possibly be relevant to any other theory of the nature of personality formation.

G. W. Allport (60) has criticized Dollard's criteria, on the ground that their choice was determined rather arbitrarily and subjectively, and because of their cultural and psychoanalytical bias. Certainly they are in need of revision, but they represent a significant attempt to make the writing of biographies more useful to psychologists. It would be worth while to examine the life histories which have appeared, or to write new ones with these criteria in mind, in order to see the extent to which they are really applicable. Dollard has already made this attempt with six biographies which are written from various points of view, but he has been concerned mainly with pointing out their limitations in respect to the criteria. It would be advisable to repeat the process without any preconceptions as to the value of the criteria which Dollard has suggested. Allport himself makes a strong case in favor of the use of biographical materials as a means toward psychological understanding, even though they frequently cannot be subjected to the customary quantitative approaches of the natural sciences.

Dollard's first criterion, namely, that the subject must be viewed as a specimen in a cultural series, raises some special problems. Granting the tremendous influence which the culture exerts on the development of personality, the question remains as to the extent to which any given individual reflects the culture of his community. Sapir (61), who was a pioneer in the analysis of the relation between culture and the individual personality, refers to a phrase which he encountered in J. O. Dorsey's *Omaha Sociology*: "Two Crows denies this." Sapir comments: "Apparently Two Crows, a perfectly good and authoritative Indian, could presume to rule out of court the very existence of a custom or an attitude or a belief vouched for by some other Indian, equally good and authoritative" (p. 240). He goes on to ask whether it is not reasonable to say that the "culture" with which Two Crows was familiar was not in all respects the same entity as that presented to some other Indian, or perhaps to all other Indians. This is an important point, and one which has not always received the attention which it deserves. The biographical material collected from various cultures throws additional light on the problem which Sapir raises.

One such personal document is represented by the autobiography of Crashing Thunder, a Winnebago Indian, recorded by Paul Radin (62), who published it with significant editorial comments. It illustrates Sapir's dichotomy between a culture pattern and the experience of the individual. The Winnebagos, in common with many other American Indian tribes, stressed the importance of the experience of "seeing the vision" as a focal point in personal development. Crashing Thunder received an education similar to that of the other young men in his tribe and was taught that fasting and prayer and careful attention to the ritual procedure would bring him the vision and the attendant blessing. It is probable that many if not most of the other members of the group did obtain a vision under such conditions; Crashing Thunder tried twice and failed. As a result he became a convert to the peyote cult, obtaining his vision under the influence of the drug.

This account indicates that some persons are unwilling or unable to accept the suggestions given by their culture. Psychologically this raises the important problem as to what there is in personality which determines deviation from the norm in this and other respects. As a matter of fact, there may be many others who deviate in the same manner and do not confess their failure. The problem necessitates the understanding of individual personalities as well as of cultures.

Many more such personal documents are now available, and those collected up to 1945 have been subjected to an excellent critical analysis by Kluckhohn (63). In many instances, comparisons between the personal documents and the general account of the culture, or between two different personal documents from the same community, have revealed the variation in the individual choices which are made from what the culture has to offer. [See, for example, Aberle (64), Hanks (65) and Titiev (66).]

We now turn to a more direct analysis of the interrelationship between culture and the individual.

SUMMARY

Although there is considerable argument regarding the *extent* to which problems of personality development enter into social psychology, there can be no doubt regarding the *fact* that social factors are important.

Personality includes aspects in which the individual is (a) like all other men, (b) like some other men, and (c) like no other men. It is not a mere sum of traits, but a dynamic integration.

Among the attempts to find a biological or organic basis for personality may be mentioned the study of physiognomy, which has some value as an aspect of expressive behavior; glandular secretions, undoubtedly of importance, although the exact nature and extent of the effects upon normal personality remain to be determined; general bodily constitution, which seems to show some relation to psychosis but has not been demonstrated to have any consistent relation to the characteristics of the normal individual. The combined evidence is to the effect that biological factors do play a part, but it should be kept in mind that some influences which appear to be hereditary may in fact be due to prenatal environment.

The child is in many respects the "father of the man," but this expression should not be taken too literally. In some cases it is clear that specific traits introduced early in childhood are directly linked to later, adult characteristics; in others, discontinuities may be found. Culture affects the individual throughout life, and not just at one stage of development.

The writing of biographies has been subjected to analysis by Dollard, who has suggested several criteria for their improvement. These include attention to the cultural background, the organic motors of action, the role of the family group, the elaboration of organic materials into social behavior, the related character of experience from childhood to adulthood, the social situation, and the organization and conceptualization of the whole life history. Although the criteria are in need of modification, they represent a step in the direction of making biographies more useful to social science.

The personal documents which have been collected from various societies reveal the manner and the extent to which the individual makes his own unique choices out of the materials present in the culture as a whole.

REFERENCES

1. Kretschmer, E. *Physique and Character*. 1925
2. Sheldon, W. H., Stevens, S. S., and Tucker, W. W. *The Varieties of Human Physique*. 1940. Sheldon and Stevens. *The Varieties of Temperament*. 1942
3. Allport, F. H. *Social Psychology*. 1924
4. Murphy, G. *Personality: A Biosocial Approach to Origins and Structure*. 1947
5. Allport, G. W. *Personality: A Psychological Interpretation*. 1937
6. Kluckhohn, C., Murray, H. A., and Schneider, D. M. (eds.). *Personality in Nature, Society, and Culture*. 1953
7. May, M. A. "The Foundations of Personality." In Achilles, P. S. (ed.), *Psychology at Work*. 1932
8. Paterson, D. G. *Physique and Intellect*. 1930
9. Healy, W. *Personality in Formation and Action*. 1938
10. Lanier, L. H., and Leedy, J. L. "Speed of Reaction in Relation to Basal Metabolism and Blood Pressure," *Psychol. Bull.*, 1933, 30: pp. 609-610
11. Steinberg, J. "The Relation Between Basal Metabolism and Mental Speed," *Arch. Psychol.*, 1934, No. 172
12. Levy, J. "A Quantitative Study of the Relationship between Basal Metabolic Rate and Children's Behavior Problems," *Amer. J. Orthopsychiat.*, 1931, 10: pp. 298-310

13. Mead, M. "The Concept of Culture and the Psychosomatic Approach," *Psychiatry,* 1947, 10: pp. 57-76

14. Halliday, J. L. *Psychosocial Medicine.* 1948

15. Draper, G. *The Human Constitution.* 1924

16. Garvey, C. R. "Comparative Body Build of Manic-Depressive and Schizophrenic Patients," *Psychol. Bull.,* 1933, 30: pp. 567-568

17. Farber, M. L. "A Critique and an Investigation of Kretschmer's Theory," *J. Abn. and Soc. Psychol.,* 1938, 33: pp. 398-404

18. Burchard, E. M. L. "Physique and Psychosis," *Comp. Psychol. Monog.,* 1936, 13, No. I

19. Klineberg, O., Asch, S. E., and Block, H. "An Experimental Study of Constitutional Types," *Genet. Psychol. Monog.,* 1934, 16, No. 3

20. Klineberg, O., Fjeld, H., and Foley, J. P. Unpublished study

21. Harsh, C. M., and Schrickel, H. G. *Personality: Development and Assessment.* 1950

22. Seltzer, C. C., Wells, F. L., and McTernan, E. B. "A Relationship between Sheldonian Somatotype and Psycho-type," *J. Personal.,* 1948, 16; pp. 431-436

23. Child, I. I., and Sheldon, W. H. "The Correlation between Components of Physique and Scores on Certain Psychological Tests," *Char. & Pers.,* 1941, 10: pp. 23-34

24. Fiske, D. W. "A Study of Relationships to Somatotype," *J. Appl. Psychol.,* 1944, 28: pp. 504-519

25. Cabot, P. S. de Q. "The Relationship between Characteristics of Personality and Physique in Adolescents," *Genet. Psychol. Monog.,* 1938, No. 20

26. Seltzer, C. C. "The Relationship Between the Masculine Component and Personality," *Am. J. Phys. Anthropol.,* 1945, 3: pp. 33-47; 84-96

27. Adler, A. *The Study of Organ Inferiority and Its Compensation.* 1917

28. Montagu, M. F. A. "Constitutional and Prenatal Factors in Infant and Child Health." In M. J. E. Senn (ed.), *Symposium on the Healthy Personality.* 1950

29. Washburn, R. W. "A Study of the Smiling and Laughing of Infants in the First Year of Life," *Genet. Psychol. Monog.,* 1939, 6: pp. 397-537

30. Bühler, C. "The Social Behavior of Children." In Murchison, C. (ed.), *Hdbk. Child Psychol.* 1933

31. Sontag, L. W. "Some Psychosomatic Aspects of Childhood." In Kluckhohn, Murray and Schneider (eds.), *Personality in Nature, Society, and Culture.* 1953

32. Bonham, M. A., and Sargent, M. K. "The Behavior of Human Infants Twenty-four and Thirty Months of Age." Unpublished Master's Essay, Catholic University, 1928

33. Jack, L. M. "An Experimental Study of Ascendant Behavior in Pre-school Children," *Univ. Iowa Stud. Child Welfare,* 1934, 9, No. 3

34. Page, M. L. "The Modification of Ascendant Behavior in Pre-school Children," *Univ. Iowa Stud. Child Welfare,* 1936, 12, No. 3

35. Davis, A., and Havighurst, R. J. *Father of the Man.* 1947

36. Goldman-Eisler, F. "Breastfeeding and Character Formation." In Kluckhohn, Murray and Schneider (eds.), *Personality in Nature, Society, and Culture.* 1953

37. Ribble, M. A. "Infantile Experience in Relation to Personality Development." In J. McV. Hunt (ed.), *Personality and the Behavior Disorders.* 1944

38. Spitz, R. "Hospitalism." In A. Freud, H. Hartmann and E. Kris (eds.), *The Psychoanalytic Study of the Child.* 1945

39. Orlansky, H. "Infant Care and Personality," *Psychol. Bull.,* 1949, 46: pp. 1-48

40. Erikson, E. H. "Growth and Crises of the Healthy Personality." In M. J. E. Senn (ed.), *Symposium on the Healthy Personality.* 1950

41. Simmons, L. *Sun Chief.* 1942

42. Eggan, D. Quoted in Slotkin, J. S., *Personality Development.* 1952

43. Goldfrank, E. "Socialization, Personality, and the Structure of Pueblo Society," *Am. Anthropol.,* 1945, 47: pp. 516-539

44. MacGregor, G. *Warriors Without Weapons.* 1946

45. Thompson, L. *Culture in Crisis: A Study of the Hopi Indians.* 1950

46. Kluckhohn, C. "Some Aspects of Navaho Infancy and Early Childhood." In G. Roheim (ed.), *Psycho-Analysis and the Social Sciences,* 1947, 1: pp. 37-86

47. Eggan, D. "The General Problem of Hopi Adjustment." In Kluckhohn, Murray and Schneider, *Personality in Nature, Society, and Culture.* 1953

48. Benedict, R. "Continuities and Discontinuities in Cultural Conditioning." In Kluckhohn, Murray and Schneider, *Personality in Nature, Society, and Culture.* 1953

49. Mead, M. *Sex and Temperament in Three Primitive Societies.* 1935

50. Schaffner, B. *Father Land.* 1948

51. Kardiner, A. *The Individual and His Society.* 1939. *The Psychological Frontiers of Society.* 1945

52. Newcomb, T. M. *Social Psychology.* 1950

53. Whiting, J. W. M., and Child, I. L. *Child Training and Personality: A Cross-Cultural Study.* 1953

54. Lewis, O. *Life in a Mexican Village: Tepoztlàn Revisited.* 1951

55. McClelland, D. C. *Personality.* 1951

56. Dollard, J. *Criteria for the Life History.* 1935

57. Latourette, K. S. *The Chinese, Their History and Culture.* 2 vols. 1934

58. Mead, M. *Coming of Age in Samoa.* 1928

59. Frazier, E. F. *The Negro Family in the United States.* 1939

60. Allport, G. W. "The Use of Personal Documents in Psychological Science," *S.S.R.C. Bull.,* 1942, 41: pp. 1-210

61. Sapir, E. "Why Cultural Anthropology Needs the Psychiatrist." In P. Mullahy (ed.), *A Study of Interpersonal Relations.* 1949

62. Radin, P. *Crashing Thunder.* 1926

63. Gottschalk, L., Kluckhohn, C., and Angell, R. "The Use of Personal Documents in History, Anthropology and Sociology," *S.S.R.C. Bull.,* 1945, 53: pp. 79-176

64. Aberle, D. F. "The Psychosocial Analysis of a Hopi Life-History," *Comp. Psych. Mono.,* 1951, 21: No. 1

65. Hanks, L. M., Jr. "The Focus of Individual Differences in Certain Primitive Cultures." In S. S. Sargent and M. W. Smith (eds.), *Culture and Personality.* 1949

66. Titiev, M. "Old Oraibi," *Papers Peabody Mus.,* 1944, 22, No. 1: pp. 1-277

13

Culture and Personality: Status, Role and the Individual

INTRODUCTION

The problem of the relation between culture and personality is involved in a great deal of what has already been discussed. The material dealing with motivation and its cultural determinants; emotions and their expression; differences between social and economic classes; behavior frequently alleged to be determined by inherited physical type but in all probability of cultural origin; the effect of cultural differences in child training procedures—all such material belongs in this general category, and many more examples could be given. There remain a number of specific problems which have not so far been discussed, and a variety of important investigations which throw further light on the relationship. In the present and the succeeding chapter the major emphasis will be on concepts and phenomena that refer more directly to the normal personality; this will be followed by an analysis of social and cultural factors in abnormality, and in delinquent and criminal behavior.

In one sense the discussion of culture *and* personality represents a false dichotomy and a spurious problem. It can be argued on the one hand that culture expresses itself in the behavior and the attitudes of persons and that it has no existence apart from the individuals who are its carriers; on the other hand, it may be urged that personality is what it is because of the process of enculturation and that the concept of personality represents at least in part the incorporation of materials from the surrounding culture. The suggestion has been made that we should rather speak of culture *in* personality, or personality *in* culture, or that we should use the hyphenated expression culture-and-personality to indicate the indivisibility of the two terms.

There are some anthropologists, notably Kroeber (*1*) and White (*2*), who have made a case for the independent existence of culture, basing their position on two main arguments. The first is that though individuals die, the culture lives on; even after the passage of centuries it may retain its recognizable character. The second argument takes its point of departure from the fact that so often in the history of a particular culture, inventions or discoveries are independently made by two or more different individuals; it almost appears, as Herskovits (*3*) puts it, that "in the thinking of these writers, man is impotent in the face of culture which, in ordering his existence, carries him as his creature as it grows, flowers, and decays" (p. 154). Herskovits goes on to point out that even these writers admit that culture cannot exist without human beings, but they treat it as if it had a life of its own. He himself insists that the locus of culture "cannot be regarded as anything other than the individuals who, responding to the enculturative process, live in accordance with the traditions of their group" (p. 156).

Granting that culture and personality are interdependent, the problem still remains as to the precise nature of the relationship. No culture is ever completely expressed in any one individual, as has already been indicated. There are in Linton's (*4*) terminology, *universals,* which apply to all normal adult members of the society; but there are also *specialties,* which are found only in distinct categories of individuals (for example, the priest or the warrior); *alternatives,* with respect to which there is free choice; and *variants,* which are specific to individuals or to small segments of the total community. The anthropologist has on the whole been more interested in the universals, the aspects in which the behavior of individuals in any given society is similar; the psychologist has directed his attention rather more to the individual, and to the variations among individuals. The focus on culture-and-personality represents the principal meeting-ground of the two disciplines.

PERSONALITY TYPES AND CULTURAL INTEGRATIONS

The anthropologist is confronted with many different cultures, and the psychologist with many varieties of individuals. Attempts have been made to introduce some order into this diversity through the description of general types or categories expressive of similarities rather than of differences. The concepts utilized have been taken from many sources, and their application has aroused considerable interest.

Nietzsche (5), for example, on the basis of his studies of Greek tragedy, spoke of two different ways of life, the Apollonian and the Dionysian. Apollo "governs the beauteous illusion of the inner world of fantasy." He represents measure, number, limitation, the mastery of everything savage and untamed. The Dionysian way represents the freeing of unmeasured instinct, nature unbridled, drunkenness in the highest sense. Although Nietzsche himself did not attempt to divide human beings on this basis, his dichotomy has been employed by others in this manner. Ruth Benedict (6) has applied this scheme to cultures, describing the Pueblo Indians of Arizona and New Mexico as Apollonian, and the surrounding tribes as Dionysian in their way of life.

There can be no doubt that for the understanding of a culture, as well as of an individual, it is of fundamental importance to realize the character of the integration, or of the inter-relationship of the parts with one another. It is clear that an act of dishonesty may not have the same meaning for two individuals, and a vision experience may have functionally a quite different significance in two cultures. This analogy between individual and culture is in many respects a valid one, but the result is that the difficulties of understanding individual personality and its integration, and of classifying individuals into types, hold also, perhaps even more markedly, in the case of cultures. Not all cultures are integrated, for instance, or at least not all to the same degree; there may be contrasts and conflicts, and the culture is not understood unless these are taken into account. A striking example is found in the Hako peace ceremony of the Pawnee Indians. This consisted of a prayer to the Great Mother (Maize), requesting children, long life, the enjoyment of plenty, happiness and peace. There was not the slightest whisper of war or dissension; numerous ceremonies of the Pawnee were directed to this same end. Among these people, however, war in its most intensive form was the main preoccupation. They were the terror of their neighbors, and mothers in the adjacent tribes would frighten their children with "The Pawnees are coming!" As Radin (7) expresses it, "only in such introspective rites could they gain peace of mind and rid themselves of the evil effect of too much preoccupation with war. Only thus could a warrior civilization become balanced and save its soul" (p. 289). A similar phenomenon is found in the prevalence of the orgy which permits a periodic relaxation of social restraints. Here the behavior may be completely at variance with that which is normal or habitual for that particular community. To mention only one example, among the Hos of northern India during the period of the orgy "servants forget their duty to masters, children their reverence for parents, men their respect for women" (8, p. 108).

This does not mean that communities are not integrated. It does mean that integration is relative, that it varies in degree, and that it cannot be assumed to exist completely in every community. This makes it possible for two different observers to obtain from the same culture varying pictures of the nature of its integration. Many of the Plains Indian tribes, for example, whom Benedict describes as Dionysian, might still give an impression of calm and serenity throughout the major portion of their activities.

The best-known psychological typology is undoubtedly that of C. G. Jung (9), who is responsible for the classification of humans as *extraverts* and *introverts*. The fundamental difference between these is that in the one case there is an outward movement of interest toward the object; in the other, a movement away from the object toward the subject and his own psychological processes. The extravert gives the object the predominant value, and the subject is relatively unimportant; for the introvert the values are reversed. Jung has often been criticized on the ground that there are no pure types, but he himself recognizes and acknowledges this fact. For him, every human being possesses both mechanisms; usually one predominates, though there may be a rhythmical alternation of the two forms of psychic activity. If the predominance of one becomes chronic or habitual, a type is produced. The other is not completely suppressed, however, and there is merely a relative predominance of one mechanism over the other. Jung considers the decisive factor to be the inherited disposition of the child, although under abnormal conditions there may be a falsification of the type by the external environment. Plant (10) believes that these attitudes may arise from inherited factors, from acquired bodily conditions producing similar factors, from the environment, or from any combination of these.

Jung interprets the psychological systems of his distinguished colleagues, Freud and Adler, from the point of view of his typology. Adler's system is essentially introvert, since it emphasizes feelings of superiority and inferiority in the ego, and subjective values in general. Freud's system is essentially extravert, the craving for the sex object constituting its central drive, whereas failures in this respect give rise to disturbances of various kinds.

There have been many experimental attempts to test Jung's theory. In a study by Heidbreder (11) a questionnaire was given to 200 students at the University of Minnesota, the items being so chosen that a positive answer meant introversion, and a negative, extraversion. There were altogether 54 items, and an individual who was completely extravert would therefore score −54; one who showed equal tendencies in both directions would have a score of 0; and so on. It was felt that the shape of the distribution curve would give evidence as to the validity of Jung's theory, since the existence of two distinct types in a population should yield a bi-modal curve. Actually, the curve obtained was a normal distribution curve, and Heidbreder therefore concludes that pure introverts or extraverts are rare, most individuals falling into an intermediate category. This conclusion is undoubtedly the correct one, but as we have seen, it does not really conflict with that adopted by Jung himself. One other interesting result of this study was that the average score was not 0 but −11.25, that is to say, the group as a whole showed a definite tendency in the extravert direction. This is probably to be expected from an American group, since the culture of the United States as a whole undoubtedly stresses extravert rather than introvert activities.

The psychoanalysts have also been concerned with the problem of personality types. Abraham (12), for example, regards early suckling habits as responsible for a distinction between two types of personality, the oral optimist and the oral pessimist. Where suckling in infancy is undisturbed and pleasurable, there develops an imperturbable optimism which may lead to carefree indifference and inactivity. Such individuals expect that they will be cared for, that the mother's breast will "flow for them eternally." Those who have had an unsatisfactory suckling period are pessimistic as a result of their failure to achieve gratification in early life. This may result in a later attitude of asking or demanding things of others and in a tendency toward dependence. Campbell (13) suggests that the great Osler may have had some premonition of this in a humorous speech which he made in honor of pediatricians. Osler stated that the efforts to encourage breast feeding had been stimulated "by an exhaustive collective investigation which has been made on the future of bottle-fed babies, in which it is clearly shown that intellectual obliquity, moral perversion and special crankiness of all kinds result directly from the early warp given to the mind of the child by the gross and unworthy deception to which it is subjected" (p. 102).

An observation by Mead (14) makes it possible to apply this concept to group differences. In her study of temperamental differences in three Melanesian communities, she found one of them, the Arapesh, similar to the oral optimist type, and another, the Mundugumor, to the oral pessimist. In the former, children were fed frequently and liberally, and were caressed by their mothers while being suckled; as adults, the Arapesh were friendly, cooperative individuals. The Mundugumor mothers, on the other hand, fed their children grudgingly, bending down so that they could take the breast for a brief period, and then drawing away; as adults, the Mundugumor were about as hostile and unfriendly a people as one could possibly find. In this type of material, however, as has already been pointed out, the difficulty lies in separating cause from effect. (See Chapter 12.) The same considerations apply to LaBarre's (15) suggestion that the Chinese may also be characterized as oral optimists.

Freud speaks also of an anal character type, developing from an unusual childish interest in the function and products of elimination. There are three personality traits which Freud explains on this basis; the first is orderliness, frequently accompanied by bodily cleanliness, reliability, conscientiousness and pedantry. Patterns of activity and work may develop on the basis of habits of elimination, so that there may be on the one hand thoroughness, persistence, general energy and on the other, inactivity, brooding, delay, postponement of work with final complete absorption and rapid productivity, and so on. A second trait is parsimony, which may become avarice. This is due to symbolization or to identification of the products of elimination with gifts or money. The third trait is obstinacy, which may become defiance and include irascibility and vindictiveness. This approach has also been applied to the understanding of a culture, in this case by Roheim (*16*) to the Australian Arunta. Roheim finds this triad of traits entirely absent among the Australians, who have at the same time a completely natural attitude toward elimination, without any taboos or restrictions whatsoever. On the other hand, LaBarre (*17*) expresses the opinion that Japanese personality structure may be understood in terms of the anal character type.

Riesman (*18*) describes three types of society—the tradition-directed, represented by the conservative cultures of the East as well as by many European peasant groups; the inner-directed, of which the Puritans are a good example; and the outer-directed, which our present American culture is in the process of becoming. Other examples of cultural typologies could be given.

Types are unsatisfactory, both in the case of individuals and in that of cultures, because so few of them actually fit the categories which the typology assumes. Probably no persons and no cultures are completely introvert or extravert, Apollonian or Dionysian. The application of tests and personality inventories has demonstrated this fact in the case of individuals; the same appears to hold true for cultures. Even when many of the elements are similar, the organization or integration is unique. As Kluckhohn (*19*) expresses it, "One may find in two individuals almost the same personality traits. Yet each has his own life style, which differentiates the constellation of traits. So, also, a culture cannot be fully understood from the most complete description of its explicit surface. The organization of each culture has the same kind of uniqueness one finds in the organization of each personality. It is a totality which must be grasped as such" (p. 97).

There is, however, a bridge between the uniqueness of a culture and the uniqueness of individual personality. Every culture makes certain demands on the individual; every society has certain expectations regarding the behavior of its members. We have already indicated (Chapter 12) some of the ways in which a child learns to become an adult; the process of socialization brings him slowly but in most cases surely to an awareness of what he must do to be accepted by his community. It also gives him a realization of the position or status which he occupies, and of the role which he is expected to play.

STATUS AND ROLE

Although, as Sargent (20) points out, the concepts of status and role, particularly the latter, have long had a place in social-science literature, the recent development of these concepts into useful tools of description and analysis probably owes most to the anthropologist Linton (4). He writes: "The place in a particular system which a certain individual occupies at a particular time will be referred to as his *status* with respect to that system" (p. 264). The term *role* is used "to designate the sum total of the culture patterns associated with a particular status. It thus includes the attitudes, values, and behavior ascribed by the society to any and all persons occupying this status. . . . In so far as it represents overt behavior, a role is the dynamic aspect of a status: what the individual has to do in order to validate his occupation of the status" (ibid.). In recent social-psychological writing the concept of role has acquired an important place; the textbooks by Sargent (21), Hartley and Hartley (22), and particularly Newcomb (23) may be mentioned as representative of this trend.

Sargent gives the following definition. "A person's role is a pattern or type of social behavior which seems situationally appropriate to him in terms of the demands and expectations of those in his group" (p. 360). He regards this concept as especially important because it gives due weight to cultural, personal and situational determinants of behavior. Newcomb believes that a society keeps itself going by a process in which individuals come to take on the role behaviors expected of them. A few examples of the manner in which status and role function in different societies should help to suggest the wide range of behaviors to which these concepts are applicable.

One of the universal phenomena associated with status and role is *age*, since all societies make some distinction in what they expect of individuals at different stages of development. These expectations may begin to exert their influence very early in life. In the case of the Manus tribe of New Guinea, as Mead (24) has pointed out, great stress is laid upon physical proficiency. The early "education" of the child accustoms him from his first years to self-reliance as well as to a large number of manual and motor activities. "He grows up to be an adult wholly admirable from a physical standpoint, skilled, alert, fearless, resourceful in the face of emergency, reliable under strain" (p. 47). On the other hand, social discipline is very loose, and the children are pampered and spoiled to a considerable degree. They have everything their own way and show no obedience or deference to their parents' wishes. If the child is physically efficient, has respect for other people's property, and shows an adequate observance of the canons of prudery and shame, no other demands are made upon him.

The lack of discipline among Manus children is in striking contrast to the African Kaffirs described by Kidd (25). Among children in this group there is little disobedience, and the first lesson they learn is politeness and consideration for others. At the same time they are almost never punished, and they seem to catch the spirit of obedience and politeness by imitation of their elders. Sociability is strongly developed. In this connection there is one type of trauma which occurs rather frequently among children in our soicety, and which is rare in a primitive community; the primitive child is never "left out." There are no social gatherings from which he is excluded, and he is rarely if ever made to feel that he is not accepted by the others in his group. This may have great significance in connection with feelings of personal security and with personality development generally.

Mead has indicated some of the factors contributing to the education of the child in Samoa (26). Responsibility is given at an early age, and a little girl of six or seven is expected to care for younger members of the family. The young child is pampered for a time, but soon it is disciplined and socialized through the task of caring for others. One of the interesting aspects of Samoan education is its condemnation of precocity. The greatest social error a child can make is to "talk above his age," or in any way show advancement over his age-mates. In strong contrast with our own society, a child is not encouraged to progress as quickly as possible, and the parents would be ashamed to find their child ahead of the average. There is only one situation in which the community permits precocity, namely, in the dances. A child may then take the limelight and will gain prestige from any special proficiency he may show.

The problem of role expectations becomes particularly important at the period of adolescence. As is well known, the behavior of the adolescent was once regarded as almost entirely explicable on the basis of the physiological changes accompanying that period of development; the name of G. Stanley Hall (27) is usually associated with this approach. Under the influence of the current doctrine of recapitulation, which sees the development of the individual as a reflection of the development of the whole human race, Hall regarded the adolescent as "neo-atavistic, prone to storm and stress" because of "ancestral prepotencies struggling with each other for predominance." He and his students circulated a large number of questionnaires dealing with the phenomena of this period and made a careful study of biographies from the same point of view. On the basis of this material ten characteristics of puberty were listed as typical—(1) inner absorption and revery, (2) the birth of imagination, illusions, dreams, etc., (3) self-criticism, skepticism, scruples, (4) the over-assertion of individuality, (5) imitation at its acme, (6) the assumption of dramatic roles, poses, affectations, (7) folly, absurdities, freakishness, (8) a new speech consciousness, (9) absorption in friendship, (10) impairment of orientation in time and place, intense fluctuations in energy, and emotional and intellectual plasticity. Hall regarded the adolescent stage as characterized especially by "a loosening of the bonds between the manifold factors of the ego." He likened the manifestations of adolescence to the symptoms of hysteria and insanity, and considered it a period particularly prone to religious conversions and other extreme personality changes.

Without denying the significance of the physiological changes characteristic of adolescence, we know that when difficulties occur, there may be many other factors operative. One of the most important problems arises out of the adolescent's uncertainty as to his status. As Gardner Murphy (28) expresses it: "Much of this could be summarized by saying that one of the chief aims of the young adult is status, and that his picture of himself as a recipient of a certain kind and degree of status is so clearly drawn that almost every aspect of it gives a fair clue to all the rest" (p. 513).

In our complex society there is no fixed age at which certain privileges are automatically obtained, and for a number of years an adolescent must fight for his independence. To take one example, a study by Butterfield (29) showed that in a relatively homogeneous community in a large city, the parents differed widely as to the age at which they permitted their daughters to go out unchaperoned; the range was from about fourteen years to twenty. Such a range might constitute a source of conflict and disappointment in all those children above the age of fourteen who were not allowed this privilege. This is one of many possible examples of variations in status and role among children of the same age which create uncertainty in the child's mind as to his true position and make "becoming an adult" a source of continual struggle.

This is not the only source of the adolescent's uncertainty regarding his status and role. With reference to many different situations, the range of possible role behaviors is very wide. There are no definite rules or expectations regarding the hour at which teen-agers are expected home at night, the number of dates permitted, the night-spots that may be visited, the use of the family car, etc. It is highly probable that the wear and tear upon both parents and children might be reduced if some code of standards could be adopted and accepted by both in order to decrease this tremendous variation. It is not being suggested that there should be a national referendum, with the decision of the majority becoming the law of the land. Codes would have to be local, and advisory rather than binding, and they would apply only to those items on which it is possible to reach agreement. If successful, this procedure might well reduce many of the strains which are due to relative frustrations even in groups which in material terms have little cause for complaint, and would make it easier for the adolescent to discover and to fulfill the role which is expected of him.

The adjustment of the child and the adolescent is made more complicated by the fact that he has to take into consideration two different sets of social norms and as a consequence two different roles, one laid down by the adult culture represented by his parents, the other by his own contemporaries. Much has been written about the so-called "peer cultures," the standards of behavior determined by children for themselves, with strong pressures toward conformity, often in conflict with the norms set by adults, and with definite sanctions against the dissenter. The phenomenon is particularly noticeable in the teens, and Talcott Parsons (30) has labeled it "youth culture." Frequently, parental expectations are subordinated to acceptance by one's peers. Blos (31) writes: "Group opinion serves, then, as a selective influence for desirable and undesirable behavior, and the approval or disapproval of peers becomes progressively the most influential force in motivating adolescent conduct" (p. 251). Many aspects of peer cultures remain obscure, but their importance in relation to feelings of personal security and worth can hardly be overestimated. They appear to be particularly influential in cultures in which the independence of young people is encouraged, as for example, in the United States and evidently also in Israel [see Wolman (32)]. In any case, uncertainty as to one's role—how much of the child, how much of the adult—certainly represents one of the most crucial factors in creating difficulties for many adolescents.

Although sex impulses, as the Freudians have amply demonstrated, play a part long before adolescence is reached, it is obvious that sex as a problem is accentuated at a period when the individual is prepared biologically for a form of behavior often denied to him by his society. We know that on the organic side there are actual tensions set up which demand some form of release, and that a psychological conflict may result from the inability to accomplish this in a satisfying manner. Even when some form of sexual satisfaction is discovered, there will be difficulties arising from the opposition between behavior on the one hand and the moral dictates of society on the other.

As Mead has shown, these difficulties need not arise in a different type of society. In her study of the adolescent girl in Samoa, she indicates that "storm and stress" during adolescence is rare. There is no conflict or revolt, no picture of neurotic or psychotic disturbance. The adolescent girl need have no worries either about her status in the community or about her sexual needs. The former is determined by rules and regulations which grant to members of certain age groups definite rights and privileges, and in these respects no one may progress more quickly than anyone else. On the sexual side, the girl engages shortly after adolescence in a series of affairs with the boys of the community, each affair lasting only a short time and being followed almost immediately by another. It is apparently rare for any girl except the "taupo," or princess, to be left out of such an arrangement. The adults in the community are of course perfectly aware of what is going on and make no attempt to interfere in any way.

Under such conditions there are no special problems characteristic of this period, and the adolescent girl differs from the non-adolescent only in the fact that certain bodily changes have taken place. Mead concludes that the difficulties associated with adolescence, whatever these may be, originate in the social situation and not in the physiological condition of the individual.

Undoubtedly this conclusion is in the main correct, but certain problems of interpretation in connection with the Samoan material still remain. There is, for instance, the fact that the adolescent girls do not engage in sex activity immediately after puberty; usually there is an interval of two or three years. Miss Mead writes that the adolescent girls were given this valuable interval in which to get accustomed to new work, greater isolation and an unfamiliar physical development. One wonders why this interval was not more often characterized by difficulties of adjustment, since the girls were now organically prepared for a form of behavior which nevertheless was postponed for a substantial period of time. The girls for whom difficulties were reported were principally, however, those who lived under missionary control, and who had special problems arising out of the imposition of foreign standards of morality. At any rate it seems clear that the situation of the Samoan adolescent girl contains much less stress and strain than Stanley Hall regarded as inevitable.

From another point of view, "coming of age" may constitute a severe trial in primitive communities. In a great many cases the appearance of puberty is the signal for special treatment which cannot fail to make a great impression upon the adolescent. Among other things, there may be change of dwelling, entrance into youth societies, ordeals, tests of skill and endurance, acquisition of a guardian spirit, separation from the family group, disappearance from home into the forest or desert, initiation into sexual life, freedom from childhood restraints, the symbolic use of decorations or mutilations as an indication of the enhanced status, ceremonies of initiation, and so on (33).

The initiation ceremonies, referred to by Van Gennep (34) as *rites de passage*, may in some cases constitute a severe ordeal, and it is certain that the initiate is not undisturbed in the process. Among the Australian tribes the ordeal was particularly trying, and might be accompanied by circumcision, subincision, the knocking out of a tooth and other physically painful experiences. Since the adolescent had to bear his trial without any complaint or any indication of suffering, it was naturally a severe test of self-control. Among the African Masai, initiation was accompanied by circumcision in the case of the boys, and clitoridectomy for girls. In the Banks Islands in Melanesia, entrance into the men's society was not the occasion for any actual mutilation of the initiate, but he underwent all sorts of trials during a probationary period of 100 days, during which others threw his food into the fire, destroyed his possessions and set him a variety of difficult tasks which he had to perform without complaining (35). Among a great number of American Indian tribes, as well as in other parts of the world, puberty in the girl resulted in her segregation as "unclean" for a varying period of time. There were, however, many primitive communities (Samoa is one example) in which adolescence was not marked in any important way, and in which coming of age was not attended by any special difficulties.

It is important to keep in mind, as Benedict has pointed out (6), that these initiation ceremonies and other activities indicating the transition from childhood to adult status, did not necessarily coincide with the period of the physical changes of puberty. They might come earlier or later, depending upon the customs of the community; they are to be regarded as a social rather than a biological coming of age. Even if they constitute periods of stress, the difficulties which they create are not to be explained by physiological instability, but by the need to meet the requirements set by custom and convention. Where these rites de passage occur, however, they perform an important function both individually and socially. They make it clear that the adolescent has now definitely entered into a new status with a clearly defined role. Unlike many of our own adolescents, he knows just where he stands and exactly what is expected of him. He experiences none of the conflicts which arise out of uncertainty as to his role in society.

At the other end of the developmental scale, the role of the aged also presents special problems. As the Lynds (36) have indicated, in our society, growing old is regarded as a calamity, largely though not entirely because of the economic insecurity which it involves. In a society like that of the native Australians, old age is on the contrary a privilege. The government of an Australian tribe is really a gerontocracy, with the authority vested in the old men. Status and prestige, as well as the economic services of the rest of the tribe, are assured to individuals as they grow old. It is obvious that the whole attitude of the individual to his future would be modified as a result. Simmons (37) has amply demonstrated the wide variety of role expectations for the aged in different cultural groups, and has shown the extent to which the effects of aging are determined by social norms as well as by the biological processes involved. The greater life expectancy in many countries, and the consequent increase in the proportion of the aged in the population, make the problem of the status and role of older people particularly important.

In connection with sex differences, we have already indicated (Chapter 10) the wide variety of role expectations for men and women in different cultures. In our own society we start early with the process of acquainting boys and girls with the fact that they are to behave differently. We remain reasonably consistent in our demands on boys, but girls may frequently be faced with the need to reconcile conflicting role expectations. This was clearly demonstrated in an investigation by Komarovsky (38), who obtained autobiographical data from undergraduate women students. The investigator concludes that there are marked contradictions between two roles simultaneously presented. The first, termed the "feminine" role, emphasizes the need to be more emotional and sympathetic than men, less dominant and aggressive, attractive to the opposite sex, interested in marriage and children, etc. The second, referred to as the "modern" role, demands of women much the same qualities, patterns of behavior, and attitudes that it does of men. Many of the girls in this study found it difficult to satisfy both these roles at the same time. As one of them expressed it: "It seemed that my family had expected me to become Eve Curie and Hedy Lamarr wrapped up in one." The girls vary in their handling of this conflict situation, but in the lives of a great many of them it introduces serious problems, which according to the investigator will persist "until the adult sex roles of women are redefined in greater harmony with the socioeconomic and ideological character of modern society" (p. 189).

Status and role are of course closely associated, in our society as in many others, with the phenomenon of socioeconomic class structure. As Warner and his associates (39) have amply demonstrated, the lines of demarcation in an American community may be quite marked, with minimal contact between members of distinct classes. Davis and Havighurst (40) go so far as to suggest that these distinctions may actually result in different cultures for different classes; "by setting up barriers to social participation, the American social-class system actually prevents the vast majority of children of the working classes, or the slums, from learning any culture but that of their own groups" (p. 309). Their study of class differences in child rearing was based on interviews with approximately 200 mothers in a large city. The results showed that middle-class mothers were more rigorous than those of the lower class in training children in feeding and cleanliness habits, expected them to take responsibility for themselves earlier in life, and placed them under a stricter regimen, with more frustration of their impulses. Although these differences emerged clearly, it seems to the writer that to speak of mutually exclusive cultures represents an exaggeration. In the first place, the results do indicate considerable overlapping in the practices reported by members of the two class-groups investigated. Secondly, "contact of cultures" does occur as the result of the fact that lower-class children are often taught by middle-class teachers, and also through the pervasive influence of the mass media.

Class status is of course related to a number of objective variables such as property or income, occupation, power, length of residence in a community, ethnic origin, etc. It also has a number of subjective aspects. This fact emerges clearly when individuals are asked to indicate the class to which they belong. A poll by the American Institute of Public Opinion in June, 1941, asked: "To what social class in this country do you feel you belong—middle class, or upper or lower?" Only 4.9% answered "upper" and 0.7%, "lower," with the rest classifying themselves in the "middle" group. Other polls in the United States have given similar results. This has sometimes been taken to mean that the United States is predominantly a "middle class" society; this may be true, but the evidence from the polls is unsatisfactory, since few people would describe themselves as "lower" class, even if they were conscious of their low economic status. When a similar poll was conducted in 1946, but with the addition of the category "working class," slightly more than 50% of the respondents chose that designation for themselves. In still another poll in 1947 the expression "laboring class" was used instead of working class, and in this case the percentage dropped to 35%, with 53% placing themselves in the "middle" class.

The problem of the subjective aspects of class was explored further in an important investigation by Centers (41), who analyzed the results obtained from interviews of 1100 persons, representing a cross section of the American adult White male population. They identified their own social class as follows: upper, 3%; middle, 43%; working, 51%; lower, 1%; don't know, 1%; don't believe in classes, 1%. Since the respondents gave information regarding their occupations, they could be classified according to objective position as well as in terms of their own subjective identification. These did not always coincide. Most manual workers, for example, regarded themselves as "working class," but a considerable minority said they were "middle class." All the respondents answered a battery of six questions designed to test radical-conservative orientations, and permitting a subdivision into conservative, intermediate and radical groups. The attitudes expressed could now be compared in terms of objective position, subjective identification, and both combined.

The results showed that both factors are important. The middle-class occupational groups (business, professional and white collar workers) are definitely more conservative than those in the working class (manual workers). In addition, those members of an occupational stratum who identify with the middle class tend to be more conservative than those of the same stratum who identify with the working class. Of these two factors, actual occupational position is a better index to attitudes than subjective class affiliation. When the two coincide, the attitude differences emerge most clearly. Centers' study may therefore be regarded as having demonstrated that subjective class identification has definite importance, but the fact remains that the objective aspects of class show a more significant relationship to attitudes.

In Australia Hammond (42) interviewed 129 adult men in a suburb of Melbourne, and like Centers found it important to make a distinction between *real* stratum position and the *subjective* stratum choices. In the actual working-class groups, one-third of the respondents placed themselves in the middle class. Although the orientation of this study was somewhat different from that of Centers, the results showed, for example, that among Labour Party supporters, those who considered themselves to be working class were somewhat more radical in their views than those who considered themselves middle class. The subjective class phenomena described by Centers appear, therefore, not to be limited to the United States.

Earlier, Hyman (43) had demonstrated that status was not only objective, but also subjective, determined by a person's conception of his own position relative to others. He found that when individuals were asked about their status, they usually compared themselves not with the population at large, but with others in their own small groups—their friends, their business associates, their neighbors, etc. These constituted the *reference groups* for their subjective determination of their own relative status. We shall return to this important concept in connection with the development and modification of attitudes of the individual in the group. (See Chapter 17.)

Our analysis of status and role has touched upon differences related to age, sex and class. There are many other phenomena of

American life which could be—and in some cases have been—treated from this standpoint. As examples might be mentioned the studies by Waller (44) of the role of the teacher, by Henry (45) of the business executive, by Merton (46) of the bureaucrat, by Sutherland (47) of the professional thief, by Parsons (48) of the physician, and by Schneider (49) of the patient. The role of the leader will be discussed further in Chapter 17. Taken together, these studies contribute to our understanding of the variety of roles which go to make up a complex society, and help to indicate how the demands of the culture, as well as of the various sub-cultures which have been identified, are related to the behavior of the individual.

CULTURE, ROLE AND PERSONALITY

Roles may be regarded as a connecting link between culture and personality. It is largely by determining the role which the individual is expected to perform that the culture influences the behavior of individual members of any community. The importance of the concept should not, however, be exaggerated. There are material and also ideational aspects of a culture which have an important influence on behavior, and which cannot easily be expressed in terms of status or role. There are also differences between individuals which cannot be attributed to their different roles, since two physicians, let us say, of the same religious background, living in the same neighborhood, belonging to the same clubs, fathers of families of similar size, etc., will still show unique and idiosyncratic organizations of behavior. Role prescriptions and expectations help us to put some order into the variety of individual personalities found within any community, but they do not tell the whole story.

As Kluckhohn and others (50) state, and as we have already indicated, the individual must be understood in terms of a combination of constitutional, cultural, role and situational determinants. We must grant to the concept of role its very real importance, but we must see it also in perspective, as a part of the total explanatory picture.

SUMMARY

The study of culture-and-personality represents the principal meeting-ground between anthropology and psychology. It is concerned with both the universals and the variations in behavior within any community.

The concept of "type" has been applied both to cultures and to individuals, and although frequently convenient as a descriptive technique, is unsatisfactory because each culture and every individual is unique. The relation between culture and personality is clarified by the application of the concepts of *status* and *role*, which influence attitudes and behavior through social expectations. Status and role are related to age, sex, class, and many other factors; they have subjective as well as objective determinants. Difficulties arise when roles are not clearly defined, as in the case of adolescents, women, and others.

The role concept has acquired great importance in recent social psychology.

REFERENCES

1. Kroeber, A. L. *Anthropology*. 1948
2. White, L. A. *The Science of Culture*. 1949
3. Herskovits, M. J. "On Cultural and Psychological Reality." In J. H. Rohrer and M. Sherif (eds.), *Social Psychology at the Crossroads*. 1951
4. Linton, R. *The Cultural Background of Personality*. 1945
5. Nietzsche, F. *The Birth of Tragedy*. 1924
6. Benedict, R. F. *Patterns of Culture*. 1934
7. Radin, P. *The Story of the American Indian*. 1934
8. Crawley, E. *Studies of Savages and Sex* (ed. by T. Besterman). 1939
9. Jung, C. G. *Psychological Types*. 1926
10. Plant, J. S. *Personality and the Cultural Pattern*. 1937
11. Heidbreder, E. "Measuring Introversion and Extroversion," *J. Abn. and Soc. Psychol.*, 1927, 21: pp. 120-134
12. Abraham, K. *Selected Papers*. 1927
13. Campbell, C. M. *Human Personality and the Environment*. 1934
14. Mead, M. *Sex and Temperament in Three Primitive Societies*. 1935
15. LaBarre, W. "Some Observations on Character Structure in the Orient; The Chinese," *Psychiatry*, 1946, 9: pp. 215-237; 375-395
16. Roheim, G. "Psychoanalysis of Primitive Cultural Types," *Internatl. J. Psychoanal.*, 1932, 13: pp. 2-224
17. LaBarre, W. "Some Observations on Character Structure in the Orient; The Japanese," *Psychiatry*, 1945, 8: pp. 319-342
18. Riesman, D. *The Lonely Crowd*. 1950. *Faces in the Crowd*. 1953
19. Kluckhohn, C. "The Study of Culture." In D. Lerner and H. D. Lasswell (eds.), *The Policy Sciences*. 1951

20. Sargent, S. S. "Conceptions of Role and Ego in Contemporary Psychology." In J. H. Rohrer and M. Sherif (eds.), *Social Psychology at the Crossroads.* 1951

21. Sargent, S. S. *Social Psychology.* 1950

22. Hartley, E. L., and Hartley, R. E. *Fundamentals of Social Psychology.* 1952

23. Newcomb, T. M. *Social Psychology.* 1950

24. Mead, M. *Growing Up in New Guinea.* 1930

25. Kidd, D. *Savage Childhood.* 1906

26. Mead, M. *Coming of Age in Samoa.* 1928

27. Hall, G. S. *Adolescence.* 2 vols. 1908

28. Murphy, G. *Personality: A Biosocial Approach to Origins and Structure.* 1947

29. Butterfield, O. McK. *Love Problems of Adolescence.* 1939

30. Parsons, T. "Age and Sex in the Social Structure of the United States." In C. Kluckhohn, H. A. Murray and D. M. Schneider (eds.), *Personality in Nature, Society and Culture.* Rev. ed. 1953

31. Blos, P. *The Adolescent Personality.* 1941

32. Wolman, B. "The Youth Movement in Israel." *Jewish Frontier.* 1949

33. Van Waters, M. "Adolescence," *Encycl. Soc. Sci.,* 1930, I: pp. 455-459

34. Van Gennep, A. *Les rites de passage.* 1909

35. Lowie, R. H. *Primitive Society.* 1925

36. Lynd, R. S., and Lynd, H. M. *Middletown in Transition.* 1937

37. Simmons, L. W. *Role of the Aged in Primitive Society.* 1945

38. Komarovsky, M. "Cultural Contradictions and Sex Roles," *Amer. J. Sociol.,* 1946, 52: pp. 184-189

39. Warner, W. L., and Lunt, P. S. *The Social Life of a Modern Community.* 1941

40. Davis, A., and Havighurst, R. J. "Social Class and Color Differences in Child-Rearing." In G. E. Swanson, T. M. Newcomb and E. L. Hartley (eds.), *Readings in Social Psychology.* Rev. ed. 1952

41. Centers, R. *The Psychology of Social Classes.* 1949. See also Swanson, Newcomb and Hartley (eds.), *Readings in Social Psychology.* Rev. ed. 1952

42. Hammond, S. B. "Stratification in an Australian City." In Swanson, Newcomb and Hartley (eds.), *Readings in Social Psychology.* Rev. ed. 1952

43. Hyman, H. "The Psychology of Status," *Arch. Psychol.,* 1942, No. 269

44. Waller, W. "The Teacher's Roles." In J. S. Roucek (ed.), *Sociological Foundations of Education.* 1942

45. Henry, W. "The Business Executive—the Psychodynamics of a Social Role," *Amer. J. Sociol.*, 1949, 54: pp. 286-291

46. Merton, R. K. "Bureaucratic Structure and Personality," *Soc. Forces*, 1950, 18: pp. 560-568

47. Sutherland, E. H. (ed.). *The Professional Thief.* 1937

48. Parsons, T. M. "Illness and the Role of the Physician." In Kluckhohn, Murray and Schneider (eds.), *Personality in Nature, Society and Culture.* Rev. ed. 1953

49. Schneider, D. M. "Social Dynamics of Physical Disability in Army Basic Training." In Kluckhohn, Murray and Schneider, *Personality in Nature, Society and Culture.* Rev. ed. 1953

50. Kluckhohn, C., Murray, H. A., and Schneider, D. M. (eds.). *Personality in Nature, Society and Culture.* Rev. ed. 1953

Culture and Personality: The Study of National Characteristics

14

INTRODUCTION

In recent years students of culture and personality have increasingly directed their attention and their techniques to the understanding of contemporary national groups. The problem is an old one, of course, and the interest in it has been continuous throughout the ages, but the approach has altered considerably not only in its character but also in its intensity. In the past it was largely the concern of historians on the one hand, and of journalists and travelers on the other. Now almost all the social sciences have begun to make their contribution to the understanding of national characteristics; not only history but also sociology, anthropology, psychology, psychiatry, psychoanalysis, political science, comparative law, the study of public opinion, and many other related disciplines. Several universities, for example Columbia and Harvard, are engaged in extensive research along interdisciplinary lines. UNESCO, in connection with its Project on Tensions Affecting International Understanding, has initiated a series of investigations of national cultures. The literature relevant to national characteristics is already extensive, and is increasing rapidly. In France a journal, *Revue de Psychologie des Peuples*, is entirely devoted to this topic.

The task of understanding the characteristics of nations remains, however, an exceedingly difficult one. A few years ago Barzun (1) began his review of two new books about the British with the words: "Of all the books that no one can write, those about nations and national character are the most impossible." He went on to say, "a people is too numerous, too various, too much an epitome of mankind, to be cited for judgment in a formula, or even in a string of formulas modifying and annulling one another" (p. 188). In spite of this critical attitude, which is shared by many other scholars, we shall make an attempt to review a portion of the relevant literature, to discuss the principal techniques which have been applied, and to assess our present position regarding this important problem.

Many of those who have written on this topic have used the expression *national character;* the present writer prefers to speak of *national characteristics.* The distinction may appear to be a trivial one, but the word *character* is used in so many different senses that it may be misleading. Popularly, and in the field of ethical philosophy it has a moral connotation; to the psychoanalyst it suggests the more deep-seated and fundamental aspects of personality. The term *characteristics* is more neutral and all-inclusive and makes no assumptions of a theoretical nature. It would seem to be preferable for our purposes if we keep in mind that what we are trying to discover is not a mere listing of separate and distinct traits, but also the manner in which these are organized and integrated into a unified structure.

The question may legitimately be raised as to whether we are justified in speaking of national character or even of national characteristics at the present stage of our knowledge. It has been argued, for example, that from certain points of view there may be more similarity between the inhabitants of Paris and New York than between either of these and a French or American farmer, respectively. What appear to be differences between two nations may turn out to be due to such factors as degree of urbanization, economic and industrial development, level of education, religion, and other variables which cut across national lines. The answer to this criticism is that of course all these factors must be taken into account. We need studies of various regions within a nation, as well as of economic classes and other subgroups; we need a comparison of similar classes in different nations as well as of different classes within the same nation. It is largely on the basis of such considerations that Linton (2) writes: "The existence of different personality norms for modern nations as wholes has not been established . . ." (p. 144). It may very well be that something specifically national may still be discovered after all the above factors have been controlled or equated. In any event, a case could be made for the existence of national characteristics, even if they may best be explained along the lines suggested. Even if a nation is relatively undeveloped economically, with its population concentrated in rural areas, a low level of literacy, etc., these conditions do not negate the fact that the nation has certain characteristics.

A second objection is that nations change, and that characteristics found at one period of history may not necessarily persist. This is also true, although there may be certain relatively constant elements. Here we need the help of historians and economists; the study of history in particular is an absolute prerequisite for a complete picture. Without it, we shall make one mistake after another. In any case, the possibility of change does not rule out the study of national characteristics at any given moment. It does impose caution in inferring from one historical period to another.

A general review of the problems involved in this area of research, with an extensive bibliography, is to be found in a recent article by Margaret Mead (3). Elsewhere the present writer (4) has discussed at some length various possible approaches to the study of national characteristics. The treatment here will therefore be limited to a rather general description of the main lines of inquiry, with some suggestions as to what remains to be done.

As far as methods are concerned, it may be convenient to distinguish three major tendencies. The first may be described as an over-all, holistic approach, directed toward establishing the general pattern of the national culture and its effect on personality. It is an attempt to see the culture as a whole, and the common personality which is its counterpart. The second tendency concerns itself with the examination of a number of individuals within a particular nation, and notes the differences as well as the similarities among such individuals. It is interested in the distribution of characteristics in the total population, and in the frequency with which certain behaviors actually occur. The third approach is intermediate between the first two, and is characterized by attention to a particular unit within the total society, or to a particular segment of the total culture. The distinction between these approaches—as well as the overlapping—will emerge more clearly in connection with the specific examples which will now be presented.

NATIONAL CULTURE AS A WHOLE

One of the major developments in the study of national characteristics has come from the attempt by certain anthropologists to apply to complex modern societies certain of the techniques and points of view which were developed in the study of relatively simple and "primitive" communities. Margaret Mead (5), for example, believes that the ethnologist has the necessary objectivity and impartiality with which to describe any complex culture including his own, because he has learned to recognize the ways in which the individual is shaped by the cultural patterns and institutions of his society. His knowledge of other communities makes it possible for him to see his own in proper perspective. With regard to American national characteristics, Mead describes the patterns of parent-child relationships, early training, forms of aggressive behavior, criteria of success, etc. We are told that Americans in one sense are all of the third generation, "our European ancestry tucked away and half forgotten, the recent steps in our wandering over America immortalized and over-emphasized." In a consideration of the American war effort it is stated that Americans fight best when the other fellow starts the fight; when the other fellow has more breaks at the start; when Americans feel that they are on the side of the Right. Americans, we are told further, start life "with a tremendous impetus toward success." Even parental love is conditioned upon successful achievement by the child.

Gorer (6) presents an analysis of American personality along similar lines. He is also impressed with the importance of recent immigrant ancestry in determining the psychological reactions of Americans, particularly the lack of respect for authority. He points out that women play an especially important part in the whole life of the community; the mother is the dominant figure in the household; the growing boy is educated by women schoolteachers and so develops a conscience or superego which Gorer describes as feminine in character.

Another important example of an interpretation of a national group by an ethnologist is the study of Japan by Ruth Benedict (7). In this book there is special stress on the importance for the Japanese of "taking his proper station," an attitude which affects the whole area of Japanese interpersonal relations. Great importance is attached also to a series of interlocking obligations or "debts" which the Japanese individual owes to his parents, to his superiors, to the Emperor, etc.

In many instances, the approach of the cultural anthropologist has been integrated with the theoretical framework supplied by psychoanalysis. (See Chapter 12.) Gorer (8), for instance, on the basis of interviews in the United States with people who had had considerable contact with the Japanese, suggested a close relationship between Japanese character structure and certain experiences of the young child. In particular, he believes that the severe and early toilet training helps us to understand the aggression displayed by the Japanese in later life, as well as their excessive fear and dislike of dirt. A further "derivative" (Gorer's term) is the compulsive emphasis on neatness and tidiness, with "a place for everything and everything in its place," with minutely regulated rituals and preoccupation with detail.

In the discussion of Russian characteristics, Gorer and Rickman (9) lean heavily on certain aspects of behavioristic psychology, in combination with a psychoanalytic approach. Many years ago John B. Watson had pointed out that one of the primary and original sources of rage in the new-born infant is restriction of movement. On this basis, Gorer argues that the tight swaddling imposed by Russian parents on infants during the first year of life, would have certain predictable consequences, and he believes that such swaddling gives a clue to much that would otherwise remain enigmatic in Russian behavior.

Psychiatrists and psychoanalysts have also tried in some cases to arrive at a generalized view of national culture and personality. Brickner makes use of a diagnostic category well-known to psychiatrists, namely *paranoia*, extending it from its customary individual application so as to describe German national culture in general. He does not state—and here he has occasionally been misinterpreted—that all or even the majority of Germans are paranoid; he is describing the culture, and not individuals, though he does indicate that in such a culture paranoid characteristics in certain persons would facilitate their choice as leaders (10).

Schaffner (11) attempted to find the basic explanation for German personality and behavior in the patterns of family relationship. Because the German boy had learned to react to his father with confidence, respect and obedience, he was ready to respond with the same attitudes to Hitler, whose manner was that of the traditional German father, and who proposed to reunite all Germans within the family fold.

In this context mention should also be made of the system developed by Kardiner (12), who sees the basic personality structure of a community as the consequence of the primary institutions which affect the developing child. Kardiner has made one attempt to apply this scheme to contemporary Western man on the basis of his analysis of the American community described by James West. More such applications are needed before we are in a position to determine the fruitfulness of this approach to modern nations.

A great many criticisms have been directed against the over-all approach described above. In the first place, are the descriptions accurate? Do they correspond to the facts? These questions are important, because the evidence on which the analyses are based, and which furnishes the starting-point for the interpretations that follow, is not always presented in such a manner as to carry conviction. Sometimes there is evidence in the opposite direction; Gorer's emphasis, for example, on the severe toilet training of the Japanese infant is not corroborated by the investigation of Mildred Sikkema into the habits of Japanese families in Hawaii (13). Her results indicate that those parents who were born in Hawaii, and who were therefore presumably more "American" in their culture, were actually stricter in the toilet training of their children than were those born in Japan.

Secondly, even if the description is accurate, to what extent is it unique? Does it adequately differentiate one national culture from another? Granting that restriction of movement through swaddling is widespread in Russia, the fact remains that similar restriction of movement is found among infants in many other cultures as well. [See P. Greenacre (14).] In that case, can swaddling really be the clue to the national characteristics of the Russians? In connection with Americans, Gorer refers to the fact that infant feeding is regulated by the clock; the infant is fed according to a strict time schedule, with little regard for his needs or wishes in the matter. In Czechoslovakia, however, a public opinion poll in 1947 also indicated that most mothers fed their infants at regular intervals. The unquestioned authority of the German father has been used [for example by Bertram Schaffner (11)] to explain many aspects of German political behavior. The authority of the traditional Chinese father, however, was at least equally unquestioned. Many other examples could be given of facts that appear to be true of one national culture but which—if we may use a medical expression—are not sufficiently specific to that culture to permit a differential diagnosis.

Finally, it is important to ask this set of questions: Is the over-all cultural pattern true of everybody in that culture? Is it universal within a particular nation? If not, to what extent, in what manner, and with what frequency, do people deviate from such a pattern? These questions have usually not been asked nor answered by those whose descriptions of national cultures we are now discussing. It is important to know whether *all* Japanese subject their children to a strict toilet training; whether *all* German fathers are authoritarian; whether *all* American mothers feed their infants according to a rigid time schedule: In the case of all three of these generalizations there are undoubtedly many exceptions, and their frequency and range require further exploration. We know that class differences may sometimes play an important part; it has been demonstrated (*15, 16*) that adherence to a time schedule for feeding is much more commonly observed in upper and middle class families in the United States than in working class families. This is only one of a number of examples that could be given of the need to take into account the range of individual and subcultural variations within any nation.

NATIONAL CHARACTERISTICS AND INDIVIDUAL VARIATIONS

This brings us to the second major approach, namely, that concerned with the examination of individuals. This has taken many forms, of which only a few will be mentioned at this point. Public opinion studies of the polling variety have begun to yield material of value. Although the information so obtained is at a rather superficial level, the method has the virtue of basing its findings on answers given by a representative cross section of the total population, with minority as well as majority views receiving consideration as part of the total picture. There are serious difficulties of interpretation in many cases. When, for example, we learn that in 1948 the question: "Do you, personally, believe in God?" was answered in the affirmative by 96% of respondents in Brazil and only 66% in France, we would first have to make sure that the words used have the same connotation in the two countries; we would also need to know the relation of this belief to the total complex of religious attitudes of Brazilians and Frenchmen respectively. Similar considerations apply to the fact that, in 1947, 68% of Canadians interviewed expressed themselves in favor of capital punishment as contrasted with only 23% of respondents in the Netherlands. Both of these differences are probably too large to be dismissed as accidental. In any case the method is useful both as a starting-point for further investigation, and also as a means of checking on statements made about "typical" French or Dutch or Brazilian views on these and other topics.

At a somewhat more intensive level, use has been made of a series of interrelated questions designed to make possible quantitative comparisons of the frequency with which certain attitudes or opinions are expressed. In one such study (17) D. V. McGranahan asked a number of interesting questions of boys of high school age in the United States and Germany. There were definite differences between the two national samples, but there was a marked degree of overlapping. The alleged German pattern of unquestioned paternal authority was in a sense borne out. To the question: "Do you think a boy is justified in running away from home if his father is cruel or brutal?" 50% of the German sample, and only 30% of the American sample said "no." More Germans than Americans, therefore, accepted the father's authority without question. From another standpoint, however, this view of the German family structure is seriously challenged; the number of those stating that the boy *is* justified in running away is 45% of the German total (the remaining 5% expressed no opinion). The apparent exceptions are almost as frequent as those who answer in the expected direction. Nor must we forget the very considerable minority of Americans (30%) who answer the question in the "German" direction. This type of quantitative comparison makes a definite addition to our understanding of the nature of the group differences.

In the book by Schaffner to which reference was made above, interesting use is made of the technique of sentence-completion. One of the sentences used was: "The opposition of a young man against his father is . . ." The completions on the whole appear to bear out Schaffner's contention that in general the authority of the German father is unquestioned; they include phrases such as "the result of poor training," "a lack of character," "to be condemned," etc. There were some completions that went in the opposite direction, though these were apparently in the minority; for example, "the natural behavior of youth," "the sign of beginning independence," etc. Unfortunately, Schaffner gives no adequate indication of the relative frequency of the two types of completions, nor does he have results from any other national group as a basis for comparison.

The Rorschach technique is finding an increasingly wide application in the study of national characteristics. One study by Abel and Hsu (18) compares Chinese-born with American-born Chinese, all now living in the United States, and finds the Rorschach to be a valuable instrument not only for the study of national differences, but also as an indication of the process of acculturation, in which a group is observed to be adopting the patterns prevalent in the country to which they or their parents have migrated.

Another variety of projective technique, Raven's Controlled Projection Test, was used by Kaldegg (19) in a study of German and English boys between the ages of eleven and fourteen. The subjects were shown the picture of a boy sitting at a table with his back to the onlooker; they were then asked questions about what the boy liked to do, whom he liked to play with, what he thought or dreamed about, what stories he told, etc. The results showed some striking differences between the two groups. The German boys disliked cowards, the English boys disliked bullies, ruffians and girls; the Germans showed a much greater acceptance of corporal punishment for wrong-doing, and were in general much more rigid and conventional in their responses. The interests and desires of the two groups were however quite similar.

Intensive interviews, modified from the psychiatric and psychoanalytic techniques in wide clinical use, have also been applied to the problem of national characteristics. Perhaps the outstanding example is that of the British psychiatrist, Henry V. Dicks (20), who interviewed a large number of German prisoners of war and described the character structure that he regarded as typical. Among the characteristics that Dicks ascribes to his German subjects are the following: earnestness, over-respect for authority, concern with status, conformity, uneasiness in unforeseen situations, etc. The major query that must be raised in this connection relates to the conditions of the investigation. The Germans were all prisoners of war; they were interviewed by a British officer. Can we be certain that the rapport that prevailed under these circumstances would be satisfactory for the purposes of such a study? In any case Dicks has adequately demonstrated the feasibility of using interviews for this purpose, although here again it would have been interesting to have similar interviews of British or American men under comparable conditions. Mention should be made also of the interviews carried out by David M. Levy (21) in Germany with a view to establishing differences in the background and personality of Nazis and anti-Nazis, respectively. His study is significant precisely because it keeps in mind the variations as well as the similarities in German national characteristics. More recently Dicks (20) has applied a similar analysis to the results of interviews of a group of Russians, but here also the problem of the selection of the sample raises serious difficulties of interpretation. The respondents were all outside their homeland, and all had for one reason or another broken with the Soviet regime.

The approach to national characteristics in terms of the study of individuals has an obvious appeal to psychologists, who are concerned with the application of methods which as far as possible should be objective, experimental, quantitative and verifiable. It must be admitted, however, that such methods also have serious limitations. The anthropologists rightly ask: What can be quantified? The answer must be that quantitative techniques can be applied to specific aspects of behavior, to attitudes or opinions, to personality constellations and value systems, but not to culture-and-personality as a unit. It may be that what we gain in precision and certainty is balanced by a lesser understanding of the total pattern or the configuration. This raises the question of the possibility of combining the two approaches in such a manner as effectively to answer the criticisms that have been directed against both. We shall return to this point later.

SEGMENTAL APPROACHES

We are using the term *segmental* to designate those techniques which are directed toward the study of a part of a large modern nation, or of a part of a complex national culture. There are two methods in this category which appear to be particularly promising. The first is the study of individual communities, an approach which is characteristic of anthropological fieldwork among relatively small, "primitive" groups, but which has come to be applied more and more to contemporary "civilized" societies.

Perhaps the best known investigations in this group are the two Middletown studies by the Lynds (22). The community selected was a midwestern American city of about 40,000 population and regarded as more or less "typical," although it is admitted that this assumption may not be entirely justified. The authors list six main activities of the individuals in this community: (1) getting a living, (2) making a home, (3) training the young, (4) leisure, play and art, (5) religion, and (6) community activities. One of the peculiar aspects of American life as contrasted with many other cultures is the fact that earning a living is the dominant problem. This is a great concern of the individual from childhood on through life; it is often the cause of pessimism and worry about the future. It attaches fear to the prospect of growing old and not being able to keep one's place in the economic scheme. It is an important factor in determining the nature of law, which is concerned largely in maintaining the sanctions of "private property," "free competition" and "individual initiative." It results in the expenditure of much time and energy upon an education, since the uncertainty of the parents about the economic future makes them wish to give their children the best possible training. The authors point to the almost universal "dominance of the dollar" and to the fact that all are "running for dear life to make the money they earn keep pace with the rapid growth of their subjective wants" (*Middletown*, p. 76).

In their second volume the Lynds give an interesting account of the ideas, values and ambitions of the average American in Middletown. There is in general a marked degree of conservatism and hostility to all radical ideas and movements, a belief in the "ladder of opportunity" and the possibility of rising above one's present position, there is a pride in the growth of one's community or of one's organization, there is a desire for prestige and the good opinion of one's neighbors, and so on. This is by no means a denial of individual differences with respect to these attitudes, but there is sufficient homogeneity to enable us to speak of the influence of the culture of Middletown upon the large majority of its citizens.

During the period of approximately 25 years since the appearance of *Middletown*, community studies in contemporary national societies have multiplied, and the relevant literature is now extensive. The critical survey by Steward (23) gives an excellent account of the contributions which can be made by this method, as well as of its defects and limitations. He believes that in too many cases the community studied has been treated as if it were a self-contained whole which could be understood in terms of itself alone; relations to the broader national—and even international—society have frequently been neglected, and there has been little attention paid to historical perspective. A second limitation as far as concerns national characteristics is that community studies in different nations have been conducted from such varied points of view, with attention focused on such different aspects of the culture, that the direct comparison of results is often difficult if not impossible. Further, the study of a single community does not permit inferences to the national culture as a whole, unless we have independent evidence regarding the extent to which this particular community is typical. We may conclude that the method may best make its contribution to the understanding of national characteristics if these criticisms are kept in mind in the design of the study; this method will be particularly effective when more than one community within the same nation is investigated, and also when communities in different countries are studied by techniques that are as similar as the differences in culture permit.

A recent study of a village in Mexico by Lewis (24) illustrates the increasing tendency to combine the traditional community study with careful statistical reporting and the application of psychological techniques like the Rorschach. The results appear to be exceedingly promising. One interesting feature of Lewis's study is that it was conducted on the same community, Tepoztlàn, which had previously been described by Redfield (25). Although in many respects the two studies are mutually corroborative, the picture which emerges of the personality characteristics of Tepoztecans differs markedly; Redfield sees them as much happier, more secure, cooperative and friendly than does Lewis. We shall not attempt to decide who is right, or whether the Tepoztecans changed in the intervening period, but the discrepancy does suggest the need for techniques in this field which do not depend too much upon the subjective judgment of even the most careful observer.

A second method which may be characterized as segmental is represented by the content analysis of cultural products; here again not the whole culture, but only a portion of it is the object of study. Content analysis, which may be either quantitative or qualitative,

has recently attracted considerable attention in the field of communications research [see Berelson (26)], and in a few noticeable instances has been applied to the question of national characteristics.

What is perhaps the first major effort along these lines is represented by Kracauer's (27) analysis of the content of German films
over a long period; one of his findings relates to the all-pervading
respect for authority which has animated German film production.
This respect for authority is so great that movie scripts which depict
any power-figure as evil (as for example the original story on which
was based *The Cabinet of Dr. Caligari*) are usually transformed in
order to fit the prevailing pattern. Kracauer sees obvious parallels
to German attitudes in general, even long before the appearance of
Hitler.

Wolfenstein and Leites (28) have examined American films from
the point of view of what they reveal about the American personality. They analyzed the pattern of relationship between the sexes
(identifying in the films the "good bad girl," who seems to be
wicked and glamorous at the outset, but who turns out to be a good
girl after all); the family background (the protagonist usually has
shadowy or absent parents; he is more closely identified with the
family he establishes than with the family from which he comes);
the relation to authority (in crime films the police, symbols of
authority, are frequently made to appear ridiculous), etc.

A comparison of German and American plays was made by Mc-
Granahan and Wayne (29), who chose for detailed analysis the
45 most popular plays in both countries during the relatively normal
year of 1927. The American plays, as contrasted with the German,
showed a greater concern with love and personal morals, and a lesser
concern with social and political problems; they more frequently
had a happy ending; they more often had a contemporary rather
than a historical setting; they included many more characters who
changed their minds or "reformed" as the plot progressed. Women
much less frequently played the central role in German plays; when
they did, they tended to be "masculine" in characteristics and type
of action. One of the interesting aspects of this study is the comparison of the results obtained by this method with those that
emerged from the application of attitude questionnaires, reactions
of Germans to American movies, etc. On the whole, the pattern
appeared to be fairly consistent.

There are a number of problems involved in the use of content analysis in the present context. If we study only one cultural product, our result may be affected by factors which determine the nature of that product, rather than by characteristics of the culture in general. The content of motion pictures, for example, may be influenced by the age of the audience (on the whole a youthful one) and by censorship of various kinds; plays will usually reach a more sophisticated and wealthier group, especially in the United States. We know little about the degree of influence exerted by the personal taste of those in control of the mass media, or by the popularity of certain actors or playwrights. At the same time the results already obtained hold out promise of increased success in the application of this technique, particularly if more than one cultural product is examined, and if proper attention is paid to more than one period of time.

A COMBINED APPROACH

We have found something to praise and something to criticize in all the techniques which have passed under review. The descriptions by the anthropologists give us integrations and patterns, but they leave many of us skeptical regarding the facts on which the interpretations are based. The techniques of experimental psychology, if applied to a representative sample of the nation, do carry conviction, but they are piecemeal and isolated. Community studies and content analysis give us a good deal of valuable information, but the results cannot safely be extrapolated to the national culture as a whole. No one technique appears capable of giving us all the answers. The obvious solution would be a combination of several different approaches, and—in the present state of our knowledge—the more the better. This will make the task expensive and time-consuming, but there is no simple way to solve such a complex problem.

As we have already indicated, there are encouraging signs that more and more scholars are realizing the need for a combined approach, in which inter-disciplinary teams cooperate in a common scientific enterprise. There is no real conflict between the ethnologist who is concerned with the *grammar* of a culture [see Mead (3)] and the psychologist who wants to know how people actually do speak. Both sets of facts are relevant to the understanding of national characteristics.

The writer feels that there is developing a welcome convergence of ideas among specialists in this area of research. Few psychologists would quarrel with the most recent statement by Mead (3) regarding the steps in the research process. These are: "(1) developing initial hypotheses in which any material which is highly patterned can be used; (2) subjecting these hypotheses to systematic scrutiny in the light of selected bodies of materials; (3) the determination by extensive sampling techniques of the prevalence and incidence of the behavior which has been identified; (4) validation of the findings through prediction and experiment" (p. 662).

It should be added, however, that without step (3)—as in studies of nations at a distance—the conclusions necessarily remain unconvincing. It is also important that changes with time be given full consideration in the study of national characteristics, and also that at every step there should be cross-cultural comparisons, so that the meaning of any particular aspect of a culture, whether it be swaddling, an authoritarian father, or milk drinking, may be seen in proper perspective.

This chapter has been largely methodological, and little has been said about the actual characteristics of national groups. The writer feels that it is preferable at this stage to look critically at what has been done and to exercise caution in accepting the conclusions that have so far been reached. Taken as hypotheses, they may usefully prepare the way for further research; taken as facts, they may be dangerous indeed.

The problem of national stereotypes, which is relevant in this connection, will be discussed in Chapter 18.

SUMMARY

The understanding of psychological similarities and differences among nations is an important but difficult task. In spite of the questions raised concerning the existence of national characteristics, there seems good reason to assume that they represent a legitimate field of inquiry. At the same time, it must be admitted that relatively little has been established as definite fact.

National characteristics have been approached in terms of the culture-as-a-whole, through a study of the distribution of characteristics among the individuals who make up a nation, and by attention to a particular unit of the society or to a segment of the culture. Among the specific methods which may be mentioned are included ethnological accounts, psychiatric and psychoanalytic approaches, public opinion and attitude studies, projective techniques, interviews, community studies, content analyses, etc. A combination of several different techniques is recommended.

REFERENCES

1. Barzun, J. "Book Reviews," *The Nation,* 1943, p. 188
2. Linton, R. "The Concept of National Character." In A. H. Stanton and S. E. Perry (eds.), *Personality and Political Crisis.* 1951
3. Mead, M. "The Study of National Character." In D. Lerner and H. D. Lasswell (eds.), *The Policy Sciences.* 1951
4. Klineberg, O. *Tensions Affecting International Understanding: A Survey of Research.* 1949
5. Mead, M. *And Keep Your Powder Dry.* 1942
6. Gorer, G. *The American People.* 1948
7. Benedict, R. *The Chrysanthemum and the Sword.* 1946
8. Gorer, C. "Themes in Japanese Culture," *Trans. N.Y. Acad. Sciences,* 1943, 5: pp. 106-124
9. Gorer, G., and Rickman, J. *The People of Great Russia.* 1949
10. Brickner, R. *Is Germany Incurable?* 1943
11. Schaffner, B. *Father Land.* 1948
12. Kardiner, A. *The Psychological Frontiers of Society.* 1945
13. Sikkema, M. "Observations on Japanese Early Training," *Psychiatry,* 1947, 10: pp. 423-432
14. Greenacre, P. "Infant Reactions to Restraint: Problems in the Fate of Infantile Aggression." In C. Kluckhohn, H. A. Murray and D. M. Schneider (eds.), *Personality in Nature, Society and Culture.* Rev. ed. 1953
15. Davis, A., and Havighurst, R. J. "Social Class and Color Differences in Child-Rearing." In Kluckhohn, Murray and Schneider, *Personality in Nature, Society and Culture.* Rev. ed. 1953
16. Ericson, M. C. "Child-Rearing and Social Status," *Amer. J. Sociol.,* 1946, 53: pp. 190-192
17. McGranahan, D. V. "A Comparison of Social Attitudes among American and German Youth," *J. Abnorm. Soc. Psychol.,* 1946, 41: pp. 245-257
18. Abel, T. M., and Hsu, F. L. K. "Some Aspects of Personality of Chinese as Revealed by the Rorschach Test," *Rorschach Res. Exch. and J. Projective Techniques,* 1949, 13: pp. 285-301

19. Kaldegg, A. "Responses of German and English Secondary School Boys to a Projection Test," *Brit. J. Psychol.*, 1948, 39: pp. 30-53

20. Dicks, H. V. "Personality Traits and National Socialist Ideology," *Hum. Rel.*, 1950, 3: pp. 111-154. "Observations on Contemporary Russian Behavior," *ibid.*, 1952, 5: pp. 111-175

21. Levy, D. M. "Anti-Nazis: Criteria of Differentiation," *Psychiatry*, 1948, 11: pp. 125-168

22. Lynd, R. S., and Lynd, H. M. *Middletown*. 1929. *Middletown in Transition*. 1937

23. Steward, J. H. *Area Research: Theory and Practice*. 1950

24. Lewis, O. *Life in a Mexican Village: Tepoztlàn Revisited*. 1951

25. Redfield, R. *Tepoztlàn: A Mexican Village*. 1930

26. Berelson, B. *Content Analysis in Communications Research*. 1952

27. Kracauer, S. *From Caligari to Hitler*. 1947

28. Wolfenstein, M., and Leites, N. *Movies: A Psychological Study*. 1950

29. McGranahan, D. G., and Wayne, I. "German and American Traits Reflected in Popular Drama," *Hum. Rel.*, 1948, 1: pp. 429-455

Social Factors
in Abnormality

15

INTRODUCTION

When Sullivan (1) defined psychiatry as "the study of interpersonal relations" he gave expression to the intimate connection between abnormal and social psychology. "Psychiatry is the study of the phenomena that occur in interpersonal situations, in configurations made up of two or more people, all but one of whom may be completely illusory" (p. 99). Abnormality is *social*, however, not only because it occurs in social situations, but also because it is embedded in the very structure of a society, and can only be understood against the background of the culture in which it occurs.

This does not mean that biological or physiological bases of abnormality are unimportant or that they should be neglected. There can be no denying that a great deal of mental disorder is determined by causes which are not directly social. There are psychological consequences of brain injury, alcoholism, drug addiction, syphilis and other physical diseases. At the same time it must not be forgotten that even these factors have a social aspect. Alcoholism and drug addiction, for example, are not only the causes but also the effects of personality difficulties; they represent in many cases an escape from a social world which is otherwise unbearable. In addition, the effects on behavior of a physical agent such as alcohol can be demonstrated to be intimately related to the phenomena of cultural patterning.

A study by Bunzel (2) of alcoholism in two American Indian communities, Chichicastenango in Guatemala, and Chamula in Mexico, makes this clear. In the former group there is excessive drinking, during which there are frequent sexual and aggressive reactions which are normally inhibited. No control is maintained by the authorities, and there are frequent "colossal sprees in which men stay drunk for days on end." In Chamula drinking is also excessive; during fiestas "the whole town is in varying degrees of intoxication for a day or a week." The effects are different, however; there is little aggression, sexual inhibitions are not released, the spree is peaceful and ends in stupor. Bunzel finds the explanation of these differences in the whole complex of economic, social and religious institutions characteristic of the two societies respectively.

Horton (3), on the basis of an extensive analysis of the drinking patterns of a large number of different communities, notes that a great many background factors are related to drinking; for example, there is more insobriety when living conditions are more difficult; and the belief in sorcery usually means that drinking will be accompanied by extreme aggression. These observations indicate how difficult and artificial would be the complete separation of biological from social factors in the causation of this particular form of abnormality.

These and allied considerations have led many social scientists to conclude that mental abnormality is to be regarded as a disease of the society rather than of the individuals who compose it. This concept of "society as the patient" or of the "sick society" has been analyzed by L. K. Frank (4). Such an approach has many advantages over the more usual emphasis upon disturbances in the individual, the most immediate gain being that of simplifying the problem.

> Instead of thinking in terms of a multiplicity of so-called social problems, each demanding special attention and a different remedy, we can view all of them as different symptoms of the same disease. . . . If, for example, we could regard crime, mental disorders, family disorganization, juvenile delinquency, prostitution and sex offenses, and much that now passes as the result of pathological processes (for example gastric ulcer) as evidence not of individual wickedness, incompetence, perversity or pathology, but as human reactions to cultural disintegration, a forward step would be taken (p. 336).

It would be a mistake, however, to disregard entirely the phenomena of individual pathology. Kallmann's (5) study of hereditary factors in schizophrenia (see Chapter 9) indicates that such phenomena probably do play an important part. In what follows, our concern will be with the social factors in abnormality, but this should not be regarded as justifying the conclusion that only social factors are responsible.

There are at least four distinct ways in which culture and abnormality may be said to be related. In the first place, the very concept of normality and abnormality may vary from one community to another. Secondly, there may be variations in the relative frequency of abnormality. Thirdly, and allied to this, the situations precipitating mental disturbance may differ because of social patterning. Finally, there may be differences in the nature of the disturbance; we might speak of "fashions in abnormality" in this connection. These various approaches to the problem are closely interrelated, but for the sake of convenience the relevant material will be presented under the four distinct headings. Certain aspects of the material have been discussed elsewhere (6) and these will here receive only brief mention.

VARIETIES OF NORMAL BEHAVIOR

A good discussion of the relativity of the concept of the abnormal is to be found in the work of Ruth Benedict (7). She points out that there are a number of societies in which the usual pattern of behavior corresponds rather closely to what in our society would be regarded as abnormality. The Kwakiutl Indians of British Columbia, for example, act in a manner which she characterizes as paranoid— they show megalomania, or "delusions of grandeur," in their self-glorification during the speeches made in the potlatch, and also "delusions of reference" in their interpretation of accidents and untoward events as deliberate "insults" directed against them by the universe. Similarly, the intricate system of taboos in Polynesia is regarded as analogous to the extension of the neurosis known in our culture as *défense de toucher*, characterized by an avoidance of certain objects. Other examples are the "normal" occurrence of trance and ecstasy among the shamans of many California tribes, and the cataleptic seizures among the Siberian shamans; the continual and excessive fear found among the Dobuans of Melanesia; and the homosexual practices of many American Indian and Siberian communities. These examples lead Benedict to the conclusion that the limits of the normal and abnormal are culturally defined and vary markedly between one group and another.

From a strictly behavioristic standpoint there can be no doubt

that the concept of the normal demands restatement for each culture. It is obvious that going about unclothed would not be diagnosed as exhibitionism in an Australian native, or strict avoidance of
the mother-in-law as a neurosis in the case of Navajo Indians.
Examples of this kind could easily be multiplied. Benedict's instances are somewhat different, since they refer to feelings and
attitudes as well as to overt behavior. Even in their case, however,
it is debatable whether terms such as *paranoid* or *catalepsy* may
legitimately be applied to the phenomena she describes. As Horney
(8) points out:

> If we regard a neurosis only from the sociological point of view as a
> mere deviation from the behavior pattern common to a certain society,
> we neglect grossly all we know about the psychological characteristics
> of a neurosis, and no psychiatrist of any school or country would rec-
> ognize the results as what he is accustomed to designate a neurosis
> (p. 27).

A deviation must be considered both in its objective or manifest
picture and in the dynamics of the psychic process. It may be that
in this latter respect there is something common in the concept of a
neurosis or other form of abnormality no matter where it is found;
it may be, as Horney suggests, that there are always fears, and
defenses against these fears, as well as attempts to find compromise
solutions for conflicting tendencies. If this is true, the similarity
between the behavior of the Kwakiutl and that of the paranoid
patient in our society may be more superficial than real, and may
not require a redefinition of the normal except in connection with
the overt behavior patterns. The same considerations apply to Franz
Alexander's (9) suggestion that the Buddhistic self-absorption of
mystics in India, accompanied by the physical phenomena of rigidity
and immobility, is to be interpreted as an artificial schizophrenia
of the catatonic type. As is well known, schizophrenia represents
among other things an extreme form of withdrawal from reality,
and the catatonic type of schizophrenia is frequently characterized
by phenomena of rigidity, stupor and immobility. Superficially there
are obvious similarities, but the ability of the mystics to control their
behavior, and their consequent rapport with the physical environment, separate them sharply from the schizophrenic patient.

This appears to be the essence of Wegrocki's (10) criticism of
Benedict. He writes that "the delusions of the psychotic and the

delusions of the Northwest Coast Indian cannot by any means be equated. Mechanisms like the conviction of grandeur are abnormal not by virtue of unique, abnormal qualia but by virtue of their *function in the total economy of the personality.* The true paranoiac reaction represents a *choice of the abnormal;* the reaction of the Haida chief represents no such choice. There is but one path for him to follow" (p. 695). It remains true that the argument of Benedict, supported by the further data of Alexander, is important as showing the variability in normal *behavior.* In those cases in which the abnormality consists entirely of a form of behavior, as in homosexuality, trance states, etc., Benedict's point is clearly proven. In those abnormalities, however, which contain subjective components of fear, maladjustment, conflict, autistic fantasy and so on, the analogy must not be pressed too far.

This material raises the interesting possibility that an individual whose personality determines him to behave in a specific manner may find his behavior accepted in one society and rejected as abnormal in another. A tendency to daydream, for example, may be looked upon as reprehensible in an American classroom, and as a sign of potential holiness in India. The occurrence of epileptic seizures has been regarded by Mohammedans as conferring a special virtue upon the individual. Among many Siberian tribes, the transformed shaman who took on the habits of the opposite sex, often to the extent of homosexuality, acquired added power as a consequence; in this case, however, the shaman was feared and disliked and apparently regarded as a deviant, even though he was accepted by the community.

A person who has a desire to withdraw from the world would find it hard to fit into our American culture. Even among Catholics, escape to a monastery or a convent is not always considered a satisfactory solution. Such a person would have a relatively simple problem if he lived in a country in which Buddhism was an accepted religion, since Buddhism regards the external world as unimportant. In the psychopathic hospital in Peking the writer observed several cases in which people suffering from a mild form of schizophrenia showed simultaneously an increased interest in Buddhism and the Buddhist classics. In one such case the physician in charge noticed a marked improvement in the symptoms whenever the patient was given an opportunity to express this interest. Although this observation could not be checked by any statistical investigation, it seems

to point to the possibility that an individual with the desire to withdraw from the world may find Buddhism, with its insistence upon
the unimportance of external reality, particularly palatable. It is
probable that many persons may actually be saved from the disease
of schizophrenia because their introvert tendencies find in Buddhism
a satisfactory outlet.

On the basis of her experience with psychotic patients in our
society, Horney (8) arrives at a similar conclusion. She points out
that in Western civilization there are few if any cultural patterns
in which the drives toward withdrawal or oblivion, regardless of
their neurotic character, may be satisfied.

> Religion, which offers such a possibility, has lost its power and appeal
> for the majority. Not only are there no effective cultural means for such
> satisfaction, but their development is actively discouraged, for in an
> individualistic culture the individual is expected to stand on his own
> feet, assert himself, and if necessary fight his way. In our culture to
> yield realistically to tendencies toward self-relinquishment involves the
> danger of ostracism (pp. 278-9).

There is suggested here a research problem of the first importance.
In India, China or Japan, there are possibilities for the careful study
of the behavior of the psychotic or neurotic from this point of view.
A psychiatrist trained to observe the significance of cultural factors
could give us valuable insight into the extent to which the religions
of the Far East afford a satisfactory diversion of these tendencies
toward oblivion.

A beginning in this direction has been made by Dhunjibhoy (11),
who reports on the incidence of schizophrenia and manic depressive
insanity in the mental hospitals of Bombay, India. In the psychiatric
institutions throughout most of the Western world, schizophrenia is
far more frequent than manic depressive insanity; in Bombay the
relative frequency is reversed. If this result is corroborated by additional statistical data, its implications are exceedingly important. It
may mean that in India, where "escape from reality" in our sense is
made possible through mystical religious experience, schizophrenia
occurs with relatively less frequency because it is less needed.

There is another possibility in this field which should not be overlooked. Granting that there are individuals who would be normal
in one society and abnormal in another, there may still be some who
would be abnormal anywhere. This is probably true of extreme cases

of feeble-mindedness, although where the demands of the culture are simple, such a defect may not be conspicuous. More important, however, is the possibility that some individuals are so constituted, whether as a result of biological factors or of early conditioning, that they rebel against the customs and dictates of their society, whatever these may be. It is conceivable, for example, that a person who has the urge to express his contempt of society, or who wishes to attract attention to himself, may indulge in precisely that form of activity which his society condemns. If further investigation proves this to be the case, we should still have to insist with Benedict that the majority of individuals are patterned by the form of their culture; we should have to add that some individuals are, by their very nature, deviants.

SITUATIONS DETERMINING ABNORMALITY

Associated with the phenomenon of cultural relativity in the meaning of abnormality is the fact that in different cultures there will be variations in the situations in which abnormality develops. This really follows from certain of the considerations discussed in the preceding section. A special defect or inhibition in the individual may escape notice if there is nothing in his social environment which demands the presence of the corresponding ability. Among the African Bantu, for example, almost every man and woman is a fluent and sustained speaker, and Gordon Brown has observed (12) that "the most prevalent mental disturbance is in youths who realize that they are unable to become finished speakers" (p. 55). It is hardly necessary to point out that in our own society such inability causes only temporary inconvenience on special occasions.

With regard to speech problems, Johnson (13) reports that his research on stuttering among Indians in Idaho encountered an unexpected difficulty when no stutterers were discovered. Teachers with as much as 25 years of experience in these communities confirmed this observation; there was not even a word for stuttering in the language of these Indian groups. This may be due to the fact that the particular tensions which give rise to speech disorders are nonexistent in these groups, or that when they do arise, they are expressed in other varieties of behavior difficulties. (See "fashions in abnormality," discussed on page 407.)

The family situation in our culture may give rise to conflict and mental disturbance in many ways (*14*). There is the usual pattern of obedience to parental authority and the consequent taboo upon criticism of parents by their children. One possible consequence is the violent revolt of the child against the parent; another is the guilt-feeling which accompanies the reflection that if the parents are necessarily right it must be the child himself who is in the wrong. In either case—and there are many other possibilities—the pattern of authority in the family may contain inherent contradictions. As has previously been pointed out, another type of family, in which the authority is not nearly so pronounced, will not precipitate the same type of conflict.

There are other contradictions in the demands and the values of our culture which constitute possible sources of disturbance. According to Horney (*8*) these contradictions are of three main types —(1) between competition and success on the one hand, and brotherly love on the other; (2) between stimulation of our needs and our factual frustrations in satisfying them; (3) between alleged freedom of the individual and all his factual limitations.

These contradictions embedded in our culture are precisely the conflicts which the neurotic struggles to reconcile: his tendencies toward aggressiveness and his tendencies toward yielding; his excessive demands and his fear of never getting anything; his striving toward self-aggrandizement and his feeling of personal helplessness. . . . It seems that the person who is likely to become neurotic is one who has experienced the culturally determined difficulties in an accentuated form. . . . (pp. 289-290).

In a changing culture the possibilities of difficulty and conflict are often increased. In pre-Communist China the transition between the old family pattern and the newer Western one constituted serious difficulty for many young people (*15*). The traditional Chinese family demanded complete submission of a young wife to her mother-in-law, and the girl brought up in the accepted Chinese fashion found little or no difficulty in adapting to such an arrangement. In those cases, however, in which there had been exposure to the Western notion of the independent small family, marriage into the large one might easily produce friction. There were some cases in the Peking psychopathic hospital in which this was apparently the precipitating cause.

Kardiner (16) cites a striking case of increase in the amount of maladjustment among the Tanala-Betsileo of Madagascar on the occasion of a change from a dry-rice to a wet-rice economy. In the former situation, there had been communal ownership of land, with control in the hands of a powerful authoritarian father. Under the wet-rice system, everyone had to shift for himself, and a premium was placed on competition and aggressiveness, attitudes which had not previously been developed. "The result was an enormous increase in a destructive form of hysterical illness accompanied by amnesia, in sexual perversions (homosexuality) and crime" (p. 166) There was also a great increase in mutual fear and distrust, in obsessional and compulsive traits, and in superstition. "There was little neurosis in the old society because the personality was effectively geared to the existing problems of adaptation; the aberrations increased when the problems of the individual were too great for the existing personality organization" (pp. 166-7).

As the result of the extensive technological changes which are now being introduced into so-called "underdeveloped" countries special attention has been directed to the human implications o such changes, and to the possible effects on individual and socia adjustment. It has become obvious that the building of a factor in a community for the first time may have consequences which greatly transcend the economic changes themselves. If, for example the withdrawal of young people from agriculture to industry involves the disruption of the patriarchal authority of the father, without any other social control to serve as an adequate substitute, ther may be considerable disorganization as a consequence. Research o this important problem is now being actively fostered in variou parts of the world, and many of the problems involved have bee reviewed in the case-books edited by Arensberg (17), Mead (18 and Spicer (19).

Within our own society, also, many examples could be given of the manner in which psychological difficulties may arise in respons to tension-producing situations. Hunt (20) has described a grou of boys who were subjected to two sets of conflicting values. In the gang life they had been taught sexual perversions, but they had als undergone a religious conversion which prohibited such behavio Hunt writes: "Those members and only those members of the neigl borhood group who experienced both these antithetical influence were later committed as psychotic" (p. 463). He concludes tha socially induced conflicts are important causes of mental disorders. He adds, however, that the fact that the boys succumbed to psychoses at various ages suggests that a constitutional factor in the form of frustration-tolerance may also have played a part.

The ecological survey by Faris and Dunham (21) of the distribution of various neuroses and psychoses in a number of American cities also suggests the importance of social factors. Schizophrenia, for instance, shows an unusually high incidence in urban slums. Unless we assume that individuals suffering from such a disorder gravitate to this particular environment, the conclusion in favor of social causation appears to be justified. Since obviously not all slum-dwellers succumb, however, individual predisposition must be included as a contributing factor.

Finally, in this connection, mention should be made of the special difficulties in the way of the adjustment of minority groups. Immigrants are faced with the problem of learning a new set of folkways; their children may be caught between two ways of living, and they find it hard to effect a compromise between the authority of their parents and their desire to be like other Americans. Negroes have the special problem of adapting to a society which may never completely accept them, and it is not surprising if, as a consequence, certain forms of maladjustment occur more frequently among them than among Whites. (See also Chapter 19.)

One important study apparently points to a conclusion which differs from that adopted here. Allport, Bruner and Jandorf (22) studied the effects of "social catastrophe," as reflected in autobiographical documents collected from German refugees on the subject of "My Life in Germany Before and After January 30, 1933." In response to an announcement of a prize competition over 200 life histories were obtained, of which 90 were subjected to detailed analysis. Many different reactions to the Nazi terror were reported. In the present context, the significant finding is that the catastrophic social changes rarely produced catastrophic alterations in the personality. "Neither our cases nor such statistics as are available reflect any such number of regressions, hysterias, or other traumatic neuroses as the gravity of the social crisis might lead one to expect. On the contrary, perhaps the most vivid impression gained by our analysts from this case history material is of the extraordinary continuity and saneness in the individual personality" (pp. 442-3). This conclusion appears somewhat surprising, especially in view of the evidence collected by Lewin and others (see Chapter 17) regarding the relationship of personality to the social field. It should be noted, however, that the study by Allport and his colleagues was conducted with documents written several years after the occurrence of the events which they described, and that retrospective falsification can therefore not be entirely ruled out. There is also the possibility that those individuals who did show "catastrophic alterations in personality" did not survive to tell the tale.

AMOUNT OF ABNORMALITY

The discussion of the situations giving rise to abnormality leads directly to a consideration of its frequency, since it appears certain that the more numerous such situations are, the more often does disturbance of one sort or another ensue. This is of course a problem of the greatest practical importance. The effect of the social environment in determining the incidence of abnormality is sometimes considered to be proven by the far greater frequency in reported cases of psychosis and neurosis in the city than in the country (23). This difference is apparently found for mental disease in general, and also for specific diseases. In Brazil, for example, Ribeiro (24) reports that the incidence of schizophrenia in the urban population is nine times as great as in the rural areas. This fact is difficult to interpret, however, since it may be due to a difference in the ease of diagnosis and of hospitalization in the city rather than to a direct increase resulting from urban living conditions (25). That the social environment is important, however, can hardly be questioned. Healy (26) reports a number of almost miraculous changes in problem children as the result of their transfer to foster homes, and Plant (27) tells of a child who gave an uneasy picture of tension in her own home as a result of competition with an elder sister, and whose symptoms cleared up entirely upon association with a group of companions of her own age. A survey of the incidence of abnormality in large cities, which was referred to above, has revealed a concentration in certain areas rather than others, and has indicated the relation of mental disease to economic factors (28).

The most striking account of a reduction in the extent of abnormality following social and economic changes is that by Frankwood Williams in the case of Russia (29). This has been discussed elsewhere (6), but it may be of interest that Williams believed that the reduction of "anxiety pressures" has meant that hundreds of thousands of people have been saved from the development of mental disturbance. Although economic worries may not be the only ones precipitating a breakdown, they are so important that their elimination will affect for the better the mental health of the community. Accurate statistics are difficult to obtain, but Williams points to the fact that hospital beds for psychotic patients are largely unoccupied and that cases of certain types of mental disease are actually difficult to discover.

This report by Williams is now out of date (1934); moreover, his conclusions have not uniformly carried conviction. It has been urged that his visit to Russia was too brief and too superficial to permit such far-reaching inferences, and that actually mental diseases may be more frequent in Russia than he believed. It has also been suggested that whereas the disturbances consequent upon economic worries may have been reduced, there are other sources of difficulty which are still present to the same or even to a greater degree; the speeding-up process in many factories, for example, may conceivably lead to an increase in neurasthenia and other fatigue neuroses, and fear of denunciation to the police for failure to live up to accepted party standards may be the source of strong anxiety feelings. If the Freudians are right in their insistence upon sex problems as the main source of neurotic disturbance, we should hardly expect these to disappear entirely in the Russian system. There is badly needed in this field a detailed statistical analysis of the incidence of mental disease in Russia, and of the specific types of disturbance which occur with greatest frequency.

According to the Freudians, a certain amount of neurotic disturbance is apparently inevitable in a civilization as complex as ours. Freud (30) regards culture as primarily the result of the action of biological urges which are denied their natural expression and consequently sublimated; the energy which would be directed to the satisfaction of biological urges is used for the production of culture. Since, however, not all individuals possess the ability to sublimate their drives in these socially valued directions, repression will in many instances lead to neurosis. If there were no repression there would be no neurosis, but at the same time there would be no culture. This is what Roheim (31) has in mind when he says the culture is produced at the expense of the woman, man's energy being diverted from her to the creation of cultural products. From this point of view, the growth of civilization necessarily implies an increase in the amount of neurosis, the more complete repression of instinctive urges being accompanied by a higher development of culture. This direct relationship between the amount of sexual repression and the level of cultural development is not, however, substantiated by the findings of anthropology. There are many "primitive" cultures, it is true, which allow a degree of freedom in sexual activity far greater than that permitted in our society. On the other hand, the Veddas of Ceylon, with an exceedingly simple material culture, are very strict in their insistence upon a rigid monogamy, and any infraction of the moral code is dealt with severely (32). Many other examples could be given. Malinowski (33) contrasts the Amphlett Islanders and the Trobrianders with respect to their sexual morality; the former are very puritanical, regard pre-nuptial intercourse with disapproval, and have no institutions to support sexual license. This apparently results in a greater incidence among them of neurasthenic and other neurotic tendencies, but it has evidently not resulted in raising their cultural level above that of the Trobrianders. The creation and development of culture certainly result from more than the sublimation of repressed sexual impulses.

In connection with the amount of disease, both physical (especially psychosomatic) and mental, Parsons (34) makes the important point that if there is more of one kind of deviation, there may be less of another. If it is true that there has been a marked increase in the incidence of mental illness in recent decades, this does not necessarily mean that there has been a corresponding increase in social disorganization generally. "It is altogether possible that an increase in mental illness may constitute a diversion of tendencies to deviance from other channels of expression into the role of illness, with consequences less dangerous to the stability of society than certain alternatives might be" (p. 61). It is difficult to find objective data in favor of this conclusion, but the hypothesis is one which deserves to be more fully investigated.

VARIETIES OF ABNORMALITY

In a previous section we discussed the variations in the concept of the normal, and the fact that behavior regarded as normal in one society may be abnormal in another. We turn now to an allied problem, namely, that of the manner in which abnormality expresses itself when it does occur. It is possible to speak of "fashions of abnormality" from this point of view, except that these manifestations have a continuity and a permanence in social life with which the concept of fashion is not usually associated.

The writer has discussed some of these phenomena in another connection (6). Familiar examples include the Arctic hysteria of the Siberian tribes, characterized by heightened suggestibility and an irresistible impulse to imitate the words or the acts of others in the vicinity; a similar disturbance among the Malays known as *latah;* running amok, also most frequent among the Malay peoples, and so on. Even in the history of our own culture, there are many instances of such fashions in abnormality. Bromberg (35) tells of an epidemic of convulsions of an erotic nature which occurred among the nuns in the Convent of Nazareth in Cologne about 1565. These nuns would lie on their backs with their eyes closed and their abdomens elevated; after the convulsion passed, they "opened their eyes with apparent expressions of shame and pain." The "charming invalid" of the Victorian era, who made up a good portion of the doctor's practice in the latter part of the nineteenth century, is another instance of this phenomenon.

> It was not uncommon for women of gentle birth to be afflicted with a mysterious ailment that kept them languishing in bed behind drawn curtains, sipping as their only nourishment some anemic fluid like skim milk or port wine diluted with water. The bizarre types of hysteria described by medical writers of seventy years ago are for some unfathomable reason almost a rarity nowadays. It is almost as if nervous diseases succumb to the rule of fashion, at least in their outer appearances (35, pp. 200-1).

The well-known examples of the dancing mania and of the various forms of religious possession and ecstasy reported throughout the Middle Ages may also be cited in this connection.

An interesting observation is reported by a psychiatrist with much experience in the German city of Weimar, the home of Goethe and Schiller and long the center of drama and opera. The patients in this city were apparently influenced by the cultural traditions of the community, and their psychotic manifestations had a theatrical and dramatic aspect which distinguished them from similar psychoses elsewhere. It was as if they "declaimed their symptoms." The doctor speaks in this connection of a "psychosis vimariensis," and states that the Weimar psychiatrists discounted these characteristics in their approach to the disease (36).

The Chinese writer Lin Yu-t'ang (37) mentions a similar phenomenon. He reports that there is a peculiarly Chinese disturbance referred to popularly as an "opera psychosis," in which the patient, apparently otherwise normal, has an impulse to sing long passages from the Chinese musical plays. Such an individual may be seen at a street corner in Peking singing and acting for hours at a time, though at other times he may be perfectly normal. During the present writer's stay in Peking no cases were observed of exactly this type, but there were some patients at the psychopathic hospital who showed this form of behavior as part of a more general disturbance. It may be added that in the psychoses of the Chinese, rich use is apparently made of mythological and traditional themes in connection with their delusions and hallucinations. Among these, possession by a fox spirit, a recurrent motif in the popular tales known to most Chinese, appears with some frequency. This is reminiscent of the "werewolf" stories in our own tradition. In this case also there were many people whose hysterical disturbance evidently took the form of the belief that they were occasionally transformed into a wolf or other animal.

Among neurotics in our own society Horney (8) finds the striving for power to be a frequent symptom of the disturbance. This also involves a cultural factor. In our society individual power and prestige play an important role; this may be achieved by wealth, and the compulsive striving for possessions occurs with some frequency among neurotics. This compulsion may disappear as soon as the anxieties determining it are diminished or removed. Wealth is, however, only one of the possible means of acquiring power, and the neurotic may use other methods to protect himself from his feeling of helplessness or humiliation. In certain other cultures such a striving for power is normally absent, and therefore plays no special part in neuroses. In an earlier discussion it was pointed out that certain communities, for example, the Pueblos, laid no particular stress upon individual prestige or power. Among such groups, Horney says, "it would be meaningless to strive for any kind of dominance as a means of reassurance. That neurotics in our culture choose this way, results from the fact that in our social structure power, prestige and possession can give a feeling of greater security" (p. 163). This raises the important problem of the manner in which neurotics in other societies may express their feelings of insecurity, and the situations which determine such feelings; this field is one in which the combination of psychiatric and ethnological analysis may make a significant contribution.

An interesting example of a "fashion in abnormality" is the windigo psychosis among the Ojibwa Indians (38). The windigo is a mythological giant made of ice, who is also an insatiable cannibal. The psychosis expresses itself as the belief that one has been transformed into a windigo. The immediate cause is usually threatened starvation, and the disease begins with a melancholia which may give way to violence and compulsive cannibalism. In this final stage the patient may kill and eat the members of his own family. Recovery may occur, but often for the protection of the community the sufferer is put to death. This disturbance, which has also been described by Cooper (39) for the northern Cree, is clearly a culturally determined variety of abnormality. One other observation made by Landes (38) is significant in this connection. "A group of women who in our culture are thought simply eccentric are regarded by the Ojibwa not as merely abnormal but as criminally abnormal. These are the women who refuse to marry, spoiling the sexual sport of men and handicapping them in gaining a livelihood" (p. 29).

Many other examples have been collected. Powdermaker (40) reports the occasional occurrence in Buka of "states of hysterical dissociation" with considerable excitement and threats to kill; this is said by the natives to be due to possession by the "urar" or spirits of the dead. It is much like amok, though apparently not so serious in most cases, and the sufferer is not "out to kill" as in the case of the amok-running Malay. The people of Buka, incidentally, are Melanesians, and racially quite distinct from the Malays among whom amok is said to occur with some frequency. Among the Saultaux of the Berens River in Manitoba, Hallowell (41) tells of a case of zoophobia which took the form of an intense fear of toads. This occurred in an Indian who had spent most of his life in the bush, and had been a good hunter apparently unafraid of the most dangerous animals, but became panic-stricken when a toad hopped toward him. Toads are evil creatures in native lore, and the old belief had returned as a cause of this disturbance under certain precipitating circumstances. In Ethiopia, Brambilla (42) has described a variety of hysteria in which the patient believes himself to be possessed by devils from whom he strives to free himself; this "devil's disease" may sometimes assume the proportions of an epidemic. In Bahia, Brazil, the writer was informed that a number of patients in the psychiatric hospitals showed delusions and hallucinations which contained elements from the religious institution of the *candomblé,*—a combination of Christian and African religious beliefs and ceremonies. In the case of Haiti, Mars (43) has described a form of religious possession, including rigidity, hallucinations, delusions of persecutions, and occasional anesthesia.

This material raises a general problem which requires study. Wells (44) writes that "a special interest of comparative psychiatry is that, in so far as symptom-pictures vary according to culture, the influence of psychogenesis might be separated from that of organic or constitutional factors" (p. 890, n.). More work is needed on the underlying mechanisms of the disturbances as distinct from the external manifestations, before such a separation is possible on the basis of comparative material. It may well be true, as Wegrocki and others have pointed out, that underlying the various "fashions" in abnormality, there are common psychological principles which operate, and common diagnostic categories which apply. Kardiner (16) expresses the opinion that the "culture supplies the *content* but not the mechanism" (p. 177), but it is not always easy to distinguish these two aspects of the abnormality. In any case, as far as the external aspects are concerned, there can be no denying the tremendous importance of cultural influences.

CONCLUSION

The material summarized in this chapter amply demonstrates the significance of cultural factors for the understanding of abnormality. Such factors aid in determining the meaning we attach to normal and abnormal, the situations giving rise to abnormality, its frequency, and the nature of its manifestations. We must again caution, however, against the generalization from this material to the effect that all abnormality is culturally determined and that the personality is entirely at the mercy of prevailing cultural patterns. As has been frequently pointed out, not all individuals react similarly to the influences of the social environment; some may accept these influences readily, while others resist them. Even in a simple laboratory situation we may never be certain that the same external stimulus has an identical meaning for two different subjects, since the whole

pattern of previous experience may contribute to the response.'
Piéron (45) speaks in this connection of an "envelope" surrounding
the personality and varying in its permeability from one individual
to another.

In his analysis of the relation between personality and culture,
Plant (27) distinguishes three contributing elements.

> There is a growing changing personality made up at any moment of
> the total of its own contributions and those of the environment. There
> is a cultural pattern which itself grows and changes in answer to the
> interests of all those personalities which make it up and in answer to
> a series of forces engendered precisely by the fact that it is made up
> of great numbers of personalities. There is a selective process occurring
> at the place where the pattern impinges upon the personality, which
> controls the material accepted . . . (p. 233).

This means that although culture does shape and mold the personality, the individual still has an effect upon his cultural and social
environment. He is not a mere passive recipient, but a reacting and
interacting organism.

In connection with both the normal and the abnormal personality,
therefore, it is important to study not only culture but also the individual. The available ethnological accounts of abnormality have
made important contributions through their analysis of cultural phenomena, but they have so far taught us little about the individual
who is considered abnormal. It may be argued that this has been
done sufficiently by psychiatrists in our own culture, but in their
case the concomitant emphasis upon the role of culture has usually
been lacking. The relative influence of the culture on the one hand,
and the attributes brought to it by the individual on the other, may
be separated only by attention to both. There is no branch of social
psychology more important as a field of potential investigation, and
the material is relatively accessible. The combination of psychiatric
and ethnological techniques in this field should yield data of the
greatest significance. In the meantime, this chapter has emphasized
the role of the culture because it is one that has not always been
recognized in the customary psychiatric approach to the individual
in our society.

SUMMARY

Without denying that many types of abnormality may be the result of organic disorders, the present emphasis is upon the influence

of social and cultural factors. This influence may be effective in various ways.

In the first place, the concept of abnormality may vary from one society to another. Behavior resembling paranoia is normal for the Kwakiutl, withdrawal from reality is permitted to a Buddhist, homosexuality and trance states are accepted in many communities. Behavioristically, therefore, the relativity of the abnormal has been demonstrated, although the possibility remains that there are underlying problems—conflicts, fears, etc.—which constitute the real nature of neurosis wherever it is found.

There are variations in the situations in which abnormality develops. These include differing types of family organization, contradictions in the demands of the culture, conflicts arising out of culture change, etc. The frequency of occurrence of such situations is at least partly responsible for the incidence of abnormality; it seems certain that points of strain, particularly with reference to economic and sexual problems, are found more often in our society than in many other communities, particularly those of relatively simple character.

There are also varieties or fashions of abnormality determined by the folkways. Among others may be mentioned the imitative mania of the Siberian natives, running amok among the Malays, the windigo psychosis of the Ojibwa, and the striving for power among neurotics in Western society.

These findings should not be interpreted as meaning that all abnormality is culturally or socially determined.

REFERENCES

1. Sullivan, H. S. *Conceptions of Modern Psychiatry.* 1947

2. Bunzel, R. "The Role of Alcoholism in Two Central American Cultures," *Psychiatry,* 1940, 3: pp. 361-387

3. Horton, D. "The Functions of Alcohol in Primitive Societies." In C. Kluckhohn, H. A. Murray, and D. M. Schneider (eds.), *Personality in Nature, Society, and Culture.* Rev. ed. 1953

4. Frank, L. "Society as the Patient," *Amer. J. Sociol.,* 1936, 42: pp. 335-344

5. Kallmann, F. J. "The Genetic Theory of Schizophrenia." In Kluckhohn, Murray, and Schneider (eds.), *Personality in Nature, Society and Culture.* Rev. ed. 1953

6. Klineberg, O. *Race Differences.* 1935

7. Benedict, R. F. *Patterns of Culture.* 1934

8. Horney, K. *The Neurotic Personality of Our Time.* 1937

9. Alexander, F. "Buddhistic Training as an Artificial Catatonia," *Psychoanal. Rev.,* 1931, 18: pp. 129-145

10. Wegrocki, H. J. "A Critique of Cultural and Statistical Concepts of Abnormality." In Kluckhohn, Murray and Schneider (eds.), *Personality in Nature, Society and Culture.* Rev. ed. 1953

11. Dhunjibhoy, J. E. "A Brief Résumé of the Types of Insanity Commonly Met with in India," *J. Ment. Sci.,* 1930, 76: pp. 254-264

12. Thomas, W. I. *Primitive Behavior.* 1937

13. Johnson, W. "The Indians Have No Word for It: Stuttering in Children," *Quart. J. Speech,* 1944. 30: pp. 330-337

14. Fromm, E. *Autorität und Familie.* 1936

15. Lamson, H. D. *Social Pathology in China.* 1935

16. Kardiner, A. "The Relation of Culture to Mental Disorder." In P. H. Hoch and J. Zubin (eds.), *Problems in Psychiatric Diagnosis.* 1953

17. Arensberg, C. M. Manuscript in preparation.

18. Mead, M. (ed.). *Cultural Patterns and Technical Change* (UNESCO). 1953

19. Spicer, E. *Human Problems in Technological Change.* 1952

20. Hunt, J. McV. "An Instance of the Social Origin of Conflict Resulting in Psychoses." In Kluckhohn, Murray and Schneider, *Personality in Nature, Society, and Culture.* Rev. ed. 1953

21. Faris, R. E., and Dunham, H. W. *Mental Disorders in Urban Areas.* 1939

22. Allport, G. W., Bruner, J. S., and Jandorf, E. M. "Personality Under Social Catastrophe: Life-Histories of the Nazi Revolution." In Kluckhohn, Murray and Schneider, *Personality in Nature, Society, and Culture.* Rev. ed. 1953

23. White, W. A. "Social Significance of Mental Disease," *Arch. Neur. and Psychiat.,* 1929, 22: pp. 873-900

24. Ribeiro, R. "The Schizophrenic," *Revista ibero—americana de neurologia e psiquiatria,* 1938, 1

25. Landis, C., and Page, J. D. *Modern Society and Mental Disease.* 1938

26. Healy, W. *Personality in Formation and Action.* 1938

27. Plant, J. S. *Personality and the Cultural Pattern.* 1937

28. Faris, R. E. *Social Psychology.* 1951

29. Williams, F. E. *Russia, Youth and the Present-Day World.* 1934

30. Freud, S. *Civilization and Its Discontents.* 1930

31. Roheim, G. "Psychoanalysis of Primitive Cultural Types," *Internatl. J. Psychoanal.,* 1932, 13: pp. 2-224

32. Seligman, C. G., and Seligman, B. Z. *The Veddas.* 1911

33. Malinowski, B. *Sex and Repression in Savage Society.* 1927

34. Parsons, T. "Illness and the Role of the Physician." In Kluckhohn, Murray and Schneider, *Personality in Nature, Society, and Culture.* Rev. ed. 1953

35. Bromberg, W. *The Mind of Man.* 1937

36. Binswanger, O. "Betrachtungen über Volksart, Rasse und Psychose in Thüringer Lande," *Archiv f. Psychiatrie u. Nervenkr.,* 1925, 74: pp. 218-240

37. Lin Yu-t'ang. *My Country and My People.* 1935

38. Landes, R. "The Abnormal Among the Ojibwa Indians," *J. Abn. and Soc. Psychol.,* 1938, 33: pp. 14-33

39. Cooper, J. M. "Mental Disease Situations in Certain Cultures: A New Field for Research," *J. Abn. and Soc. Psychol.,* 1934, 29: pp. 10-18

40. Powdermaker, H. *Life in Lesu.* 1933

41. Hallowell, A. I. "Culture and Mental Disorder," *J. Abn. and Soc. Psychol.,* 1934-35, 24: pp. 1-9

42. Brambilla, S. "Contributo allo studio delle manifestazioni psicopatologiche delle popolazioni dell' Impero," *Rivista di patologia nervosa e mentale,* 1939, 53: pp. 187-206

43. Mars, L. P. "Culture et Psychiatrie," *Union méd. du Canada,* 1941, 70: pp. 244-253

44. Wells, F. L. "Social Maladjustments." In C. Murchison (ed.), *Hdbk. Soc. Psychol.* 1935

45. Piéron, H. *Principles of Experimental Psychology.* 1929

Social Factors
in Delinquency and
Crime

16

INTRODUCTION

Crime has been variously defined. It has sometimes been identified with behavior which is immoral, or which results in some harm to society. Actually, the one common characteristic of all crime is the fact that it is prohibited by the criminal code. It follows, as Michael and Adler (1) have pointed out, that the criminal law is the formal cause of crime; if there were no law, crime would automatically disappear. In establishing our criminal law therefore, we are at the same time deciding what kinds of crime we wish to cause, paradoxical as this may sound. Delinquency has the same meaning, except that it refers to offenses against the law committed by persons below a certain age, this age being determined by law and varying from one society to another. Delinquency and crime do not differ with regard to the seriousness of the act, in spite of popular belief to this effect, although the delinquency may be regarded less seriously by the court in view of the youth of the offender.[1]

It is clear from the above definition that crime is relative, and that an act regarded as criminal in one society may be unobjectionable in another. Offenders against the prohibition law in the United States furnish an example of behavior which is criminal at one time and later ceases to be so. An amusing incident is reported of a man convicted, at the very end of the prohibition era, for making and selling beer. Before he could be summoned to receive his sentence, the prohibition amendment had been repealed. A fine was imposed,

[1] The term *delinquency* is used in other senses as well, but the meaning here ascribed to it is the customary one.

415

but the man was freed on parole so that he could earn enough money to pay the fine. This he planned to do by making and selling beer.

Ethnological material is rich in examples of this variation. Parricide and matricide are among the most heinous crimes in our society, but under the influence of certain religious beliefs as in the Fijian notion of the virtue of an early death, killing a parent may be a pious act. Homosexuality is no crime among the Siberian Chuckchee, and "stealing" ceases to occur in a community with no notion of private property. This consideration in itself throws doubt upon the possibility of arriving at a general psychology of the criminal, since no single type of behavior may be taken as a universal characteristic.

This difficulty is also reflected in the study of the criminal in our own society. As Osborne (2) expresses it:

> To list men who commit all sorts of different crimes arbitrarily in a group and proceed to generalize about them, is as ridiculous as it would be to generalize about the habits and character of any chance assortment of men—legislators or theater-goers; or to draw conclusions as to the psychological characteristics of blue-eyed men, or those who wear tan shoes. "The criminal," as he is usually described, has about as much real existence as the equator (p. 19).

Osborne's rich and varied experience with all types of criminals in the penal institution of which he was in charge lends added weight to this conclusion.

Corroboration is to be found also in the study by Gillin (3), who reports that the social background and personality of a group of sex offenders in the Wisconsin State Prison were markedly different from those in the same institution who had been convicted of murder or of offenses against property.

The line of demarcation between the criminal and the "normal" cannot always be drawn with any clarity or definiteness. Porterfield (4), for example, found that college students frequently indulged in the same kind of behavior for which delinquents were arrested and convicted; Wallerstein and Wyle (5) report that 99% of a sample of people questioned admitted having committed one or more of the forty-nine offenses listed in the penal law of New York State. In commenting on this and related material, Rouke (6) states that the difference seems to lie mainly in being caught.

It is almost universally assumed that crime represents a serious disease of society which should at all costs be eradicated. The problem of crime is in essence that of crime prevention. Dunlap (7) has, however, argued that crime is a necessary characteristic of a progressive civilization.

Social progress . . . seems possible through two procedures. 1. The violation of conventions, leading to the formation of new conventions. 2. Where the conventions have the form of law, there crime (the breaking of law) is the indispensable method of progress. All great reformers have been law breakers, and wherever laws limit progress, the systematic and conscientious infraction of law is the only possible progressive method. Flouting of conventions and infraction of laws seem to constitute the essential spirit of civilization. Where a population shall have become universally law-abiding, civilization will have died (p. 58).

Adoption of this extreme position would necessitate a radical change in the usual attitude toward crime. It seems, however, to be something of an exaggeration. Admitting that there are certain infractions of the law which do point the way to an improvement in society, it is hard to justify the majority of them on the same ground. To most of us the elimination of crime would seem desirable even if this should impede slightly the process of social change.

PHYSICAL CHARACTERISTICS OF THE CRIMINAL

In spite of the relativity of the concept of crime and the consequent variability in the nature of the individual criminal, there have been many attempts to discover general features typical of the criminal as such. The theory which has aroused the greatest comment and controversy is that of the Italian criminologist Cesare Lombroso (8), who in the latter part of the nineteenth century developed his view of the relation between criminality and physical or anatomical characteristics. In his early years Lombroso was in the medical service of the Italian army, and he noted the prevalence of tatooing among criminals; this appeared to indicate their greater degree of physical insensibility, and Lombroso concluded that moral insensibility is the result of its physical counterpart. Later he had occasion to make a post mortem examination of the brain of a brigand and he found that in certain respects it was like that of the lower vertebrates. This gave rise to the general theory of the atavistic nature of the criminal. Among the characteristics indicative of this atavism, Lombroso listed prognathism, woolly hair, a scant beard, oxycephaly (high, pointed head), oblique eyes, prominent cheek-bones, prominent supraorbital ridges, a receding forehead, an unusually large or unusually small head, a long or narrow head, a high pointed palate, large ears, characteristics of the opposite sex type, and asymmetries of the skull, face or body. When several of these features are found combined in the same individual, the diagnosis of criminality may be made with some assurance. These features were spoken of as "stigmata of degeneration."

It is often stated that Lombroso failed to make any adequate comparison between criminals and non-criminals in the population. One such comparison was, however, made by Ferri (9) working under Lombroso's direction, and it was discovered that about 10% of prisoners and 37% of soldiers were without these stigmata. This result shows that even though the stigmata may occur more frequently among criminals, the exceptions are numerous. Lombroso attempted to explain this fact by the suggestion that when the stigmata "are found in honest men and women, we may be dealing with criminal natures who have not yet committed the overt act because the circumstances in which they have lived protected them against temptation." This is of course an admission that the social environment may play an important part in the occurrence of crime, and to that extent doubt is thrown upon the validity of the original theory.

Lombroso's work attracted great attention and at the same time bitter opposition. He himself suggested a crucial experiment which would determine whether he or his critics were right; he proposed a selection by his antagonists of one hundred criminals and one hundred honest men whose anatomical characteristics should be carefully studied. It would seem to us now that this was an exceedingly small number of cases with which to test a theory of such scope. In any event, the comparison was never made because no agreement could be reached as to the manner of selection of the individuals to be examined. Such a study was carried out, however, by Charles Goring (10) in England, with the cooperation of the biometrician Karl Pearson, and the results were published in *The English Convict* in 1913. Goring made a large number of measurements on 3000 prisoners, all recidivists, and compared them with groups of students and army men. He reported that stigmata of degeneration were just as frequent in Oxford and Cambridge as in the penal institutions of London. The only difference noted was that criminals were inferior in height and weight, and this was attributed to their lower economic status and inferior opportunities for bodily development.

There have been other attempts to describe the criminal in terms of physical features (1). Galet speaks of degenerative defects in the ears; Vervaeck states that criminals are taller and stronger than others. There have been many suggestions that the criminal may be distinguished by his glandular make-up; Schlapp speaks of a glandular imbalance, Reynolds of the presence of abnormal thyroids in murderers, and Berman goes so far as to attach specific criminal propensities to varying glandular diagnoses. In his scheme, for example, thieves, hoboes, and liars are of the pituitary type; perverts and exhibitionists are thymus-adrenal; cases of impulsive assault are due to excessive activity of the parathyroid, and so on. It seems clear that these characterizations in terms of endocrine activity are made on insufficient evidence and are not to be accepted as valid until further proof is forthcoming.

In recent times the consensus has been against the point of view represented by Lombroso and his followers. His theory has, however, been revived as the result of an extensive investigation by E. A. Hooton (11) of Harvard, who regards it as probable that the physical and mental features of an individual, both due to heredity, may be associated with each other, and that physical features may therefore afford clues as to mentality and disposition. If such a relationship could be established, it would be of practical benefit in the apprehension and identification of criminals, in the examination of persons suspected because of their bodily form, and in providing a better basis for the selection of immigrants. In connection with the study there were examined 17,680 inmates of penal institutions and 1,976 non-criminals. On each individual a large variety of anthropometric measurements was made, as well as a visual appraisal of morphological features. The results showed significant differences between the criminal and civilian populations. One portion of the study dealt with "old Americans," that is, persons whose parents were American-born. In this group the comparison revealed "the smaller size of the felon, his inferior weight and poorer body build, his smaller head, straighter hair, absolutely shorter and relatively broader face, with prominent but short and often snubbed nose, his narrow jaws and his rather small, and relatively broad, ears" (p. 128). Hooton points out, however, that there is considerable overlapping, and that no single feature is peculiar to the criminals. He concludes nevertheless that "whatever the crime may be, it ordinarily arises from a deteriorated organism. . . . You may say that this is tantamount to a declaration that the primary cause of crime is biological inferiority—and that is exactly what I mean" (p. 130).

This conclusion is exceedingly important, and if verified it would have the most far-reaching implications for the attitude toward crime and the treatment of the criminal. There is, however, a fatal methodological defect in the whole approach which relieves us of the necessity of taking the results seriously. In any comparison between two groups, it is essential that they be equated for all characteristics except those in which they are being compared—in this case, criminality and physical characteristics. Since apparent biological inferiority may be due to socioeconomic conditions, the two groups must at least come from comparable backgrounds. Actually, the "old American" criminals were taken from a number of different states and represent in general a selection at a low economic level. The civilian "controls" included 146 firemen from Nashville, Tennessee, who were "inclined to be fat" (!), and a heterogeneous Massachusetts sample taken from hospitals, drill-halls and beaches, and representative of the "lower and lower middle economic classes." No more precise indication is given of their comparability with the criminal group, though we are told that they have had more schooling, and the indications are that in other respects also the differences between the two groups are marked. For this reason, Hooton's study fails entirely to carry conviction; his conclusions may be correct, but they have not been demonstrated.

These criticisms do not apply in the same degree to Hooton's discussion of physical variations within the criminal population itself according to the kinds of crime committed. One is struck, however, by the inconsistencies in these results for the separate racial and ethnic groups studied. For one thing the differences between criminals and non-criminals noted for the White population do not hold in the case of Negroes; Negro homicides do not show the greater stature and more powerful physique said to be characteristic of Whites in the same category. It seems unlikely, if Lombroso is right in his contention that physique and criminality are somehow related, that such a relationship should hold for one ethnic group and not for the other. The writer is inclined to feel that the differences which Hooton has noted have no far-reaching significance.

There is, however, an indirect manner in which physical "stigmata" may be related to criminality. As Sutherland (12) and others have pointed out, personal appearance may play an important part in determining whether an individual will make a satisfactory social adjustment, or will seek gratification by devious and frequently illegal methods. This is probably true especially of women. Obvious deformities and asymmetries might therefore occur with greater frequency in criminal groups, not because of the relationship postulated by Lombroso, but because of the social and individual attitudes toward these defects. "It is easy to imagine the rebuffs and failures which offensive-looking individuals are likely to encounter in attempting to pursue many of the socially desirable walks of life and to understand why such individuals are prone to gravitate to the 'underworld' " (13, p. 122.)

Sheldon (14), whose constitutional typology was discussed above (Chapter 12), has also sought and found a structural or anatomical basis for delinquent behavior. His study of 200 delinquent boys at a detention home in Boston revealed a marked predominance of mesomorphy in this group as compared with the normal controls. The chronic offenders were almost invariably high in the mesomorphic component, and correspondingly low in endomorphy and ectomorphy. Sheldon describes these individuals as having low control over their expressive activity, with little warmth or need for companionship. As has already been indicated, there are certain methodological difficulties in Sheldon's approach which impose caution until the theory has been independently validated.

SOCIAL AND PSYCHOLOGICAL FACTORS

Many studies have been made of the social and psychological characteristics of criminals and of their families. A report of the U.S. Census Bureau for 1923, for example, indicates that there is a much larger proportion of illiteracy in the criminal group and a far greater frequency of divorce among the parents. This finding that crime is related to broken homes has been verified in some subsequent investigations, but not in all. After a review of the available evidence on this point, Sutherland (12) concludes that the break in the home is less important than was previously believed. There is considerable indication also that criminals and delinquents include a rather large proportion of neurotic and psychopathic individuals. Anderson (15), for instance, found that in his mental hygiene survey of 4,326 school children in Cincinnati, only 2.6% were psychopathic, whereas among the juvenile delinquents there were 31.2% who could be so described. Slawson (16) reports the occurrence among delinquent boys of a tendency to morbid depression and similar abnormal phenomena, together with an overwhelming preponderance of psychoneurotic responses to the questions on the Matthews revision of the Woodworth Personal Data Sheet.

One of the most careful and significant of the studies of psychiatric aspects of delinquency has been made by Healy and Bronner (17) in their survey of cases brought before the child guidance clinics of Boston, New Haven and Detroit from 1929 to 1933. They made an intensive examination of 105 pairs of seriously delinquent and non-delinquent siblings; that is to say, the delinquents were compared with their own siblings so that factors of heredity and socioeconomic environment were adequately controlled. They report that about 91% of the delinquents showed major emotional disturbances, such as feelings of insecurity in affectional relationships, deep feelings of being thwarted, emotional disturbances over family discipline, marked feelings of inferiority, sibling jealousy or rivalry, deep-set internal emotional conflicts, and unconscious feelings of guilt and the need for punishment. Among the control group, on the other hand, only 13% of the cases showed similar evidences of inner stress.

Alexander and Staub (18) also speak of a neurotic type of criminal whose transgressions are often of a compulsive nature and carried out under the strong pressure of unconscious motives. One type, for example, may have a sense of guilt of unknown origin; a crime is committed and the sense of guilt is then connected with it and becomes easier to bear as a consequence. In the case of such a criminal, punishment has of course no deterrent effect, since the expected punishment is the main motive for the transgression.[2] According to these writers, however, not all criminals are neurotic, and they distinguish three additional types. (1) Those who commit crimes as the result of toxic or other organic destructive processes, for instance,

---

[2] It is probable, as Healy (19) and others have pointed out, that punishment is no great deterrent in the majority of cases of criminal behavior, since the possibility of apprehension is rarely contemplated.

idiots, sufferers from organic mental disease, alcoholics and drug addicts. (2) Normal, non-neurotic criminals, including tramps, beggars, gangsters, professional criminals like pickpockets and burglars, etc. (3) Genuine criminals without any inhibitions whatsoever. In addition, there are crimes resulting from temporary emotional conditions, and usually forgiven by the community. The psychoanalytic approach to the neurotic criminal deserves careful consideration, since there can be little doubt that many criminals require psychiatric help rather than incarceration in a penal institution.

Among the many studies dealing with social factors determining the incidence and the nature of criminal and delinquent behavior, those of Shaw and his co-workers (20) in Chicago have attracted the greatest attention. In a careful survey of juvenile delinquency in Chicago among boys from 11 to 17 years of age, it was found that the city could be divided into a number of zones or delinquency areas, starting with the central or Loop district and progressing to the residential suburbs In all, seven such zones were mapped at one-mile intervals from the center. It was found that there was a progressive decrease in the proportion of delinquency from the center to the periphery of the city. The study extended over a considerable period of years during which the population of the central area changed completely without affecting this relationship. There were, for example, successive waves of migration from various European countries, as well as of Mexicans and Negroes, but the delinquency rate remained substantially the same. This has usually been interpreted as meaning that the social and economic setting, rather than the nature of the people concerned, has a definitive influence upon the delinquency rate. The technique has been applied to other cities as well, although not all of them lend themselves geographically to this same regular division into concentric zones. In New York, for example, the careful surveys by Maller (21) have shown a number of distinct delinquency areas rather than a single center; there is, however, a close relationship between delinquency and such factors as density of population and economic level. In London, Burt (22) demonstrated a correlation of +.77 between delinquency and density of population, and of +.67 between delinquency and poverty. It should be added, however, that the approach to this problem represented by the analysis of delinquency areas has been criticized by Robison (23) because of the difficulty involved in obtaining adequate and reliable data, and by Landor (24) on the ground that more complete analysis reveals that the original formulation was oversimplified. It seems clear, however, in spite of these strictures, that some degree of relationship between delinquency and economic status can be regarded as proven.

There are other studies whose conclusions point in the same direction. Bonger (25) noted that in Italy between 1887 and 1889, 60 percent of the population was classified as indigent or poor and this group contributed 88 percent of the convicts in the Italian prisons at that time. Shaw and McKay (26) in connection with the Chicago delinquency area study found that when the city was divided into square mile areas, the delinquency rate (in 1931) correlated +.74 with the rates of financial aid to families. There was also a correlation of +.82 between the number of delinquency cases and dependency cases in the juvenile court, and +.63 between delinquency cases and mother's pension cases. These correlations are all high and indicate the close correspondence between economic conditions and crime. This is shown also (27) by the fact that criminality tends to increase during periods of depression and to decrease when there is relative prosperity. Sellin's research memorandum on crime in the depression demonstrates this relationship very clearly. It is pertinent also in this connection that in the *Studies in Deceit* by Hartshorne and May (28), dishonesty in the tests used was found to increase regularly with a decrease in economic level.

In the study made by Dollard, Doob and others (13), it is suggested that the high rate of crime in underprivileged groups as well as its increase during bad times is to be understood as a reaction to frustration. Their theory is that frustration inevitably leads to aggression, and that acts of crime represent merely one of the possible types of aggressive behavior. There is considerable plausibility to this hypothesis, but it must be borne in mind that economic crimes may in part result directly from economic disabilities, rather than indirectly as a more general response to a dissatisfied or frustrated condition.

In the same connection, these writers refer to the preponderance of males in the criminal population. Although the proportion varies markedly from one country to another—3:1 in Belgium to 22.5:1 in Finland—there is a consistent difference in this direction (12). It is barely possible that biological factors are responsible, but in the light of the earlier discussion (see Chapter 10), it seems more probable that the cause is to be found in social and educational influences. For one thing, aggressiveness is regarded as a legitimate masculine trait, but as highly undesirable in a woman, and it has been suggested that this may be the underlying factor.

A fundamental causative factor seems to be our socially conditioned concepts regarding masculinity and femininity. Thus, passivity is felt to be feminine, aggressivity, masculine. A male needs to fight off any sense of femininity by physical activity—a masculine trait (29, p. 408).

Crime and Ethnic Origin. The problem of the relation between crime and ethnic origin has attracted considerable attention and has given rise to many popular misconceptions. It is commonly believed that the foreign-born contribute much more than their share to the crime in this country; actually, the opposite is true. The figures for Negroes are far in excess of those for Whites, but as Woofter (30) and others have indicated, there is such a great discrepancy in the readiness with which Negroes and Whites, respectively, are accused and convicted that the statistics as such are meaningless. Even if the Negro rate is actually higher, the interpretation of this fact would have to include the consideration of economic status, and some allowance would have to be made for the consequent difference in the predisposing factors. It seems unlikely that ethnic origin as such plays any significant part.

There is, however, a definite problem arising from the status of the native-born of foreign parentage. Glueck (31) has pointed out that the crime and delinquency rates for this group are certainly higher than those for comparable groups with native-born parents. The explanation cannot be a biological one, since the foreign-born parents themselves have a relatively low incidence of crime, and Glueck suggests the hypothesis of "conflict of cultures" as responsible. A case history of one such instance was reported by Shaw (32) in 1930; the subject of the study, Stanley, was born into a disorganized community situation where the *mores* of his family of Polish origin could not be maintained. The result, according to Shaw, was the freeing of the boy from traditional controls, making him accessible to delinquency patterns. Many similar cases have been reported, with the suggestion that where the conflict between the old European culture pattern and the new American one is great, delinquent behavior is a frequent consequence.

A careful study by Taft (33) gives an analysis of crime-rate data from 26 states and indicates that for these 26 states as a whole, the sons of immigrants actually show lower commitment rates than the sons of natives; in nine of these states, however, the rate is higher. These nine states are relatively more industrial, are concentrated in the northeast section of the country, except for Illinois, and are much more highly urbanized. They contain also a larger number of foreign-born, and these foreign-born come mainly from southern and eastern Europe. The cause, therefore, of the higher delinquency rate is not the fact of having foreign parents, but the degree of conflict between the two cultures as well as the attendant economic circumstances. This interpretation is supported by the finding of Carlson (34) that in Iowa the native-born of foreign-born parents have less than the expected proportion of delinquency. As he points out, "the process of assimilation has probably been smoother and more gradual in Iowa than in more industrial states." We must agree, therefore, with Sellin (35) that the concept of culture conflict by itself is not sufficient as an explanation of variations in crime rate, but that it must be seen within the total complex of social and economic factors. This does not mean, however, that culture conflict may not play an important part within the complex.

Apart from the question of culture conflict it is certain that the folkways of any particular group also contribute to the amount and the nature of the crimes committed. This is indicated by the statistics for homicide in various European countries. The following table gives the number of deaths by homicide per hundred thousand persons of all ages (36, p. 241).

Year	England and Wales	Scotland	Germany
1921	.7	.4	2.71
1922	.5	.4	2.50
1923	.6	.4	2.60
1924	.6	.5	2.22
1925	.7	.4	2.29
1926	.7	.4	2.17
1927	.5	.4	2.06
1928	.5	.7	1.99
1929	.5	.4	1.84
1930	.5	.5	1.91
1931	.5	.5	2.07
1932	.5	.5	

The remarkable consistency from year to year within any one country, and in spite of undoubted variations in economic conditions, indicates that there must be certain attitudes toward homicide prevalent in a community and that these are to be explained by the folkways or the culture generally.

A similar consistency is found in the case of statistics for suicide. An analysis of census data by Dublin and Bunzel (37) indicates that in the years 1924 to 1930, for example, Canada never had fewer than 8 suicides per 100,000 population, and never more than 10. During this same period, the Irish Free State never had less than 3 nor more than 4, whereas Japan varied between 19 and 22, and Austria, between 31 and 40. The interpretation of these figures would have to take into account socioeconomic factors, rural-urban distribution, religious beliefs, etc., but it seems highly probable that national patterns of behavior also play a part.

In the Wickersham report (38) on crime in New York State in 1930, it was noted that Mexicans were convicted in great numbers of the crime of carrying concealed weapons; it is obvious that the habits of many Mexicans in their own country have merely been transferred to this one. Beynon's (39) study of Hungarians in Detroit illustrates a similar mechanism. The Hungarian peasants have transferred to coal-stealing from the railroad their old attitude toward the stealing of firewood from a nobleman's estate. Gangs of boys who steal coal receive therefore a sort of social approval in the community, even though this form of behavior may get them into trouble with the authorities. An additional example is represented by the case of Yugoslav immigrants on the west coast of the United States. Mirkowich (40) reports that at one time during the prohibition era as many as 80% of adult male Yugoslavs in Spokane, Washington, were engaged in the illegal production and distribution of liquor. As farmers in their own country, they had been accustomed to making liquor for their own consumption, and they continued the practice here. They were also frequently convicted of the violation of tax laws of various kinds; here the explanation may be found in the historical fact that in Yugoslavia taxes were usually levied by conquerors who occupied the country, and the inhabitants took every advantage of opportunities to evade them. These crime statistics indicate the need to look at the whole background of national culture for their explanation.

With the passage of time and the consequent acceptance of American *mores* there is a change in the social patterning of crime. Stofflet (41) has indicated that American-born sons of Italian parents commit homicide less frequently than do their fathers, and for different reasons. Whereas in the immigrant group, homicide often results from family quarrels or from threats to the family honor, in the next generation it is more likely to be a concomitant of predatory crimes like robbery or burglary.

It is not easy to separate the cultural from the more directly economic factors operating in this field. Ross (42) points out that rural areas have a lower crime rate than cities, independently of whether they are populated by foreign groups or children of immigrants or by native Americans. He concludes that the broad socio-economic environment rather than the characteristics of the culture is mainly responsible for crime. It is his hypothesis that all peoples on the same socio-economic level have approximately the same crime rate.

> The second generation is not a group culturally adrift with neither the culture of their parents nor of their new environment to guide them, but is a group with a very definite culture, a culture of a socio-economic level that is determined by irregular, poorly paid employment and results in broken homes, inadequate education and recreational opportunity and a general stunted environment (p. 208).

Without quarreling with this emphasis upon economic factors, we must still point out that they do not serve as a universal principle of explanation. The economic approach fails, for example, to explain those crimes which are committed by people in the most favored economic circumstances, and these constitute a substantial minority of all crimes. As was suggested at the beginning of this chapter there are so many different kinds of crime and criminals that it is exceedingly doubtful whether any one explanation will serve for all of them [we have already referred to the classification by Alexander and Staub (18)]. Along these lines, Hopkins (43) attempted a classification into four varieties—(1) political crimes, or those regarded as treasonable by the state, (2) civic crimes, such as being drunk and disorderly, or failing to take out a driver's license, (3) economic crimes, due to want, and (4) psychological crimes, due to passion, sex and other emotional drives. Hopkins, whose approach is primarily psychoanalytic, believes that in all of these, with the possible exception of the third, psychological causes are the determining factors. It is certain that his emphasis goes too strongly in this direction, but there can be no doubt of the reality of those crimes which are psychological rather than primarily economic in their etiology. Both the socio-economic and the psychological approaches must receive adequate consideration. It may be that Dollard and his collaborators (13) are right in their assumption that the frustration-aggression hypothesis applies to all cases of criminal behavior, but it seems more reasonable and more in keeping with the known facts to look upon crime as heterogeneous in nature and subject to multiple causation.

A MULTI-CAUSAL APPROACH

The conviction has grown that no one cause is adequate to explain the varied and complex behavior included under the category of crime or delinquency. The studies by Bowlby (44) in England and Abrahamsen (45) in the United States, although both oriented toward personality factors, show a very definite appreciation of sociological variables. What is perhaps the most extensive and thorough investigation representing the multi-causal approach is that by Glueck and Glueck (16) of delinquency in the area of Greater Boston; 500 boys from correctional schools were matched with 500 "normal" boys with regard to age (14-15 years), residence (in underprivileged areas), the delinquency rate of the neighborhood in which they lived, ethnic origin, general neighborhood factors, and tested intelligence. Data on both groups were gathered and interpreted at four levels, (1) the sociocultural, (2) the somatic, (3) the intellectual, and (4) the emotional-temperamental. Many of the items analyzed did not distinguish between the delinquents and the controls; many others did. In the words of the investigators: "The delinquents as a group are distinguishable from the non-delinquents: (1) *physically*, in being essentially mesomorphic in constitution (solid, closely knit, muscular); (2) *temperamentally*, in being restlessly energetic, impulsive, extroverted, aggressive, destructive . . . ; (3) *in attitude*, by being hostile, defiant, resentful, suspicious, stubborn, socially assertive, adventurous, unconventional, non-submissive to authority; (4) *psychologically*, in tending to direct and concrete, rather than symbolic, intellectual expression, and in being less methodical in their approach to problems; (5) *socioculturally*, in having been reared to a far greater extent than the control group in homes of little understanding, affection, stability, or moral fibre by parents usually unfit to be effective guides and protectors . . ." (p. 361). The important fact to note, they add, is that in general "the high probability of delinquency is dependent upon the interplay of the conditions and forces from all these areas" (p. 361).

One of the striking features of this study is the indication that an analysis of the various factors involved may make it possible to predict which boys will be more likely to become delinquent as they grow older. Such social factors as over-strict or erratic discipline of the boy by the father, unsuitable supervision by the mother, indifference or hostility on the part of the parents, lack of cohesiveness in the family, are all found in greater frequency among the delinquent boys than among the normal controls. The investigators have developed prediction tables based on these factors in the social background, as well as on the character traits revealed in the Rorschach and in the psychiatric interviews. The prediction tables are not to be used mechanically, but as tentative indications not only of the likelihood of delinquency in general, but also of the particular sources of disturbance which may make the occurrence of delinquency more probable.

If successfully used in this fashion, the prediction tables may prepare the way for adequate and effective prevention or therapy. This is of course the crux of the problem and the aspect which is most in need of development. The techniques so far applied to the reduction of delinquency have not been conspicuous for their success; the Cambridge-Somerville Youth Study (47), a carefully-controlled ten-year experiment, showed no significant reduction of delinquency among the teen-agers involved. The approach of the Gluecks, if validated by subsequent application, offers some hope that the techniques of prevention may be improved. It is too early to express optimism, but the trend appears to be in a promising direction. [The application of group psychotherapy to "children who hate" by Redl and Wiseman (48) gives us an indication of methods that could be more widely applied.]

SUMMARY

The relativity of crime to the laws of a particular society, and the variations in the nature of behavior which is termed criminal, make it impossible to speak of *the criminal* as such, or to ascribe specific characteristics to him. The attempt by Lombroso to relate criminality to physical appearance may be regarded as a failure. The recent revival of the theory by Hooton is unconvincing, mainly because the two groups compared, namely, the criminal and civilian populations, were not adequately equated. Certain "stigmata" may be related indirectly to crime, not because they are signs of biological inferiority, but because of the attitudes which such defects may arouse. There is evidence that many delinquents and criminals show signs of neurotic disturbance, and that they require psychiatric assistance rather than punishment.

Among the social factors related to criminal and delinquent behavior, the demonstration of the existence of delinquency areas and of the relation to crowding and poverty may be regarded as particularly significant. Ethnic groups probably do not differ in innate criminal propensities, although there may be differences in crime rate because of economic and cultural backgrounds. The cultural conflicts in the native-born of foreign parentage contribute to the greater incidence of crime and delinquency in this group, although other factors undoubtedly enter. A combined, multi-dimensional approach is necessary.

REFERENCES

1. Michael, J., and Adler, M. J. *Crime, Law and Social Science.* 1933
2. Osborne, T. M. *Society and Prisons.* 1924
3. Gillin, J. L. *The Wisconsin Prisoner.* 1946
4. Porterfield, A. L. *Youth in Trouble.* 1946
5. Wallerstein, J. S., and Wyle, C. J. "Our Law-abiding Law-breakers," *Probation,* 1947, 25: pp. 107-112
6. Rouke, F. L., "Delinquency." In E. L. Hartley and R. E. Hartley, *Fundamentals of Social Psychology.* 1952
7. Dunlap, K. *Civilized Life.* 1934
8. Lombroso, C. *Crime, Its Causes and Remedies.* 1911
9. Ferri, E. *Criminal Sociology.* 1917
10. Goring, C. *The English Convict.* 1913
11. Hooton, E. A. *Crime and the Man.* 1939
12. Sutherland, E. H. *Principles of Criminology.* 3d ed. 1939
13. Dollard, J., et al. *Frustration and Aggression.* 1939
14. Sheldon, W. H., et al. *Varieties of Delinquent Youth.* 1949
15. Anderson, V. V. "Feeblemindedness as Seen in Court," *Ment. Hygiene,* 1917, I: pp. 260-265
16. Slawson, J. *The Delinquent Boy.* 1926
17. Healy, W., and Bronner, A. F. *New Light on Delinquency and Its Treatment.* 1936

18. Alexander, F., and Staub, H. *The Criminal, the Judge and the Public.* 1931

19. Healy, W. *The Individual Delinquent.* 1915

20. Shaw, C. R., et al. *Delinquency Areas.* 1929

21. Maller, J. B. "The Trend of Juvenile Delinquency in New York City," *J. Juv. Res.,* 1933, 17: pp. 10-18

22. Burt, C. *The Young Delinquent.* 1925

23. Robison, S. *Can Delinquency be Measured?* 1939

24. Landor, B. Unpublished Ph.D. Dissertation, Columbia University

25. Bonger, W. A. *Criminality and Economic Conditions.* 1916

26. Shaw, C. R., and McKay, H. D. "Social Factors in Juvenile Delinquency," *Report on the Causes of Crime,* No. 13, Vol. II

27. Sellin, T. *Research Memorandum on Crime in the Depression.* N.Y. Social Science Research Council, 1937

28. Hartshorne, H., and May, M. A. *Studies in Deceit.* 1928

29. Bender, L., Keiser, S., and Schilder, P. "Studies in Aggressiveness," *Genet. Psychol. Monog.,* 1936, 18: pp. 357-564

30. Woofter, T. J., Jr. "The Status of Racial and Ethnic Groups." In *Recent Social Trends,* N.Y., 1933, Vol. I, Chap. II: pp. 553-601

31. Glueck, E. T. *One Thousand Juvenile Delinquents.* 1934. "Culture, Conflict and Delinquency," *Ment. Hyg.,* 1937, 21: pp. 46-66

32. Shaw, C. R. *The Jack-Roller.* 1930

33. Taft, D. R. "Nationality and Crime," *Amer. Sociol. Rev.,* 1936, I: pp. 724-736

34. Carlson, H. S. "The Incidence of Certain Etiological and Symptomatic Factors Among a Group of Iowa Delinquents and Felons," *Univ. Ia. Stud. Child Welf.,* 1937, 13, No. 4: pp. 61-98

35. Sellin, T. "Culture Conflict and Crime," *Amer. J. Sociol.,* 1938, 44: pp. 97-103

36. Huxley, J. S., and Haddon, A. C. *We Europeans.* 1935

37. Dublin, L., and Bunzel, B. *To Be or Not to Be.* 1933

38. Wickersham, G. W., et al. *National Commission on Law Observance and Law Enforcement.* Report No. 10, Washington, 1933

39. Beynon, E. D. "Crime and Custom of the Hungarians of Detroit," *J. Crim. Law Criminol.,* 1934-1935, 25: pp. 755-774

40. Mirkowich, N. "Yugoslavs and Criminality," *Sociol. and Social Res.,* 1940, 25: pp. 29-34

41. Stofflet, E. H. "A Study of National and Cultural Differences in Criminal Tendencies," *Arch. Psychol.,* 1935, No. 185

42. Ross, H. "Crime and the Native-born Sons of European Immigrants," *J. Crim. Law Criminol.,* 1937-1938, 28: pp. 202-209

43. Hopkins, P. *The Psychology of Social Movements.* 1938

44. Bowlby, J. *Forty-four Juvenile Thieves: Their Character and Home Life.* 1946

45. Abrahamsen, D. *Who Are the Guilty?* 1952

46. Glueck, S., and Glueck, E. T. *Unraveling Juvenile Delinquency.* 1950

47. Powers, E., and Witmer, H. *An Experiment in the Prevention of Delinquency: The Cambridge-Somerville Youth Study.* 1951

48. Redl, F., and Wiseman, D. *Children Who Hate.* 1951

Part Five

SOCIAL INTERACTION

17

The Individual in the Group

INTRODUCTION

We have entitled this last section of the book *Social Interaction*, but the term is so inclusive as to be appropriate to a large proportion of the topics already discussed. Motives and emotions are examples of social interaction; so is the relation between culture and personality, and the performance of the various roles which a community assigns to its members. Our present concern is with some of the more direct and immediate phenomena of interaction, which represent perhaps the core problems of the social psychologist. It would be more accurate, however, to characterize the present section as dealing with some additional, important phenomena of social interaction which have not so far been discussed.

The same considerations apply to this particular chapter, *The Individual in the Group*. It is concerned mainly with the question of the manner and the degree in which the behavior of an individual is altered by the actual presence of others. In terms of our definition of social psychology, this may be regarded as one of our central problems. It represents one of the oldest and at the same time one of the most active approaches in this field, involving on the one hand the ancient problem of crowd mentality, and on the other, a series of important studies which have laid the modern foundation for an experimental social psychology. Such an approach has already been included in our analysis of the formation of social norms in perception, the phenomena of rumor, problems of communication, etc. It would therefore again be more accurate to say that in this chapter we shall carry further the discussion of the relation of the individual to the group, even though this relation has entered, both implicitly and explicitly, into what has preceded.

Many of the phenomena to which attention will now be directed occur in what has been termed the *face-to-face group*. We have preferred not to use this expression, because it is somewhat too narrow for our purposes; the discussion of leadership, for example, extends beyond these limits. It remains true that most of the studies which will be reviewed in this chapter do deal with the *face-to-face* group.

The problems to be discussed have a close relation to what many sociologists have called the *primary group*. Cooley (1), who first used the expression in this context, wrote: "By primary groups I mean those characterized by intimate face-to-face association and cooperation. They are primary in several senses, but chiefly in that they are fundamental in forming the social nature and ideals of the individual" (p. 23). Cooley's concept, however, leaves out many groups which also deserve consideration. He was primarily interested in groups that are "practically universal, belonging to all times and all stages of development"; they constitute "a chief basis of what is universal in human nature and in human ideals" (p. 24). We shall be dealing with many groupings that are not nearly so universal nor so permanent as Cooley's view would demand.

Homans (2) defines a group as "a number of persons who communicate with one another often over a span of time, and who are few enough so that each person is able to communicate with all the others, not at second hand, through other people, but face to face" (p. 1). Here, too, an undue limitation appears to be imposed on the concept by the use of words such as "often over a span of time." If two or more individuals are together briefly, but interact and influence one another, they constitute, if only for a time, a real group. As we shall see, many of the experimental studies of group phenomena make use of just such temporary forms of interaction, as well as of the more lasting variety.

Sometimes the groups are artificial, brought together through the agency of the experimenter; sometimes they are studied as they are found "in nature." There are arguments in favor of both varieties of investigation. Festinger (3), for example, in one of his studies writes: "We have thus succeeded in setting up a situation which it would be impossible to find in everyday life" (p. 38). He believes that this procedure has real value, because it enables the investigator to isolate and single out for study the changes in behavior due to one and only one variable. Sherif's (4) important study of intergroup hostility in a boys' camp examined the behavior of two groups especially constituted for the purposes of this particular experiment; the same holds for the well-known study of leadership by Lewin, Lippitt and White (5). On the other hand, Arensberg (6), referring to studies of industrial behavior, writes: ':'The study of such small groups in their real-life daily activity has meant a new realism, objectivity, and fidelity to fact in the social and psychological sciences" (p. 325). There is no need to choose between these two approaches; as we shall see, both have their uses and their limitations.

A final caution is required in connection with the focusing of attention on small groups. Obviously they are more accessible and easier to study. They should be seen, however, in the context of the whole society in which they are found. Whyte (7), who has himself conducted one of the most important investigations of a real-life group, a street-corner gang, correctly points out that: "Studies of small groups and of large organizations should necessarily fit together. There is no point to studying the over-all organizational structure unless we can trace out its impact upon particular individuals and groups. Nor is there any point in studying the small group as if it operated in a vacuum" (p. 311). Leighton's (8) description of the group solidarity of Japanese-Americans in wartime relocation centers would clearly have been meaningless except against the background of the total war situation and the measures taken by the Federal Administration. Not only is a small group affected by the larger organization of which it is a part, but the individuals in the group bring to it reactions which have been, and continue to be, influenced by their wider group membership.

IMITATION

What might seem at first glance to be the most obvious manner in which one person may be affected by another is through imitation, or through the direct and usually immediate reproduction of behavior occurring in one's environment. There has been considerable discussion in the literature as to the true nature of this process. William James and Baldwin regarded it as instinctive. McDougall believed that it should not be regarded as instinctive, since there are no specific forms of behavior characteristic of it, and the mode of expression varies according to the external situation.

Historically the most important use of imitation in the field of social psychology is that of Gabriel Tarde (9) who built upon it a theory of the nature of society. Himself a criminologist, Tarde rejected the current theory of Lombroso that crime is based upon the biological nature of the individual, and looked rather for a social explanation of this and allied phenomena. He was influenced by the psychiatry of his day, particularly by the growing knowledge of hypnotism, and of the suggestible and imitative behavior characteristic of the hypnotic state. He studied the nature of "crime waves" and "crime epidemics" from this point of view, and extended the theory to other forms of social behavior. Imitation was for him the fundamental social fact, and there were laws which described its nature and its effect. Social change is possible because people imitate the novel and the striking. Society without imitation is unthinkable.

It is doubtful, however, whether imitation can ever be used as a principle of explanation. Even among animals, imitation apparently occurs only under specific conditions and in response to definite goals; that is to say, the animal imitates when something is to be gained by it, when it enables him to reach food, and so on. Similarly, among human beings, there seems always to be a selection from a great many possibilities, and imitation occurs only when it brings some kind of additional satisfaction. As Brown (10) expresses it:

> Humans imitate when this type of behavior enables them to arrive at certain goals in the psychological field. The underlying dynamic situation creates the imitation, rather than a force called imitation creating these goals. Whenever a shopgirl cuts her hair in a Garbo bob, she does this, not because imitation as a force causes her to do it, but rather because she perceives it as means towards arriving at the type of life that either Garbo or one of the heroines she portrays lives (p. 92).

Freeman (11) also insists that imitation can occur only in so far as the imitated act already possesses meaning and functional significance to the mimic, and only to the extent that one desires to imitate. Behavior may be imitated because it appears to have brought success to others, or because we approve of it, as in the familiar saying that "imitation is the sincerest form of flattery." As a result, we follow the customs of the "best people," of our hero or heroine, and children repeat the words and actions of their elders, particularly of their own parents. F. H. Allport (12) adopts a similar position. It seems clear that imitation is not in itself a sufficient explanation of uniformities of behavior, since such uniformities appear to develop only under certain conditions and not under others.

An important series of investigations into the conditions under which imitation occurs was conducted by Miller and Dollard (13), who applied to the problem the principles and techniques associated with learning theory. One of the simplest, and at the same time most convincing, of their experiments dealt with a situation in which two six-year-old children were brought into a room in which there were two identical wooden boxes with their contents concealed. One child, the "leader," was told whether to go to the right or left box on any given trial, and he always found a piece of candy in his box. The second child was now told to choose a box. Would he imitate the leader or not? On the first trial, 77% of the children went to the box different from the one the leader had chosen. Twenty children obtained the candy when they went to the same box as did the leader; they quickly learned (with an average of 1.7 errors) to "imitate." Another twenty were successful when they chose the other box; they learned even more quickly (with an average of 0.4 errors) to "non-imitate." The investigators concluded that we do not learn by imitation; we learn to imitate. Further experiments were directed toward discovering the conditions under which imitation was more easily learned, and those which made such learning more difficult.

In commenting on these experiments Asch (14) indicates that the learning involved here may not be as mechanical and indiscriminate as the investigators believe. Citing an unpublished study by A. Field, he suggests that the children tried out various assumptions and hypotheses, attempting to find some meaning in the curious situation with which they were confronted. They solved the problem by noting the relevant features. Asch insists that "learning from others is possible only when the observer has understood the sense of the action he has followed and when he has noted its relevance to the given conditions. Imitation of this order is an intelligent process, not wholly different from the insight required for the independent solution of a problem" (p. 390). It is however possible that once imitation has been found successful as a solution to one problem, it may be extended to other individuals and to new situations.

The point has also been made that what appears to be imitative behavior may be due to the similarity in the conditions affecting different individuals at the same time. The fact, for example, that when one guest leaves the others follow, does not necessarily indicate imitation, since they may all feel that it is about time to go. When a theater audience laughs at a humorous situation on the stage, the individuals are all responding to the same external stimulus rather than imitating one another; at the same time, there is the additional phenomenon of interaction between individuals which contributes to the final result.

We may conclude that the behavior described as imitative can be explained in a variety of ways, and represents a variety of different phenomena. At one time it is a form of conditioned response; at another it merely represents similar reactions of several individuals to the same external situation. When imitation of a direct character does take place, it is to be understood as a means to an end, and occurs because value is ascribed to the act which is imitated or to the person who has performed the act, or because the act which is "imitated" is seen as the correct solution to a problem. There is no drive to imitate.

SUGGESTION

It is difficult to draw a sharp line between suggestion and imitation, and as we have seen, Tarde's laws of imitation were based upon the facts of suggestion and hypnosis described by the psychiatrists. William Stern (15) has attempted to distinguish between the two concepts on the ground that suggestion is a higher and more complicated stage of behavior which includes some degree of interpretation. If someone claps his hands, for example, and a child repeats the action, it is imitation; if someone weeps, and the child realizes that this person is unhappy and therefore himself begins to cry, it is suggestion. It is doubtful, however, whether the distinction can be validly drawn in terms of the interpretation involved. In the case in which the subject is told, under conditions of waking suggestion, that he is falling forward, he may accept this idea and react accordingly, without interpreting it in any way. It is precisely the *unreasoned* acceptance, to use F. H. Allport's (12) phrase, which is essential to the phenomenon of suggestion.

Murphy, Murphy, and Newcomb (16) indicate that the term

"suggestion" has been used for three quite distinct human tendencies which have been confused.

1. The tendency to make a response which has been previously made in a similar situation, whether appropriate or inappropriate at the time. This includes habit and the response by analogy (the "transferred conditioned response").

2. The tendency to go on doing what one has started doing. This is said to be due to suggestion if the experimenter believes that the tendency to go on with the act involves gross failure to realize its inappropriateness.

3. The tendency to believe or to do what one is told because of social motives such as dependence upon, or fear of, or fondness for, some person. This includes hypnosis.

The first two of these are not always distinct, however, and there are many cases in which both operate at the same time. In the well-known test of progressive lines devised by Binet (17), the fact that successive lines presented to the subject regularly increase in size for a time, appears to produce a set in the subject so that he continues to report the increase even when the size of the lines is kept constant. In this case there is habit and the response by analogy, but also the tendency to go on doing what one has started doing. There is still an important distinction between these first two types which together constitute what Aveling and Hargreaves (18) call ideo-motor suggestion, and "the tendency to believe what one is told" which they call prestige suggestion. In the former case the suggestion or idea comes from the nature of the material or of the act previously performed, whereas in the latter it depends upon the relation to some other individual or group of individuals.

There are many experiments which illustrate the effect of ideo-motor suggestion. Binet's illusion of progressive lines belongs in this category, as well as the similar illusion of progressive weights. In the field of social psychology, however, prestige suggestion is by far the more important. Experiments in this field range from simple conjuring tricks in which the experimenter tells a group of children that he is about to throw a ball into the air (and finds that about fifty percent of them see him do it) to the complicated relationships found in hypnosis and in the mechanisms underlying propaganda and public opinion. This is a phenomenon which differs in important respects from ideo-motor suggestion, since it is affected by a host of social and emotional attitudes. The marked difference between the two types of suggestion probably accounts to a considerable degree for the low correlations reported between the different tests of suggestibility, and makes it impossible to speak of suggestibility as a trait of character or personality.

The use of "leading questions" in connection with testimony is frequently also an example of prestige suggestion. When a picture is shown and the subject later questioned as to the kind of hat the man was wearing, it is difficult to resist the suggestion that he was wearing one, even though actually he was not. There have been so many experiments which have demonstrated this tendency that one can certainly understand the insistence of the judge in a law court upon eliminating such questions as far as possible.

In connection with the prestige phenomenon, there are many tests of waking suggestion such as the instruction to a subject that he is about to fall forward, used with considerable effect by Hull (19) in selecting suitable subjects for hypnosis. Aveling and Hargreaves (18) suggested to their subjects that their hand would remain rigid, and found that about 46 percent of them responded positively; in the case of hand levitation ("Your hand is getting lighter. It is rising in the air."), 42 percent accepted the suggestion. In these experiments the interesting phenomenon of "negative" or "contrary" suggestion enters, some of the subjects responding in a manner opposite to that suggested by the experimenter. On the statistical side this is shown by the fact that in the ideo-motor type of test there is an approximately normal distribution of responses, whereas in prestige suggestion the curve is U-shaped, indicating that subjects tend to fall into two distinct groups, the suggestible and the negatively suggestible. This has obvious significance in the social field; as we shall see later, in the experiments on propaganda there are always some subjects who react in a manner opposite to that anticipated by the propagandist. We are dealing here with personality characteristics of a complicated and obscure type, and further research is needed upon the factors operative in situations of this kind.

The phenomenon of hypnosis is one of the most striking in this whole field. As is well known, the use of hypnotism received its greatest impetus through Anton Mesmer's theory and practice of animal magnetism. His notion of animal magnetism as a kind of impalpable gas or fluid which could be manipulated and transported has been entirely discredited, but his work led to the discovery of the artificial somnambulism which we call the hypnotic state, and which includes phenomena of great scientific interest. Although the French psychiatrist Charcot in part revived the notion of animal magnetism, it was proved beyond any possible doubt by Liébeault and Bernheim of the Nancy school that the hypnotic trance state could be explained as an extreme form of suggestion. It is important for social psychology precisely because it represents in marked form phenomena similar to those found under normal conditions. As in ordinary prestige suggestion, the subject in an hypnotic trance is willing to accept the ideas presented to him; in both cases, however, there appears to be some control and criticism left, so that for example the subject in a trance will commit an imaginary murder with a paper knife, but will not actually do harm to anyone.

This commonly accepted view has in part been challenged in an investigation by Rowland (20). There were some subjects who under deep hypnosis reached out toward a coiled rattlesnake when told it was a rubber rope, and who after some urging threw sulphuric acid at the experimenter, protected by an invisible sheet of glass. Most of the subjects were, however, frightened at the appearance of the snake and would not come close to the box.

A serious danger in connection with prestige suggestion lies in the assumption that a person of outstanding ability in one field is also to be taken seriously in another. In connection with advertising and propaganda, this becomes especially dangerous; an important baseball player endorses a candidate for the Presidency, a physicist expresses his belief in spiritualism or in one particular type of economic system, a movie star endorses a new automobile, an aviator analyzes the international situation. The legitimate acceptance of a man's pre-eminence in one field leads to an unwarranted assumption that he also has authority elsewhere. The prestige effect of large numbers is a similar one. Since the classical experiment of Moore (21) on the effect of knowledge of popular opinion upon the attitudes of the individual, many investigators have demonstrated a similar influence in a variety of situations.

It is important to keep in mind, however, that the nature of the group may make a real difference, and Lewis (22) has clearly shown that majority opinion does not always have the same prestige effect. In one experiment she presented to a group of students a list of ten political slogans, chiefly of contemporary political interest, and asked them to rank these for their "social significance," "author's intelligence," and so forth. The slogans included: "Give me liberty or give me death," "Balance the Budget," "Workers of the world, unite," and seven other expressions used by conservative and radical leaders. Another group of students was then given the same task, but this time with the knowledge of the rank order for "author's intelligence" presumably obtained from 500 college students. The results showed for the various rankings a definite shift in the direction of the "prestige suggestion" for those subjects who were political liberals but not for those who were political radicals (there were no conservatives in this group). It seems probable that for the radical subjects the opinions of the majority have little or no prestige, since the radicals know that their own views differ from those generally accepted.

In a further study a similar procedure was followed, but the ratings for "author's intelligence" were presumably made by Franklin D. Roosevelt, Herbert Hoover, and Earl Browder respectively. It was felt by the experimenter that the views of the General Secretary of the Communist Party in the United States might have true prestige for the radical students. The rankings ascribed to Browder were inversely related to those which the radical students had previously given. The results still showed little shift in the direction of the new ratings, in spite of the prestige with which they were presumably associated for the radical students. This indicates that prestige works very differently under different conditions. Interviews with the subjects showed, for example, that most of the radicals refused to believe that the given rankings correctly represented Mr. Browder's opinions. The author concludes that:

> Radicals do not shift their judgments markedly under the influence of a most authoritative, but conflicting standard. . . . The authoritativeness of a standard, i.e., its effectiveness, requires as a minimum condition the presence of some point of integration between it and the subject's opinions. . . . The operation of prestige suggestion is confined to ambiguous, ill-defined situations.

Lorge (23) gave to his subjects the following statement by Thomas Jefferson: "I hold that a little rebellion, now and then, is a good thing, and as necessary in the political world as storms are in the physical." The task of the subjects was to indicate their degree of agreement with this statement. Later they were given the same statement, but told that its author was Lenin; again they indicated their degree of agreement, which turned out to be related to the subjects' acceptance of Jefferson and Lenin, respectively. Lorge concludes that changes of evaluation or judgment can be produced regardless of the merit of the issue involved.

Asch (*14*) modified this procedure somewhat, and reached a different conclusion as to the nature of the phenomenon. He gave the same passage to his subjects, ascribed to the same two authors, but he also asked them to write down in their own words what the statement meant. One subject, for example, interpreted Jefferson as follows: "By rebellion he means alertness and the exercise of political rights." Another subject, who thought that Lenin was the author, wrote: "Lenin is justifying the Russian revolution, and probably all revolutions as a potential source of good." Asch comments: "The outstanding fact about the reactions is that the statement is not simply the 'same' under the two conditions, at least not for most persons. The effect of changing the authorship has been to alter the cognitive content of the statement" (p. 422). He regards this as an instance of the general Gestalt proposition about the interaction between part and whole. His analysis introduces an important qualification into the interpretation of a good deal of the research into prestige suggestion, but does not alter the fact that frequently people will be influenced by the opinions of others, accept or reject them—often quite uncritically—and perceive reality differently as a consequence. This effect may be confined, as Lewis suggests, to ambiguous, ill-defined situations, but there are enough of these to make the effect an important one.

It is of course unjustifiable to attribute all kinds of consequences to suggestion as if it were some force or entity which caused things to happen. If we use the term, however, as a convenient shorthand for the effects produced by the literal and unreasoned acceptance of beliefs presented to us by a prestige figure, or by majority opinion of the group to which we belong, it can be applied to a large number of different situations.

Suggestion has been used as an explanation of many phenomena of an otherwise mysterious nature, examples of which have been reported with some frequency, particularly in ethnological literature. It helps to explain the case of the Polynesian native who died when he discovered that he had eaten food touched by the chief;

belief in the potency of the taboo is apparently sufficient, at least in some cases, to bring about this extreme result. The fact that a Crow Indian sees a vision after four days of prayer and fasting, or that natives all over the world are reported to succumb to witchcraft, may be similarly understood. It is probable that suggestion also operates to ensure a reasonable amount of success in the use of oaths and ordeals as part of the legal procedure of the Africans; the belief, for example, that the guilty man will be destroyed by the "poison" which he is given, is often strong enough to cause the death of the man who knows he is guilty. Not all the ordeals lend themselves to this interpretation, and it is certain that they do not always result in freeing the innocent, but in many instances the effect of suggestion will be in the "right" direction. Similar examples might be multiplied. It is important, however, not to go too far in using this mode of explanation. There is some tendency to account for everything from seasickness to paralysis in these terms, and although suggestion may play an important part in many cases, we must not assume that it is always responsible. The exact manner in which suggestion works to influence organic functions is not always clear, but it seems probable that beliefs and emotions may have a direct effect upon the autonomic nervous system, which in turn acts upon the viscera. In spite of the wide variations in their specific character, these examples all belong in the category of prestige suggestion, the prestige being located in an individual (as in the case of the hypnotist) or less tangibly in the folk beliefs of a community (as in the ethnological examples cited).

The usual assumption that one of the essential characteristics of suggestion is that an idea or stimulus comes to the individual from the outside, seems to conflict with the existence of the phenomenon of auto-suggestion. This form of suggestion, popularized by Coué, appears to demonstrate that the idea may also come from within, and in that case the process would seem to be an unreasoned and uncritical acceptance of one's own ideas. This is probably an incorrect way of looking at the matter, however, since it is certain that in a great many of the cases of auto-suggestion the idea actually comes from outside. Coué taught his patients certain formulae which they could use in his absence, but actually it was his ideas and suggestions which were operative. Phenomena of this type do not necessitate any restatement of the essential nature of suggestion.

THE CROWD AND THE GROUP

The problem of the relation of the individual to the group comes into clear focus in connection with the study of crowds and crowd behavior. This field of social psychology is usually regarded as having its principal origin in the work of Gustave LeBon (24), who insisted upon the unique nature of the crowd and its distinctness from the individuals of which it is composed.

> Whoever be the individuals that compose it, however like or unlike be their mode of life, their occupations, their character, or their intelligence, the fact that they have been transformed into a crowd puts them in possession of a sort of collective mind which makes them feel, think, and act in a manner quite different from that in which each individual of them would feel, think, and act were he in a state of isolation. There are certain ideas and feelings which do not come into being, or do not transform themselves into acts except in the case of individuals forming a crowd (pp. 29-30).

The crowd therefore is not a mere sum or average of its component individuals, but a different entity.

According to LeBon there are three causes which predispose to the phenomena of crowd behavior. First there is the feeling of invincible power, which makes the crowd more primitive and less subject to control by conscience or by fear of punishment; second, the fact of contagion or imitation; and third, allied to this, heightened suggestibility. These factors help to make of the crowd a single being, less civilized, less intelligent, and more dangerous, though potentially also more heroic, than individuals in isolation.

There have been other attempts to define the characteristics of the crowd. Scott (25) thinks of the crowd as highly emotional and suggestible with complete absence of any feeling of individual responsibility, without ability to reason or to be critical of the ideas suggested to it, and at a more primitive level than that of its component individuals. Everett Dean Martin (26) has attempted a description of the crowd in terms of psychopathic behavior. As in psychopathic cases, there may be a release of repressed impulses, delusions of grandeur and of persecution, lack of awareness of the true motives for the behavior, and a regression to a more primitive level. These descriptions do not differ markedly from those of LeBon.

At the other extreme F. H. Allport (*12*) has insisted that there is no real difference in the nature of the individuals when they are in a crowd and when in isolation. "The individual in the crowd behaves just as he would behave alone, *only more so*" (p. 295). This means that there may be at the most a facilitation in the crowd of certain activities, but not the creation of any that are really foreign to the nature of the individuals. Allport admits, however, that emotional reactions in the crowd are increased by the expressive behavior of others, and also that there is prestige suggestion resulting from the presence of a large group of persons, and an attitude of compliance in the individual as a consequence. He agrees also that acts may be performed in a crowd because the individuals in it go unperceived, or at least unpunished. In spite of these points of agreement with LeBon, there is a real distinction between the two positions. Allport would admit that individuals are affected by others in the vicinity, but this would not constitute the formation of a new entity called the "crowd mind." Two crowds composed of entirely different individuals would differ because of the nature of their components.

This conclusion is on the whole supported by an experimental study of mob behavior by Meier, Mennenga and Stoltz (*27*). Groups of students were told of an imaginary kidnaping which had presumably just taken place; the incident was presented dramatically, culminating in information that a crowd was forming to go after the "criminals," who had been located nearby. The students indicated whether they would join the crowd immediately; would be unwilling to be actually involved, but would go along to assist the others; would not participate in any way; or would attempt to reason with the mob to avoid hasty action. Only then were the subjects told that the story was a hoax, which apparently very few had suspected up to that point. On the whole, those who were prepared to participate in the mob action tended to be younger, more extraverted, less frequently members of a church and included relatively more men than women. The investigators comment that "in the crowd setting the individual will behave in accord with the dominance of previously established habits, attitudes and behavior patterns" (p. 524), but they add that the nature of the situation is of course also important. It remains true, however, that in certain respects the individual is altered by his presence in the group situation. As we have seen, there appears to be a greater degree of emotional reactivity, and a lessening of the inhibitions due to the fear of discovery or of punishment. There is the tendency to accept the notions current in the crowd or group—the familiar phenomenon of prestige suggestion. There is further the fact of interaction between individuals, so that they mutually affect one another. As Lewin (28) has correctly pointed out we must not look upon the individual as a static entity, but rather as a dynamic being whose characteristics and actions change under the varying influence of external situations, or "the social field." The crowd constitutes one such social field and we would expect the behavior of the individual to be modified as a consequence. We may even go one step further with the Gestalt psychologists and agree that the whole is always different from the sum of its parts, that it even determines the nature of the parts, and that a group therefore has a reality different from that of the sum of its individual members. At the same time, just as the Gestalt psychologists would admit the importance of the elements which constitute the totality, we must not lose sight of the nature of the individuals who constitute a group. As individuals they have a background and a set of folkways and traditions which they retain even in the crowd situation. There are many people, for example, who probably never under any conditions would become members of a lynching mob.

This position is in agreement with the conclusions reached in the analysis by Cantril, Gaudet and Hertzog (29) of the panic which followed the Orson Welles broadcast on the evening of October 30, 1938, on the invasion from Mars. It is estimated that at least six million people heard the broadcast and that no less than one million of them were frightened and disturbed. The excitement was great, and many of the phenomena of mob reaction occurred, but not in all people. The investigators state that the problem is "to determine why some people are suggestible, or . . . why some people lack critical ability" (p. 204). The important point in the present context is that the previously existing personality characteristics played an important part in determining who would succumb to the panic. In the case, however, of those who were suggestible, bewildered, uncertain of the future, worried about war and economic insecurity, there can be no doubt that behavior was greatly influenced by the crowd situation.

Our compromise position is therefore in agreement with Allport that the crowd is not entirely distinct from the individuals, and that these latter do not entirely lose their identity within it; on the other hand, the phenomena of increased emotionality, heightened suggestibility and the effect of certain individuals upon others lend support at least to that part of LeBon's theory which insists that the group is more than the sum of its parts and that the individual is altered by his presence in it.

The phenomena of "crowd behavior" may not be confined to the actual crowd situation in the narrower sense, in which a number of individuals congregate in one place at the same time and in a more or less unorganized manner. The various so-called "mental epidemics" belong in the same general category. There have been many historical instances in which the factors of suggestion and interaction have resulted in the widespread occurrence of striking and bizarre forms of behavior over an area much larger than a single locality or a single group. Kimball Young (30) mentions among these the various crusades and pilgrimages between the years 1000 and 1270 which became a universal mania and even caused children in many cases to claim to be prophets and to join in the crusades despite the protests of their parents; the spread of the practice of flagellation from Italy in 1260 as an expression of remorse for real or fancied transgressions; the demonophobia or fear of the devil which took the form of persecution of alleged witches, lasting a century and a half, and causing the torture and death of an untold number of innocent persons; the tulipomania in Holland in the seventeenth century resulting from the mad scramble for tulips in the belief that fortunes could be made by their cultivation; the many religious revivals throughout history and lasting up to the present time, etc. These all indicate the manner and the degree of "crowd behavior" on the widest possible scale. In this general category also we may put the phenomenon of fashion, not only in dress but in other forms of activity as well; there is the same spread from a center of origin or a leader, the contagion or imitation determined by the prestige of certain individuals or of the group as a whole, and usually an uncritical acceptance of the new form of behavior. There is even the same lack of individual responsibility, since a new fashion, no matter how bizarre or irrational, may be accepted without fear of ridicule as long as it is common to a great many individuals.

SOCIAL FACILITATION

A more direct attack upon the problem of the individual in the group situation and the manner in which the group affects the behavior of the individual, has been made by means of a series of ingenious experimental techniques. This approach originated in the work of Mayer (31) and Schmidt (32), who were interested in the difference between work done by school children in the class-room situation and when they were alone in their own homes; the procedure was crude, but it suggested the presence in the former situation of a "social increment" which has been made the basis of many further studies. The most important of the early investigations in this field is that by Moede (33), who showed the effect of the group on the individual in a variety of situations. He found in the first place that in an experiment involving the ability to bear pain, the boys who were his subjects always accepted a great deal more pain without complaining when they were in the presence of others. This was all the more marked when two boys who were rivals were tested together. This result is not so difficult to understand since the pain sensation is to a considerable degree subjective; as we know from the phenomena of hypnotic anesthesia as well as from the reputed ability of certain groups like the Plains Indians to bear pain without complaining, the majority of us can probably stand a great deal more pain than we willingly accept under normal conditions. A second experiment of Moede's raises a more interesting problem. His subjects pressed upon a dynamometer, which measures the strength of grip in the hand, presumably as hard as they possibly could. This "maximum" was, however, exceeded in the group situation, the improvement being most marked again when rivalry was introduced. We have here apparently some form of dynamogenesis, or the liberation of additional energy, as a result of the changed conditions. This effect is probably analogous to that which occurs in conditions of emotional excitement, in which certain physiological changes occur which enable the organism to put forward more energy than under normal circumstances.

Other experiments by Moede included the use of cancellation tests in the individual and in the group situation, the results indicating that work in the presence of others tended on the whole to be quicker but less accurate than when it was done individually;

the benefit of the group situation appeared to be greater for the poorer subjects whose work was stimulated as a consequence, whereas the efficiency of the best workers was lowered.

One of the most significant experiments in this whole field was conducted by F. H. Allport (12). In a series of simple motor tasks there was noted a social increment of the type reported by Moede, most marked in the case of the slowest subjects. In judgments of an esthetic nature, in connection with the pleasantness and unpleasantness of odors, there was the important finding that there were more extreme judgments in the individual situation, and that the presence of others tended to bring the extremes somewhat closer together. We have here therefore an experimental indication of the process of conformity resulting from the group situation. In another part of the experiment Allport had his subjects produce as many word associations as possible within a given period of time, and found a definite facilitation under group conditions. Finally, the subjects were asked to write arguments for and against excerpts from Marcus Aurelius which were presented to them for discussion, and Allport states that whereas more arguments were produced in the group than in the individual situation, they were on the average not of such good quality. In other words, there appears to be a social increment for quantity, but a social decrement for quality of production in this complicated intellectual activity. This final result has undoubted practical significance, since it points to the necessity of varying the nature of the conditions, whether group or individual, depending upon the kind of work which is being performed.

In most of the experiments of Moede and Allport the effect of the group situation may be twofold, that is to say, there may be a direct social facilitation and there may also be the factor of competition. If, for example, there is an increase in speed in a cancellation test when others are present, it is not clear whether this is due to seeing others work, or to the fact that one is competing with others, or to both. The attempt was made by Dashiell (34) to separate these two factors by having one experimental situation in which each individual worked separately but knew that he was competing with others, and another situation in which he worked with others but at slightly different tasks so that the competitive factor could not enter. There were in addition the usual "group" and "individual" conditions of the former experiments. The results showed that the competitive effect alone was greater than the social or ideo-motor effect. In other words, working by oneself becomes a special situation when it is known that others are competing at the same time. It would seem that much of Allport's "social facilitation" effect is really due to the facilitating factor of competition.

A somewhat different variety of social facilitation is found in an investigation by Pepitone (35), who set up experimental groups in which two kinds of work were performed with varying degrees of importance attached to each. The output was studied under three conditions, with the task to be performed described to the subjects as having high, medium and low importance, respectively. The results showed that those who perceived their task as having high importance did more work and made fewer errors. This is interpreted as being due to different degrees of feeling of responsibility to the group as a whole. We shall return to the question of increased output under different social conditions in connection with the survey of group dynamics.

It should be clear from the discussion of motivation and particularly of the prestige drive in Chapter 5 that any generalization from these results to what might be expected in other cultures is quite impossible. In our own society the drive to excel others is so great and so intimately bound up with many aspects of our social and economic organization that it seems safe to assume its operation in any experimental situation of the type we have been reviewing. The careful analysis of competitive and cooperative habits in a number of different communities by Margaret Mead (36) and her associates reveals very wide variations between cultures in this respect. There is reason to believe that in certain American Indian communities we would be much more likely to obtain a social decrement in many situations of this kind; these same communities might, however, show social facilitation in the ability to bear pain, since this is an important value in the group and there is a tradition of competition in this respect. This means that we would have to revise our inferences as to the effect of social and competitive factors in other cultures from two points of view, first with reference to the amount of facilitation present, and second as related to the specific situations in which the facilitative effect might be expected to occur. There is need here for a series of experiments, the results of which would undoubtedly be of great interest in this whole field, particularly if they could be carried out in a number of widely different communities. It is probable that the Zuñi at the one extreme and a Melanesian tribe like the Mundugumor at the other, would make particularly interesting subjects for these experiments. Failing these, it would still be worth while to repeat them upon any other non-Western groups available.

Even within our own culture such differences can be demonstrated under certain conditions. Travis (37) repeated a portion of Allport's study of social facilitation, but used as his subjects American college students who stuttered. The task was to write down successive words as rapidly as they came to mind. This was done individually, and also in groups of five persons. Allport had found that fourteen out of fifteen of his subjects produced more associations in the group situation; in the case of the stutterers, eight out of ten produced more when they were alone. The group operated to cause a "social decrement" in the case of subjects for whom the social situation represented a traumatic experience. Mintz (38) was also able to demonstrate that competition between individuals could be disruptive and produce inferior results, when the situation required cooperation in finding a solution to the problem.

CONFORMITY

Allport found, as one of the consequences of the group situation, a tendency to conform; Sherif's experiments on social norms point in the same direction. Many additional examples could be given of the pressure to conformity which a group exerts on its members. Newcomb (39), for example, found marked changes in the direction of more liberal economic and political attitudes on the part of many students during their four years at Bennington College; he interprets the changes as due in most cases to just such pressures. Patrick and Sims (40) demonstrated that northern students who attended southern universities tended with time to approximate the attitude toward Negroes characteristic of southern students. Roethlisberger and Dickson (41) showed how a group of workers in a factory set up standards for output, and even those among them who could work much faster adapted their rate to the group standard. The gangs described by Thrasher (42) and Whyte (7) insisted on conformity to their rules of behavior, and imposed severe sanctions on those who dared to deviate.

The observed variations in degrees of conformity have been explained in a number of different ways. Cartwright and Zander (43)

suggest that in the face-to-face group the major factors responsible
may be personality characteristics, group pressures exerted differentially, the liked person, for example, receiving more of such pressures
than the one who is not liked; differential perception of the amount
of pressure, some members being more aware of it than others;
greater attraction of the group to some members than to others.

As for the wider culture, few persons really refuse to conform;
when they do rebel, it is only against a tiny part of the total complex. Herskovits (44) makes this point clear: "The political revolutionary does not refuse to cast his revolutionary songs in the modal
structure and scale progressions of the culture he is in process of
changing; his formations, if his organized forces are strong enough,
will operate in terms of accepted patterns of military procedure. The
one who rebels against the religious and moral system of his time
will couch his appeals in the linguistic patterns of his people, use
established affect symbols, and employ accepted esthetic standards
in heightening the responses of his followers" (p. 153). Even non-
conformists conform most of the time. The important question arises
as to why the individual is almost always willing to accept uncritically the customary behavior of his community. There are of
course dissenters, but they are on the whole rare. The sociologist
Bagehot (45) speaks of the "cake of custom" in this connection,
and seems to regard it as literally difficult, if not impossible, for the
individual to break through. There are probably four main reasons
for this customary conformity. There is first the phenomenon of
prestige suggestion to which we have already referred, and which
in this case is associated with the fact that the group has power and
importance, and ideas coming from it will therefore tend to be
accepted. There is in the second place the fact that the individual
often knows no other customs than those of his own community;
this is of course true only of relatively small isolated groups, but
among them it is highly probable that they act as they do because
they are unfamiliar with any alternative. A third important factor is
that the individual who does not practice the customary behavior
related to the social and economic life of the group will soon be
regarded as outside the system of reciprocal rights and duties upon
which life in the community may depend; if there is a system of
gift exchange, for example, and he fails to return an equivalent
value, he will simply not be included in the next round of gifts, and
will not be able to obtain what he wishes in exchange. Finally, and

allied to this last, there may be punishment for transgression. This punishment may be violent and coercive in nature, but much more frequently in small communities it takes the form of ridicule. These four factors together make it possible to understand why individuals conform, without the necessity of assuming that custom in itself has power and authority.

F. H. Allport (46) has indicated some of the special features of conformity behavior. The reactions of individuals to the social institutions of their community show a different distribution from that characteristic of most psychological phenomena. Instead of fitting into the pattern of the normal probability curve, with the frequencies gradually tapering off in either direction from the mode or other measure of central tendency, conformity behavior tends to take the form of the J-curve. This means that there is an asymmetrical piling up of most cases at one end—the conformity end—of the distribution, with a small number of cases showing the opposite type of behavior. Most individuals conform more or less closely, and there are only a few deviants. Allport's examples include the reactions of automobile drivers to a red light, the time of arrival of employees at their work, and the performance of ritualistic acts upon entering a place of worship. It is still uncertain whether this finding holds for all social institutions, but it is important to realize that at least in some cases the customary "normal distribution" does not operate.

SOCIOMETRY

An important approach to the study of the structure of groups and of some of the interrelationships of their members is represented by sociometry, which stresses the significance of *choice* in human behavior. Its principal technique, the sociometric test, has been defined by its originator, Moreno (47), as "an instrument to measure the amount of organization shown by social groups" (p. 432). As applied to a classroom, for example, the method consists in finding out from each child which members of the class he would like to have sit near him. The experimenter is enabled to draw a chart or *sociogram* which indicates the positive and negative attitudes of these children to one another. Such sociograms usually indicate that there are certain key individuals, or leaders, who have a positive attraction for a great many others in the class; others who are "isolates," not wanted by anyone; and others in between. This method makes it possible to rearrange the seating so that most children have neighbors whom they like, instead of being placed in a haphazard manner. The technique may be used not only in a classroom, but also in helping to create any harmonious community. One of the interesting results is that a person who is an isolate, and therefore very unhappy in one group, may find himself fairly well liked in another, and his whole behavior will undergo a consequent change for the better. In the placement of girls in the cottages of the New York State Training School for Girls, excellent results were obtained by this method in reducing the possibilities of friction and increasing the cohesiveness and compatibility of the groups. The technique has been used to study the development of sex cleavage, which starts about the fourth grade (age nine) and extends to the eighth grade (about age thirteen), thus providing some experimental verification for Freud's latency theory. It has also been applied to a study of cleavage in a classroom between White and Negro pupils, and Criswell (48) was able to show statistically how early such cleavage develops, and to describe some of the factors related to the phenomenon. The technique, because of its simplicity and naturalness, is well adapted to comparisons of ethnic cleavages in different communities, or in the same community at different times.

An interesting application of the method was made by Jenkins (49) in his study of the morale of two flying squadrons during World War II. The men were asked whom they would like to have with them, and whom they would reject as flying partners. The choices in one (low morale) squadron showed that the group was made up of two separate cliques; the officers were almost never chosen; many choices were made of men outside the squadron, and there were many rejections of men within it. In the other (high morale) group, there was no cleavage, the officers were chosen frequently, and most of the dislikes were directed against individuals outside the squadron. Jennings (50) has made use of this technique in an important study of leadership, which will be discussed later.

Another aspect of sociometry which has attracted considerable attention is the *psychodrama,* used by Moreno as a therapeutic technique. The subjects (or patients) take part in a dramatic play in which they express various emotional attitudes, or act out their own problems and conflicts. This may serve as a form of abreaction or catharsis, and it may also give the therapist information about the degree to which particular situations or emotions affect the reactions of the individual. The technique of *role playing* has aroused particular interest. Occasionally in a conflict situation, roles may be reversed, with each protagonist taking on the role of the other; this may give much-needed insight into the position of one's opponents, and serve as a valuable device for changing attitudes, and bringing conflicts closer to solution. Lippitt (51) has made good use of this technique in connection with relations between Negroes and Whites, and it has been incorporated into the field known as Group Dynamics.

GROUP DYNAMICS

It is not easy to define or delimit the important area of group dynamics. From one point of view it represents a field of inquiry, a series of interrelated problems; from another, it includes a set of techniques; from a third, a theory of the nature of groups and of interaction within groups. The Research Center for Group Dynamics was founded in 1945 at the Massachusetts Institute of Technology, and moved to the University of Michigan in 1948. Its founder, Kurt Lewin, who gave the center its name, was convinced, in the words of Cartwright (52) "that laws of group behavior could be established independently of the purposes or the specific activities of the group. Thus it would be possible to study a group's productivity as a phenomenon whether it be in the committee room, factory, or classroom. Further, one would be able to specify the determinants of friendship or hostility between groups whether they be formed on the basis of race, religion, sex, or nationality. Common problems of group operation or leadership in boys' clubs, work teams, hospital staffs or families which produce frustration or growth of the group, would also be revealed" (p. 6).

Although a good deal of the research in this field takes its impetus and its inspiration from the work of Lewin, studies of the same and related problems, with the use of similar or related techniques, are now going on in many different laboratories, which have arisen independently. Many of them are represented in the collection of studies in group dynamics edited by Cartwright and Zander (43). The theories of Gestalt psychology, the earlier investigations of social facilitation, the approach of sociometry, the work in industrial psychology and sociology, in communications research, in the analysis of the nature and modification of attitudes, etc., all have played a part in giving shape and substance to this broad field. In what follows we shall limit ourselves to identifying certain key areas of research, and describing a few of the many investigations related to group dynamics in its wider sense.

Group Decision. In a series of important studies Lewin and his associates (43) compared the effects of group decision and lectures or individual instruction in changing food habits. In a first experiment the objective was to increase the use of beef hearts, sweetbreads and kidneys. The subjects included three groups of housewives, thirteen to seventeen in each group, who were given 45-minute lectures which emphasized the vitamin content and mineral value of these meats, the techniques by which they could most appetizingly be prepared for the table, etc.; a follow-up showed that three percent of the women in these groups later served one of these meats in their own homes. Another three groups of similar size spent the time in a group discussion of the problems faced by "housewives like themselves," with the nutrition expert answering questions as they arose instead of presenting the material in lecture form. Thirty two percent of these women later made use of one of the meats discussed. Group discussion and decision evidently resulted in a much greater degree of ego-involvement, with a more marked effect on behavior as a consequence. In a second investigation, involving the increase of home consumption of milk, group decision again resulted in a much greater change than did a lecture, and the increased consumption persisted during a four-week follow-up period. In a third study, group decision was compared with individual instruction of farm mothers regarding the use of orange juice and cod-liver oil in the care of their children; the group decision method proved far superior, and again the superiority persisted over a four-week period.

Group Productivity. The processes of group decision and the consequent ego-involvement enter directly into a series of investigations concerned with the problem of modifying methods of work with the objective of increasing productivity. The study by Coch and French (53) may be cited as representative. It was conducted in the plant of the Harwood Manufacturing Corporation, which produces pajamas, employing mostly women, who work on an individual incentive system. When it becomes necessary in this plant to change an operator from one kind of work to another, a bonus is given, but in spite of this there is considerable resistance to such change, which is usually accompanied by a drop in output. The investigators were interested in discovering the most appropriate methods for overcoming this resistance to change. The experiment involved different degrees of participation by the employees in planning the changes. In the control group, there was no such participation, although an explanation was given. In a second group there was participation through a few chosen representatives of the workers in designing the required changes. Finally, in the third the procedure was followed in which there was total participation by all members of the group. Though the changes were actually of a minor character, the control group (no participation) showed marked resistance, expressions of hostility, lack of cooperation, and a consistently low production rate. The representation group performed much better, and showed definite improvement after an initial drop. The total participation group recovered faster than the others, and soon reached a level about fourteen percent higher than that before the change was introduced. The investigators conclude: "It is possible for management to modify greatly or to remove completely group resistance to changes in methods of work. . . . This change can be accomplished by the use of group meetings in which management effectively communicates the need for change and stimulates group participation in planning the changes" (p. 279). We may add that the more "democratic" the procedures, the less resistance there is to change, and the greater the productivity. A number of other studies point in the same direction. [See for example Roethlisberger and Dickson (41), Jacques (54).] The practical as well as the theoretical importance of these findings is clear, and has been accepted in many industrial establishments.

Group Interaction. In the phenomena included under the general heading of group dynamics, the manner in which the face-to-face group is structured, and the processes by which individuals interact with one another, have received considerable attention. The sociometrists have been particularly alert to these aspects of group behavior. Another significant approach in this area is represented by Bales (55), who has developed specific techniques for the observation and recording of what he calls "interaction process analysis." He defines a small group as "any number of persons engaged in interaction with one another in a single face-to-face meeting or a series of such meetings, in which each member receives some impression or perception of each other member distinct enough so that he can, either at the time or in later questioning, give some reaction to each of the others as an individual person, even though it be only to recall that the other was present" (p. 30).

In keeping records of the process of interaction according to the technique devised by Bales, the observer classifies the behavior of individuals within the group according to twelve different categories, ranging from "(1) *shows solidarity,* raises others' status, gives help, reward;" and "(2) *shows tension release,* jokes, laughs, shows satisfaction" to "(11) *shows tension,* asks for help, withdraws out of field" and "(12) *shows antagonism,* deflates others' status, defends or asserts self." Records are also kept of the amount of participation by different individuals. Groups may then be compared in terms of the kinds of interaction which occurred, the degree to which the attitudes of individuals were positive and friendly or negative and hostile, the consistency of interaction patterns from day to day, the relative participation of different individuals, etc. The method makes possible the study of different groups, or of the same group at different times, with a degree of objectivity and quantification which takes such judgments out of the class of purely subjective impressions. Other techniques for this purpose have been developed by Chapple and Arensberg (56).

An approach to group interaction in terms of the functional roles of group members has been suggested by Benne and Sheats (57) as a result of their work with the First National Training Laboratory in Group Development. Three categories of group roles are described: The first includes those related to the group task, that is, those participants who facilitate or coordinate the group effort; examples are the *initiator-contributor,* who suggests new ideas or new procedures and solutions; the *information seeker,* who asks for clarification or additional facts, etc. A second category of roles includes those pertaining to group building or maintenance, and to the functioning of the group as a group; here there are the *encourager,* the *harmonizer,* the *follower,* etc. In the third category are the roles directed toward the satisfaction of the individual needs of the participants; there may be an *aggressor,* a *recognition-seeker,* a *playboy,* etc. The application of this technique of analysis may help in the understanding of why some groups fail to find a solution to their problems and others succeed; it may also prepare the way for training members to take more constructive roles as a consequence of insight into the manner in which they have been reacting.

Group Locomotion. Here we are concerned with the question as to where the group succeeds in going and the extent to which it makes progress in reaching its goal. Considerable research has been devoted to determining the factors which lead to success or failure, respectively, of group discussions and conferences. This issue is implicit in a number of aspects of group dynamics to which reference has already been made. A more direct approach is represented in the study by Fouriezos, Hutt and Guetzkow (58), who analyzed no less than 72 actual decision-making conferences in governmental and industrial organizations. In one portion of this extensive study the investigators were concerned with the effect of self-oriented needs, classified under the heads of dependency, status, dominance, aggression, and catharsis (defined as the need for personal unburdening). Each conference was rated on an over-all scale which indicated the extent to which such needs predominated in the discussion. It was found that those groups which ranked high on self-orientated needs were on the whole least satisfied with the meetings in general, with the decisions reached and the manner in which they had been reached, with the conduct of the meeting by the chairman; they tended to get less work done; they showed more group conflict. This study is an interesting example of an attempt to put some order into a complex and relatively inaccessible area of investigation. In view of the part played by conferences in determining important issues at the local, national and even international levels, it is to be hoped that further information regarding the improvement of conference procedures will soon be forthcoming. (See Chapter 20.)

Group Cohesiveness. A significant characteristic of a group is the degree to which the members feel identified with it, work with others toward a common goal, are loyal to their fellow members, and are willing to defend them and the group against outside attack. It is this last aspect which particularly impressed sociologists like Sumner, who spoke of the in-group in this same connection. A cohesive group is one to which the individual members feel they belong; we may speak of group-belongingness and of group-cohesiveness as reciprocals.

Festinger (59) has indicated some of the sources of attraction which individuals may feel toward a group. It may help to make possible the attainment of important individual goals; it may engage in activities which are attractive to its members; it may help to satisfy those individual needs which require personal relationship to other people. A person may be expected to move—if he can —into groups which satisfy his particular needs, and to move out of them when they no longer do so. Sometimes, however, involuntary and even accidental factors play an important part. Festinger, Schachter and Back (60), for instance, found that in a housing project occupied by married veterans who were students at a university, the friendships which were formed were a direct function of (a) sheer distance between houses and (b) the direction in which a house faced. As the distance between houses increased, the number of friendships fell off rapidly. The investigators also noted that those units in which a great many friendships had developed tended to have uniform attitudes on a number of problems which arose in the housing project. It is striking that such marked effects can be produced by topography alone.

Group Communication. Festinger (43) and his colleagues have also conducted a series of investigations into the manner in which informal communication occurs within groups, and have suggested several hypotheses. Communication may result from pressures toward uniformity in a group, in which case there will be more communication regarding a particular item in connection with which there is greater discrepancy of opinion, and also when such an item has greater relevance to the functioning of the group. The more cohesive the group, the greater the pressure on members to communicate. There will be less urge to communicate to a particular person if he is not wanted as a member of the group. These and other hypotheses help to explain some of the findings by Festinger and Cartwright (61) in their study of the spread of a rumor within a community.

This sampling of studies and theoretical approaches should give some idea of the variety, range and vitality of the field of group dynamics. As has already been indicated, many of the problems involved enter into areas of investigation and practice which have different labels and another orientation, but which also are concerned with an understanding of what goes on in the face-to-face group. Such an understanding is of the greatest importance for those psychiatrists and psychologists who are engaged in group therapy, for the important subdivision of social work known as

Group Work, and for educators who are concerned with improving the methods and techniques of adult education. When one looks at these various approaches, one is struck by the frequency with which the same processes are studied under different names or in a different theoretical framework. An important contribution to inter-professional clarification and collaboration in this area has been made through the publication of one number of the *Journal of Social Issues*, edited by Lerner and Kelman (62), in which the similarities and differences in these various approaches are analyzed in some detail.

There remains at least one important problem in connection with group activity, namely, that of the characteristics and the role of the leader, and the nature of leadership.

LEADERS AND LEADERSHIP

The story is told of an uprising in Paris in 1848 during which the police had made a number of arrests. One of those who had been halted cried out, "Let me go. I must follow that crowd over there. I am their leader." In spite of the anecdotal nature of this incident, and the time at which it is alleged to have occurred, it may be taken as symbolic of the present attitude of social psychologists to the phenomenon of leadership. The emphasis has shifted from the attempt to discover the characteristics of *the* leader, to an understanding of the leader-follower relationship.

A major reason for this shift in emphasis is to be found in the failure of investigators to agree on the characteristics of leaders. A survey by Bird (63) in 1940 found a total of 79 different traits attributed to leaders in twenty studies of high-school and college groups. The agreement was very small, only 28 of these traits appearing in more than a single list. Gouldner (64) in a recent review of the relevant literature also concludes that the attempts to discover the traits associated with leadership in general have so far resulted in failure. As Jennings (50) expresses it on the basis of her own investigation of leadership among adolescent girls: "It is necessary to ask, leadership in what respect? For whom? In what sort of group?"

This does not mean that there is no relationship whatsoever between leadership in one situation and another, or in one group and another. Carter and Nixon (65) report a correlation of +.64 between

leadership in an intellectual task and in a clerical task. There was
on the other hand very little relationship between leadership in a
series of such tasks, and leadership as measured by election to office
in clubs and recreation groups. In the OSS study (66), leadership
was estimated in a series of specific situations, and also through
interviews and ratings by associates; the intercorrelations of the
various measures were fairly high and all positive, ranging from
+.24 to +.79. There was some generality, therefore, in the trait of
leadership, at least within the situations included in this particular
study. (It should be added that there was only a very low correlation, +.11, between the leadership grades assigned during the assessment sessions and the subsequent appraisal of performance in
real-life situations.) On the basis of all the available evidence, therefore, some individuals appear to emerge as leaders in a number of
different situations, others rarely or never do so, and still others—
probably the majority—play the role of leader only on certain occasions and in certain groups.

The role of leadership in group phenomena is demonstrated in
the important investigation by Lewin, Lippitt and White (5), who
were interested in the different patterns of behavior which were
found in various experimentally created "social climates." These
climates differed in the nature of the leadership provided, and
were of three main types: authoritarian, democratic and laissez-
faire. Clubs were formed of boys who, to begin with, were carefully equated, and who were then placed in one of the three experimental groups. In the authoritarian group, for example, all
policies were determined by the leader, techniques and activities
being indicated by him one at a time so that future steps were
always uncertain, and the "dictator" remained aloof from active
group participation except when demonstrating to the others what
they were to do. In the democratic group all policies were determined by group discussion, the members were free to work with
whomever they chose, and the division of tasks was determined by
the group. In the third situation there was complete freedom for
group or individual decision, and the leader supplied the information, but took no other part in group discussions. The factor
of personality differences in the boys was controlled by having each
group pass through autocracy and then democracy, or vice versa.
The factor of the leader's personality was controlled by having each

of four leaders play the role of autocrat and the role of democratic leader at least once.

In one experiment, hostility was thirty times as frequent in the autocratic as in the democratic group. Much of the aggression was directed toward two successive scapegoats within the group; none was directed against the autocrat. In a second experiment, the boys in the autocratic groups showed less aggressiveness, but their behavior was of an apathetic type. This lack of aggression is interpreted as due to the repressive influence of the autocrat. Among the boys in these groups there were outbursts of aggression on the days of transition to a freer atmosphere, and a sharp rise of aggression when the autocrat left the room. Nineteen out of twenty boys liked their democratic leader better than their autocratic leader, and seven out of ten also preferred their laissez-faire leader.

This study is of special interest, because it submits to experimentally controlled procedures some of the hypotheses which have been suggested as to the effects of various kinds of leadership and political organization on the behavior of the individual. Students of politics, for example, have observed that fascist dictatorships are frequently characterized by the appearance of a scapegoat upon whom all ills may be blamed. This study has revealed that even in an artificial dictatorship of this type such a scapegoat mechanism may easily be elicited. Although value judgments are not usually regarded as within the province of a social psychologist, the apparent superiority of the democratic over the autocratic form of society may be mentioned as one of the important findings of this study.

Genius. The search for characteristic qualities of outstanding individuals has been conducted with special attention directed toward that variety of leadership to which the term *genius* has been given. This term was first used in the religions of ancient Italy to refer to the god-like personification of the procreative power in general and was considered responsible in particular for any activity of a rare and extraordinary character. It has been defined as "the highest conceivable form of original ability, something altogether extraordinary and beyond even supreme educational prowess, and differing, in kind apparently, from 'talent,' which is usually distinguishable as marked intellectual capacity short only of the inexplicable and unique endowment to which the term 'genius' is confined" (67). We can distinguish two entirely different trends of opinion in connection with the nature of genius. The first regards the genius as differing only quantitatively from the normal or average person; the second insists upon a fundamental difference in kind. Of the first view Francis Galton (68) is perhaps the most outstanding exponent. His discussion of "Hereditary Genius" makes use of a strictly statistical criterion. The tremendous differences in human abilities represented by the idiot and the great man are to be regarded as deviations from the average ability. The genius represents one extreme of the normal probability curve. In this sense Galton defines an "eminent" man as one who has achieved a position attained by only 250 persons in each million of men, or by one person in each four thousand; an "illustrious" man is literally one in a million.

Terman (69) has adopted a similar viewpoint. He defines genius as meaning the very exceptional, superior grades of ability, whether the ability in question be general or special. Talent refers to a superior grade of ability, exceptional, but less so than the grade constituting genius. The difference from the average is quantitative, not qualitative. "The genius and the moron are explained by the same psychological laws. Neither has any trait which the other, also, does not in some degree possess" (p. 406). In this sense the word "genius" has been applied to children with very high scores on intelligence tests, an I.Q. of 140 or more usually being regarded as the dividing line. In connection with the *Genetic Studies of Genius* by Terman and his collaborators (70), this criterion has been used in order to select those children in whom the characteristics of "genius" may be studied. In the follow-up studies which Terman and his collaborators (71) have conducted on these children in later life, there is clear evidence of their superiority to the average of the general population, but little indication that as a group they should be included under the category of genius. At the other extreme, the opinion is held that genius is qualitatively different from normality. This opinion is usually associated with the name of Lombroso (72), who carried further than anyone else the notion of the essential identity of genius and insanity. As Hirsch (73) has shown, Lombroso's theory was not new. Aristotle observed that many persons become poets, prophets and sibyls, and are fairly good poets while they are maniacal, but when cured can no longer write verse. Lamartine referred to "la maladie mentale qu'on appelle génie." Dryden wrote, "Great wits are sure to madness near allied." The immediate stimulus to Lombroso's theory came from the work of Moreau de Tours, who in his *Psychologie Morbide* in 1859 stated that all genius is a neurosis and often a psychosis. It was this thesis which was expanded by Lombroso and supported by much biographical material tending to show the frequency with which men of genius suffer from insanity. His theory received wide attention, and most of the succeeding books on the psychology of men of genius find their starting point in a discussion of his thesis.

Among the later books in this field, one of the most interesting is that of Lange-Eichbaum (74), who brings modified support to Lombroso's theory. Geniuses may be healthy, and he mentions Titian, Raphael, Andrea del Sarto, Rubens, Leibnitz and a few others. These are a small minority. Among the very great geniuses more than 30 percent were psychotic at some time during their lifetime; more than 83 percent were, if not psychotic, at least markedly psychopathic, that is to say, they had a mental disorder less severe than a definite psychosis. About 10 percent of the remainder were slightly psychopathic, and only about 6.5 percent were healthy. Among those with genuine psychoses, Baudelaire and Donizetti had general paralysis of the insane, Tasso and Newton had schizophrenia, and so on. In general, however, it is not psychosis but psychopathy which is found most frequently among men of genius.

According to this theory, psychopathy tends toward genius for three main reasons. In the first place, it increases the strength of the emotional life and with it the responsiveness to minute stimuli; this, plus the lack of self-control, may result in experiences which average people do not have. In the second place, psychopaths may undergo great suffering and pain and a consequent feeling of inferiority which leads them to attempt some adjustment. This is accompanied finally by a tendency to dream and a rich fantasy life in which the creations of the genius find expression.

Kretschmer (75) holds similarly that mental diseases, especially psychopathic borderline cases, are definitely more common among men of genius than among ordinary men. People who are unadapted to their environment and who feel uncomfortable in it are more likely to do important things because they find their environment unbearable. There must of course be ability, but in genius there must also be the "daimonion," which has principally a psychopathic origin. "If we take the psychopathic factor, the ferment of demonic unrest and psychic tension away from the constitution of the genius, nothing but an ordinary gifted man would remain" (p. 28). Kretschmer goes on to apply his constitutional typology to men of genius, pointing to the qualitative differences in the achieve-ment of pyknics and leptosomes. Among poets, for example, the cyclothyme pyknic will write narrative epic poems and the schizo-thyme leptosome will write subjective lyrics.

The psychoanalysts have attempted to carry further this notion of unrest or psychic tension in the genius. Freud (76), for example, writes: "Happy people never make fantasies, only unsatisfied ones. Unsatisfied wishes are the driving power behind fantasies; every separate fantasy contains a fulfillment of a wish and improves an unsatisfactory reality" (p. 176). Similarly Healy (77) states that "many of the world's great achievements have come from those who were by no means happy about their own personality characteristics and responses—perhaps because in them burned the flame of divine discontent" (p. 138). Freud admits, however, that the fantasies may be transformed into artistic creations only if the individual who is displeased with reality is in possession of that artistic talent which is still a psychological riddle. While this general position of the Freudians seems essentially reasonable, the specific attempts made by psychoanalysts to explain the activity of individual geniuses seem in many cases far-fetched to the extreme. Jekels (78), for example, finds in the Oedipus complex a satisfactory explanation of the aims of Napoleon. "That astounding ambition that causes one half of the world to heap his memory with execrations and the other half to surround it with expressions of admiration," is explained as due to his wish to be in full possession of his mother—Mother Earth. Simi-larly, in an article "On Dante's Unconscious Soul Life" by Sperber (79), it is argued that Dante clung to authority in the form of the Church because of his love and reverence for his parents; his mild and non-interfering father aroused no revolt in him, and Dante had therefore no impulse to emancipate himself.

The Freudian emphasis on the unconscious has also been directed toward an explanation of the products of genius, at least in certain fields. There have been many instances in which literature of the greatest value has been produced in a state resembling that of the trance; Coleridge's "Kubla Khan" is an outstanding example. Many writers certainly have the impression that their work is produced to some degree without conscious volition on their part. Henry James speaks of dropping an idea for a time "into the deep well of uncon-scious cerebration; not without the hope, doubtless, that it might eventually emerge from that reservoir . . . with a firm iridescent surface and a notable increase of weight" (80, p. 327). Nietzsche wrote, "If one had the least vestige of superstition, one could hardly refrain from supposing himself to be merely the incarnation, merely the mouthpiece, merely the medium of higher forces. . . . One hears, one does not search; one receives, one does not ask who gives; like lightning an idea flashes out, appearing as something necessary" (80, p. 329). The frequent accounts of literary production in the form of "automatic writing," the precise content of which is unknown to the writer until it has been completed, also testify to the importance of unconscious factors. This of course does not mean that creation is entirely unconscious; we know, for example, that even those of Tennyson's lyrics with the greatest air of spontaneity were worked over and polished before their publication. It is probable that the relative roles of conscious and unconscious factors vary in different individuals and with different kinds of creation.

An interesting attempt to apply psychoanalytic principles to the interpretation of one particular type of creation has been made by Herzberg (81) in his *The Psychology of Philosophers*. After an examination of the biographical details in the life of the most important philosophers, Herzberg finds certain characteristics which he regards as typical. The philosophers were for the most part unadapted to their environment, found it difficult to earn a living, rarely made a satisfactory marital adjustment, and were in general dissatisfied with the reality in which they lived. As a consequence they found greater satisfaction in the constructs of their philosophical systems than in the world around them. Their philosophy may in the majority of instances be regarded as an escape. The "idealistic" philosophers went much further in this respect, since they denied the existence of the real or phenomenal world, insisting that the only reality was that of ideas. In this way they achieved the comforting conviction that the world in which they were unsuccessful was really non-existent. This theory leaves unexplained the philosophic activity of men like Bacon and others who were also successful men of affairs.

The Adlerians regard significant achievements to be in many cases the product of over-compensation for organ inferiority. We have already referred to the classical example of Demosthenes, who stuttered as a child and became one of the greatest orators the world has ever known. Wexberg (82) suggests that Beethoven's important works were composed after he became hard of hearing and that even in early life he probably had hearing difficulties. "We may be certain that Beethoven focused his interest on auditory experiences from his earliest days, and that he began a process of intense training culminating in his remarkable success as a musician" (p. 119). Many other cases of such over-compensation have been cited; Theodore Roosevelt, for instance, was a sickly boy and developed in the direction of a "he-man." It is known that Glenn Cunningham, one of the greatest mile-runners of all time, suffered an accident in early life which left his legs in bad condition. He took to running to overcome this defect and achieved outstanding success.

Wexberg insists that there is absolutely no hereditary basis for genius. "It has been the experience of individual psychology that attainment is not the result of inherited talent, but a product of courage and training" (p. 142). Genius is not the product of the superman, but results from industry and drive of a compensatory nature. "The so-called 'genius' cannot be damaged by knowing that others can accomplish what he has done under certain circumstances" (p. 151). Differences in native ability do not exist; there are only differences in what one does with one's ability.

This is certainly an extreme position, and one which would be accepted by few psychologists. It leaves unexplained the large majority of cases of outstanding achievement. For one great musician who was deaf, there are easily a hundred with no known impairment of hearing; for one orator who stuttered in his childhood, there are many who never had any perceptible speech defect. On the other hand, hosts of people have poor hearing without developing into Beethovens, and few stuttering children later become famous orators. There must be some other factor differentiating the genius from the average individual. Exactly what this factor may be is in Freud's words "a psychological riddle," but it is apparently an ability which is in part inborn, and not to be explained entirely in terms of early training and experience or organ inferiority.

Leadership, whether of a boys' club, a new movement in art, or of a nation, has a common denominator; it requires followers. This is an apparently self-evident and even tautological statement, but it expresses the need to keep constantly in mind the interdependence of the leader and those whom he leads. Hitler's motivation may perhaps be explained, as Bychowski (83) has done, by describing the

Oedipal reactions involved, but we cannot explain Hitler's success in winning support without taking into account the hopes and aspirations, the frustrations, as well as the habitual modes of response, of the German people. [In this connection, see Fromm (84) and Gilbert (85).] No one can deny the importance of Hitler, but he would not have been important if no one had accepted him as leader. Leadership is perhaps in part a quality, but it is also a role and a relationship. (See also Chapter 20.)

REFERENCE GROUPS

We have suggested that most members of a group, including the leader, tend to follow their group, to conform to its rules and regulations. The results of experimental research as well as of common experience support this conclusion. Less obvious, but no less important, is the fact that we often pattern our behavior and our attitudes in terms of standards laid down not by the group to which we belong, but by a group which serves as our frame of reference. Such reference groups may be our membership groups as well, but not necessarily; they may be groups to which we aspire, or groups which we use as a reference point in making evaluations of ourselves or others. Kelley (86), who makes this distinction, speaks in the first case of the *normative function,* and in the second of the *comparison function* of reference groups.

Many examples of this phenomenon could be given. Hyman (87), who first used the term reference group in this connection, showed how an individual's judgment of his own status varies according to the group which he uses as a basis for comparison. In Newcomb's Bennington study (39) changes in attitude frequently occurred in response to the desire of the students to be accepted by the college community; they moved in the direction which they thought would bring them closer to the general norm. Merton and Kitt (88) find reference group theory useful in explaining some of the results in the study titled *The American Soldier* (89). Fresh replacement troops, for example, gradually took over the value-systems of combat veterans with whom they were associated, even to the extent of applying to themselves the rather unflattering estimate of their leadership capacity which was held by the veterans.

Reference groups may even be *imaginary.* When we behave in a manner which we regard as typical of the "best people " we may be entirely mistaken as to the manner in which those to whom we refer really act. When we, in a foreign country, "do as the Romans do," our national stereotypes may be sufficiently false and misleading to keep our behavior from approximating that of most "Romans." In matters as important as our moral standards, or as trivial as the manner in which we hold our tea-cups, we may be influenced by reference groups which are nonexistent, or at least which do not possess the standards which we attribute to them.

Reference groups may also be *negative*. There are groups which we may wish to approach more closely, and others from which we may wish to be as far removed as possible. In the latter case, knowing that such a group supports a particular policy, or accepts a certain value, may cause us to move in the opposite direction. At the present moment in our history, it seems clear that for most Americans the Soviet Union represents a negative reference group, and vice versa. This has the obvious danger of leading to judgments which may be divorced from reality; one side is automatically for what the other is against, irrespective of the merits of the case. It may be well to remind ourselves occasionally that two and two remain four even if all the Communists in the world are of the same opinion, and that peace is a value even if advocated by the Soviet leaders.

Reference group theory has acquired an important place in social psychology, and represents a useful conceptual tool for the understanding of certain important aspects of human relations. [See Newcomb (90) and Sherif (4).]

SUMMARY

One of the core problems of social psychology is the understanding of interaction in the face-to-face group. Many different social phenomena have been investigated under this heading.

Imitation is not a force or an instinct, but occurs when the action or the person imitated has value for the subject. In some cases it is a form of conditioned response. It is closely related to suggestion, which consists essentially of the unreasoned acceptance of an idea presented to the subject from an outside source. Of the various types of suggestion, the most important for social psychology is "prestige suggestion," in which the relation to some other individual or group of individuals determines the response. The phenomenon of hypnosis belongs in this category, as does also the prestige effect of large numbers and of folk-beliefs and superstitions.

The crowd has been regarded by LeBon and others as an entity different from that of the individuals of which it is composed, and with a specific mentality. Although F. H. Allport correctly attacks this position, it remains true that the phenomenon of social interaction (the social field) does have a marked effect upon behavior.

The behavior of the individual conforms to custom for four main reasons: (1) the effect of prestige suggestion; (2) lack of knowledge of contrasting customs; (3) the practical need to participate in the social and economic exchanges of the community; (4) punishment for transgression. Even the leader or the genius must in a sense "follow" the group, though he is not without influence upon its future course.

Experimental studies of the effect of the group on the individual have demonstrated social facilitation in the ability to bear pain, in the output of energy and in speed of response in a variety of situations. These effects are evidently due more to the phenomenon of competition than to the mere presence of others. There is some evidence also that the group situation increases the amount of conformity among individuals, and produces a "social decrement" in the quality of intellectual activity. Comparative studies in other cultures are needed in order to check the universality of these phenomena.

The fields of sociometry and group dynamics have made important contributions to the understanding of group processes. Research in group dynamics has focussed on decision-making, productivity, interaction, locomotion, cohesiveness, and communication.

Reference groups, which may or may not coincide with membership groups, aid in the understanding of the behavior and attitudes of the individual.

REFERENCES

1. Cooley, C. H. *Social Organization.* 1909
2. Homans, G. C. *The Human Group.* 1950
3. Festinger, L. "Laboratory Experiments: The Role of Group Belongingness." In J. G. Miller (ed.), *Experiments in Social Process.* 1950
4. Sherif, M., and Sherif, C. W. *Groups in Harmony and Tension.* 1953
5. Lewin, K. A., Lippitt, R., and White, R. K. "Patterns of Aggressive

Behavior in Experimentally Created 'Social Climates,' " *J. Soc. Psychol.*, 1939, 10: pp. 271-299

6. Arensberg, C. H. "Behavior and Organization: Industrial Studies." In J. H. Rohrer and M. Sherif (eds.), *Social Psychology at the Crossroads*. 1951

7. Whyte, W. F. "Small Groups and Large Organizations." In Rohrer and Sherif (eds.), *Social Psychology at the Crossroads*. 1951. Also *Street Corner Society*. 1943

8. Leighton, A. H. *The Governing of Men*. 1945

9. Tarde, G. *Les lois de l'imitation*. 1890

10. Brown, J. F. *Psychology and the Social Order*. 1936

11. Freeman, E. *Social Psychology*. 1936

12. Allport, F. H. *Social Psychology*. 1924

13. Miller, N. E., and Dollard, J. *Social Learning and Imitation*. 1941

14. Asch, S. L. *Social Psychology*. 1952

15. Stern, W. *Psychology of Early Childhood*. 2d ed. 1930

16. Murphy, G., Murphy, L. B., and Newcomb, T. M. *Experimental Social Psychology*. Rev. ed. 1937

17. Binet, A. *La suggestibilité*. 1900

18. Aveling, F., and Hargreaves, H. L. "Suggestibility with and without Prestige in Children," *Brit. J. Psychol.*, 1921, 18: pp. 362-388

19. Hull, C. L. *Hypnosis and Suggestibility*. 1933

20. Rowland, L. W. "Will Hypnotized Persons Try to Harm Themselves or Others?" *J. Abn. and Soc. Psychol.*, 1939, 34: pp. 114-117

21. Moore, H. T. "The Comparative Influence of Majority and Expert Opinion," *Amer. J. Psychol.*, 1921, 32: pp. 16-20

22. Lewis, H. B. "An Approach to Attitude Measurement," *Psychol. League J.*, 1938, 2: pp. 64-67

23. Lorge, I. "Prestige, Suggestion and Attitudes," *J. Social Psychol.*, 1936, 7, pp. 386-402

24. LeBon, G. *The Crowd*. 1896

25. Scott, W. D. *The Psychology of Public Speaking*. 1907

26. Martin, E. D. *The Behavior of Crowds*. 1920

27. Meier, N. C., Mennenga, G. H., and Stoltz, H. J. "An Experimental Approach to the Study of Mob Behavior," *J. Abnorm. Soc. Psychol.*, 1941, 36: pp. 506-534

28. Lewin, K. A. *A Dynamic Theory of Personality*. 1935

29. Cantril, H., Gaudet, H., and Hertzog, H. *The Invasion from Mars*. 1940. See G. E. Swanson, T. M. Newcomb and E. L. Hartley (eds.), *Readings in Social Psychology*. Rev. ed. 1952

30. Young, K. *Social Psychology*. 1930

31. Mayer, A. "Uber Einzel- und Gesamtleistung des Schulkindes," *Arch. f.d. ges. Psychol.*, 1903, I: pp. 276-416

32. Schmidt, F. "Experimentelle Untersuchungen über die Hausaufgaben des Schulkindes," *Arch. f. d. ges. Psychol.*, 1904, 3: pp. 33-152

33. Moede, W. *Experimentelle Massenpsychologie*. 1920

34. Dashiell, J. F. "An Experimental Analysis of Some Group Effects," *J. Abn. and Soc. Psychol.*, 1930, 25: pp. 190-199

35. Pepitone, E. A. "Responsibility to the Group and Its Effects on the Performance of Members." Unpublished Ph.D. Dissertation, Univ. of Mich. See D. Cartwright and A. Zander (eds.), *Group Dynamics: Research and Theory*. 1953

36. Mead, M., et al. *Cooperation and Competition Among Primitive Peoples*. 1937

37. Travis, E. L. "The Influence of the Group upon the Stutterer's Speed in Free Association," *J. Abn. and Soc. Psychol.*, 1928, 23: pp. 44-52

38. Mintz, A. "Nonadaptive Group Behavior." In Swanson, Newcomb and Hartley, *Readings in Social Psychology*. Rev. ed. 1952

39. Newcomb, T. M. *Personality and Social Change*. 1943

40. Patrick, J. R., and Sims, V. M. "Personality Differences between Negro and White College Students, North and South," *J. Abn. and Soc. Psychol.*, 1934, 29: pp. 181-201

41. Roethlisberger, F. J., and Dickson, W. J. *Management and the Worker*. 1934

42. Thrasher, F. M. *The Gang*. 2nd ed. 1937

43. Cartwright, D., and Zander, A. (eds.). *Group Dynamics*. 1953

44. Herskovits, M. J. "On Cultural and Psychological Reality." In Rohrer and Sherif (eds.), *Social Psychology at the Crossroads*. 1951

45. Bagehot, W. *The Works of Walter Bagehot* (ed. by F. Morgan). 5 vols. 1889

46. Allport, F. H. "The J-Curve Hypothesis of Conforming Behavior," *J. Soc. Psychol.*, 1934, 5: pp. 141-183

47. Moreno, J. L. *Who Shall Survive?* 1934

48. Criswell, J. H. "A Sociometric Study of Racial Cleavage in the Classroom," *Archives of Psychol.*, 1939, No. 235

49. Jenkins, J. G. "Nominating Technique as a Method of Evaluating Air Group Morale," *J. Aviation Med.*, 1948, 19: pp. 12-19

50. Jennings, H. H. *Leadership and Isolation*. 1943

51. Lippitt, R. *Training in Community Relations*. 1949

52. Cartwright, D. *The Research Center for Group Dynamics*. 1950

53. Coch, L., and French, J. P., Jr. "Overcoming Resistance to Change." In Cartwright and Zander (eds.), *Group Dynamics: Research and Theory*. 1953, and Swanson, Newcomb and Hartley, *Readings in Social Psychology*. Rev. ed. 1952

54. Jacques, E. *The Changing Culture of a Factory*. 1951

55. Bales, R. F. *Interaction Process Analysis*. 1950

56. Chapple, E. D. (with the collaboration of C. M. Arensberg). *Measuring Human Relations.* 1940

57. Benne, K. D., and Sheats, P. "Functional Roles of Group Members," *J. Soc. Issues,* 1948, 4: pp. 41-49

58. Fouriezos, N. T., Hutt, M. L., and Guetzkow, H. "Self-oriented Needs in Discussion Groups." In Cartwright and Zander (eds.), *Group Dynamics: Research and Theory.* 1953

59. Festinger, L. "Group Attraction and Membership." In Cartwright and Zander (eds.), *Group Dynamics: Research and Theory.* 1953

60. Festinger, L., Schachter, S., and Back, K. *Social Pressures in Informal Groups.* 1950

61. Festinger, L., Cartwright, D., et al. "A Study of Rumor: Its Origin and Spread," *Human Relations,* 1948, 1: pp. 464-486

62. Lerner, H. H., and Kelman, H. C. (eds.). "Group Methods in Psychotherapy, Social Work and Adult Education," *J. Soc. Issues,* 1952, 8, No. 2

63. Bird, C. *Social Psychology.* 1940

64. Gouldner, A. W. (ed.). *Studies in Leadership.* 1950

65. Carter, L. F., and Nixon, M. "Investigation of the Relationship Between Four Criteria of Leadership Ability for Three Different Tasks," *J. Psychol.,* 1949, 27: pp. 245-261

66. OSS Staff. *Assessment of Men.* 1948

67. "Genius," *Encycl. Britannica,* 1936, 14th ed., 10: p. 116

68. Galton, F. *Hereditary Genius.* 1869

69. Terman, L. M. "Talent and Genius in Children." In V. F. Calverton and S. D. Schmalhausen (eds.), *The New Generation.* 1930

70. Terman, L. M., et al. *Genetic Studies of Genius.* 3 vols. 1925-1930

71. Terman, L. M., et al. *The Gifted Child Grows Up.* 1947

72. Lombroso, C. *The Man of Genius.* 1891

73. Hirsch, N. D. M. *Creative Intelligence.* 1931

74. Lange-Eichbaum, W. *The Problem of Genius.* 1932

75. Kretschmer, E. *The Psychology of Men of Genius.* 1931

76. Freud, S. "The Relation of the Poet to Day-Dreaming," *Collected Papers,* 1925, Vol. IV

77. Healy, W. *Personality in Formation and Action.* 1938

78. Jekels, L. "The Turning Point in the Life of Napoleon I," *Imago,* 1914, 3: pp. 313-381

79. Sperber, A. "Dante's Unconscious Soul-Life," *Imago,* 1914, 3: pp. 205-249

80. Chandler, A. R. *Beauty and Human Nature.* 1934

81. Herzberg, A. *The Psychology of Philosophers.* 1929

82. Wexberg, W. B. *Individual Psychology.* 1929

83. Bychowski, C. *Dictators and Disciples.* 1948

84. Fromm, E. *Escape from Freedom.* 1941

85. Gilbert, G. M. *The Psychology of Dictatorship.* 1950

86. Kelley, H. H. "Two Functions of Reference Groups." In Swanson, Newcomb and Hartley (eds.), *Readings in Social Psychology.* Rev. ed. 1952

87. Hyman, H. H. "The Psychology of Status," *Arch. Psychol.*, 1942, No. 269

88. Merton, R. K., and Kitt, A. S. "Contributions to the Theory of Reference Group Behavior." In Swanson, Newcomb and Hartley (eds.), *Readings in Social Psychology.* Rev. ed. 1952

89. Stouffer, S. A., et al. *The American Soldier.* 1949

90. Newcomb, T. M. *Social Psychology.* 1950

18

Attitudes and Opinions

In a significant article written by G. W. Allport (*1*) in 1935, the view was expressed that the concept of attitude "is probably the most distinctive and indispensable concept in contemporary American social psychology." Although almost twenty years have elapsed in the meantime, the study of attitudes has remained a major area of investigation. Several writers have in fact defined social psychology as the scientific study of attitudes. The first important use of the concept as a central characteristic of sociological problems was made by Thomas and Znaniecki (*2*), who in their study of the Polish peasant in America in 1918 concerned themselves largely with the question of his adjustment to the changed social environment in America. They saw the problem in terms of the substitution of new values for old, and its main feature was therefore the question of attitude, which they defined as *a state of mind of the individual toward a value.* Bogardus (*3*) and Folsom (*4*) have also described social psychology as concerned mainly with the question of attitudes.

Allport suggests that one reason for the popularity of the concept of attitude in social psychology is that it escapes the ancient controversy concerning the relative influence of heredity and environment. Attitudes can be and have been studied without any direct reference to their possible biological origins. There have been investigations, however, which have concerned themselves with this question of origins. Moore (*5*), for example, made an attempt to discover some relationship between radical and conservative attitudes on the one hand, and the supposed hereditary temperamental make-up of the individual on the other. The problem of prejudice is sometimes stated in terms of a direct, biologically determined hostility or aggressiveness between different ethnic groups. In these cases we have not escaped the nature-nurture problem, and it would seem therefore that Allport's explanation of the popularity of the concept is only relatively, not absolutely, correct. It is much more probable that the concept has come into such wide use because within its confines are included fundamental relationships to the problems of public opinion, propaganda, hostility between groups, economic rivalries, religious beliefs, and other issues of practical as well as theoretical importance in the field of social relationships.

Allport gives the following definition: "An attitude is a mental and neural state of readiness, organized through experience, exerting a directive or dynamic influence upon the individual's response to all objects and situations with which it is related" (p. 810). It connotes "a neuropsychic state of readiness for mental and physical activity"; that is to say, the presence of an attitude prepares the individual for a certain response. An attitude of hostility against the Negro, for example, predisposes the individual to participate in activities in which such hostility is expressed, whether it be merely the perception and recollection of unfavorable news items in the newspapers, the expression of arguments against the Negro, or actual participation in some violent overt act. Even when such a person is engaged in some perfectly harmless activity which does not concern the Negro in any way, we still speak of him as having an anti-Negro attitude because of his readiness to respond in a hostile manner.

Newcomb (6) similarly speaks of attitude as "a state of readiness for motive arousal"; an individual's attitude toward something "is his predisposition to perform, perceive, think and feel in relation to it" (pp. 118-119). It is a readiness to respond. *Opinions* are closely related to attitudes, since what we believe to be true regarding an object or a group will obviously play a part in determining our readiness to respond to it in certain ways rather than others. It would be desirable to reserve the word *attitude* to indicate what we are prepared to do, and *opinion* to represent what we believe or regard to be true. These usually go together, but not necessarily. In a good deal of current research and practice, the two terms have been used interchangeably; studies of public opinion, for example, have sometimes been referred to as studies of attitudes. It is highly probable that this usage has contributed to the uncertainty as to what is meant by *attitude*, and has resulted in conflicting definitions of the two terms. We shall be concerned with both attitudes and opinions in this chapter.

In connection with the formation of attitudes, Allport mentions four common conditions. There is first the accretion of experience—that is, the integration of numerous specific responses of a similar type. Our hypothetical anti-Negro, for example, may have had so much experience with Negroes as servants that he cannot accustom himself to seeing them in any other relationship. This is supplemented, in the second place, by individuation, differentiation, and segregation; further experiences make the attitude more specific and distinguish it from other allied attitudes. A third possible cause of the formation of an attitude is a trauma or a dramatic experience. Again to take our hypothetical case, a particular crime committed by a Negro against a member of one's family may determine a hostile attitude; conversely, being saved from danger by a Negro may be responsible for a favorable attitude toward all members of the group. Finally, an attitude may be adopted ready-made by imitation of parents, teachers, playmates, etc. Allport does not decide the order of importance or of the frequency of these four conditions in the formation of attitudes. It is probable, however, that the last one named far exceeds the others in significance; as we shall see more clearly later, attitudes appear to depend much less upon individual experience than upon the ready acceptance of viewpoints already current in the community. The problem then becomes one of understanding the origin and spread of these opinions in the community, in addition to the manner in which the individual integrates these with his own personality.

Another possible source of attitude formation should be considered in addition to those mentioned by Allport. The psychoanalysts have suggested that certain attitudes may be a direct or indirect reflection of family relationships: to take a specific example, anarchism or any other form of radicalism may be due to a revolt against authority in general, resulting from the revolt against the father in particular. Lasswell (7) has made use of this method of interpretation in his analysis of the life histories of radical leaders, and Fromm (8) has shown how the pattern of family authority may shape the reactions to political movements. There have been attempts to check this hypothesis quantitatively, but the results are inconclusive.

STEREOTYPES

In connection with the study of opinions, the nature and the content of stereotypes are of the greatest importance. In his book on *Public Opinion,* Walter Lippmann (9) refers to the influence upon our behavior of these stereotypes or "pictures in our heads." Only part of our concept of an object consists of immediate or stored sense impressions. The rest is "filled out" with ideas about the class to which the object, perhaps on insufficient evidence, has been referred. Our concept becomes therefore a composite of the real and the imputed character of the object. As expressed by Stuart Rice (10), the "element in the composite which is pre-existent or stored—which does not consist of immediate sense impressions—may be regarded as a stereotype" (p. 54). It is clear that to certain groups or individuals the mention of words like "politician," "capitalist," "senator," "cowboy," "gigolo," as well as all terms referring to racial and national groups, elicit stereotypes the correctness of which has never been demonstrated.

In connection with the stereotype of the "criminal," there were several classical experiments performed by Sir Charles Goring (11), the British criminologist who led the opposition to the theories of Lombroso (12). The latter, as is well-known, believed that a criminal could be recognized by the presence of certain definite physical characteristics, spoken of as "stigmata of degeneration" (see Chapter 16). Without using the term "stereotype," Goring believed that some such mechanism was responsible for the belief in the criminal type. He had an artist draw from memory the portraits of a great many inmates of a penal institution in London. He made a composite photograph of these drawings, and found that this did look very much like the usual conception of the criminal. Then he took actual photographs of these same criminals and made another composite photograph out of these. This showed no trace of the familiar "criminal type" and was quite unlike the one based upon the drawings. The effect of the stereotype on the artist is clear. In another experiment a warden and a prison physician were told to rate the intelligence of 300 convicts, and also to estimate roughly the height of their foreheads. The results showed that those who were regarded as highly intelligent were also "seen" as having high foreheads, and conversely, the unintelligent as having low brows. The foreheads were then actually measured, and it was found that as a matter of fact those who were judged to be "unintelligent," "weak-minded" and "imbeciles" had on the average higher foreheads than those who were judged "intelligent." Here the stereotype of the "high brow" as a concomitant of superior intellectual ability determined the judgments. It may be added that a study by Sherman under the direction of Clark Hull (*13*) showed a slight *negative* correlation between height of forehead and scholastic achievement.

A careful experimental study of stereotypes was made by Stuart Rice (*10*), who used as his material nine portraits which appeared in the *Boston Herald* for December 15, 1924. These portraits were of Edouard Herriot, the French political leader; James Duncan, then Vice-President of the A. F. of L.; Leonid Krassin, the first Soviet Ambassador to Paris; Joseph W. McIntosh, then Deputy-Comptroller of Currency; Martin H. Glynn, a former Governor of New York State; Max Agel, a bootlegger; Charles M. Schwab, the industrialist; Howard Heinz of the 57 varieties; and Senator Pepper of Pennsylvania. In the first portion of the experiment, the subjects were 141 students who were told which occupations were represented among the men whose photographs were shown to them. If the photographs were identified entirely by chance, there would be 168 correct identifications out of a possible total of 1224. Actually, 337 identifications were correct, or about twice as many as the chance expectation. The photograph of the Communist Krassin yielded a result far below chance, as his well-groomed appearance and short Van Dyke beard gave him an aristocratic air, quite different from the usual Communist stereotype. The photographs of McIntosh and Pepper were also judged below chance, whereas all the others were judged better than chance. In the second portion of the experiment the subjects were Grange members and they gave similar stereotypes. The only important difference was that they showed a higher concentration of results, that is, greater agreement among the subjects and therefore greater strength of the stereotypes. The experiment as a whole has two interesting results, first, it gives evidence that stereotypes may and do distort judgments to a considerable degree, but second, that they may not be mere chance products, and they may contain some truth.

It has sometimes been suggested that stereotypes must be at least partly true; otherwise, it is argued, it would be impossible to understand their occurrence and widespread acceptance. Plausible as this may sound, actual investigation has demonstrated that stereotypes can and do develop without any basis in objective reality. Striking evidence against the "kernel of truth" hypothesis is to be found in the investigation by Schoenfeld (*14*), who was interested in the occurrence of stereotypes related to proper names. He asked a group of 120 male students to "match" 8 masculine names with 8 personal characteristics. Out of the 120, 63 matched Richard with good-looking; 58 matched Herman with stupid, and 71 judged Adrian to be artistic. In a comparable experiment with female names, 58 out of 120 students stated that Maisie was talkative, and 73 said that Agatha was middle-aged. These stereotypes have, of course, a cause; but the cause is more likely to be found in characterizations in novels or the cinema than in actual experience. Schoenfeld's study indicates that stereotypes can and do develop without any "kernel of truth." The safest conclusion to be drawn in this connection is that every stereotype must be examined in order to determine its relation to objective reality, and that no stereotype may be regarded as even partially true simply because it exists.

A study of ethnic stereotypes was made by Katz and Braly (*15*). The ethnic groups were first ranked for preference by 60 students, with results somewhat similar to those obtained in earlier studies by Bogardus (*16*) and others. In a second part of the experiment one group of students listed what they regarded as the typical psychological characteristics of each race or nationality, a total of 84 traits being named in this manner. Another group of 100 students chose from this list the five traits which they regarded as the "most typical" of each of the ten ethnic groups. The investigators were interested in the definiteness of the stereotype as measured by the degree of agreement between the judges; they used as their measure the smallest number of traits of the five checked which had to be included to find 50% of the 500 checks made by the subjects. The possible range is therefore from 2.5 at the one extreme, indicating that every one of the subjects chose the same five traits for the same ethnic group, to 42 at the other, which means that all the 84 traits were used in the characterization of the group. The results were as follows:

Negroes	4.6
Germans	5.0
Jews	5.5
Italians	6.9

English	7.0
Irish	8.5
Americans	8.8
Japanese	10.9
Chinese	12.0
Turks	15.9

The first interesting result is that there appears to be little direct relation between the definiteness of the stereotype and the amount of prejudice against any group. The Negroes, with the most definite stereotype, and the Turks with the least, were both responded to unfavorably in the first portion of the experiment. The results cannot be explained in terms of familiarity either, since presumably the subjects were most familiar with Americans, who occupy an intermediate position. It is possible, however, as Murphy, Murphy, and Newcomb (17) suggest, that stereotypes are most definite toward nationalities with whom one's own group is or has recently been in conflict; least definite for distant and unfamiliar peoples; and intermediate for one's own and related groups. The investigators conclude that prejudice involves a generalized set of stereotypes of a high degree of consistency, which includes emotional responses to "race" names, a belief in typical characteristics associated with such names, and an evaluation of the typical traits.

With regard to the content of these ethnic stereotypes, Katz and Braly report that out of 100 Princeton University students who were the subjects of the investigation, 78 described the Germans as "scientifically minded" and 65 described them as "industrious"; 53 students used the adjective "artistic" for the Italians; 84 considered Negroes as "superstitious" and 75 regarded them as "lazy"; 53 described the English as "sportsmanlike"; 79 said the Jews were "shrewd"; 54 that the Turks were "cruel." We may summarize the results somewhat differently by indicating the characteristics most commonly ascribed to each nationality. These included, for the Germans, scientifically minded, industrious, stolid; the Italians, artistic, impulsive, passionate; the Negroes, superstitious, lazy, happy-go-lucky, ignorant; the Irish, pugnacious, quick-tempered, witty; the English, sportsmanlike, intelligent, conventional; the Jews, shrewd, mercenary, industrious; the Americans, industrious, intelligent, materialistic, ambitious; the Chinese, superstitious, sly, conservative; the Japanese, intelligent, industrious, progressive; the Turks, cruel, religious, treacherous.

The Katz and Braly study was conducted in 1932. In 1950 G. M. Gilbert (18) repeated the study, using exactly the same techniques on a new generation of Princeton University students, 333 in number. Gilbert noted a very important change which he describes as a "fading effect." There was in general much less agreement among the students in 1950 than in 1932; any specific trait was usually checked by a much smaller proportion of students in the later study, even though there was little change in the characteristics which were most frequently attributed. The percentage of students who described Negroes as lazy dropped from 84 in 1932 to 31; those describing the Jews as shrewd dropped from 79% to 47%. The description of Italians as artistic dropped from 83% to 28%, of the Japanese as industrious from 43% to 12%, of Americans as progressive from 27% to 5%. Gilbert concludes that there has been a very marked reduction in the extent to which these stereotypes prevail, as well as in the willingness of the university students to generalize about ethnic groups. He suggests a number of possible reasons for this change—among others, "the gradual disappearance of stereotyped characterizations in all entertainment and communication media." The study is of very real importance as indicating that, with time, stereotypes may not only change their character, but may also become considerably less definite and less sweeping in scope. There is also the possibility, however—and this was not explored by Gilbert— that certain other stereotypes, for example that of the Russians, may have become more rather than less definite with the passage of time. (See Chapter 19 for a further discussion of ethnic stereotypes.)

It is difficult to overestimate the strength and importance of stereotypes. In Chapter 8 we noted how they affected perception and memory. With regard to ethnic differences (Chapter 11), reference was made to the "discovery" by Bean of certain characteristics of the Negro brain indicating its inferiority. It seems clear in the light of the negative results obtained in the more careful study by Mall that Bean was influenced by the "picture in his head" or stereotype of the Negro. The study by E. L. and R. E. Horowitz (19) points in the same direction. When they presented pictures to White children and asked for an interpretation, the stereotype of the Negro entered to a considerable extent. For instance, when the children were shown an attractive house and grounds and asked what the colored woman was doing, many of them said she was cleaning up the place, although there was actually no colored woman in the picture. Given the stereotype of the Negro as a domestic servant, it was difficult for the children to imagine her in such a fine house in any other capacity. The existence of such a stereotype may play an important part in preventing any improvement in race relations on the basis of increased contact between two conflicting groups. It may result in a literal inability to see those things which do not fit into the stereotype.

The part which words play in the formation of stereotypes is illustrated by an interesting experiment of Stagner's (20) on fascist attitudes. Stagner found that 73% of his subjects disapproved strongly of fascist Germany and its policies. At the same time many of the subjects made very favorable scores on a questionnaire which had been carefully prepared to include the actual components of fascism. Such word stereotypes may have an important influence upon the success or failure of various types of propaganda.

THE MEASUREMENT OF ATTITUDES AND OPINIONS

Many different techniques have been devised for the study and, whenever possible, for the measurement of attitudes and opinions. There has been warm, and sometimes even acrimonious, discussion as to the possibility of measurement in this field and as to the merits of the various techniques which have been proposed. We shall be helped to arrive at a reasonable judgment if we first determine what we want to know about attitudes, and then examine the suggested procedures for arriving at that knowledge.

Attitudes may be regarded as having various attributes or dimensions. [See Newcomb (6), Hartley and Hartley (21), Krech and Crutchfield (22).] These may briefly be described and illustrated as follows:

(a) *Direction.* Are we *for* or *against* a particular candidate for office, or equal rights for Negroes, or participation in the United Nations?

(b) *Degree.* Do we favor equality for Negroes in all situations, or would we restrict such equality to economic opportunities? Do we think candidate A is a little better than his opponent, or much better?

(c) *Intensity.* How strongly do we feel about equal rights for Negroes? Degree and intensity of attitudes are undoubtedly related, but it is possible to feel intensely about a situation even when our position is by no means an extreme one. There have been many southerners, for example, who devoted themselves with energy and enthusiasm to obtaining educational opportunities for Negroes, even though they were unwilling to extend equality beyond a very limited area. The attitudes in this case might be described as intense, although they are far from extreme in degree.

(d) *Consistency*. If we believe in freedom of speech for certain groups, would we extend the same privilege to others? If we favor trade unionism for miners, would we also approve of it for school teachers?

(e) *Salience*. How ready are we to express any particular attitude? If we are opposed to the political party at present in power, how easily and how quickly do we speak of our opposition even when we are not being questioned about our politics?

There are perhaps some other ways in which attitudes vary, but these five are probably the most important.

Public Opinion Polls. The technique which has received the greatest publicity, and has aroused the greatest controversy, is undoubtedly the public opinion poll. Identified in the popular mind with pre-election predictions, the polls achieved their most spectacular success when Gallup, Roper, Crossley and others successfully forecast the results of the Roosevelt-Landon contest in 1936. As is well known, the *Literary Digest*, on the basis of more than 2,000,000 ballots, and with a record of successful predictions in 1928 and 1932, gave Landon 370 electoral votes out of 531; actually Roosevelt was elected with 523. The pollsters were able to point to their more accurate sampling procedures as the reason for their success, and they were widely hailed as having set the foundation for a "science" of public opinion. This is where matters stood until the polls suffered their most outstanding failure in 1948, with their prediction that Dewey would be elected president.

As Gallup and Rae (23) have pointed out, the pre-election polls are not really important in themselves, since the outcome of an election is determined by the actual voting, and not by the results obtained from the sample interviewed. Such polls are exceedingly important, however, from the standpoint of methodology. The common criticism of any investigation based on verbal responses has been expressed in the question, how does anyone know whether the respondents are telling the truth? The most convincing answer— until 1948—was the fact that the pre-election polls were apparently capable of successfully predicting the outcome of an election. The outcome could therefore be considered a validation of the method; people evidently voted as they said they would vote.

Although in scientific circles many questions had been raised concerning the polls even before 1948, Truman's unexpected victory resulted in a particularly critical examination of polling methods. The reasons for the failure of the polls are discussed in considerable detail in a report by a Social Science Research Council Committee (24) and in a conference on Attitude and Opinion Research at Iowa State University (25). Among the factors held to be responsible were faulty sampling, inadequate attention to those respondents who answered "don't know," a failure to take into account last-minute shifts in voting intentions, and lack of knowledge as to who would actually go out to vote.

This last point raises the question of the *intensity* of the attitude, in this case the preference for Truman and Dewey, respectively. Katz (26) has suggested that in the voting contest intensity might be measured by having the respondents indicate on a scale or "thermometer" how intensely they feel about the election; the lower end might then be worded "don't plan to vote," and the upper end "going to vote even if I have to be carried to the polling booth on a stretcher." Without some such measure of intensity, there is no way to take into account the likelihood with which the supporters of one or the other candidate will actually cast their ballots on election day.

Public opinion polls usually make use of only one question, which requires a *yes* or *no* answer, or which presents the respondent with a set of fixed choices, for example a list of candidates for election, or of suggested procedures to be followed, etc. This means that although the *direction* of the attitude may be ascertained, little information is available concerning the other dimensions which have been described. Another defect of the single question is that if it is misinterpreted, or interpreted differently by different respondents, the final percentages may be misleading. Cantril and his colleagues (27) have given a number of examples of this possibility. Crutchfield and Gordon (28) studied the interpretations given to a question used by the American Institute of Public Opinion in 1943: "After the war, would you like to see many changes or reforms made in the United States, or would you rather have the country remain pretty much the way it was before the war?" They found that some persons thought the question referred to "domestic changes or reforms"; others, "technological changes"; others, changes in the "basic political-economic structure of the United States"; and still others to changes in "foreign affairs of the United States."

Another problem in connection with the polls results from the degree to which the attitude of the interviewers ("interviewer bias") may affect the nature of the responses obtained. Cantril and his associates (27) have demonstrated that interviewers who were in favor of aid to Britain during the early days of World War II found a larger proportion of their respondents sharing that view than did interviewers with the opposite attitude. Stember and Hyman (29) indicate that not only the attitude held by the interviewer, but his expectations regarding the attitudes held by his respondents, may also play an important part in his findings.

One further criticism of the poll should be mentioned. It has frequently been suggested that there is danger, particularly in pre-election polls, resulting from the presumed bandwagon effect. If people believe, on the basis of the polls, that candidate A is sure to be elected, they will be more likely—so the argument runs—to vote for that candidate, to jump on the bandwagon. In that case, the predictions would actually influence the outcome. Gallup and Rae (23) have presented data which throw considerable doubt on the validity of this criticism. Not only did the *Literary Digest* poll, in spite of its prestige at the time, fail to elect Landon, but analysis of the results obtained in successive polls taken in connection with a number of different political contests failed to reveal any consistent trend in favor of either candidate. It is of course possible that there may be both a bandwagon and a reverse bandwagon effect which cancel each other.

The criticisms which we have listed—and there are others which could be added—should not be regarded as justifying the conclusion that the polls are useless. On the contrary, they can perform a valuable function when the questions asked are clear and unambiguous, and when conclusions are drawn with due regard for the nature of the sample, the possibility of interviewer bias, and the probable error of the obtained percentages.

This last point is especially important. If the polls contain a probable error of four percentage points, that means that if one candidate or one issue is supported by 51% of the respondents, the true picture is represented by a range from 47 to 55%; the minority view, in this case 49%, will really be held by a percentage ranging between 45 and 53%. This makes the statistical basis for predictions clearer, and shows how dangerous it is to draw any conclusions when the difference is as small as in this hypothetical case. Since many elections are close, the fact that the polls have predicted the outcome successfully in 80% of the contests [Gallup and Rae (23)] demonstrates that the method does have real merit.

We shall return to the question of sampling in connection with the discussion of interview surveys.

Attitude Scales. A single question is usually incapable of yielding information regarding the *degree* of the attitude, and for that purpose attitude scales have been devised. They are designed to tell us not only whether an individual is for or against something (*direction*), but how he compares with others in degree. Two individuals may both be in favor of trade unionism but to different degrees, and the scales make it possible to establish their position in relation to the rest of the population studied.

One method which has been used in this connection is represented by the construction of an *a priori* scale, that is to say, a scale ranging between two extremes, but constructed on a logical rather than an empirical basis. In this method the scoring is arbitrary and depends upon the investigator's judgment of what steps or intervals should be included. The best-known example of this type is the Bogardus Social Distance Scale (*16*), which was constructed in order to measure ethnic attitudes. The subjects were asked to indicate on a scale at what "distance" they wished to keep members of various racial and national groups. At one end of the scale the groups were to be kept out of the country altogether; at the other, they would be permitted to intermarry with members of one's own family. The intervening steps included admission to the country, but not to citizenship; to citizenship, but not to one's own vocation, and so on. This type of scale involves the assumption that the acceptance of any one point automatically includes the other points below it.

A second approach is sometimes described as the *psycho-physical* or *rational scale*, and is mainly the result of the work of Thurstone and his collaborators (*30*). In the best-known of the Thurstone techniques, the procedure takes the following form. A large number of statements, sometimes as many as several hundred, are gathered, which are presumed to be related to the attitude in question.

These are presented to a hundred or more judges who classify the statements into eleven categories ranging from most to least favorable. The scale value of each statement is determined by the median position to which it has been assigned by the judges; those statements which have been placed in many different categories are discarded. Finally, the scale is made up of statements spread out evenly between the two extremes, and duplicate forms may be constructed which can then be used to test the reliability of the method, which incidentally is usually high. A score is assigned to each respondent based on the items with which he expresses agreement. Scales have been devised in this fashion to measure attitudes toward various ethnic groups, toward internationalism, war, religion, prohibition, birth control, socioeconomic issues, etc.

A third technique, much simpler than that of Thurstone, is associated with the name of Likert (31). Here the investigator himself collects a large number of statements which he considers relevant, and presents these to a group of subjects who indicate with regard to each item whether they (1) strongly approve, (2) approve, (3) are undecided, (4) disapprove, or (5) strongly disapprove. These responses are given values from 1 to 5, with the higher values indicating a greater degree of favorableness to the attitude under investigation. The sum of these values is the total score for each individual. Those items which yield low correlation with the total score are eliminated, in order that the scale as a whole may be internally consistent.

Other scaling methods which have recently been developed include the Scale-Discrimination Technique of Edwards and Kilpatrick (32), the Scale Analysis or the Scalogram Method of Guttman (33) and the Latent Structure Method of Lazarsfeld (34). The last two were utilized in connection with the studies of attitudes of American soldiers during World War II. For a detailed critical review of these various techniques, see Jahoda, Deutsch and Cook (35).

The objections that have been raised against the measurement of attitudes are similar to those directed against the use of questionnaires and interviews in general. The problems of the reliability of the scale can usually be handled successfully, since care in the selection and phrasing of the items usually gives high reliabilities, by both the split-half and the repeat methods. The problem of validity is a much more serious one. We mean by validity the success with which the attitude scale measures what it purports to measure. This is usually taken to refer to the correspondence between what the subject describes as his attitude, and the actual overt activities in which he participates. To be more specific, a valid scale of attitudes toward the Negro would indicate, from this point of view, not only how the subject *talks* about the Negro but also how he *acts* in the same connection. This approach would regard verbal behavior as significant only to the extent that it gives information about overt behavior. An alternative and more correct view would regard verbal behavior as important in its own right, since the attitudes of a person as expressed in his speech and in his writings may also have direct practical consequences for himself and for his social relationships. In that case the attitude scale would be valid if the subject told the truth as well as he could, and understood the questions correctly. Incidentally, the subject can falsify his actions just as he can his words.

It is important to know, however, whether the verbal and overt behavior are consistent, and many investigations have been directed to this end. The usual method has been to validate the scale against ratings by teachers and associates, and although this may often be the only method available, it has all the drawbacks inherent in the rating method. By far the better procedure is to validate against the actual stand taken by the subjects, or by the behavior which they have already exhibited. In some instances this can be done successfully. The validity of a scale for the measurement of economic radicalism, for example, may be indicated by its ability to differentiate between members of the Communist and the Republican parties. It may be possible also to validate a scale of attitudes toward the Negro by comparing the results with actual behavior in a mixed "racial" situation.

This problem of consistency or inconsistency is a particularly important one; it was referred to above as one of the significant dimensions of attitudes. The scales which we have briefly described can give us information regarding consistency *within* the verbal responses; they tell us whether the answers to some questions are consistent with the answers to others. The problem becomes more complicated when we inquire further into the relation between the verbal responses and other aspects of behavior. [See Chein and others (36).]

An early study by LaPiere illustrates the difficulty involved. Together with a young Chinese student and his wife, LaPiere traveled extensively throughout the United States, visiting 184 restaurants and cafés and 66 hotels, auto camps and tourist homes. They were almost invariably treated with courtesy and consideration, and only on one occasion were they definitely refused service. Six months later a questionnaire was mailed to the same establishments, asking: "Will you accept members of the Chinese race as guests in your establishment?" Answers were obtained from 128 of the establishments visited, and the results showed that 91% of them answered the question in the negative. (About the same proportion of establishments which had *not* been visited answered similarly.) The discrepancy between "attitudes" and "actions" is striking (37).

At the same time it would be unfair to conclude that the study of attitudes as verbally expressed is a waste of time and effort. Frequently there is consistency, both internal and external. LaPiere's results may be a function of rather specific circumstances and therefore not applicable to attitude measurement in general. It may very well be that the proprietors of these hotels and restaurants thought it would be safer to answer the question in the negative, since they knew nothing about the kind of people they might be required to serve, nor could they anticipate the reactions of other guests who happened to be present at the time. When confronted with pleasant, attractive Chinese accompanied by a White man (this is probably important), they saw no reason to refuse service. LaPiere's study does, however, indicate the need for further efforts to increase our understanding of the conditions under which attitudes are consistent or inconsistent, respectively.

Katz (38) makes an interesting suggestion for a possible use of attitude measurement as "the accurate and reliable recording of the ideologies or attributes of people." He regards this as the best method of arriving at the content of a culture, and believes it may be used as an adjunct to anthropological research. It has in his opinion many advantages over the usual approach, since anthropologists bring back a description of a culture as a whole, and tell very little of the range and frequency of the attitudes held by the individuals in the community. When any particular belief is mentioned as current among the members of a primitive culture, little is said about its extent, or about the number and variety of deviations from it. Katz is correct in his suggestion that a knowledge of the range of attitudes would add valuable material to the reports of the anthropologists. In actual practice, however, it is probable that the measurement of attitudes within a primitive culture will be beset by many more difficulties than a similar study in our own society. There will be not only the customary problems, but the additional one of stating the questions in terms sufficiently devoid of ambiguity so that they will have the same meaning to the subjects and to the investigator. The difficulty of placing oneself at the standpoint of another culture becomes intensified with the necessity of asking questions of all informants in exactly the same form. Some knowledge of the variations within a community would be gained, however, and would in part compensate for a definite deficiency in much anthropological writing.

Survey Research. A significant attempt to develop techniques which should avoid some of the difficulties of both public opinion polls and attitude scales is represented by the Sample Interview Survey. Likert (39), for example, points out that the scores obtained from attitude scales give little insight into cause-and-effect relationships; in addition, they have usually been standardized on student groups, and are not always applicable to the adult population in general. As for the polls, Likert's criticisms follow the lines already indicated, but include one additional important point, namely, that the method of sampling is inadequate.

As expressed by Newcomb (6), all sampling methods are based upon "one fundamental requirement—namely that every person in the total population should have an equal chance to be included in the sample" (p. 184). There are three main methods of drawing a sample. (1) In *file* sampling, the investigator lists all the people in the "population" and in random fashion chooses the sample which he requires. If, for example, there are 2000 students in a university, and a sample of 200 is required, all that may be necessary is to list the student body alphabetically, select a number from 1 to 10 by chance, then start with that number and select every tenth name following it. If the number so chosen is three, then the sample will consist of the third, thirteenth, twenty-third, etc., names on the list. This method is excellent if the total population is sufficiently small and accessible.

For large populations, where there is no list of names, other methods must be used. Most public opinion polls utilize what is known as (2) *quota* sampling. If we are making a pre-election poll and require a sample of the total American adult population, our sample must be like the total population with respect to those variables which may play a part in voting behavior. These will include such factors as age, education, economic status, size of community, region, sex, ethnic origin, religious background, political party membership, etc. On the basis of the distribution of these factors in any particular community, for example, an interviewer may be told to obtain a definite percentage of males and females (usually 50-50); Whites and Negroes; Protestants, Catholics and Jews; upper, middle, and lower income groups; college, high-school, and grade-school education; under 30 years of age, between 30 and 50, over 50, etc. Apart from these general instructions, the interviewer is left relatively free; he may find his respondents—provided they fulfill the above requirements—wherever he wishes. What may happen is that he may unconsciously bias the sample, if he is unwilling to enter slums and alleyways, or houses which are unattractive and dirty. Katz (*40*) has demonstrated that this method of sampling has played an important part in producing constant errors in many pre-election polls, mainly because of the under-representation of respondents at the lowest economic levels.

The essence of the method known as (3) *area* sampling (sometimes referred to as *probability* sampling) is that the choice of respondents is not left to the discretion of the interviewer. A sample is chosen by those responsible for the investigation; the places to be visited may be marked on an aerial photograph, or designated according to specific street and house numbers; the people to be interviewed are exactly indicated. This method is much more expensive and time-consuming, since the interviewer may have to return many times to the same address before he finds his respondent at home. The final sample is, however, much more nearly representative of the total population from which it is drawn.

The Sample Interview Survey utilizes area sampling, which appears to be definitely superior to other techniques for this purpose. In addition, careful attention is paid to the design of the study as a whole, the construction of the questionnaire and its pre-testing, the training and supervision of the interviewers, and the coding and analysis of the responses. Reliance is not placed on a single question, but rather on an interrelated series of questions which attempts to get at opinions, the reasons for them, the relevant background of information, any changes which have occurred, plans for future action, etc. The questions are usually *open-ended,* that is, instead of fixed alternatives among which the respondent must choose, opportunity is given for a free expression of opinion. An example of an open-end question would be: "What do you think of the job the United Nations is doing?" This will usually be followed by a *probe,* such as "Why do you say that?" or "What do you mean by that?" etc.

A special feature of open-ended questions is their frequent arrangement in a *funnel* structure, which proceeds gradually from the more general to the more specific. A hypothetical series of questions structured in this fashion might be the following:

1. How are things going in your community?
2. Does your community have any special problems?
3. How do the various groups in your community get along together?
4. How about the Negroes?

This technique is especially adapted to measure that dimension of attitude which has been termed *salience.* In the case of a respondent for whom Negro-White relations have high salience, the Negro might be mentioned in the answer to the very first question; the greater the salience, the greater the ease with which a particular response is elicited. It is sometimes possible to arrive at some notion of salience through the use of a single question. A *Fortune* Survey in September, 1939, asked the following question: "Is there any one group—racial, religious, economic or social—in your city which represents an important problem?" In the sample from the South Atlantic and eastern South Central states, 12.8% mentioned Negroes; in the Mountain and Pacific states, none of the respondents did so (*41*). It is clear that the salience of the Negro problem differs markedly in different regions of the country.

Likert (*39*) has given a striking example of the practical application of the Sample Interview Survey in connection with a series of studies conducted for the U.S. Treasury Department in 1943 on the buying of war bonds. From the analysis of the results obtained from a national sample of about 1800 persons, it was found that personal solicitation played a much more significant part than had previously been realized. In every occupational and regional group, there were about 35% more bond buyers among those who had been personally approached. "Of all the different factors influencing bond-buying behavior, personal solicitation appeared to be one of the most important" (p. 244). As a direct result of this survey, individual solicitation was greatly increased in the next bond drive; 59% of those personally approached bought more bonds than usual, as compared with 17% of those who were not so approached.

One further example of the relation of surveys to economic behavior may be mentioned. Katona (42) has been particularly concerned with the influence of expectations on such behavior. In one of his studies he demonstrated that those who expected an increase in their income actually spent more, as a group, on the purchase of durable goods than those who expected their income to go down; this latter group were motivated to increase their savings. "Optimistic attitudes, on the other hand, influenced people to make large, unusual expenditures and even to 'dissave' (spend more than their income through drawing on assets or borrowing). In brief, expectations influenced behavior" (p. 226). Katona's investigation may be regarded, incidentally, as contributing to the validation of the survey method, since the expressed attitudes—in this case the expectations—were on the whole consistent with the subsequent activities of the respondents.

For a critical review of many of the problems involved in measuring public opinion and attitudes, see Campbell and others (43).

The Panel Method. In many cases it may be important to know not only the present distribution of attitudes, but the direction in which attitudes are moving. It is possible to make trend studies, as Cantril (27) has shown, by analyzing the results of successive public opinion polls on a series of representative samples of the same population. The panel method makes use of repeated interviews of the *same* individuals over a period of time. [See Lazarsfeld (44).] This has the great advantage of discovering not only the general trend, but also of locating precisely those individuals who change or remain constant, and discovering the reasons for the change or the consistency respectively. An excellent example of this method is to be found in a study by Lazarsfeld, Berelson, and Gaudet (45) in which the same 600 people were interviewed on seven different occasions concerning their opinions on political questions and voting behavior.

Projective Techniques. The extensive use of projective techniques such as the Rorschach, the Thematic-Apperception Test, and others, in the study of personality has suggested the possibility of their application to the attitude field as well, particularly when it seems desirable not to question the respondent directly, but to arrive at an indirect expression of the attitude. To mention one example, Proshansky (46) studied attitudes toward labor as expressed in the stories supplied by subjects in response to pictures which showed working people in conflict situations. The same picture, for example, shown to two different subjects elicited such contrasting responses as (1) "Why don't the government provide for these people? The ordinary worker is always forgotten and allowed to rot"; and (2) "They seem to be messy, sloppy people, who seem to enjoy dwelling in their own trash." Cobliner (47) has suggested further applications of projective techniques in this field. Much more work will have to be done on the problem of validation before such techniques can be used with confidence, but they appear to have promise in the study of attitudes which are not accessible to direct questioning.

PROPAGANDA

Lumley (48) points out that the term "propaganda" is related to the Latin *propagare*, meaning to fasten down layers, shoots or slips of plants for the purpose of reproduction, hence to generate, reproduce, and generally to extend or increase. Etymologically, therefore, "propaganda is not a breeding that would take place of itself; it is a forced generation" (p. 186). Kimball Young (49) defines it as "the propagation of ideas, opinions and attitudes, the real purpose of which is not made clear to the hearer or reader" (p. 653). Doob (50) describes propaganda as "a systematic attempt by an interested individual (or individuals) to control the attitudes of groups of individuals through the use of suggestion and, consequently, to control their actions" (pp. 75-76).

In spite of its respectable etymological origin, the term "propaganda" is in bad repute. It suggests a manipulation of opinions for ulterior purposes. There is in many quarters, however, a frank recognition of its importance, and as is well known it achieved a position of respectability in Germany where one of the most important members of the Government was titled "Minister of Propaganda and Enlightenment." In America it is customary to distinguish it from education, on the general ground that education is concerned with truth, whereas propaganda is indifferent to truth. Doob states that the essence of education is its objectivity in the light of the scientific truths prevalent at the time, whereas propaganda intentionally or unintentionally is an attempt to control the attitudes of the people. In this sense propaganda should receive a stigma only when its social effects are harmful. Whether propaganda is good or bad depends not upon the fact that it is propaganda, but on the uses to which it is put.

In practice, the distinction between propaganda and education is difficult to maintain. Freeman (51), in an interesting discussion of "impartiality," shows how in a text as harmless in appearance and as far removed from the social scene (apparently) as a book on arithmetic there may still be an unintentional manipulation of attitudes. He takes as an example Thorndike's *Arithmetic*, Book II, which appeared in 1917. In less than 200 pages, says Freeman, there are 643 problems which not only deal with, but accept and stress the concepts of capitalism and of our familiar commercial practices. These problems in one obvious way or another lay stress on commercial transactions depending upon the profit motive. There is selling, buying and re-selling, rent, working for wages, employing others for wages and interest on loans. As an indication of what he means by arithmetic problems which do not stress the profit motive and which therefore do not contribute to the perpetuation of attitudes favoring the present economic system, Freeman suggests the following. If a family needs fifteen dollars a week for food, but receives five dollars on the dole, what is the percentage of undernourishment? If in a southern cotton mill, one out of every hundred has pellagra, how many new cases will appear when the mill expands by one thousand employees? If in a modern war there were ten million combatants and two million casualties annually, what are the probabilities of remaining unscathed during four years of participation? "Books containing such problems, although they taught the abstract relationship of numbers as well as any others, would be dismissed as propagandistic and unworthy of the dignity of pure arithmetic" (p. 265). It goes without saying that Thorndike is here not accused of deliberate propaganda, but merely of taking for granted existing economic practices and unwittingly helping to keep them alive by the examples he uses. In this connection it is interesting to note that Russian educators have been disturbed by the frequency with which the profit motive has persisted in their arithmetic books, and have taken steps to make the necessary alterations in the direction of their own economic ideology. Erika

Mann (52) has collected a number of striking examples of the manner in which the Nazis used arithmetic textbooks in order to convey the militaristic and chauvinistic attitudes which formed an essential part of their philosophy.

The case of Thorndike's *Arithmetic* raises the general question as to whether the term "propaganda" is legitimately used in those cases in which there is no intention to control the opinions or attitudes of anyone. Is there any meaning, in other words, to "unintentional propaganda"? There is a legitimate difference of opinion on this point, some writers contending that propaganda is defined by its effect, and others by its motive. In the interests of a satisfactory terminology it would seem advisable to use the word in those cases in which there is a deliberate attempt to control opinions and attitudes. When this control is unwittingly exercised the results may be the same, but the effect is accidental.

The Principles of Propaganda. For this reason we are not inclined to lay much stress upon the first among the "principles of propaganda," which Doob develops. This is termed the Principle of the Intention of the Propagandist; Doob states that "in intentional propaganda, the propagandist is aware of his interested aim; in unintentional propaganda he does not appreciate the social effect of his own actions" (p. 90). This is as a matter of fact in conflict with Doob's own definition of propaganda as a "systematic attempt" to control attitudes.

The second principle is that of Perception. "The propagandist makes his stimulus-situation stand out from its competing ground," that is to say, he wishes his message to be perceived and tries to give it some stimulus value which sets it off from the general background of sense impressions in the environment of the individual at the time. Various methods may be used to accomplish this end. Auxiliary attitudes may be called in which have nothing to do with the final act, as when an advertiser of tomato juice shows it being drunk by a pretty girl; or the stimulus may be repeated many times to increase the probability that it will be perceived, as when a radio announcer brings in the name of his product continually; or use may be made of the principle of simplification, in which the stimulus situation is simplified so as to bring it within the range of the average individual, as when scientific statements about the nature of vitamins are reduced to their simplest terms in order to help sell a particular product. These various methods serve just as well in political as in advertising propaganda.

The third principle is that of the Type of Propaganda. "The propagandist employs any one or all of the following types of propaganda: revealed, delayed-revealed, and concealed propaganda." In the first of these, use is made of direct suggestion, and the aim of the propagandist is clear from the beginning. In delayed-revealed propaganda an interval of time elapses which is presumably long enough to enable related and auxiliary attitudes to be aroused; for example, during a war the attempt may first be made to arouse patriotic motives in general, and only later will young men be directly induced to enlist. Although this was the aim in the first place, it is not brought out into the open until the ground has been properly prepared. In the concealed type, the propaganda is indirect, and the propagandist refrains from stating his aim at any time. This may be illustrated by the celebrations in honor of Edison conducted by certain electric power companies, in which the primary aim of persuading people to use electric power was left to indirect suggestion.

There is fourth the Principle of Related Attitudes. "In the process of suggestion, the propagandist arouses related attitudes that are instrumental in bringing about the desired integration." There are many ways in which this is done. Not long ago opponents of the Roosevelt administration, for example, tried their best to make use of the general attitude of "fear of dictatorships" in order to win support for candidates and a platform quite irrelevant to this issue. A politician may try to win the favor of a group of lawyers by telling them that their profession contributes to civilization, or an automobile company may provide beautiful symphonic music in order to attract favorable response to their product. The propagandist may also vary the content of his stimulus-situation to appeal to people of many different interests, as when a hotel simultaneously advertises accessibility to the downtown shopping district, a radio in every room, garage facilities, etc.

A fifth principle is that of the Desired Integration. "The propagandist secures a desired integration that predisposes people toward his aim." This should really be expressed as a hope rather than as a method, since of course the desired integration or activity does not always follow. In this connection Doob discusses the theory of Biddle (53) to the effect that the desired action may be brought about by a process of emotional conditioning. If, for example, the florists wish to increase their sales they develop Mother's Day and relate the thought of purchasing flowers to existing emotions attached to the mother. Biddle believes that "theoretically any emotion can be drained off into any activity by skillful manipulation." It is Doob's contention, on the other hand, that it is only when the two emotions are related that any conditioning occurs; in other cases, the secondary stimulus-situation has value only in attracting attention. In the familiar example of the pretty girl drinking tomato juice, Biddle would expect the favorable attitude towards the attractiveness of the girl to determine a favorable attitude to the tomato juice; Doob would regard her function as that of making certain that the tomato-juice advertisement is perceived. Both points of view appear to be correct in part. Biddle's idea that any emotion can be drained off into any activity is undoubtedly extreme; on the other hand, if the tomato-juice advertisement were presented in a particularly unattractive or even repulsive setting, it would probably be perceived without any difficulty, but the desired integration would certainly not follow. The girl undoubtedly functions both as a method of attracting attention and of arousing a favorable attitude. In summary and criticism it may be said that this principle of the Desired Integration should really not be listed with the others, which refer to methods, whereas Integration or action is rather the goal. Several of the other principles describe the means used to achieve the Desired Integration.

The sixth principle is that of the Sphere of Unpredictability.

> Before the desired integration is achieved between the related attitudes and, except in the case of concealed propaganda, the comprehension of the propagandist's aim and before it leads to action, there is a sphere of unpredictability due to the temporal character of the propaganda, the presence of competing propagandists, and the complexity of the person in the group with which the propagandist must deal.

Various methods are suggested for reducing this unpredictability and for making it more probable that action in the desired direction will take place. The phenomenon of prestige suggestion, for example, is very important in this connection, and may enter through the use of slogans or objects of positive social value, such as the American flag, "100% American," etc., or by creating the impression of universality—"everybody's doing it." In the case of groups which have complete control of all the organs of propaganda the sphere of unpredictability may be reduced by limitation of the kind of material available to the individual, as in the Nazi or Soviet censorship not only of their own newspapers and radios but also of foreign sources of information. Unpredictability may also be reduced by means of primacy, that is to say, by reaching children at a very early age before conflicting integrations can possibly be formed; early education by some religious groups or by the Nazi and Communist parties is an instance of this technique. There can be little doubt that the earliest impressions are the most stable and the most difficult to eradicate, and any system of propaganda which achieves such an early start is difficult to combat.

Doob's seventh principle is that of Counter-propaganda. "The propagandist uses counter-propaganda when conflicting attitudes tend to prevent the desired integration from emerging." It was not enough for the German propaganda to be pro-Nazi; it was also anti-communist, anti-Jew, and anti-democratic; and these negative suggestions with reference to outside groups and organizations helped to solidify the more positive ones toward the Germans. It is reported that leaders of Nazi meetings were instructed to let no occasion pass without attacking something, the idea apparently being that the in-group is strengthened by clear and definite denunciation of the enemy. This principle is used in a somewhat different manner in advertising; cigarette manufacturers, for example, employ counter-propaganda against the notion that smoking is harmful, that it shortens the wind, etc. Here the advertising in many cases stresses as virtues those effects which contrast directly with the arguments usually directed against smoking.

Finally Doob mentions the Principle of Persuasion. "The propagandist uses persuasion as a supplementary method." Persuasion here refers to the process of getting some prominent person to endorse a particular program or product in the expectation that the prestige suggestion will attract very many followers. In the case of advertising, the prominent movie actress who endorses a cosmetic preparation is usually "persuaded" to do so by some direct material gain; in other cases a program of propaganda may be required to persuade the individual before his name in turn may be used to propagandize others.

We have discussed these principles at some length, because they represent the most logical and systematic attempt so far made to reduce propaganda to its essentials. They are equally applicable to many different fields, and in spite of the criticisms which may be leveled against the details, the principles are of help in the understanding of what happens when attempts are made to mold and modify the opinions of others.

There arises the important problem of the limitations which are to be placed on the possible effects of propaganda. Many who witnessed the occurrences in Nazi Germany came away with the feeling that propaganda is all-powerful. There can be no doubt that its use was directed there with a thorough effectiveness which would be difficult to overestimate. The fact remains, however, that the efficient propaganda campaign of the Nazis in Germany was only part of the reason for their success. The historian who wishes to understand the factors which were responsible for the Third Reich will have to take into consideration the whole political and socioeconomic condition of Germany in 1933. The defeat in the World War, the conditions of the Versailles Treaty, the multiplicity of political parties and the consequent frequency of elections, the gradually lowered standard of living, the tragic effects of inflation—all prepared the way. Without them, and without the actual use of force, it is not probable that the propaganda would have achieved its goal. In the absence of efficient propaganda, on the other hand, the exact nature of the "solution" to these problems might have been quite different, and Hitler would probably not have had the support which finally persuaded Hindenburg to appoint him Chancellor. In other words, propaganda can be successful only under certain conditions, and with a state of readiness for it in the pre-existing attitudes of the people. This still leaves to it a tremendous influence in modifying these attitudes and directing them into certain channels rather than into others.

Other problems and experimental techniques related to the modification of attitudes are treated in connection with the analysis of prejudice in the following chapter.

SUMMARY

An attitude is defined as a state of readiness for certain types of response. It may be adopted ready-made by imitation of others, or it may be due to personal experiences of various kinds. It expresses itself frequently in the form of a stereotype or "picture in our heads," which may have a marked influence upon perception and behavior; such stereotypes may apply to single individuals or to groups.

Attitudes may be characterized in terms of various dimensions, namely, direction, degree, intensity, consistency and salience. Methods that have been applied include public opinion polls, attitude scales of different variety and construction, survey research, panel techniques, and projective techniques.

The control or manipulation of attitudes is known as propaganda. It is usually distinguished from education, which is concerned with truth, whereas propaganda is indifferent to truth; in actual practice this distinction is often difficult to maintain. The principles of propaganda include: (1) the Intention of the Propagandist, (2) Perception, (3) Type of Propaganda, (4) Related Attitudes, (5) Desired Integration, (6) Sphere of Unpredictability, (7) Counter-propaganda, (8) Persuasion. Propaganda has great influence in modifying attitudes, but it can be successful only under certain conditions.

REFERENCES

1. Allport, G. W. "Attitudes." In C. Murchison (ed.). *Hdbk. Soc. Psychol.* 1935

2. Thomas, W. I., and Znaniecki, F. *The Polish Peasant in Europe and America.* 5 vols. 1918-20

3. Bogardus, E. S. *Social Psychology.* 4th ed. 1923

4. Folsom, J. K. *Social Psychology.* 1931

• 5. Moore, H. T. "Innate Factors in Radicalism and Conservatism," *J. Abn. and Soc. Psychol.*, 1929, 35: pp. 220-238

6. Newcomb, T. M. *Social Psychology.* 1950

7. Lasswell, H. D. *Psychopathology and Politics.* 1930

8. Fromm, E. *Autorität und Familie.* 1936

9. Lippmann, W. *Public Opinion.* 1922

10. Rice, S. A. *Quantitative Methods in Politics.* 1928

11. Goring, C. *The English Convict.* 1913

12. Lombroso, C. *Crime, Its Causes and Remedies.* 1911

13. Hull, C. L. *Aptitude Testing.* 1928

14. Schoenfeld, W. N. "An Experimental Study of Some Problems Relating to Stereotypes," *Arch. Psychol.*, 1942, No. 270

15. Katz, D., and Braly, K. "Racial Stereotypes of 100 College Students," *J. Abn. and Soc. Psychol.*, 1933, 28: pp. 280-290

16. Bogardus, E. S. "A Social Distance Scale," *Sociol. and Soc. Res.*, 1933, 17: pp. 265-271

17. Murphy, G., Murphy, L. B., and Newcomb, T. M. *Experimental Social Psychology.* Rev. ed. 1937

18. Gilbert, G. M. "Stereotype Persistence and Change Among College Students," *J. Abn. and Social Psychol.,* 1951, 46: pp. 245-254

19. Horowitz, E. L., and Horowitz, R. E. "Development of Social Attitudes in Children," *Sociometry,* 1937-38, I: pp. 301-338

20. Stagner, R. "Fascist Attitudes: An Exploratory Study," *J. Soc. Psychol.,* 1936, 7: pp. 309-319

21. Hartley, E. L., and Hartley, R. E. *Fundamentals of Social Psychology.* 1952

22. Krech, D., and Crutchfield, R. S. *Theory and Problems of Social Psychology.* 1948

23. Gallup, G., and Rae, S. F. *The Pulse of Democracy.* 1940

24. Mosteller, F., et al. *The Pre-election Polls of 1948.* 1949

25. Meier, N. C., and Saunders, H. W. (eds.). *The Polls and Public Opinion.* 1949

26. See Reference 27,

27. Cantril, H. (ed.). *Gauging Public Opinion.* 1944

28. Crutchfield, R. S., and Gordon, D. A. "Variations in Respondents' Interpretations of an Opinion-poll Question," *Int. J. Opinion and Attitude Res.,* 1947, 1, No. 3: pp. 1-12

29. Stember, H., and Hyman, H. "How Interviewer Effects Operate Through Question Form," *Int. J. Opinion and Attitude Res.,* 1949, 3: pp. 493-512

30. Thurstone, L. L., and Chave, E. J. *The Measurement of Attitude.* 1929

31. Likert, R. "A Technique for the Measurement of Attitudes," *Arch. Psychol.,* 1932, No. 140

32. Edwards, A. L., and Kilpatrick, F. P. "A Technique for the Construction of Attitude Scales," *J. Appl. Psychol.,* 1948, 32: pp. 374-384

33. Guttman, L. See S. A. Stouffer (ed.). *The American Soldier.* v. IV. 1949. Summarized in M. Jahoda, M. Deutsch, and S. W. Cook (eds.). *Research Methods in Social Relations.* 1951

34. Lazarsfeld, P. L. In Jahoda, Deutsch and Cook (eds.), *Research Methods in Social Relations.* 1951

35. Jahoda, M., Deutsch, M., and Cook, S. W. (eds.). *Research Methods in Social Relations.* 1951

36. Chein, I., et al. "Consistency and Inconsistency in Intergroup Relations," *J. Soc. Issues,* 1949, 5, No. 3

37. LaPiere, R. T. "Attitudes and Actions," *Social Forces,* 1934, 13: pp. 230-237

38. Katz, D. "Attitude Measurement as a Method in Social Psychology," *Soc. Forces,* 1937, 15: pp. 479-482

39. Likert, R. "The Sample Interview Survey." In D. Lerner and H. D. Lasswell (eds.), *The Policy Sciences*. 1951

40. Katz, D. "The Public Opinion Polls and the 1940 Election," *Public Opinion Quarterly*, 1941, 5: pp. 52-78. "The Polls and the 1944 Election," *ibid.*, 1944, 8: pp. 468-482

41. Klineberg, O. (ed.). *Characteristics of the American Negro*. 1944

42. Katona, G. "Expectations and Decisions in Economic Behavior." In Lerner and Lasswell (eds.). *The Policy Sciences*. 1951

43. Campbell, A. (ed.). "Measuring Public Attitudes," *J. Soc. Issues*, 1946, 2, No. 2

44. Lazarsfeld, P. F. "Panel Studies," *Public Opinion Quarterly*, 1940, 4: pp. 122-128. See also Jahoda, Deutsch and Cook (eds.), *Research Methods in Social Relations*. 1951

45. Lazarsfeld, P. F., Berelson, B., and Gaudet, H. *The People's Choice*. 1944

46. Proshansky, H. M. "A Projective Method for the Study of Attitudes," *J. Abn. and Social Psychol.*, 1943, 38: pp. 393-395

47. Cobliner, W. G. "On the Place of Projective Tests in Opinion and Attitude Surveys," *Int. J. Opin. and Attitude Res.*, 1951, 5: pp. 480-490

48. Lumley, F. E. *The Propaganda Menace*. 1933

49. Young, K. *Social Psychology*. 1930

50. Doob, L. W. *Propaganda*. 1935

51. Freeman, E. *Social Psychology*. 1930

52. Mann, E. *School for Barbarians*. 1938

53. Biddle, W. W. "A Psychological Definition of Propaganda," *J. Abn. and Soc. Psychol.*, 1931, 26: pp. 283-295

Prejudice

19

INTRODUCTION

Prejudice refers to pre-judgment, a feeling or response to persons or things which is prior to, and therefore not based upon, actual experience. It may be either positive or negative, and it may be directed to any one of a large variety of objects. One may be prejudiced in favor of modern music or Norwegians, or against oysters or Englishmen. In the present context we shall consider only prejudice against ethnic groups. This is the form of prejudice which is of the greatest practical concern to all of us, and which represents one of the most active areas of research in contemporary social psychology and sociology.

Although popularly and in many scientific texts the problem is discussed under the head of "race" prejudice, this expression is misleading, since the type of group conflict which is being considered is not necessarily restricted to groups which differ in inherited physical type. (See Chapter 11.) In the United States, some of the minorities against whom prejudice is directed may perhaps be characterized in this fashion—for example, Negroes and Orientals. Even in the case of the Negro, however, prejudice may extend to many persons who are much less Negro than White, and who differ very little "racially" from the majority group. On the other hand, the prejudices of non-Jew against Jew, of American-born against immigrant, of one religious group against another, show essentially the same psychological mechanisms even though "race" in the strict sense plays no part. In some countries, such as the United States and South Africa, physical differences are important; in the Near East, as Dodd (1) has shown, the essential distinctions and hostilities occur between groups of different religions, and physical features are of relatively little significance.

Prejudice has been explained in many ways, and from many different points of view.

PREJUDICE AS "NATURAL"

One of the oldest approaches to this problem has taken the form of an explanation in terms of the nature of man, or of certain inevitable features of human society. According to this theory, prejudice cannot be avoided when two groups come into contact; the inference is clear that in a heterogeneous world prejudice will always be with us.

One view of the origin of prejudice lays stress upon a consciousness of kind, a feeling of solidarity with those like oneself and an accompanying "dislike of the unlike." It is the American sociologist Giddings who is mainly responsible for this concept and its use as a principle of explanation (2). The philosopher Royce (3) also spoke of a "natural antipathy" against those who differ from us. A similar point of view is expressed in the distinction between the in-group and the out-group, as well as by Sumner's (4) reference to ethnocentrism, or the feeling of loyalty to one's own group and of hostility against all who seem to threaten it in any way.

The phrase "consciousness of kind" has little practical meaning until the term "kind" is adequately defined. Until we know the basis of similarity or likeness, we cannot use it as the explanation of actual group hostilities. The most common interpretation is the identification of kind with physical type, and the "high visibility" of the Negro, or the ease with which he is recognized, is often mentioned as a sufficient reason for the prejudice against him. This is certainly an oversimplification. It is much more likely that the external visible characteristics are merely made the excuse or the occasion for the manifestations of a pre-existing prejudice.

The case of the Jews makes this clear. In spite of the fact that a certain proportion among them may be recognized as such, it remains true that in a very large number of cases they cannot be distinguished from the non-Jews among whom they live. As was indicated in Chapter 11, anthropologists do not regard the Jews as a distinct race, and usually explain this degree of recognizability on the basis of cultural and social factors. Even Houston Stewart Chamberlain (5), who was certain of the existence of a distinctive

Jewish race, admitted the frequent difficulties of identification, and fell back upon a childlike intuition as a means to that end. He wrote:

> Very small children, especially girls, frequently have a quite marked instinct for race. It frequently happens that children who have no conception of what "Jew" means, or that there is such a thing in the world, begin to cry as soon as a genuine Jew or Jewess comes near them. The learned frequently cannot tell a Jew from a non-Jew; a child that scarcely knows how to speak notices the difference (Vol. I, p. 537).

As is well known, visibility can be artificially manufactured when it does not exist in nature. During the Middle Ages Jews were required to wear a distinctive cloak, sometimes marked with a yellow badge, so that they could be easily recognized. During the Nazi regime a German edict required Jews to use distinctive personal names for the same purpose. There were of course many cases in which Jewish identity was unknown until brought to light by the painstaking investigations of the authorities. The fact that there is no Jewish race and no dependable visibility did not lessen the severity of the prejudice.

Even between groups of different physical characteristics a consciousness of kind may not always be presumed to exist. Pearl Buck tells an interesting story about being informed by her little daughter that a lady wished to see her. "Is it a Chinese or an American lady?" she asked. "I don't know, Mother," was the reply. "I didn't ask her." Mrs. Buck's explanation is that in a social environment in which racial differences mean nothing, they simply go unnoticed. Perhaps the child did notice the features of the visitor, but did not classify them in the usual manner. This experience has been duplicated by many persons who have had intimate contact with another race, the members of which then become distinguishable as individuals rather than as an alien group.

We live in a society in which skin color has often been the basis for distinguishing between groups, and in consequence we notice differences of this kind more readily than others. As was pointed out previously, however, at least one anthropologist, Sergi (6), regarded shape of the head as a more significant characteristic. Fouillée (7), a French writer, went so far as to say that in the future millions would be at each other's throats because of one or two points' difference in their cephalic index. If this point of view were generally accepted, we would in all probability notice first the head shape of a new acquaintance instead of the color of his skin. Visibility depends largely on habit.

A special turn to the theory of the dislike of the unlike has been given by Embree (8) and Reuter (9), who interpret it as a kind of narcissism. It is because we like and admire ourselves so much that we react with hostility against those who differ from us. This still leaves open the question as to what kinds of differences between individuals are important, and what criterion we are to use for likeness and unlikeness.

The best indication, however, that dislike of the unlike is not a natural but an acquired trait comes from the fact that it is entirely absent in young children. Even in those parts of the South in which the color line is quite rigidly drawn, there is the most intimate association between children of both groups until that is prevented by parents or teachers. An observation by Horowitz (10) is pertinent here. During the investigation of intergroup relations in a small Tennessee community, it was noticed that not only did White and Negro children play together until the former were forbidden to do so, but that they even attempted to continue the friendships in spite of parental opposition. There were many instances in which the White children had to be punished more than once before they finally accepted the mores of the group. In the sociometric studies of Moreno (11) in which children in school were asked which of their classmates they would like to have seated next to them, there was no noticeable "racial" cleavage in the first three or four grades; here, too, it is evident that prejudice is acquired and is not native to the child. This result proves clearly that the theory of the instinctive nature of intergroup hostility has no basis in fact.

It has been suggested that the dislike of the unlike may express itself in connection with cultural rather than physical differences. It is probably true that in some cases a difference in folkways and in values may create certain misunderstandings that contribute to hostility. Lafcadio Hearn (12) goes so far as to suggest that the contrast between the emotional folkways of the Japanese and the Whites has played a large part in developing hostility between them, the Japanese smile appearing to the Whites to be insincere, whereas the White face in turn seems to the Japanese to be in a state of constant irritation. This is rather a small point upon which to base hostility, although it may play a part in individual cases. In general, cultural differences do not afford a satisfactory basis of explanation.

In the South there appears to be the greatest hostility between Negroes and poor Whites between whom cultural differences are at a minimum, and the extent to which Jews in Germany identified themselves with German culture and made their contributions to it did not protect them from the development of animosity.

To the psychologist the whole notion of dislike of the unlike fails to carry conviction for the reason that most individuals show a desire for new experience, and curiosity and interest in what is novel. This tendency should at least counteract some of the opposition which Giddings regarded as natural under these conditions. Further, it should be kept in mind that between two scientists of different ethnic background we would expect more consciousness of kind than between either of these and an uneducated laborer of the same physical type or even of the same nationality. We cannot use the concept without further definition, and this further definition removes from it any exclusively "racial" significance.

Ethnocentrism is a fact, in the sense that we do regard ourselves as belonging to one group and that we often show a certain amount of hostility against others. Huxley and Haddon (13) write: "A 'nation' has been cynically but not inaptly defined as a 'society united by a common error as to its origin and a common aversion to its neighbors'" (p. 5). This may have nothing to do, however, with any biological affinity, since we know of many instances both among animals and human beings in which the in-group is composed of dissimilar elements. Murphy, Murphy and Newcomb (14) point out that "unless barriers imposed by social stratification are present, friendships as deep as any can grow where there is physical dissimilarity" (p. 43). These authors suggest that the major clue to the formation of these in-groups is familiarity, but it must be understood that this does not always overcome the effect of pre-existing lines of demarcation established by society.

A final reason for rejecting this theory as an explanation of prejudice is that it is by no means present in all groups. Hooton (15) states:

Primitive peoples are probably not race conscious to the deplorable or laudable extent which is characteristic of civilized populations. I mean that they are rather naively free from race prejudice until they have learned it from bitter experience. The American Indian was quite ready to take the European literally to his arms until he found out that a civilized embrace was inevitably throttling (p. 143).

This of course does not mean that primitive groups never showed hostility against outsiders, but this hostility did not take a "racial" form, and apparently was just as frequently directed against those who were physically similar to themselves. It is probable that in most cases there was fear of the unfamiliar, rather than dislike of the unlike.

Even in more complex societies, it is evident that the amount of prejudice varies greatly from individual to individual and from group to group. There is much less prejudice against Negroes in Brazil than there is in the southern part of the United States; there is more prejudice against Orientals in California than in Hawaii. Such variations are difficult to reconcile with the theory that prejudice is natural and therefore inevitable.

Similar considerations apply to the thesis that prejudice may best be explained on the basis of native aggressiveness. The notion of the instinctivist psychologist that pugnacity or aggressiveness is a part of human nature has been revived in somewhat different form by the psychoanalysts. Freud speaks of a "death instinct" as referring to a universal need to express hostility against someone, and Dr. Karl Menninger (16) has used it also as an explanation of many cases of suicide, in which the aggression, although ostensibly directed against oneself, is really a means of revenge against some other person.

Other psychoanalysts, although accepting the notion of the existence of these aggressive tendencies, find their explanation in the actual life experiences of the individual. Franz Alexander (17), for example, believes that the early frustrations of childhood create such emotional tensions that most individuals in later life tend to develop greater resentments and aggressions than are warranted by their actual life situations. A frequent result is projection of the hostile aggression upon others, that is to say, an ascription to others of the aggressive attitudes held by oneself. As Alexander puts it, "it is not that I hate him, it is not that I want to attack him, but he hates me and he wants to attack me. This projection leads to fear and mistrust of others and eventually to hate and supposedly self-protective aggressions" (p. 810).

This interpretation, which has direct implications for the problem of intergroup hostility, is applied by Dollard (18) to the question of Negro-White relations in the South. He accepts the notion that in all individuals there is frustration due to the very fact of growing up in a culture. There are many things which the child is not permitted to do and the resulting frustration calls into action an aggressive tendency. It is probable that as a consequence every mature person carries some generalized hostility toward his environment, but is unable to find a legitimate object on which the hostility may be directed. The aggressive tendencies are kept in check by the folkways of the group as well as by a direct fear of punishment. In the case of the southern White, however, there is presented in the person of the Negro a socially acceptable means for the expression of this latent hostility. "It is suggested that, when society does indicate an object, like the Negro whom one may detest with a good conscience, much of this irrational affect is drained off" (p. 442). In this case the visibility of the Negro serves as a sign which tells the prejudiced person whom to hate and makes easy and consistent discrimination possible.

This approach, in spite of its wide use by psychoanalysts and others who have been influenced by them, is in reality based upon a circular argument. It takes for granted the existence of the very phenomenon which it presumably sets out to explain. If society does indicate the Negro as a legitimate object of hostility, that hostility must be there before it may offer to the Whites a satisfactory outlet for their latent aggressiveness. We cannot make use of the concept of latent aggressiveness in order to explain prejudice, and at the same time assume the existence of prejudice to start with. We are left with the fundamental problem of explaining how the prejudice originated, and how it happened to be there as a socially acceptable means of draining off the stored hostility.

Dollard's theory, therefore, is not to be accepted as an explanation of the existence of prejudice. It may, however, to a certain degree account for the variations in its intensity. As has already been indicated, even when intergroup hostility exists in a society, it is not present equally in all regions or in all individuals. It seems highly probable that where frustration has been great, there would be an increased readiness to seek that outlet for aggressiveness of which Dollard speaks. Studies of the relation between frustration and aggression by Dollard and his colleagues (19) supply considerable evidence in this direction. There appears to be, for example, an intimate relationship between economic frustration, as represented by the level of real wages and the success of the cotton crop, and the number of acts of hostility against southern Negroes. When conditions are bad someone must be blamed for them, and the Negroes are convenient victims. Hovland and Sears (20) computed the annual per-acre value of cotton for fourteen southern states for the years 1882 to 1930. The correlation between this index and the number of lynchings in these same fourteen states was $-.67$, that is, the aggression increased as the economic frustrations became more severe. Mintz (21) has criticized the statistical techniques used in this study, but there remains a substantial degree of relationship after the necessary corrections have been made. Gallagher (22) comes to a similar conclusion on the basis of his examination of the relevant data.

In an experimental study of the frustration-aggression relationship, Miller and Bugelski (23) suggest the importance of irrational aggression resulting from the mechanism of displacement. Thirty-one young men at a summer camp were asked to rate Japanese (this was before the war) and Mexicans before and after a frustrating experience. Although they had expected to go to the theater, they were suddenly told they would have to work in camp instead. The ratings showed a marked diminution in the number of favorable traits, and an increase in the unfavorable traits, attributed to the two groups after the frustration. These results suggest at least a partial explanation of variations in the amount and severity of intergroup prejudice.

It would be a mistake, however, to regard the frustration-aggression hypothesis as telling the whole story. There is, for example, more economic frustration among White Brazilians than among White Americans on the average; there are fluctuations in economic conditions in Brazil just as there are in the United States. There are, however, no lynchings of Brazilian Negroes; there is apparently no need for that particular kind of displacement. It is therefore impossible to explain ethnic hostilities entirely in terms of the aggressive impulses which result from frustration.

The theory of aggressiveness as a *native* trait is even less acceptable as an explanation of the phenomenon we are here discussing. The Freudians have made use of this concept not only to account for race prejudice, but also as a basis for the understanding of war as well as of class conflict. War, at least from this point of view, becomes inevitable. In our discussion of warfare and aggressiveness in connection with the classical instinct theory, we had occasion to point out not only that there are many communities in which war is unknown, but also that when it does occur adequate causes are usually to be found in the general life conditions in the social and geographical environment. Aggressiveness appears to be an effect and not a cause. As for class conflict, it seems highly probable that the underprivileged are influenced more by the actual inequalities and their consequences than by a native impulse to kill and to destroy. This is by no means a denial of the strength of aggressiveness as a motive in individual cases, nor of its possible influence in the behavior of whole communities or groups, but it is a denial of its universal and innate character.

PREJUDICE AS "LEARNED"

A second, and much more convincing, approach sees prejudice as an aspect of the learning process, subject to the same principles of explanation that apply to any attitudes or value systems which we acquire in the course of experience. In connection with intergroup relations we have already discussed the effect on perception of the stereotype "Negroes use open razors" (see Chapter 8); it will be remembered that the distortion in reproduction did not occur in the case of very young children, who had not yet "learned" to make such an association. We must now broaden our inquiry to include some of the many different ways in which this kind of learning occurs.

What undoubtedly impresses many people as the most obvious possibility is that we develop friendly or unfriendly attitudes toward other groups as the result of our experience with them. With reference to Allport's theory (24) of the formation of attitudes, it was pointed out that three of the four conditions mentioned refer to personal experiences, either of a long-continued or of a traumatic nature. Allport admits, however, that they may be conditioned by the acceptance of pre-existing attitudes current in the community. In the study by Lasker (25) of the development of racial attitudes, many cases are cited in which individuals explain their racial dislikes and preferences in terms of their own experience with members of a particular ethnic group. A distinguished professor of sociology accounts for his own favorable attitude toward Norwegians as the result of his pleasant memories of a childhood nurse.

This whole approach is made explicit in the suggestion by House (26) of a method for the study of race relations.

. . . it is in the experience of individuals, their *subjective* experience
as known to them and susceptible of being reported by them, that the
data for the study of race relations . . . may be found. In other words,
race relations, conceived as cultural, may profitably be studied from
"life-history" documents, or by the method of "case-study," in the best
scientific sense of the term (p. 3).

It is highly probable that in the case of many individuals personal
experiences may play a definitive part in the formation of attitudes.
It is also probable that the study proposed by House would yield
valuable information as to the manner in which individuals consciously react to members of other groups, as to regional and community differences, and as to the changes which have taken place
in this respect. Such an investigation would be of little value, however, for the discovery of the motives underlying the prejudice or
of its exact origin.

This is indicated by the results of one of the experiments on
"social distance" by Bogardus (27), to which reference has previously been made. The results showed that the students had the
greatest prejudice against the Turks, although actually most of them
had never seen a Turk, and had had no experiences which could
account for their attitude. In his analysis of the reasons for the attitudes, Bogardus mentions first the acceptance of traditions and
current opinions, second the personal experiences of childhood, and
third the personal experiences of adult life. There can be no doubt
that in the case of the Turks, at least, personal experiences played
no important part. The investigation was conducted at a time when
the stories of the Armenian massacres were receiving much space
in the newspapers, and when the notions of the brutalities of the
"unspeakable Turk" were prevalent. Without any direct knowledge
of their own, the students who were subjects in these experiments
merely adopted the current stereotypes.

Another example of the existence of prejudice apart from any
direct personal experience is given by Bilgray (28), who was one
of the guides at the Jewish Exhibit at the Chicago World's Fair in
1933. He writes that visitors stared open-mouthed at the replica of
the synagogue, and requested in a whisper to see the knives used
for sacrifice. Some of them wished to know whether Jews really
sacrifice children before the Passover. Many stared at him because
they had never seen a Jew before. A village pastor from northern
Wisconsin said: "I have been teaching the Gospel for 30 years and

I have often mentioned the Pharisees; but until now I never knew what a Pharisee looked like. When my congregation asked me whether there were any Pharisees left, I told them I had heard there were some in New York" (p. 176).

What is probably the most convincing demonstration of the possibility that prejudice may develop without any personal experience whatsoever with the groups concerned is to be found in a study by Hartley (29), who applied a modified social distance test to students at eight different colleges. The subjects were asked to indicate their degree of acceptance or rejection of 35 ethnic groups, but included among these were the names of three fictitious groups, the Danerians, Pirenians and Wallonians. Some of the students were unwilling to answer questions about these groups, but many others had no such hesitation. There was on the whole a considerable degree of social distance in relation to these groups, more marked than toward a large majority of the other groups included in the study. It is obvious that this attitude cannot be related to any experience with them. No one could have been attacked by a Pirenian or robbed by a Wallonian; for many of the subjects it was apparently enough that they "looked" foreign and different.

The discussion of stereotypes in the preceding chapter has also indicated the frequent discrepancy between our actual experience and the "pictures in our heads." LaPiere (30) makes this clear in connection with prevailing attitudes toward Armenian immigrants to Fresno County in California. He states correctly that it is safe to disregard the explanation given by members of an in-group for their antipathy toward the members of an out-group. Such explanation is in his opinion more in the nature of a justification than a reason for antipathy. It was alleged, for example, that the Armenians are "dishonest, lying, deceitful," but the records of the Merchants' Association give them as good a credit rating on the average as Americans. The Armenians were described as "parasitic," but they apply much more rarely for charity to the County Welfare Bureau. They were also said to have an inferior code of social morality and to show frequent cases of social friction, yet they appear in fewer legal cases than their numbers would lead one to expect. LaPiere concludes: ". . . these explanations for the antipathy towards the Armenians have this in common: they point to a cultural difference between the in-group and the out-group.

But all have this further trait in common as well: they are not verifiable; in fact, they are definitely false" (p. 236).

Historical material also gives clear evidence of the extent to which prejudice may develop without any clear relationship to the real characteristics of minority groups. In connection with immigration, for instance, it is illuminating to note the occurrence of the same type of prejudice even though the ethnic composition of the new arrivals changes with the passage of time. There is a tendency (*31*) to hold our immigrants responsible for a great deal of the crime of the country and to regard them as representing the lowest elements in their respective mother countries. One reason given is that the character of the migration has changed in recent years and that at least until the latest immigration restrictions, the "inferior" counries of southern and central Europe were contributing a major share. As Schrieke (*32*) points out, however, in the early days of immigration there was also apprehension when the "bands of homeless, houseless mendicants" from Ireland invaded the country, and "the deluge of paupers from Germany," "the sweepings of English poorhouses and prisons" were deposited upon American shores. In a speech before the House of Representatives during the immigration debate of 1924, Congressman Meyer Jacobstein said:

> You contend that the present foreign element is less desirable than that of forty, fifty, sixty years ago. I call your attention to a report made to the House by a select congressional committee in 1838. It charged that "the country is being flooded with the outcasts of the jails, almshouses, and slums of pauper-ridden Europe." It asserted that at the time the jails of the capital were filled with these foreign-born people. It described them as "the most idle and vicious classes, in personal appearance most offensive and loathsome." But who were these "offensive and loathsome paupers and criminals"? Why, they were the scrappy Irishmen and Germans and British whose children today fear the influx of new "foreign hordes" (*33*, p. 136).

Still earlier, in a letter dated May 9, 1753, Benjamin Franklin expressed his opinion of the Germans who were then migrating into Pennsylvania.

> Those who come hither are generally the most stupid of their nation, and as ignorance is often attended with great credulity, when knavery would mislead it . . . it is almost impossible to remove any prejudice they may entertain. . . . Not being used to liberty, they know not how

to make modest use of it. . . . I remember when they modestly declined intermeddling with our elections; but now they come in droves and carry all before them (33, p. 134).

Earlier still it was the Irish who were the objects of the hostility of the previous settlers. By 1720 there were many Irish in Massachusetts, and the General Court passed an ordinance directing that "certain families recently arrived from Ireland be warned to move off" (33, p. 89). The hostile attitude against the Irish was by no means restricted to this period, and it has flared up on many occasions throughout American history.

These various incidents show that in all probability it is not the characteristics of the immigrants which cause them to be disliked, but rather that those characteristics are ascribed to them which give the dislike an apparent justification. There may of course be differences in folkways which cause a certain degree of suspicion and distrust, but it is unlikely that these by themselves could ever lead to open and violent antagonisms. From this point of view it is illuminating to observe that the very groups which are scorned on their first arrival quickly join in the hostility against any newcomers.

These facts indicate that personal experiences with minority groups are not necessary for the development of prejudice; such facts do not mean that experiences never play a part. The occurrence of stereotypes without any kernel of truth does not permit us to conclude that they never contain any truth. This point is made by Allport (34), who suggests that one of the most important research tasks that we should undertake is the discovery of the actual characteristics of the groups against whom prejudice is directed.

In connection with anti-Semitism, the presence of alleged Jewish characteristics of behavior and mentality is frequently held responsible for the hostility. Whatever these characteristics may be, it is clear from our previous discussion in Chapter 11 that we cannot regard them as racial or hereditary. First, the Jews are not a race and their behavior cannot be explained on a racial basis. Second, the so-called Jewish characteristics are by no means universally found among Jews, yet the hostility often extends to those who show no trace of them. Finally, and most important, the characteristics of the Jews as of other minority groups are much more probably the effect than the cause of prejudice. If it is true, for example, that aggressive behavior manifests itself more frequently among Jews than others, by far the most probable explanation is to be found in the need for self-assertion in a group that has suffered consistent discrimination. The same phenomenon appears among southern Negroes who experience for the first time the relative freedom of the North. If it is true that Jews play a comparatively large part in radical movements, this is certainly not due to any special genes for radicalism in their heredity, but is a reaction against a socioeconomic system in which they or their ancestors have been oppressed. Even the economic distribution of the Jews, and their preponderance in the cities, are to be explained by the former legal restrictions against their ownership of land and their resulting concentration in trade and the professions.

It is frequently suggested that the Jewish case is peculiar because of the religious issues involved. The story of the Crucifixion is part of the education of all Christian children, and it is sometimes told in such a way as to leave the impression that the Jews were responsible; the resulting attitude of hostility may never be overcome. Even this, however, presupposes some prejudice in the interpretation, since otherwise the decisive part played by the Romans, and the Jewishness of Jesus, could be emphasized. Allport makes a similar point. "It goes without saying that if accusations against minority groups should turn out to be justified to an appreciable degree the problem would still remain whether the traits in question were the cause or the consequence of public prejudice" (p. 8). This may be regarded as an example of what has been aptly called the "self-fulfilling prophecy": Negroes are regarded as inferior, therefore they are not given adequate educational opportunities, therefore they do in fact become inferior—not in potentialities, of course, but in terms of their average accomplishments.

The relation is therefore a circular one. As Myrdal (35) expresses it: "White prejudice and discrimination keep the Negro low in standards of living, health, education, manners and morals. This, in its turn, gives support to White prejudice. White prejudice and Negro standards thus mutually 'cause' each other . . ." (p. 75).

At the same time we must not overemphasize the importance of the objective facts of which Allport speaks. Two individuals may look at the same Negro slum; one of them may condemn the Negroes for their low standard of living; the other may blame the Whites for denying to Negroes the opportunity to improve that standard. In any case, as we have seen, prejudice may be found in individuals who have never seen a Negro slum, or who for that matter have never seen a Negro. Hartley and Hartley (36) write: "Attitudes toward Negroes are now chiefly determined not by contact with Negroes, but by contact with the prevalent attitude toward Negroes" (p. 705). How are these "prevalent attitudes" acquired?

There can be no doubt as to the importance of two dominant institutions, the home and the school. What we learn from our parents and our teachers exerts its influence precisely because it enters our lives at the most impressionable period, when the pronouncements of adults are surrounded by an aura of omniscience. A study by Remmers and Weltman (37) in which the Purdue Public Opinion Poll for young people was administered to high school students, their parents and their teachers, indicated that parents and children are more similar than are teachers and children. The school is by no means a negligible factor, however. The results showed a tendency for older children to be less like their parents in the attitudes studied than were the younger ones. This suggests that the schools may have a cumulative effect which becomes progressively more marked as children grow older.

The important part played by the teacher is demonstrated by Manske (38), who studied the effects of high school courses which included factual material dealing with minority problems. The same material was used by all the teachers. When the teacher was friendly and tolerant toward minorities, her pupils showed a change in attitude of greater friendliness; when the teacher was prejudiced, there was no such change. Presumably the same material was "taught" differently in the two cases, and the responses of the children were differentially affected as a consequence.

The mass media may also aid the process of learning the prevailing attitudes. This fact is well documented in the analysis of American magazine fiction by Berelson and Salter (39). They made a quantitative content analysis of 198 short stories published in eight of the magazines most widely read in the United States in 1937 and 1943. The results indicated a substantial difference in the presentation of "Americans" as contrasted with that of members of minority groups or of foreigners. In general these latter groups were described in terms of stereotypes, so that the Italian was frequently a gangster, the Negro amusingly ignorant, the Jew sly and shrewd, the Irish emotional, etc. The authors believe that the effect of such magazine fiction would be to increase the tendency on the part of readers to assign stereotype descriptions to foreign groups and minorities, and to give the readers the impression that they had found "proof" of the stereotype traits. Studies of school textbooks have yielded similar, though not nearly so striking, results. There is good reason to believe that such stereotyping occurs less frequently now than it did even a few years ago, but the phenomenon has by no means disappeared completely.

The prevailing attitudes, which constitute an aspect of the folkways or culture of a particular nation, region, or community, may also be transmitted through what Krech and Crutchfield (40) call the "environmental supports" of prejudice. These include many of the factors already considered; the inferior living conditions of minority groups such as Negroes or Mexicans, differences in the behavior of various ethnic groups (in many cases the result of prejudice, as in the circular relationship described above), the manner in which minority groups are depicted in the mass media, the beliefs and attitudes current in the community, etc. In addition Krech and Crutchfield identify a group of sociological environmental supports resulting from the segregation of various ethnic groups in such a manner and to such a degree as to create the impression that they are not only different but also inferior. Segregation may be sanctioned by law or by custom; it is found in education, housing, labor unions, churches, the armed forces (until recently), facilities for health and recreation, etc. It applies particularly to Negroes, but in certain parts of the country and under certain conditions may affect other minorities as well; it may be sanctioned by force or by "gentlemen's agreements." Whenever it occurs as a result of the action of the majority, it is interpreted to mean that the minority is in some way inferior. It serves as a constant reminder that others are not as we are. Acts of discrimination, by serving as environmental supports for prejudice, make the prevailing attitudes clear to all.

We have still to ask, why such discrimination? What is gained by it?

PREJUDICE AS A MEANS TO PRACTICAL ENDS

In part at least, these questions are not too difficult to answer. The existence of prejudice and discrimination confers certain very definite and practical advantages upon the dominant majority. One gain which emerges clearly and unmistakably is the economic. In the period of colonial expansion, the European nations who conquered a large section of the world's territory and placed a considerable portion of the world's population under their tutelage, obviously made great economic gains through the denial of equal rights and equal pay to the natives. The case of slavery in the Americas is also clear from this standpoint. Economic factors still play a dominant part in Negro-White relations, the Negro being kept in a position of inferiority so that he will not become an active rival of the Whites. As Dollard (18) points out, there have been frequent cases of aggression against Negroes entirely as a consequence of their economic success, even when they are willing to "keep their place." As for the Jews in Nazi Germany, the economic motive for their suppression is clear; long before the Nazis came into power they promised their followers the jobs held by the Jews, and to a certain extent that promise was fulfilled. Owing to the relatively small number of Jews in the country the Nazis were forced to extend the concept of "Jew" to those who were unable to prove a pure "Aryan" ancestry as far back as January 1, 1800, in order to increase the possible economic rewards to their supporters. The actual expropriation of Jewish wealth was a further step in the same direction. Although the economic motive is not the only one, it is certainly an important factor determining the origin and the extent of prejudice. Where the weaker group has "high visibility," as in the case of the Negro or the Oriental, physical characteristics serve as a convenient distinguishing mark between the members of the two groups; they indicate at a glance those whom one may with impunity eliminate from the field of competition. Where there is no such visibility, as in the case of the Jews, the same purpose may be obtained by other means. The motive of the dominant group, although not realized by all its members, is to appropriate the best positions and the greatest wealth for itself.

Such a direct economic motive is rarely admitted by members of the dominant group; they feel the need to justify their behavior in nobler terms. Among the mechanisms which the psychoanalysts have brought to our attention, none is more important in the present connection that that of rationalization. There seems to be in most of us a definite urge to give good reasons in support of our attitudes or behavior, though these reasons may not be the true ones.

In the field of intergroup relations this means in practice that the exploitation of a weaker group by a strong one is always justified by the latter, either in terms of the characteristics of the weaker people, or on the grounds that they will be benefited thereby. As Hooton (15) expresses it:

Man incessantly seeks to compromise with his conscience or with his innate humanitarianism, by rationalizing his predatory behavior. He must convince himself that the act of grabbing is somehow noble and beautiful, that he can rape in righteousness and murder in magnanimity. He insists upon playing the game, not only with an ace up his sleeve, but with the smug conviction that God has put it there (p. 151).

A survey of the historical material pertinent to the problem of ethnic contacts supplies a great many examples of this mechanism. When the Spaniards first came to America, several of their apologists, particularly Quevedo and Sepulveda, supplied them with the proper excuses for taking the land away from the Indians, and for treating them with complete lack of consideration. They developed the theory that the Indians had an entirely different origin from that of the Spaniards, that they were not human in the same sense, and that there was therefore no need to accord to them the same treatment as to one's fellow human beings. The familiar refrain of the "White Man's Burden," which was mainly of British manufacture and found its literary expression in the writings of Carlyle, Froude, Kingsley, and most strongly and clearly in those of Kipling, made of imperialism a noble activity destined to bring civilization to the benighted members of other "races." What the British stood to gain as a result was never mentioned.

One of the best examples of the mechanism of rationalization is to be found in the case of the Chinese on our own West Coast. Schrieke (32) has collected many of the descriptive phrases applied to them during the course of their residence in California. In the beginning, the Chinese were among "the most worthy of our newly adopted citizens," "our most orderly and industrious citizens," "the best immigrants in California"; they were spoken of as thrifty, sober, tractable, inoffensive, law-abiding. They showed an "all-round ability" and an "adaptability beyond praise." This was at a time when the Chinese were needed in California. Most of the White immigrants from other parts of the United States were anxious to make money quickly; they had no patience with domestic labor or with working in cigar factories or making boots and shoes. The Chinese were welcomed into these occupations, particularly during the hectic gold-rush period. Then came competition in the fields which the Chinese were occupying. In the elections of 1867 both political parties pledged themselves to enact legislation protecting Californians against Mongolian competition. The following phrases were now applied to the Chinese—"a distinct people," "unassimilable," "keeping to their own customs and laws," "they did not settle in America," "they carried back gold to their homes," "their presence lowered the plane of living," "they shut out White labor." They were spoken of as clannish, dangerous because of their secret societies, criminal, secretive in their actions, debased and servile, deceitful and vicious, inferior from a mental and moral point of view. They smuggled opium and spread the use of it, and Chinatowns were full of prostitution and gambling. They were "filthy and loathsome in their habits." They were "undesirable as workers and as residents of the country" (pp. 10-12). Here is an instance of a diametrical change in the alleged characteristics of a group without any actual change in the nature of the population. There were no new personal experiences to account for the contrast. There was no increase in native aggressiveness on the part of the White group. There was no heightening of an instinctive consciousness of kind. There was, however, a change in the economic conditions in California which made it to the advantage of the Whites to eliminate the Chinese as a factor in competition, and the attitude toward them was an effect of this situation.

Strong (41) points out an essentially similar mechanism operating in the case of the Japanese at a time when hostility against them had developed in California.

> Every significant thing about the Japanese, whether favorable or unfavorable, was seized upon and twisted about until it made a suitable weapon for injuring the newcomers. Hence, if they asked less than the going wage, they were threatening the American standard of living; if they demanded better wages, they were avaricious; if they were successful in farming and saved enough to buy their own ranch, they were driving the whites out; if they were unsuccessful, they were "wearing out the land" (p. 125).

In the case of the Negro many different types of rationalization have been used. The customary excuse for not giving to Negroes an equivalent occupational status to that of the Whites is that the Negro is constitutionally inferior. Charles Johnson (42) cites in this connection the fact that during slavery many skilled mechanical tasks were in the hands of Negro slaves, whose masters were quite content to entrust them with this work. After Emancipation, there was competition between Negroes and Whites for paid positions of this type. There followed the gradual growth of the idea that Negroes are fitted only for the simplest manual tasks and that complicated mechanical activity is outside the scope of their intelligence.

A second purpose served by prejudice is allied to the economic motive, but sufficiently distinct from it to deserve special attention, namely, finding a scapegoat to blame for all hardships and calamities. This mechanism is probably clearer in the case of anti-Semitism than in any other variety of prejudice. In a play by S. N. Behrman, *Rain from Heaven,* one of the characters is a German expatriate who has been forced to leave the country for writing a pamphlet, "The Last Jew." He says:

> With the extermination of the Jews, the millennium has been promised the people. And with the efficiency of a well-organized machine the purpose is all but accomplished. They are all dead—but one—the last Jew. He is about to commit suicide when an excited deputation from the All-Highest comes to see him. There has been a meeting in the sanctum of the Minister of Propaganda. This expert and clever man has seen that the surviving Jew is the most valuable man in the Kingdom. He points to the Council their dilemma. Let this man die and their policy is bankrupt. They are left naked, without an issue, without a programme, without a scapegoat. The Jews gone and still no millennium. They are in a panic—till finally a committee is dispatched —and the last Jew is given a handsome subsidy to propagate. . . .

The economic motive sometimes underlying the need for a scapegoat is illustrated in a story reported by Gessner (43). During the Nazi regime, two German workers are reading an official bulletin. "I see where another anti-Jewish campaign begins on Monday," says one. The other replies, "That means another wage-cut on Saturday." They knew from experience that if conditions became worse so that another wage-cut was necessary, the blame would again be placed upon the Jews.

It is perhaps unnecessary to state that the writer is not using these stories and anecdotes to prove, but rather to illustrate, the scapegoat theory. There can be little doubt that this mechanism plays an important part in many of the manifestations of group hostility. Gessner has made a strong case for the theory that the famous forgery known as *The Protocols of the Elders of Zion* was published anew whenever a scapegoat was needed. It appeared in Russia in 1905 to prove that the Jews were responsible for the disaster of the war with Japan; in 1919 in England at a time of severe industrial distress; in 1921 in Damascus in connection with Arab-Jewish riots; and it was outlined in twenty pages of *Mein Kampf* to aid the campaign of the National Socialists. (The previously reviewed research on the relation between economic conditions and the frequency of lynchings is also relevant to the scapegoat mechanism, which can in fact best be explained in terms of the frustration-aggression theory.)

This mechanism does not always have a direct economic basis. It has frequently been used as a means for re-establishing feelings of national self-importance. Not only in the Germany of our own generation, but also in France after the defeat of 1870 there was the need to find someone to blame for the disaster. As Barzun (44) points out, the insecurity and relative helplessness of the French were expressed in the wave of anti-Jewish feeling which followed the Dreyfus Affair, and which was extended at times to include Protestants, atheists, Freemasons and all foreigners.

> The Dreyfus affair . . . exhibited the full force of racial hysteria that we have come to associate with Nazi Germany. The only difference was that the anti-Semitic, anti-foreign, anti-Protestant group did not fully control the government (p. 206).

We discover in this example a third gain resulting from prejudice, namely, a gain in status, self-confidence, feelings of importance. The inferior position of poor Whites in the South is made more bearable by the knowledge that Negroes are worse off than they are; their prestige is heightened, in their own eyes at least, through the fact that the most educated and successful Negroes occupy in some respects a position lower than their own. Many Germans, after defeat in World War I, were undoubtedly comforted by the Nazi message that they were really of a super-race, destined for supremacy, with the right and even the duty to dominate the lesser peoples of the world. There is one other gain which may result from the existence of race prejudice or a "caste" situation, namely, the sex gain. In the

contact between two different groups the usual pattern is for the
men of the stronger to have access to the women of the weaker, and
to resist violently any attempt by the men of the weaker group
to obtain reciprocal privileges. As Dollard (18) and others have
pointed out, this is the typical pattern in race relations in the South.
"It may indeed be one of the functions of the caste situation to keep
the Negro woman without a protector and therefore more accessible" (p. 146). It is difficult to estimate the importance of this gain
in keeping the caste situation alive, but it undoubtedly enters to
some degree.

These various gains and advantages undoubtedly play an important part in the development of prejudice and discrimination,
although as we have seen they are rarely admitted by the prejudiced to be their real motives, and are usually disguised in order
to appear more ethical and justifiable. We have still not reached a
full explanation of prejudice, however. Two individuals in the same
community may be equally poor, equally in need of a job, equally
low in status; one of them may blame Negroes or Jews for his failures, and do everything possible to keep these groups in a position of
inferiority; the other may blame himself or his lack of training and
experience. We turn now to a consideration of the relationship
between prejudice and personality.

PREJUDICE AS A DIMENSION OF PERSONALITY

In recent years significant research evidence has accumulated
which demonstrates the important part played by personality in the
development of prejudice. Murphy and Likert (45) were able to
show, for example, that anti-Jewish, anti-Negro, and other prejudices were as a rule found together. These attitudes also appear to
be found more frequently in persons who have conservative or reactionary opinions on domestic and international issues. The inference that there is a bigoted or prejudiced personality has been the
subject of several important investigations.

Hartley (29), in a study to which reference has already been
made, indicates also that when an attitude of unfriendliness toward
"foreigners" has developed, it is usually extended indiscriminately
to all groups. In his analysis of the student responses, he divided his
thirty-two ethnic groups into "odd" and "even" lists of sixteen each,
and gave tolerance scores to each subject based separately on re-

actions to the two lists. Correlation coefficients were computed for these scores, and they were remarkably high, averaging about +.95. He also computed the correlation coefficients for the social distance scores referring to the thirty-two real ethnic groups on the one hand, and the three imaginary ones on the other. Once again the coefficients were high and positive, ranging from +.78 to +.85. In most cases therefore those who were prejudiced against existing groups extended that attitude to groups with which they could have had no experience whatsoever. Hartley concludes that "there is evidence to suggest that the degree of tolerance expressed by individuals is a generalized function of the individual and is not completely determined by the specific group toward which the attitude is directed" (p. 25).

The most extensive and thorough investigation of the relationship between prejudice and personality was conducted by Adorno, Frenkel-Brunswik, Levinson, and Sanford (16), who administered attitude scales to over two thousand subjects in California and Oregon, although not all the subjects responded to all the questionnaires utilized. The results showed once again the extent to which attitudes cluster together. For their Total Ethnocentrism Scale, which included items dealing with Negroes, other minorities, and "patriotism," the split-half reliability, obtained by correlating the sum of the scores on the even-numbered with the odd-numbered items, was +.91. The sub-scales on Negroes and other minorities correlated +.74; attitudes toward Negroes and "patriotism" correlated +.76; attitudes toward "patriotism" and minorities, +.83. A special scale constructed for the measurement of anti-Semitism correlated +.80 with the Total Ethnocentrism Scale. The general conclusion is inescapable that on the whole those subjects who dislike Jews also dislike Negroes and other minorities, and show excessive patriotic responses [the investigators correctly point out that: "The term 'patriotism' as used here does not mean 'love of country.' Rather, the present concept involves blind attachment to certain national cultural values, uncritical conformity with the prevailing group ways, and rejection of other nations as outgroups. It might better be termed *pseudopatriotism* . . ." (p. 107).].

This evidence to the effect that certain kinds of persons are prejudiced has been upheld by further investigation. There was a smaller, but still substantial positive correlation of +.57 between Ethnocentrism and the scores obtained on a scale of Politico-Economic

Conservatism. Finally, there was a correlation of +.73 between Ethnocentrism and the scores on the fascism scale, which included items dealing with conventionalism, authoritarianism, preoccupation with power and "toughness," generalized hostility, etc. There emerges the portrait of the prejudiced individual as one who tends to be indiscriminately hostile to all minorities, who is super-patriotic, conservative in politics and economics, and "fascist."

In addition to the investigation of large numbers of subjects by means of intercorrelations between the results of the attitude scales, detailed interviews were conducted with eighty individuals, twenty men and twenty-five women with extremely high scores, and twenty men and fifteen women with extremely low scores on the Ethnocentrism scale. Flowerman (47), who was a co-editor of the series which included this investigation, believes that the findings justify the following composite portrait of the authoritarian (and prejudiced) man: he is a supreme conformist, he sees the world as menacing and unfriendly, he is a loyal camp-follower as long as the leader remains strong, he is rigid and shows limited imagination; he is herd-minded, exalting his own group and disliking many out-groups; he is a "phony conservative," waving the flag, but showing many anti-democratic tendencies; he is a moral purist. On the basis of the original report we may add that the prejudiced individuals often are on the surface poised, self-confident and well-adjusted, but fundamentally anxious and insecure; they appear to worship their parents but have strong repressed hostility against them; they blame others for their own faults and misfortunes. Those who obtain low scores on the Ethnocentrism scale in general show the opposite constellation of characteristics.

On the basis of a questionnaire administered to 437 college undergraduates, Allport and Kramer (48) conclude that those who cling most strongly to parental patterns are most prejudiced, whereas a critical attitude toward such patterns more frequently accompanies friendliness to other groups. The prejudiced on the whole have a "jungle" philosophy of life, viewing the world as a hazardous place, where men are basically evil and dangerous; they are authoritarian, status-conscious, and with little or no sympathy for the underdog. Ackerman and Jahoda (49) examined the psychoanalytic case histories of forty anti-Semitic patients and, while admitting the highly selective nature of their sample, suggest the frequent occurrence of a diffuse and pervasive anxiety, a confused and vague self-image, difficulty in establishing satisfactory interpersonal relationships, a strong emphasis on conformity, poor adaptation to reality, and an inadequate and unreliable conscience.

Other studies could be cited. Although differing in methodology and in their specific findings, they agree in demonstrating that there are personality characteristics which distinguish the prejudiced from the unprejudiced individual; they are in substantial agreement, also, as to the nature of these characteristics. There can be no doubt that personality represents an important factor in the understanding of the nature and development of prejudice.

A MULTI-DIMENSIONAL APPROACH

The preceding discussion has made it clear that the writer is not prepared to accept any one explanation of prejudice as entirely adequate. Prejudice may satisfy a number of different motives, it may be learned in a variety of different ways. It may be adopted as a reflection of the folkways, or in response to deep-seated personality needs. Even in the same individual it may be the result of several different factors operating together. Our approach must therefore be multi-dimensional. It must also recognize that these factors are interdependent, that they influence one another.

An example should make this interdependence clearer. As was pointed out above, prejudice may result in economic gain; one might therefore expect less prejudice among those who are economically successful. This possibility was explored by Campbell (50) who analyzed the responses of a nationwide cross section of 316 White, non-Jewish Americans who were interviewed regarding their attitudes toward Jews. He reports that there is no consistent relationship between amount of anti-Semitism and level of income. The respondents were also rated, however, for their degree of satisfaction or dissatisfaction with their own personal economic situation; now a clear relationship emerged. "Those persons classified as dissatisfied with their own economic situation expressed hostility toward Jews more frequently than those who were economically satisfied" (p. 605). Not the economic fact itself, but this fact as interpreted psychologically, turned out to be the important variable.

In another investigation, Bettelheim and Janowitz (51) interviewed 150 Chicago veterans of World War II as to their attitudes toward Jews and Negroes. There was no statistically significant relation between income or socioeconomic status on the one hand and the intensity of anti-Semitic or anti-Negro responses on the other. The hypothesis was then explored that not social *status* but rather social *mobility* might be the important factor. The veterans were rated in terms of whether they had gone *up* or *down* the socioeconomic scale as compared with their previous civilian employment. The results showed "that ethnic hostility was most highly concentrated in the downwardly mobile group, while the pattern was significantly reversed for those who had risen in their social position. Those who had experienced no change presented a picture somewhat in the middle . . ." (p. 596). The conclusion appears justified that in this case we are dealing not with economic or psychological factors acting separately, but with the two in intimate interdependence.

In the important article by Allport (34) to which reference has already been made, it is suggested that there are six different valid levels of causal analysis. There is (1) the approach *via* the stimulus object, represented by the actual characteristics of various ethnic groups; (2) the phenomenological level, which refers to the manner in which the individual perceives the stimulus object; (3) personality dynamics and structure; (4) the situational approach, represented by the "outer forces that act upon the individual," such as unemployment, contact between different ethnic groups, etc.; (5) the influence of culture and sub-culture; and finally (6) the historical approach. Allport concludes: "A social scientist is free to select his own level of approach, but he should be respectfully aware of the whole etiological sweep" (p. 23).

The writer finds himself in very substantial agreement with Allport's analysis, but feels that more stress should be laid on the interdependence of the various levels. To take one example, Allport quotes an observation by Malherbe (52) who asked candidates on a public service examination in South Africa to "underline the percentage that you think Jews constitute of the whole population of South Africa: 1 per cent, 5 . . . 10 . . . 15 . . . 20 . . . 25 . . . 30 per cent." The modal estimate was 20 percent; the correct answer is slightly over 1 percent. Allport cites this as an example of how prejudice accentuates features within the phenomenal world. In that case, does phenomenology represent a "level of causal analysis"? Or is it an effect, rather than a cause? It would seem desirable to emphasize the reciprocal relationship among all the factors which have been identified.

Keeping in mind, therefore, that there are many factors, and that they are interdependent, we turn now to a brief discussion of what can be done about prejudice.

THE REDUCTION OF PREJUDICE

In what follows we shall limit ourselves to some rather general observations, and a few relevant examples. More detailed presentation of the problems and techniques involved may be found in the publications by Williams (53), MacIver (54), Rose (55), Watson (56), Saenger (57), and Klineberg (58). A valuable account of methods of conducting research in this important field is presented by Jahoda, Deutsch and Cook (59).

There are three basic principles which appear to be logical inferences from our analysis of prejudice. The first is that if there are many causes, we can hardly expect to find any one cure; if prejudice is multi-dimensional, the reduction of prejudice will have to be approached from many different directions. The second is that techniques for reduction should as far as possible be directly related to our understanding of the causes. The third is that since the causes are interdependent, various techniques for reduction should be used simultaneously.

An example should make the application of these principles clearer. There has been much discussion as to whether we can successfully legislate against prejudice and discrimination, for example, through Fair Employment Practices Commissions, anti-segregation statutes regarding the use of public facilities, housing, education, etc. On the one hand it is argued that laws do not work unless the people are prepared to accept them, and that an educational campaign must therefore precede any attempt to bring about the desired changes through legislation. On the other hand it is urged that although we cannot legislate against prejudice, we can outlaw discrimination, and that an attack on the environmental supports of prejudice will not only make life easier for the minority group, but will also in time change the attitudes of the majority.

On the basis of our preceding discussion, the second line of argument carries much more conviction. In a country in which most citizens are after all relatively law-abiding, legislation against discrimination can usually be expected to have the anticipated consequences. This may sometimes be due to the fact that a particular community may actually be less prejudiced than is commonly believed. When as a result of the Supreme Court decisions the graduate schools of some Southern universities were opened to Negro students, there were dire predictions as to what would happen; the Whites would never stand for it, there would be violence and rioting, it would never work, etc. Nothing of the sort occurred; the transition was relatively smooth and easy, and there were none of the unpleasant consequences which had been anticipated. We have here an excellent example of what F. H. Allport (60) in another context labeled "pluralistic ignorance"; all those concerned were apparently ready to accept the proposed change, but they believed that *others* would object violently. This is not very different from the "pseudo-community" which Cameron (61) has described in connection with paranoia; the patient's world is made up of people to whom he ascribes motives and viewpoints which they do not in fact possess. The phenomenon is by no means restricted to the paranoid.

If legislation, therefore, is effective in reducing the environmental supports of prejudice, it represents a technique of the greatest potential usefulness. Where there is real opposition to it on the part of the people directly concerned, the legislation may be difficult to enforce, and ways may be found to circumvent its intent and reduce its effectiveness. In those cases in which legislation is under the control of local or regional groups, it is obvious that it will never be passed if the people are not prepared for it. In both these situations, what Myrdal (36) calls an "educational offensive" should first be undertaken. The fact remains that some of the greatest gains that have been achieved in the position of the American Negro in recent years are to be attributed directly to this technique, either in the form of new legislation, or through the appeal to civil rights as guaranteed by the American Constitution.

It must be remembered, however, that not all the environmental supports of prejudice are of the kind which are susceptible to legislation. There are the customs, the folkways of ethnic relations —not sanctioned by law, but by tradition. Such folkways also change, however, sometimes slowly and gradually, sometimes in a comparatively short time. There was no law against Negroes playing big league baseball, but tradition was opposed to it until a small number of courageous individuals dared to break the tradition. In this case, too, there was less opposition than had been anticipated, and quite probably it represented another example of pluralistic ignorance.

In the preceding chapter reference was made to Gilbert's (62) view that the observed decrease in stereotyped thinking may be due in part to the effect of college courses in the social sciences; these have introduced caution and a critical attitude toward ethnic generalizations. It does seem highly probable that some at least of the findings of the social scientists with regard to ethnic characteristics have influenced the thinking not only of college students but of educated people generally. The writer had occasion to testify as a witness for the National Association for the Advancement of Colored People in a suit to compel a municipal school system in a border state to admit Negro children to schools previously restricted to Whites. He was questioned regarding the problem of inherited differences in intelligence and personality, and his testimony followed the lines indicated in Chapter 11 of this volume. To his great surprise he was not cross-examined; his evidence was not questioned by the attorney for the State. In essence this meant that what he said was admitted as fact.

This raises the whole question of the extent to which information can be utilized to change attitudes in the direction of better ethnic relations. The assumption that the presentation of facts will always have the desired result has rightly been questioned. We have already seen (Chapter 8) to what extent perception and memory are affected by many factors independent of the stimulus which is presented. Katz (63) speaks of "psychological barriers to communication," and Hyman and Sheatsley (64) analyze a number of reasons "why information campaigns fail." Lazarsfeld (65) reports that when radio broadcasts were utilized in an attempt to increase information regarding ethnic groups in the United States, for the most part each broadcast was listened to by members of the particular group described, rather than by the other groups to whom the broadcast was directed.

These results should certainly temper whatever faith we may have in the power of information to solve all problems, but they do not justify a completely pessimistic conclusion. In a survey of the results of eleven studies on the effect of school courses dealing with intergroup relations, Rose (55) finds in six of them a change in the anticipated direction, in four cases no change, and ambiguous results in the remaining one. Information is evidently effective more often than not. Green (66) reports a favorable change in attitude toward Negroes on the part of White children in southern schools who had received information regarding the Negro. These investigations all dealt with "captive audiences" who were not in a position to leave the classroom or turn off the radio, but they indicate that at least under certain conditions information may be effective. We need to know more about the circumstances under which information is successful in changing attitudes, and those under which it is unsuccessful. This is an important area for future research.

The mass media may of course be used to present not only information, but also emotionally toned situations involving different ethnic groups. To mention one example, the effect of moving pictures on attitudes has been studied by Thurstone (67) in a series of experiments. The five films used included one favorable to and one unfavorable to the Chinese, a pro-German film, an anti-gambling film, and one illustrating the evils of bootlegging. The subjects were high school children in small towns not far from Chicago, and they answered the attitude questionnaires before and after seeing the pictures. In the case of the pro-Chinese film the change was 16.98 times its probable error; the other films were less effective, but in their case also some change was reported. Two films with the same type of propaganda were more effective than one, and three were more effective than two. Thurstone reports that most groups retain a large percentage of the change after intervals of time varying from 2½ to 19 months.

The effect of contact between different groups has also been extensively investigated. It is obvious that contact will not change attitudes when it is of a kind congruent with existing stereotypes, for example, the contact of a White plantation owner with Negro field hands, or of an American employer and his Mexican laborers. It is much more likely to be successful if the contact is between individuals of equal status with similar problems and goals. In one such investigation F. T. Smith (68), instead of merely telling his subjects, who were 46 Teachers College students, about Negroes and the reasons for developing a more favorable attitude toward them, exposed them to two consecutive week-ends in Harlem. With the cooperation of Negro artists, writers and business men, he showed his White subjects the inadequacy of their stereotypes and brought them into contact with Negroes of a kind quite foreign to their previous experience. The change was marked and persistent.

Contact has been found to be very effective in improving attitudes when it occurs between ethnic groups working together in a trade union (69), fighting side by side in the army (70), or living in close proximity in a housing project (71). In connection with housing, it is important to note that the results of the investigation by Deutsch and Collins (71) led to at least a partial change in the folkways. Mr. Louis Dantzig, Executive Director of the Housing Authority of the City of Newark, wrote in a postscript to the Deutsch-Collins volume that the partial segregation which characterized public housing in Newark would be abandoned. "Instead of Negroes and Whites being kept in separate buildings, they are being assigned to apartments in the same buildings without regard to their race. In large measure, this change in fundamental policy reflects the impact of the study reported in this book" (p. 103). It is also significant that in all these instances the individuals involved —trade unionists, soldiers, apartment dwellers—were not asked to consent to such contact. They were presented with a *fait accompli* by the respective authorities, who took the responsibility for the change, and carried it through successfully. There is a place here for leadership wisely exercised [see Saenger (57)].

We have seen that if prejudice can be learned, it can also be unlearned. It would of course be more efficient if the original learning process for which parents and teachers are responsible were directed more effectively and more consistently toward friendliness rather than toward intolerance. Implicit in what we have said is the need to direct an educational offensive to all groups in the population, and not to school children or college students alone.

What of the gains resulting from prejudice? These gains, particularly the economic, have sometimes been regarded as playing such an important part as to lead to the conclusion that prejudice can be eliminated only when competition between individuals is replaced by a classless society. Without for a moment denying the importance of economic factors, we must insist that an explanation in economic terms alone does not carry conviction. Hawaii and California are both within the American economic system; there is much less prejudice against Orientals in the former. Both Brazil and the Union of South Africa have economic competition, but whereas the former does not discriminate against Negroes to any appreciable degree, the latter is in the process of extending such discrimination to the extreme.

Even as between France and England, the attitude toward Negroes differs markedly. In a comparative study by LaPiere (72) of race prejudice in these two countries, it was noted that out of 360 people questioned in France, 279 of them were apparently free from prejudice; the figures for England were 14 out of 315. Out of 31 French hotels, 24 admitted Negroes, whereas only 4 out of 20 English hotels admitted Negroes. LaPiere was careful to make the comparison between people of similar socioeconomic status in the two countries. It may be added that the difference in French and English attitudes extends also to the colonization policies of the two countries, and that there has been much more intermarriage in the French than in the British colonial Empire. Bunche (73) indicates that this did not prevent the same degree of exploitation of African Negroes by the French as by the British administrators. As far as race is concerned, however, the French attitude is undoubtedly less prejudiced.

This means that there are customs and folkways which create regional and national differences in intergroup relations not understandable in terms of economics alone. To that extent they are subject to change even under relatively constant economic conditions. The Soviet Union for a time appeared to have markedly reduced prejudice within its borders, but recently anti-Semitism has been either encouraged or suppressed, depending on the national or international policy of the moment. We are reminded again that prejudice has many causes and that no one of them tells the whole story.

It should be remembered also that prejudice results in losses as well as in gains. Rose (74) speaks of the direct economic waste resulting from the failure to use the full productivity of manpower; the aggravation of social problems; the increase of fear and anxiety; the loss of good will between nations, etc. The presence in any nation of large sections of the population who are prevented from achieving equal status with the majority, inevitably results in a marked degree of social pathology. For obvious reasons, discrimination helps to develop in the minority group lower standards of living, more broken homes, greater dependency, an increase in disease rates, in crime and delinquency, and in the need for institutions to care for the maladjusted and the destitute. All of this represents a great cost to the community as a whole—a cost which is to be reckoned not only in economic terms but in social terms as well.

Deutscher and Chein (75) summarize the opinions of social scientists regarding the psychological effects of segregation and other forms of discrimination. Over 90% of those who answered the questionnaire were certain that the effects on members of minority groups were exceedingly detrimental. The typical effects listed in the answers received could be classified as follows: first, special stresses created by the discrepancy between democratic ideals of equality and the practice of discrimination; second, the development of feelings of inferiority and of not being wanted; third, submissiveness, feelings of persecution, tendencies toward withdrawal, and aggression; fourth, distortion in the sense of reality. More than 82% of these social scientists also indicated their conviction that prejudice was harmful to the mental health of those who discriminate. There may be inner conflicts and guilt feelings; increased hostility, the deterioration of moral values, an unreal attitude toward one's own capacities and those of others, etc. Rose believes that if people could be made more aware of these and other "costs" of discrimination, they might be better prepared to substitute for it an attitude of cooperation and friendliness.

Finally, what can be done about the prejudice which has its roots in personality dynamics? In one sense, this is a part of the general problem of mental health. Whatever increases feelings of personal security, acceptance of oneself and of others, adaptation to reality, should at the same time reduce the need for prejudice, or for status obtained at the expense of others. Mental hygiene and psychotherapy may be indicated in many cases, but their application obviously presents great difficulties.

There are some aspects of the personality of the prejudiced, however, which give grounds for hope. He is a conformist; he may therefore accept the folkways even when they prescribe acceptance of others. He respects power; he may therefore follow the lead of prestige figures who condemn discrimination. He has a great need of approval; he may change his attitudes if the group to which he belongs adopts attitudes different from his own. There were undoubtedly some authoritarian students at Bennington College who, as Newcomb demonstrated (76), became more liberal in order to fit into the atmosphere by which they were surrounded.

Considerable progress has been made in intergroup relations in this country in recent years. Although much remains to be done, there is good reason to be optimistic regarding future developments, particularly if the findings of the social sciences are increasingly accepted and applied.

SUMMARY

The phenomenon of prejudice, or negative prejudgment, is found between groups which differ from one another in various ways; it is not limited to groups of different "race" or inherited physical type. The explanation in terms of a natural antipathy must be rejected, primarily because an awareness of difference may be absent in those individuals who have not learned from others that the differences are to be taken seriously, and also because in-groups are frequently formed independently of physical characteristics. The notion of a native aggressiveness which finds an outlet in group hostility is also unsatisfactory. It is highly probable, however, that when frustrations are great, there is more readiness to engage in aggressive behavior, and fluctuations in the amount of group hostility may be accounted for on this basis.

Prejudice is "learned," as the result of personal experience, or the influence of parents and teachers, or through the acceptance of attitudes current in the social environment. It seems certain that in a large number of instances the nature of one's experiences with members of another group will be determined by the pre-existing attitude, rather than the attitude being determined by the experiences.

Prejudice is also to be explained in part as a means to an end. It may arise from economic motives, or out of a need to find a scapegoat, or as a way of enhancing self-esteem.

Personality also plays an important part in the development of prejudice. Evidence has accumulated which shows the existence of a bigoted or prejudiced personality, with a fairly well defined cluster of characteristics.

Prejudice is multi-dimensional, in the sense that it may arise from a number of different causes and satisfy a variety of motives. Both the understanding and the treatment of prejudice require an integrated approach from a number of directions. Positive effects have been obtained through information programs, contact, changes in cultural patterns (particularly through the attack on environmental supports of discrimination and prejudice), psychotherapy, and other means. The developments of recent years give grounds for optimism regarding the future.

REFERENCES

1. Dodd, S. C. "A Social Distance Test in the Near East," *Am. J. Sociol.,* 1935, 41: pp. 194-204

2. Giddings, F. H. *The Principles of Sociology.* 1896

3. Royce, J. *Race Questions, Provincialism and Other American Problems.* 1908

4. Sumner, W. G. *Folkways.* 1906

5. Chamberlain, H. S. *The Foundations of the Nineteenth Century.* 2 vols. 1911

6. Sergi, G. *L'Uomo, secondo le origini, l'antichità, le variazioni e la distribuzione geografica.* 1911

7. Fouillée, A. *Tempérament et caractère selon les individus, les sexes et les races.* 1893

8. Embree, E. R. *Brown America.* 1931

9. Reuter, E. B. *The Mulatto in the United States.* 1918

10. Horowitz, E. L., and Horowitz, R. E. "Development of Social Attitudes in Children," *Sociometry,* 1938, I: pp. 301-338

11. Moreno, J. L. *Who Shall Survive?* Rev. ed. 1953

12. Hearn, L. *Glimpses of Unfamiliar Japan.* 2 vols. 1894

13. Huxley, J. S., and Haddon, A. C. *We Europeans.* 1935

14. Murphy, G., Murphy, L. B., and Newcomb, T. M. *Experimental Social Psychology.* Rev. ed. 1937

15. Hooton, E. A. *Apes, Men and Morons.* 1937

16. Menninger, K. A. *Man Against Himself.* 1938

17. Alexander, F. "Psychoanalysis and Social Disorganization," *Amer. J. Sociol.,* 1937, 42: pp. 781-813

18. Dollard, J. *Caste and Class in a Southern Town.* 1937

19. Dollard, J., et al. *Frustration and Aggression.* 1939

20. Hovland, C. I., and Sears, R. R. "Minor Studies of Aggression: VI. Correlation of Lynchings with Economic Indices," *J. Psychol.,* 1938-9: pp. 301-310

21. Mintz, A. "A Re-examination of Correlations between Lynchings and Economic Indices," *J. Abn. and Social Psychol.,* 1946, 41: pp. 154-160

22. Gallagher, B. G. *American Caste and the Negro College.* 1938

23. Miller, N. E., and Bugelski, R. "Minor Studies of Aggression: II. The Influence of Frustration Imposed by the In-group on Attitudes Expressed Toward Out-groups," *J. Psychol.,* 1948, 25: pp. 437-452

24. Allport, G. W. "Attitudes." In C. Murchison (ed.), *Hdbk. Soc. Psychol.* 1935

25. Lasker, B. *Race Attitudes in Children.* 1929

26. House, F. N. "Some Methods of Studying Race and Culture," *Soc. Forces,* 1936, 15: pp. 1-5

27. Bogardus, E. S. *Immigration and Race Attitudes.* 1928

28. Bilgray, A. T. "Alas, Poor Goy," *Hebrew Union College Monthly.* Oct. 1933

29. Hartley, E. L. *Problems in Prejudice.* 1946

30. LaPiere, R. T. "Type-Rationalizations of Group Antipathy," *Soc. Forces,* 1936, 15: pp. 232-237

31. Armstrong, C. P. "Juvenile Delinquency as Related to Immigration," *School and Soc.,* 1933, 38: pp. 61-64

32. Schrieke, B. *Alien Americans.* 1936

33. Feldman, H. *Racial Factors in American Industry.* 1931

34. Allport, G. W. "Prejudice: A Problem in Psychological and Social Causation," *J. Soc. Issues,* 1950, Supplement Series No. 4, pp. 1-25

35. Myrdal, G. *An American Dilemma.* 1944

36. Hartley, E. L., and Hartley, R. E. *Fundamentals of Social Psychology.* 1952

37. Remmers, H. H., and Weltman, N. "Attitude Inter-Relationships of Youth, Their Parents, and Their Teachers," *J. Social Psychol.,* 1947, 26: pp. 61-68

38. Manske, A. J. Unpublished Ph.D. Dissertation, Teachers College, Columbia University, 1935. See D. Krech and R. S. Crutchfield, *Theory and Problems of Social Psychology.* 1948

39. Berelson, B., and Salter, P. J. "Majority and Minority Americans: An Analysis of Magazine Fiction," *Public Opinion Quarterly,* 1946, 10: pp. 168-190

40. Krech, D., and Crutchfield, R. S. *Theory and Problems of Social Psychology.* 1948

41. Strong, E. K., Jr. *The Second-Generation Japanese Problem.* 1933

42. Weatherford, W. D., and Johnson, C. S. *Race Relations.* 1934

43. Gessner, R. *Some of My Best Friends Are Jews.* 1936

44. Barzun, J. *Race: A Study in Modern Superstition.* 1937

45. Murphy, G., and Likert, R. *Public Opinion and the Individual.* 1938

46. Adorno, T. W., Frenkel-Brunswik, E., Levinson, D. J., and Sanford, R. N. *The Authoritarian Personality.* 1950

47. Flowerman, S. H. "Portrait of the Authoritarian Man," *N.Y. Times Mag.,* April 23, 1950

48. Allport, G. W., and Kramer, B. W. "Some Roots of Prejudice," *J. Psychol.,* 1946, 22: pp. 9-39

49. Ackerman, N. W., and Jahoda, M. *Anti-Semitism and Emotional Disorder.* 1950

50. Campbell, A. "Factors Associated with Attitudes Toward Jews." In G. E. Swanson, T. M. Newcomb, and E. L. Hartley (eds.), *Readings in Social Psychology,* Rev. ed. 1952

51. Bettelheim, B., and Janowitz, M. *The Dynamics of Prejudice.* 1950. Summarized in Swanson, Newcomb, and Hartley, *Readings in Social Psychology.* Rev. ed. 1952

52. Malherbe, E. G. *Race Attitudes and Education.* 1946

53. Williams, R. M., Jr. *The Reduction of Intergroup Tensions* (Social Science Research Council). 1947

54. MacIver, R. M. *More Perfect Union.* 1948

55. Rose, A. *Studies in Reduction of Prejudice.* 1947

56. Watson, G. *Action for Unity.* 1947

57. Saenger, G. *The Social Psychology of Prejudice.* 1953

58. Klineberg, O. *Tensions Affecting International Understanding: A Survey of Research* (Social Science Research Council). 1950

59. Jahoda, M., Deutsch, M., and Cook, S. W. *Research Methods in Social Relations.* 1951

60. Allport, F. H. *Social Psychology.* 1924

61. Cameron, N. *The Psychology of Behavior Disorders.* 1947

62. Gilbert, G. M. "Stereotype Persistence and Change Among College Students," *J. Abn. and Social Psychol.,* 1951, 46: pp. 245-254

63. Katz, D. "Psychological Barriers to Communication," *Ann. Amer. Acad. Polit. Soc. Sci.,* 1947, 250: pp. 17-25

64. Hyman, H., and Sheatsley, P. B. "Some Reasons Why Information Campaigns Fail," *Public Opinion Quarterly,* 1947, 11: pp. 412-423

65. Lazarsfeld, P. F. *The People Look at Radio.* 1946

66. Green, M. W. Unpublished Ph.D. Dissertation, Teachers College, Columbia University

67. Peterson, R. C., and Thurstone, L. L. *Motion Pictures and the Social Attitudes of Children.* 1933

68. Smith, F. T. "An Experiment in Modifying Attitudes toward the Negro," *Teachers College Contribs. to Ed.,* 1943, No. 887

69. Brophy, I. N. "The Luxury of Anti-Negro Prejudice," *Public Opinion Quarterly,* 1946, 9: pp. 456-466

70. Hovland, C. I., et al. *Experiments on Mass Communication.* Studies in Social Psychology in World War II, Volume 3. 1948

71. Deutsch, M., and Collins, M. E. *Interracial Housing: A Psychological Evaluation of a Social Experiment.* 1951

72. LaPiere, R. T. "Race Prejudice: France and England," *Soc. Forces,* 1928, 7: pp. 102-111

73. Bunche, R. J. *A World View of Race.* 1937

74. Rose, A. *The Roots of Prejudice* (Unesco). 1951

75. Deutscher, M., and Chein, I. "The Psychological Effects of Enforced Segregation," *J. Psychol.*, 1948, 26: pp. 259-287

76. Newcomb, T. M. *Personality and Social Change.* 1943

Psychology and International Relations

20

INTRODUCTION

Since wars begin in the minds of men, it is in the minds of men that the defenses of peace must be constructed." This famous sentence from the preamble to UNESCO's constitution has aroused great discussion and argument. There are some who have hailed it as an inspiration, and others who have dismissed it as nonsense. If the statement is true, it represents a tremendous challenge to the social sciences, and particularly to psychology. The "minds of men" are after all the special concern of the psychologist—his presumed area of competence. If it is really there that wars begin, the world may legitimately expect help of the psychologist in solving the complicated international problems of our time.

Those who have doubted the accuracy of the UNESCO statement have often done so on the ground that psychological factors remain at the fringe of international relations, and that politicians are moved by impersonal, objective forces beyond their control. These forces are variously defined as economic, demographic, ideological, cultural, etc., acting singly or in combination; in comparison with these the motives of individual men are sometimes regarded as trivial in their consequences, or judged to be effects rather than causes.

This dichotomy between objective and subjective factors does not seem to be justified, not only because dualism of this variety is now considered to be outmoded, but because so-called objective factors exert their effects in and through individuals. An economic "fact" operates through a *person* whose reaction to the "fact" will vary in part according to his character and his previous history. This was demonstrated, for example, by Campbell (1), whose study was summarized in the preceding chapter; prejudice against minority groups was related not to economic success, but to the degree of satisfaction with one's economic success. It is not the economic fact alone, but the psychological meaning of that fact which is apparently of primary importance.

In a field more directly related to international politics, it has frequently been suggested that demographic factors, particularly the fact of overpopulation, play an important part in leading to tension between nations, and even to war. We all remember the cry of *Lebensraum* which the Nazis used in an attempt to justify their expansionist policies. An analysis by Waller (2) of population pressures as a cause of war reaches the conclusion that such pressures by themselves cannot be regarded as responsible. For one thing, overpopulated countries like India, at least in recent times, have shown no great inclination to wage war. Further, the very nations that have claimed to need more space for their existing populations were paradoxically at the same time most anxious to keep up their birth rate, and went to great lengths to encourage larger families. Germany, which certainly started the last war, was not really overpopulated; by any measure of population density it was much better off than many of the countries which it attacked.

At the same time, it is true that many Germans accepted the myth of their country's overpopulation. It would appear to be more accurate, therefore, to stress the importance of the *feeling* of overpopulation, rather than the fact, in helping to explain why nations go to war. Perhaps these examples may suffice to make the point that the so-called impersonal and objective factors in international relations are by no means lacking in a strong and pervasive psychological component.

It is a far cry, however, from recognizing the existence of the psychological aspects of international relations, on the one hand, to understanding their nature or controlling their influence on the other. Have psychologists anything vital to say in this context? Do we have any knowledge that is relevant? Do we have any techniques that we can apply? There are undoubtedly many people—some within our profession, more outside it—who would unhesitatingly answer all these questions in the negative.

They can make a reasonably good case for this position. They can point to the fact that psychology as a science shows little permanence, that theories accepted only yesterday are today in limbo. When Graham Wallas wrote his *Human Nature and Politics* (3) in

1914, he applied the psychology current at that time to the understanding of political problems, but it was a psychology based almost exclusively upon McDougall's instinct theory, and it has for all of us today a decidedly antiquated flavor. All this is true. But it is also true for chemistry, for physics, and for many of the branches of medicine, all of which have undergone great transformations in recent years, without having suffered general repudiation as a result.

A second argument against the application of psychology to politics is based on the fact that there is not one psychology, but many. If the doctors disagree, how can a diagnosis be made, or a cure effected? Who will decide between the schools and systems now competing for acceptance? The confusion is worse confounded as the result of our having not only different psychological systems, but even subdivisions within the systems—not only psychoanalysis and behaviorism, but varieties of psychoanalysis and forms of behaviorism. This also is true. A fundamental question remains, granting the diversity of theory, is there any substantial agreement as to fact? Is there enough such agreement to make it possible for any of us to speak out, in the name of our science, concerning political problems? To this question we shall return later.

Related to the above is a point of view which, in one form or another, has found frequent expression in recent years, particularly since the creation and use of the first atomic bomb. According to this point of view the trouble with the world today resides in the fact that the physical sciences have progressed too fast, and the sciences of man, including psychology, too slowly. The physicists have split the atom, and in so doing have let loose forces which could cause incalculable destruction; if the psychologists knew enough about man—so the argument runs—they could tell him how to control these forces, or rather, how to control his relations with his fellow men so that such forces need never be used for destructive purposes; it is because the sciences of man cannot do this that we are now face to face with the possibility of the greatest catastrophe the world has ever known. It has even been suggested that it might be a good idea to declare a moratorium or a period of inactivity for the physical sciences in order to give the human sciences a chance to catch up.

This is a very serious indictment of our science, and of the neighboring sciences of man. We have all had some contact with this point of view, and it has brought to many of us a kind of occupational soul-searching, and some discouragement. Have we really learned so little in all these years? Are we still at the place from which we started? Or is our progress restricted to the relatively more accessible problems which we can handle in the laboratory—the principles of learning, perhaps, or the nature of dark-adaptation, or the construction of tests? Or is the indictment unfounded?

Let us look at the problem from another standpoint. Let us imagine a situation in which all political decisions are taken in accordance with facts established or accepted by psychologists, either because politicians request psychological guidance, or because the facts are universally known and taken into consideration. What would be the result?

THE IMPLICATIONS OF PSYCHOLOGICAL FINDINGS

We shall take as our first example the conclusions reached in the survey of materials relating to the problem of inherited psychological differences among ethnic groups (Chapter 11). The position of the overwhelming majority of psychologists on this point has been made abundantly clear; during the war statements to the effect that there is no proof of inborn psychological differences between such groups and therefore no scientific basis for "racial" discrimination were issued by several psychological bodies, including the Society for the Psychological Study of Social Issues, as well as by professional organizations in the field of anthropology and genetics. Even those few psychologists who still believe in such innate differences would agree that the *overlapping* of abilities between groups is so great that putting *all* members of one ethnic group in a superior category, and *all* members of another in an inferior category, has clearly no justification in psychological science. We may therefore assume practical unanimity among psychologists against any political action based on racialism.

Acceptance of this "fact," and action based upon it, would produce a revolution in human relations which would transform some of the most important aspects of international politics. Let us consider what it would have done in the recent past. It would have removed one of the basic props of Hitler's political program, erected upon a mystical bond between Germans everywhere because of a community of "blood," and directed toward the extermination of those in Germany and elsewhere whose "blood" was different. It might have saved the lives of millions of Jews, Poles, Czechs and others who were regarded as unfit to live. It might have reduced Hitler's appeal sufficiently so that he could never have come to power. In that case, it might have meant that there would not have been a war.

Think what it would have meant in our own recent history. Our Oriental Exclusion Act, based on the assumption that Japanese and Chinese were different and unassimilable, clearly contributed toward the atmosphere of hostility and resentment which characterized Japan's attitude toward the United States. It was a gratuitious insult to a people for whom international "face" is all-important. It may have been one of the steps on the road to Pearl Harbor.

Think what it would mean today. In South Africa the policy of segregation or "apartheid" is creating a situation which may have catastrophic consequences for the whole African continent. It has already produced strained relations between South Africa and India. It has virtually deprived millions of African Negroes of their citizenship, and has created deep resentments which continue to spread far beyond the borders of the country. It is contributing to the possibility of a "race war" in the not-too-distant future. If our "facts" concerning race had been accepted and *used*, none of this could have developed. The whole atmosphere in Africa would be entirely different.

Think what it would mean in our own country. We would have no Negro problem. We would have no southern Senators filibustering against an F.E.P.C.; in fact we would need no F.E.P.C. We would have no second-class citizens. In our international relations we would no longer have to try to explain away or justify to our critics in other countries the glaring inconsistency in our democratic tradition. (Here it may be said parenthetically that all over the world, the same question is asked over and over again, not only by our enemies, but also by our friends. How does it happen that in a democracy, minority groups are still so badly treated? Everywhere one hears the statement: "America is wonderful but . . .," and the "but" almost invariably refers to the status of Negroes. Children in France, England and Germany, asked to complete the sentence: "America is the land where . . ." frequently brought in a reference to the race problem. Many other examples could be given.) We would take away from Communists one of their most effective arguments in their attack upon our way of life. Our stock would go up immeasurably among all the so-called "colored peoples" of the world. All this would happen if what psychologists *know* were accepted by others and made a part of their thinking and feeling and acting.

The next example comes from an entirely different area of psychological competence. We have heard a great deal in recent years, particularly as a result of our experience with the Nazis, of the phenomenon of pathological leadership, of the accession to power of men who are personally maladjusted. Psychologists who have specialized in the clinical field or in the study of personality (and also, of course, psychiatrists) are presumably able to distinguish between normal and maladjusted individuals. There are doubtful borderline cases, and errors will occasionally be made, but it seems clear that if a panel of three to five well-trained psychologists and psychiatrists agreed in their diagnosis, there would be little room for doubt. What would happen if this knowledge were utilized, both in domestic and in international politics? What would happen if no man were permitted to attain a position of national leadership unless he were certified as "normal" by a panel of experts appointed by an independent organization such as the World Health Organization, the World Federation for Mental Health, or an International Association of Psychologists? At the local level, we frequently insist that candidates for our Police Department successfully pass certain tests of physical and mental capacity. Is it any less logical to take similar precautions at a higher level of leadership? We have the knowledge. What would happen if this knowledge were utilized?

For one thing, many of the Nazi leaders would never have been permitted to take office. The study by G. M. Gilbert on *The Psychology of Dictatorship* (4) makes it clear that not all the top Nazis could be correctly diagnosed as psychopathic. His clinical observations do permit the conclusion, however, that at least Hitler, Goering, Himmler, Hess, Streicher, and probably Goebbels, would not have passed the psychological or psychiatric test which has been suggested. The difference that their absence would have made in the international situation can hardly be overestimated. The point is that we *had* the means, the knowledge, the techniques, which would have permitted (and to a certain extent did permit) the diagnosis to be made before the damage had been done. There was, of course, no application of this knowledge.

At a slightly less dramatic but still very important level, it has been suggested by Brock Chisholm, former Director-General of the

THE IMPLICATIONS OF PSYCHOLOGICAL FINDINGS

World Health Organization (5), as well as by a Committee of the World Federation for Mental Health (6), that those who represent their countries abroad, and particularly those who participate in international conferences, must be people with healthy mental adjustment. Those of us who have had some experience with international conferences can testify to the fact that not a few have been wrecked by the presence of one or more participants who were insecure, oversensitive, suspicious, or resentful to a degree which indicated that they were not psychologically healthy individuals. In an article by Walter R. Sharp on *The Scientific Study of International Conferences* (7), the suggestion is made that the cultural and psychological aspects of conference experience be subjected to systematic study. Sharp goes on to suggest that this might lead to "improvement in the educational preparation *and selection* (italics supplied) of future delegates, as well as of the international secretarial staff. Nor is it inconceivable that certain governments might be led to review the criteria by which delegates are now chosen and give some attention to personality traits as they relate to particularly delicate multilateral negotiations. Many such a negotiation—indeed, the work of not a few technical committees—has been jeopardized by the 'immature' reactions of 'immature' representatives who can't stand the stress and strain!" (p. 113). We are not suggesting, and neither is Sharp, that this is the only reason why conferences may fail; it is, however, one of the possible reasons, and it could be eliminated by judicious use of knowledge now available. In view of the great part now played by international conferences, the result might be a very important one.

Our next example relates to the phenomenon of national stereotypes (Chapter 18) and to the part they play in determining our relations with other nations. Those who hold such stereotypes and act upon them—and that undoubtedly includes the overwhelming majority of human beings—are usually unaware of the tenuous foundation on which they rest and the frequency with which they deviate from reality. Most people have no hesitation in stating that of course *the* French, *the* Germans, *the* Irish are thus and so. The objective investigations which we have summarized indicate that frequently, though not always, such stereotypes may develop without any demonstrable "kernel of truth" whatsoever. Here again a knowledge and acceptance of such facts might effect something of a transformation in our relations with other people. Similarly, the fact that ethnic attitudes may develop without any factual basis, as in the social distance shown toward the Pirenians and the Wallonians (Chapter 19), might also help to destroy the myth that if we dislike a particular group, that group must necessarily have done something to deserve it. In this whole area, the development of a truly scientific approach to national characteristics, with factual data to replace hearsay and popular impressions, should go a long way toward placing our contacts with others on a more objective and realistic foundation. Such data should include not only the differences, but also—and perhaps even more important—the fundamental similarities and uniformities in the aspirations, practices and beliefs of the peoples of the world. [See Allport (8).]

Another series of investigations with practical implications in this context is that relating to social factors in perception (Chapter 8). Discussion and experimentation are continuing in order to determine the specific nature and the limits of social influence upon perceptual processes, but no one can doubt that social factors, and specifically group membership, do play a part. In the international field we may speak of *ethnocentric perception* to designate the tendency for an individual to see and judge external phenomena in terms of his membership in a particular national group. The same item of behavior, objectively considered, has an entirely different meaning depending upon whether it is one's own or another nation which is responsible for it. A suggestion made in a conference will be seen as a constructive solution if it comes from one side of the table, or as an example of Machiavellian double-dealing if it comes from the other. Aid to a hungry people will be humanitarian or merely propagandistic, depending on our attitude toward the nation supplying the food. Military aid to a government faced with the danger of revolt may be interpreted as strengthening the hand of the legitimate authorities or as suppressing the legitimate aspirations of the people. In these cases there is rarely what Lasswell (9) calls *reality testing;* on the contrary, reality is subordinated to ethnocentric perception. Again we may speculate regarding the extent to which international relations might be transformed if adequate consideration were given to this phenomenon, and if both sides in any controversy could be led to see how their actions look to others. One is reminded of the technique of role playing, and particularly of role reversal, which has been applied by sociometry and group dynamics to the area of interpersonal conflict (Chapter 17). The understanding of the socially determined perceptions found in others might be an important preliminary to reaching agreement at the international level.

Still another fact related to the above must not be overlooked. Gordon Allport, in a chapter of a book edited by Cantril for UNESCO (10), has rightly stressed the role of *expectancy* in the production of events. If we expect war, we are more likely to get it. There is nothing mysterious about this phenomenon. It would not operate in those cases in which expectancy had no effect on our actions, or where the event anticipated could not be influenced by what we do. To take an obvious example, even if every human being in the world expected rain tomorrow, the actual event would not be affected in any way. Where expectancy determines what we do, however, or refrain from doing, the consequences may be significant indeed. (See Chapter 18.) Expectancy—real expectancy—of war means that we no longer do everything in our power to avert it; we are discouraged from looking for peaceful alternatives.

If this fact were accepted, understood, and kept in mind by public spokesmen and by those who direct the operations of the mass media, and if as a consequence we spoke less of the probability of war and more of the possibility of peace, less about the routes by which we or the Soviet Union could be attacked and more of our faith in the United Nations—these things too would reduce by a little the threat of war. Obviously, the same would have to be done from the other direction. Talk of the "American capitalistic Wall Street imperialist fascist warmongers" is hardly conducive to an atmosphere in Russia which could be characterized as an "expectancy of peace." If, as we believe, Americans do not want war, and if, as we hope, the Russians do not want war either, an understanding on both sides of the role of expectancy would very probably change the situation for the better.

These few examples are obviously inadequate for an analysis of the political situation, nor do they do justice to the relevant content of psychology. They are taken out of a large body of psychological knowledge and understanding which is available to those who want it, and capable of transforming human relations if it were accepted and applied.

Many other examples could be given. Data regarding the important part played by semantics in the whole area of international communication (Chapter 3), the nature of aggressive attitudes

[Chapter 5; see also Eysenck (11)], the methods by which attitudes may be modified (Chapters 18 and 19), techniques for improving group procedures (Chapters 17)—all of these have a contribution to make in this important field.

THE UTILIZATION OF PSYCHOLOGY

If the preceding analysis is sound, psychology has much more to
offer than is usually realized. The difficulty lies not so much in the
lack of accomplishment as in the lack of general acceptance or
recognition of the accomplishment. Psychologists have built a good
house, but they have not been able to sell it. In a sense, they have
never tried. It may seem undignified to exchange an attitude of
scholarly detachment for the activities of a salesman, and in this
case it is somewhat dangerous as well; there is the danger of over-
selling, of undertaking more than we can accomplish; there is the
danger of selling the wrong product, one which may later turn out
to be defective. There are, however, scientific safeguards that can
be introduced so that when we speak, we will speak with authority
and will be certain of our ground. There is nothing undignified
about that kind of salesmanship.

There are several encouraging signs. In the past few years psychologists have shown an increasing concern with international
problems and with the potential contribution which psychologists
might make for their solution. The Society for the Psychological
Study of Social Issues devoted one of its yearbooks, under the editorship of Gardner Murphy, to Human Nature and Enduring Peace
(12). As a direct outgrowth of work on the Tensions Project in the
Department of Social Sciences of UNESCO, two volumes were published, one under the editorship of Hadley Cantril, Tensions That
Cause Wars (10), and a second by the present writer on Tensions
Affecting International Understanding (13). Another psychologist,
Kisker, edited a symposium on World Tension (14). Psychologists
have collaborated with others, as in Personality and Political Crisis,
edited by Stanton and Perry (15). Scholars identified with other
disciplines have occasionally made use of psychological data, as in
Dunn's War and the Minds of Men (16), and Jackson's The Meeting of Minds (17). Psychologists have served, and continue to serve,
on the secretariats of the United Nations and of UNESCO. The latter
organization has also embarked on an extensive program of dissemi-

nation of relevant scientific information. The series of UNESCO publications on *The Race Question in Modern Science* (18) is an outstanding instance. Many other examples could be given.

This does not mean that psychologists have all the answers. There are still great lacunae in our knowledge, and these can be filled only by the most careful and painstaking research. Here, too, there are signs of increased activity, at both the national and the international level. Allport (8) has made a valuable listing of many of the problems that require investigation, and has suggested some of the means by which this might be accomplished.

We turn now to a brief consideration of another kind of contribution which psychologists, and social scientists in general, can make. Often when a psychologist is asked for information in the international field, for example, regarding the nature of tensions between two peoples, or whether attitudes are changing in one direction or another, his answer is in essence: "I don't know, but I can find out." In other words, even if he does not have the answers, he may have at his disposal the techniques by which the answers may be discovered. This is particularly true in the field of attitudes and opinions, a field which the psychologist shares with sociologists and other social scientists.

One example of the manner in which such technical skills have been utilized is to be found in the study conducted by Gardner Murphy (19) for the government of India. The Indian Ministry of Education was interested in knowing more about tensions among the various groups which make up the population of India, and the Department of Social Sciences at UNESCO was asked for guidance in making the survey. UNESCO in turn invited Professor Murphy to spend some time in India in organizing the research, working with Indian colleagues, and integrating and coordinating the study as a whole. The result is an encouraging indication of what can be done under these conditions, and although it is too early to assess the practical consequences on Indian intergroup tensions, there can be no doubt of the definite contribution toward clarifying the issues and preparing the way for a solution. It is to be hoped that this pattern will be followed again in the future.

We are not making a plea for psychological imperialism in the field of international relations. There are many aspects of the problem with which specialists in other disciplines are better qualified to deal. The fact remains that psychological factors do enter; the minds of men do play a part. There is a great deal that psychologists do not yet know; there is need for further research and study, and for the development of better and more efficient techniques for extending the area of psychological competence. It remains true that with the knowledge already available, important steps can be taken in the direction of improving international relations by basing our behavior on sound psychological principles. The task is difficult and complicated, but there is no task which is more significant.

SUMMARY

There is an important psychological component in international relations. Economic, demographic and other factors exert their influence in and through "the minds of men." The apparent failure of psychological science to solve the problems of peace and war is due not so much to the lack of available facts, but to unwillingness to accept and apply the facts. As examples may be mentioned the conclusions of psychologists and others regarding race, the diagnosis of pathological leadership, the dangers arising from the use of national stereotypes, the effects of ethnocentric perception, the role of expectancy, etc. It is suggested that psychology has much to offer, in terms both of data and of method. There are encouraging indications of the increasing application of psychology in this area.

REFERENCES

1. Campbell, A. "Factors Associated with Attitudes Toward Jews." In G. E. Swanson, T. M. Newcomb and E. L. Hartley (eds.), *Readings in Social Psychology*. Rev. ed. 1952

2. Waller, W. "War in the Twentieth Century." In J. E. Nordskog, E. C. McDonegh and M. J. Vincent (eds.), *Analyzing Social Problems*. 1950

3. Wallas, G. *Human Nature in Politics*. 3rd ed. 1929

4. Gilbert, G. M. *The Psychology of Dictatorship*. 1950

5. Chisholm, G. B. "Social Responsibility," *J. Soc. Issues*, Supplement Series No. 1, 1947

6. *Mental Health and World Citizenship*. World Federation for Mental Health. 1948

7. Sharp, W. R. *The Technique of International Conferences*. UNESCO Document, 55/3. See also *Int. Social Science Bull.*, 1953, vol. 5

8. Allport, G. W. "Guide Lines for Research in International Cooperation." In T. H. Pear (ed.), *Psychological Factors of Peace and War.* 1950

9. Lasswell, H. D. "Propaganda and Mass Insecurity," *Psychiatry,* 1950, 13: pp. 283-299

10. Allport, G. W. "The Role of Expectancy." In H. Cantril (ed.), *Tensions That Cause Wars.* 1950

11. Eysenck, E. G. "War and Aggressiveness." In T. H. Pear (ed.), *Psychological Factors of Peace and War.* 1950

12. Murphy, G. (ed.). *Human Nature and Enduring Peace.* 1945

13. Klineberg, O. *Tensions Affecting International Understanding: A Survey of Research* (Social Science Research Council). 1950

14. Kisker, G. W. (ed.). *World Tension.* 1951

15. Stanton, A. H., and Perry, S. E. (eds.). *Personality and Political Crisis.* 1951

16. Dunn, F. S. *War and the Minds of Men.* 1950

17. Jackson, E. *Meeting of Minds.* 1952

18. *The Race Question in Modern Science* (UNESCO), Publications include Dunn, L. C. *Race and Biology;* Rose, A. *The Roots of Prejudice;* Klineberg, O. *Race and Psychology;* Leiris, M. *Race and Culture;* Comas, J. *Racial Myths;* Lévi-Strauss, C. *Race and History.* Other publications are to follow.

19. Murphy, G. *In the Minds of Men.* 1953

Index of Names

Index of Subjects